The Blackwell Companion to Religious Ethics

Edited by

William Schweiker

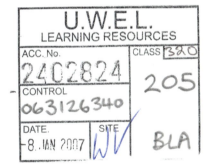

Blackwell
Publishing

BLACKWELL PUBLISHING
350 Main Street, Malden, MA 02148-5020, USA
9600 Garsington Road, Oxford OX4 2DQ, UK
550 Swanston Street, Carlton, Victoria 3053, Australia

First published 2005 by Blackwell Publishing Ltd

4   2007

Library of Congress Cataloging-in-Publication Data

The Blackwell companion to religious ethics / edited by William Schweiker.
p. cm. — (Blackwell companions to religion)
Includes bibliographical references and index.
ISBN 0-631-21634-0 (hardback: alk. paper)
1. Religious ethics. I. Schweiker, William. II. Series.
BJ1188.B57 2005
205 — dc22

                                        2004008958

ISBN-13: 978-0-631-21634-6 (hardback: alk. paper)

A catalogue record for this title is available from the British Library.

Set in 10 on 12.5 pt Photina
by SNP Best-set Typesetter Ltd., Hong Kong
Printed and bound in Singapore
by COS Printers Pte Ltd

The publisher's policy is to use permanent paper from mills that operate a sustainable forestry policy, and which has been manufactured from pulp processed using acid-free and elementary chlorine-free practices. Furthermore, the publisher ensures that the text paper and cover board used have met acceptable environmental accreditation standards.

For further information on
Blackwell Publishing, visit our website:
www.blackwellpublishing.com

Contents

Notes on Contributors

Svend Andersen is Professor of Ethics and Philosophy of Religion, and Director of the Center for Bioethics in the University of Aarhus, Denmark. He was a member of the Danish Council of Ethics 1988–93 and also President of Societas Ethica, European Society for Research in Ethics 1999–2003. She is the author of *Ideal und Singularität. Über die Funktion des Gottesbegriffes in Kants theoretischer Philosophie* (1983), *Sprog og skabelse. Fænomenologisk sprogopfattelse i lyset af analytisk sprogfilosofi med henblik på det religiøse sprog* (1989), and *Bioetik* (co-editor, 1999).

Maria Antonaccio is Associate Professor of Religion and currently holds the NEH Chair in the Humanities at Bucknell University. She is the author of *Picturing the Human: The Moral Thought of Iris Murdoch* (2000), co-editor of *Iris Murdoch and the Search for Human Goodness* (1996), and author of numerous articles in moral theory.

Mark Berkson is Assistant Professor in the Department of Religion at Hamline University. He teaches courses in the religious traditions of East and South Asia, as well as comparative religion. He has published articles on Confucian and Daoist thought and interfaith dialogue. His current scholarly work focuses on Chinese conceptions of the self and understandings of death.

Don S. Browning is Alexander Campbell Professor Emeritus of Religious Ethics and the Social Sciences in the Divinity School, the University of Chicago. He is the co-author of *From Culture Wars to Common Ground: Religion and the American Family Debate* (1997, 2000) and *Reweaving the Social Tapestry: Toward a Public Philosophy and Policy of Families* (2001). He is also the author of *Marriage and Modernization: How Globalization Threatens Marriage and What to Do about It* (2003).

Bénézet Bujo is Professor of Moral Theology in the Department of Moral Theology and Ethics at the University of Freiburg. He has also served as Vice-Rector at the University of Freiburg (2000–3). His many works include *Morale africaine et foi chrétienne* (1980), *Afrikanische Theologie in ihrem gesellschaftlichen Kontext* (1986), and *African Christian Morality at the Age of Inculturation* (1990, 1998).

John Ross Carter is Professor of Philosophy and Religion and Robert Ho Professor in Asian Studies at Colgate University. He has published on the Theravāda tradition, especially in Sri Lanka, and more recently has contributed numerous articles on the Pure Land tradition in Japan, while editing works and writing on issues of religious pluralism. He has also served as Director of Chapel House at Colgate.

Francisca Cho is Associate Professor of Buddhist Studies, Georgetown University, and works in the area of East Asian Buddhism and culture, particularly through literature and film. She is the author of *Embracing Illusion: Truth and Fiction in The Dream of the Nine Clouds* (1996) as well as articles on comparative studies and comparative religious ethics.

David A. Clairmont is a PhD candidate in religious ethics at the Divinity School, the University of Chicago. He is an adjunct instructor in the Department of Religious Studies at De Paul University. Recipient of a Newcombe Fellowship, he is completing a dissertation entitled, "Moral Motivation and Comparative Ethics: Bonaventure, Buddhaghosa and the Problem of Material Simplicity."

Francis X. Clooney, SJ, is Professor of Comparative Theology at Boston College and (during 2002–4) Academic Director of the Oxford Centre for Hindu Studies. His most recent books are *Hindu God, Christian God: How Reason Helps Break Down the Boundaries Between Religions* (2001) and *Divine Mother, Blessed Mother: Hindu Goddesses and the Blessed Virgin Mary* (forthcoming).

Mark Csikszentmihalyi is Associate Professor in East Asian Languages and Literature and Religious Studies at the University of Wisconsin-Madison. His works include *Virtue: Material Ethics and the Body in Early China* (2004) and *Religious and Philosophical Aspects of the Laozi* (co-edited with Philip J. Ivanhoe, 1999). His current research concerns Han dynasty detectives and early Chinese notions of fate and contingency.

Vine Deloria, Jr. is a member of Standing Rock Sioux Tribe of North Dakota. He was Professor of Political Science at the University of Arizona 1978–90 and Professor of History at the University of Colorado 1990–2000. His books include *Custer Died for Your Sins* (1969), *God is Red* (1973), *Red Earth White Lies* (1996), *Evolution, and Creationism and Other Modern Myths* (2002).

Frederick Mathewson Denny is Professor of Islamic Studies and the History of Religions in the Religious Studies Department at the University of Colorado at Boulder. He has studied Islamic ritual and devotional practices and Muslim communities in Egypt, Indonesia, Malaysia, and North America. His publications include the widely used textbook *An Introduction to Islam* (2nd edn., 1994).

Jean Bethke Elshtain is the Laura Spelman Rockefeller Professor of Social and Political Ethics at the Divinity School, the University of Chicago. She is the recipient of many awards and the author of many books, including *Democracy on Trial* (1995), *Augustine and the Limits of Politics* (1998), *Jane Addams and the Dream of American Politics* (2002), and *Just War Against Terror: The Burden of American Power in a Violent World* (2003).

Darrell J. Fasching teaches comparative religious ethics at the University of South Florida. His books focus primarily on issues of violence and non-violence and include *The Ethical Challenge of Auschwitz and Hiroshima* (1993), *The Coming of the Millennium* (1996), and (with Dell de Chant) *Comparative Religious Ethics: A Narrative Approach* (2001).

Michael Fishbane is Nathan Cummings Professor of Jewish Studies and Chair of the Committee on Jewish Studies at the Divinity School, the University of Chicago. He is the author of many books, including *The Exegetical Imagination* (1988), *Biblical Text and Texture* (1998), and *Biblical Myth and Rabbinic Mythmaking* (2003).

William French is Associate Professor in the Theology Department of Loyola University, Chicago and teaches in Loyola's environmental studies program. He has written widely on environmental issues in numerous books and journals.

Franklin I. Gamwell is Shailer Mathews Professor of Religious Ethics at the Divinity School, the University of Chicago. His publications include *The Divine Good: Modern Moral Theory and the Necessity of God* (1996), *The Meaning of Religious Freedom: Modern Politics and the Democratic Resolution* (1995), and *Democracy on Purpose: Justice and the Reality of God* (2000).

Segun Gbadegesin is Professor of Philosophy at Howard University, Washington, DC where he teaches African philosophy, ethics, and bioethics. His publications include *African Philosophy: Traditional Yoruba Philosophy and Contemporary African Realities* (1991) and he is the co-author of *Ethics, Higher Education and Social Responsibility* (1996).

Robin Gill is Michael Ramsey Professor of Modern Theology at the University of Kent. He is the author of *A Textbook of Christian Ethics* (2nd edn., 1995) and editor of *The Cambridge Companion to Christian Ethics* (2001). He is also series editor and contributor to New Studies in Christian Ethics (1992–).

Ronald M. Green is Eunice and Julian Cohen Professor for the Study of Ethics and Human Values, and Director of the Ethics Institute and Chair of the Department of Religion at Dartmouth College. From 1998–9 he was President of the Society of Christian Ethics, and he has served two elected terms as Secretary of the American Academy of Religion. He is the author of *Religious Reason* (1978), *Religion and Moral Reason* (1988), and *Human Embryo Research Debate* (2001).

Bruce Grelle is Professor in the Department of Religious Studies and Director of the Religion and Public Education Resource Center at California State University, Chico. He is co-editor of *Explorations in Global Ethics: Comparative Religious Ethics and Interreligious Dialogue* (1998).

Laura Grillo, a historian of religions, teaches at Pacifica Graduate Institute. With grants from the National Endowment for the Humanities, the American Academy of Religion, and the West African Research Association, she was able to return to Côte d'Ivoire to conduct the field research on which her work is partially based.

Vigen Guroian is Professor of Theology and Ethics at Loyola College in Maryland. An Armenian Orthodox theologian, his books include *Incarnate Love: Essays in Orthodox Ethics* (2nd edn., 2002), *Tending the Heart of Virtue: How Classic Stories Awaken the Child's Moral Imagination* (1998), and *Life's Living Toward Dying* (1996).

Barry Hallen is Professor of Philosophy and Chairman of the Department of Philosophy and Religion at Morehouse College and Fellow of the W. E. B. Du Bois Institute for Afro-American Research at Harvard University. He is the author of *The Good, the Bad, and the Beautiful: Discourse About Values in Yoruba Culture* (2001) and *A Short History of African Ethics* (2001).

Charles Hallisey is Associate Professor in the Department of Languages and Cultures of Asia and in the Religious Studies Program at the University of Wisconsin-Madison. Working in the Asian humanities, with a special focus on the cultural history of Theravāda Buddhism, he has recently published "Works and Persons in Sinhala Literary Culture" in *Literary Cultures in History: Some Reconstructions from South Asia* (2003).

Maria Heim is Assistant Professor of Religion at Amherst College. She has also taught at California State University, Long Beach. She is the author of *Theories of the Gift in Medieval South Asia* (2004).

Simeon O. Ilesanmi is Zachary T. Smith Associate Professor of Religion at Wake Forest University. He writes and teaches in the areas of comparative ethics, political theory, and religion and law. His publications have appeared in numerous journals and his current research projects focus on human rights, war crimes, and constitutional theories of religion in Africa.

Philip J. Ivanhoe is the John Findlay Visiting Professor of Philosophy at Boston University. He teaches East Asian and Western Philosophy and specializes in the history of East Asian religious thought and its potential for contemporary ethics. Among his publications are *The Daodejing of Laozi* (2003) and *Ethics in the Confucian Tradition: The Thought of Mengzi and Wang Yangming* (2002). He is co-editor of the anthology *Working Virtue: Virtue Ethics and Contemporary Moral Problems* (forthcoming).

Albert R. Jonsen is Professor Emeritus of Ethics in Medicine in the Department of Medical History and Ethics, University of Washington, Seattle. He received the McGovern Award of the American Osler Society, the Annual Award of the Society for Health and Human Values, and the Davies Award of the American College of Physicians. He is the author of *A Short History of Medical Ethics* (1999), co-author of *The Abuse of Casuistry* (1988), and co-editor of *Source Book in Bioethics: A Documentary History* (1998).

Thomas P. Kasulis is Professor of Comparative Cultural Studies at Ohio State University. His field of specialization is the comparative study of philosophy and religion, with a special Asian focus on Japan. He has written and edited seven books, including *Zen Action/Zen Person* (1990) and *Intimacy or Integrity: Philosophy and Cultural Difference* (2002).

John Kelsay is Richard L. Rubenstein Professor of Religion at Florida State University. He is the author of *Islam and War: A Study in Comparative Ethics* (1993) and other works dealing with religion and war. He is the co-editor of the *Journal of Religious Ethics*.

Damien Keown is Reader in Buddhism at Goldsmiths College, University of London, and founding co-editor of the *Journal of Buddhist Ethics*. His publications include *The Nature of Buddhist Ethics* (1992), *Buddhism and Bioethics* (1995), *Buddhism and Abortion* (1999), and *Contemporary Buddhist Ethics* (2000).

Sallie B. King is Professor of Philosophy and Religion at James Madison University. A former President of the Society for Buddhist–Christian Studies, she is the author of *Buddha Nature* (1991), co-editor of *Engaged Buddhism: Buddhist Liberation Movements in Asia* (1996), and author of numerous articles in cross-cultural philosophy of religion.

Nancy Levene is Assistant Professor of Religious Studies at Indiana University. She is the author of *Spinoza's Revelation: Religion, Democracy, and Reason* (2004) and co-editor (with Peter Ochs) of *Textual Reasonings: Jewish Philosophy and Text Study at the End of the Twentieth Century* (2002). Her recent research is on religion, politics, and interpretations of modernity.

Robin W. Lovin is Cary Maguire University Professor of Ethics at Southern Methodist University and a former President of the Society of Christian Ethics. His writings include two studies of twentieth-century Christian social ethics: *Christian Faith and Public Choices: The Social Ethics of Barth, Brunner, and Bonhoeffer* (1984) and *Reinhold Niebuhr and Christian Realism* (1994). He is also the author of *Christian Ethics: An Essential Guide* (2000).

Gerald P. McKenny is Associate Professor of Theological Ethics at the University of Notre Dame. He is the author of *To Relieve the Human Condition* (1997), a Choice Outstanding Book, and co-editor of *The Ethical* (2003), a collection of essays on Continental moral philosophy. He is currently co-principal investigator of a multi-year collaborative project on "Altering Nature: How Religions Assess Biotechnology," sponsored by the Ford Foundation.

Shaul Magid is Associate Professor of Jewish Philosophy at Indiana University. He is the author of *Hasidism on the Margin: Reconciliation, Messianism and Antinomianism in Izbica/Radzin Hasidism* (2003), editor of *God's Voice From the Void* (2001), and co-editor of *Beginning/Again: Toward a Hermeneutics of Jewish Texts* (2001). He has written numerous scholarly and popular articles in the field of Jewish mysticism and modern Jewish philosophy.

Eske Møllgaard studied Chinese, philosophy, and literature at the University of Copenhagen and at Harvard University. He has taught at universities in the United States and published articles on Chinese philosophy.

Anne E. Monius is Assistant Professor of South Asian Religious Traditions at Harvard Divinity School. She is the author of *Imagining a Place for Buddhism: Literary Culture and Religious Community in Tamil-Speaking South India* (2001).

Ebrahim Moosa is Associate University Research Professor in the Department of Religion and Co-Director of the Center for the Study of Muslim Networks at Duke University. His interests are in the history of Muslim ethics, Islamic law, and theology, as well as modern Muslim narratives in ethics, especially the formation of Muslim selfhood in encounters with modernity. As a scholar of early Islam, he also studies the impact and contribution of Abu Hamid al-Ghazali and his paradigmatic value for ongoing questions in contemporary Muslim thought.

Thomas W. Ogletree is Professor of Theological Ethics at Yale University Divinity School and the Graduate Department of Religious Studies. He is a past President of the Society of Christian Ethics. He is the author of *Christian Faith and History: A Critical Comparison of Ernst Troeltsch and Karl Barth* (1965), *The Use of the Bible in Christian Ethics* (1983), and *Hospitality to the Stranger: Dimensions of Moral Understanding* (1985).

Gene Outka is Dwight Professor of Philosophy and Christian Ethics at Yale University and a former President of the Society of Christian Ethics. He is the author of *Agape: An Ethical Analysis* (1972) and co-editor and contributor to *Norm and Context in Christian Ethics* (1968), *Religion and Morality* (1973), and *Prospects for a Common Morality* (1993).

Roy W. Perrett is Professor of Philosophy at the University of Hawai'i. His publications include *Death and Immortality* (1987), *Indian Philosophy of Religion* (ed., 1989), *Justice, Ethics and New Zealand Society* (co-ed., 1992), *Hindu Ethics: A Philosophical Study* (1998), and *Indian Philosophy: A Collection of Readings* (ed., 2001).

Jean Porter is O'Brien Professor of Theological Ethics at the University of Notre Dame. She has also been President of the Society of Christian Ethics. Her recent publications include *Natural and Divine Law* (1999), *Nature As Reason* (2005), and *The Recovery of Virtue* (1990).

Joseph Prabhu is Professor of Philosophy and Religion at California State University, Los Angeles and co-editor of the journal *ReVision*. He has been a visiting professor at many universities in Germany, India, and the US and a Senior Fellow at Harvard Divinity School. He is editor of *The Intercultural Challenge of Raimon Panikkar* (1996) and *Indian Ethics: Classical Traditions and Contemporary Challenges* (2004).

Hilary Putnam is Cogan University Professor Emeritus at Harvard University. His books include *Reason, Truth and History* (1981), *Pragmatism: An Open Question* (1995), *The Threefold Cord* (1999), *Renewing Philosophy* (1992), *Realism with a Human Face* (1990), and *Ethics Without Ontology* (2004).

Regina Ammicht-Quinn is Privatdozentin for Theological Ethics at the Center for Ethics in the Sciences, Tübingen. Her main publications are *Von Lissabon bis Auschwitz. Zum Paradigmawechsel in der Theodizeefrage* (1992) and *Körper – Religion – Sexualität. Reflexionen zur Ethik der Geschlechter* (2003).

A. Kevin Reinhart is Associate Professor of Islamic Studies in the Religion Department at Dartmouth College. His research interests are in Islamic law and ethics, Islamic ritual practices, and Late Ottoman Islamic ideologies. He is the author of *Before Revelation: The Boundaries of Muslim Moral Thought* (1995).

Frank E. Reynolds is Emeritus Professor of History of Religions and Buddhist Studies in the Divinity School and Department of South Asian Languages and Civilizations at the University of Chicago. He is the co-editor with Robin Lovin of *Cosmogony and Ethical Order* (1985) and the author of several essays on Buddhist ethics.

Abdulaziz Sachedina is Professor of Religious Studies at the University of Virginia, Charlottesville. He works in the field of Islamic law and theology, concentrating on social and political ethics, including Islamic biomedical ethics. His publications include *Islamic Messianism* (1981), *The Just Ruler in Shiite Islam* (1988), and *The Islamic Roots of Democratic Pluralism* (2001).

Lamin Sanneh is D. Willis James Professor of World Christianity and Professor of History at Yale. He is an Honorary Research Professor at the School of Oriental and African Studies in the University of London, and is a life member of Clare Hall, Cambridge University. He was awarded an honorary doctorate at the University of Edinburgh. For his academic work he was made Commandeur de l'Ordre National du Lion, Senegal's highest national honor. His many works include *The Crown and the Turban: Muslims and West African Pluralism* (1997) and *Whose Religion is Christianity?: The Gospel Beyond the West* (2003).

Jonathan W. Schofer is the Assistant Professor of Classical Rabbinic Literature in the Department of Hebrew and Semitic Studies at the University of Wisconsin-Madison. His primary area of research is in classical rabbinic ethics, and he has a longstanding interest in comparative ethics, including a study of early Confucian thought. He is the author of *The Making of a Sage: A Study in Rabbinic Ethics* (2005).

William Schweiker is Professor of Theological Ethics at the Divinity School, the University of Chicago. An award-wining author and lecturer in many universities, he is the author of *Responsibility and Christian Ethics* (1995), *Power, Value and Conviction: Theological Ethics in the Postmodern Age* (1998), and *Theological Ethics and Global Dynamics: In the Time of Many Worlds* (2004). He is also the editor of many volumes, including *Having: Property and Possession in Religious and Social Life* (2004).

Max L. Stackhouse is the Stephen Colwell Professor of Christian Ethics at Princeton Theological Seminary. He is the primary author of *On Moral Business* (1995), *Creeds, Society and Human Rights* (1984), and the new series, *God and Globalization* (2000–). He argues that Christian ethics requires a "public theology" to address the common life. He is a former President of the Society of Christian Ethics.

Winnifred Fallers Sullivan is Dean of Students and Senior Lecturer at the Divinity School, the University of Chicago. She teaches and writes in the area of the comparative study of law and religion and is the author of *Paying the Words Extra: Religious Discourse in the Supreme Court of the United States* (1994) and *Cemetery Anarchy or "Talking Theology" in Federal Court* (forthcoming).

Donald K. Swearer is the Charles and Harriet Cox McDowell Professor of Religion at Swarthmore College, where he teaches courses in Asian and comparative religions. His main field of research is Buddhism in Southeast Asia, with special attention to Thailand. His recent publications include *Becoming the Buddha: The Ritual of Image Consecration in Thailand* (2004), *The Sacred Mountains of Northern Thailand and Their Legends* (with Sommai Premchit and Phaitun Dokibuakaew) (2004), *The Legend of Queen Cama* (with Sommai Premchit) (1998), and *The Buddhist World of Southeast Asia* (1995).

Sumner B. Twiss is Distinguished Professor of Human Rights, Ethics, and Religion at Florida State University. His scholarship focuses on comparative ethics, human rights, and the role of religion in human rights abuses and preventing crimes against humanity. He is co-editor of the *Journal of Religious Ethics* and *Explorations in Global Ethics: Comparative Ethics and Interreligious Dialogue* (2000), and co-author of *Comparative Religious Ethics* (1978). His forthcoming co-edited volume is *Advancing Human Rights*.

Jef Van Gerwen was a member of the Jesuit faculty of the University of Antwerp. His research focused on the Roman Catholic social justice tradition, the ethics of early Christian communities, and contemporary issues in business ethics. His works include *Niet uit eigen macht. De kerk als morele gemeenschap* (1987), *More Europe? A Critical Christian Inquiry Into the Process of European Integration* (co-ed., 1997), *Business en ethiek: spelregels voor het ethisch ondernemen* (2nd edn., 2002), and *Onderweg. Over de navolging van Christus in de 21ste eeuw* (2003).

Lee Yearley is Professor and Chairman in the Department of Religious Studies at Stanford University. He was the Henry Luce Professor of Comparative Religious Ethics at Amherst College in 1987–8 and a Luce Fellow at the Institute for the Advanced Study of Religion at the University of Chicago in 1990–1. His specialty is comparative religious ethics, especially classical Greek, Christian, Confucian, and Taoist traditions. His many works include *The Ideas of Newman: Christianity and Human Religiosity* (1978) and his renowned *Mencius and Aquinas: Theories of Virtue and Conceptions of Courage* (1990).

Katherine K. Young is Professor of Hinduism in the Department of Religious Studies at McGill University. Her scholarly expertise includes Hinduism, the religions of Tamil Nadu, Hindu ethics, and gender and religion. Her many works include *Hermeneutical Paths to the Sacred Worlds of India* (1994). She is the co-editor of *Today's Woman in the World Religions* (1993) and *Feminism and World Religions* (1998).

Preface

The Blackwell Companion to Religious Ethics provides a comprehensive account of issues and themes in current religious ethics as well as substantive treatments of the moral outlook and practices of the world's religions. With the dawning of present global realities, the religions are, for good and ill, some of the most dominant forces on this planet. Increasing cultural and religious interaction makes it imperative that scholars working within "religious ethics" understand the impact of traditions and communities on each other. For those theorists and community leaders undertaking constructive and normative moral reflection within their own traditions, critical awareness of the interactions among the world's religions seems extremely important as well. This volume, then, is meant for anyone interested in the moral beliefs and practices of the world's religions and their meaning and significance for current life. It aims to provide for scholars, teachers, religious leaders, and students at all levels needed resources and tools for the study of the world's religions.

The volume is structured into three parts, each of which has subdivisions. Part I: Moral Inquiry provides an account of basic conceptual issues in religious ethics. The chapters explore (1) the elements of moral reflection, (2) the mechanisms of transmission and innovation in traditions, and (3) questions about how to carry out comparison among traditions. Part II: Moral Traditions is the largest section of the volume, realizing that the very idea of a "tradition" is perhaps too ambiguous to capture the complexities of these religious realities. Major moral traditions are explored under four interlocking rubrics. The treatment of each tradition begins with the question of the appropriateness of the idea of "ethics" for exploring its moral teaching. This enables scholars of religion to clarify the form of thinking found in a specific moral community or tradition. This initial treatment is followed by chapters that explore the origin, historical differentiations, and present trajectories of a tradition. To be sure, no volume can capture the entire scope of any religion; no single volume can address every religious form found in history or present life. Limitations noted, the hope is that a fairly comprehensive vision of a religious tradition will be presented, a vision that specifies its historical complexity. Finally, Part III: Moral Issues turns directly to contemporary questions of worldwide import. In each of these chapters, the author draws comparatively on the resources of traditions to address present challenges. These are roughly divided between moral problems arising within social and natural "systems" and those that bear more directly on the lives of "persons," again realizing the ambiguities of these ideas. Between the covers of this book, the reader will find superb accounts of the moral beliefs and practices of the world's religions, inquiry into the structure of religious ethics, and comparative treatments of some of the most pressing issues confronting peoples around the world.

Several concerns have guided the development of this volume. First, the terminology and conceptuality of "religion" and "ethics" is admittedly Western. More than once the editor and authors have been warned about the problem of presenting a companion to "ethics" with respect to the "religions." Scholars interested in the "moral" life of communities and traditions must address questions about basic categories. Mindful of this challenge, we have included essays in Part I of the volume to address this issue. Additionally, each of the "moral traditions" sections starts with an essay that addresses the problem (e.g., "Buddhist Ethics?"). This matter is also addressed in an introductory chapter.

Another concern that has guided the development of this Companion is found within current academic debates but may in fact be rather longstanding. One might put it like this: how deep does morality go? Some authors argue that morality is free from claims about "reality" and thus conceptions, beliefs, and practices for guiding life develop with respect to distinctive social purposes, languages, and communities. Other scholars argue from within a tradition or on strictly conceptual grounds that the good and the real are intertwined. This debate has taken various forms: anti-realism and realism in moral theory; questions in hermeneutical theory; ideas about social constructivism and identity formation, and the like. If the first concern that has structured the development of this book was about concepts, at issue here are matters of validity and religious diversity. The purpose of the volume is not to resolve these debates. Mindful of the importance of this many-sided debate, we have tried to conceive the volume and select authors who provide a range of answers within the discussion.

Final scholarly concerns can be noted. It seems clear that questions about sexuality and gender as well as issues of race, ethnicity, and class are being debated around the world and within each tradition. The worldwide women's movement has offered profound insights into traditions and beliefs. Attention to race and class provides new means to understand and analyze traditional beliefs, social structures, and questions of human rights. Likewise, there are debates about identity formation within the dynamics of global cultural flows, economic forces, and political realities. While not dominating any one specific essay, these matters are in fact addressed throughout the volume. Again, the purpose of the book is not to propose one answer to these matters. It is to see how and why they arise naturally within reflection on the moral thought and practices of the religions. Lastly, given the diversity of languages used in this volume, we have followed standard scholarly conventions for the transliteration of terms (e.g. Kṛṣṇa; Qur'ān). A list of the most commonly used terms and their standardized English forms is appended to the volume.

Mindful of these concerns now found in scholarly work and, more importantly, among peoples around the world, *The Blackwell Companion to Religious Ethics* seeks most basically to aid in understanding and assessing the moral beliefs, values, and practices of the world's religions. As the work of renowned scholars, it is our deepest intention that this work will help to define the tasks and purposes of the developing field of "religious ethics."

William Schweiker
Chicago

Acknowledgments

I would like to thank several people without whom *The Blackwell Companion to Religious Ethics* would not have been conceived or completed. At the early stages of imagining the project I was greatly aided by the insight of several people, including Lee Yearley, Frank Reynolds, Robin Lovin, and especially Charles Hallisey. As the labor of this volume unfolded – all too slowly I admit – I was greatly aided by the work of assistants Joyce Shin, Kevin Jung, Michael Johnson, Elizabeth Bucar, and Jamie Schillinger and also my secretary, Sandra Crane. All of this assistance would not have been possible without the support of the University of Chicago Divinity School. A special word of gratitude is due Rebecca Harkin of Blackwell Publishing for her wide capacity of mind and also constant encouragement of the project.

Of course, this book would not have been possible without the untold hours of labor and sheer brilliance of the authors whose work is presented here. During the production of such a work, many changes occur in the lives of authors. Most sadly, Professor Jef Van Gerwen died unexpectedly in 2002. He was mourned by many, including the contributors to this Companion. An "In memoriam" by Johan Verstraeten was published in *Ethische Perspectieven* (2002).

Finally, my deepest gratitude goes to David Clairmont, my assistant throughout this project, for his incredible diligence, good humor, capacious mind, and scholarly insight.

William Schweiker

On Religious Ethics

William Schweiker

The publication of this Companion represents a defining moment for religious ethics. Ethicists, historians of religion, theologians, philosophers, political theorists, and other experts have explored the moral outlooks and practices of the world's religions. Drawing on and revising religious resources, basic themes in moral theory as well as a host of contemporary moral and political problems are treated. Given the comprehensive nature of this volume, the purpose of the present chapter is not to provide a detailed "introduction" to the book. Such an introduction is not possible given the sheer size of this volume and insofar as this is a collective work rather than a single line of argument. A few words about the book's structure can be found in the preface. This chapter is meant to provide orientation to the range of questions and kinds of thinking found in the various parts of *The Blackwell Companion to Religious Ethics*.

Religious Ethics?

Anyone who works in religious ethics confronts an immediate and obvious problem. "Ethics" or "moral philosophy" is not indigenous to the world's religions. Inspired by Socrates and other sages, Greek and Roman thinkers engaged in the rational analysis and justification of norms, practices, forms of character, and ways of life believed to secure human happiness or well-being (*eudaimonia*). The inspiration of Socrates, and the memory of his conviction and execution on the charge of impiety, meant that ethics was also a challenge to the authority of religious beliefs. What is more, the conception of a good human life advocated by Hellenistic philosophers is foreign to the religions. Religious traditions obviously sustain reflection on human well-being, happiness. However, these accounts are set within an order defined by beings, realms, ideals, purposes, and practices not limited to human life and happiness. The scope of concern found in the world's religions is thereby wider than the discourse of ethics and Hellenistic ideas about human well-being. It is quite unremarkable, then, that the world's religions have generally not used the idea of ethics to specify the character of their outlooks on what defines a good life, right conduct, and proper social relations.

Similar problems surround the idea of "religion." None of the historical legacies explored in this Companion initially defined themselves as a religion. The term seems to have arisen from the Latin *religare*, meaning to tie or to bind. Religion specified how one was bound to the origins of the city of Rome as itself a sacred reality. Other ideas of religion developed, especially during the seventeenth to twentieth centuries, in order to facilitate the study of the beliefs, practices, values, and histories of human communities. Definitions range from religion as belief in gods or one God, claims about sacred power, ultimate concern, to the charge that religion is about concealed mechanisms of domination. Most scholars agree that a religion includes several features: convictions about what is most important in life (experiences like birth and death, sex and sorrow), ritual actions, beliefs about the whence and whither of existence, codes of conduct, communal life, and also experiences of transcendence (e.g., enlightenment, redemption, mystical insight). However, these features of religion are disputed and bear different meanings in cultures and traditions.

The idea of "religion," just like "ethics," is a scholarly invention. As rightly noted in the various parts of this volume, these ideas are not native to traditions, much less necessary categories of the human mind. They are tools for inquiry and reflection. What is more, one must keep distinct, if sometimes related, the morality or ethic of a religion (the actual ways of life, beliefs, values, norms, and outlooks of a people) from the intellectual labor of scholars and thinkers called "religious ethics." What is sought in this volume and this chapter is an account of the intellectual enterprise of religious ethics mindful of complex connections to ways of religious and moral living.

Given the conceptual problems surrounding religion and ethics, it is not surprising that one finds different options in the intellectual pursuit of religious ethics. Some distinct approaches have typified the field, although there are manifold subtypes and variations (see Part I; also Schweiker 1998; Twiss and Grelle 1998: 11–33). First, some religious ethicists have sought to specify a unique concept, phenomenon, rational structure, or set of practices called religion more or less manifest in what are conventionally seen as the "religions." Often called the *formalist* approach to religious ethics, the task is to show the place and import of religion for the moral life (see Green 1978; Gamwell 1990). Others adopt, second, a *sociolinguistic* approach. These thinkers explore specific action guides recommended by communities and/or how communities specify through ritual, myth, discourse, and belief often incommensurable ways of life (see Little and Twiss 1978; Stout 1988). Third, there are scholars who develop versions of *ethical naturalism*. This approach is concerned with the particularity of moral outlooks, but also "treats a system of beliefs as a whole and refuses to isolate moral propositions for analysis from propositions about how things are in the world and how they come to be that way" (Lovin and Reynolds 1985: 3). Each of these approaches in religious ethics, as well as various permutations on them, can be found in this book. No attempt, thankfully, has been made to demand agreement among them.

Another way of conceiving religious ethics is now coming into view and also finds expression throughout this Companion. The remainder of this chapter gives an account of this emerging *hermeneutical* and *multidimensional* option alongside other approaches to the field. Like formalists, a multidimensional approach specifies a structure for ethical thinking necessary to examine specific traditions, but is not reducible to their distinctive languages and practices. Yet, as shown below, it moves beyond most formalist proposals in terms of how knowledge and disciplines are conceived. With the sociolinguistic and naturalistic options, a hermeneutical approach to religious ethics examines the distinctive outlooks of traditions. However, precisely as hermeneutical in character, religious ethics labors between and among traditions rather than focuses on the incommensurability of language-games, distinct action guides, or even moral worldviews. "Religious ethics," on this new account, is defined in terms of critical, comparative, and constructive *tasks* of moral inquiry into religious resources undertaken from a hermeneutical *standpoint* and with respect to interlocking *dimensions* of reflection. My contention is that this account captures something of the scope and spirit of this book.

Of course, it must be immediately stressed that what follows is a *proposal* for religious ethics, developed in view of this volume. There is no assumption that every author will agree or even ought to agree with this depiction or, for that matter, any other depiction of religious ethics. As a field of inquiry, part of the vitality of religious ethics is precisely that it must constantly engage in appraisals of its purposes, methods, and criteria of adequacy. In fact, this Companion must partly be seen as engaged in that kind of appraisal.

We turn next to the question of how to characterize the *tasks* and *dimensions* of religious ethics in order that the full import of this volume can be grasped.

Tasks and Multidimensional Inquiry

There are many ways to define ethics and also many ways to carry out ethical reflection. Contemporary scholarship in religious ethics undertakes to a greater or lesser extent several related *tasks*. Religious ethics entails the *critical* inquiry into complex ways of religious and moral life, but often also indicates the *constructive* use of religious sources in meeting current problems. Each of those tasks, the critical and constructive, is usually bound to the work of *comparison*. As found in Part II, a scholar critically explores a tradition by comparing its expressions through time and/or seeing it in relation to other cultural and social dynamics, including other religions. Constructive work, like that undertaken in Part III, compares accounts of how to live with other proposals in order to assess duties and values binding on people. The question – explored in Part I – becomes: how ought we to define religious ethics as a discipline, an intellectual practice?

With the rise of the modern Western world there were extensive debates about what constituted a discipline of thought. There emerged the conviction that any genuine discipline must have a distinct subject matter, even as there was the need to define a "system of the sciences" around a fundamental principle or scientific method in order to ensure the coherence of knowledge. The core of the modern project was to understand the world and free human beings from ignorance and illusion. One did so by specifying the method, purpose, and criteria of various disciplines in such a way that each was *autonomous* and yet consistent with all others because they shared a *rational* structure. As Stephen Toulmin has noted: "In the underlying European worldview, then, the value of a single all-embracing system of theories, into which phenomena of all kinds could eventually be fitted, was taken for granted right up until the twentieth century" (Toulmin 2001: 87). Ethics, for instance, had to be about a distinctive domain of human conduct, say, about obligation or utility, which was different than other sciences, and yet founded rationally or empirically in the same way as other sciences. This led to the radical distinction between ethics as a *normative* discipline and other *descriptive* approaches to human behavior. One finds, interestingly enough, residues of this modern outlook in formalistic approaches to religious ethics. Even those who reject the modern enterprise, from the Romantics to some sociolinguistic thinkers and ethical naturalists, assume that definition of a discipline only to deny it. They contest the modern account through ad hoc or unsystematic approaches to inquiry.

This book aptly shows that the aspiration to isolate one formal structure of reason built on a single principle or to specify one scientific method as alone adequate for research is insufficient given genuine moral, religious, and cognitive diversity. Still, as formalists have long seen, there is also the need to define and characterize the discipline of religious ethics as an intellectual pursuit. Further, the modernist desire to establish the autonomy of ethics around some *sui generis* dimension at action (e.g., the ought) fails to indicate how moral reflection can and must interact with other intellectual practices in order to address exceedingly complex problems and phenomena. A crucial aspiration of much contemporary discourse is to move beyond the formal rationalism of the modern project, as well as its denial by Romantics and others. It is to grasp a more humane, practical form of reasonableness. Yet in order to be apt for religious ethics, this construal of ethics must also, as naturalists and sociolinguistic approaches show, explore the connections among "moral" beliefs and actions and other convictions and practices of actual living communities.

There is an important new turn in providing an account of knowledge that bears promise for religious ethics. This is what I have called *multidimensional* thinking. What is rejected by a range of thinkers in various fields is a depiction of knowledge gained and justified through autonomous disciplines tenuously held together by one formal rational structure or method of inquiry. As Mary Midgley has astutely noted:

> We exist, in fact, as interdependent parts of a complex network, not as isolated items that must be supported in a void. As for our knowledge, it too is a network involving all kinds of lateral links, a system in which the most varied kinds of connection may be relevant for helping us to meet various kinds of questions. (Midgley 2003: 25)

In this light, the burden placed on any intellectual practice aimed at knowledge is to specify those points at which it is linked to other disciplines given shared interests. Knowledge is a complex, reflexive network; it is a space of warranted intelligibility or reasonability. This depiction of knowledge is important not just for addressing shared interests. It is basic to the determination of the cogency, scope, and integrity of a discipline. Rather than focusing on the *autonomy* of a "discipline," one will be interested in the *lateral links* wherein reflection and information move in and out of an intellectual practice (see Gustafson 2004). *Scope*, rather than *autonomy*, will be essential in deciding the validity of claims. Accordingly, a discipline is best defined in terms of the basic questions it seeks to answer. When carefully examined these basic questions naturally pose other questions that, if answered, implicate a form of reflection in other modes of inquiry pursuing their own questions. A method must be devised not on one formal model but in order to match the problems and questions that need answering.

A multidimensional account of inquiry seems particularly apt for religious ethics. In very different ways, what scholars call the religions provide guidance for human living through rituals, myths, exemplars, doctrines, and teachings that answer a range of questions surrounding human existence. These questions demarcate a space of human existence determined by the problem of how one ought to live religiously – say, live as a Protestant Christian or a Tibetan Buddhist. "Morality," the religious ethicist can insist, is a term for the space or network of questions within which human life transpires and the answers a community gives to those questions in order to shape character and guide conduct. From the perspective of actual traditions, religious ethics must be conceived as examining various features of how the moral space of life is conceived and enacted in life. Viewed as a whole, this book can be seen to enact just this kind of examination of religious moralities.

If one takes seriously recurring questions found in the legacies of religions and formulates them at an appropriate level of generality, it is possible to adduce the multidimensional shape of religious ethics (see Schweiker 1995). At least five deeply interrelated questions ground the dimensions of inquiry used to engage in its comparative, critical, and constructive tasks. These questions are not related in a sequential or deductive manner; they are not a check-list to be applied to thinkers, texts, or practices. They constitute the interacting "dimensions" of ethics that aim to explicate a religion's account of and directions for orienting existence and conduct in the moral space of life. And insofar as religions use stories, rituals, and exemplary characters in order to guide life, these dimensions explicate and analyze the moral meaning of these phenomena. Further, the dimensions are important for the reader of this volume to understand what questions a scholar is answering, even as the religious ethicist is held accountable for questions not answered but which are in the background of a religious outlook.

This account of moral inquiry articulates an approach for religious ethics that labors alongside *formalists* and those working *sociolinguistically* and *naturalistically* with religious traditions and communities. The account admits with formalists that a construal of "ethics" is an intellectual construct, but it denies that one dimension alone defines "ethics" and it specifies, like the other approaches, questions and answers of ethics from within the resources of real traditions. In this way religious ethics escapes the modernist reduction of a discipline to one rational principle or method, while also avoiding relativistic forms of postmodernism. What, then, are the multiple and interacting dimensions of inquiry that represent a new option for religious ethics and can provide orientation for reading this volume?

The descriptive dimension

Human beings live and act in specific places, times, and sets of relations. How a situation is described and defined has implications for the possibilities and limits on actions and relations. In its widest compass, some construal is given of the moral context of the entirety of human life, often enough through myths, ideologies, or a moral world-view. Specific moral situations will be described and defined with reference to the wider outlook. So when, for example, a Buddhist practitioner must decide in a situation what to do, there is the need to answer a basic question, "what is going on?" This is a diffi-cult question not only because of the complexity of any situation, its openness to mul-tiple interpretations, and the limitations of human perception and attention. The question is rendered all the more difficult because someone (authority figure, practi-tioner) must sort out what reality or perspective on reality is at issue, one marked by conventional truth or one rooted in *Dharma*. A devout Muslim too must determine "what is going on" in a specific situation. This requires not only a description of that case, but also knowledge of how Allāh is acting, the import of *Sharī'a*, and also specific reasoning skills.

While each tradition provides answers to the question "what is going on?" they do so in wildly complex and different ways. Ethics has a *descriptive* dimension that is linked to other interpretive disciplines, ranging from studies of myth to specific analyses of events and situations that provide ways to construe and understand moral situations. Religious ethics draws on a range of resources, experiences, types of discernment, and even beliefs about reality. These resources provide the means to describe and analyze a situation in terms of its moral meaning.

The normative dimension

Deciding "what is going on" in any concrete situation is never a disinterested activity. The descriptive dimension of ethics is necessarily related to some norms and values that orient thinking and action. These norms and values allow some realities to appear within moral perception; they also can conceal. Christian ideas about neighbor love, for instance, might allow a perception of human worth and vulnerability even for those deemed enemies. This depends, of course, on how neighbor and love are normatively understood. "What norms and values ought to guide human life?" That too seems to be a basic question asked repeatedly in the legacies of religious traditions. A religious ethics has a *normative* dimension.

A bewildering diversity is found among the religions on the normative question. In many traditions there are distinct and sometimes conflicting *sources* for defining what norms and values ought to guide life. One source is the native intelligence of human beings struggling to live together; it is reason. The other source is the ultimate binding claims and teachings, the revelation, of the community. Consider aspects of Jewish thought. Rooted in the so-called Noahide covenant, Jewish thinkers have long insisted that every person can at some level grasp moral principles. Yet, for the Jewish commu-nity, this knowledge is rudimentary in light of the revelation of the divine will in Torah. Not surprisingly, there are debates within religious traditions about the relative author-ity of the various *sources* of norms and values and how these ought to relate in living religiously. The sources drawn upon in moral thinking also link to other intellectual practices, especially ones interested in human valuing, social norms and goods, and debates about moral intelligence.

Disputes about the sources of moral norms and values also turn on the *content* of and *relations* among norms and values. Generally speaking, religious traditions acknowledge and seek to sustain a range of goods, like bodily integrity, family, education, art, and, at the highest level, moral excellence and righteousness (see Finnis 1983; Nussbaum 2000). How these goods are understood differs between traditions and even within a tradition; they constitute another link to disciplines, from economics to anthropology, which explore basic goods. Classical Hindu accounts of caste show, for example, that the meaning of bodily integrity shifts between the warrior caste (Kṣatriyas) and the priestly caste (Brahmans). Nevertheless, some domain of goods or values is protected and promoted by living morally. There are also debates about the norms for deciding how to respect and enhance goods. African beliefs about what is owed ancestors as the norm for human choice are decidedly different than, say, the Ten Commandments in the Hebrew and Christian Bibles. In each case, norms protect and promote goods within religious living.

Normative and descriptive dimensions of inquiry are reflexively related at the level of perception and decision making. They link ethics to other ways of articulating, describing, and valuing human actions and relations. Adducing these dimensions from widespread questions in no way blinds us to the stark differences between and within traditions. Attention to these dimensions facilitates critical, comparative, and constructive work.

The practical dimension

When people ask about what is going on and what are the norms and values that ought to orient their living, they do so for practical rather than merely theoretical reasons. While the ethicist or religious thinker will develop complex epistemological theories or debate the nature of value and the validity of some conception of a norm, this is not the concern of most people. As the Bhagavad Gītā opens Arjuna, standing beside Kṛṣṇa, watches a bloody battle unfold between members of his family. Should he join the battle? In the struggle of decision, a host of forces might be active, the advice of a god (Kṛṣṇa), duties bound to class or social role, bonds of love. Here too is a basic question: "what ought I or we to do?"

Religious ethics has a decidedly *practical* dimension, no matter how theoretical and speculative moral inquiry becomes. It is related to other disciplines that focus on decision making and judgment. Little wonder that so many religions link their ethics to law as well as the demand to imitate moral saints or to participate in practices of divination or study and commentary. Traditions develop complex and subtle patterns of moral reasoning in order to answer the practical questions of life. Confucian teachings about how to live the scholarly life are decidedly different than Jewish patterns of Halakhic reasoning. Each is, nevertheless, a response to the practical question "what ought I or we to do?" Of course, it might be illuminating to explore how Halakhah throws light on Confucian practices of moral reasoning and vice versa. Comparison is always possible in religious ethics.

It is also clear that this "I" is never some kind of isolated and ghostly being, but someone in relation to others. What I ought to do is related to what we ought to do. While certain traditions have emphasized a radical individualism in moral action, by and large there is profound awareness that moral quandaries find people amid others. Therewith develop patterns of communal reasoning and judgment; that is, the formation of a political ethics. The point is that some form of practical reasoning and judgment will be found. The work of scholars in other fields (law, social analysis, rhetoric) can aid the religious ethicist. Noting the practical dimension of ethics facilitates, rather than delimits, critical, comparative, and constructive thinking.

The fundamental dimension

Insofar as individuals and communities confront questions about how to orient life, something is asserted about the moral structure of reality and human beings as creatures with the power to act and choose in concert with others and thereby influence reality, themselves, and others. Human beings can be and ought to be aware of themselves in relations to others, the context of life, and with respect to norms and values about how rightly to live. Any ethics aims, thereby, to answer a question seemingly presupposed in other moral questions: "what does it mean to be a moral agent within the wider compass of reality?" From philosophy to neuroscience, religious ethics is linked with others fields of inquiry into human being and doing and the very nature of reality.

Religions present fantastically complex accounts of agency and the moral context of life. This is what is meant by a *fundamental* dimension of ethics. A good deal of modern Western ethics defined an "agent" as a being with reason and will who can act intentionally, bring about changes in reality, others, and the agent's self, and have accountability for actions imputed and/or ascribed to him or her (see Gewirth 1978). The scope of the moral world is determined by the interactions, cooperatively or not, among these agents. Each of the defining attributes of agency has of course been hotly debated. What do we mean by reason or will or intentionality or accountability or moral ascription? How do we best understand the formation of moral character, say through the virtues? There has been reflection on the limitations of agency, the nature of corporate agency, and questions about moral self-understanding.

Work in religious ethics is challenging and amending modern Western conceptions of agency by attending to non-human powers and also the wider realms of reality. In the Christian tradition, what it means to be an agent is defined not only in terms of the power to act and to be held accountable. It is also defined by patterns of relation in which the self exists in God and in others through faith and love before God's kingdom. Further, faith and love are understood with reference to the divine activity, and this means, paradoxically, that at least two agents, the human and the divine, act in any genuinely good action. Sin, or a broken relation to God and others, is marked not just by wrong acts, but, more profoundly, by an estrangement in which one must act alone and for one's own purposes and good. God's judgment on sin is really the withdrawal of the divine presence such that the agent is left to his or her own devices. In traditional African ethics what it means to be an agent is rendered complex by the fact that the ancestors are operative forces in the world. This is also why, as noted above, practical and normative issues in Buddhism hinge in part on the distinction between conventional and Dharmic truth and so on a distinction between "self" and "person." Insofar as the root problem is craving that gives rise to suffering, one can only speak of an agent or person through conventional terms. In the light of the teachings of the Buddha, ultimately, there is no-self.

In the religions, forces other than self, insofar as we can speak of a self, are at work in the world and in the individual. Each of the religious traditions, furthermore, examines complex psychological and sociological mechanisms that lead to moral failure, delusion, and conflict – mechanisms like inordinate craving (Buddhism), distorted loves (Christianity), ritual impurity (Hinduism), violation of ancestral bonds (African and Native-American ethics), and systemic, social distortion. An agent is set amid forces that must be considered in attaining valid understanding. Inquiry into what it means to be an agent within these rich accounts of moral reality is the fundamental dimension of religious ethics simply because these ideas are presupposed in all other moral questions.

The metaethical dimension

If one looks at the legacies of religion, there seems to be one further general question that helps to constitute the shape of religious ethics. The Buddha insisted that anyone could test the truth of his teaching in actual life. Jesus is reported to have said, "I am the way, the truth, and the life." Hindu ways of life claim to accord with the truth about the cosmos and also the specific tenor and form of individual life. Muslims believe that the Qur'ān gives the final and ultimate revelation of the will of God. Every religion, despite what modern critics hold, purports to be truth seeking. Communities and traditions implicitly pose the question and provide some account of the truth of their morality, their picture of how to orient existence in the moral space of life. Of course, claims to truth differ and so too the means for showing their validity (experience, teaching, revelation, etc.). To enter into this kind of reflection is to engage in what is often called, somewhat unhappily, "metaethics." Reflection centers on clarifying moral concepts, strategies of validating claims, and forming judgments about the relative weight the evidence and interpretations from other fields of inquiry can and ought to have in guiding life. The question of validity or truth is posed from within the religions. This too is a dimension of religious ethics.

The question of the truth of a moral outlook is without doubt one of the most vexing issues for religious ethics. While the ethicist might explore dimensions of a tradition's morality, how does one judge the truth of an entire religion? On one level, the religious ethicist can address this question comparatively and critically. In Part II of this volume, readers will see scholars examine the ways in which one or several traditions go about showing the truth of their moral beliefs and practices. Further, if the religious ethicist is working within a specific tradition, say, Shī'ite Islam or Zen Buddhism, then, presumably, its strategies of validation will be in play, a matter also explored in parts of this Companion. When the ethical task is to speak critically, comparatively, and constructively across traditions about shared human problems, matters become pressing. It poses a question implied in the very undertaking of religious ethics: from what *standpoint* is inquiry carried out and what criteria of adequacy pertain to its work?

Hermeneutical Standpoint

The *dimensions* of inquiry gleaned from persistent questions aim to provide a coherent way to undertake, singularly or together, the comparative, critical, and constructive *tasks* of religious ethics. They also signal the kinds of questions engaged by scholars represented in every part of this book. Moral knowledge is thereby depicted as a network of intelligibility, a space of reasons, about how rightly to orient life that is held and enacted by some tradition or community and examined by the scholar through multidimensional reflection. The religious ethicist might also make constructive claims about how rightly to live. This is, again, a proposal for religious ethics that is responsive to the complexity of the "religions" and also to shifts in the way knowledge and disciplines are conceived. The account of the scholarly labor of religious ethics does not prejudice one set of moral beliefs over another, say Confucian over African; nor does it specify only one kind of ethics, say virtue ethics, as best for a normative understanding of the religions and meeting present day challenges. It is an inductively developed *method* for, or *approach* to, religious ethics. Working alongside other options in the field, this proposal is, hopefully, subtle enough to facilitate the examination of the moral outlooks and practices of the world's religions. Through its dimensions, religious ethics interacts with many fields of inquiry.

We have been led to the thorny question of the standpoint and criteria of religious ethics. For those who take a *formalist* approach, the contention is that despite empirical differences among religions one can discern or articulate philosophically a basic structure shared by the religions that facilitates critical, comparative, and constructive work. One seeks to develop an ethics outside of substantive connections to any tradition or the surrounding life-world (see Benhabib 1992). The criterion of adequacy must be determined with respect to moral rationality itself or through a metaphysical vision. Those who pursue a *sociolinguistic* approach in the discipline insist that the sheer diversity among religions and cultures means that material differences rather than formal similarities must be basic to method in religious ethics. Moral rationality, on this account, is tradition-constituted rationality (see MacIntyre 1990). The means to validate a position are internal to a tradition or they emerge at the intersection of competing traditions. *Ethical naturalists*, for their part, insist that norms and values must be grasped and evaluated in terms of their place in a whole outlook on life. The standpoint of the religious ethicist, thereby, is to engage in the examination of a community's moral worldview even while acknowledging the substantive outlook that backs her or his inquiry.

Shifts in how to describe knowledge enable one to conceptualize religious ethics in a new way. Similarly, there are developments afoot that demand a standpoint in religious ethics somewhat different than other approaches in the field. While the method of religious ethics is aptly described as multidimensional, its standpoint can also be conceived as fully *hermeneutical* in character conjoined to specific criteria of adequacy. The importance of this standpoint is found in the moral significance of recent global developments which parallel shifts in the construal of knowledge.

Recent developments

Developments that characterize the present age warrant a hermeneutical standpoint in religious ethics. These recent developments, and others too, are charted throughout this volume. A prominent one is the growing awareness around the world of the diversity of religious and moral beliefs, practices, and convictions. A good deal of modern moral theory seemed to efface the particularity of outlooks from a concern to isolate general features of human existence deemed of universal ethical relevance. The need nowadays is to understand and to explain the moral vision of communities and cultures on their own terms without an initial judgment of truth or goodness. This requires interpretive engagement with the forms of thought, types of texts, practices, rituals, and organization of religions and societies.

The present awareness of global diversity has spawned the critical and comparative tasks of religious ethics, both in formulating more adequate categories of thought (Part I) and by exploring the legacies of traditions (Part II). However, understanding beliefs and practices, no matter how critical that might be, is not the same as justifying them, determining their truth. In a world in which the religions too often and too readily sanction violence and hatred of others, neglect or denigration of the environment, and also back excessive preoccupation with one's religious condition, judgments about what counts as a valid policy for living are required. Present worries about moral diversity provoke inquiry into how one is to establish norms that transcend particular systems of authority in order to address shared human concerns (Part III). This seems to require that the standpoint of religious ethics neither be so formal as to efface differences nor so historically particularistic that normative judgment across moralities becomes impossible.

The awareness of diversity is just one development in the current situation that challenges how one conceives of the standpoint of religious ethics. The age of "globality," as it is called, is marked by multiple forms of reflexivity, ranging from economic processes to cultural and informational flows (see Schweiker 2004). Reflexivity is the ability of an acting entity to respond to information coming from elsewhere and to adjust its actions in this light. Human persons can respond to recommendations and judgments on their actions, say, from others, a sage, moral saint, or a god, and then seek to live and act better. Increasingly, one is aware of the ways in which social systems, cultures, and religious traditions are, analogically, reflexive or learning beings. Global reflexivity works through economic, cultural, imaginary, and legal mechanisms shaping human and non-human life.

The reflexive dynamic of global flows has brought with it new and unexpected developments. During the twentieth century, many scholars of religion defined their work in terms of secularism. The modern world was supposedly a time in which all ideas and experiences of religion or transcendence or the sacred were being effaced by the pressure of differentiated social structures and the march of science to demystify the world.

Similarly, the legacies of colonialism demanded that peoples around the world adjust their lives and cultures to the secular order (see Appadurai 1996). Throughout this Companion, and especially Part II, one can trace the ways religious traditions have responded to secularism, colonialism, and modernism.

The dawn of the secular world never really came, or it only appeared in faint glimmers. The present age is characterized by nothing so much as the force and movement of the religions on the global scene. Global reflexivity, the ways in which communities appear in the "gaze of the other," is of great moral import. One can witness the transformation of traditions in and through interactions with and resistance to other global forces, including other religious traditions, rather than the pressure of secularization. This also seems to require a hermeneutical standpoint in religious ethics insofar as hermeneutics examines the dynamics of human understanding through encounters with divergent claims to meaning, encounters in which transformation as well as conflict is possible.

The awareness and worries about moral diversity and global reflexivity arising out of the contours of the emerging age are deeply intertwined with shifts in moral sensibilities. These shifts in sensibility, examined especially in Parts I and III, are other developments which impinge on the standpoint of religious ethics. The modern world saw the apotheosis of human power in technology, political organization, the media, and economic systems, and with these developments an exclusive concentration on human flourishing. Ironically, modern anthropocentrism turned against itself. Holocausts, genocides, terrorism, grinding poverty, and horrific wars scarred the twentieth century and now too the twenty-first century. Massive suffering and violence have sparked deeper sensitivity to the vulnerability and preciousness of persons (see Gaita 2000; Glover 2000). Conjointly, there is growing awareness of the interdependence of life on this planet. People around the world are imaging the scope of moral value to include but also to exceed human well-being. This ecological sensibility has challenged longstanding beliefs about moral value and standing. In various ways, moral sensibilities for the worth of all realms of life are spreading around the world. This is sorely needed insofar as the religions continue to take violent expression and to foster ignorance and the neglect of finite, planetary resources. Emerging sensibilities can and must aid in the transformation of the traditions that spawn but also thwart moral aspirations.

The realities of moral diversity, global reflexivity, and emerging moral sensibilities are obviously interrelated developments. Taken together, these demarcate some of the contours of the current moral space of life. In order to understand and respond to them, religious ethics must carry out critical, comparative, and constructive work. Because of the deeply interrelated nature of current dynamics, religious ethics obviously needs to be defined beyond modern conceptions of what constitutes a discipline or intellectual practice. Furthermore, something important is at stake in an account of an ethical standpoint once the reflexive dynamics of cultural interactions amid human diversity in global times is seriously considered. The religious ethicist does not simply exist within or outside actual traditions. She or he is always thinking at the *lateral connections* among communities, traditions, and intellectual practices. What does this fact mean for the standpoint of religious ethics?

Standpoint and criteria

In order to specify the standpoint of religious ethics in the light of current global developments, one can reclaim terminology from the Hellenistic world that arose within its religious and cultural imagination *prior* to the development of "ethics." The standpoint of religious ethics is *hermeneutical*. Derived from the Greek god Hermes, hermeneutics is reflection on the possibilities and limits of understanding ambiguous meanings won through the act of interpretation and thereby how meanings are conveyed from one realm to another. In the Homeric texts, the virtual sacred literature of that culture, Hermes conveyed meanings from the gods to mortals. Other religions, as found in this volume, explore the conveyance of meanings across boundaries in revelations, divinizations, rituals, exegetical strategies, and mystical insights.

The point is not to reclaim Greek ideas in order to define the standpoint of religious ethics. The insight is that religious ethics conceived as a hermeneutical enterprise moves between traditions or among expressions of one tradition, seeking understanding and orientation. No doubt that movement will always be marked by the ethicist's "home tradition," religious or secular. One remains a Chinese or Japanese Buddhist religious ethicist or an African Christian or a postmodern European Aristotelian. No one (thankfully) must necessarily sacrifice their identity for the sake of undertaking religious ethics. Yet the standpoint, the posture of thinking, takes place at the reflexive connections of traditions and other forces working in the world. The religious ethicist on this picture enacts the lateral links among the dimensions of ethics and other forms of inquiry into the moral beliefs and practices of the religions. In the process some degree of knowledge and understanding is attained, a shared world of meaning is partly disclosed, even as identities can be confirmed or tentatively transformed. The religious ethicist participates in the enacting of a complex network of moral knowledge, never complete yet nonetheless attained. This hermeneutic action is achieved by undertaking the adventure of thought signified through the various dimensions of religious ethics.

How then are we to judge the work of a religious ethicist? This is a question hotly debated in the pages of this Companion, particularly in Part I. Generally stated, two *criteria* bear on a hermeneutical standpoint in ethics. First, any adequate ethical claim, whether about the beliefs and practices of a specific tradition or a proposal for meeting a current moral problem, must prove its great adequacy to relevant material in argumentative exchange. A position is truer than some other insofar as it answers more comprehensively and coherently the range of questions specified in the dimensions of ethics. It must, accordingly, meet demands entailed in the act of multidimensional inquiry, as well as be error reducing with respect to rival positions or interpretations (see Taylor 1990). Again, scope rather than autonomy is basic to the adequacy of an ethics. This is a *procedural* criterion. It means that a religious ethics is never justified prior to lively engagement with other positions. Additionally, a position must afford some advance in thinking by provoking or providing deeper insight into a moral problem or way of life. This second *heuristic* criterion is more illusive than the procedural one. What counts as insight, let alone "deeper" insight? Nevertheless, a moral position can claim greater adequacy, greater truth, if it enables one to apprehend, understand, and respond to factors really pressing on human lives but missed by other moral positions. *Heuristic* and *procedural* criteria are applicable to the scholarly labor of criticism and comparison as well as to constructive ethics.

There are good reasons within the religions as well as those found in global dynamics to adopt a hermeneutic standpoint in moral inquiry. The religious ethicist can isolate and articulate these various reasons as backing for her or his work. Abiding by the criteria of a hermeneutical standpoint within multidimensional inquiry, religious ethics can, but need not, aid in the reconstruction of religious identities around criteria of ethical truth, rather than subjecting the question of truth to communal identity. In this way, a thinker critically and comparatively releases the resources of traditions and communities for constructive thought about how rightly to orient human life.

Conclusion

This chapter has sought to address terminological, methodological, and also criteriological issues within the ongoing work of religious ethics. It has sketched an approach to the discipline working alongside others in terms of *tasks*, *dimensions*, and *standpoint*. This proposal is meant to aid the reader in exploring the richness of the thought represented in this volume, as well as to outline a new possibility for religious ethics itself. One should not expect all scholars represented here to use this proposal, nor is that needed. As noted before, part of the vitality of the field is to keep constantly in play the appraisal of its work and adequacy. Yet by enlisting a vast range of renowned scholars from various disciplines, traditions, and cultures, the labor of religious ethics now crosses disciplinary boundaries that have for too long inhibited its development. *The Blackwell Companion to Religious Ethics* presents an exciting vision of moral inquiry engaged with the fantastic resources of the world's religions, open to other fields of reflection on the human adventure, and dedicated to understanding and addressing moral challenges and possibilities emergent in our global times.

Bibliography

Appadurai, Arjun. 1996: *Modernity at Large: Cultural Dimensions of Globalization*. Minneapolis: University of Minnesota Press.

Benhabib, Seyla. 1992: *Situating the Self: Gender, Community, and Postmodernism in Contemporary Ethics*. New York: Routledge.

Finnis, John. 1983: *Fundamentals of Ethics*. Washington, DC: Georgetown University Press.

Gaita, Raymond. 2000: *A Common Humanity: Thinking About Love and Truth and Justice*. New York: Routledge.

Gamwell, Franklin I. 1990: *The Divine Good: Modern Moral Theory and the Necessity of God*. San Francisco: Harper San Francisco.

Gewirth, Alan. 1978: *Reason and Morality*. Chicago: University of Chicago Press.

Glover, Jonathan. 2000: *Humanity: A Moral History of the Twentieth Century*. New Haven, CT: Yale University Press.

Green, Ronald. 1978: *Religious Reason*. New York: Oxford University Press.

Gustafson, James M. 2004: *An Examined Faith: The Grace of Self-Doubt*. Minneapolis, MN: Fortress Press.

Little, David and Twiss, Sumner B. (eds.) 1978: *Comparative Religious Ethics*. New York: Harper & Row.

Lovin, Robin W. and Reynolds, Frank E. (eds.) 1985: *Cosmogony and Ethical Order: New Studies in Comparative Ethics*. Chicago: University of Chicago Press.

MacIntyre, Alasdair. 1990: *Three Rival Versions of Moral Enquiry: Encyclopaedia, Genealogy, and Tradition: Being Gifford Lectures Delivered in the University of Edinburgh in 1988*. Notre Dame, IN: University of Notre Dame Press.

Midgley, Mary. 2003: *The Myths We Live By*. New York: Routledge.

Nussbaum, Martha C. 2000: *Women and Human Development: The Capabilities Approach*. New York: Cambridge University Press.

Schweiker, William. 1995: *Responsibility and Christian Ethics*. Cambridge: Cambridge University Press.

—— 1998: *Power, Value and Conviction: Theological Ethics in the Postmodern Age*. Cleveland, OH: Pilgrim Press.

—— 2004: *Theological Ethics and Global Dynamics: In the Time of Many Worlds*. Oxford: Blackwell.

Stout, Jeffrey. 1988: *Ethics After Babel: The Languages of Morals and their Discontents*. Boston, MA: Beacon Press.

Taylor, Charles. 1990: *Sources of the Self: The Making of Modern Identity*. Cambridge, MA: Harvard University Press.

Toulmin, Stephen. 2001: *Return to Reason*. Cambridge, MA: Harvard University Press.

Twiss, Sumner B. and Grelle, Bruce. 1998: *Explorations in Global Ethics: Comparative Ethics and Interreligious Dialogue*. Boulder, CO: Westview Press.

PART I
Moral Inquiry

1 Reflection

CHAPTER 1

Moral Theories

Robin W. Lovin

Moral Life and Moral Theory

Every religious tradition offers guidance for living a moral life. At the most basic level, this guidance is simply woven into the fabric of observances, beliefs, and expectations that shape a way of life we identify as Hindu, or Christian, or Ibo, or Confucian. In most cases, traditions also give rise to teachers, prophets, and philosophers who provide a critical assessment of these everyday expectations. Aristotle (384–322 BCE) gave a systematic account of the virtues that were honored in Greek culture. The Hebrew prophets identified principles of justice and mercy that explained the requirements of the Law (Torah) and sometimes criticized the ways the Law was generally observed. Confucius (551–479 BCE), Lao Tzu (sixth or fourth century BCE), and Chuang Tzu (399–295 BCE) showed the right way to observe Chinese traditional virtues by relating them to the demands of social harmony or to the patterns of an underlying natural order. Such reflections may be called "moral philosophy." By identifying principles on which practices rest, these reflections systematize prevailing expectations, and they also provide a basis for criticizing and revising them. Most religions have had moral philosophy, in this general sense, for a very long time (Donagan 1977).

Modern moral theory, however, has a more comprehensive critical purpose. Moral theory is less about how to live a particular way and more about why we ought to be moral and what it means to say that a rule, an action, or an ideal is moral. Western philosophers, beginning in the seventeenth century with Descartes, Spinoza, Hobbes, and Locke, attempted to answer these critical questions by establishing the rational requirements for any sort of morality. A moral theory in this modern sense may also give rational arguments for specific moral commands and prohibitions. Some moral theorists begin with this normative task. Others concentrate first on the questions of moral authority and moral meaning. In either case, the theorist develops a comprehensive basis for explaining, comparing, and criticizing existing ways of life or systems of moral philosophy, including religious moralities. On the basis of the moral theory, the theorist can make judgments about whether the requirements a religion or a way of life imposes are morally justifiable. The theorist also appears to have in principle a powerful tool for comparative study by assessing diverse systems of belief and practice in light of the structure of morality that the theory provides. At the beginning of the modern period in Western thought, these theoretical tools were believed to hold great promise for adjudicating religious conflicts and settling disputes about morality (see chapter 16).

Moral Theory and Religion

The earliest use of moral theory in religious ethics, then, was by Western philosophers who used their theories for a critical evaluation of traditional Christian ethics. This theoretical assessment of prevailing moral traditions has been repeated, with important variations, by other philosophers in relation to other traditions around the world (Cho 1998). Extensive use of moral theory as a tool in the comparative study of religious ethics is a more recent development (Little and Twiss 1978).

The way that a modern moral theory can relate to a religious tradition is well illustrated by the work of Immanuel Kant (1724–1804). Kant based his moral theory on a *categorical imperative*, an exceptionless moral rule that requires us to act only on those reasons that we can also make into universal laws, governing the choices of others as well as our own. Thus, lying is morally wrong because we cannot rationally formulate a rule that would require it as a universal practice. We choose to tell a lie only by allowing ourselves an exception to a rule that we acknowledge in the very act of breaking it (Kant 1964).

Kant's moral theory overturned several understandings of the moral life that have been common in Western Christianity. A Kantian could not argue that God has implanted certain ends and purposes in human beings by nature, so that all people share certain moral aims. Desire for a goal, even if it is universally shared, does not explain why we are morally required to pursue it. Kant's theory thus disposes of a pattern of argument, based on the universal human desire for peace, or happiness, or blessedness, that Catholic Christian writers had learned early from Greek philosophy and built over the centuries into an elaborate theory of natural law, given special prominence in the work of Thomas Aquinas (1125–1274). Likewise, Kant calls into question the claim, more common among Protestant theologians, that we are obliged to obey God's commandments simply and solely because it is God who commands us. Even when God is the lawgiver, the rational person cannot accept the command as a *moral* law unless it meets the test Kant sets out in the categorical imperative (see chapter 21).

While there is little left of some religious ways of thinking about morality in Kant's moral theory, Kant preserved what many people regarded as central to the practice of Christian ethics. Other theories raised more radical questions about conventional moral expectations. Friedrich Nietzsche (1844–1900) devised a moral theory in which the basic principle is the development of a person's capacities for creativity and control over the circumstances of life, so that when we ask what we are required to do, the answer must be closely tied to the possibilities inherent in our individual personalities. When viewed from this theoretical perspective, many prevailing moral expectations and the religious beliefs that support them have no moral justification (Nietzsche 1998). In this case, the theory does not provide a rational basis for traditional moral requirements, but offers instead a moral justification for setting traditional morality aside. Nietzsche understood his task to be the destruction of traditional Christian morality, so that something new might arise in its place.

Varieties of Moral Theory

Kant and Nietzsche are two of the most important moral theorists in terms of their impact on religious thought, but they hardly exhaust the possibilities for moral theory. The study of moral theory in the West since the seventeenth century has produced a variety of competing accounts of the basic principle of morality, rather than a single, dominant theory. While all of the theories aim to provide a basis for ethics that is independent of existing moral beliefs and particular religious traditions, they establish that starting point for morality in different ways, and their assessments of religious beliefs and practices vary accordingly. In this section, we will briefly survey the main types of moral theory and consider the general implications of each for our thinking about religious ethics.

There is no universally accepted taxonomy of ethical theories, nor even any strict conventions about how to name them. Nevertheless, the main types of moral theory are generally recognized, and we can follow an outline that allows us to consider the implications of each for thinking about religious ethics. The terminology used here appears, with some modifications, elsewhere in this volume and more widely in the contemporary literature of philosophy and religious ethics.

We have already noted that moral theory has two basic tasks. The first is to make sense of the multitude of rules, proverbs, parables, tales of moral heroes, lists of virtues, and descriptions of moral ideals that guide the moral life as we are supposed to be living it. "Normative ethics" develops theories that systematize moral expectations and explain how a living moral tradition can be understood as a consistent system of moral requirements. The second task of moral theory is to explain why a certain kind of discourse is, or appears to be, uniquely authoritative for conduct. Why is it that when we use moral language, we make a claim on someone's behavior that is more demanding than when we recommend a restaurant or a movie? Why should we expect other people to concur in our moral judgments and act in ways that support the moral claim? Philosophers have given the study of these questions about the meaning and authority of moral language the name "metaethics." (The term is coined by analogy to "metaphysics," which inquires into the nature of reality, while physics systematizes the laws that govern how reality behaves.)

Metaethics and normative ethics, then, are two main divisions of ethical theory which answer rather different questions about the nature of moral claims in general and about the norms that guide specific moral choices. Each of these questions, in turn, has elicited a variety of answers that become the main types of ethical theory.

about facts (Hare 1952). Moral language expresses the commitments of persons and groups to ways of acting. It does not make sense to ask whether such a commitment is "true."

Non-cognitivist moral theories have proved most useful in thinking about ways of life that are radically separated by time and distance. It is not altogether plausible to say that two persons locked in a face-to-face moral dispute are not really making any claims about what is the case. By contrast, attempts to settle the differences between, say, the Aztec culture of warrior virtues and the European bourgeois values of individualism and moderation by assessing their views of human flourishing from some supposedly neutral standpoint often leave us with a sense of irrelevance (Williams 1985). The differences are just too great to think that they can be reduced to right or wrong ideas about some set of facts. We will understand them better, the non-cognitivist suggests, if we recognize that these alternative moral worlds are not built on views of the facts at all.

Non-cognitivism may seem an unpromising moral theory for religious ethics, useful primarily to those who reject religious claims to moral knowledge. Non-cognitivism does, however, offer a strong alternative to all forms of naturalism and rationalism for theologians who seek to build their moral systems directly on divine revelation. A religious thinker who finds no secure basis for morality in human experience and believes that obedience to God's command is what makes an action right or wrong will find an interesting ally in the non-cognitivist, who will at least join in demonstrating that none of the languages of morality actually make the universal claims about the world and our knowledge of it that they appear to be making at the outset.

Criticism of Moral Theories

Recent developments in philosophy have called into question the construction of moral theories. Critics suggest that a principle of morality cannot be isolated from the way of life in which it is embedded. Normative theories at their best are accounts of the central convictions that shape a particular way of life. Metaethics, however, is largely useless. The effort to build a general theory of morality, critics charge, distorts the religious and cultural systems to which the theory is applied, and the accounts which emerge reflect more of the theorist's own ideas than of real moral life.

In religious ethics, the criticism of moral theory has often been received as good news, freeing religious thinkers to explore a multitude of relationships between religious beliefs and moral practice, unconstrained by a rigid philosophical system that seeks a logic of morality independent of its practices (Stout 1981). Use of moral theory as a tool for comparative religious ethics has also been criticized for privileging a set of Western philosophical questions and then making these the basis for comparison (Cho 1998).

These criticisms are important, but they suggest caution in the use of moral theory, rather than an entire rejection of it. Several centuries of effort have failed to produce a general theory of morality that could function in the way that theory functions in the natural sciences. It would be a mistake to use a moral theory as a standard against which religious ethics could be measured, or as a system by which all religious ethics might be organized. The questions of moral theory do reflect the modern, Western philosophical context in which they emerged, and there are no doubt other questions in traditional religious thinking which are important to those traditions, and which the moral theory may miss entirely.

Nevertheless, the questions of moral theory are important, if only to those who have been trained by Western philosophy to ask them. To give up on the creation of an authoritative standpoint from which to view all possible traditions does not invalidate the more modest project of asking how different traditions look when we try to examine them carefully from our own partial point of view. Precisely because the moral life as lived does not come with a theory attached to it, the possibility of systematic comparisons between lived traditions will often depend on having some theory to guide the study (see chapter "on Religious Ethics"). The task, especially in comparative religious ethics, is to determine which theory least distorts the experience of persons in the tradition, while best enabling the investigator – from his or her own distinctive standpoint – to make meaningful connections between the traditions.

Bibliography

Cho, F. 1998: "Leaping into the Boundless: A Daoist Reading of Comparative Religious Ethics." *Journal of Religious Ethics* 26, 139–65.

Donagan, A. 1977: *The Theory of Morality*. Chicago: University of Chicago Press.

Gewirth, A. 1978: *Reason and Morality*. Chicago: University of Chicago Press.

Green, R. M. 1988: *Religion and Moral Reason: A New Method for Comparative Study*. New York: Oxford University Press.

Hare, R. M. 1952: *The Language of Morals*. Oxford: Oxford University Press.

Kant, I. 1960: *Religion Within the Limits of Reason Alone*, trans. T. M. Greene and H. H. Hudson. New York: Harper & Row.

—— 1964: *Groundwork of the Metaphysics of Morals*, trans. H. J. Paton. New York: Harper & Row.

Little, D. and Twiss, S. B. (eds.) 1978: *Comparative Religious Ethics: A New Method*. San Francisco: Harper & Row.

Lovin, Robin W. and Reynolds, Frank E. (eds.) 1985: *Cosmogony and Ethical Order: New Studies in Comparative Ethics*. Chicago: University of Chicago Press.

Nietzsche, F. 1998: *Beyond Good and Evil*, trans. M. Faber. New York: Oxford University Press.

Porter, J. 1999: *Natural and Divine Law: Reclaiming the Tradition for Christian Ethics*. Grand Rapids, MI: William B. Eerdmanns.

Stout, J. 1981: *The Flight from Authority*. Notre Dame, IN: University of Notre Dame Press.

Williams, B. 1985: *Ethics and the Limits of Philosophy*. Cambridge, MA: Harvard University Press.

CHAPTER 2

Moral Truth

Maria Antonaccio

Moral Truth and Moral Realism

All religions make moral claims that are considered binding on their adherents: claims about what moral beliefs to hold, what moral values to pursue, and what forms of moral character and conduct to cultivate. Insofar as a religious community embeds its moral claims within a larger vision of reality and human life and expects its members to conform their lives to that vision, some notion of "moral truth" seems to be presupposed in every such community. Religions differ, of course, in the content of what they regard as morally true and in their methods of validating or sanctioning their moral claims. And the scholar or moral theorist may regard the validity of a community's moral claims in quite different terms than its members do. But religious communities are implicitly "realistic" about their moral claims: those claims are considered true in the sense that they refer to and provide access to some notion of "the real."

Philosophers have made a similar point about the practice of morality generally: some notion of moral truth seems to be presupposed in everyday moral practice (Smith 1991). The fact that persons routinely argue about moral claims, appraise actions as right or wrong, and seek resolutions to moral conflicts, suggests that persons engaged in moral argument are trying to avoid a mistaken judgment or course of action. Common moral practice thus seems to assume some version of moral realism – the view "that there are correct answers to moral questions to be had" and that "there exists a domain of moral facts about which we can form beliefs and about which we may be mistaken" (Smith 1991: 399; Brink 1989).

Nevertheless, the notion of moral truth is one of the most contested subjects in ethical theory. In an age of awesome scientific advances, acute recognition of moral and religious diversity, and persistent global conflict over moral claims, the idea of moral truth seems hard to sustain, perhaps even dangerous. How is the religious ethicist to make sense of a community's moral truth claims in an age of moral skepticism?

Normative Ethics

Religious traditions usually offer a variety of guides for specific moral choices. They teach moral rules. They use stories and parables to show how the moral life is lived in specific situations. They identify saints and heroes or produce lists of virtues to explain the goals of the moral life. Normative theories generally try to establish one type of guide as primary. The rule or the goal becomes the key to understanding the varieties of traditional moral advice. A theory may try to show, for example, that a large body of cautionary tales, commandments, and proverbs all express a small number of basic rules. Alternatively, a theory may argue that rules, laws, and virtues a tradition teaches all point to a single goal, or perhaps to a small number of primary goals.

Deontology presents normative ethics as a system of rules. (The term derives from the Greek *deon*, meaning that which is necessary or obligatory.) A deontological theory might, for example, give an account of Jewish ethics that emphasizes the centrality of obedience to the Law. A deontological theory of Confucian ethics would stress the rules governing relationships to parents, rulers, patrons, or teachers that are essential to the Confucian way of life. A comparison of two different religious traditions based on deontological theory would identify the key moral rules in each tradition and compare the patterns of action expected from believers who follow these rules. Deontological theories give less attention to consequences and focus more on choices and actions when deciding the right thing to do.

Teleology, from the Greek *telos*, or goal, focuses the decision about whether an act is right or wrong on the results which it is intended to achieve. A teleological theory of religious ethics evaluates actions in terms of how they contribute to a goal, rather than how they conform to a rule or commandment. The goal might be a characteristic of a community of believers, such as being organized to welcome strangers and provide hospitality for their needs. It might be a state of affairs in society, such as having a system of justice that treats rich and poor equally. Or the goal might be a virtue of persons, valued habits they acquire by repeated patterns of choice and action. A teleological theory may include a number of important goals, or it may propose that the variety of our goals can be understood in terms of a single goal – "happiness," "blessedness," or "love," for example – to which all the rest are subordinate. In any case, a teleological theory evaluates choices and actions in terms of whether they sincerely intend and effectively achieve the goal.

Because every religious tradition probably includes both rules and goals, devising a deontological or teleological theory that accounts for how a tradition guides moral choice inevitably involves a decision about which parts of that guidance are most basic and most important. This can be controversial. Christian ethics, for instance, regularly sees new versions of the argument between deontological thinkers, who insist on doing what the rules require, and teleological thinkers, who are prepared to ignore familiar moral rules to achieve the most loving results. Hindu ethics can be interpreted either as a set of rules governing an elaborate hierarchy of specific relationships, or as a set of virtues that characterize the person who knows how to order life well within those relationships.

Metaethics

Religious traditions do more than provide normative guidance. They also explain why we are required to do what the moral norms prescribe. Moral theories provide several types of frameworks for understanding these explanations. We will focus here on three of them: rationalism, naturalism, and non-cognitivism.

Rationalism

Kant's ethical theory is an example of ethical rationalism. Failure to follow the requirements of morality always involves us in the contradiction of willing to do something that we are unwilling to make into a general rule that human beings ought to follow. What ethical rationalism shows us is that moral requirements are not imposed on us by outside authorities to test our obedience. We impose moral requirements on ourselves, if we think rationally about our conduct. We are required to act morally because acting against the basic principle of morality is self-contradictory (Gewirth 1978).

Rationalist moral theories can develop in close connection with traditional religious ethics. Rationalist moral theories often offer as the basic principle of morality some version of the requirement that we treat others consistently with the ways we would expect to be treated ourselves (Green 1988). The same principle appears in more traditional form in many religions, including the "Golden Rule" of Christianity (Matthew 7:12). On the other hand, the close resemblance between the basic principle of morality and a traditional religious precept that requires us to "do to others as you would have them do to you" does not imply that the moral theorist will find every requirement of traditional morality logically consistent with this basic principle. Ample opportunity remains for philosophical critique of conventional moral expectations that are not obviously consistent with the basic moral principle. Also, even with respect to central moral principles, the moral theorist may conclude that treasured religious language about persons as children of God or as individuals with a sacred dignity is superfluous once the logical point is clearly understood.

Naturalism

Where rationalism grounds moral requirements in reason, naturalism seeks that ground in the regularities of nature and human experience. While these would seem to be more difficult to state precisely than the requirements of reason, there is no doubt that nature imposes some constraints on all of us. We all have basic physical needs. Physical security requires that we live in society, and although societies vary greatly in the ways they are organized, they must all restrain and support us in some of the same ways, or their promises of security will be in vain. Every moral system offers some account of what we have to do to live a good human life within these constraints of nature and society.

Ethical naturalism makes understanding of the human good the key to ethical theory. What we are required to do, morally speaking, is the thing that allows us to flourish as human beings under the particular constraints with which we live. The set of requirements we develop may vary considerably as individuals with different talents and needs seek to make their way in societies that differ a great deal in the resources and opportunities they offer. The classical philosophers who first gave us versions of ethical naturalism did not always experience or appreciate that variety, but the task of building a moral theory calls our attention to the common project that underlies many quite different ways of talking about the things that make a life worth living. A great variety of moral and religious traditions share the thought that claims about what we ought to do are based on the persons we want to be, and on what it takes to become that sort of person. The proof that we have it right, for this kind of moral theory, is not that our rules do not contradict themselves, but that they point us toward becoming recognizably good people.

Naturalism provides a moral theory that is well suited to religious traditions that speak about ethics in stories of saints, heroes, and other exemplary lives, or that recount the natural constraints on human life in myths about the creation of the cosmic order (Lovin and Reynolds 1985). In Western religion and philosophy, it provides a way to link contemporary philosophical ethics to the discussions of virtue and human excellence that run from Aristotle through Thomas Aquinas to modern Roman Catholic moral theology (Porter 1999).

However, a naturalistic moral theory may also suggest that the traditional language of religious morality is superfluous or misleading. If we learn by careful observation what human flourishing requires, what sense does it make for a religious tradition to tell us that the requirements of morality are God's commands? Moral theorists who adopt a thoroughgoing naturalism often regard religious language with suspicion, suggesting that the supposed commands of God are really expressions of the self-interest of the preachers, and proposing that we might all see that more clearly if we insisted that the case for a moral requirement be made only in naturalistic terms.

Non-cognitivism

For all the differences between them, rationalism and naturalism agree that sound moral judgments rest on knowing something that is universally true, whether that knowledge is about moral reason or about human nature. Each type of theory struggles to make this claim to universality credible in spite of obvious human diversity, and to accommodate diversity in spite of the claim that moral truths are universal. Some moral theorists, however, have sought to resolve this tension by abandoning the claim to universality. Indeed, they deny that our claims about what morality requires rest on any knowledge at all.

For the non-cognitivist, moral language is a way to praise the sorts of action we call moral and a way to express our commitment to acting morally, even if we find it difficult to do so. We can avoid arguments about whether the world really is the way our moral language says it is by recognizing that moral language does not make claims

The aim of this chapter is metaethical, namely, to provide the conceptual tools needed to understand how religious traditions validate moral claims. The chapter begins by addressing some background assumptions that have shaped contemporary discussions of the idea of moral truth. It then presents a typology of metaethical theories and critically assesses them in relation to the task of religious ethics.

Moral Truth: Background Assumptions

Ordinary notions of "truth" seem to assume that truth claims can be tested by their conformity to some knowable fact. Purported statements of fact (e.g., "The cat is on the mat") can be tested by comparing what is asserted to the reality or state of affairs to which the statement refers ("Is the cat really on the mat?"). But when it comes to assertions purporting to state truths of a moral nature (e.g., "Murder is wrong"), difficulties arise. While one can test an assertion such as "The cat is on the mat" by looking to see whether this is in fact the case, there is no analogous procedure for testing whether the assertion "Murder is wrong" is true (i.e., nothing in the act of murder itself from which we can *directly* determine its "wrongness"). The problem seems even more acute in the case of moral imperatives, such as "Thou shalt not kill" or "Love your enemies." What kind of "fact," if any, can determine the truth status of such commands?

Many moral theorists of the twentieth century took the difficulty just noted as indicating a fundamental difference between moral discourse and factual or "value-free" science. Unlike scientific inquiry, there seem to be no empirical facts in relation to which the truth status of moral statements can be assessed, and hence no "truth" to be discovered about morality. The distinction between facts, which tell us how things objectively "are," and values, which tell us how things "ought to be," underlies one of the most influential arguments in modern moral philosophy – the so-called naturalistic fallacy. In its basic form, the argument logically prohibits the deriving of evaluative conclusions from factual premises. But in practice, it carries far-reaching implications for ethics. One of its effects was to sever the deep connection between moral claims and a wider vision of reality that had been traditionally affirmed by many metaphysical systems and religious traditions. Moral – as well as religious, political, and aesthetic – beliefs were no longer regarded as genuine insights into the character of reality, but as the subjective attitudes or recommendations of the thinker who proposed them (Murdoch 1960). Values were seen as the product of human choice, rather than as perceptions of the real.

Given these assumptions, much twentieth-century moral theory was inhospitable to moral realism, and thus to religion as well. The traditional realist claim that there are moral facts (or "correct answers to moral questions") discoverable by human reason was thought to violate the fact–value distinction, which defines "facts" as morally neutral. The perceived failure of moral realism spurred the growth of antirealism in ethics. But the extremes of realism and antirealism do not exhaust all of the available options in metaethics. New forms of moral realism have emerged which reject both the empiricist assumptions of modern moral theory and traditional realist views about how to validate moral claims. The following section presents a spectrum of metaethical theories and considers their implications for the study of religious ethics.

Varieties of Moral Realism

Metaethical positions may be distinguished by their answers to three fundamental questions: (1) Do moral facts exist? (2) Do moral statements have truth value? (3) Can moral claims be rationally validated? These three questions may be called ontological, semantic, and epistemic, respectively. The ontological question is usually answered by referring to theories as "realist" or "antirealist"; the semantic question, by referring to theories as "naturalist" or "non-naturalist"; and the epistemic question, in terms of whether theories are "cognitivist" or "non-cognitivist." Forms of moral realism generally give a positive answer to both the ontological and the semantic questions. However, different forms of moral realism provide different accounts of what *makes* moral statements "true" (or meaningful) as well as how their truth can be known. In its strongest (traditional) form, moral realism holds that moral facts exist independently of our beliefs and theories about morality (Brink 1989: 7), that is, independently of our "mental machinery" or our cognitive frameworks. But what, exactly, are "moral facts"?

Ethical non-naturalism

Some theorists, called "intuitionists," held that moral facts have a unique mode of existence: they are "non-natural" properties perceived through a special kind of moral knowledge (i.e., intuition). The intuitionist G. E. Moore argued that moral terms such as "good" and "right" refer to some really existing property of persons, actions, or institutions. But that property cannot be identified with or reduced to any other property or state of affairs (e.g., happiness); it is *sui generis*. Moore was, in this respect, a non-naturalist. Non-naturalists deny that moral values can be derived from any determinate account of non-moral nature. Kant, for example, held that the ground of obligation must be sought not in the nature of the moral agent or the agent's circumstances, but *a priori* in the concepts of pure reason. Although non-naturalists can be moral realists (like Moore), all non-naturalists leave the fact–value distinction intact: moral values are distinct from non-moral facts.

Some scholars argue that divine command theory is a form of non-naturalist moral realism. The Christian theologian Karl Barth, for example, held that the command of God defines a revealed morality that may differ radically from what reason can discover. The Jewish philosopher Emmanuel Levinas made a similar point about the function of valid ethical commands. In both cases, the domain of moral value, defined by a command or duty, is discontinuous with the realm of non-moral "nature."

Ethical naturalism

Other moral realists, called "naturalists," reject the claim that moral facts are unique non-natural properties known by intuition or revealed by God's command. There are no distinctive moral facts and properties "over and above the facts and properties that can be specified using non-moral terminology" (Pigden 1991: 421). Many moral and religious traditions are "naturalist" in this sense. Thinkers like Thomas Aquinas, in

Christian ethics, and Moses Maimonides, in Jewish ethics, held that moral terms like "good" or "right" can be predicated of actions and beliefs that conform to the principles of natural law. Some scholars of Buddhism have argued that dharma functions similarly to natural law, representing both the principle of order and regularity in nature and the idea of universal moral law (Keown 1996). Other forms of naturalism hold that "good" and "right" can be predicated of those forms of excellent human character and conduct whose cultivation leads to human flourishing. In each case, goodness or rightness is not seen as a *sui generis* moral property. Rather, to call something "good" or "right" is to say that some particular set of facts or state of affairs warrants the attribution "moral."

From the perspective of a non-naturalist like Moore, naturalist moral theories (by definition) commit the naturalistic fallacy: they identify moral value with a description of certain features of reality, thus confusing "is" and "ought." But this judgment is misleading. Naturalists reject the distinctions on which the so-called naturalistic fallacy rests: the distinction between moral (i.e., non-natural) and non-moral (i.e., natural) reality. While strict naturalists hold that moral claims are coterminous with claims about reality and human existence, other naturalists (sometimes called "non-reductive" naturalists) are more sensitive to Moore's charge. They contend that the domain of morality must include but is not reducible to natural goods; the latter are ordered by a principle of assessment that is relatively independent of natural goods (Schweiker 1995).

Naturalism is well suited to describe religious views that stress the connection between beliefs about reality and claims about moral goodness. An influential paradigm in the study of comparative religious ethics adopts the perspective of ethical naturalism to analyze the relation between cosmogony and ethical order (Lovin and Reynolds 1985), and the correlation between "worldview" and "ethos" (Geertz 1973) in diverse traditions.

The remaining two versions of moral realism seek to revise the metaphysical claim of traditional moral realism that moral facts exist independently of our beliefs and theories. They also qualify the assumption that moral facts are known and validated through intuition, commands, or natural moral knowledge.

Reflexive realism

"Reflexive realism" argues that moral claims are validated with respect to some feature of human experience understood as morally basic (Schweiker 1995; Antonaccio 2000). Although reflexive realists contend that the *source* of moral truth lies in some reality that exists prior to or independently of our knowledge of it (e.g., nature, God, the Good), our *grasp* of moral truth is mediated and rendered meaningful through some feature of human existence. Versions of reflexive realism identify different aspects of human experience as the medium through which moral claims resonate in human life. Some religious thinkers argue that moral claims impinge on human life through various "senses" (e.g., of gratitude, dependence, obligation, etc.) (Gustafson 1984). Others are more rationalistic, claiming that there is a "deep structure" of religious

Conclusions: Moral Theory and Religious Ethics

The metaethical theories presented here, while often technical, address a set of questions that are crucially important to religious communities. Does the validity of moral claims rest on their connection with some notion of "the real," as moral realism holds? Does their validity derive from their practical force in motivating human conduct toward particular ends, as antirealism argues?

Much current academic discourse is "antirealist" in sensibility. It holds that moral beliefs (as well as other human ideas and social practices) are "social constructions"; they have no validity beyond what human beings attribute to them to further their interests. Scholars of religious ethics often share this view. Yet for many members of religious communities, morality is not a contingent matter of human preference or social convention. It is a force that is as deep and often recalcitrant to human preference as the notion of "reality" itself. Faced with this apparent disparity between current critical discourse and the lived experience of moral communities, how should the scholar of religious ethics proceed?

Theories of moral realism challenge both the view that reality is value neutral, as well as the constructivist claim that reality is infinitely malleable to human purpose, by insisting on the connection between moral beliefs and claims about reality. Even if the scholar rejects this connection, realist theories remain indispensable to the study of religious ethics because they clarify why and how moral claims exert the force they do *on those who actually believe them to be true*. The danger of assuming an exclusively antirealist methodology is that the substantive claims of a tradition may be subordinated to the methodological commitments of the scholar rather than illuminated in their own terms.

At the same time, religious ethicists should be wary of relying exclusively on moral realism as the metaethical theory best suited to the study of religious communities. Academic study presupposes the need for critical distance between the scholar's perspective and his or her subject matter. An exclusively realist perspective threatens this distinction by allowing the scholar to accept the claims of the tradition as the last word on the validity of its beliefs and practices. Moreover, the claim of some realists that moral truth is immediately apprehended (e.g., revealed by divine command, or discovered in the regularities of nature) understates the ambiguity of moral and religious experience as well as the strenuousness and fallibility of human understanding. Theories of antirealism, almost by definition, presuppose some reflective distance from a tradition's own (realistic) account of its moral claims. They require the scholar to ask how moral discourse functions and how truth claims are actually validated in the life of communities.

Revised forms of moral realism may strike an appropriate balance between theoretical rigor and appreciative understanding of religious traditions. Reflexive and internal realism recognize that moral knowledge is mediated by the particular institutions, beliefs, and vocabularies of historic religious communities, and that members of those communities may grasp its moral truths only in a partial or distorted fashion. Yet both positions retain the realist insistence that the validity of moral claims must be assessed in terms of some general notion of intelligibility – some notion of "the real" – rather than being confined to the preferences of individuals, the claims of communities, or the scholar's own theoretical commitments.

Bibliography

Antonaccio, M. 2000: *Picturing the Human: The Moral Thought of Iris Murdoch*. New York: Oxford University Press.

Brink, D. O. 1989: *Moral Realism and the Foundations of Ethics*. Cambridge: Cambridge University Press.

Geertz, C. 1973: *The Interpretation of Cultures*. New York: Basic Books.

Green, R. 1988: *Religion and Moral Reason*. New York: Oxford University Press.

Gustafson, J. M. 1984: *Ethics from a Theocentric Perspective*, Vol. 1. Chicago: University of Chicago Press.

Hare, R. M. 1991: "Universal Prescriptivism" in *A Companion to Ethics*, ed. P. Singer, 451–63. Cambridge, MA: Blackwell.

Hauerwas, Stanley. 1981: *A Community of Character: Toward a Constructive Christian Social Ethic*. Notre Dame, IN: University of Notre Dame Press.

Keown, D. 1996: *Buddhism: A Very Short Introduction*. New York: Oxford University Press.

Little, D. and Twiss, S. B. 1978: *Comparative Religious Ethics*. New York: Harper & Row.

Lovin, R. W. and Reynolds, F. E. (eds.) 1985: *Cosmogony and Ethical Order: New Studies in Comparative Ethics*. Chicago: University of Chicago Press.

Murdoch, Iris. 1960: "Metaphysics and Ethics" in *The Nature of Metaphysics*, ed. D. F. Pears, 99–123. London: Macmillan.

Pigden, C. R. 1991: "Naturalism" in *A Companion to Ethics*, ed. P. Singer, 421–30. Cambridge, MA: Blackwell.

Putnam, H. 1987: *The Many Faces of Realism*. LaSalle, IL: Open Court.

Rachels, J. 1991: "Subjectivism" in *A Companion to Ethics*, ed. P. Singer, 147–57. Cambridge, MA: Blackwell.

Schneewind, J. B. 1991: "Modern Moral Philosophy" in *A Companion to Ethics*, ed. P. Singer. Cambridge, MA: Blackwell.

Schweiker, W. 1995: *Responsibility and Christian Ethics*. Cambridge: Cambridge University Press.

Smith, M. 1991: "Realism" in *A Companion to Ethics*, ed. P. Singer, 399–410. Cambridge, MA: Blackwell.

Stout, J. 1988: *Ethics after Babel: The Languages of Morals and their Discontents*. Boston, MA: Beacon Press.

CHAPTER 3
Agents and Moral Formation

Thomas W. Ogletree

Accounts of moral agency usually address three subjects: (1) a primal *disposition* to live a moral life; (2) the *capacity* to act morally; and (3) sound *moral judgment*. I will focus on classic Christian and Western philosophical treatments of these subjects, though there are corollaries in other religions and cultures. I will then note contemporary resources that enrich the classic traditions.

Classical Accounts of Agency

Classic Christian discussions of moral agency follow two major trajectories. The first employs a theory of natural law for articulating the moral requisites of human flourishing. Drawing upon Aristotle's work, Thomas Aquinas (1966) gave this approach its definitive theological expression. His thought remains pivotal in Roman Catholic moral theology. The second trajectory stresses the intrinsic authority of the moral law. Protestant reformers Martin Luther (1966) and John Calvin (1957) exemplify this trajectory in tradition-dependent forms, focusing on biblical accounts of divine commands. Immanuel Kant (1996, 1998) offered a philosophical parallel, stressing the human capacity to formulate universally binding moral principles. His inquiries have influenced Reformed Judaism and Protestant Christianity. Augustine's (1955a, 1955b) ideas are manifest in both trajectories, especially his attention to original sin, and to the human aspiration for union with God.

Moral disposition

Interest in a *primal moral disposition* presumes that moral responsibility is integral to human life. Thomas Aquinas linked this disposition to natural human desires for happiness. We achieve happiness, he argued, when we live in accord with natural law reason keyed to specific features of human moral experience and expectation (Green 1988). Still others identify the call of conscience as morally basic (Schweiker 1995). In each case, the locus of the validity of moral claims shifts from direct knowledge of "moral facts" to some feature of human experience. Moral knowledge is not simply a matter of "discovering" moral truth, as traditional moral realism holds. Rather, the moral life requires human beings to engage in the creative work of interpreting what moral claims mean as they impinge on human experience in particular circumstances.

Reflexive realism illuminates a feature of religious traditions that traditional moral realism often obscures: the *difficulty* of acquiring truthful moral knowledge. Even when a tradition posits a paradigmatic moment when moral truth is apprehended (e.g., when the moral law is revealed to the community, or the sacred manifests itself in the natural order), this is only the beginning of moral knowledge, not the end. Religious traditions contain complex forms of textual interpretation, patterns of moral and legal reasoning, rules for ritual practice, techniques of prayer and meditation, discourses of great moral teachers, etc., in order to further the process of moral education. In thus depicting moral insight as a struggle requiring moral effort, religious traditions may present a subtler version of moral realism than the idea of "discovering moral facts" suggests. Moral truth is not passively apprehended, but creatively refracted through human experience and understanding.

Internal realism

"Internal realism" also revises certain features of traditional moral realism. It argues that moral claims are validated not by reference to an empirically knowable set of independently existing "moral facts," but with respect to some cognitive framework, such as a community's moral beliefs. The truth or falsity of moral claims can only be established in relation to the total system of cultural meanings of which they are a part, rather than in relation to some metaphysical account of "moral facts" *tout court*. This has led some theorists to classify this position as a form of "ethical constructivism" or "idealism" rather than realism (Brink 1989: 19). For example, Christian narrative ethicists argue that the Christian community's vision of life is constituted by beliefs and narratives that cannot be translated into the general language of "natural" or "public" morality (Hauerwas 1981). Attempting to warrant Christian truth claims in terms of some general notion of intelligibility is unfaithful to the biblical witness. Fidelity means taking the moral claims of the community as true; no extra-communal warrant is needed.

Other accounts of internal realism, however, stress that it is still a form of *realism* (Putnam 1987; Stout 1988). They acknowledge that a certain "conceptual relativity" is unavoidable in moral theory. Yet these positions leave open the possibility of a convergence of moral truth claims between communities. A comparative analysis of moral communities informed by internal realism would proceed "holistically." Rather than asking whether a particular community affirms the belief that "Murder is wrong," the theorist asks what the concept of "murder" (or its closest analogue) means in that cultural context: how it is defined, under what conditions it applies, and to what other beliefs and practices of the community it is related. The identification of cross-cultural moral truths is possible as long as the theorist recognizes that the meaning of moral claims is dependent on a wider framework of cultural beliefs.

The Challenge of Antirealism

Despite these revisions of traditional moral realism, many theorists remain unconvinced. Recalling the three questions noted above, antirealists give a negative answer to the ontological question about moral facts; they deny that moral statements have truth value; and they usually embrace some form of non-cognitivism in ethics. But forms of antirealism differ over what a moral statement means once its truth status is undercut, and whether reason has any role to play in ethics under these conditions.

If one assumes that all religions start from "realist" premises, then antirealism seems to threaten the very idea of religious ethics. Antirealists advance a different notion of the "validity" of moral claims than the idea of conformity to a set of moral facts (as in moral realism) by highlighting the practical dimension of morality. Moral values are human constructions meant to serve practical purposes. Although moral statements are not fact stating, they are not meaningless. Their aim is practical or action guiding rather than cognitive.

Moral nihilism

The most radical form of antirealism, moral nihilism, claims that there are no moral facts, and hence no "truth" about morality. While other antirealists hold that ethics can continue without the notion of moral truth, nihilists believe that the whole project of morality and its rational justification is a "sham" (Smith 1991: 35). The paradigmatic case of moral nihilism is Nietzsche's critique of Western (and especially Christian) ethics, whose moral claims he saw as a disguised form of the human will to power. Morality had nothing to do with finding the right answers to moral questions, but with "the struggle for mastery, and envy and resentment of those who achieved it" (Schneewind 1991: 154). Nietzsche's method of unmasking moral claims to lay bare the psychological and political interests that drive them, seems to be aimed at the traditional realist claim that moral values are rooted in reality. But a revised form of moral realism, such as reflexive realism, recognizes that distortions and abuses of morality are inevitable given the fallible, mediated character of human understanding.

Emotivism

Although emotivism, like other forms of antirealism, denies that moral statements can be judged in terms of truth and falsity, it does not regard ethics as a sham, as nihilists do. As developed by the American philosopher C. L. Stevenson, emotivism articulated a novel theory of moral language. Moral statements do not make truth claims or provide any factual information whatsoever; they express the subjective attitudes of the speaker who utters them. The statement "Murder is wrong" does not purport to state a moral truth, or even a fact about the speaker's disapproval of murder (Rachels 1991). Rather, moral statements are "emotive"; they *express* the speaker's moral disapproval ("I'm against murder!"). The purpose of such statements is to persuade others to share the speaker's attitude, and thereby to influence their conduct.

Many theorists today reject emotivism as irrational (i.e., as denying the place of reason in ethics). Yet emotivism may still be a useful theoretical tool for religious ethics insofar as it shifts attention away from the emphasis on "moral reasoning" and the rational validation of moral claims characteristic of much (Western) modern moral theory, and suggests that there may be other (emotive or expressive) functions of moral language besides the statement of purported truths. Instead of testing the validity of moral claims in relation to a set of moral "facts" (as in traditional moral realism), a constitutive feature of experience (reflexive realism), or a community's beliefs (internal realism), emotivism insists that the function of moral discourse is expressive and persuasive. This insight expands the range of available options in analyzing the function of moral discourse both within and across traditions.

Prescriptivism

Prescriptivism, associated with the British moral philosopher R. M. Hare, builds on some of the insights of emotivism and was developed in part to answer its deficiencies. Like emotivism, prescriptivism shifts the debate in metaethics away from the ontological question of "whether moral facts exist" toward the semantic question about the meaning of moral statements. Against the view of many moral realists that moral statements are *wholly* descriptive (i.e., fact stating), prescriptivists contend that moral statements may also contain a "prescriptive" element (formerly called "emotive") (Hare 1991: 452). In fact, there are many kinds of sentences whose meaning is not determined by "truth conditions" at all. Imperatives are a case in point. The meaning of the sentence "Shut the door" is not dependent on establishing its truth conditions (it has none), yet we still understand its meaning (Hare 1991: 452). Where prescriptivism departs from emotivism is its insistence that the presence of the action-guiding element in moral discourse does not necessarily mean that one cannot reason about ethics. "Universal" prescriptivism holds that "there are rules of reasoning which govern nondescriptive as well as descriptive speech acts" (Hare 1991: 455). Imperatives associated with "ought" statements are governed by the rule of universalizability (Hare 1991: 456).

Prescriptivism influenced one of the earliest methodological approaches to comparative religious ethics. David Little and Sumner Twiss (1978) adopted the conceptual terminology of "action guides" in order to stress the practical and prescriptive force of moral and religious discourse in influencing human behaviors and attitudes.

principles that exemplify the kinds of beings we are. The first principle, *synderesis* or "conscience," founds moral agency. It is the human disposition to do what is right and to refuse to do what is wrong.

Aquinas embraced Augustine's earlier contention that the quest for happiness, though rooted in the goodness of creation, has been corrupted by humanity's lapse into sin. We seek happiness, but we no longer know what truly brings happiness, so we grasp after ephemeral pleasures that are finally worthless. It is by loving God for God's own sake, and by loving all creatures in conjunction with our love for God, that we know blessedness. "Thou hast made us for Thyself," Augustine confessed, "and our souls are restless until they find their rest in Thee" (1955a). In conjunction with this vision of ultimate fulfillment, Aquinas emphasized as well the role "natural" human dispositions play in moral formation. Augustine qualified his own sweeping dismissals of the illusory quest for earthly happiness. The human need for social order and for meaningful participation in community, he conceded, does require worldly approximations of "justice" and "peoplehood." Still, his primary concern was to contrast the "justice" of this world with true justice, where all things are ordered according to God's purposes.

Luther and Calvin traced the human disposition to do what is right and good to the goodness of creation, in particular, the creation of human beings in the image of God. They too stressed the broken state of humanity. Only fragments of God's righteous decrees survived the "fall" into sin. Yet these fragments suffice to hold us accountable for our wickedness. In Paul's words, we are "without excuse." The good news is that God renews our hunger to do what is right and good.

Immanuel Kant sought to demonstrate the authority of the moral law in the context of the European Enlightenment. He saw no possibility of basing the moral law upon the "happiness principle." This principle is the "death of morals"! It highlights human drives to satisfy bodily needs and to gratify selfish desires. Such behavior is in no case free. Kant stressed the "freedom principle" instead. Free acts require rational beings who can formulate the moral law for themselves. We act freely when we resolve to do what the moral law requires, not because we must or because of some advantage we might gain, but out of respect for its intrinsic rightness. Kant described the *supreme maxim* of the moral life as an agent's *resolve* to subject all actions to the dictates of the moral law. This maxim is equivalent to Aquinas' notion of *synderesis.* Kant lifted up the promise of a transcendent version of happiness, not as a foundation for the moral life, but as an affective accompaniment of moral virtue. Though we cannot prove God's existence, moral awareness gives us grounds for "postulating" God's existence, and for affirming a congruence between God's will and the moral law. These beliefs awaken hope that moral virtue will lead to blessedness.

Moral capacity

To function as moral agents, we need more than good intentions. We require strength to implement our intentions in practice. All human capabilities are relevant to the moral life: physical vitality, the ability to communicate, cognitive capacities, artistic gifts. Kant argued that we are morally obliged to develop our "powers" so that we can manage our lives. With regard to *moral* capabilities, classic sources stressed control over bodily appetites: hunger, thirst, sexual desire, combative energy. These appetites, which are common to all animals, are perfectly natural, and they have positive import for human well-being. Hunger and thirst impel us to secure the food and drink we need for survival. Sexual desire assures the propagation of the species. Combative impulses equip us to defend ourselves against assaults, or perhaps to escape our attackers. The same appetites can also be destructive. Hunger can lead to gluttony; thirst, to drunkenness. Erotic desires can drive us to promiscuity, adultery, rape. Combative impulses can unleash explosive fits of temper or unjustified acts of violence. Aristotle stressed a balanced response to bodily appetites. Guided by wise mentors, we adopt practices that form habits. These habits become a "second nature," enduring over a lifetime. Good habits are "virtues." They represent a "golden mean" between excess and defect. They channel bodily appetites in morally sound ways while constraining their destructive tendencies. Bad habits are "vices." They manifest the extremes: a lack of control over the appetites, or their suppression, until they can no longer energize action.

Aquinas applied Aristotle's model to the four "cardinal" virtues: temperance, courage, justice, and prudence. Temperance is the golden mean with regard to bodily desires, especially for food, drink, and sexual gratification; courage is the golden mean with regard to our combative impulses. Justice and prudence are virtues governed by reason. Justice is the readiness to give each person what he or she is due, recognizing the dignity of all human beings. Prudence is the employment of practical reason in exercising moral judgments. Justice and prudence presuppose temperance and courage. Without these latter virtues, we cannot discern what is right and good.

Aquinas then subordinated the natural virtues to supernatural virtues infused in us by divine grace: faith, hope, and love. Faith is cognitive assent to church teaching. It marks the starting point in the human quest for understanding. Hope expresses confidence that God's purposes will be realized. Love is human aspiration toward union with God. We can properly love others and ourselves only in relation to our love for God. Supernatural virtues alone qualify as genuine virtues, and they have no limits. They can even override the "balance" of natural virtues, calling for times of fasting, for lifelong commitments to celibacy, for a readiness to suffer and die for Christ's sake. Yet they bestow qualified significance on the natural virtues as well.

Protestant thinkers, following Luther and Calvin, stressed the primacy of the will and volitional control over the passions. They did not believe that human sin resided in the passions, still less in malformed habits that Aristotle labeled vices. The root of sin is a disobedient will, the refusal to do what God commands. Because of our rebellion, our passions spin out of control, becoming destructive "works of the flesh." The result is the "bondage of the will," rendering us incapable of doing God's will. Our hope rests in God alone, who forgives us and empowers us to do his will. Luther spoke of how God's love flows through us and moves outward toward our neighbors, enabling us to love them truly. Calvin stressed growth in faith, which transforms our hearts. A new heart is the mark of God's healing presence.

Kant's account of moral virtue also centered in volitional control, the resolve to obey the moral law for its own sake. Only the good will, he argued, is good without qualification. Yet a good will must still contend with passions. The underlying problem is that natural inclinations get a head start over rational capabilities. Inclinations are present from birth, but we require time to develop practical reason. In *The Doctrine of Virtue*, Kant (1996) acknowledges that some emotions, which he calls moral dispositions, can furnish the *subjective conditions* of our receptiveness to duty. He cites good feelings that accompany actions consistent with duty, and bad feelings that follow violations of duty. He portrays love as a caring feeling for fellow human beings. We are obliged to help our fellow human beings achieve happiness whether we love them or not. Where love is present, however, our obligations become more bearable. Kant also mentions self-esteem, a positive feeling about oneself. Self-esteem invigorates duties to self, such as the duty to preserve one's life. Kant does not believe we are obliged to cultivate moral feelings, though they can support a good will. True virtue is solely my ability to do my duty. I acquire virtue by exalting the moral law and consistently doing my duty.

Moral judgment

Classic traditions stress the human capacity to exercise sound moral judgment. For Aquinas, we first consider the things we have in common with other creatures; we then examine our distinctive qualities. Based on these reflections, we determine principles of natural law that will sustain conditions necessary for human well-being. Ideally, laws of the state will reinforce these principles. Laws revealed in scripture supplement and correct deficiencies in natural law reasoning. Luther and Calvin begin with scripture, focusing on the Ten Commandments and the summary commands to love God and neighbor. Neither was content merely to apply the "letter of the law" to particular human practices. They sought deeper meanings in the commandments. Thus, the prohibition of stealing stimulates reflection on the significance of personal property within God's providential care for human life. It leads the faithful to claim their obligations toward others, especially the poor and the marginal, so that all might have resources to live in decency. Recognizing the social necessity of holding sin in check, Luther and Calvin urged magistrates to construct human laws informed by biblical wisdom. Calvin stressed growth toward righteousness through reflections on the divine commands. Our ultimate destiny is to glorify God and to enjoy God forever.

Kant called for formulations of moral imperatives that are universally binding upon all rational beings. He distinguished "strict" and "broad" imperatives. The former prohibit inherently contradictory acts, such as lying or suicide. The latter state broad obligations, though with few specifics (e.g., to develop one's capacities, and to promote the happiness of others). Broad imperatives have affinities with Aquinas' account of natural law (i.e., obligations that foster human flourishing). Kant offered the "principle of humanity" as an all-encompassing "secondary formulation" of the moral law: "Act so as to treat humanity, whether in your own person or in that of any other, as an end in itself, never as a means only." This formulation facilitated a shift in moral discourse from the classic focus on duty to the modern interest in human rights. Broad imperatives can in principle be elaborated in rules that govern more particular social practices. The Protestant theologian Paul Ramsey (1965) pressed for "exceptionless moral rules" for applying the commandment of neighbor love to particular practices. Kant's method furnished a useful model for his reflections.

Recurring ethical controversies involve disputes about concrete applications of basic moral principles. Aquinas addressed this problem directly. The closer we move to particulars, he acknowledged, the more inexact our judgments become. Why? Natural laws address specific facets of human life, while concrete cases often involve multiple considerations that cannot be combined under a single principle. Aquinas gives many examples. We are normally obliged, for example, to return lost property to its owner, *unless* the property is a dangerous weapon, and the owner an enemy invader. Aquinas' reflections have been expanded as *casuistry* and *proportionalism* (see chapter 5). Casuistry involves the examination of particular cases in light of accumulated experiences in dealing with similar cases. Proportionalism stresses the quest for optimal balance in ordering competing values in concrete situations. Critics resist both strategies. They press for strict applications of natural law principles to concrete cases, lest the authority of the moral law be undermined by flawed reasoning.

Challenges to Classic Understandings of Agency

Contemporary additions to the classic traditions involve reflections on human sociality: the import of interpersonal relationships, established social structures, and prevailing cultural values for moral formation. The human sciences have made substantial contributions: ego psychology, object-relations theory, socialization theory. Contemporary theologians and philosophers also place greater emphasis on the relational composition of human persons.

Psychology and identity formation

Classic accounts of moral formation focused on basic human faculties: the will, practical reason, bodily appetites. Contemporary psychological studies direct attention to the self, and to relational processes that facilitate an emerging sense of personal identity (see chapter 56). These studies suggest that the human disposition to do what is good and right cannot be derived simply from a general desire for happiness, or from a basic capacity for rational judgment. Instead, these dispositions arise from a child's feelings of "secure attachment" to an attentive caregiver, usually the mother, during the first months of life (Ainsworth et al. 1978; Bowlby 1982). Securely attached children begin to create a "coherent, enduring self-narrative" by the age of five. Simultaneously, their sensitivity to the feelings of others and their recognition of the "reciprocal nature of relational transactions" expands significantly (Thompson 2000).

Adolescence marks the turning point in the formation of identity (Erikson 1963, 1968). A stable personal identity is essential for purposive action and for critical moral judgment. It is only when we know who we are and what we stand for that we can act on our own. The primary threat to adolescent identity is "role confusion," not knowing who you are or how you fit into the world. Notions of "the will" or of "virtuous habits" are not obsolete, but they can no longer be abstracted from the complex processes that give rise to personal identity. In Erikson's theory, the attainment of identity positions young adults to form intimate relationships, and to establish homes of their own. Here the threat is isolation and loneliness. To flourish, human beings require highly personal, life-sustaining relationships. Nancy Chodorow's (1999) studies of adolescent girls disclose a complex interplay between an emerging sense of self and growing sensitivity to the feelings of others. She attributes this dynamic to the fact that females differentiate themselves from their mothers while also continuing to identify with them strongly. In contrast, boys tend to differentiate themselves from their mothers while competing with their fathers. Gender differences in studies of moral formation largely reflect times when mothers were the primary caregivers for infants, children, and even youths. One can anticipate changes in those patterns in a world of working mothers where fathers frequently play more active parenting roles.

These studies all give prominence to feelings: trust, attachment, self-confidence, empathy, self-esteem. Just as passions remind us that we are embodied selves, so feelings and affections bear witness to our social composition. Because feelings are closely bound to human relationships, they cannot be treated merely as secondary reinforcements of moral volition. Attitudes of respect and acts of beneficence toward others are cold and heartless if they are devoid of feeling. They can even be undermined by negative or ambivalent feelings that contradict their intended purposes: resentment, envy, disdain, contempt. Classic Christian theological perspectives took note of feelings: remorse, release from guilt, a new heart, hunger for God, blessedness. Such feelings were taken as signs of God's presence. Virtually exclusive attention was given, however, to the God relation, with little thought for the place of human relationships in moral formation. Yet caring human relationships are integral to the moral life, and they can serve as media for the redemptive purposes of God.

Cognitive development

Studies of *cognitive* moral development parallel accounts of identity formation. Using hypothetical moral dilemmas to stimulate conversations, Lawrence Kohlberg (1971) charted the patterns of moral reasoning that children and youth employ at various ages. His results reflect Kant's view of moral reasoning. In early childhood, children talk about avoiding pain and securing pleasure. In the middle years, they speak of conventional expectations for proper behavior. Adolescents and young adults stress mutual agreements, and a few appeal to principles of justice. For Kohlberg, the last response marks the highest stage of moral reasoning, a level males appeared more likely to attain than females. Carol Gilligan (1982) expanded Kohlberg's work by focusing on female subjects. She too found that females do not typically assess moral dilemmas by abstract appeals to justice. Instead, they strive to negotiate new arrangements that will overcome problems posed by the dilemmas. The moral reasoning of females, she suggested, is driven by "care" rather than justice, and it involves the give and take of discourse. Care presumes justice. Persons are to be given what they are due. Yet care moves beyond formal respect toward collaborative human relationships. Seyla Benhabib (1992) stresses principles of mutual respect that make discourse possible. Discourse enables us to honor human differences, even to cultivate shared understandings that reach across differences. In pluralistic societies, care and discourse are indispensable for civility.

In Erikson's theory, human development finally moves toward "ego integrity," where a maturing self gathers the experiences, insights, and discoveries of a lifetime into a more coherent whole. At this stage, the ultimate threat is "despair," where life appears empty and without meaning. Erikson's account of ego integrity calls to mind Augustine's portrait of the faith pilgrimage. God's eternity, Augustine reminded us, is not timelessness, but timefulness. God is able to encompass all of the moments and details of our lives, bestowing value upon them all. Our evil acts, our virtuous deeds, our sinful impulses, our spiritual hungers, our experiences of pain and loss, our moments of joy and fulfillment: all play roles in our formation as unique, irreplaceable individuals. Alfred North Whitehead (1929) elegantly captures Augustine's vision: "God is a tender care that nothing be lost."

Social theory and cultural values

Socialization theory displays the transmission from generation to generation of established cultural values and institutionalized social practices (see chapter 50). We internalize these values and practices through our interactions with parents, teachers, and mentors, until they become self-evident "givens" in our own perceptions of the world. This theory raises cautions about human claims to grasp moral standards that are absolute and universal in import. Our moral and religious convictions are inevitably filtered through taken-for-granted beliefs that reside in familiar social practices. Deeply entrenched racial, ethnic, religious, and gender prejudices can distort our moral judgments, though without our awareness.

In democratic societies, our lives are no longer framed by an encompassing, cohesive culture grounded in a religious establishment. We have a political culture that privileges individual freedoms and an economy that celebrates personal preferences. Beyond these common values, we live amid a rich plurality of communities and associations offering diverse, even conflicting, visions of human well-being. For many people, this new order has been liberating, opening the way for social mobility, and for bold new experiments in the quest for human fulfillment. It has facilitated movement beyond the racism of the past, and opened new opportunities for women to employ their capabilities in a wider social world. The same circumstances have also been destabilizing, weakening communal bonds that are essential for moral formation: strong families, close neighborhoods, vital religious communities, and overlapping associations that compose civil society.

A world of diversity and change has inspired renewed interest in substantive moral traditions. Alastair MacIntyre (1984) has given philosophical attention to the importance of tradition, narrative, and stable social practices for cultivating moral virtue. Stanley Hauerwas (1981) has emphasized a common faith narrative and shared communal practices in the formation of Christian character. The option of living in a closed, self-subsisting community is open to few. We normally participate in multiple social arenas, interacting daily with fellow human beings whose personal convictions and value priorities cover a wide spectrum of possibilities. The challenge is to uphold with integrity our own deepest convictions while honoring others who hold different views; it is to rebuild and renew our particular moral communities, while fostering broad social commitments to the common good.

Emmanuel Levinas (1969) traces the roots of moral formation to the "gracious face" of the feminine. At the same time, he contends that the full realization of moral responsibility requires the "radical face" of "the Other," the stranger who exposes our prejudices, and jolts our confidence that we have all the right answers. The radical Other is also vulnerable, a person who cannot get a hearing unless we are prepared to listen. Openness to the Other becomes a pivotal feature of moral responsibility. It corrects our arrogant attempts to construct comprehensive views that render all things intelligible. It expresses our openness to the ultimate mystery of God, in whom all beings realize their destiny. Levinas displays moral maturity as a combination of personal integrity and respect for human plurality.

Bibliography

Ainsworth, M. D., et al. (eds.) 1978: *Patterns of Attachment: A Psychological Study of the Strange Situation*. Hillsdale, NJ: Lawrence Erlbaum Associates.

Aquinas, T. 1966: *Treatise on the Virtues*, trans. J. A. Oesterle. Englewood Cliffs, NJ: Prentice-Hall.

Augustine. 1955a: *Augustine: Confessions and Enchiridion*, trans. A. C. Outler. Vol. 7, Library of Christian Classics. Philadelphia, PA: Westminster Press.

——1955b: *Augustine: Later Works*, trans. J. Burnaby. Vol. 8, Library of Christian Classics. Philadelphia, PA: Westminster Press.

Benhabib, S. 1992: *Situating the Self: Gender, Community, and Postmodernism in Contemporary Ethics*. Cambridge, MA: Polity Press.

Bowlby, J. 1982: *Attachment and Loss*, 2nd edn. New York: Basic Books.

Calvin, J. 1957: *Institutes of the Christian Religion*, Vol. 2, trans. H. Beveridge. Grand Rapids, MI: William B. Eerdmans.

Chodorow, N. 1999: *The Reproduction of Mothering: Psychoanalysis and the Sociology of Gender*. Berkeley: University of California Press.

Erikson, E. H. 1963: *Childhood and Society*, 2nd revd. edn. New York: W. W. Norton.

——1968: *Identity: Youth and Crisis*. New York: W. W. Norton.

Gilligan, C. 1982: *In a Different Voice: Psychological Theory and Women's Development*. Cambridge, MA: Harvard University Press.

Hauerwas, S. 1981: *A Community of Character: Toward a Constructive Social Ethic*. Notre Dame, IN: Notre Dame University Press.

Kant, I. 1996: *The Doctrine of Virtue*, trans. and ed. M. Gregor. Vol. 2, *The Metaphysics of Morals*. Cambridge: Cambridge University Press.

——1998: *Critique of Practical Reason*, trans. H. W. Cassirer, ed. G. H. King and R. Weitzman. Milwaukee, WI: Marquette University Press.

Kohlberg, L. 1971: "Stages of Moral Development as a Basis for Moral Education" in *Moral Education: Interdisciplinary Perspectives*, ed. C. M. Beck et al. New York: Newman Press.

Levinas, E. 1969: *Totality and Infinity: An Essay on Exteriority*, trans. A. Lingis. Pittsburgh, PA: Dusquesne University Press.

Luther, M. 1966: "Treatise on Good Works" in *The Christian in Society*, ed. J. Atkinson. Vol. 44, *Luther's Works*. Philadelphia, PA: Fortress Press.

MacIntyre, A. 1984: *After Virtue*, 2nd edn. Notre Dame, IN: University of Notre Dame Press.

Ramsey, P. 1965: "Deeds and Rules in Christian Ethics." *Scottish Journal of Theology. Occasional Papers No. 11*. Edinburgh: Oliver and Boyd.

Thompson, R. 2000: "The Legacy of Early Attachments." *Child Development* 71 (1), 145–52.

Whitehead, A. N. 1929: *Process and Reality*. New York: Macmillan.

CHAPTER 4
Ideas of Ethical Excellence

Lee Yearley

Humor, much less humility, may not be central to most notions of human excellence, but they surely must inform the efforts of anyone who attempts to write briefly about the notion. One reason is that dramatically diverse practices have been taken to exemplify such excellence; for example, the purported excellences of celibacy and of parenthood. Another is that a significant if perhaps less dramatic diversity attends theoretical accounts of what excellence consists in and how, therefore, it is to be attained; for example, by the dogged nurture of inchoate capacities or by the abandonment of all dogged activities. Finally, no single person can grasp well all the various kinds of human excellence that humans have displayed in their practices and manifested in their theories. (The ignorance of this writer about areas outside East Asia and the West is vast enough to make his imperfect knowledge of those two areas seem substantial.)

To emphasize the diversity of the phenomenon and scholarly ignorance ought not, however, lead the reader to query the worth, or even viability, of an endeavor like this one. Not only can some things be said with reasonable assurance, but the subject is also as important a topic of inquiry as we have: if inquiry into ideas about human excellence is not important, what is important? Indeed, the character of the subject means any treatment must contain a normative dimension; it must not just describe what people have thought about human excellence, but also examine what those thoughts may mean for us today. An examination of those normative considerations will appear in due time, but let us now turn to certain general observations about human excellence, focusing on how the notion of virtue and those subjects that follow in its wake, most notably conceptions of the self, help us to understand it.

Features of Human Excellence

The specific features of human excellence can best be described as virtues: perfections of discrete human functionings that manifest the distinctive aspects of the laudatory state (Yearley 1990). (The notion of virtue has, of course, a specific set of meanings inside the Western tradition, but all traditions or groups of which I know have terms that resemble, sometimes closely, Western uses of the term.) To treat fully such specific excellences we must also, and more controversially, speak not only about ordinary virtues but also about religious virtues. That is, we need to differentiate the sphere of virtues into two realms – realms that share some characteristics and have others that sharply divide them. But let us begin with what is shared.

In virtually all cultures, those specific features that exemplify human excellence could fit within a list of virtues that is ordered in a hierarchical fashion. The list defines what qualities are virtues, are instances of human excellence, and by implication what qualities are not. The list tells us, for instance, that courage is a human excellence and cowardliness is not. The hierarchical rank helps a person determine in which situations one or another virtue should be manifested. That is, it allows a person to know, for example, that being patient rather than assertive, ironic rather than flamboyant, is the correct behavior when you are told a friend has been slandered. Grasping how the hierarchy operates and fluently manifesting that grasp can be a difficult task – especially for a beginner – but it is often fairly easy for members of the culture and is crucial to the full expression of human excellence.

Even granting that virtues do operate in this way, we must also realize that for many today the word virtue has an even more archaic ring than does the notion of human excellence. It often seems to be associated with problematic ideas like priggish scrupulosity; or to be restricted to narrow areas like sexual activity; or to reflect fixed unjust social hierarchies like the ones found in virtually all traditional societies. (The old saying puts such concerns pungently: "When they begin to talk about virtue it's time to emigrate.") Nevertheless, the idea has the significance it does because virtues seem to be necessary if humans are to operate well in the various areas in which human excellence must function. It is unsurprising, given this, that we find certain virtues in the lists of many cultures. Individuals need qualities such as courage or self-control if they are to thrive, and probably even survive, and societies need people to have them if they are to survive, much less thrive.

This illustrates how many, perhaps even all virtues, and thus notions of human excellence, can productively be thought of as being *corrective*. Ideas of virtue, and thus of human excellence, rest on pictures of human weakness and need. Virtues correct some difficulty thought to be natural to human beings, some temptation that needs to be resisted or some motivation that needs to be made good. Industry, for example, can be said to correct a propensity to idleness; perseverance a tendency to give up before it is necessary to do so; and courage the inclination to be dissuaded by fear from doing what should be done. Virtues, to put it more abstractly, display some characteristic pattern of desire and motivation, some disposition toward action. They are not simple thoughts that occur and pass. I do not manifest a virtue if I think how compassionate it would be to invite those lonely people to dinner as I walk on past them. Nor are they emotional states that pass quickly. I am not virtuous if I feel very strongly that I should at least talk to my troubled relative but realize the movie is about to start and leave.

A virtue, then, is a human excellence or an example of human flourishing. It is a permanent addition to the self, part of what makes people who they are, a feature of what we call character (see chapter 10). Unlike some character traits, however, there must be evidence of what we can call "thought and will" if a quality is to count as a virtue, and that is true even within perspectives that emphasize the problems that beset ordinary thinking and willing. Most agree, of course, that they may not be conscious – "to think a little and then act" is an absurd picture of human behavior even if we are talking only about academics. Nevertheless, judgment or thinking occurs in the sense that, at minimum, I can explain (at some point, in some fashion) to myself or another person why I do something or value some trait. A virtue, then, is a disposition to act, desire, and feel that involves the exercise of judgment.

Motives and Models

Virtuous activity also involves choosing virtue for itself. I do not possess the virtue of generosity, but a semblance (or even counterfeit) of it if I act because of some ulterior motive such as that if I help specific people now they will think well of me, or help me later, or convince their rich relatives to give me money. Indeed, the differences between *semblances* of virtue and true virtue are crucial in almost all theories of human excellence. That is, semblances generate activities that resemble the activities of real virtue but lack important elements in it. People who manifest semblances do a virtuous act not for its own sake but for consequences that a non-virtuous person would desire. Or they choose it not for their own reasons but because of some secondhand support such as custom, unexamined authority, or the inertia provided by accepted, routine reactions.

This difference also illustrates how virtuous activity involves choosing specific virtues in light of some justifiable life plan. I believe, for example, the best kind of human life involves generosity not selfishness, giving not just taking and possessing. I have a general view, and good reasons (of some sort) for it, that lead me to think that kind of life is better than one that lacks it. The significance of such an overall view of life underlies our last theoretical comment about those features of human excellence we call virtues: virtuous behavior, that is, has not only *acquisitive* but also *expressive* motives.

People choose a virtuous action not only because it contributes to goods they want to acquire, but also because it expresses their conception of human excellence. (The latter motive, as we will see, underlies many forms of religious virtue.) The essential characteristic of expressive virtue, then, is its response to one basic question: Why might, or even should, people embrace an ideal of excellence if they have severe doubts that it will have the kind of effects in the world they hope it will? The answer is that the best kind of human excellence simply demands such activity, and therefore no further questions about its contributions to the agent's or anyone else's happiness need to be raised. This does not mean such choices are made recklessly; indeed, they must be well considered if they are to be fully expressive. Nevertheless, it is not the good benefits received or given but the good expressed that is the crucial motivating force.

These common features in ideas about virtue and thus human excellence ought not to mask the fact that the substantive variety we mentioned earlier is also present. We have already noted some dramatic differences in practice, but here I want to consider two significantly different theories about human excellence. One rests on a *developmental* model, the other on a *discovery* model. Each model defines the end of a continuum and the many variants in the middle of the continuum mix some qualities that are discovered and others that are developed.

The developmental model is common in many traditions and can have either religious or non-religious forms. In this model, human nature has an innate constitution that manifests itself in processes of growth and culminates in specifiable forms. That fulfillment occurs, however, only if the organism is both uninjured and properly nurtured. The basic conceptual mode is, then, relatively simple and it draws on a biological framework. A basic set of capacities exists and their unhindered, nurtured development generates qualities that lead to specifiable actions or characteristic forms. Those, in turn, provide the standard that allows an observer to determine a being's nature and to judge whether any specific action represents its nature in normal, exemplary, or defective fashion.

A fundamentally different model is a discovery model; somewhat less common, it also rests squarely within a religious framework. That framework is "monistic" in its purest form and "theistic" in its more mixed or muted forms. In a discovery model, true human nature contains a permanent set of dispositions that is coextensive, in some way, with a sacred being. Those dispositions are obscured by ordinary human qualities, but they may be discovered and then contacted in a fashion that allows them to animate a person. People do not, as in a developmental model, cultivate inchoate capacities. Rather, they discover a hidden ontological reality with sacred characteristics that truly defines them, whatever may be the apparently defining, regnant social ideas about human excellence.

The two models differ, then, both in the character of the ontological and religious ideas they rely on and in the ways in which their notions of human perfection depend on those ideas. The ideas of human excellence in a discovery model are much more deeply embedded in specific ontological and religious ideas than are those in a developmental model. The level of embedding is especially important today because many moderns think it difficult to imagine a discovery model generating a lively notion of pluralism or separating itself from specific, and questionable, cultural guidelines about what human excellence is.

A development model and the weaker forms of a discovery model generate an important question – to some people the most important question – we can ask about general notions of human excellence. What kind of training or cultivation, either by other people or by the individual, can best help people achieve human excellence? Answers to that question are many, but most important here is that those answers affect the character of many of the most significant social institutions (like schools or families), and therefore connect their characters closely to one or another ideal of human excellence.

Religious Notions and Human Excellence

The distinctions between these two models highlight the difference religious notions can make when we consider human excellence. That difference is also highlighted, and in a more concrete way, when we consider the role normal ideas of human functioning play in our understanding of excellence. "Normal" here means those kinds of ideas most people in a society would accept without much thought: for example, possessing some materials goods; feeling acute emotions at certain kinds of loss or failure; participating both in a family and in various aspects of a culture's social life. Religious ideas of human excellence, in contrast, often manifest a perspective in which these normal ideals appear to be either insignificant or relatively unimportant. For example, these perspectives contain ideals like voluntary poverty, complete equanimity, and celibate withdrawal from society. Indeed, the disjunction seen here is pronounced enough that some people have said that religious perspectives may manifest excellences, but they seem to be the excellences of a species other than the human species.

Even given this, some people may still think that distinguishing between religious and ordinary virtues is either problematic or wrong-headed because those distinctions are not made by many traditions or groups. In several cases, in fact, a tradition's general conceptual framework not only does *not* lead to, but also literally *could* not allow for what in, say, Christianity, are called natural and supernatural virtues. Nevertheless, many people believe, even if inchoately, that some virtues have a very special "religious" character.

These religious virtues produce actions and attitudes that both differ from normal virtues and change a range of normal actions in profoundly important ways. Sharp distinctions are made, for instance, among the kinds of objects pursued, among the goals of the intentions manifested, among the precise forms of behavior produced, and among the kinds of empowerment displayed. On the one hand, then, religious virtues are virtues where one cannot draw on too many normal presumptions and arguments (about the importance of, say, possessions, family, or a minimal concern for others) to defend, or even to make plausible, the virtue or else it ceases to be a religious virtue. On the other hand, one cannot simply disregard normal presumptions or else the virtue ceases to be a human virtue, and thus a plausible human option.

Adopting the needed, delicate balancing of ordinary and religious ideas about human excellence seems to occur reasonably easily when people think about topics like the significance of possessions, family, or a minimal concern for others. But other and more pronounced difficulties appear when we turn to the possible effect of some religious beliefs on the idea of human excellence. Probably the most significant example of this effect is the question of whether considerations of human excellence need to take account of the past or future lives that a person either may have lived or may live after a "natural" death. In thinking about the human excellence of a person, that is, must we attend closely not just to the features of the, say, 85-year life Sally lives, but also to the features of her past or future lives?

Proponents of the strongest version of the view that we must attend to those other lives argue that Sally's excellence can be adequately judged only by focusing on them. They argue her excellences either were caused by acts she performed before her present appearance or can be truly evaluated only from the perspective of the life she will live after her "natural" death. Adopting the strong version of this position involves, of course, a robust claim about what one can know with assurance, namely, that Sally's future life will be of a certain sort or that her past lives were not only of a certain sort but also formed her present life. Some religious people have not shied away from making such claims, but others, who firmly believe in the idea of past or future lives, have also thought lack of clarity about the exact characteristics of those past or future states (and perhaps the causal links among them) meant that our ideas about human excellence will not be much affected.

Excellence and Identity

More could, of course, be said about the implications of distinctions among religious and normal kinds of human excellence, but let me end by considering abstractly a crucial normative issue (at least for many moderns) raised by the notion of human excellence. What true variety of excellences, if any, can such a notion allow? A muted recognition of diverse kinds of excellences (even if they are ranked hierarchically) will, it seems, accompany any culture or group's ideal of human excellence. Most common and benign is the calibration of excellence to stages in life; for example, praiseworthy judgment or courage will differ in a 5-year old, in a 25-year old, and in a 50-year old. Also common is the calibration of excellence to temperament or character, qualities that may in turn be said to manifest a person's "class," and even perhaps the effects of a person's past lives. The excellences of the warrior, the teacher, and the religious recluse may indeed all be excellences yet still differ considerably, with the differences reflecting the distinctions inherent in the material from which the excellences spring. This remains true even if some general excellences, such as courage, appear in each.

This last kind of calibration, with its notion that a person "is a warrior," reflects the ideas that people have what can be called *necessary identities*, and that those identities control the kind and level of excellence available to them. The notion of necessary identities usually combines with the ideas, first, that very few people have an identity that allows them to reach the highest excellence, and, second, that most groups cannot reach the most valuable excellence. The former notion is defensible, but only in the sense that it reflects the obvious fact that only a few actually do attain to certain especially valuable states. Even granting that notion, however, we can still doubt both that the ability to attain such states is the privilege of only one class and that the causal accounts used to explain people's capacities are adequate.

The notion that some groups have limited abilities seems to be completely indefensible especially because, in almost all cases, one group with severe limits on its possible achievements is that half of the human race identified as woman. This situation can lead us, as it has led many moderns, to question the whole notion of human excellence; that is, to bring the notion under the purview of ideas about justice and then to analyze how and why it functions as it does. One can, for example, argue that models of the self and ideas about human excellence relate closely, but that the models always distinguish and order opaque or inherently disorderly phenomena that provide us with neither decisive tests nor impartially collected evidence. People cannot, of course, invent any model of the self they might happen to want, due to the constraints of so-called "natural facts" and current webs of belief. Nevertheless, the models appear to be theoretical inventions, constructions made in order to achieve specific goals.

The importance of the purposes that guide the construction of these models becomes clear when we attend to how both the distinctions among human powers and the hierarchical arrangement of them (matters crucial to the idea of human excellence) usually match the prevailing social structure and its justifying ideology. Perhaps the most striking example of this is the traditional Western model of the subordination of raw desire to reason, the most familiar and notorious instance of which occurs in Aristotle. For Aristotle, reason should control the other elements in the self, and it will if the person is a full human being who has been well formed by a proper upbringing. Those who lack reason's control can never attain real human excellence and therefore also can never lead the society. That unfortunate group includes three subgroups: (1) those who completely lack the capacity to reason, such as natural slaves; (2) those who lack the full capacity to reason, such as women; and (3) those whose capacities were undeveloped by proper upbringing, such as most other people in the society.

Examples like Aristotle's draw on what can be called the fallacy of false fixity. Fixed features of the self are seen as part of the nature of things. They cannot be other than they are and therefore they limit human deliberation because sensible people do not attempt to deliberate about what cannot be changed; one thinks in terms of them, one does not think about them. Human history is, of course, littered with examples of false fixities, ideas that in retrospect we realize were social myths that protected specific ways of life. Our present thinking, however, is no less liable to be formed by them and searching them out is, I believe, an essential if painful part of examining ideas of human excellence. Indeed, the need to identify them is a major reason why it is helpful, perhaps even necessary, for any such examination to have both historical depth and comparative range.

The Current Demand

All this means, I think, that religious ethics must critically question and then develop traditional notions of human excellence if they are to be applicable today. Crucial to this development is a process that involves two enterprises: *elaboration* and *emendation*. Each of these enterprises draws on the results of modern scholarship and reflection, but they differ in noteworthy ways.

Elaboration, a relatively benign activity, utilizes modern historical and textual scholarship to understand the language and context of texts and practices. It is especially important with examples of human excellence that appear in forms that either make them easily misunderstood or allow their challenge to be easily overlooked.

Emendation, a complicated and possibly dangerous activity, utilizes modern theoretical analyses to clarify, test, and reformulate traditional ideas and practices relevant to human excellence. It must reformulate these ideas and practices in a way that is appropriate to, shows appreciative fidelity toward, their meanings as judged by the most basic norms found in the tradition. But it must also reformulate them in a way that is credible to (meets the conditions of plausibility found in) our common contemporary experience, informed as that experience is by modern scientific explanations, historical consciousness, and ideas about the rights of all humans. Meeting both demands is difficult, and it may in some cases be impossible. It is, however, what is needed if most notions of human excellence are to remain alive.

Bibliography

Yearley, L. H. (1990): *Mencius and Aquinas: Theories of Virtue and Conceptions of Courage.* Albany, NY: State University of New York Press.

CHAPTER 5

Practical Reasoning and Moral Casuistry

Albert R. Jonsen

Practical reasoning is a phrase used in Western moral philosophy to designate the intellectual process whereby an agent deliberates and decides about a particular course of
action. Since moral decision and action is formulated in the light of some sort of general
principles, applicable to all similarly situated agents, particular agents must determine
how those general principles apply to the specific situation in which they will act (see
chapter "On Religious Ethics"). The logic of practical reasoning has been a topic of
interest since Aristotle delineated his views in the *Nicomachean Ethics*, pointing out how
deliberation and decision about practice differs from speculative or scientific reasoning
(1994: III, iii). Modern philosophers have studied how reasons serve to explain, evaluate, and justify intentional decisions and have analyzed the forms of inference involved
in statements containing such words as "ought," "should," etc. (Audi 1989; Gauthier
1963; Raz 1978). Since real moral agents decide and act in relation to specific, attainable ends and in the context of concrete circumstances, practical reasoning can be said
to be about "cases," that is, "instances" (in Latin, *casus*), in which the particular agent's
specific purposes and motives, as well as the extant circumstances of time, place, prob-
ability, and possibility, etc., can be described. Thus, the term "casuistry," although it has
a more particular meaning to be noted below, may be used as somewhat synonymous
with practical reasoning, and will so be used in this chapter about practical reasoning
in religious ethics.

  While diverse manners of practical reasoning appear in different traditions and
cultures, this chapter will attend particularly to the forms of casuistic reasoning that
have a prominent place in the ethical traditions of three historic religions: Judaism,
Christianity, and Islam. This review of the casuistic traditions aims at a general account
of casuistic reasoning, with recognition of some problems inherent in this form of
practical reasoning.

Textual Sources for Casuistry

Judaism finds the source of divine revelation in the five books of the Law given by Yahweh to Moses: Genesis, Exodus, Leviticus, Numbers, and Deuteronomy, called collectively the Torah. Christianity accepts the same five books, together with another 34 books of the Hebrew scriptures, called collectively the Old Testament, and the four gospels and 23 other writings, called the New Testament. Muḥammed designated Jews and Christians as "People of the Book," meaning that they had received a divine revelation contained in the written words of an inspired text, the Bible. Islam also has its Book, the Qur'ān, in which Allāh conveys to humankind a vision of the meaning of life and commands about how to live it.

Thus, in each of these historic faiths, a written text incorporates the fundamentals of belief, not in abstract terms, but in the specific communications of the Lord, Creator, and Redeemer. The form of that communication, in each of the holy books, is varied: stories about divine creation and providence, poetry about divine mercy and justice, and extensive rules about worship and about the behavior of believers in every aspect of their lives.

The faithful, who are guided by the sacred texts, also live in times and societies not exactly like those in which the divine words were spoken to the inspired scribes. Thus, while the commands are clearly in universal form and are intended to bind the faithful through all time, the differences in cultural, social, and linguistic settings of the faithful through history, require additional interpretation, beyond the casuistry found within the text itself (see chapter 7). Further, there is the theological question about inspired scripture itself: Does it represent the literal words of the divine source or does the human intermediary necessarily introduce the human elements of fallibility or cultural relativity and, if so, to what extent? Faced with these questions, each of the three faiths, through their long history, developed institutions for interpretation and commentary on the originating texts. Over many centuries, theological, moral, and legal commentary accumulated into elaborate systems of scholarly theory and method and of rules and opinions taught to the faithful.

Jewish Casuistry

Judaism reveres Torah as the primary source of revelation (see chapter 17). These books contain not only the Decalogue but also, according to Jewish tradition, another 613 commandments applicable to Jewish life. A scholarly class, the rabbis, reflected on every word of those books to reveal their deepest meaning and their relevance for observant Jews. Schools of interpretation, with differing emphases but a common purpose of elucidating the sacred text, grew up in Palestine, Babylon, and the Diaspora; the vast literary collection of their reflections constitute Talmud. The Talmudic literature, incorporating the commentary of a multitude of rabbis over many centuries, becomes the major secondary source of Jewish Law. Codes, composed for the most part during the Middle Ages, systematize the multifarious reflections of the rabbis. In general, the sum of Torah, Talmud, and Mishnaic commentaries and Codes make up Halakhah, the law of Jewish life, in its ritual and moral dimensions. However, all these sources are themselves written works, in need of continual interpretation for current times and problems. Rabbinic activity includes a dynamic process: responses to particular questions posed by the observant Jew facing a situation in which some aspect of the tradition seems challenged by previously unfamiliar circumstances. These responses, called Teshuva, (often given the Latin name *Responsa*), are directed to the immediate question but reflect the entire tradition and become part of the tradition (Freehof 1955).

The responding rabbi (or rabbinical council) first examines the texts of Torah and of Talmudic and Mishnaic commentary and the Codes for the most relevant guidance, notes any contradictions or obscurity in these sources, then attempts to reconcile these difficulties in order to find a way toward a resolution appropriate to the immediate case. In the most orthodox view, rabbinic resolution is more than advice; it binds the conscience of the questioner. These responses, which are given in the course of daily life, are often private but are sometimes recorded and collected, particularly if they issue from a rabbi of renowned piety and scholarship. The responses then enter the stream of interpretation of the Law and are used by subsequent rabbis as sources of wisdom. Among the vast number of known Teshuva (estimated at around 250,000 dating from several centuries before the Common Era), a recent collection is most poignant and revealing of rabbinic method and wisdom: responses issued during the Holocaust to Jewish questioners under the most extreme circumstances. One eloquent and heartrending response, issued by the Chief Rabbi in the Warsaw ghetto, considers whether an infant's crying might be stifled as Nazi stormtroopers hunted for hidden Jews, even if the stifling might smother the child. The rabbi answers in a long, scholarly review of the tradition about endangering life, which is almost uncompromising about protecting life, yet he comes to the conclusion that, although the child might not be killed, its life might be endangered to save the hidden Jews, for its own life would certainly be extinguished if the parents were discovered. This casuistry manifests how a tradition with the highest respect for the preservation of life might find grounds for an exception (Kirschner 1985).

Christian Casuistry

Christianity accepts the same first five books of the Hebrew Bible (see chapter 21). At the same time, the moral imperatives of Jesus announced in the gospels and the teachings of the first disciples reported in the rest of the New Testament, provide extensive teachings about the moral life, many of which, in Christian eyes, surpassed the Jewish Law in rigor and in sublimity. Early Christians endeavored to put into practice some of the "hard teachings" of Jesus, such as the imperative to leave father and mother to follow him, to turn the other cheek and put up the sword when attacked, and to refrain from marriage, and were forced to interpret these commands within the demands of daily life. In the early church, distinctions between counsels of perfection, as enunciated in the words of Jesus, and moral imperatives, stated in the Decalogue, marked the beginnings of casuistry. Clement, Bishop of Alexandria, for example, wrote extensive treatises to advise his Christian flock about how to live in the pagan surroundings of that great metropolis. When the church was officially recognized within the empire, the strict pacifism that appeared to be the teaching of Jesus had to accommodate the needs of civil defense. Christians served as soldiers and could not be simply told to put up the sword. St. Augustine, formulating the theology of church and state, initiated a casuistry of "just war," an idea already adumbrated in Roman authors, such as Cicero, in which the conditions of legitimate self-defense of person and nation allowed Christians to shed blood. A large casuistry developed around these questions (Kelsay and Johnson 1991).

A practice of confession of sins by a believer to a priest appeared in the late middle ages. Practiced in different ways in different churches, the church in the British Isles, particularly in Ireland, imposed on the faithful a particularly demanding regimen. Moral offenses were catalogued in detail and penances for each specified in books entitled Penitentials. Despite the detail, priests had to consider the grounds for excuse or mitigation and so a rudimentary casuistry developed that was carried by monks from Ireland onto the Continent. Toward the end of the eleventh century, there appeared a movement to organize church law and practice, which had developed largely out of the decrees of local bishops and regional counsels. Collections of these "canons," or rules, were made, inspired by the desire to order and reconcile them. As canonists, the lawyers of the church, performed these tasks, they encountered the many cases that had given rise, over time, to the decrees they were reconciling and, in so doing, formulated certain rules for the interpretation of cases. In 1215 a major church council, Lateran IV, promoted the practice of personal, private confession to a central place in Christian life, requiring all Christians to confess to a priest at least once a year. In the wake of this decree, the need arose to educate clergy throughout Europe about how to judge the seriousness of the sins confessed to them and to make discretionary decisions about penance and absolution. Much more sophisticated Penitentials were produced, often by the theological scholars of the new universities, in which the nature of virtues and vices was analyzed and the circumstances that rendered them more or less serious, that is, as mortal or venial sins, were explained, usually under the general heading of the Ten Commandments. These explanations were illustrated by "for examples," that is, "cases." These cases were sometimes reports of actual ones familiar to confessors or were fictitious ones used for didactic purposes.

The work of canonists and theologians drew on several sources. They not only referenced the precepts of the Bible, the comments of the Fathers, and the decrees of councils. They also utilized the rational techniques of scholastic thought, inspired by the Aristotelian renaissance in the thirteenth century. Also, a theory of natural law, inspired by Roman law and Ciceronian and Stoic philosophy, provided a conceptual framework for ethics which was not dependant on revelation. Christian casuistry, unlike Talmudic or Islamic, could proceed with wide ranging exploration of rational ethics and only peripheral references to revealed sources.

In the sixteenth century, casuistry emerged as a special branch of moral theology and a multitude of books, analyzing every conceivable moral act, appeared. The authors of these books were frequently members of the newly founded Jesuit order, whose interest in the education of young Catholics and in the ministry of the confessional made them the casuists *par excellence*. In 1656 the mathematical genius Blaise Pascal published *The Provincial Letters*, a scathing criticism of Jesuit casuistry in which he claimed that the techniques of rational analysis had been carried to extremes, justifying by clever reasoning the most outrageous violations of Christian morals and submerging the gospel message under sophistry. His criticism gave casuistry a bad reputation for centuries, and ascribed to the word "casuistry" an almost entirely pejorative meaning – a cynical, sophistic, deceptive distortion of moral rules in order to avoid obeying them through specious rationalization (Pascal 1967; Jonsen 1993). Despite Pascal's criticism and the temptation to abuse, a sound, serious practice of casuistry continued within the Catholic and Anglican, and to some extent, Lutheran and Calvinist, churches (Jonsen and Toulmin 1988; Mahoney 1987; Keenan and Shannon 1995).

During and after the Reformation, casuistry also came in for severe criticism from the Protestant reformers. As Protestantism developed, the formal techniques of casuistry withered, although all moral judgment required some sort of practical reasoning. In Anglicanism alone, a vigorous scholarly casuistry prevailed, closely resembling Roman Catholic casuistry, although notably more liberated from hierarchical doctrine (Kirk 1999).

Islamic Casuistry

Islam holds the Qur'ān to have been dictated to Mohammed by Allāh and to contain the substance of divine prescriptions for life (see chapter 25). In addition, the Ḥadīth, or traditions ascribing certain words and practices to the Prophet, and to his first companions, was also held in high esteem as a guide to the moral life. Islam, within the first century of its existence, became sovereign over a wide region of the Near East and North Africa. Its military and political dominance prevailed over Persian, Syrian, Byzantine, and Hellenistic states where substantial systems of law and moral custom already existed. Islamic rulers desired to bring those legal and customary systems into some conformity with the divine law expressed in Qur'ān. Early in Islamic history, then, judges (*quadis*) were appointed not simply to decide cases but to reinterpret them in light of Qur'ān and Ḥadīth, and out of these judicial activities arose Sharī'a, the law of Islam which contained both legal norms for social life and ethical norms for personal behavior, which were not sharply distinguished: all life for the believer, as well as all rules for the state, were included in Sharī'a. The task of interpreting Sharī'a, the jurisprudence and ethics of Islam, is called *Ficq* (Schacht 1964; Hourani 1971).

The daily life of the faithful encounters difficulties with the familiar norms of Sharī'a and those who wish to fulfill the law are encouraged to seek the opinion of scholars of Ficq. These scholars, *mufti*, devote themselves to the study of Qur'ān, Ḥadīth, and the traditions of interpretation. Organized in many schools of thought over centuries, these divided into traditionalists and rationalists: the former adhere closely to text and traditions, the latter allow the use of logic and rational methods, derived, as in medieval Christianity, from Aristotelian thought, to guide interpretation. Unlike Christian thinkers, Islamic scholars, even the rationalists, did not develop a formal theory of natural law ethics, although they left a large place for customary moral practices in their interpretation of Sharī'a. The mufti, either as individual scholars or in schools, consider cases submitted to them, formulate their opinion, *Ra'y*, and issue advice, called *Fatwā*, about behavior that would most closely conform to Sharī'a. The format of a Fatwā resembles the format of the Jewish Teshuva: reference to relevant scriptural texts, examination of scholarly opinion, rational efforts to interpret and reconcile opinions, allusion to analogies and formulation of advice. Fatwā can address political or personal problems. The consensus or agreement of the scholars, in a particular place or of a particular school or in all of the lands of Islam, provides an important criterion for the reliability of opinion. In the latter centuries of the Ottoman empire a bureaucracy was established, headed by a Grand Mufti of Istanbul, devoted entirely to the preparation of Fatwā for the guidance of government and of individual behavior.

Among the earliest and most fundamental moves of Islamic casuistry is the distinction of all moral law into five categories: obligatory, recommended, permitted, disapproved, and forbidden (there is debate about whether any acts are neutral). Working within these categories, mufti can draw careful distinctions about how stringently laws bind the believer. Thus, the ominous words of Qur'ān, "Fight in the cause of Allāh those who fight you . . . and slay them wherever you catch them" (S. 2, 190) can be interpreted as permissive, not obligatory, and it can be recommended that women, children, old men, and other non-combatants can be left unmolested. The words "those who fight you" can be interpreted to exclude these parties but if they, although non-combatants, give aid to the enemies of Allāh, it is permitted, perhaps obligatory, to execute them. It is disapproved to slay any conquered person who may be of use to Islam and it is forbidden to slay those who convert to Islam. Principles of mercy and moderation temper literal fulfillment of the law in the light of circumstances (Khadduri 1955).

Casuistic Method

The casuistries of these three faiths, while different in content and inspiration, are remarkably similar in their fundamental methodology. Crucial to each form of casuistry is the move between revealed text or universal ethical principle and the particular decision. The revealed text itself is rarely specific enough to meet the perplexity of the presented case and the texts themselves often seem to the uninitiated rather peripheral to the problem. For example, a text of the Book of Leviticus (19:16), "thou shalt not stand by the blood of your neighbor," serves as the starting point for a rich Talmudic casuistry about the duty to heal the sick. These words are certainly not an explicit command to heal, but one of the greatest Talmudists, Moses Maimonides (also a physician), reads them to say that anyone capable of rescuing another from drowning, from marauders, or from attacking beasts, who fails to do so, transgresses this command (Maimonides, *Hilkhot* 1.14). Maimonides clearly goes beyond the words of the text to what he considers its meaning. Modern Jewish bioethicists still reflect on cases of withholding technological life-support in the light of this text and its interpretations over time. Drawing any text close to an actual case demands both reverence for the text as well as intellectual ingenuity. It is this intellectual ingenuity that forms the heart of any casuistry.

However, intellectual ingenuity may also challenge reverence for the text or the principle. The human intellect is capable not only of reasoning but also of rationalization:

thus, scholars may utilize the techniques of reasoning, such as definition of terms, distinction and division of concepts and the subtle, often fallacious, steps of logic to reach any conclusion dictated by their preferences. Religious casuistry attempts to reign in the unfettered use of rational techniques by embedding the reasoning within the tradition of scholarship. Many casuists have considered similar cases and frequently come up with similar conclusions, sometimes even by different routes of reasoning. Their opinions are to be respected and the divergent opinions that may also appear are to be carefully analyzed, in order to discern the grounds for the differences and to reconcile them, insofar as possible. If reconciliation is not possible and a genuine difference of defensible opinion remains, the questioner is free to act in accord with various opinions. Here the reputation of the competing casuists and the reasonableness of the various opinions must be weighed. In each casuistic tradition, rules for this weighing of opinion are devised.

Reference to the tradition of scholarly casuists involves reference to the cases that those scholarly predecessors and contemporaries have decided. The cases are, as noted above, "similar" to the instant case and their conclusions are "similar." Again, the casuistries of the three faiths utilize reasoning by analogy as an indispensable technique. Reasoning by analogy involves identification of a case that seems similar to the present case and then carefully distinguishing the precise ways in which the present case resembles the former one, in expectation of finding some feature that allows the casuist to claim that this previously decided case is similar enough to the present case that the prior decision, or consensus of decisions, should be taken as the key to the resolution of the present case. It is, however, only the key, for the circumstances of the present case are likely to differ from the former one, or the circumstances of the former one might be too sketchily described to allow direct comparison. Thus, the importance of the circumstances must be carefully specified and their bearing on diverse resolutions evaluated.

These are central activities of casuistry: use of analogical reasoning and evaluation of circumstances. They too are open to abuse, since the choice of appropriate analogies and the description of circumstances may be very subjective. Here, the recourse to tradition is of less value, since at this point in the analysis, the casuist is on his own. He has been able to check his subjectivity by placing himself within the long conversation of his casuistic colleagues, but only up to the point where he must choose the appropriate analogy and weigh the current circumstances. Here the "prudence" or "practical wisdom" of the casuist, his ability to consider fairly and comprehensively the circumstances of this case, in light of relevant principles, becomes central. It is a virtue or talent of the experienced casuist. Casuistry, then, is both conservative and creative: it places cases within a tradition and then moves the tradition ahead by the decision in the present case. The primary check on unfettered ingenuity now becomes the response of the contemporary casuistic community, and the broader community of believers, to the new resolution of the new case.

Religious casuistry, then, is the practical reasoning of communities of faith. In the background always stand the scripture and traditional beliefs of the community. In the foreground stand the scholarly communities who interpret that scriptural and traditional background and teach it to the faithful. They use common rational methods of interpretation and, in addition, refer that interpretation to the preceding tradition of scholarship. They not only theorize but also respond to actual cases in which the faithful may face perplexity in acting according to their faith in current circumstances. They utilize to a high degree analogical reasoning, working from case to case, in order to reach a resolution that is both traditional and novel.

Bibliography

Aristotle. 1994: *The Nicomachean Ethics*, ed. H. Rackham. Cambridge, MA: Harvard University Press.

Audi, R. 1989: *Practical Reasoning*. London: Routledge.

Freehof, S. B. 1955: *The Responsa Literature*. Philadelphia, PA: Jewish Publication Society of America.

Gauthier, D. P. 1963: *Practical Reasoning: The Structure and Foundations of Prudential and Moral Arguments and their Exemplification in Discourse*. Oxford: Clarendon Press.

Hourani, G. F. 1971: *Islamic Rationalism: The Ethics of 'Abd al-Jabbar*. Oxford: Clarendon Press.

Jonsen, A. R. 1993: "Casuistical." *Common Knowledge* 2 (2), 48–66.

Jonsen, A. R. and Toulmin, S. E. 1988: *The Abuse of Casuistry: A History of Moral Reasoning*. Berkeley: University of California Press.

Keenan, J. F. and Shannon, T. A. (eds.) 1995: *The Context of Casuistry*. Washington, DC: Georgetown University Press.

Kelsay, J. and Johnson, J. T. (eds.) 1991: *Just War and Jihad: Historical and Theoretical Perspectives on War and Peace in Western and Islamic Traditions*. New York: Greenwood Press.

Khadduri, M. 1955: *War and Peace in the Law of Islam*. Baltimore, MD: Johns Hopkins University Press.

Kirk, K. E. 1999: *Conscience and Its Problems: An Introduction to Casuistry*, ed. D. H. Smith. Louisville, KT: John Knox/Westminster Press.

Kirschner, R. 1985: *Rabbinic Responsa of the Holocaust Era*. New York: Schocken Books.

Mahoney, J. 1987: *The Making of Moral Theology: A Study of the Roman Catholic Tradition*. Oxford: Oxford University Press.

Pascal, B. 1967: *The Provincial Letters*, trans. A. J. Krailsheimer. London: Penguin Books.

Raz, J. 1978: *Practical Reasoning*. New York: Oxford University Press.

Schacht, J. 1964: *An Introduction to Islamic Law*. Oxford: Clarendon Press.

CHAPTER 6

Authority and Religious Experience

Darrell J. Fasching

Ethics and Authority: The Twentieth-Century Crisis

The question of the relationship between ethics and authority is as old as civilization, but the events of the nineteenth and twentieth centuries seem to have raised our consciousness of it to a new level and in ways that make us sensitive to issues of cultural diversity. For the nineteenth century brought the colonial conquest of the globe in the name of Western religious and cultural "superiority" and was followed by the twentieth century, which brought us the global tragedy of two world wars, culminating in the attempted Nazi genocide of the Jews and numerous lesser wars since, intent on "ethnic cleansing." Fascism, Nazism, colonialism, racism, sexism, and religious prejudice are part and parcel of the human journey through these centuries.

What was learned from the Nuremberg trials after World War II is emblematic of these centuries, namely, that morality can be dangerous. For the crimes of war perpetrated in the death camps and elsewhere were too often "crimes of obedience." These were crimes in which the humanity of others was violated in the name of a morality of unquestioning obedience to higher authority that defined its victims as less than human and not worthy of life. In the aftermath of World War II, reacting to these crimes, the nations of the world took the unprecedented step of establishing a covenant of nations pledged to an ethic of human dignity and human rights – an ethic that makes a claim to be binding on persons of all religions and cultures. The founding of the United Nations in 1946 and the creation of the Declaration of Human Rights in 1948 were major milestones in the global history of human morality, marking an ethical revolution that declared limits on all authority, especially political authority.

In the aftermath of World War II, a microcosm of this global revolution in religion and ethics took place in the United States. A community of ethical revolutionaries inspired by the example of Mahatma Gandhi and led by M. L. King, Jr., Abraham Joshua Heschel, Thich Nhat Hanh, and others of the Civil Rights/Vietnam War era demonstrated that it was possible for persons of diverse religions and cultures to share a common ethic of human dignity, human rights, and human liberation (see chapter 51). It was an ethic not of unquestioning obedience to authority, but of disobedience – civil disobedience in defense of our common humanity across religious, cultural, and racial divisions. What such social activists from diverse religious traditions have demonstrated is that there can be ethical cooperation while sustaining religious diversity and that the essence of the ethical life lies in challenging authority in order to promote justice and compassion for all. What is striking is that each could find precedents for this understanding of the essence of ethics not only in their own traditions (in figures like the Buddha and Abraham) but also in each other's traditions, and all found inspiration in the life and death of Socrates. The story of the trial and execution of Socrates attracted these social activists because it offered them an ancient and authoritative example of the ethical life as a challenge to authority.

Our words "morality" and "ethics" are derived from Latin (*mos, mores*) and Greek (*ethos, ethike*) terms which originally meant the "customs" of the people – the sacred customs. It was Socrates who gave new meaning to the term "ethics," for his religious experiences led him to practice philosophy as the pursuit of wisdom through the questioning of such customs (see chapter "On Religious Ethics"). Although the terms "ethics" and "morality" are often used interchangeably, I find it useful to give privileged status to the Socratic usage for the term "ethics" while reserving for the term "morality" the pre-Socratic meaning of "sacred customs." Thus we shall understand sacred customs as the traditional morality of a community and ethics precisely as the questioning of that morality.

Ethics as the Religious Compulsion to Question Sacred Morality

If, as is likely, the Latin root (*religio*) for our word "religion" comes from *religare* (to tie or bind), it is because the Romans used the term to refer to their sense of being "tied" or "bound" in relations of ritual obligation to those powers they believed governed their destiny. In their case these were the gods and goddesses who ruled the forces of nature.

Just what powers (or power) a people believe themselves to be "tied and bound" to, and what these powers expect of them, is defined through the myths (stories) and rituals (obligatory actions) passed from one generation to the next (see chapters 8 and 9). Religion is always about a sacred way of life. Humans tend to treat as sacred whatever power or powers they believe govern their destiny and the way of life these powers originate. In primal societies, the right way to live is the rite way. And in all societies myth and ritual deeply influence the customs or way of life that ties and binds a people to its sacred ancestors and/or gods. Through myths and rituals such sacred powers speak with authority and are taken with utmost seriousness.

To speak with authority, according to the *Oxford English Dictionary*, is to speak with a "godlike manner" – a manner which is commanding, imperial, perhaps even dictatorial. To speak with authority is to speak as (or for) the author, the originator. In the beginning were the ancestors, the spirits, and the gods who authored a sacred way of life and provided an originating model of how things ought to be.

Since the beginning of recorded history there has been an intimate connection between religion and authority. In primal cultures authority seems to be primarily tied and bound up with stories and rituals of creation or originating power (see chapter 13). The gods and the sacred ancestors speak with authority because they defeated the forces of chaos and death and created the sacred order of the cosmos that makes life possible. Priests and shamans mediate that authority. There is a taboo that surrounds the sacred that forbids all questioning. The way things are, as reflected in the sacred customs of the people, mirrors their sacred origins. Consequently, the hierarchy of status, power, and authority in a society is given and not open to debate. One cannot argue with "the way things are." The way things are is the way they ought to be (Is = Ought). In such societies we have morality but not yet ethics (see chapters 1 and 2).

Throughout the history of the use of the term "authority" there has been an ambivalent tension between the "authoritative" and "authoritarian" as aspects of its meaning. Authoritative power, we could say, is that power which commands through the spontaneous respect it elicits from others, whereas authoritarian power is that power which commands through raw force, even at the price of respect. This distinction has led to the common contrast of authority with power (as coercion). From this perspective, authoritarianism as a resort to power is really the reaction of one who has lost authority and so is no longer accepted spontaneously by others as worthy of respect. In such cases, respect is replaced by fear as the motivation for taking a command seriously.

Socrates, however, insisted that no one could be ethical who succumbs to the final fear – the threat of death. For Socrates, ethics involved questioning the authority of Athenian sacred customs by asking: Is what people call "good" really the good? Socrates was put on trial and executed for "impiety towards the gods" and "corrupting the youth" because he dared to question and teach others to question the sacred way of life of Athenian society.

Socrates' goal was not to demean the Athenian way of life but to raise it to a higher level. The paradox of Socrates' criticism of the sacred morality of Athenian society was that it was rooted in religious experience – an alternative form of religious experience to that which had shaped Athenian society. Responding to his accusers, Socrates insisted that he was neither irreligious nor an atheist. On the contrary, he said he was commanded to doubt and to question the Athenian way of life by his own "daimon." This God, he said, sent him as a "gadfly" to the citizens of Athens to teach them to lead virtuous lives and seek justice. To doubt, and to teach others to doubt and to question, he says, "is what my God commands; and it is my belief that no greater good has ever befallen you in this city than my service to my God" (Plato 1969: 62).

The trial of Socrates represents an important moment in the history of Western religious ethics in relation to the question of authority. Socrates' challenge to the religiously grounded polity of Athenian society presents one of the first recorded acts of civil disobedience. Here, the sacred law and order of Athenian society was called into question in the name of a type of religious experience that claimed the authority to *transcend* (in the literal sense of "going beyond") a given sacred way of life and offer a "higher" vision of the good life. In the Socratic model "the way things are" is challenged in the name of the way they ought to be (Ought vs. Is), where the "ought" appeals to an authority that transcends sacred order – namely, the god who compels him to question. Socrates suggests that the authoritativeness of this divine compulsion is testified to by his poverty – that he was willing to sacrifice personal advantage (even his life) to respond to this call.

Model Ethical Activists

It is significant that the social activists of the mid-twentieth century, the spiritual children of Gandhi from diverse religious religions and cultures, who challenged the authoritarian systems of their time, cited Socrates as a model. But Socrates was not the only such model, nor the earliest. They also had other examples of the religious challenge to sacred authority available to them from both East and West. Martin Luther King, Jr., cited Jesus and the prophets. Abraham Joshua Heschel cited not only the prophets but especially the biblical patriarch Abraham as a model for challenging the authority of President Lyndon Johnson to conduct the Vietnam War. When Abraham fears that God will slay the innocent along with the guilty in the city of Sodom, he has the audacity to say: "Will you indeed sweep away the righteous with the wicked? . . . Shall not the Judge of all the earth do what is just?" (Genesis 18:23, 25). If Abraham did not shrink from challenging God in the name of justice then the president, said Heschel, was hardly above questioning. For Abraham and for Heschel, authority is authoritative only when it meets the requirements of justice.

Gandhi and Thich Nhat Hanh could also find inspiration in the life of the Buddha, who insisted that even his own teachings be questioned by his followers: "Just as the experts test gold by burning it, cutting it and applying it on a touchstone, my statements should be accepted only after critical examination and not out of respect for me" (Unno 1988: 129–47; quoting *Tattvasamgraha* 1926: 3588). The internal structure of the Buddha's monastic community took the form of a democracy in which each monk had an equal vote. This community expressed the Buddhist consciousness of the equality of all selves (for all selves are empty) and stood in stark contrast to the hierarchy of the caste-structured sacred society of India. The authoritativeness of the Buddha's teaching is attested to by his refusal to be authoritarian.

All religious communities (indeed, all human communities) embody a morality, but the emergence of an ethic requires a further step. The relation to authority is not just a problem for ethics to solve, it goes to the heart of what ethics is. Ethics involves the transcendence of morality through the questioning of the authority upon which that morality is founded. As with the story of Socrates, so with those of Jesus, Abraham, and Siddhartha: ethics begins with a type of religious experience that questions sacred authority and its expression in traditional morality. Ethics, so conceived, is paradoxically both a religious and an impious desacralizing activity at the same time. In my work (Fasching 1993; Fasching and deChant 2001) I have called this category of religious experiences, experiences of the holy in contrast to the experiences of the sacred.

Following a suggestion made by French sociologist Jacques Ellul (1975) in his analysis of the social dynamics of religion, the terms "sacred" and "holy" are used here as antonyms rather than synonyms. This deliberately goes against the common practice of using the two terms interchangeably. Separating the uses of "sacred" and "holy," and in a parallel manner "morality" and "ethics," in this way makes it clear that the collection of social behaviors that are generally labeled "religious" are not all religious in the same way. As Max Weber pointed out, religious experience has the power to sacralize but also to desacralize. Giving separate meanings to terms that have been used interchangeably accents these different functions of religion.

In a sacred order the way things are (as established by sacred origins) is the way they ought to be and so persons are defined by and confined to their place in the sacred hierarchy of society as legitimated by myth and ritual. Religious experiences fit the category of the holy when they prompt the questioning of the authority of such sacred ways of life. The difference between the sacred and the holy is not a difference to be found between religions, as if some were pure models of one and some pure models of the other. The sacred and the holy should be seen as opposing tendencies, or ways of experiencing life, to be found in all persons and all communities. Every actual culture and religion is likely to embody aspects of both the sacred and the holy in a complex and sometimes self-contradictory way of life.

Ethical Consciousness: Authoritative or Authoritarian?

Wherever ethical consciousness emerges, sacred order is called into question. It is legitimate to ask "by what authority" is existing sacred authority questioned? The answer, of course, can hardly be found by appealing to some "authority," but only by appealing to the authoritativeness of ethical experience itself. Wherever ethical consciousness emerges, the authority of sacred order will come to be seen as authoritarian if it is not modified by the authoritative ideal of selfless compassion. It is selfless compassion which authoritatively puts sacred order/authority in question. A good society must be more than the "cosmos writ small" providing an orderly world in which to dwell; it must also provide an order that is just and compassionate for all its members.

Nathan's challenge to King David's authority

A story of the ethical confrontation with authority of comparable importance to that of Socrates is found in 2 Samuel 11 of the Tanach, the Jewish Bible (later incorporated into Christianity as the Old Testament). It is the story of how David, King of Israel (ca. 1000 BCE) lusted after Bathsheba, the wife of one of his soldiers, Uriah. David had Uriah sent to the front lines of battle so that he would be killed, allowing David to take Bathsheba for himself. According to the story, the God of Israel then sent the prophet Nathan to confront David by telling him a story about a rich man who owned a very large herd of sheep. But when a guest came he took the only lamb of a poor man (for whom the lamb was as if a member of the family, loved like one of his own children), slaughtered it, and fed it to his guest. When David heard the story his anger flared and he said: " 'As God lives, the man who did this deserves to die. He must make fourfold restitution for the lamb, for doing such a thing and showing no compassion.' Then Nathan said to David, 'You are the man'" (2 Samuel 12:5–7).

Because the story Nathan tells David is a "story" – either fictive or at least about someone else – it disarms David. It places David in the situation philosophers would typically identify as the ethical point of view, that of the "disinterested observer" who can be objective because he is not personally involved. From this perspective, David sees immediately that an injustice has been done. But then, in a second step, the story quickly moves David emotionally from disinterestedness to empathy. That is, it creates in him a sense of identification with the victim which outrages him and compels him to act. Only then is David prepared to reason "objectively" about what is good and what is evil and unwittingly stand in judgment of himself. For Nathan's abrupt turning of the story into an allegory for David's own situation forces David to confront his own actions. Ethical insight occurs when David identifies with the pain of another. Genuine ethical insight occurs when we see and judge our own actions through the eyes of the one who will be affected by our actions, as if we were that person. This is what Nathan's story enables David to do.

As king, David had the power to impose his own morality on the situation and yet he is unable to excuse his own actions with either the authoritarian claim that the king decides what is right and wrong, or with the libertarian claim that every individual has a right to make their own rules, deciding for themselves what is right and what is wrong. He tried that and failed. He failed because the story seduced him into identifying with the victim of his actions, which enabled him to see the injustice of his actions by enabling him to empathically identify with the victim's experience of injustice – of being wrongfully violated. The ethical point of view induced in David by Nathan's story transcends both authoritarianism and libertarianism and speaks authoritatively. As such it leads David to condemn himself in spite of himself. When David identifies with the victim, he realizes that what he has violated is not a rule or a principle but another person like himself. He recognizes the humanity of the stranger and the authoritative claim that humanity makes on his own conscience.

Ethical consciousness as authoritative

What separates religious ethics from purely philosophical ethics is the notion that our ordinary state of consciousness is distorted and disoriented by deeply (unconscious) selfish emotions (see chapter 12). Therefore, until the self has undergone a profound spiritual transformation of personality, it is not capable of seeing, understanding, and reasoning correctly. Thus, unlike philosophical ethics, religious ethics usually entails engagement in rituals and spiritual practices in combination with powerful orienting stories (stories of saints and heroes, parables of ethical insight, etc.) intended to bring about such a reorienting transformation through which the individual, like David under the influence of Nathan's story, comes to identify with the pain and suffering of the other.

That kind of awakening of ethical compassion is not unique to any one religious tradition. It is, for instance, described in Mahāyāna Buddhism as "becoming the other." According to the *Bodhicharyavatara* of Santideva: "All have the same sorrows, the same joys as I . . . so likewise this manifold universe has its sorrow and its joy in common

. . . Why should I not conceive my fellow's body as my own self? . . . I will cease to live as self, and will take as my self my fellow-creatures" (Burtt 1955: 139–40). A similar sense is expressed in the writings of Paul in Christianity, when he says that in Christ the whole of creation forms one body and the faithful community are those who are aware that all are "members of one another" such that if one experiences pain, so do all and likewise with joy (1 Corinthians 12).

Gandhi's challenge to authority: A model of ethical consciousness

Finally, nowhere is the link between such compassion and ethics as the challenging of authority clearer than in the teachings of Gandhi on the *Bhagavad Gītā* and non-violence. The *Gītā* tells the story of Arjuna and his brothers, who are about to enter into battle against their cousins who attempted to cheat them out of their fair share of their deceased father's kingdom. As the *Gītā* opens, Arjuna is on the battlefield in his chariot with his driver, Kṛṣṇa, awaiting the beginning of the battle. Arjuna confesses to Kṛṣṇa that he has no taste for the fight. He wishes neither to kill nor be killed. Much of the *Gītā* is then taken up with Kṛṣṇa attempting to persuade Arjuna that it is his caste duty to fight and even kill. Killing another, he is instructed, will not lead to negative karma or moral culpability, if he does so out of selfless duty rather than attachment to personal gain. Then in chapter 11 Kṛṣṇa reveals his true identity as the all highest deity, Viṣṇu, lord of life and death. In a rather violent vision he is shown that not he (Arjuna) but Viṣṇu decides who lives and who dies. By the time the *Gītā* reaches its conclusion, Arjuna is ready to stand up and fight in obedience to the authority of the all highest power, Viṣṇu.

A literal reading of the *Gītā* seems to lead to a morality of unquestioning obedience. What is astonishing is that Gandhi found authorization for just the opposite, the questioning of authority and the practice of non-violent civil disobedience. He accomplished this through a three-point strategy. First, he insisted that the *Gītā* must be read spiritually rather than literally. It was, he said, an allegory of the struggle of good and evil within the self. Second, he argued that the spiritual essence of the *Gītā*'s teaching (and of Hinduism) is the "oneness" of all humanity. His practice of *satyagraha* was a spiritual clinging to the truth of this oneness. Such a clinging gives birth to compassionate identification with the suffering of all others and leads to *ahiṃsā* or non-violence. Non-violence, here, does not mean a passive surrender to suffering and injustice, but an active transformative mode of civil disobedience as a strategy for alleviating them. Third, he argued that the test of all authority, including sacred scripture, was ethics derived from authoritative experiential insight. He recognized that there were other interpretations of the *Gītā*, but argued that forty years of putting his life on the line, endeavoring to live by the deep truths of the *Gītā*, gave him the authority to call more superficial or literal readings into question.

Like Socrates, Gandhi offered his own life of poverty and self-sacrifice (*brahmacharya*) as an authoritative justification of his challenge to all authority (whether of sacred Hindu scriptures or of British political domination). In this way Gandhi offers us our final dramatic example of religious ethics as the power of ethical consciousness, through identification with the other (becoming the other), as the authoritative basis for challenging authority.

Bibliography

Burtt, E. A. (ed.) 1955: *The Teachings of the Compassionate Buddha*. New York: Mentor, New American Library.

Ellul, J. 1975: *The New Demons*. New York: Seabury Press.

Fasching, D. J. 1993: *The Ethical Challenge of Auschwitz and Hiroshima: Apocalypse or Utopia?* Albany: State University of New York Press.

Fasching, D. J. and deChant, D. 2001: *Comparative Religious Ethics: A Narrative Approach*. Oxford: Blackwell.

Plato. 1969: "The Trial of Socrates: The Apology" in *The Last Days of Socrates*, trans. H. Tredennick. London: Penguin Books.

Tattvasamgraha. 1926. Baroda: Gaekwad Oriental Series.

Unno, T. 1988: "Personal Rights and Contemporary Buddhism" in *Human Rights and World Religions*, ed. L. S. Rouner. Notre Dame, IN: University of Notre Dame Press.

2 Transmission

CHAPTER 7
Text and Canon

Michael Fishbane

Introductory Considerations

A characteristic feature of the great historical religions is the formulation of their teachings, laws, and norms into collections of authoritative teachings. The status of these diverse instructions varies, depending upon the status of the teacher (e.g., prophet, priest, or wise man) and their putative source (in divine revelation, guild esoterica, or experience and tradition). Moreover, these "text ensembles" (be they oral or written) are variously deemed to be sealed and sacred by their societal stewards, such that their classical content is closed and their transcription or recitation are part of the ritual order. Hence, distinctions are regularly made between the primary or foundational sources of authority and subsequent secondary traditions that deal with their meaning and ongoing significance (see chapter 6). The closure of the initial teachings gives them all a fixed, canonical status, and whatever the form of their initial presentation (oral or written), the end result is the emergence of a written scripture which has the status of a holy object, to which nothing may in principle be added or removed. On the other hand, the secondary traditions remain theoretically open and subject to ongoing modifications or revisions through interpretation; though, in time, these oral instructions are also written down and develop their own canonical status, thus requiring explications of both their own meanings as well as how they are assumed to explicate the scriptures (see chapter 5). Such is the recurrent dialectic, and it produces a type of sensibility that we may well call "canon consciousness." Its effect upon religion, and upon the ethical life practiced within its contours, is considerable and merits reflection and analysis.

Among the Western religions, the Hebrew Bible is a paradigm example of the processes just noted. It is a massive anthology of foundational instructions, memories, and traditions from ancient Israel, recording in written form a variety of divine and human teachings, as well as a large assortment of practices both official and popular (and rooted in physical or verbal performance) that in one way or another were preserved and deemed worthy of transmission. In the process of tradition-building that developed, diverse narratives, laws, and practices were variously integrated, wherever possible, or were collected in self-contained units. The editorial result preserves a great mass of materials, even on the same subject, covering a time expanse of a millennium and more, and collated from various cultic, legal, and royal centers, as well as from a variety of scribal schools and wisdom traditions. Certainly, hierarchies of authority and instruction may readily be observed (in both the category of divine revelation and in the category of human wisdom): the teachings vouchsafed to Moses and the prophets were topmost; and below them come any number of legists and priests who claimed to teach the older laws, as well as individuals whose proverbs and reflections were grounded in reason or experience. The upshot is a welter of instructions, quite often tangled and contradictory. This is particularly evident from the internal evidence of scripture itself, where authoritative teachings were interpolated with secondary instructions – for further clarification, qualification, or harmonization of the histori- cally diverse materials; or for purposes of revisions and correction on the basis of new or competing values (see Fishbane 1985).

We might therefore note the existence of modes of canon consciousness within the canon-in-formation. Much was at stake. Insofar as the separate teachings all provided warrants (of different types and authority) for action, or their enforcement, the precise meaning of these teachings would have to be clear, as well as their interrelationships (insofar as they were complementary, supplementary, or contradictory). Interpretation is therefore an inherent component of the emergent biblical "text culture," though matters are much more simple when the traditions were still open to change and cir- culated in separate units. With the closure of the canon, the multiplicity of teachings on any subject increased, raising the thorny issue of just what the warrant of scripture was on any given point. Conversely, the delimitation of a canon fixed the formulations themselves, but these then required interpretation to make them livable – either because the received formulation was too loose and ambiguous, or because its values appeared to be problematic to later eyes and sensibilities. The sources were thus under- stood to project certain legal or ethical standards and values that could be variously accepted, rejected, or transformed on the basis of the norms, standards, or values of later readers. These intersecting "value vectors" are of immense hermeneutical and cultural importance. Paradoxically, the linguistic conditions for one set of ethical values and action (the canon) may also provide the site for their exegetical revision – in whole or in part. In this way, the authority of the ancient canon is both sustained and honored in the breach. One might even contend that the strength of a traditional culture (or one rooted in the language of precedents) depends upon its capacities to utilize the inherited formulations of a canon, without sacrificing its ongoing ethical will or judgment.

In the ensuing discussion, Jewish law and ethics will provide the paradigmatic cases to illustrate modalities of how certain Western religions have negotiated their values in and around an authoritative scripture. They will hopefully also provide a paradigm for a certain mentality and sensibility in which ethical action is part and parcel of a larger realm of religious duties – be these authorized by divine revelation or human reason, or both. In the present discussion, texts will be chosen largely from the classical collections of ancient rabbinic Bible interpretation, called Midrash, during the second to fourth centuries CE. Their explicit hermeneutical character will best allow us to see how scriptural exegesis negotiated the vectors of values just noted – deftly authorizing the new as a species of the old, and the old as encoding ensuing meaning. The following examples are meant to serve as models only, and not by any means to characterize the full range of types of ancient Jewish religious ethics and values. Rooted in the canon of Hebrew scripture, we find here a privileged witness to a mode of moral reasoning or justification through textual exegesis.

Models and Cases

Reactions and revisions

Among the "hard cases" bequeathed to later tradition is the rule found in Deuteronomy 21: 18–21 concerning a "wayward and rebellious son who does not listen to the voice of his father and the voice of his mother." It goes on to state that "they reprove him," but he heeds them not; and then "they seize him and take him out" to the local elders at the gate. They say to these persons that their son is rebellious, does not heed them, and indulges in gluttony. The sentence for this crime is that all the men of the city shall stone the guilty son to death, so that this evil will be eradicated and "all Israel will heed and fear." Clearly, a certain measure of procedure is presented in the conditions that are to ensue before and during the trial. Presumably, the issue of rebellion is deemed a repeated offense of insubordination that also includes reproval or warning before the son is taken to the judges; and it is notable that the offense is unspecified and that it is against both the father and the mother (probably intended to mean either one of the family order, and not just the father). However, at the trial itself, the matter of reproval is not specified, leaving the impression that this is not a separate condition, but a feature of the repeated attempts of the parents to make the son obey; and further, the vague category of rebellion is supplemented by references to gluttony, suggesting that this represents the need to specify the type of rebellion, and probably not to delimit it entirely. Withal, we see that the son has no judicial say or defense in his trial – possibly because he is a minor or because the parents have complete hegemony. Either way, the parents have total discretion about whether the offense is actionable, and can press charges without prior restraint or subsequent court investigation. Moreover, it is notable that the penalty of death is executed by all "the men of the city" and does not specify the parents at all (and it certainly does not include the mother); and that this harsh verdict is intended to serve as a public deterrent to such misdemeanors.

The rule as formulated is thus puzzling and problematic in many places, even on its own terms. Later commentators accentuated these matters in their discussions of the canonical rule, and their different attempts to justify or delimit it reveal aspects of their moral concerns and sensibilities (Halbertal 1997). The rule in this religious source thus sets the template for certain features of ethics bearing on family law, whereas the cases of exegetical reasoning revise the absolute warrant of the text and refocus the ethical issues involved. A spectrum of issues emerges.

The first matter to be noted in the earliest stratum is moral outrage at the gap between crime and punishment: "And because [the son] ate and drank [a specified overdose of] meat and wine he is to be stoned [to death]?!" (Finkelstein 1966: 253 [pisqa 220]). Such a query sharply exposes an unethical dimension of the law, and thus requires a response. One tack is to protect the law and its overall moral purpose, and this is done by transforming the initial exclamation into a rhetorical question. Since for this position the unethical character of the law is unthinkable, the solution is to see the law not as dealing simply with a rude and uncontrollable son, but with an offender whose sociopathic character has hereby been revealed, such that the law must impose a harsh penalty at the outset (when the person is relatively innocent) in order to prevent a more dangerous crime in the future (Hoffmann 1908–19: 131). The tactics of proof offered vary: in some cases they are simply asserted or presented (Hoffmann 1908–19: 131), in other instances the procedure is exegetical and uses traditional forms of hermeneutical logic (Finkelstein 1966: 251 [pisqa 218]). In both cases the underlying ethical concern of the ruling is clear and firm, its intention being to protect the social fabric as a whole through a precautionary action: just as one may kill a real attacker in self-defense, so must the law protect the people from the real or imminent danger of a rebellious son. The culprit is thus moved out of the category of a family nuisance into one that justifies the use of preemptive legal force to protect society. Through this reasoning, the punishment of death is made to fit the crime. But in the effort to provide an ethical justification for the authoritative divine law, the new rule becomes readily subject to abuse by less than omniscient human legislators. The paradox is here pressing, and may serve to highlight a danger for religious ethics when it settles on strategies of exegetical justification – rather than taking on the language of difficult laws and defanging their force.

More decisive in this regard are those interpreters who turn the formulations of the old rule into pawns of their new moral purpose. Several strategies occur. One of these is to take on the term "son" and so delimit its age range (between youngster and pubescent young adult) as to make it of fleeting applicability (M. Sanhedrin 8.1). A second strategy is to pick up on the apparently redundant phrase "the voice of his father and the voice of his mother" and turn this into a razor's edge to reduce the applicability of the law. Thus the clever interpreters said that this clause means that the son has to be warned by the voice of both parents – which has to be identical; and just as their voice must be identical, so also must their size and appearance be the same (M. Sanhedrin 8.4; B.T. Sanhedrin 71a). Clearly, this is an absurdity, and only marks the need to take an offensive but ineradicable law and make it practically inapplicable and void. A similar tack is taken by others who so define the nature of this gluttony (in terms of consuming vast quantities of meat and wine simultaneously) as to make the conditions for its performance humanly impossible to execute. Indeed, in all this, the moral will of the later tradition subverts the rule entirely. Perhaps for this reason, if not just for reasons of absolute outrage, the opinion is even given that the law of the rebellious son was never meant to be applied, but was only given as an exercise for exegesis – and that just this is the sole merit of the rule and the sole basis for a divine reward for its fulfillment (B.T. Sanhedrin 71a). Hence, if at one end of the foregoing spectrum of interpretations we saw an attempt to discern the deeper divine purpose in a rule whose punishment does not seem to fit the crime, at the other is an attempt to see a divine pedagogy that confirms the moral will of the interpreters themselves. Indeed, herewith the canon has itself provided the culture with a case that can be used to teach exegetes how to subvert its own applications when these are deemed ethically improper. Thus, while the canon of divine scripture is formally honored, the canon of traditional interpretations shows repeated attempts to displace its effectiveness through a casuistry that honors the moral will of the sages even more. In the process, the canon can even become the site of ethical reflection and reform.

Delimitation or expansion of operative conditions

The ensuing cases continue some aspects of the preceding model, but show in a unique manner how the formal features of a law can be applied in ways that promote certain moral values or alleviate certain immoral situations (see chapters 11 and 14). In these instances, the moral will of the interpreter provides new warrants and conditions that allow the law to rise to its highest value potential. I choose two polar instances from the rules of witness: the case of the abandoned wife (*agunah*) and the cases of capital crimes. The legislators revise the same rules of testimony in two opposite directions in order to safeguard and even serve moral values of the legal culture as a whole. Indeed, they show the potential flexibility of a canonical culture where the moral will is determined to be flexible for the sake of the dignity of its citizens and the value of life as a whole.

Biblical legislation is absolutely clear on the requirement of two witnesses to produce valid testimony; and a great amount of rabbinic discussion attempts to determine just how the witnesses are deemed to complement one another. With respect to married women, rabbinic law is also precise and clear on the point that a woman is permitted to remarry only if she has received a valid writ of divorce, or if there is valid testimony that her first husband is dead. An *agunah* is a married woman in a limbo and potentially irremediable situation, insofar as she may have been abandoned by her husband, or otherwise put in an intolerable predicament by virtue of the fact that she has no divorce document (either because the man cannot be found or refuses to do so); or because there is no valid testimony from two witnesses that her husband is dead (as, for example, in cases of soldiers missing in action, or as was recently the case with unconfirmed deaths at the World Trade Center). This rule notwithstanding, rabbinic law went to exceptional lengths to protect a woman from a life of solitude due to the circumstances just noted. With respect to a missing husband, the normally rigorous application of the rules of testimony by courts that had no means of proving the death of the husband were relaxed and made more lenient. For example, Rabban Gamliel the Elder (first century CE) resolved the problem by adjusting the rules of evidence themselves, and he gave a rule (now codified in the Mishnah) that in cases of no legally certain evidence of death, the testimony of one witness was sufficient, even if that testimony was hearsay only, or even if the testimony was brought by persons normally deemed invalid to give legal evidence (like a bondswoman or a slave) (M. Yebamot 16.7). Thus, hereby, a difficult rule was suspended owing to circumstances, and canonical law (of written scripture and rabbinic tradition) was revised owing to a certain moral temperament. And once that happened, a permanent loophole was left open so that judges could remedy other difficult cases of a similar kind. An example from a millennium later proves the point, for we have at hand a *responsum* of Maimonides (thirteenth century CE) concerning a case where there was only the testimony of a non-Jewish woman that a certain man had been killed, and this testimony was brought to the court as hearsay evidence. Maimonides decided that this testimony was sufficient and that the Jewish woman was free to remarry. In support of his ruling, he articulated a fundamental principle that came to serve as a canon for moral rectitude in such cases thereafter. He noted: "We do not enter into lengthy and detailed examinations of the testimony offered on behalf of an *agunah*. Moreover, whoever adopts a stringent position in such cases, and subjects the evidence offered to a detailed investigation and examination, *does not behave properly*. [Indeed,] our sages are displeased with this conduct, since it was their specific rule that we are to take the most lenient position with respect to an *agunah*" (Maimonides 1934: 157 [no. 159]).

Clearly, the application of the canon is left to judicial discretion, and Maimonides not only made his own moral position clear, but also gave it further warrant by attributing this sensibility to the early sages, whose revision of the rule was taken as a sign of moral probity as well as the warrant for further remedies in the same spirit. The complex dialectics of text, canon, and morality are fully played out in this case.

But the wheel of testimony can turn in the opposite direction as well, when the values of life impose themselves on the will of a custodian of the canon. For example, as against the maximalist relaxation of rules of testimony just noted, cases involving capital punishment could produce highly stringent applications of the rule in order to minimize, if not eradicate, the possibilities of issuing a verdict of death. Indeed, in some circles, antipathy to the death penalty was so severe that the details required for valid testimony were taken to extreme lengths. Normally, the need for two eyewitnesses to produce absolutely congruent testimony established a very high judicial standard, and it was very rigorously enforced. But while this procedure ensured the probity of the court, in certain hands the rules were also used to subvert the process itself. Such is the case when Rabbi Yoḥanan ben Zakkai (first century CE) was faced with a murder case, and he required the witnesses to provide detailed descriptions of the stalks of the figs on the tree near which the murder was alleged to have taken place (M. Sanhedrin 5.2). This made the application of the testimony virtually impossible, for the judicial conditions he imposed were in fact a razor's edge for the sage to cut off the necessary testimony at its root.

What can be learned from these contrary cases, which bear on cultures that are locked into canonical formulations of rules that one would not want to tamper with, but are faced with potential and actual instances where these rules might produce or aggravate some unwanted situation? These formulations not being readily amenable to exegetical revision, they were variously suspended or reformulated in order to remedy difficult instances, or they were so applied as to produce the desired result. The point to stress is that the requirement to save and conserve the authority of the canonical law need not prevent or frustrate the cultivation or application of moral values and value judgments that might contradict the normal or formal enforcement of a rule. These values may cóme from within the canonical system itself or from the outside, but their bold applications show that a cultural system remains alive by virtue of the vigor and manner with which it addresses difficult issues and allows the same text to provide the warrant for alternate actions. It is in the arena of this debate that religious laws and ethics are tested and proved. One might even say that the received formulations of a canon provide a framework for an ongoing cultural pedagogy, whereby the conservation or cultivation of the laws may be ethically enacted and evaluated.

Tensions between ethics and norms

Another significant dimension of the relationship between text, canon, and ethics is where there are tensions between the strict formulation of a rule and the guiding ethical dimension that may be overridden by comporting with such a formalism. Indeed, it brings to the fore the fact that ethical principles must guide the application of the law in order to safeguard the overarching norms of justice and equity. We may take an example from the law of sales, where the basic rule is that one does not acquire proper title to moveable property, even if money has been exchanged, until the purchaser of the goods performs an act of drawing the object (actually or symbolically) into his possession. Such an action derives from an older customary stratum of sales, but it was retained as a component of gaining title. However, in the process, a gap could arise of a moral nature, as when two persons enter into a verbal agreement and even exchange money, but the buyer has not performed the requisite ritual of "drawing" the goods into his domain. Now in the rule as canonized in the Mishnah, the vendor formally has the right to withdraw from the purchase agreement with no penalty (M. Baba Metzi'a 4.2). But the Mishnah goes on to say that it is improper for anyone to take advantage of this loophole simply on formal grounds; one may have a legal right, but this is not the morally right thing to do. To stress the point, the text states that God will curse such a person "who does not stand by his word" (M. Baba Metzi'a 4.2). The higher principle is therefore stressed, in order to strike down a narrow application of the law. Maimonides summarizes the case a thousand years later, and gives a further moral dimension in his codification of it. He says that a person "who changes his mind" after an agreement has been struck, be he the vendor or the buyer, "has not acted in a manner befitting a Jew" (M. Torah, Hilkhot Mekhirah 7.1).

This becomes the standard, and introduces a principle of ethical rectitude that overrides the strict letter of the law. A more specific articulation of what that principle might be is stated in a commentary on Deuteronomy 6:18. The words "you shall do what is right and good (ha-yashar veha-ṭov) in God's eyes" seem initially puzzling, since they appear both too vague, on the one hand, and apparently irrelevant on the other (since the biblical canon is full of very specific rules of behavior). But this is exactly the point, says Nahmanides (thirteenth century CE). On the one hand, scripture (the textual canon) could not state every single possible rule of behavior that might arise; hence, the phrase is not empty, but a statement of the overarching principle for all unspecified actions. Moreover, this same phrase is actually a specific formulation of the principle with which one should enact every rule and law; namely, with a spirit of equity and compromise and decency. Absent such a standard, and one can justify improper actions by appealing to the law itself. Elsewhere, in a trenchant rebuke, Nahmanides acidly states that a person who exploits gaps in the law without any principle of restraint is simply "a crass vulgarian with the permission of the Torah" (Leviticus 19:2). Clearly, in the tension between formalism and virtue, religious ethics must condition and set the standard of action. In the Mishnah itself, and subsequent Talmudic discourse, this guiding principle is referred to variously as "the ways of peace" or "the ways of pleasantness." (The Hebrew idioms are *darkhei shalom* and *darkhei no'am*, respectively. For examples, see M. Gittin 5.8–9 and BT. Sukkah 32b and BT. Yebamot 15a.) Hence, the canon may teach the law and even ethics, but it is also clear that the overall moral tone that a religious ethics propagates may have much to say to some specific laws, and to the spirit or manner by which they should be applied. These are seen as the higher warrants of behavior, and become the measures of justice itself.

Some Conclusions and Considerations

Religious ethics finds its duties and their warrants in authoritative texts, of divine and human authorship; it also finds ongoing duties and their warrants in ongoing reflection on the meaning and implications of these texts, thus producing new texts and traditions of various degrees of authority (see chapter 6). This process is at the core of traditional societies, grounded in scriptural canons; and the measures of cultural strength are directly related to the comprehensive authority of the primary canon, on the one hand, and the correlative boldness and assertiveness of its cultural inheritors on the other. The tension is necessary for the ethical matters to retain a transcendent and *a priori* claim upon those who accept the canon as one stamped with a divine and traditional imprimatur, even as this latter is subject to creative transformations based on ethical imperatives which impose themselves upon the cultural conscience. Hence, the heteronomous character of canons does not subvert the play and power of autonomous reason, but rather subordinates its activities to itself through acts of legitimate exegesis, which uphold the canonical sources while revising their contents in often bold and radical ways. Canonical cultures thus have various voices of authority. The ongoing ethical voice of the interpreters speaks through the shape of the authoritative words of scripture, so that by donning the mask of exegesis the authoritative texts speak anew, as the old and ever-new world of moral and religious authority. Split the sacred bond between a scripture and its interpreters, and the scripture becomes a historical relic and its interpreters mere rhetoricians. Joined together, the imperatives of the canon may be renewed in unexpected ways.

The canonical texts and their ethical teachings and values provide the framework and terms of an ongoing moral pedagogy that variously imposes itself upon and challenges the conscience of the interpreters. The mark of a culture is the nature and substance of its ongoing responses to its authoritative teachings, and how these are carried over or changed for new generations. Indeed, readers provide the canon with new moral valences and warrants for action. "Normativity" thus emerges as a negotiated and constructed entity. For whatever be the content of the original norms imposed by the canonical sources, their normative force cannot be separated from the power and character of their reinterpretation. Ethical freedom is thus conditioned by the content of canonical texts and constrained by the modes of exegesis available. But it is repeatedly clear that where there is a will there is a moral way. Canonical cultures meet the challenge and raise their traditions to the standard of their new ethical insights through the instruments of exegesis and unwavering integrity. Mere (legal) formalism is repeatedly resisted.

We thus acknowledge a paradox: the coexistence of "hegemonic texts" and "hegemonic interpreters." Strong texts can withstand strong readers; and strong readers can withstand strong texts. Authority and integrity are at both poles of the dialectic, as also are ethical imperatives and their cultural challenges. But in the end, ethical readers are the true "spirit" of the law, animating it and giving it vitality for new generations. In this way, the present recreates its past for the sake of its future.

Bibliography

All references to the Mishnah (M) are by tractate and citation. References to the Babylonian Talmud (BT) follow traditional pagination; for an English rendition, see the edition by I. Epstein (London: Soncino Press, 1938–52).

Finkelstein, L. (ed.) 1966: *Sifre on Deuteronomy*. New York: Jewish Theological Seminary of America.

Fishbane, M. A. 1985: *Biblical Interpretation in Ancient Israel*. Oxford: Clarendon Press.

—— "Canonical Text, Covenantal Communities, and the Patterns of Exegetical Culture: Reflections on the Past Century" in *Covenant as Context: Essays in Honour of E. W. Nicholson*, ed. A. D. H. Mayes and R. B. Salters. Oxford: Oxford University Press, 2003.

Halbertal, M. 1997: *Intrepretative Revolutions in the Making*. Jerusalem: Magnes Press [in Hebrew].

Hoffmann, D. T. (ed.) 1908–19: *Midrash Tana'im 'al Sefer Devarim : meluqqat mi-tokh Midrash Ha-gadol ketav yad . . . Berlin : ve-nilvu-'elav hearot u-mar'eh meqomot*. Berlin: I. H. Itskovski.

Maimonides, M. 1934: *Teshubot ha-Rambam*, ed. J. Blau. Jerusalem: Mekize Nirdamim.

CHAPTER 8
Practices

Francis X. Clooney

Practices and Moral Change

Theory follows upon practice, theories are rethought in order to undergird practices to which a community remains committed, and ethical analysis is primarily about practices generative of theories, not theories eventuating in practices.

People normally do not determine first what they think and see as their values and then, on that basis, decide what to do. Most of the time, they instead articulate ideas and values in conformity with what they already do; they begin with and do not merely conclude to expectations about proper ways of acting religiously (see chapters "On Religious Ethics" and 2). They belong to traditions already in place; concepts, explanations, and modes of behavior have been settled in the past. The boldest thoughts and most consistent logical conclusions are constrained to conform to what people already do and want to keep doing. Radical change, as distinct from claims about the desirability of radical change, is unlikely, and conclusions about the rightness of particular actions become predictable once we attend to the requirements generated by practices already in place before the reflection begins.

These persistent patterns of action, understood and explained within communities, are what I mean by *practices* – not merely actions, but actions as invested with explanatory and supportive meaning through continuity of tradition (as prior to their current practitioners), habit (as regular, insinuated deeply enough so as to function smoothly without overt attention on the part of their agents), and interpretation (as plausibly explaining actions in discourses which are in some way public). As practices, such actions survive changes in justification by generating new explanations allowing for continuity even when other factors might commend other practices. While practices change over time, most often explanations change to support of persisting practices (MacIntyre 1981; Bourdieu 1977, 1990; Reynolds and Tracy 1992; Yearley 1990).

As traditional, habitual, and (even if open to new interpretations) already explained sufficiently well, practices require little by way of explicit comment. Evident to their practitioners, they remain unspoken in conversations about communal values and function perfectly well without overt attention. Perhaps inadvertently, their very centrality may be concealed from the view of newcomers, because other things with less foundation in tradition require more discussion. The persistence of practices may be all the more unnoticed in a comparative context where explanation and practice are both unfamiliar, and where it may be tempting to treat explanations – available in conversation, in books – as determinative of behavior, causes rather than results. While causal inquiries are useful, realizing that conceptions and words normally follow upon practice illumines how people act, how they think in relation to what they do, and how we can best assess both practice and theory.

It is in times of controversy that the justifications attached to practices become explicit, vulnerable to review, and available for an analysis able to distinguish theories from underlying practices (see chapter 6). Proposing new explanations calls practices into question by threatening the reasons traditionally supportive of them. Proponents of established practices may merely defend contested theories but, since the practices are more important than the theories, such proponents may also invent new explanations able to support old practices in a new situation. Innovators may lay claim to older and truer versions of the practices in dispute, and to more honest explanations, but in order to gain credence for their new ideas they may have to attenuate those ideas' effectiveness and diminish their potential actually to change practices. Accordingly, it is a key area of ethical reflection to notice how practices are debated and explained in times of stress when (at first) new practices seem likely but when (in the end, most of the time) established practices endure.

This chapter elucidates the preceding reflections on practice by pointing to three controversies highlighting how religious practices resist change and stimulate new supporting theories when the practices are under stress and seemingly about to change. First, I consider a familiar Reformation dispute: the argument over meritorious works, justification, and atonement as argued by Lutheran Philipp Melanchthon (1497–1560) and Roman Catholic Tommaso de Vio Cajetan (1469–1534). Second, I turn to the south Indian Hindu context and examine differing views on the religious significance of birth status and religious class – "caste" – according to Piḷḷai Lokācārya (1205–1311) and Vedānta Deśika (1270–1369). Third, in a sense combining the preceding cases, I consider how Roberto de Nobili (1577–1656), a Jesuit intellectual missionary in south India, chose to characterize caste as cultural but not religious practice in order to make it compatible with conversion understood as religious but not cultural practice. These instances of practice – religious works (such as the confession of sins, the Mass, the veneration of relics); caste behavior (such as restricted patterns of marriage and dining, and of the study of sacred scriptures) resignified in light of divine love; conversion (as abolishing caste practices and replacing them with alternative Christian patterns of behavior, or as complementary to caste) – are complex and require much more detailed analysis than is offered here. My aim is simply to exemplify how thinkers moderate new ideas to make them consonant with practices likely to endure whatever the supporting reasons.

Does the Death of Christ Make Good Works Unnecessary?

The early Catholic–Lutheran debate over faith, merit, and good works was a fierce contest with broad social, political, and religious roots (see chapter 23). It was also a serious theological dispute about how traditionally esteemed good works might be relevant to the accomplishment of human salvation if, as Protestants and then Catholics came to admit, salvation is achieved through the death of Christ and not by human accomplishment. In the Catholic–Lutheran context the debate was also a delicate negotiation in which both sides had already decided not to drop the key practices in question, but sought ways to accommodate those practices to the logic of new supporting theories (for this section, see Melanchthon 2000; Cajetan 1978).

In "The Lutheran Apology of the Augsburg Confession" Melanchthon argued for a realignment of the language of salvation, so that primacy is accorded to justification by faith. God's saving initiative is primary; humans must simply recognize this and take it to heart, rejecting notions of self-salvation and also the related merits of works and other forms of self-justification. He repeatedly emphasized God's initiative in Christ and the role of faith as the proper human response to God, and he denounced Roman Catholic defenses of merit and satisfaction as perverse justifications of self-aggrandizing actions merely portrayed as pious. Despite the rancor, however, Melanchthon's overall agenda was conservative. He respected tradition and ecclesial structures, and left no room for a life lived so purely by faith that there would no longer be any recognizable normative Christian practices. If reliance on faith is the foundation of the Christian life, it can also yield a proper sense of the worship, duties, and pieties that continue to be obligatory. Although Melanchthon called for a radical recalculation of values, he left no room for truly radical innovation in the living of the Christian life. Confession and absolution are to be retained even if they occur in the context of God's activity and not as signs of the human achievement of sinlessness; baptism, the Mass, prayers, alms giving and other acts of charity, all were to be maintained in the new Lutheran dispensation. A new theology in fact confirms much of what was already in place.

In "Faith and Works" Cardinal Cajetan refuted Melanchthon's "poisonous" charges about superfluous customs and superstitions in the Catholic community. To safeguard the faithful from doubts about or laxity in the performance of Catholic practices, Cajetan shifted the argument away from Melanchthon's appeals to personal experience and conviction, emphasizing instead the faith of the church and its tradition. However satisfying personal convictions may be, the church is a more reliable guide to the Christian life. In an ecclesially regulated context one will be able to understand clearly the dynamic of salvation: God's love works in particular persons who are transformed in ways that become evident as they perform good deeds approved by God and the church. Even a person mired in mortal sin, if he or she has some inkling of the better life arising in repentance, can profit from performing good deeds which make one more responsive to the divine initiative.

Although Cajetan could not bring himself to dismiss any of the disputed church practices, he actually aimed for a middle ground that accommodates Melanchthon's concerns. He refused to base practices merely on authority or the sheer fact of tradition; instead, he revalued meritorious works, purifying them of the appearance of merit construction or the incremental achievement of salvation. Like Melanchthon, he forged a more spiritual and Christocentric foundation for his position, adducing scripture texts acknowledging divine grace while confirming traditional practice. It is true, he said, that scripture, tradition, and the revered practice of the church all testify that it is Christ who offers salvation by his singular and perfect self-giving action; good works are a response to Christ's salvific act. Works are important, but they remain essentially secondary to the work of Christ. Catholic practices are reinterpreted in order to preserve them.

Differences aside, Melanchthon and Cajetan agreed that scripture and ecclesial authority had to be respected and important practices preserved. Both reject (real or hypothetical) antinomian alternatives leading to radically truly different ways of acting. Meritorious works are not conceded primary status, but the notion of merit is adjusted so that key practices are allowed to continue. This compromise worked in the Catholic–Lutheran context – old practices, new theories – because the theories about good works and merit were not the cause of the debated practices; rather, theory was for the most part conformed to already-existing practices which were to endure, even if purified in some way or another. For Lutherans and Catholics alike, just as practices provoke debates, they also marked off boundaries within which reflection should rightly begin and end. Changes in theology did not necessarily change practice in any radical fashion, and more often preserved it. There were surely some Catholics who did simply repeat old explanations in favor of the debated practices; some Reformation theorists and practitioners did adopt more radical stances which led to the abolition of hitherto settled practices. But the classic argument between Melanchthon and Cajetan more modestly and typically clarified debated issues and eliminated abuses in order to preserve practices central to both the Catholic and Lutheran traditions.

Does Love of God Make Caste Irrelevant?

Like other Hindu theorists writing in Sanskrit or in heavily Sanskritized vernaculars in medieval India, the thirteenth and fourteenth-century Śrīvaiṣṇava theologians of south India sought to combine new religious values – such as devotion to Lord Nārāyana (Viṣṇu, Rāma, Kṛṣṇa) – with the traditional and pan-Indian elite practices connected with brahmanical orthodoxy, including the caste practices calculated according to birth status (*jāti*) and religious class (*varṇa*). Birth status, assumed to be innate, regulated "natural social" activities related to birth, dining, marriage, and education; the theory of religious class served as a theoretical explanation of these regulations. Birth status was understood to mirror the reality of the universe, and the categories of religious class articulated the meaning of the innate differences. The system of *varṇa-āśrama* (class, state of life) *dharma* framed in ideal terms the life of the male according to stages of life (āśrama) and class hierarchy (varṇa), reaching from (theoretically) religiously and intellectually privileged elite brahmans down to (theoretically) inferior and uneducated manual laborers, *śūdras* (for this section, see Lokācārya 1979: vv. 194–233; Ayyangar 1956; Mumme 1988).

Along with the observance of caste practices, however, new devotional movements brought to the fore a new theistic and interpersonal religious calculus, according to which relationship to God was the first and foremost measure of relevance (see chapters 34 and 35). Pillai Lokacarya, a founding leader of the emerging Teṅkalai sect of Śrīvaiṣṇavism, was a foremost proponent of the new turn to a theistic perspective. In his *Śrīvacanabhūṣaṇam* he established the absolute priority of love of God and divine favor over against any other criteria for religious value, superseding previously settled orthodox standards for religious value, including caste. Were divine love really to become the sole measure of social practice, then caste would be stripped of its significance and its practices would lose support. Pillai Lokācārya did not go so far, since he also implanted religious values in a context of settled religious practices, and accordingly maintained a delicate balance between new religious insights, radical rhetoric, and traditional practices. On the one hand, he argued as vigorously as possible that radical dependence on God is indeed the core value by which actions are rendered religiously significant; religious identity and prestige within the community of believers can no longer depend on birth status and religious class. On the other, he in fact also remained committed to caste practices. While he valued exceptions to caste rules, he offered no comprehensive alternative; he seemed interested more simply in insisting that divine love is primary while status and class are secondary. Norms for purity, eating, ritual performances, etc., were not discarded, but only treated as secondary, and as liable to important and occasional exceptions. In his *Śrīvacanabhūṣaṇam* he moderated a potentially radical language of devotion which might have overturned caste entirely by replacing it with stress on the interior quality of individuals surrendered entirely to God; the overall impact of Pillai Lokācārya's argument was to suggest that devotees should learn to live in an ordered world where caste differences did not really matter but were still to be observed. Devotion triumphs, but caste practice endures.

Vedānta Désika, a theologian of the next generation and of the reputedly more conservative Vatakalai sect, placed stronger emphasis on the value of caste practices. He may have had Pillai Lokācārya's arguments in mind when he strongly defended caste in several of his writings, particularly in chapter 25 of his *Śrīmadrahasyatrayasāra*. As he saw the matter, even if overly excited devotees suggest that there is some conflict between devotion and caste, there is in fact no real problem, once devotion and caste are properly understood. Just as Cajetan accommodated Melanchthon, Désika conceded much of the ground contested by Pillai Lokācārya, agreeing that devotion and relationship to the Lord are the primary religious criteria – but he then used the new values to support the old practices. Caste was not religiously odious, but existed according to the will of God. People who love God should have no problem in adhering to practices which continue to please God. Old practices were thus preserved, precisely by a cooptation of the originally troubling logic of devotion. For Lokācārya, the new devotional calculus did not actually change caste practices, but simply moved them to a secondary position; for Désika, those practices were maintained by investing them with new religious values. Both of them, even in the heat of debate, agreed to exclude the possibility that practices such as marrying, dining, or studying would really change, as if to occur entirely without consideration for caste.

Does Conversion to Christianity Make Caste Objectionable?
A Debate Among Missionaries

The third example builds on the first two. Roberto de Nobili, an Italian Jesuit and missionary in Madurai, south India, brought the concerns and questions of Reformation Europe to brahmanical south India; traditional practices and their (new and old) religious justifications were already an issue in de Nobili's mind before he arrived in India. By 1610, a few short years after his arrival, he had decided that the major obstacle to the conversion of Hindus was the reluctance of brahmans to become interested in the gospel; in turn, the major reason for their disinclination was their reluctance to give up the practices marking brahman status (e.g., the wearing of the brahman thread, sectarian markings on the forehead, distinctive hats, certain ablutions, and even their certainty that the Sanskrit language was intellectually and spiritually superior) (for this section, see de Nobili 2000; for general background on de Nobili, see Saulière 1995; for the controversy over caste and conversions, see Zupanov 1999).

Most missionaries seem to have had no interest in caste values, and assumed that converts should abandon them. Indeed, among practices which might be considered prototypically radical, conversion practices – promoting it, undergoing it – would certainly be among the more prominent. Brahmans opposed the missionary agenda not primarily because of any particular Christian doctrines, but rather because conversion would entail a radical departure from caste values, the mingling of castes, and a pernicious disregard for obligatory practices. They were right; most missionaries were interested in conversion and not in caste, and perhaps assumed that converts would abandon the old brahmanical practices for the new Christian ones.

In the face of seemingly conflicting practices, de Nobili sought a middle ground. He did so because he prized the practice of conversion, and did not want to see it stymied by theories of culture that would unnecessarily (in his view) encumber it. Missionaries would make no progress in converting brahmans as long as conversion entailed the rejection of deeply embedded caste practices, so a new theory was required: it had to be the case that those practices were not actually contrary to Christian identity, and it had to be the case that conversion could be lived in such a way as to not interfere with caste. To further his own religious project, conversion, he had to develop a consonant theory of caste which reinterpreted caste practices as cultural and not religious.

For this purpose he wrote his *Report Concerning Certain Customs of the Indian Nation* in order to defend the conclusion that key brahman practices were social and not essentially religious (de Nobili 2000). Insisting that such practices were not incompatible with Christian values, de Nobili hoped to persuade both missionaries and brahmans that cultural caste practices could be combined with the religious practices of the Christian community. Both conversion and caste practices could be reinterpreted, to preserve both.

Although currently available sources do not warrant conclusions about all sides of this debate – we have only missionary writings – we can recognize at least how the several agendas overlapped in this trilateral dispute involving de Nobili, other missionaries, and brahmans. For their own reasons, brahmans defended caste and missionaries defended conversion; for his own reasons, de Nobili defended both caste and conversion. He prized conversion to the extent of stripping it of its cultural force, reconceiving it as a religious discourse compatible with Indian caste practices. Neither caste nor conversion would any longer mean quite what it had meant previously, yet the practices involved would continue. Out of necessity de Nobili thus invented the "Christian Brahman," preserving both Christian and brahman practices.

From Classic Controversy to Contemporary Ethics

In the preceding sections we have explored three moments of controversy where practices were attacked, rethought, and resignified, but still enacted: the death of Christ is recognized as central, but pious and meritorious actions are still performed; divine love is recognized as superior to practices related to birth and class, but those practices persist, for new reasons; conversion is recognized by missionaries as a foremost religious practice, but with the proviso that it not interfere with caste practices. Criticisms of works, caste, and conversion had endangered traditional practices, but at the moment of resolution potentially radical ideas and words were refashioned in order to resignify and thus preserve the practices undergoing critique. All our disputants portrayed themselves as rejecting more extreme lines of thought such as would have totally overthrown traditional values; likewise, they all rejected more stubborn defenses of tradition which would have bound practices exclusively to particular theories. Rather, particular theories are dispensable and can be adjusted or replaced so that practices could be maintained (see chapters 7 and 9).

Practices are not eternal, however agile their defenders may be in improvising new theories to justify them. Even the most skillfully reinterpreted practices may eventually decline and fall out of favor. If supporting explanations fail, and fail to be replaced by more convincing ones, it may become impossible to continue acting in certain ways, however valuable the traditions involved. Powerfully intrusive new practices do sometimes overwhelm and eradicate older, settled ones. There are certainly instances, too, when cherished theories become in effect verbal practices to be preserved by the discovery of still further additional justifications. Nonetheless, I suggest, the fact that practices endure while justifications change is the ordinary state of affairs and rightly a primary object of ethical analysis. We need to keep asking which practices are at stake when theories are being explained, adjusted, or replaced in arguments about what is morally and religiously acceptable (see chapter 15). Hear the words, but search out the practices.

The three examples adduced here are safely located in premodern and early modern times, and remind us of concerns to be kept in mind while studying controversies from the past. But they also illustrate patterns still operative in actual ethical decision making and central to the study of those decisions by ethicists. Today, it remains necessary to step back and identify the dominant practices likely to remain in force even after a debate about ideas and values, since what is debated is not identical with what is at stake. We must examine how theories, however radical, often simply revalue practices rather than change what people do. Debates over liturgical norms and jurisdictional control within a church, prohibitions of stem cell research and euthanasia, the relief of third world debt, and the abolition of the death penalty, etc. – all entail important theoretical issues, but we must remember to seek out the enduring practices at stake "beneath" the issues explicitly debated. We must notice how behavior does not change, while new reasons are enlisted to defend established practices. It is useful to attend to new theories which, if implemented, would change everything, but not primarily because in a few cases such theories might actually take effect. Rather, their novelty prods those with vested interests to stake out moderate positions couched in the language of the new concepts and values, to situate these positions as prudent alternatives to real or imagined extreme positions, and thus, in the long run, to maintain traditional practices by promoting new reasons for still doing them.

Bibliography

Ayyangar, M. R. R. (trans.) 1956: *Sri Vedanta Desika*. Salem: Literary Press.

Bourdieu, P. 1977: *Outline of a Theory of Practice*. New York: Cambridge University Press.

—— 1990: *The Logic of Practice*. Stanford, CA: Stanford University Press.

Cajetan, T. d. V. 1978: "Faith and Works – Against the Lutherans (1532)" in *Cajetan Responds: A Reader in Reformation Controversy*, ed. J. Wicks, 219–39. Washington, DC: Catholic University of America Press.

de Nobili, R. 2000: "Report Concerning Certain Customs of the Indian Nation" in *Preaching Wisdom to the Wise: Three Treatises by Roberto de Nobili, SJ, Missionary and Scholar in 17th Century India*, ed. A. Amaladass, SJ and F. X. Clooney, SJ. St. Louis: Institute of Jesuit Sources.

Lokacarya, P. 1979: *Srivacana Bhusanam*, trans. R. Lester. Chennai: Kuppuswamy Sastri Research Institute.

MacIntyre, A. C. 1981: *After Virtue: A Study in Moral Theory*. Notre Dame, IN: University of Notre Dame Press.

Melanchthon. 2000: "The Lutheran Apology of the Evangelical Church" in *The Book of Concord: The Confessions of the Evangelical Lutheran Church*, ed. R. Kolb, T. J. Wengert, and C. P. Arand, 107–294. Minneapolis, MN: Fortress Press.

Mumme, P. Y. 1988: *The Srivaisnava Theological Dispute: Manavalamamuni and Vedanta Desika*. Madras: New Era Publications.

Reynolds, F. and Tracy, D. (eds.) 1992: *Discourse and Practice*. Albany: State University of New York Press.

Saulière, A. 1995: *His Star in the East*, revd. edn., ed. S. Rajamanickam. Madras: De Nobili Research Institute.

Yearley, L. H. 1990: *Mencius and Aquinas: Theories of Virtue and Conceptions of Courage*. Albany: State University of New York Press.

Zupanov, I. G. 1999: *Disputed Mission: Jesuit Experiments and Brahmanical Knowledge in Seventeenth-Century India*. New Delhi: Oxford University Press.

CHAPTER 9

Ritual

Francisca Cho

Ritual and Moral Action

In common parlance, the term "ritual" – both religious and secular – denotes a pattern of regularly performed or scripted behavior, usually in a ceremonial context. At first blush, rituals seem to have little to do with moral actions, if the latter are understood as deeds that are guided by principles that help people to negotiate their way through everyday life (see chapter 1). A link between ritual action and moral action has been suggested, however, by historians of religion who see rituals as outward expressions or enactments of myths. Myths, in turn, are understood to be narrative accounts of a society's most profound beliefs about the world – such as the way it came into existence, our personal roles in relation to it, and the ultimate destiny or purpose of existence in such a world (see chapter 10). These beliefs, in turn, comprise the fundamental principles that help us to see what is moral. Moral acts can be expressed in specific ritual behaviors, such as the custom of widow burning (*sati*) in India, based on beliefs about the identity and duty of a wife in relation to her husband. Or they can be negotiated day to day based on the reasoning supplied by the mythological worldview. One might decide against an abortion, for example, based on the reasoning that all matters of life and death should be left to the will of a creator God.

This way of linking ritual to myth participates in a longstanding interpretive strategy that sees religion as primarily an intellectual activity. Myth, ritual, and even morality are outgrowths, in this view, of the human need to make sense of the world. Sense making, in turn, is a function of making propositions about the world that will allow us to act meaningfully and properly within it. In the recent history of ritual studies, however, scholars have become more interested in ritual as a qualitative experience in and of itself, rather than as the mere physical execution of an intellectual text. In this view, ritual is "pure activity," completely meaningless with respect to intellectual propositions, but quite meaningful relative to itself. Ritual and ritual players may be sustained through time as a social institution or fact, but the viability of ritual is a matter of the sensual, aesthetic, psychological, and neurological satisfaction attained by the participants. Hence, rituals have no objectives external to themselves, such as making sense of the world or even building collective solidarity. Contrary to functionalist interpretations, ritual is its own aim and its own value (Staal 1979: 9).

The focus on ritual as an experience to be enjoyed rather than as a text to be displays the influence of performance theory, which is the study of theater, and the work of sociologist Erving Goffman, who extends the concept of performance to social and cultural action. Victor Turner, for example, extends the category of ritual from discrete ceremonial settings to larger social dramas in which historical tensions and ruptures are negotiated and social change is brought about. Contrary to the prior reading of ritual as socially conservative, always acting to preserve existing ideologies and worldviews, Turner suggests ritual is a form of cultural performance that negotiates reality in an ongoing manner. This nexus between ritual performance and social innovation suggests a new way of tying together the categories of ritual action and moral action. The new link can be forged upon the basis of a qualitative experience rather than an intellectual operation. The focus on experience and performance allows one to encompass the possibility of social change and, more importantly, predicates such social evolution on the transformation of the individual. And to the degree that ritual action can be transformative of the individual, it is also a moral practice (see chapter 8). It will help to examine specific historical expressions of these ideas.

The lack of precise linguistic equivalents to the terms "morality" or "ethics" in comparative religious traditions points out, of course, the cultural specificity of these words and their traditions of inquiry (see chapter "On Religious Ethics"). More importantly, however, this problem of translation opens up an opportunity to enhance our moral investigations by forcing us to accept rough terminological equivalents from other cultures, with the result that new connotations and meanings of morality come into view. Hence, this chapter on the role of ritual in moral inquiry will draw upon the examples of Chinese religions – particularly the articulate and text-based traditions of Confucianism and Daoism. Although neither of these traditions has a history of discussions that parallel the Western discourse on morality, both of them, by virtue of their religious goals, are profoundly concerned with how people should behave. The goals of sagehood and unity with the *Dao* ("the Way"), respectively, may be described as forms of spiritual realization that are predicated on proper conduct within the social and natural spheres. This conduct is a matter of ritual action, which is expressed as forms of cultural and physical performance. And like the recent moves in ritual studies, performance is a matter of a qualitative experience that is self-referentially "holy" and which expresses a level of skillfulness that is a form of transformative and "great" knowledge (*dazhi*).

These Asian paths, to be sure, are embellished by their own mythologies and systems of meaning-making – they are, after all, highly literate traditions. This chapter will draw upon their meaning systems in order to help the reader make sense of their practices. These texts, however, repeatedly aver that intellectual knowledge is inferior to the embodied knowledge of action – a point we would do well to keep in mind.

Ritual Action in Confucianism

The conflation of ritual and moral action is superlatively expressed in the Confucian concept of *li*, or "rites." For the philosopher Confucius, the goal of sagehood, which entailed the rectification of one's mind (*xin*), first presumed the mastery of formal social behavior, codified in the rites (see chapters 38 and 39). The rites originally derived from the highly formalized court rituals of the Zhou dynasty (1046–221 BCE). In the hands of Confucius, however, the rites were centered on social behavior, and hence came to signify "propriety." The specific rules of social interactions derived from the five major social relationships recognized by Confucianism, which are posed as reciprocal, though mostly hierarchical, relational pairs: ruler and minister, father and son, elder and younger brother, husband and wife, friend and friend (*Doctrine of the Mean* 20). These "universal ways" of Confucianism define a social and moral world. As a social–ethical system of thought, the emphasis on *li* evinces the belief that order and harmony depend on the ability of every individual – especially the ruler – to play his social role to perfection. Role playing consists of action that is observable to all: "Look at the means a man employs, observe the path he takes and examine where he feels at home. In what way is a man's true character hidden from view?" (Lau 1979: 64). Proper social performance was a matter of attaining an intuitive knowledge of the appropriate words and actions in every social situation. No act was exempt from this demand. As Confucius states:

> Do not look unless it is in accordance with the rites; do not listen unless it is in accordance with the rites; do not speak unless it is in accordance with the rites; do not move unless it is in accordance with the rites. (Lau 1979: 112)

To be sure, Chinese history has demonstrated that the principle of the rites/propriety, with its attendant value of righteousness (*yi*), is perhaps more conducive to the rule of an oppressive social conformity than to the production of sages. In addition, given the hierarchical nature of most social relationships, the actual practice of Confucian moralism has tended to be expressed in the oppression of those on the low end of the power scale. The Confucian fixation on outer appearances as a reliable indicator of moral worth has also encouraged an ethos of "saving face" that values ceremonial behavior in its most pejorative, empty sense rather than sincere action. History demonstrates that it is easy to reduce Confucianism to formalism and political advantage. Such practice neglects the religious and cosmological sides of Confucius, which cherish ritual social action as a method of completing the individual and bringing her into harmony with society, as well as the natural world.

The religious ideal of sagehood is grounded in a cosmological view that unites human action to the larger natural environment. The Confucian "heaven" (*tian*) is an amalgamation of both nature and a moral consciousness that does not entail supernatural agency or will. Heaven is better described as the principle of synchronous activity so prevalent in Chinese correlative cosmology. The body politic, as well as the individual human body, are microcosms of the natural universe, and all three work in sympathy. As one text states, humans form a triad with heaven and earth. Individual cultivation leads to the cultivation of others, to the development of the nature of things, and ultimately to the nourishing of heaven and earth (*Doctrine of the Mean* 22). Socially prescribed action does not take society as its end; rather, it is the means by which individuals can actualize the Way (*Dao*) that ultimately unites all things. Ritual action is therefore more than an arbitrary set of rules and social customs. On the other hand, the value of ritual action does not lie in its enactment of metaphysical principles or truths, but rather in its very performance – in its qualitative experience that actualizes the ideal of becoming fully human.

The Confucian concept of humanity, or humanness (*ren*), is the linchpin of its moral system in that it is entirely focused on human interrelationships (see chapter 37 and 40). The teaching can be reduced to "love your fellow men" (Lau 1979: 116), and an inverse rendition of the Golden Rule: "Do not impose on others what you yourself do not desire" (Lau 1979: 135). These familiar injunctions do not flow from an omnipotent lawgiver, or from rational principles. They articulate the fact that it is only in the course of social and familial interactions that one can experience the grace and fulsomeness of the *Dao*. Significantly, the rites include the meanings of "etiquette" and "refinement," which are more matters of ritual norms than rational discernment. It is primarily by appropriating the external forms of culture that humans can attain the experience of graciousness. Social rules both define and create such harmony because without them, we do not know "where to put hand and foot" (Lau 1979: 118); we do not know what to say, or what to do, and as a result, others cannot know our meaning nor our intentions.

Ritual performance is a key element of peak religious states such as ecstasy, trance, and meditation. The quality of consciousness denoted by these states is usually induced by ritual contexts and practices. This connection between ritual performance and qualitative experience is also present in the secular arenas of theater and the kind of social performances specified by *li*. What ritual induces, ideally, is the reality of what is symbolized, so that "the invisible world referred to in ritual is made manifest and the subject placed within it" (Myerhoff 1990: 246). Such states, to be sure, cannot be scripted or willed, and may hinge on the triggering of certain neurological activity – an event more easily subject to direct physiological than social manipulation. More important, however, is the observation that ritual actions pack a punch precisely because they are embodied – literally performed by the body to create distinctive spaces and experiences, all within the moral course of human interaction. The terminology of "performance" indicates the priority of embodied action in determining the nature of our thinking as well as our emotions. The social choreography of the Confucian rites is certainly liable to affectation, but it nevertheless forms the necessary condition for the fusion of symbol and consciousness that paradoxically transforms choreography into sincere action.

Contrary to some cultural tendencies to separate the rational faculties from the "baser" instincts of the body, Chinese traditions might be described as practices of self-cultivation that view the body as foundational. The generalization can be sustained across disparate Chinese practices such as Confucianism and Daoism, in spite of their significant intellectual disagreements. Confucianism, as we have seen, is primarily enamored of the social body, with its emphasis on the proper enactment of hierarchical, rule-governed relationships. This social play, however, rests upon the cultivation of individual physical performance, with much emphasis on propriety of appearance, physical comportment, and speech. The rites go beyond a system of action guides and hold out the ideal of ritualizing every social interaction so that each encounter is fully moral and humanizing. Daoism, on the other hand, with its severe allergy to systems of rule-governed behavior, is pointedly critical of the rites but nevertheless in harmony with the Confucian focus on physical self-cultivation. Indeed, its textual references to "concentrating the breath in order to become supple like the babe" (Lau 1963: 66) and making the body like a "withered tree" and the mind like "dead ashes" (*Zhuangzi* ch. 2) attest to the cultivation practices broadly known as "inner alchemy" (*neidan*) that make up a large part of Daoist tradition. Perhaps more literally embodied than Confucian action, this vast system of exercise, breath control, meditation, sexual yoga, and dietary practices are rituals in the most specific sense. Concomitant with its rejection of the rites, Daoism turns to concrete physical forms of self-cultivation as a path to moral excellence (see chapter 4).

Daoist Ritual Action

The reputation of Daoism, both in the eyes of its Confucian critics and in much of Western scholarship, is that it is an amoral (if not downright immoral) philosophy that laughs at social obligations and, indeed, at civilization itself in an anarchistic pursuit of individual freedom and spontaneity (*ziran*). Daoism turns the Confucian faith in social rituals upside down by envisioning a path of action that arises effortlessly (*wuwei*) when the mind has been released from conventional discriminations. Daoism has not been appreciated as a moral system because of a prevalent tendency, across cultures, to associate morality with value discriminations between "good" and "bad" that are encoded in specific rules of behavior (see chapter 2). This emphasis on the discriminating mind as the basis of right action is evident in contemporary Western concerns with moral reason (Cho 1998), as well as in the Confucian principle of the "rectification of names" (*zhengming*).

Daoist morality, on the other hand, challenges us to imagine right action in the space beyond value distinctions and certainties. This goal is anchored in the observation that values, in and of themselves, are never self-sustaining. Both aesthetic and moral distinctions are defined relative to each other in some particular social context, rather than signifying absolute properties. In modern terminology, we might say that perceptions of beauty and goodness are notoriously culture and time specific (see chapter 14). Cultural conventions, however, develop an aura of absoluteness and weaken our ability to respond appropriately to evolving circumstances. "Therefore the sage keeps to the deed that consists in taking no action and practices the teaching that uses no words" (Lau 1963: 58). Besides expressing Daoism's minimalist ethic, this passage counsels detachment from fixed moral conventions.

Daoism addresses the apparent contradiction of a morality outside the boundaries of fixed values and rules by exchanging social rituals for the rituals of self-cultivation. Perhaps even more pervasive than its reputation for amorality, Daoism is portrayed as a madcap, bohemian way of life that values individual freedom above all else. This picture obscures the centrality of inner alchemy practices that are governed by all of the disciplines and exactions of ritual. To be sure, there is nothing overtly other regarding, and hence morally inclined, about yogic disciplines and the pursuit of physical immortality. The current popularity in the West of Daoist practices such as *taijiquan* might be attributed to a highly self-regarding interest in health and fitness, in fact, and seems to betray a similar self-centeredness on the part of Daoist adepts. This conclusion is predicated, however, on the large assumption that physical and moral cultivation are strictly autonomous, or even mutually exclusive. Rational traditions that see the body as inimical to the superior functions of the mind may advocate a physical regimen designed to constrict bodily desires and gratification, but certainly not a system of cultivation that seeks to enhance physical energy and longevity. In *neidan* practice, in contrast, union with the *Dao* most immediately meant conforming the body to the larger patterns of the seasons so that physical life was fully enhanced:

> The sages followed the laws [of nature] and therefore their bodies were free from strange diseases; they did not lose anything (which they had received by nature) and their spirit of life was never exhausted. (Veith 1972: 104)

Following the patterns of nature entailed conformity to very specific seasonal rules of living, expressing the belief that the body is essentially parallel to and an extension of the forces and energies found in nature:

> Those who rebel against the basic rules of the universe sever their own roots and ruin their true selves. Yin and Yang, the two principles in nature, and the four seasons are the beginning and the end of everything and they are also the cause of life and death. (Veith 1972: 104)

Chinese correlative thinking is demonstrated in the Daoist conception of the body, with its four main arteries and twelve subsidiary vessels, which correspond with the four seasons and twelve months. The tremendously detailed elaboration of bodily organs, mapped to Yin and Yang energies, forms the basis of seasonal practices, diet, and medicine. Harmonizing one's physical life to the cycling energies of nature brings good health and long life, but, most importantly, it also leads to the moral and spiritual perfection of sages:

> Their spirit followed in harmony and obedience; everything was satisfactory to their wishes and they could achieve whatever they wished. Any kind of food was beautiful [to them]; and any kind of clothing was satisfactory. They felt happy under any condition. To them it did not matter whether a man held a high or a low position in life. These men can be called pure at heart. No kind of desire can tempt the eyes of those pure people and their mind cannot be misled by excessiveness and evil. (Veith 1972: 98)

To cultivate one's physical life, one must ritually integrate oneself with the macrocosmic patterns and movements that are the *Dao*. This discipline naturally results in the regulation of desires and the ability to find satisfaction in all things. Hence, physical, moral, and spiritual health are different facets of the same "way." More specifically, physical self-cultivation precedes mental cultivation in a direct cause and effect relationship. This principle is put into practice across various Asian traditions of spiritual training. The regulation of posture and breath in Indian yoga form the basis of mental cultivation, for example, and the Buddhist use of the arts (including martial arts) in East Asia uses physical discipline in the same way. Hence, in contrast to the assumption that the mind should rule over the body,

> the tradition of Eastern self-cultivation places importance on entering the mind from the body or form. That is, it attempts to train the mind by training the body. Consequently, the mind is not simply consciousness, nor is it constant and unchangeable, but rather it is that which is *transformed* through training the body. (Yuasa 1993: 26)

Hence, the discriminating mind is not the basis of moral knowledge, but rather the obstacle that is overcome by physical training. The Daoist aim of effortless action is a prerogative of those who, after considerable discipline, can throw away the rules because they have gone beyond the need to rely on mental calculation and effort. The fact that these sages can be found among an indiscriminate variety of laborers and the leisured – a cook, a wheelwright, a hunchbacked cicada catcher, a ferryman, a woodworker, a swimmer, an illustrator (*Zhuangzi* chs. 3, 19) – suggests that all common activities, much like all human interactions for Confucius, can be the actual moments of, rather than simply the means to, self-transformation.

Ritual Action and Morality

Chinese traditions move religious ethics significantly beyond the view of ritual as action that is made meaningful only by virtue of an interpretive reading. Confucian and Daoist rituals may be aligned with cosmological maps, to be sure, but their *doing* is an intrinsic value, one which instantiates the *Dao* rather than merely referring to it. In Confucianism, ritual actions are performed within the social body, and morality is expressed in the full attainment of humanness in interaction with others. In Daoism, ritual actions are performed within the physical body, and morality is expressed in the full cultivation of the self that eliminates all injury to self and others. As ritual actions, both paths give priority to the body, and, by extension, to physical performance (see chapter 54).

Performances are not just the stuff of formal theater or ceremonial event, but are also the making of meaning and identity in everyday public as well as private life. In this respect, the moral person may also be seen as a performer, not in the sense of one who "puts on" an act, but of one who attains morality in the moment of action. Action is the primary context in which moral consciousness and experience materialize:

> Cultures are most fully expressed in and made conscious of themselves in their ritual and theatrical performances. A performance is a dialectic of "flow," that is, spontaneous movement in which action and awareness are one, and "reflexivity," in which the central meanings, values, and goals of a culture are seen "in action," as they shape and explain behavior. (Schechner and Appel 1990: 1)

The absence of a direct linguistic equivalent to "morality" in traditional Chinese thought has led us to look at other terms with family resemblances. Confucian *li* and *ren*, and Daoist *neidan* practice, which seek to "nurture life" (*yangsheng*), all point us in the direction of ritual action. Their compatibility with the explanations of performance theory creates a marriage between the Asian tradition and contemporary scholarship, both of which encourage us to push back the boundaries of moral discourse. Specifically, we are encouraged to see the links between morality and aesthetics by paying attention to the phenomenological qualities of the former. Confucian benevolence and Daoist "great knowledge" (*dazhi*) and daimonic skill (*shen*) bear a great resemblance to the "flow," "concentration," and "presence" attained in performance, and inspire us to imagine morality as a similar quality, or aesthetic, of experience.

Bibliography

Cho, F. 1998: "Leaping into the Boundless: A Daoist Reading of Comparative Religious Ethics." *Journal of Religious Ethics* 26 (1), 139–65.

Lau, D. C. T. 1963: *Lao Tzu: Tao Te Ching*. London: Penguin Books.

——1979: *Confucius: The Analects*. London: Penguin Books.

Myerhoff, B. 1990: "The Transformation of Consciousness in Ritual Performances: Some Thoughts and Questions" in *By Means of Performance: Intercultural Studies of Theatre and Ritual*, ed. R. Schechner and W. Appel. Cambridge: Cambridge University Press.

Schechner, R. and Appel, W. (eds.) 1990: *By Means of Performance: Intercultural Studies of Theatre and Ritual*. Cambridge: Cambridge University Press.

Staal, F. 1979: "The Meaninglessness of Ritual." *Numen* 26 (1), 2–22.

Veith, I. T. 1972: *The Yellow Emperor's Classic of Internal Medicine*. Berkeley: University of California Press.

Yuasa, Y. 1993: *The Body, Self-Cultivation and Ki-Energy*, trans. S. Nagatomo and M. S. Hull. Albany: State University of New York Press.

CHAPTER 10
Saints and Exemplars

Lamin Sanneh

Saints and moral exemplars are an important subject in religious traditions, for they define and demonstrate the hopes, desires, practices, and moral ideals of their community. The lives of these persons provide inspiration and guidance, typically providing devotees with help on complex moral demands and personal struggles. This chapter expounds the subject of saints and exemplars with detailed attention to the Muslim tradition and its encounter with indigenous African ideas. Every tradition, it is true, has its own saints and moral exemplars, but it is hoped that attention here to the particular examples in one tradition may provide more general insight into the importance of saints and moral exemplars in religious ethics broadly conceived. The cases discussed in this chapter may be viewed as exemplary of the larger theme.

A substantive distinction is drawn in the Muslim tradition between "saintship" (*wilāya*) and "sainthood" (*walāya*). Saintship concerns the organization and expression of saintly power, while sainthood relates to the personality of the saint and the dynamics of personal saintly power. Saintship is bequeathed and perpetuated in an organized fashion, whereas sainthood is acquired by individuals. Sainthood is personal charisma, while saintship is institutional charisma. Both concepts are related to the idea of *baraka* ("favor," "grace," "virtue").

The common Arabic word for saint is *walī*, strictly speaking a friend or patron. It occurs numerous times in the Qur'ān with this meaning, often with God being the friend or patron (Qur'ān 2:258; 3:61; 6:51, 69; 17:111; 41:34; 42:7, 27; 45:18; 2:101, 114; 9:75, 117; 13:37; 18:25; 29:21; 32:3; 42:6, 30, 42; 4:77, 122, 173; 6:14; 18:16; 33:17, etc.). The Qur'ān's major stress is on God as the only *walī* worthy of trust and dependence (*tawakkul*) (Qur'ān 7:2, 11:22, 115; 13:17; 17:99; 18:48, 102; 25:19; 29:49; 39:4; 42:4, 7, 45; 45:9; 60:1). A special place is also reserved for those whom God regards as his friends (*awliyā'*) (Qur'ān 3:27; 4:91, 138, 143; 5:56, 62, 84; 7:28; 9:23; 10:63; 60:9). A further step is taken when a forensic meaning is applied to the term and human patrons are given a status in contract law such that they may act as deputies for their clients (Qur'ān 2:282) (see chapter 11).

There is Qur'ānic justification for the claim made by and about many of the saints of Islam that God may enter into a relationship of special intimacy with his creatures, so that they hold the status of "friendship" or "nearness in favor" to God. They are close to him: "near ones" (*al-muqarrabūn*), who will receive the superlative reward of Paradise (Qur'ān 61:11; 83:21, 28). The word for "near ones" is from the same root (q.r.b.) that is at the base of the standard terms for a relative or kin (*qurbā*). Making up for the abolition of natural kinship in Islam (Levy 1969: 55–6; Qur'ān 49:13; Baydāwī 1848: 276), the Qur'ān assures believers that God will provide for them a next-of-kin, and the word used is the same as that for nearness (Qur'ān 19:5). Perhaps the most striking image of God's closeness to human beings occurs in this trenchant verse:

> We indeed created man, and We know
> what his soul whispers within him,
> and We are nearer to him [*aqrabu ilayhi*] than the
> jugular vein. (Qur'ān 50:15; Arberry 1967: 234)

Súfís interpret "nearness to God" as a life marked by prayer and supererogatory devotion. The "saint" is one who leads a life of religious devotion, keeping close to God in prayer, praise, supplication, and attentiveness, and to the people in various acts of guidance, mediation, and intercession. When he or she becomes manifest to people after receiving the inner assurance of divine "friendship," the saint becomes worldly exemplar, although often the public manifestation of sainthood precedes confirmation of inner assurance.

The Holy and the Sacred

A word or two may be in order on general notions of the holy and sacred in African traditional religions. African notions of the holy and sacred are infused by a sense of danger and avoidance. The sacred is contagious, and it renders persons vulnerable to invasion by spirit forces, a contamination that can spread from contact. Muslim notions of the saint and sanctity are influenced by ideas of merit and reward at the hands of the elect. Ordinary people receive protection through the mediation of saints and exemplars. Holy men and holy women, accordingly, have their social function defined for them as brokers of popular religion.

North African impulses

In contrast to the tradition of Christian saints, saintly virtue in Muslim Africa was typically cultivated with a worldly end in view rather than as solitary retreat. For example, in the military redoubts of Northwest Africa saints emerged committed to defying the world with sacred word and consecrated sword. Ascetic practice (*zuhd*) developed alongside the study of law (*fiqh*), and together they helped sharpen the instruments of armed struggle (*jihād*). The religious recluse occupied their time with studying juridical sources, often with an eye to reforming society and local practice. The exemplary religious life made little distinction between worldly means and spiritual ends. One writer observes that whereas elsewhere in the Muslim world the ascetics (*zuhhād*) who abandoned all worldly contact were pitted against the jurists (*fuqahā'*) who were immersed in worldly affairs, in North Africa they made common cause, and many religious figures combined the two functions.

> In Ifriqiya, *fuqahā'* became *zuhhād* without ceasing the study of *fiqh*, or cutting off relations with the *fuqahā'* who demonstrated no interest in asceticism. As *zuhhād*, however, they did not become detached from the world, and they remained in constant communication with the people. They were guardians of the common people's interests, and challenged the rulers to show regard for these considerations. They were admired by the people for their piety, devotion, and independence with respect to rulers. They were not marginal to the mainstream of Islam in Ifriqiya, but rather its core. They were the true leaders of the people (Levtzion 1979: 80)

Through jurisprudence and asceticism the *jihād* tradition was strengthened, and holy personages carried their call into the citadels of power. In the numerous eruptions of reform and renewal the saintly ideal – that is, the exemplary force of the holy and learned figure – was the ideological trigger and guide for action. Struggle against the flesh (*nafs*) was matched by struggle against the unbelieving world (*dunya*), a double role that qualified the saint for political and spiritual leadership at the same time (see chapter 6).

An example was 'Abd Allāh ibn Yasīn (d. 1059), who in 1040 CE launched the religious revolution in North Africa that led to the creation of the Almoravid empire. Ibn Yasīn was a commanding, ascetic figure. He was rewarded with miracles as God's recognition of his saintly stature. The seal of *baraka*, of efficacious virtue, came to be attached to his person, and after his death he became a transmitter of blessings for people who came to his tomb seeking rescue from various pains and obstacles in ordinary life. The Arab chronicler al-Bakrī, writing in 1068 CE, recounts how a cult grew up around the tomb of Ibn Yasīn:

> On his tomb stands today a mausoleum, which is well frequented, and a hospice [*ribāṭ*] always full of people . . . Even now a group of them [the Almoravids] would choose to lead them in prayer only a man who prayed behind 'Abd Allāh, even though a more meritorious and more pious person, who had never prayed under the guidance of 'Abd Allāh, was among them. (Al-Bakrī 1913: 168; Hopkins and Levtzion 1981: 74)

Yet Al-Bakrī was scornful of Ibn Yasīn and his followers, scrutinizing the man's heritage with the unsparing eye of a rigorist. Along with the scholars ('*ulamā'*), al-Bakrī held the saintly heritage (*wilāya*) in Islam, defined as a synthesis of *zuhd* and *fiqh*, of renunciation and the code, to be in excess of accepted guidance. Yet the saints (*awliyā'*) have been the real architects of the changes that the 'ulamā idealized in doctrine; they gave practical expression to the aims of the code (see chapter 8).

The successors of the Almoravids failed the challenge of living in the world and against it at the same time. These were the Almohads, whose leader, Ibn Tumart (d. 1130), claimed the title of Mahdī, meaning Messiah, in 1127. Ibn Tumart sought to make a firm distinction between *fiqh* and *zuhd*, between religious legalism and free-wheeling experimentalism – a legalism that stressed the binding authority of received tradition, and an experimentalism that narrowed down to the individual and his culti-vated insights, including direct access to truth. In that cleavage he asserted his own towering authority, burdened by few scruples and buoyed by the single idea of a victo-rious monotheism. For Ibn Tumart, too, worldly reward was a natural appurtenance of religious virtue. (For a brief but authoritative account of Ibn Tumart, see Macdonald 1965.)

The Almoravid movement and its Almohad sequel together combined to transmit an enduring element of devotion to jurisprudential sources (*uṣūl al-fiqh*) into the stream of religious life and practice, with an impact on Muslims of sub-Saharan Africa. By that channel, *fiqh* and *zuhd* arrived in sub-Saharan Africa.

Cenobitic overtures in West African Islam

The Almohad empire eventually collapsed, in Spain first (1235) and then in North Africa (1269), although Hafsid rule in Tunisia continued the Almohad line. The religio-political unity of North Africa virtually ceased after the Almohads; the only carryover was the tradition of saintship, which continued unabated. The Sūfī orders, inspired by Qādirī devotional materials and by interest in *fiqh* and *tafsīr* (exegesis), grew in power and influence. The Qādirī order, founded after the twelfth-century scholar and mystic 'Abd al Qādir al-Jīlānī, was transmitted widely in many parts of the Muslim world, spawning a number of smaller orders that developed their own autonomous rules. One such order was the Shādilīyah, founded after Abū'l-Ḥasan al-Shādhilī (1196–1258), although it was his disciple, Ibn Aṭa'Allāh (ca. 1250–ca. 1310), who established and popularized the order in the Maghrib. It had its base in Fez, and in the eighteenth century it was taken from there to sub-Saharan Africa by a returning student.

We only have fragmentary knowledge of the Shādilīya in West Africa. Bits and pieces of information, picked up from a disparate spread of sources, are strung together in many accounts without a central figure or idea. The man responsible for introduc-ing the Shādilīya to West Africa was 'Alī al-Sūfī, described in the sources as "the apostle of Shādhilism" in his part of Africa. He received the *wird*, the office of initia-tion, from a Moroccan spiritual director (*murshid*) in Fez and subsequently brought it in the eighteenth century to the plateau area of Futa Jallon in Guinea. His litanies emphasized attachment to Fez as his spiritual birthplace, and his disciples went on to give it a veneration second in importance only to Mecca and Medina. A disciple of 'Alī al-Sūfī, Modi Sellu (1760–1813), the political head (*alfa*) of the district of Labé in Futa Jallon, expanded Shādhilism in Labé.

Tcherno Isma'īla, a student of 'Alī al-Sūfī, made the order a political success. At first he concentrated on broadening and deepening the spiritual resources of the movement, creating a religious center he called Diawia (*zāwiya*). Its focal point was the *missidi*, the word for "mosque" in the Fula language. The *missidi* was then replicated in numerous adjacent communities, resulting in a network of ideologically related centers. At the head of *missidi* was the *walī*, reassuring symbol of virtue and its reward, and under his authority the devotees bound and consecrated themselves in service. The *missidi* was the vanguard of virtue, and the *walī* the unique spiritual commissar who wafted over his motley amalgam of *refuseniks* the breath of felicity. Diawia, in Labé, became the prototype, and from there sympathizers ranged far and wide.

Diawia came under a cloud following the death of Tcherno 'Isma'īla, although Shádhilism continued to expand in other areas. With the accession of Tcherno Mamadou Sharif, the youngest son of Tcherno Isma'īla, however, the center underwent a revival. Shādhilism regained the initiative and the *diarorē* rites, for a while interrupted, were reintroduced on an organized basis. All the Labé country was now engulfed by the rites, and the flame of devotion spread from there to numerous important locations in the Fula country and beyond. One leader, Tcherno Jaw (d. 1865), chief of the district of Ndama in Labé, gave the rites a strong political basis by refashioning his subjects into the butt of military operations against adjacent non-Muslim populations. The attacks combined religious ardor with political boldness. Tcherno Jaw, at the head of such attacks, achieved an elevated status through it and was accordingly ascribed the title "*walī* of Ndama" – another worldly exemplar.

Tcherno Jaw's initiative was inherited by his second son, Tcherno Ibrahima, whose influence extended far beyond Futa Jallon. The French, recognizing that fact, wooed him in a gambit to exploit his influence, but in 1899 the two sides collided over a conflict of interest. French involvement compounded an incendiary urge that Shādhilism had exploited so successfully in an earlier era, and gave local grievances a new external focus.

The man whose career brought matters to a head was Tcherno Aliou (ca. 1828–1912) – frail, lame, and partly blind, but so considerable a force in the area that he was given the title *walī* of Goumba, whose *baraka* transfused the whole region. His retreat center at Goumba, situated on the lower escarpment of the Futa Jallon plateau, was perceived as a challenge to the French, who responded by according him the treasonable status of Mahdī – Messiah. The French soon controlled the area and captured the centers of Shādhilī influence. Shādhilism had reached a watershed in Muslim West Africa, and the saintly virtue that propelled it, for so long a force to be reckoned with in the rarefied political atmosphere of the plateau, was driven to the low ground of accommodation with the French colonial authorities.

The history of Shādhilism shows there were real and enduring links between West African and North African Islam. The synthesis of law and devotion and of involvement and retreat had assumed a firm basis in West Africa as well. In neither area did the *awliyā'* avoid controversy. On the contrary, they often became the public focus of social and political unrest, and, by their own claims, the channels and instruments of divine sanction. They perceived no dichotomy between the word of God and the world of politics, and showed little hesitation in looking to crowds to take command of events. For them, saintly virtue had a robust, worldly face to it; they viewed worldly success as the proof and validation of personal virtue. In their minds, faith and works, form and content, dogma and practice, harmonized naturally.

Virtue and Spells

It is instructive to set this understanding of the saint alongside indigenous African conceptions (see chapters 42 and 44). Unlike his counterpart in the indigenous culture who specializes in spells, incantations, and other forms of divinatory control, the *walī* is distinguished by *baraka*, understood as social capital rather than as spirit power that one fears and, thus, one has to avoid. *Baraka*, for this reason, can be institutionalized and organized with public following and support, centered in the *walī* and ratified in his devotees. The structural and social dimension of saintly power is integral to the Muslim tradition: sainthood – individual charisma – is buttressed by saintship, a historically transmitted line of personal succession. In traditional divination, *baraka* existed as potent power that could harm the uninitiated. The code regulating it emphasized avoidance and the negative results of breaches. In effect, *baraka* in traditional Africa was a magical force possessed by unusual individuals who developed a specialized art for it. In such circles the magician is answerable primarily to his or her art, not to any public or popular accreditation. Thus, if the evil eye is potent enough to accomplish its objective, then it does its work irrespective of whether or not the harm being inflicted is ethically justified. Magicians are vindicated by the intrinsic potency of their art, not by public social approbation. This tradition is quite different from the Muslim notion of *baraka*, or at least from the Islamic transformation of the notion, which implies both personal virtue (the saint is "the blessed person," *al-mubārak*) and efficacious power. The ultimate source of *baraka* is God, not magical power.

Sainthood and saint veneration: The Mourides of Senegal

The founder of the Mouride (Arb. *murīd*, "disciple") brotherhood of Senegal was Shaykh Amadou Bamba (ca. 1852–1927), a man deeply influenced by the interior devotion of the Tijānī order of Sūfīs, although his own roots lay in Qādirī soil (Dumont 1975: 71–2). Over the course of time, his Mouride brotherhood outpaced its counterparts in vigorously cultivating the unthinking obeisance of rank-and-file neophytes, called by the Mourides themselves *tálibés* (Arb. *ṭullāb*, sing. *ṭalib*). Wrapping themselves in the mantle of *baraka*, the Mouride leaders' claim over the bodies of their disciples came to be complete and total, so much so that, after a point, religious instruction, with its accompanying initiation into grades of spiritual enlightenment, was almost entirely missing in the otherwise close relationship between the postulant and his spiritual axis. Instead, the shaykh mounted the disciples like cavalry, driving them into virgin fields of submission and physical labor on the peanut plantations of the brotherhood, a cash-crop enterprise conducted for the exclusive benefit of the *shuyūkh*. At its extreme form this submission may in fact, if not in theory, substitute for submission to God, with *baraka* investing the *shuyūkh* with a semi-divine status.

The manifestation of this kind of enthusiastic *baraka* over crowds of illiterates brought the Mourides to the hostile attention of the French colonial power. Paul Marty, whose acute analysis of the Mourides remains a classic, describes the extraordinary appeal of Amadou Bamba. Describing what he saw in 1913, Marty wrote:

The mere sight of Amadou Bamba at prayer or giving his blessing with a stream of saliva on the prostrate faithful plunges some into hysterical outbursts which everyone wants to share. They roll at the feet of the saint, they kiss his sandals and the hem of his robe, they hold out their hands to him. With compunction he lets fall a stream of saliva on the open palms, which close up, clasp together, and spasmodically rub the face and body. Then there are shudderings, fainting fits, epileptic convulsions, followed by contortions and extraordinary leaps, all this accompanied by a horrible yelling. Madness finally takes hold of everyone. (Marty 1913: 52–3; cited in O'Brien 1971: 53)

The French took strong measures to curb Amadou Bamba's power, or what was perceived as his power. He and his followers were harassed. Having first installed themselves at the village of Mbake-Baol in the rural hinterland of Senegal, the shaykh and his followers moved to a new center he built at Touba, also in Senegal, in 1887. Since there was no abatement in the hostility of local commandants, Amadou Bamba and his disciples removed to St. Louis, then the capital of colonial Senegal, in 1891. But proximity to power merely served to inflame official sensibilities further, and the shaykh was apprehended by French troops. He was sentenced to imprisonment and exile in Gabon from 1895 to 1902 on charges of political subversion. His *baraka* guaranteed his popularity with the crowds. In turn, that cast him into a feared political figure in the eyes of the French. Furthermore, Amadou Bamba's association with the *Tijānīyá*, which was regarded in colonial circles as inherently subversive, established his culpability as needing no further proof. Amadou Bamba returned to Senegal in November 1902, but he was arrested again the following year and condemned to a fresh term of exile, this time in Mauritania, from 1903 to 1907.

The tenacity of *baraka* has roots in pre-Muslim society. The spontaneous and overwhelming nature of the response to Amadou Bamba as *séringe* (Wolof for holy man, saint) cannot, therefore, be explained solely on the grounds of strong Islamic influence. Most of his followers were ignorant of even the most basic tenets of the faith. For them, Amadou Bamba cut the figure of the familiar charismatic personality, which in the pre-Islamic era was designated as *borom bayré*, a Wolof phrase meaning the possessor of success and fame. The Muslim saint, when he appeared, was assimilated to this traditional African paradigm as both *borom bayré* and *borom barké*, a man of both worldly and spiritual achievement (Dumont 1975: 21–2).

This double level of understanding allowed Amadou Bamba's influence to grow among his disciples, who transmitted it to surrounding areas. In his own mind Bamba was a devout, humble Muslim, eager to behave and think in strict accordance with orthodox requirements. Indeed, when first approached by an overzealous disciple who saw in him the marks of greatness, Amadou Bamba rebuffed him as unsound, sending him packing with the advice that he put his mind to better and more useful pursuits (O'Brien 1971: 143). Even later in his career he forbade his disciples to render him obeisance that he deemed properly due to God (O'Brien 1971: 54). In his rules for novices he stressed submission to God above all else (Dumont 1975: 85), and in his prolific writings, the theme of obedience to God is persistent and unyielding. He spoke with sincerity about his unworthiness and expressed distress at evidence of his weakness. Praying to God, he said:

I desire your help in the midst of terror and vengeance. Today my heart is overburdened with sadness. My being is too weak to bear what I face. Forgive. My misfortune is plain, and my heart is anguished. (Dumont 1975: 123)

These words were spoken shortly before his first exile, an exile that was to resonate with the rising chorus of popular adulation.

Whatever his inner feelings of inadequacy, Amadou Bamba responded eagerly to the undeniable strength of his support among the peasant populations, and, reacting to the chaos around him, he tried to form order by moving in the direction of undisputed authority. In one of his devotional manuals he listed four qualities as necessary in the disciple: (1) a sincere and unshakable love for the shaykh, (2) unquestioning obedience to the commands of the shaykh, (3) abandonment of all opposition, including inward resistance, to the shaykh, and (4) the giving up of any preference for the disciple's own private thoughts (Dumont 1975: 88). Elsewhere, he wrote that he who does not have a shaykh for his training will come to grief, "for he who does not have a shaykh for his guide will have Satan for his shaykh" (Dumont 1975: 90). "Truth," he said, "consists in the love for one's shaykh" (Dumont 1975: 90). In another work Amadou Bamba says that the *walí* inherits the power of miracles from the Prophet to whom the *walí* is attached by a mystical chain of initiation (Dumont 1975: 95). "Saints," he wrote, "are the authentic signs of the Prophet's religion, and of his truth . . . Saints are preserved from error and invested with honor" (Dumont 1975: 96). This point of devotion to the Prophet is stressed in the numerous details on performing the *dhikr*. At its height, the *dhikr* is nothing but the imitation of the Prophet, the Perfect Man (*insān al-kāmil*) or the true intercessor (*shafī', mushaffa'*) (Dumont 1975: 112) (see chapter 4).

Recognizing that his disciples needed the iron hand of discipline more than the persuasive pen of the scholar, Amadou Bamba elevated physical labor to the status of a religious obligation. "Work," he contended, "is a part of true religion. The human body, since its creation, exists only to accomplish the work ordered by God" (Dumont 1975: 114). It would be unfair to blame Séringe Bamba entirely for the coarse bearing of his followers, for he was following where they led. Amar Sambe, a local Senegalese scholar, testified to the compelling interior impetus produced in the shaykh by his following when he recalled that in his youth, wandering, drunken *awliyā'* were a familiar sight; yet their followers remained undaunted. He writes:

> When I was a child in Koranic school at Kébémer [Senegal], a marabout passed frequently in front of the school, staggering, held upright by his *tálibés*. The *séringe* always had a foot in the vineyard of the Lord. Despite this fact, his followers liked to maintain that their shaykh had so much *baraka* that strong liquor transformed itself into milk when it reached his stomach. (Sambe 1964: 185; cited in O'Brien 1971: 89)

Such marabouts were the early precursors of the confluence of pre-Islamic ideas on *baraka* with their Muslim analogues. Amadou Bamba was not nearly that idiosyncratic, mainly because by the time he arrived on the scene there had occurred a general elevation in the practice and understanding of Islam. However, as it stands, the anecdote suggests the wide margin of credulity available to the local *walī* if he wished to avail himself of it. The central importance of discipleship per se in Mouride practice is dramatized in the nature of its simple initiation ritual, which has supreme value for the Mouride *tálibé*. It is called *njebbel* in Wolof (Arb. *bay'a, talqīn*), meaning personal and physical surrender, and is the crux of Mouride life and philosophy. In the *njebbel* the neophyte declares to his master, "I surrender to you my body and soul. What you forbid, I refrain from, and what you command I obey" (O'Brien 1971: 85). That unadorned formula binds the disciple to the shaykh in a relationship that is, for all practical purposes, indissoluble, though in theory the disciple can repudiate the link in an extreme crisis (O'Brien 1971: 88). The neophyte is told by the shaykh to make unquestioning obedience his watchword. *Del deglu ndiggel*, he says: "You must hear words as commands" (O'Brien 1971: 85). *Baraka* became muscular piety.

Disciple and exemplar

We need a broader perspective to understand the wider connections of Mouride extremism. Its counterpart in the wide spectrum of Súfí spirituality is the call to physical renunciation, an arming of the soul with the weapons of struggle and vigilance against the lures of the carnal body. This, essentially, is *zuhd*, and it was powerfully preached in the Tijániyá brotherhood, with which the Mourides had some affinity. There the devotee was urged to beat the carnal self

> with the whip of the Book, bind it with the halter of reproach and judgment, set limits upon it with conscientious rebuke and reprimand, and place the saddle of firm intention upon it with the girth of determination. Then mount it with the profession of the holy law [Sharī'a] and ride it into the fields of Truth [*al-Ḥaqq*, a Ṣūfī term for God]. (Tcherno Bokar Salifu Taal (ca. 1883–1940), as quoted by Brenner 1984: 114)

Even for the seasoned adept the challenges of genuine spirituality demand superhuman resources. The Mouride instinct to have recourse to saintly intercession is fed from this reality. Unaided human effort is too bedeviled by uncertainty to guarantee success. Through the servile channel of farm labor the Mouride masters have taken individual responsibility out of the hands of ignorant crowds and offered instead the duty of collective subservience and the privilege of the blessed assurance they as leaders can give. *Baraka* is in the eye of the beholder, but especially in the face of the beholden one.

The power of the shaykh in the Mouride tradition is a function of the adulation of the disciples. As Mouride theology affirms, the *shuyūkh* occupy the ranks of honor (Arb. *maqām*) to which their followers' faith and enthusiasm carry them. It seems, therefore, that the cultivation of saintly eminence is but a shorthand for the cultivation of society. Today, despite a number of premature jeremiads, the Mourides number well over a million, and at the Grand Maqál, their annual pilgrimage to Touba, up to half the total membership may attend. One could scarcely ask for a more impressive demonstration of group and religious solidarity, of tangible expression of charisma, of what has been called the "versatility" of charisma. (See, for example, O'Brien 1971, who later revised his own position; see O'Brien 1977.)

Conclusion

"Sainthood" is personal charisma, and represents the social production of *barakah*. "Saintship," on the other hand, is the structural expression of saintly power and influence. The two complement each other as when disciples, infused with the *barakah* of the saint, acknowledge their master as guide and exemplar. It is by virtue of assured popular adulation that the true mettle of *barakah* is proved. The Mouride case is an outstanding example, the extreme, wild point of a broad spectrum that includes at a different point the more sober Shádhilí *awliyā'* and other moral exemplars.

Bibliography

Al-Bakrī. 1913: *Kitāb al-Masālik wa'l-Mamālik* (Book of Routes and Realms), ed. M. G. de Slane. Algiers: A. Jourdan.

Anawati, G. C. and Gardet, L. 1961: *Mystique musulmane; aspects et tendances, expériences et techniques.* Paris: J. Vrin.

Arberry, A. J. 1967: *The Koran Interpreted.* New York: Macmillan.

Baydāwī. 1848: *Anwār al-Tanzīl*, Vol. 2, ed. H. O. Fleischer. Leipzig: F. C. G. Vogel.

Brenner, L. 1984: *West African Sufi: The Religious Heritage and Spiritual Search of Cerno Bokar Saalif Taal.* London: Christopher Hurst.

Dumont, F. 1975: *La Pensée religieuse d'Amadou Bamba.* Dakar: Nouvelles éditions africaines.

Fisher, H. J. 1979: "Dreams and Conversion in Black Africa" in *Conversion to Islam*, ed. N. Levtzion. New York: Holmes and Meier.

Hopkins, J. F. P. and Levtzion, N. 1981: *Corpus of Early Arabic Sources for West African History.* New York: Cambridge University Press.

Levtzion, N. 1979: "Abd Allah ibn Yasin and the Almoravids" in *Studies in West African Islamic History*, Vol. 1, ed. J. R. Willis. London: Frank Cass.

Levy, R. 1969: *The Social Structure of Islam: Being the Second Edition of the Sociology of Islam.* Cambridge: Cambridge University Press.

Macdonald, D. B. 1965: *Development of Muslim Theology, Jurisprudence and Constitutional Theory.* Beirut: Khayats.

Marty, E. 1913: *Les Mourides d'Amadou Bamba: rapport a M. le Gouverneur Général de l'Afrique Occidentale.* Paris: E. Leroux.

Marty, P. 1921: *L'Islam en Guinée: Fouta-Diallon.* Paris: E. Leroux.

Monteil, V. 1964: *L'Islam noir.* Paris: Éditions du Seuil.

—— 1969: "Marabouts" in *Islam in Africa*, ed. J. Kritzeck and W. H. Lewis. New York: Van-Nostrand.

O'Brien, D. B. 1971: *The Mourides of Senegal: The Political and Economic Organization of an Islamic Brotherhood.* Oxford: Clarendon Press.

—— 1977: "A Versatile Charisma: The Mouride Brotherhood 1967–1975." *Archives europeenes de sociologie* 18, 84–106.

Sambe, A. 1964: *Diplôme d'études supérieures.* Paris: Faculté des Lettres, Université de Paris.

Sanneh, Lamin. 1989: *The Jakhanke Muslim Clerics: A Religious and Historical Study of Islam in Senegambia.* Lanham, MD: University Press of America.

—— 1997: *The Crown and the Turban: Muslims and West African Pluralism.* Denver, CO: Westview Press.

Trimingham, J. Spencer. 1959: *Islam in West Africa.* Oxford: Clarendon Press.

CHAPTER 11

Law and Religion

Winnifred Fallers Sullivan

Law is an expansive concept with resonance not only in political institutions, but also in religious traditions. The fact that "law" is found across these diverse domains of human social life raises profound questions for religious ethics. Whether law should be in the business simply of creating the conditions for peace or of producing morality has been a central debate from Confucian China to the modern West. Should law leave individual behavior unregulated if it does not affect others, as John Stuart Mill would have it, or should law attempt to establish a moral regime as well? Is human flourishing (if that is indeed the appropriate goal of human activity) best served through guarantees of individual freedom and autonomy or through the coercive agency of laws prescribing appropriate behavior, public and private? And, if the second is desirable, can it be done effectively? What is the relationship between international law, state law, and more local or informal systems of regulating morality? Is law, politically defined, separate from, dependent on, or an expression of "religion"? This chapter concerns "law": "law" in relation to "religion" and to "morality."

Law, religion, and ethics are cultural complexes that, however different in many ways, share an engagement with the problem of how one ought to live. They might be seen, in fact, as alternative systems, or structures, in a sense, within which to reflect on the appropriate occupation of humankind. These alternatives are differentiated depending on whether people are to be understood to be defined primarily by their relationship to the state, to their gods, or to each other. To be sure, rarely, if ever, do particular individuals live exclusively within one of these systems. An individual human being inhabits these various realities simultaneously, fielding the competing demands of the systems in different ways. Individuals and communities both shape and are shaped by various and often multiple blendings of law, religion, and moral traditions. From a structural point of view, however, and for the purposes of discursive clarity, the three may be held apart and be seen as having had varying relationships to one another and to have taken various forms at various times in history and in various places. Law, institutionally and culturally, may at times be seen as the carrier of moral principles, which in turn may or may not be expressed in a religious idiom. Or law may be seen as autonomous, independent of the other two. Religion and morality likewise. Religion in some contexts may be expressed through law or prescribe rules of morality. In others, religion seems to be both antinomian and amoral, leaving law *and* ethics to the secular domain. Morality may be embodied in law, or not. It may be explicitly religious, or not, in its foundation and expression.

If religion is taken to represent the obligations of humans to a larger reality and morality to represent the obligations of humans to one another, it is not immediately obvious what necessary relationship these two have to one another. Indeed, ethical systems exist without any explicit religious component. And religions exist without any explicit moral component. However, for many, perhaps for most, the two are intimately related and can only be understood in relation to each other. Some would entirely collapse the two. Religion might collapse into morality such that moral behavior is seen as the only true expression of the former. In other words, the obligations to a transcendent reality are identical to and defined by the obligations to one another. Thus, to obey the "love command" of Christian theological thinking by caring for one's neighbor would at the same time be to obey God. Morality might also collapse into religion. God might make demands, such as demands to offer sacrifices or prayers, in which the horizontal component is, at best, only sketchily implied. To the extent then that one considers ethical systems that are explicitly religious, law may be seen as an expression of or a partner in that system or, as is more and more often the case in modern states, as a neutral secular system against the backdrop of which or in varying degrees of tension with which, plural religious and non-religious ethical systems contend.

Law, the rule of law, if you will, has a very high value in the modern West. It seems at times that only law – law represented by legislators, judges, police officers, and prison guards – stands between us and chaos. But "law" is a deceptively easy little word, one that is worth pausing to reflect on. What is law? Is law a list of rules made and enforced by an always essentially violent and ideologically oppressive sovereign power? Is the sovereign itself subject to law, or not? If so, where is the law to be found that governs the sovereign? What about the sovereignty of God? Is coercion a necessary component of law? Is law better understood as a particular kind of process, rather than as a list of rules – a culturally specific system for handling disputes? What is the relationship of law to justice? (see chapter 14).

Law and Culture

The Massachusetts Bay Colony was founded in 1629 on what was to be the east coast of the United States. The English men and women who constituted the members of the colony struggled over the first few generations of their corporate existence to construct a society founded in a religious vision *and* governed by law. Determined to leave behind them a corrupt British establishment, they sought, using little more than the Bible and human reason, to create a Christian place governed by Christian laws and ethics. The initial shape of the colonial government was theocratic. There were distinct religious and civil institutions, but men who claimed to know God's will ruled the community (see chapter 6). The right to vote depended on proof of religious conversion. Law, religion, and ethics were contained in the Bible for these New England Puritans. But they had endless debates as to whether the Bible was self-interpreting or whether it could be interpreted by men, and, if it could be interpreted by men, who was the appropriate interpreter and what was the appropriate method of interpretation (see chapters 7 and 8). Several different positions contended for supremacy, and these various positions are revealed in the legal controversies of the young colony. Whether debating the presence of the cross in the colony's flag or of Anne Hutchinson's legitimacy as a religious leader, the rulers of Massachusetts Bay simply could not agree. They also had debates about the jurisdictional reach of their governing institutions, church and state – the Ten Commandments, for example. Should both tablets be enforced by the civil authorities, in other words, by "law," or only the second? The first four were commandments as to one's duty to God. The remaining six expressed one's duties to other people. There were also different opinions as to the advisability of referring to English common law.

Legal historians have been fascinated with the history of this small band of idealists and of their efforts to invent a new legal system. They now trace what seems to have been a gradual abandonment of the rule of God in the face of, not simply the difficulties of biblical interpretation, but also of growing diversity within the population. Within the first twenty years of the colony's history the theocratic ideal was discarded in favor of a government of laws, not of men of God. Law was secularized while religion and morality were gradually privatized.

What is obvious from this historical example is that how one understands "law" affects how one understands its relation to religion and ethics. For some, law is to be understood as a humanistic discipline, a set of practices and language of persuasion and argumentation that is continuous with other social and cultural institutions such as theological and moral reflection and debate. If law is seen as rhetorical, as James Boyd White and others would argue, then it engages religion and ethics as other such cultural discourses, an engagement that can range across time and place but is always embedded in local culture. For others, law is to be understood as autonomous, either as universally ordained by God (in which case the role of the human is to discern God's purpose), or as a tool of social engineering, one that should be governed by "scientific" principles. If law is about social control then religion and ethics tend to be excluded from discussions of law or to be simply employed in service of what are understood to be essentially utilitarian ends. Autonomous law has no culture and no history except as a laboratory for what does and does not work. A study of law in Massachusetts Bay can teach us how better to understand American Puritans, or the early history of American government, or it can help us to understand when law is or is not successful.

Exemplary also for students of law and religious ethics is the history and experience of the Jewish Diaspora. Since the first century of the common era, Jews have lived in most countries as self-governing enclaves, tolerated more or less by various state authorities, from the Roman to the Ottoman empire and then to early modern Europe. But, as Natalie Dohrmann and others have pointed out, Jews did not simply live in a world defined by Jewish law and ethics, in some kind of timeless sense. The early rabbis, largely without political or police power with which to effect enforcement of their rulings, beginning in the Roman empire, elaborated a legal and religious system with one ear out for state law, modifying their rulings to enable their people to live both apart from and within the cultures in which they lived. Eighteen centuries later, one sees the same dynamic at work in Isaac Bashevis Singer's description of his father's law court in early twentieth-century Warsaw. His father's jurisdiction is greatly circumscribed. His cases concern the regulation of ritual activity and marriage, for the most part. A delicate balance is achieved in the family and in the community between assimilation and conformity to Russian law, on the one hand, and, on the other, fidelity to an ever-adapting Jewish law.

Through most of human history and in most places, law, religion, and ethics have shared a largely common anthropology, culture, and cosmology, whether religious or secular. So, roughly speaking, law in Morocco speaks a language that assumes Moroccan Muslim ethical principles, Moroccan Muslim understandings of the motivations and capacities of the human person, and a Moroccan Muslim picture of the universe and of causation. Law in Thailand speaks a language that assumes Theravāda Buddhist ethical teachings, notions of what it is to be human, and understandings of the nature of the universe and of causation. Within a particular society, of course, different segments, distinguished by gender, class, occupation, etc., may be understood to inhabit different legio-religio-ethical subcultures depending on their social and geographic location. So, for example, a poor woman in nineteenth-century New York City may have lived a life structured by very different notions of the nature of the human person and of causation than her well-to-do counterpart, but the identity and choices of each were largely circumscribed by an integrated legal, religious, and ethical system particular to her social location.

As noted in the context of the modern West, however, law, religion, and ethics have been progressively differentiated, being understood, both socially and rhetorically, to inhabit different domains, while debates about their interrelationship have provided the framework for an ongoing conversation about how society ought to be governed. Problematic as it is to draw bright lines between East and West, between modern and pre-modern, it is peculiarly appropriate when talking about law because of the distinctive development of law in the modern West. Law has been a prime mover in the production of a modern secular consciousness, whether of the repressive or of the liberating sort. Outside the modern West, law has taken a different and less important independent role. Western observers may distinguish institutions and ideas that parallel modern secular legal ideas and institutions but, by and large, law in premodern societies was, to a greater or lesser degree, subsumed within and served what might be termed a religious worldview. Of course, even in the West, the separation is far from universally acknowledged. Religious anthropologies and ethical systems may there too be seen either to undergird or to inhibit law, depending on your perspective, but "law" in a transcendent sense, the "rule of law," law as the successor to religion, is a Western invention.

In the economy of the Western academy, law, religion, and morality may, roughly speaking, be considered from a philosophical or an historical/anthropological perspective, depending on whether one wishes to argue abstractly about law as a part of the nature of things or whether one wishes to understand and describe law as embedded in human society and culture, now and in the past, in all its messiness. In either case, at the beginning of the twenty-first century, law, religion, and morality, and reflection upon them are, by and large, seen by most scholars to have plural forms. It is not enough to understand the relationship of a single system of law, a single religion, and a single moral tradition in one place and time. One must seek to understand how they relate in a state of radical pluralism and rapid change. And one must ask whether pluralism and radical change are modern phenomena or whether they characterize all of human history, so that cultural essentialism is inappropriate in understanding the past as well.

The Study and Practice of Law Today

The academic study of law today is in the midst of extremely unsettling times. Modern understandings of law in the West, arguably achieving their high water mark in the work of H. L. A Hart and others, were, beginning in early modernity, increasingly positivist. That is, law was understood to be a deliberate human construction. Legal authority was understood to reside solely with the sovereign. Law was what the sovereign said it was. Law had no debt to religion and had no morality of its own. Law was understood to be autonomous. Law functioned as a closed system and was studied as a closed system. It had its own modes of thinking and a specialized profession of those experts in such thinking. Its goal was largely utilitarian, efficient social control producing the greatest good for the greatest number. Law that did not fulfill these criteria – religious law, for example – was simply not regarded as law.

Over the last half century there have been a number of different critiques of legal positivism. Beginning with legal realists who imported social scientific thinking into the study of law, but more rapidly thereafter with rights theory and critical legal studies, among others, the modernist pretensions of the law have been devastatingly deconstructed. Law, and the study of law, is in considerable disarray. It becomes difficult, then, when relating law to another academic discipline such as religious ethics, to know of which "law" to speak. When the internal Western critique of law is combined with the enormous expansion of "law" through a globalizing of legal practice and scholarship, it is a daunting task indeed. It is one that also faces an academy that largely assumes an irreversible secularization of law.

The necessary and progressive secularization of law in the modern West has been taken for granted until very recently. Beginning in early modernity, law, like politics, business, and education, was gradually divided from the workings of the church. There were different theories as to how the relationship should be understood, and the extent to which law depended on religion for its moral foundation and anthropology, but law gradually developed a life of its own. Such a separation continues to unfold around the world, for the most part, particularly with respect to international and commercial law. (Family and criminal law remain, however, in many places, still heavily indebted to religious understandings of the human.)

A notable and sustained critique of this growing separation has come from several quarters in the last 25 years. Religious thinkers and actors across religious traditions seek to reverse the trend and to link explicitly religious values to state law. They seek to reintegrate what they see as a dangerously atomized and degenerate society around shared creeds and structures. Some Muslim thinkers build such a theory on the idea of Sharī'a. Sharī'a, for them, serves as a complete legal system, religiously sanctioned and more than sufficient, appropriate for the governing of a modern society in all its aspects, private and public. Some Jewish and Christian and Hindu thinkers make similar arguments. On the other hand, some religious thinkers have seen the employment of law as the antithesis of true religious conduct. Law, for these people, constitutes a threat to moral values and to the duty one voluntarily owes to God. Discipline should be internal.

Other challenges to modernist notions of law as universal, transcending social and cultural boundaries, come from critical theorists who see law as always implicated in exercises of power and/or as always local, embedded in and particular to the realities, religious and otherwise, of a single community. International human rights conventions and other transnational agreements struggle to express universal human values while protecting self-determination, religious and cultural. Martha Nussbaum and others have attempted to justify universal human rights philosophically, while critics argue that universality is impossible, that most international law simply encodes concealed Western assumptions, religious and secular, about anthropology and cosmology. These critics would have modern Western law acknowledge its religious and cultural bias, coming to the international negotiating table as a local, rather than as a universal, system.

Complicating the multiple legal, religious, and ethical layers of contemporary life is rapid technological and scientific development. Increasingly, a serious and thoughtful theory concerning the relationship between religion, law, and morality depends on a defensible scientific theory of human behavior. Why and how do people do what they do? How do laws work? Why do people obey laws? Do they, in fact, "obey" them? Is nature and/or culture and/or religion a more significant element in determining human behavior? And are law, religion, and ethics to be thought of as nature or culture? Is religion to be understood as a universal aspect of human culture structuring the human imagination or as a narrative in service of ideology?

A rapidly evolving science of human behavior suggests a continuum of possibilities. Evolutionary psychologists may argue that human behavior is largely programmed by longstanding species adaptations to survival (see chapter 3). On this reading, law, religion, and morality are simply epiphenomenal, ways of explaining or describing what would be done in any event. Those on the nurture end of the spectrum would argue for a heavy environmental component as a conditioner of human behavior. People are not simply born hardwired for life; rather, their behavior is molded and shaped by their experience, both external and internal, intentional and not. Law, religion, and ethics would for the environmentalists assume a more important role in actually structuring and changing human activity (see chapter 47). Law's own self-understanding, for the most part, falls into the environmental end of the spectrum. It assumes that law is an important conditioner of human behavior, that it does affect what people do and can be used as a tool of societal reform, because people obey the law out of fear of sanctions. Religion works with a range of explanations for human behavior. Religion may or may not assume free will. It may have access to force as a means of ensuring compliance with its norms, or it may rely on promises or threats to be enacted in future lives. Systems of morality depend on the reality of human intentionality and, when they cannot rely on law and religion, must depend on exhortation and persuasion.

In the United States today, one issue that falls at the intersection of the three systems we are discussing is the regulation, or not, of sexual behavior, particularly of homosexual behavior. The laws of the various states have until recently pro-hibited sexual relations between members of the same sex and have limited marriage to one man and one woman. Can these laws be defended in purely secular terms? Are they rather grounded in a particular Christian anthropology which under-stands homosexual activity to be sinful and marriage as ordained by God? If the latter is the case, does the Constitution prohibit such arguments for laws? Must laws be publicly justified, whatever the motivation of the legislators, on purely secular grounds?

In *Bowers vs. Hardwick* (1986) the Supreme Court of the United States held that there was no Constitutional right to privacy protecting homosexual behavior. In response to the argument by the challengers of the statute that it had no rational basis, Justice White, for the majority, said: "The law . . . is constantly based on notions of morality, and if all laws representing essentially moral choices are to be invalidated under the Due Process Clause, the courts will be very busy indeed." Concurring, Justice Burger added: "Condemnation of those practices is firmly rooted in Judeo-Christian moral and ethical standards . . . To hold that the act of homosexual sodomy is somehow protected as a fundamental right would be to cast aside millennia of moral teaching." In dissent, Justice Blackmun, citing the ecclesiastical origins of anti-sodomy laws, argued: "The legitimacy of secular legislation depends . . . on whether the State can advance some justification for its law beyond its conformity to religious doctrine . . . A State can no more punish private behavior because of religious intolerance than it can punish such behavior because of racial animus."

In part the debate in the court, and in American public discourse generally, reveals a community split about basic issues. Is homosexual identity biologically based? Can homosexual identity be modified through law, religion, or ethical exhortation? Should modern secular state law in a pluralistic nation be justified in "scientific" or in religious or ethical terms? Is it possible to somehow craft a law which simply "keeps the peace" and leaves religious and ethical choices to the individual and her chosen community? This is a loud and contentious debate, one that is magnified at a global level.

Today's many migrants face the competing demands of several legal, religious, and ethical cultures and multiple layers of authority – local, national, and international. A Laotian man is imprisoned in the United States for abduction when he attempts to enact his tradition's way of marriage through engaging in bride capture. Muslim schoolgirls in France were dismissed from school for covering their heads. In Israel religious ortho-doxy controls the marriage laws and mixed marriage is prohibited. Christian conver-sion may curtail the civil rights of Indian dalits. But all of these essentially cultural ways of understanding human identity, however different, contend with materialist explanations as a basis for law.

Bibliography

Berman, H. J. 1983: *Law and Revolution: The Formation of the Western Legal Tradition*. Cambridge, MA: Harvard University Press.

Fuller, L. L. 1964: *The Morality of Law*. New Haven, CT: Yale University Press.

Huxley, A. 2002: *Religion, Law and Language: Comparative Studies in Religious Law*. New York: Routledge Curzon Press.

Kelley, D. R. 1990: *The Human Measure: Social Thought in the Western Legal Tradition*. Cambridge, MA: Harvard University Press.

Morrison, W. 1997: *Jurisprudence: From the Greeks to Postmodernism*. London: Cavendish.

Murphy, T. 1997: *The Oldest Social Science?: Configurations of Law and Modernity*. Oxford: Clarendon Press.

Perry, M. J. 1988: *Morality, Politics, and Law: A Bicentennial Essay*. New York: Oxford University Press.

Sarat, A. and Kearns, T. R. 1994: *The Rhetoric of Law*. Ann Arbor: University of Michigan Press.

3   Comparison

CHAPTER 12

Norms, Values, and Metaphysics

Franklin I. Gamwell

What is the relation between norms and values in religious ethics? Critical reflection addressed to this question should include a clarification of the key terms involved: "norms," "values," and "religious." In discussions of morality and religion, each of these terms may be used in differing ways, the merits of which are part of the discussion. This chapter seeks philosophically to explicate the distinctive nature of religious ethics and, in that respect, the basis for comparing the ethics of differing religions. Meanings of the three key terms will be stipulated in the course of that pursuit and thus will be commended only insofar as they permit a coherent and useful statement of the character common to all religious ethics. The term "ethics" is also used in differing ways, sometimes to mean a critical theory of the moral life. In contrast, "ethics" will here designate sets or systems of moral beliefs or prescriptions in terms of which humans explicitly seek to lead their lives, and I will use "moral theory" to mean critical reflection on the validity of such moral systems.

Given this use of "ethics," the three key terms will be so defined that they are connected in the following way: Distinctively religious ethics are those that ground all valid norms in a comprehensive value or set of values (see chapters "On Religious Ethics" and 2). On this account, as I will seek to show, religious ethics presuppose a certain conception of human decision and imply that moral theory, including the study of comparative religious ethics, is incomplete without metaphysics, that is, critical reflection on the character of reality and human purpose as such. The discussion here proceeds in the context of theoretical thought in the West. This restraint does not, I think, prevent valid conclusions about religious ethics generally, but it does mean that full confirmation of those conclusions waits on attention to comparative inquiries not pursued here (see chapters 15 and 16).

Defining the Terms

In the present discussion, "values" designates the ends or states of affairs that human activities seek to realize or promote. Given the limits its situation sets, a human activity becomes what it is through pursuit of some end or ends. This follows from the evident fact that distinctively human life occurs with self-understanding. The object of a self-understanding must be the self inclusively and thus can only be the purpose in or by which all aspects of the self or all relations to its situation are integrated or unified. In understanding itself, then, an activity understands the difference it makes to the realization of some state of affairs. This initial description, we might note, does not explicitly say whether human life involves a substantial self that persists throughout some extended time, a conception some religions or religious thinkers deny (see chapter 29). The self that is understood in a self-understanding is the present activity, and the relation of this activity to what appears as a human individual is another question.

A self-understanding, moreover, must be chosen. Although every activity is caused in greater or lesser measure by its situation, self-awareness means an understanding of those determinations and, therefore, cannot be simply another product of external causes. The ends or states of affairs we pursue are properly called values because each activity chooses from among alternatives for purposes the situation allows, and taking this choice with understanding means an affirmation of the chosen alternative. Because human activities understand themselves, we live by way of decision for some or other end we take to be good. So interpreted, Aristotle's dictum cannot be surpassed: "The good has rightly been declared to be that at which all [human] things aim" (Aristotle 1941: *Nicomachean Ethics* 1094a: 2–3).

Religious ethics, I propose, are distinguished from other moral systems by the affirmation of some comprehensive value or values or by taking something to be comprehensively good. Such a value or set of values defines an all-inclusive end, to which all specific purposes ought to contribute or of which all other values ought to be specifications. Each religious understanding of the moral life, then, asserts something as the comprehensive purpose that every decision for a self-understanding ought to exemplify or the comprehensive telos by which strictly all human activity ought to be directed, although differing religions may disagree about the character of the comprehensive good. On many conceptions of morality, the notion of a comprehensive good is finally not sensible, so that religious ethics as here understood are impossible. For this reason, a coherent theory of values and norms in religious ethics must show that such an ethic can be valid, and I will argue below that there is a comprehensive purpose or, what comes to the same thing, that the conception of human decision presupposed by all religious ethics is valid. It will be useful further to explicate that conception here.

Religious ethics presuppose that every decision for a self-understanding includes an awareness of the comprehensive good, which we either pursue authentically or violate by also taking something else to be the comprehensive telos. This follows because "ought implies can." No human can be morally bound to decide in accord with a principle of which she or he is ignorant, and a religious ethic asserts that all human activities ought to exemplify the comprehensive purpose. Since the decision for an authentic or duplicitous understanding of this purpose is taken in a particular situation, this choice is simultaneously a choice among the specific possible purposes available; that is, the former determines how the specific alternatives are evaluated (see chapter 5). Thus, we can say that activity by way of self-understanding is a decision for some answer to the question of our ultimate worth, and this question is "we ourselves" (Tillich 1951: 62).

I do not mean that all human activity is religious. "Religion" designates the primary form of culture in terms of which we humans *explicitly* ask and answer the question of life's ultimate worth (cf. Ogden 1992: ch. 1), a definition more or less clearly illustrated by the so-called world religions or the principal differentiations within them. In contrast, the decision for a self-understanding is implicit in consciousness, in the background rather than the center of attention, because this decision integrates the activity as a whole, and clear consciousness can focus only on a fragment of what is understood. The function of a religion, then, is to represent explicitly in concepts and symbols, including ritual practices, an answer to the question of ultimate worth and, thereby, to mediate or cultivate implicit decisions for that answer in the lives of those who participate in the given religious community.

This is the point in saying that religion is the *primary* form of culture in terms of which the question of ultimate worth is explicitly asked and answered. We may also speak of a secondary form or forms of culture in terms of which the same question is addressed, namely, concepts and symbols that allow theology and philosophy critically or theoretically to interpret and assess answers to this question (see chapter 14). In distinction from both our implicit decisions and our moral theory, then, a religious ethic is an account of the comprehensive good, and of moral principles and prescriptions grounded by it, in terms of which adherents of the religion in question seek explicitly to lead their lives. So understanding religious ethics is, naturally, controversial, and this underscores that the definition stipulated here is not sensible unless the presupposed understanding of human decision is valid.

The remaining term to be clarified is "norms." It is often used broadly to mean all more-or-less general moral prescriptions, and this meaning accords with our frequent designation of moral systems as normative systems. But our present discussion will be served by using the term in a more narrow sense, namely, to designate rules or principles of human interaction that prescribe constraints on the values of given actors or the ways in which values may be pursued. Norms, in other words, constitute social practices or prescribe reciprocal rights and responsibilities in some pattern of interaction. Although such prescriptions may be legal in character, all institutions or enduring associations are constituted by norms. Still, rules and principles in this sense presuppose that actors have other values they pursue even while they participate in a given social practice, and thus no norm or set of norms defines an all-inclusive good.

Religious ethics have sometimes been criticized as inconsistent with fundamental norms of this kind. Stated in terms of a traditional distinction, the indictment asserts that a comprehensive telos excludes all perfect duties, duties "not to do, or not to omit, an action of a certain [specific] kind," whatever the consequences, because all specific duties can be canceled by the imperfect duty "to promote a certain general end" (Donagan 1997: 154). For this reason, it is said, the affirmation of such a telos implies the absence of any inviolable human rights, including basic rights to life and bodily integrity. Rights are at best provisional because subject to rebuttal by the overriding obligation to create the best consequences.

The objection further concludes that religious ethics finally prevent any social practices at all, because all rules of social interaction can be overridden by the imperfect duty to pursue a comprehensive end. Since no individual can have settled expectations about the circumstances in which others will make their choices, it follows that she or he cannot have settled expectations about what others will do. For instance, one cannot count on another keeping a promise because circumstances when the promise falls due may require or permit some other action in service to the best consequences. Further, this unpredictability is, as it were, cumulative. If the promiser finds, at the time when keeping it arrives, that the future she or he faces is less settled, then it becomes less likely that keeping the promise is required in order to maximize the good. Hence, no one would have reason to participate in social practices or institutions in which reciprocal duties are to be observed whatever the consequences. One can even say that a religious ethic self-destructs. On any plausible account of the comprehensive telos, maximizing the good requires the social coordination and cooperation that an ethic of this kind prevents.

Although the issues raised by this criticism are complex, it cannot succeed against all religious ethics without the following assumption: An ethic based on some comprehensive value or values prescribes "looking at each calculation in isolation, and not taking adequate account of the effects on a society's capacity to function of its being known that all actions are taken on the basis of such calculations" (Barry 1995: 219). But whether a religious ethic so prescribes depends on what comprehensive value or values it affirms. If taking each act separately means that the ethic self-destructs, then the comprehensive telos in question insofar implies that cases should *not* be so taken, precisely for the reasons on which the criticism depends. It is one thing to apply a comprehensive purpose directly to every human activity and something else to apply it indirectly through social practices required to maximize the good. Moreover, such a purpose may prescribe its indirect application through certain inviolable human rights presupposed by all permissible social practices, and whether a religious ethic does so consistently cannot be determined without attention to its understanding of the comprehensive good.

In sum, a religious ethic asserts that a comprehensive value or set of values grounds all valid norms. Recent moral theorists have often distinguished between teleological and deontological ethics. On a typical account, the former grounds morality in some good to be maximized, and the latter asserts moral principles that are independent of any such telos. I believe that religious ethics require a more nuanced set of terms, in which two conceptions of norms are differentiated. Principles said to be independent of any inclusive good to be maximized should be called non-teleological. Accordingly, a non-teleological ethic asserts that the supreme moral principle is a norm or set of norms. In distinction, deontological principles prescribe duties to be honored whatever the consequences. In a given ethic, these norms may or may not be non-teleological, depending on whether they are said to apply indirectly a comprehensive purpose.

Defending Religious Ethics

Contemporary Western moral theory widely denies that any religious ethic, as here conceived, can be valid (see chapter 1). Behind this denial is the recognition that a comprehensive purpose depends or would depend on the fundamental nature of reality. If there is a good by which all human activities ought to be directed, it follows that every possible object of human attention must implicate this good, so that its character cannot be defined independently of the common character of all things. For this reason, religions relate comprehensive value to ultimate reality. In presenting an explicit answer to the question of ultimate worth, a particular religion includes an account of both reality and human purpose as such. Thus, a theoretical explication of any given religious ethic is inseparable from metaphysics, and the similarities and differences among the ethics of differing religions cannot be fully explicated without a metaphysical comparison.

But contemporary Western moral theory widely holds, at least by implication, that no metaphysics can be validated and, therefore, a valid ethic cannot depend on a conception of ultimate reality. In this respect, moral theory since Kant has been convinced by his arguments against the possibility of metaphysical knowledge. He, too, recognized that a comprehensive purpose could only be defined by reality as such and argued that the moral law must, therefore, be radically non-teleological. It cannot be determined by any possible values and thus can be defined only by the formal universality of practical reason. Few contemporary moral theorists endorse non-teleology in this radical sense. Most are convinced that Kant's categorical imperative is empty; that is, no distinction between moral and immoral actions or maxims can be derived from it. Nonetheless, there is a dominant consensus that moral theory is properly independent of metaphysics.

Within this consensus, some who also reject Kant's moral theory conclude that there are no moral values or norms. Only understandings of value-free facts can be valid, and critical reason can only be scientific in the empirical sense. Fundamental values are determined by an individual's subrational decision, and norms are merely prior agreements that themselves depend finally on subrational value affirmations. More persuasive among philosophers earlier in the twentieth century, this theory continues to influence practical thought, notably in the social sciences (especially economics) and in wider political debates. But this view contradicts the conception of self-understanding given above. If the self is a choice with understanding among alternatives for purpose, then the alternatives must be compared evaluatively. A merely descriptive or factual comparison would not understand them *with respect to choosing* or would not understand the self as the decision. It then follows that a human activity necessarily is or involves a claim to validity for its evaluation, because, were the choice subrational, the comparative understanding of possible ends could only be descriptive or factual. In sum, no human could consistently believe that there are no moral values or norms.

If we set that view aside, theories of morality without a comprehensive good are largely framed by two principal projects. Following widespread usage, we may call these neo-Aristotelian and neo-Kantian types of moral theory. If Kant held that an ethic of values implies an understanding of reality as such and concluded that the moral law must be radically non-teleological, these theorists typically seek to escape the apparent dilemma by denying the first or the second of these two assertions. One project has affinities with Aristotelian teleology. Rejecting whatever influence Aristotle's metaphysics may have had on his own moral theory, these neo-Aristotelians conceive of practical reason independently of strictly universal values and define the moral life by some ethos that is in all respects contingent on some specific tradition or culture. Thereby, moral teleology is affirmed without a comprehensive value and thus independently of metaphysics. Some hold that such an ethic is required by Wittgenstein's account of language as presupposing a specific form of life or by Gadamer's analysis of the "pre-understanding" involved in all hermeneutics, and some so-called communitarians and neo-pragmatic theorists illustrate the type.

I am persuaded that a theory of ethics as thoroughly tradition-specific cannot avoid a kind of moral relativism and, against itself, thereby implies that values and norms are determined finally by subrational decision. Every assertion that morality is historically specific in all respects implicitly claims validity for a comparison of moral traditions, namely, that their differences are historically specific in all respects. Since it cannot consistently depend on one of the moral traditions in question, this comparison can only purport to be a value-free fact. But saying that all differences between or among moral traditions are merely factual implies that no given such tradition can be valid. The same conclusion is reached by noting that a person who understands two or more historically or culturally specific moralities is thereby given a decision between differing sets of values or norms with which to evaluate her or his alternatives for purpose. If this decision cannot involve an evaluative comparison and thus a claim to moral validity, it cannot be taken with understanding.

For reasons similar to these, others who share the dominant consensus hold, with Kant, that a teleological ethic requires a telos defined by reality as such. Their project, then, denies the second assertion creating the dilemma Kant's legacy seems to offer, namely, that a non-teleological moral law can only be the formal universality of freedom as he conceived it. These theorists may be called neo-Kantians because, with him, they claim universal validity for some or other non-teleological principle or norm, even while they seek so to revise Kant that this principle or norm does indeed ground distinctions between moral and immoral action. More often than not, perhaps, the result is a theory of human rights, respect for which constrains or overrides any conflicting values that might direct an individual's decision (e.g., Apel 1979; Gewirth 1996; see also chapter 51).

I believe that a non-teleological ethic is also finally indefensible. As prescribing constraint on the pursuit of values, a norm evaluates alternatives for purpose in one respect. If it is independent of a comprehensive purpose, a universal norm or set of norms implies that differences among the alternatives in other respects are morally indifferent or make no difference with respect to choosing. But this implication *is* a moral evaluation of the alternatives in those other respects. The conclusion that something about possible choices is morally indifferent is not itself morally indifferent, since any of those choices is insofar said to be morally permissible. Hence, the norm in question implies, against itself, another moral principle in terms of which possible purposes in all respects are evaluated.

One can also make the point this way: to understand one's alternatives with respect to choosing is not simply to compare them as similar or different in one respect but, rather, to compare them inclusively, because the choice is among them as complete things. Hence, a norm can obligate the choice only by presupposing an inclusive evaluation with which that norm is consistent. Were there no such inclusive principle, there could be no norms at all, and the chooser would be obligated only hypothetically by whatever purpose she or he has chosen. But this, too, asserts the view that values and norms are determined finally by subrational decision, and that assertion contradicts the fact that humans live with self-understanding.

Naturally, these summary comments on the two principal projects in contemporary Western moral theory can do no more than suggest how the dominant consensus might be challenged. But if a more thorough treatment can sustain such criticisms, they provide a negative argument for an ethic based on a comprehensive value. If, against neo-Aristotelians, an ethic requires some or other universally valid principle, and if, against neo-Kantians, this principle cannot be a non-teleological norm, then there can be no morality at all without a comprehensive purpose. Success in this negative argument will insofar vindicate Kant's lucidity in this respect: a valid ethic either depends on a comprehensive good or is independent of all possible values. But the sound option is the one that both he and most Western moral theory since him have rejected.

Religious Ethics and Metaphysics

The above review of contemporary moral theory also includes the elements of a positive, although summary, argument for the validity of some or other possible religious ethic. On this argument, a comprehensive purpose is implied by the distinctive character of human life. Activity with self-understanding is a decision with understanding among alternatives for purpose. It is, therefore, a comparison of the alternatives with respect to choosing, and, since there could be no such understanding except as a claim to moral validity, there must be a valid principle of morality. The supreme principle of morality must be universally valid because it could not be understood as historically specific without thereby becoming one among many alternatives for choice that must themselves be evaluated. Finally, this universally valid principle of morality must be teleological because the alternatives must be inclusively compared.

Assuming that this argument can be upheld in a more extensive examination, we can say that every human in every moment of her or his life is aware of the comprehensive good, at least implicitly, because "ought implies can." Life with self-understanding is constituted by asking and answering the question we ourselves are. Sustaining this conclusion requires a more or less complete moral theory in which the character of our comprehensive telos is formulated and defended. Among other things, that theory must explicate how this purpose consistently requires its indirect application in or through deontological norms or social practices, including a principle of human rights.

These demands cannot be met without the critical pursuit of a more or less complete metaphysics. Still, we can offer here a reason for thinking that a valid metaphysics and, therefore, religious ethic, will be theistic. The specific values that humans in diverse particular situations ought to pursue will be realized, insofar as they are, in diverse actual states of affairs. It makes no sense to speak of maximizing a comprehensive good unless these diverse actualizations, as they occur, constitute a totality of realizations. But this implies an actual totality and, thereby, a universal individual whose activities include completely all realizations of value. Charles Hartshorne (1948) makes the point in saying that human life implies "the divine relativity," an individual whose activities are completely relative to every other reality. Since this divine totality is itself the realization of value that increases everlastingly as value is realized in the world, the moral life is properly defined as the pursuit of values that maximize the divine good.

Saying that a comprehensive purpose and thus a valid religious ethic implies or presupposes a universal individual more or less obviously takes exception to some among the world religions. By this fact alone, some may think, that assertion is discredited. But ultimate reality cannot have more than one character. However impossible it may be in the final analysis fully to formulate and defend a metaphysics, it remains that metaphysical theism and its denial cannot both be true. To be sure, two or more differing religions may all affirm valid moral principles, even while they disagree about reality as such. But if a comprehensive purpose is inseparable from the nature of ultimate reality, then the common ground found in differing religious ethics either does or does not presuppose a divine individual, and the beliefs of a given religion cannot be false in this respect without introducing incoherence into its understanding of ultimate worth. This simply repeats that, however difficult the task and thus however tentatively conclusions should be held, the study of comparative religious ethics is incomplete without a metaphysical comparison. It also underscores that metaphysical comparisons, as those in moral theory, are finally inseparable from pursuit of the truth about reality and human purpose as such.

Bibliography

Apel, K.-O. 1979: "The Common Presuppositions of Hermeneutics and Ethics: Types of Rationality Beyond Science and Technology." *Research in Phenomenology* 9, 35–53.

Aristotle. 1941: *The Basic Works of Aristotle*, ed. R. McKeon. New York: Random House.

Barry, B. 1995: *Justice as Impartiality*. Oxford: Clarendon Press.

Donagan, A. 1997: *The Theory of Morality*. Chicago: University of Chicago Press.

Gewirth, A. 1996: *The Community of Rights*. Chicago: University of Chicago Press.

Hartshorne, C. 1948: *The Divine Relativity: A Social Conception of God*. New Haven, CT: Yale University Press.

Ogden, S. M. 1992: *Is There Only One True Religion or Are There Many?* Dallas, TX: Southern Methodist University Press.

Tillich, P. 1951: *Systematic Theology*, Vol. 1. Chicago: University of Chicago Press.

CHAPTER 13

Cosmology

Frank E. Reynolds and Jonathan W. Schofer

Introduction

Throughout history human beings have developed and deployed cosmologies representing their environment and their own place within it. Cosmologies generally depict temporal and spatial dynamics at the broadest scales: the full expanse of the universe, with a time span from creation to end or radical transformation. With the exception of those developed by modern science, most cosmologies have been explicitly religious. Some have given a prominent position to one or more divinities that transcend cosmic time and space. Some have affirmed the importance of sacred beings, forces, and/or processes that operate within the cosmic milieu itself. Some have done both. All of these distinctively religious cosmologies have focused attention on various connections between the structure and dynamics of cosmic realities on the one hand and the meaning and direction of human life on the other (see chapter 12).

Religious cosmologies exhibit tremendous variations, not only in their contents but also in the modes through which they have been expressed, which may include myth, narratives, poetic expressions, and visual images (both two dimensional and three dimensional). In addition, cosmological insights have been conveyed, developed, and appropriated through ritual performance, divination, philosophical reflection, and other means.

The ways in which specific cosmologies have been correlated with ethical orientations are clearly a matter for empirical study (see chapter 15). In each case there are at least three issues that need to be considered. First, virtually all established cosmologies set out background understandings of the world and human nature that provide contexts for ethical claims concerning social organization, communal activity, and individual character. Second, these cosmologies delineate various levels of reality (divine, natural, social, and individual) that condition norms for action and character, specifying their relative importance and modes of interaction. Third, most cosmologies have also included discussion of ethical attitudes and behavior, identifying unethical attitudes and activities and setting out sanctions that encourage ethical compliance.

This chapter examines three examples of the relations between cosmology and ethics in traditional religious contexts, each highlighting a particular issue: multiple cosmologies within a given tradition, the degree of order in a given cosmology, and practices of divination. In the final section we will consider the split that developed between cosmology and ethics during and after the European Enlightenment, and also the recent surge of interest in new ways of understanding the relationship between them.

Overlapping Cosmologies, Overlapping Ethics

Many religious traditions affirm multiple cosmologies. Among these traditions there are a few in which overlapping cosmo-ethical orientations, taken together, reveal important aspects of religio-ethical structure and dynamics. In Christianity, for example, cosmo-ethical orientations preserved in the Hebrew Bible are maintained in creative relationships with related but quite different cosmo-ethical orientations associated with the life, death, and resurrection of Jesus Christ. A comparable but quite different example of this pattern is found in the Buddhist tradition in which an ethically oriented "samsaric" cosmology coexists with an ethically oriented "Buddhic" cosmos brought into being by the achievements and teachings of the Gautama Buddha. Though these two cosmo-ethical orientations coexist in most Buddhist communities, we will here focus attention on the Theravāda tradition that developed in Sri Lanka and Southeast Asia (see Reynolds 1985).

The samsaric cosmology of Theravāda teaching affirms that all phenomenal realities arise from the co-dependent interaction of a set of twelve different components (ignorance, dispositions, consciousness, name and form, the six gateways, contact, craving, grasping, becoming, birth, old age, and death). In the many individual world systems that come into being within this all-encompassing samsaric universe (particularly our own), human beings occupy a central position. They have the capacity, through meditation and various forms of moral action, to generate a great deal of happiness and pleasure while minimizing the extent of their pain and suffering in their present life and in their future lives as well. This samsaric ethic has several different dimensions. It includes an emphasis on the mitigation of vices and the cultivation of virtues. It includes a notion of karmic retribution for evil deeds and karmic reward for good deeds. It includes a sense of social responsibility that involves generally applicable rules of individual behavior, as well as specific responsibilities associated with particular social functions. It also includes an ethic of care that places great value on care for Buddhist teachings and institutions, as well as care for human persons and other sentient beings (see chapter 49).

However, Theravādins have also affirmed the reality of another, closely correlated cosmology. It includes the samsaric cosmo-ethical order but also recognizes the availability of a higher level of religio-ethical practice. Ignorance is overcome by wisdom, craving is replaced by compassion, and the ongoing experience of impermanence and suffering gives way to liberation. Theravādins often characterize this higher level of ethical practice as the Noble Eightfold Path – a mode of religio-ethical activity that includes right view, right thought, right speech, right conduct, right effort, right mindfulness, and right meditation. Nibbana is the name for the final liberation that is achieved when the practice of the Noble Eightfold Path is perfected.

Within the Buddhic cosmology where its samsaric component and its distinctive soteriological component overlap, the relevant ethical tensions and continuities for individuals and for society are legion. For example, there are actions that are directed toward the proper acquisition of wealth and the proper exercise of political power that are positively valued in the context of samsaric ethics. Yet they are irrelevant, if not antithetical, to the life that is to lead as quickly as possible to the transcendence of samsaric limitations. Conversely, there are other aspects of samsaric ethics, the rooting out of vices and the cultivation of virtues, that are given particular salience because, in addition to their positive contribution to human flourishing within the samsaric process, they also serve as appropriate preparation for future entry into the Noble Path that culminates in liberation.

Some Theravāda practitioners take a more negative ethical approach that focuses on rooting out samsaric vices, the practice of a version of the Noble Path that emphasizes a radical form of ascetic withdrawal, and an interpretation of the goal of nibbana as cessation. A far larger group takes a much more positive approach that involves the cultivation of samsaric virtues, the practice of a version of the Noble Path that features more moderate forms of ascetic practice, and an understanding of nibbana as liberating fulfillment.

Despite (or perhaps because of) the complicated pattern of overlapping cosmologies with different but closely correlated ethical implications, this Theravāda approach has – over the centuries – proved to be remarkably flexible and resilient.

Cosmologies of Ethical Order

One very pervasive cosmological concern is setting out some form of order in the universe. This order can appear in a number of variations. One type, common in Indian and European religions, asserts that there exist homologies between the individual, the society, and the cosmos, and right action consists in maintaining and reinforcing those correspondences. A second type argues that a harmony between individuals, society, and cosmos can be earned, either through individual attunement with the cosmos (as in forms of Daoism) or through communal and ritual alignment (in forms of Confucianism). A third type of order, our focus in this context, concerns not structure but process. The cosmos is presented as being just, such that good actions bring good results and bad actions bring bad results. This kind of account is expressed through the concept of karma in Hinduism and Buddhism, and through images of divine justice in the Hebrew Bible and the religions that have emerged in relation to that corpus, including Judaism, Christianity, and Islam. Within and across these groupings there is of course a wide range of cosmological images and concepts, and a given religion or person may maintain more than one.

Accounts of cosmic justice assert human notions of good and bad, just and unjust, are somehow embedded in the nature of existence. The ethical order may be preserved by one or more deities or by impersonal forces, but a key feature is that human actions or character states generate consequences according to a normative assessment. From this relatively simple starting point, many variations and debates appear: the relative significance of actions and intentions, the possibilities for transfer of merit and culpability, whether or not an individual may receive the reward or punishment of a larger community, whether the consequences of an action appear during life or after death, and others.

We can focus on notions of justice in rabbinic Jewish literature, which classical or late ancient develop various cosmologies from the Hebrew Bible (see Knight 1985). In rabbinic accounts of divine justice or "reward and punishment," cosmology and theology intertwine. In many cases rabbis present God as central to the maintenance of justice, at the center of a perfect heavenly judicial system that includes an honest judge along with witnesses and attorneys. Other passages present consequences as emerging from an action, without any specific mention of direct divine involvement. In such ethically charged cosmological contexts, human action does not consist of singular, discrete events, but rather each action brings results that come at some point in the future. One is placed in a constant state of anticipation, always looking ahead to the possible consequences of one's actions. Such an anticipatory state can be maintained indefinitely, particularly when the ultimate consequences are deferred to an existence after death.

The consequence of a given action may have varying degrees of correspondence to the act itself. In some cases, rabbis assert that there exists an exact correspondence, such that the results match the act "measure for measure." In other cases, God's excess compassion and mercy can mean that punishment is suspended or annulled. A third possibility is when an apparently trivial sin brings great consequences. A rabbi may claim "malicious speech" is a greater transgression than the three paradigmatic sins of rabbinic culture (idolatry, incest, and murder), or that a moment of arrogance can bring death. Such hyperbolic claims exhort the reader or listener not to ignore the seemingly small aspects of religious and communal life. In these cases and others, scholars need to address the pedagogical and homiletic features of claims concerning the workings of the cosmos (Schofer 2005).

Cosmic order is a far from universal feature of religious ethics. Many cosmologies portray flawed or conflicting gods, or impersonal forces, shaping the world and impacting human life. One of the great distinguishing features of modernity, in fact, is the break with ideals of order (Nietzsche 1967; Foucault 1977). From these latter perspectives, notions of cosmic homologies, harmony, or justice may appear naive or problematic. However, with all their difficulties, cosmologies of ethical order represent a creative attempt to highlight human action as immensely significant, and to assert, despite great evidence to the contrary, that the world reinforces and upholds notions of what is right and wrong.

Cosmic Divination

When cosmology is prominent in ethical outlooks and practices, a key question emerges in situations of conflict and ambiguity: how can the cosmos be interpreted in order to find guidance? In many cultures, philosophical and casuistic modes of inquiry have become highly legitimated approaches for resolving such conflicts (see chapter 5). However, in numerous religious frameworks, hermeneutic methods broadly character- ized as "divination" have been (and remain today) crucial for deciding questions of ethical import (see chapter 44).

Scholars have discussed the links between divination and ethics, characterizing divination as an attempt to align human action with divine intent, or a way of thought that interprets a given person's situation and clarifies relationships with other individ- uals, the community, and cosmic powers (Turner 1975; Sullivan 1985; Grillo 1992). One can illustrate links between divination and ethical behavior through the case of the Quiché of Guatemala.

The act of consulting the universe through divination is on occasions modeled as an essential element in cosmogony itself. In the opening chapter of the great Mayan account of cosmogony, the Council Book or Popol Vuh, the gods strive to form human beings as creatures who can walk, work, talk, visit shrines, give offerings, and call upon their creators by name. After their first two attempts fail, they consult a divine elderly couple who are both "daykeepers," versed in the skills of divination. This couple counts out the days according to the Mayan calendar, sets out lots of corn or coral seeds, and asks if the gods' plans for creating humans will succeed. The reading is affirmative, and creation moves forward.

Today, Quiché divination centers on methods associated with the elderly divine couple of the cosmogonic myth. The full process is called "understanding" (ch'obonic) and the subject matter may include any of a wide range of problems concerning right action. Some clearly concern ethical matters, such as whether one owes work or a favor to another person. Others are initially diagnostic (what is the cause of a given illness) or concern decisions that may not be primarily ethical (whether or not to take a trip), though even in these cases, the conclusion of the divination may be ethically significant.

The process of understanding centers upon the diviner's experience of internal "lightning" (coyopa), a sensation that has been described as tingling, jumping, or twitching in the blood or muscles. This lightning is seen as similar to the sheet light- ning that occurs over sacred lakes in the four directions of east, west, north, and south, and these lakes are invoked in given acts of divination. A diviner interprets the light- ning through a complex system based on where it occurs in the body. Internal light- ning at the front of the body indicates a present or future event, while that on the back indicates the past. Movement on the left side of the body concerns a female, while that on the right concerns a male. As a daykeeper, the diviner's expertise stems from knowing the Mayan calendar and the particular meanings and powers associated with each day. In the divining process the daykeeper counts out the days of the calendar, and when lightning occurs in the blood, the day that is counted becomes significant for the daykeeper's counsel. In addition, the daykeeper sorts lots that mirror the authority of the municipal hierarchy.

The cosmological symbolism of this divination is multi-layered. Spatially, the diviner's body is a microcosm of the natural world, drawing upon its powers. Tempo- rally, cycles of time are invoked through the counting of days, and the movement from past to future is examined through the location of the internal lightning. The social world, moreover, is integrated into the process, whether through the lots representing the community, or through the place in the body where lightning appears (Tedlock 1992; Tedlock 1993, 1996).

Cosmic divination is a process in which the diviner works at the intersection of her or his body and intuition, knowledge of the client and the case at hand, and rituals such as counting the days and the sorting of lots. Divination is an interpretive, homiletic practice of making cosmo-ethical orientations and particular objects or texts "speak" to a given situation in order to generate knowledge and guidance for action in practical real life situations (Smith 1982).

Developments in the Modern Context

For many contemporary thinkers this discussion of ethics as intertwined with cosmology may seem odd. Or, if not odd, at least seemingly unconnected to normative ethical reflection viable in an intellectual community influenced by the European Enlightenment. This section discusses the turn away from religiously oriented cosmologies that has characterized influential ethical approaches that have emerged in the Enlightenment and post-Enlightenment context. We will then go on to consider the work of one outstanding contemporary philosophical ethicist who has been a leading figure in *The Return to Cosmology* (Toulmin 1982).

The rejection of cosmology

There are at least two very powerful factors in Western European history that have contributed to the severing of the traditional bonds between cosmological understandings and ethical orientations. One factor has been the decline in the ethical legitimacy that the various European religions (and their teachings) have suffered, beginning with their involvement in the wars that tore the continent apart during the fifteenth and sixteenth centuries. A second factor has been the somewhat later emergence and rise to prominence of a powerful and convincing scientific cosmology that is devoid of any intrinsic ethical significance.

In the face of these developments a number of Western thinkers in the seventeenth century began a search to find a new basis for philosophical reasoning that would not depend on accounts of the cosmos (Toulmin 1990). During the last four centuries the many influential ethicists who have participated in this Enlightenment project have focused their attention almost exclusively on interactions among human beings and have grounded their characterizations of ethical action in various forms of rational formalism and/or the exercise of practical reason (see chapter 2). Though it is true that the presence of positively oriented cosmological thought and imagery has never been completely eclipsed, it has definitely been relegated to the periphery.

A more recent departure from traditional religious cosmologies and the ethical orientations associated with them came to the fore in the existentialist movement that flourished, particularly in France, during the middle decades of the twentieth century.

Most existentialist thinkers did not reject the connection between cosmology and ethics. Quite to the contrary, they had a cosmological orientation of their own and affirmed an ethical orientation that was directly correlated with it. From the existentialist perspective the cosmological environment in which human beings are inextricably trapped, including both its natural dimensions and its social dimensions, was characterized by nastiness, meaninglessness, and absurdity. The ethical response that they called for, the only one that seems at all viable in the kind of cosmos that they experienced and portrayed, was an individual assertion of human freedom and defiance made with the full knowledge of its ultimate futility.

Within the past several decades there has been a remarkable resurgence of interest in cosmological orientations associated with very different kinds of ethical imperatives. These more recent cosmological orientations are distinguished by ways in which they set the stage for mutually beneficial interactions between human beings and the natural world in which they are situated (see chapter 47). In some instances this interest is focused on the way in which human interactions with the natural world can provide an antidote to the spiritual and ethical malaise that characterizes so much of modern life. In other instances this interest is focused on the formulation of a new kind of environmental ethic designed to assist in the effort to stem the ever-rising tide of non-sustainable "development" that is wrecking havoc in the natural world on which human life depends. In many cases these two closely related foci of interest are addressed jointly by a single author.

A return to ethical cosmology

The writings of the Czech philosopher Erazim Kohák provide a powerful example of a bifocal approach. In *The Embers and the Stars* (1984) Kohák sets forth a two-staged interpretation of the development of the spiritual and ethical malaise that pervades late modern experience. The first stage involves the formulation of what he calls "theoretical nature-constructs," a process that he associates with the rise of the natural sciences. The second stage is characterized by the development of a world of technologically developed artifacts that embodies these theoretical constructs (the world of denatured, dehumanized, depersonalized experience that is so vividly depicted by existentialist authors) (see chapter 46).

In response to this situation Kohák evokes for his readers a cosmologically oriented philosophy of personalism that has, as its central component, the recovery of a moral sense of nature. The approach involves a phenomenological "bracketing" that suspends the impersonal world of theoretical constructs and technologically generated artifacts. This process of bracketing opens the way for the recovery of a direct experience of the natural environment within which we live. The natural world that he claims to uncover through this strategy is a cosmos of personalized interactions within and between various levels of being that are ordered in ways that are rich with moral significance.

Kohák is not proposing to replace the modern scientific cosmology with the cosmo-ethical orientation. Rather, he advocates a dually structured cosmological understanding that has certain affinities with the paired cosmologies in the Theravāda Buddhist context (see above). In Kohák's case, the dual understanding encompasses a primary religio-ethical cosmology that can be discerned through a direct experiential interaction with the natural world. It also encompasses a secondary cosmology that is associated with the abstract constructs of the natural sciences and the world of technological artifacts that they have generated. Certain areas of overlap are envisioned between the two cosmologies as well as tensions between them. In the areas where there is overlap he affirms that the personalistic and moral orientation of the primary cosmology must take precedence over the highly useful but essentially amoral and impersonal orientation of the secondary cosmology.

In a postscript in which he identifies his own approach to ecological ethics, Kohák affirms the fundamental need "to think through and live through the whole philosophical question about the place of humans in the cosmos and in nature" (Kohák 2000: 161). This is required in order to evoke the sense of cosmic belonging that provides the experiential basis for an ethic of human frugality and environmental sensitivity. Though rejecting the notion that technologies can solve the ecological problems that we presently face, he does recognize that they have an important secondary contribution to make.

In addition to Erazim Kohák, there are many other ethicists, including many who work in the context of major religious traditions, who are now creatively involved in the effort to relate viable cosmological understandings with urgent ethical concerns. There is every reason to believe that this is a trend that will continue far into the future.

Bibliography

Foucault, M. 1977: *Discipline and Punish: The Birth of the Prison*. New York: Vintage Books.

Grillo, L. 1992: "Dogon Divination as an Ethic of Nature." *Journal of Religious Ethics* 20 (2): 309–20.

Knight, D. 1985: "Cosmogony and Order in the Hebrew Tradition" in *Cosmogony and Ethical Order: Studies in Comparative Ethics*, ed. R. W. Lovin and F. Reynolds. Chicago: University of Chicago Press.

Kohák, E. V. 1984: *The Embers and the Stars: A Philosophical Inquiry into the Moral Sense of Nature*. Chicago: University of Chicago Press.

——2000: *The Green Halo: A Bird's-Eye View of Ecological Ethics*. Chicago: Open Court.

Nietzsche, F. W. 1967: *On the Genealogy of Morals*, trans. W. Kaufman. New York: Vintage Books.

Reynolds, F. 1985: "Multiple Cosmogonies and Ethics: The Case of Theravāda Buddhism" in *Cosmogony and Ethical Order: Studies in Comparative Ethics*, ed. R. W. Lovin and F. Reynolds. Chicago: University of Chicago Press.

Schofer, J. 2005. *The Making of a Sage: A study in Rabbinic Ethics*. Madison: University of Wisconsin Press.

Smith, J. Z. 1982: *Imagining Religion: From Babylon to Jonestown*. Chicago: University of Chicago Press.

Sullivan, L. 1985: "Above, Below, or Far Away: Andean Cosmogony and Ethical Order" in *Cosmogony and Ethical Order: Studies in Comparative Ethics*, ed. R. W. Lovin and F. Reynolds. Chicago: University of Chicago Press.

Tedlock, B. 1992: *Time and the Highland Maya*, revd. edn. Albuquerque: University of New Mexico Press.

Tedlock, D. 1993: *Breath on the Mirror: Mythic Voices and Visions of the Living Maya*, 1st edn. San Francisco: Harper San Francisco.

——1996: *Popol Vuh: The Mayan Book of the Dawn of Life*, revd. edn. New York: Simon & Schuster.

Toulmin, S. E. 1982: *The Return to Cosmology: Postmodern Science and the Theology of Nature*. Berkeley: University of California Press.

——1990: *Cosmopolis: The Hidden Agenda of Modernity*. New York: Free Press.

Turner, V. W. 1975: *Revelation and Divination in Ndembu Ritual*. Ithaca, NY: Cornell University Press.

CHAPTER 14

Culture and Moral Pluralism

Bruce Grelle

Many pressing issues upon which religious ethicists reflect involve disagreements or conflicts among competing social groups that hold and act upon disparate worldviews and values (see chapter 49). Such conflicts occur not only *between* groups that hold opposing worldviews and values, but also *within* groups where there may be disagreement about the meaning of shared beliefs and values or about priorities among them. The concept of culture is an inevitable part of efforts to understand such conflicts, just as it must be an inevitable part of efforts to find possible resolutions to them. Likewise, the social-historical reality of "cultural pluralism" is the inevitable context for religious and moral reflection in this era of globalization, with its unprecedented degree of inter-action between the diverse peoples and cultures of the world. In this chapter I will briefly discuss the concept of culture and its significance for religious ethics.

The Concept of Culture

There are many excellent accounts of the origins and development of the concept of culture (see Eagleton 2000; Lincoln 2000; Masuzawa 1998; Tanner 1997; Williams 1981). Scholars typically remind us that "culture" was initially a noun of process, having to do with the cultivation and tending of crops, the rearing and breeding of animals, and the active culture or cultivation of the human mind. In the eighteenth century, "culture" became a more general designation for the "spirit" (whether ideal, religious, or national) that informed the "whole way of life" of a distinct people. This "spirit" was believed to be manifest in all human activities, but was most evident in specifically "cultural" activities such as language, morals, and styles of art. It was in this connection that Herder first used the plural "cultures" in deliberate distinction from a singular sense of "civilization." This broad pluralistic usage of "culture" became central in the development of comparative anthropology, where it continued to desig-nate a whole and distinctive way of life (Williams 1981: 10–11).

Understood as ways of life, cultures include language and modes of verbal and non-verbal communication, technologies and material artifacts, learned and customary patterns of behavior and social organization, and so on. Cultures also consist of socially inherited and community-specific "ideas about what is true, good, beautiful, and efficient" (Shweder 2000: 163). The terms "worldview" and "ethos" best describe the aspects of culture that religious ethicists are typically most interested in. As Geertz has explained these concepts,

> A people's *ethos* is the tone, character, and quality of their life, its *moral and aesthetic style and mood*; it is the underlying attitude toward themselves and their world that life reflects. Their *worldview* is their *picture of the way things in sheer actuality are*, their *concept of nature, of self, of society*. It contains their most comprehensive ideas of order. (Geertz 1973: 127; emphasis added)

The idea that cultures are whole ways of life constituted by a unity of worldview and ethos is important because it helps us to see that moralities themselves must be understood as cultural systems (see Bird 1981). Recognition that "moral concepts are embodied in and are partially constitutive of forms of social life" (MacIntyre 1973: 1) underscores the historicity and cultural specificity of moralities and acknowledges the importance of contextual understanding. It is not only a mistake to isolate the analysis of moral reasoning from the analysis of moralities as a whole, it is also a mistake to isolate ethics from the study of history, society, and culture (Gustafson 1972: 52) (see chapters 15 and 16). On this view, the study of religious ethics should focus not only on forms of moral reasoning but also on forms of life, not only on moral argument and justification but also on the full range of "normative activity that creates and sustains an ethos" (Reynolds 1979: 23) (see chapter "On Religious Ethics").

Culture, Ideology, and Hegemony

Thus far we have focused on cultures as whole ways of life characterized by distinctive blends of intellectual, moral, and aesthetic sensibilities, values, and behaviors that are shared in common by particular groups of people in specific times and places. Yet a problem with this way of thinking about cultures is that it tends to obscure the political uses and ideological functions of religions, cultures, and moralities. We can begin to move beyond an overly romantic conception of culture as a seamless whole way of life by viewing cultures in the context of struggles between competing groups over who is going to exercise intellectual and moral leadership (or hegemony) in society. According to Gramsci (1971), the supremacy of a social group is exercised and maintained not only through the exercise of coercion and force, but also and more commonly through the exercise of intellectual and moral persuasion. Through its occupation of positions of leadership in the religious, educational, and other "cultural" institutions of society, the dominant group's "view of reality" informs all tastes, morality, customs, religious, political and legal principles, and all social relations, particularly in their intellectual and moral connotations (Femia 1975: 30–1). It comes to constitute the "common sense" of the majority of the population – "the conception of the world absorbed uncritically from the various social and cultural environments in which the moral individuality of the average man develops" (Gramsci, cited in Counihan 1986: 5).

Many traditional "anthropological" approaches to culture tend to emphasize the role played by religious and moral ideas in the collective self-expression of human communities and in the intellectual and moral integration of social systems. Recall here Durkheim's famous definition of religion as a "unified system of beliefs and practices . . . which unite into one single moral community . . . all those who adhere to them" (1965: 62). By contrast, the concept of hegemony shifts our attention to a consideration of the extent to which cultural formations are characterized by conflicting interests and by lived patterns of domination. It focuses our attention on the heterogeneity that typically exists within a society (subcultures, counter-cultures, etc.) and upon the political interplay between dominant and oppositional cultural expressions (Williams 1978: 110).

Whether or not this recognition of an inevitable connection between moralities and cultures on the one hand, and the interests of social groups and the exercise of domination on the other hand, commits us to viewing moralities as nothing more than rationalizations or reflections of group self-interest is a question to which we will return below (see chapter 2).

Cultural Pluralism

At this point I want to shift from the concept of culture to a discussion of *cultural pluralism* as a chief context for, and approach to, the study of religious ethics. More specifically, we return to the comments made at the outset of this chapter regarding conflicts of worldviews and values between and within cultures. Whether described as "culture wars," "clashes of civilizations," or "struggles for hegemony," such conflicts are a fact of religious and moral life.

Though "pluralism" and "diversity" are often used interchangeably, "pluralism" understood as a philosophical and ethical–political stance toward diversity must be distinguished from "pluralism" understood as the sheer fact of diversity. *As an approach to cultural and moral diversity,* "pluralism" is conscious that "many legitimate goods exist and that whatever goods you pursue, they are but one among many possible sets of goods" (Yearley 1994: 9). This approach contends that while it is possible and useful to compare alternative cultures and ideals of human flourishing, it is not possible to rank them according to a single universal standard or make them fit into a single comprehensive conception of the good and virtuous life (Yearley 1994; Fiorenza 2001). "The Greek hero, the Christian ascetic, [the] Nietzschean critic, the twentieth-century analytical philosopher, the Buddhist monk, the capitalist entrepreneur, and the Confucian scholar . . . stand alongside one another as alternative visions of the virtuous life" (Fiorenza 2001: 81).

Anthropologist R. A. Shweder (2000) has articulated a persuasive yet problematic example of a pluralistic approach to cultural and moral diversity by contrasting pluralism with "cultural developmentalism." Shweder contends cultural develop-mentalism is favored by many first world economists and policy makers; by various agencies promoting Western-style globalization and by the international human rights movement; by "monocultural feminists" for whom traditional and non-Western forms of family life, gender relations, and reproductive practices should not be tolerated; and by a growing number of anthropologists who take an interest in other cultures "mainly as objects of scorn" rather than as sources of illumination (Shweder 2000: 159, 161–2). Cultural developmentalism believes there is only one way (the West's) to lead a morally decent and rational life. The goal of the cultural developmentalists is to lift cultures, civilizations, and religions "up from error, igno-rance, bad habits, immorality, and squalor, and refashion them to be more progres-sive, more democratic, more scientific, more civic-minded, more industrious, more entrepreneurial, more reliable, more rational, and more like (the ideal) us" (Shweder 2000: 160–2; see Harrison and Huntington, 2000, for examples of "cultural developmentalism").

By contrast, Shweder's own ethical–political project as a cultural pluralist seeks (1) to defend the idea that there are a variety of ways of living as rational and morally decent human beings; (2) to defend diverse cultures against ethnocentrism and chau-vinism; and (3) to maintain that other cultures should be viewed, at least initially and potentially, as sources of illumination rather than as obstacles to the spread of Western beliefs, values, and styles of life. He wants to resist the idea that either "we" or "they" have implemented the only credible and morally legitimate manifestation of a good human life. According to this position, it is simply not possible simultaneously to max-imize all the good things in life, "which is why there are different traditions of values (i.e., cultures) and why no one cultural tradition has ever been able to honor everything that is good." This is why we frequently find ourselves in situations where "it is possible for morally decent and fully rational people to look at each other and at each other's practices and say, 'Yuck!'" (Shweder 2000: 61, 164, 315).

Even so, it remains possible to make evaluative judgments regarding the moral progress or decline of various cultures. "Progress means having more and more of something that is 'desirable' (i.e., something that should be desired because it is 'good'). Decline means having less and less of it" (Shweder 2000: 165). The problem is that before we can make evaluative judgments we must first select some specific good to measure, and which good to select is not always self-evident. For example, if we choose maximization of child survival during the first nine months after birth as the good by which to measure a culture's success, then the United States is objectively more advanced than Africa or India. But if "maximizing the likelihood of child survival during the first nine months after conception (in the womb) is the measure of success, then Africa and India (where abortion rates are relatively low) are objectively more advanced than the United States (where abortion rates are relatively high)." There is "much that is discretionary (i.e., not dictated by either logic or evidence) in any deci-sion about how to name and identify specific 'goods' and thus morally map the world . . . And when it comes to constructing narratives about progress . . . there is lots of room for discretion (and ideology) in how one tells the story of who is better and who is worse" (Shweder 2000: 165–6).

Cultural Pluralism, Ideology, and the Common Good

Along with many scholars in religious studies, I continue to believe, like Shweder, that it is important to resist ethnocentrism as far as possible. The cultivation of a "dispassionate capacity to comprehend and explain other people's experience of their worlds without interjecting one's own preferences" (Paden 1992: 73–4) remains basic to the practice of comparative scholarship. Likewise, I accept pluralism's claims that human goods are multiple and irreducible to one another, that there are a variety of ways of being rational and morally decent human beings, and that these multiple ways are nurtured in and embodied by different cultures in different times and places. Moreover, I concur with the idea that it is best to view other cultures as potential sources of illumination rather than primarily as obstacles to one's own values or ideology. There are both existential and practical benefits to be gained through sympathetic engagement with diverse cultures and ideals of human flourishing (see Schilbrack 2002; Twiss and Grelle 1998; Yearley 1994).

But Shweder seems to believe that a genuinely pluralistic stance toward cultural and moral diversity necessitates the abandonment of efforts to articulate a common or "universal" moral language that is applicable within and across multiple cultures. For example, he implies that efforts to promulgate a moral language of universal human rights inevitably involve the imposition of a uniform and imperialistic approach to moral values that is inconsistent with genuine respect for cultural diversity. Thus, he applauds the decision of the executive board of the American Anthropological Association (1947) not to endorse the United Nations "Declaration on the Rights of Man" on the grounds that it was an ethnocentric document, adding: "in 1947, anthropologists were still proud of their anti-colonialist defense of alternative ways of life" (Shweder 2000: 164). Shweder is not alone in this view. One can find human rights skeptics among representatives of particular cultural traditions and among some scholars of those traditions who believe that the language of human rights represents a Western moral ideology intended to supplant the moral perspectives of diverse cultural traditions (Twiss and Grelle 1995: 30).

But this is an incomplete and misleading picture of the nature, source, and function of contemporary human rights discourse and of the relationship between human rights norms and particular cultural moral traditions (see chapter 51). It is a mistake to conclude from this that a pluralistic approach necessitates the abandonment of efforts to develop moral languages that both recognize the irreducibility of cultural and moral diversity while also seeking to identify values that can be shared in common across cultures.

Through cross-cultural dialogue and negotiation about problems that they face in common – tyranny, torture, starvation, lack of access to education and healthcare, discrimination and violence along religious, racial, and ethnic lines – increasing numbers of people around the world have begun to employ the language of human rights as one way of speaking about certain core moral values that appear to be shared by a number of different cultural traditions (see Kelsay and Twiss 1994; Evans 1998). Indeed, the language of human rights has increasingly become a kind of "moral creole" that people from a variety of cultural backgrounds have found to be very useful for communicating with one another in an effort to stake out a practical moral consensus among diverse traditions regarding basic conditions necessary for the respect of human dignity (Stout 1988: 243, 294).

The language of human rights has gradually developed alongside and sometimes been combined with the variety of more particular moral languages traditionally spoken by people from different cultures around the world. This does not mean that human rights can substitute for or replace these richer, more specific and complex moral languages. The discourse of rights is too minimal, too thin, to provide the motivation and sense of direction necessary for the pursuit of human fulfillment. While the human rights movement has sought to establish principles by which all people – regardless of their identity as members of particular communities and traditions – ought to live in order to render social life as peaceful and beneficial as possible, it has necessarily been associated with a relatively narrow conception of morality-as-constraint – a morality of rights, duties, and obligations.

By contrast, the world's cultural and religious traditions offer broader conceptions of morality that set forth concrete visions of human fulfillment and that focus on the cultivation of virtue and the formation of character (see chapters 4 and 10). Far from being autonomous from the particularities of traditions and cultures, such visions and virtues are intimately linked to one's identity as a member of a specific community. Among themselves, members of particular cultures will continue to speak their native moral languages, translating the subject matter of "human rights" into the richer more variegated and nuanced moral idioms that are rooted in their own specific cultural conceptions of human nature, community, and moral rationality. Likewise, they will translate elements of these moral idioms into the more generic language of "rights" when they seek to communicate with "others" who do not share the same cultural conceptions (Twiss and Grelle 1995: 33–5). What one describes and justifies as "human rights" in international and cross-cultural settings when speaking moral creole will likely be described and justified differently when speaking a moral language indigenous to one's own local culture or religion.

This is not to suggest that the consensus regarding basic human rights (in the form of international treaties and covenants) that has emerged over the past fifty years is complete. There remain tensions and disagreements between the particular moralities of cultures and the "universal" morality of human rights – especially with regard to the rights of women, children, and homosexuals – just as there remain tensions within human rights discourse itself between civil-political rights, social-economic rights, and cultural-developmental rights (see Okin 1999; Kelsay and Twiss 1994: 31–59).

This ongoing contestation regarding human rights suggests several things about the relationship between morality, ideology, and culture. It reminds us that all moral ideas and discourses are employed by particular people in specific times and places and are inevitably linked to the interests of those who employ them (see chapter 15). But this does not mean that religious ethics should abandon efforts to identify a common good shared by multiple social groups and by diverse traditions within and across cultures. Some moral discourses are more "universal" than others, in the sense that they do not simply reflect or rationalize the narrow self-interest of the groups that employ them but actually do succeed, at least *to some degree*, in encompassing and representing broader human interests. In other words, the mere existence of an ideological connection between moral discourses and sectional interests does not necessarily mean that all claims to moral universality are a mere pretense or form of deception (Grelle 1995). Likewise, while there are undeniable tensions and conflicts between the ideal of universality and the reality of cultural diversity, this does not mean that it is impossible to find common ground between traditions and cultures (An-Na'im 1992). The international human rights movement illustrates that it is sometimes possible, through dialogue and negotiation (rather than through some form of *a priori* philosophical analysis), to identify common interests shared by disparate groups with alternative cultural and moral orientations.

In this world of competing and conflicting worldviews and values, one of the main tasks of religious ethics must be to assess and compare the *degrees of universality* that are embodied in the moral discourses of diverse cultures and traditions. To what extent do they reflect or rationalize the narrow sectional interests of particular social groups? To what extent do they succeed in identifying or creating and expressing what might be regarded as "universal human interests" that are shared by disparate groups in a given society or historical epoch? Which discussions are more and which are less inclusive of the interests of the widest number of human beings – whatever their religion, race, class, gender, ethnicity, sexual orientation, and so on?

Rather than oppose efforts to develop common, "universal," cross-cultural moral languages in general – whether human rights or similar efforts, such as the interfaith movement's attempts to articulate a "global ethic" (Küng and Kuschel 1995) – cultural pluralists should look at how these languages are being used in specific times and places, by whom, and for what purposes. When such avowedly "universal" moral languages are employed in self-serving, ethnocentric, imperialistic fashions, they should be opposed. But when they are employed to help find common moral ground in the midst of conflict and competition between social groups and amid cultural and religious diversity, they should be promoted as a basis for uniting people in the task of building a world where the human dignity of both individuals and cultures is more fully respected.

An approach to religious ethics that takes culture seriously must seek to analyze moral discourses in the context of cultures as a whole, in the context of struggles for hegemony among competing social groups within and between cultures, and in the context of a recognition of the practical need to develop ways of speaking about a common good even while recognizing the irreducible cultural and moral diversity of the world in which we live.

Bibliography

American Anthropological Association 1947: "Statement on Human Rights." *American Anthropologist* 49 (4), 539–43.

An-Na'im, A. A. 1992: "Introduction" in *Human Rights in Cross-Cultural Perspectives: A Quest for Consensus*, ed. A. A. An-Na'im. Philadelphia: University of Pennsylvania Press.

Bird, F. 1981: "Paradigms and Parameters for the Comparative Study of Religious Ethics." *Journal of Religious Ethics* 9 (2), 157–85.

Counihan, C. 1986: "Antonio Gramsci and Social Science." *Dialectical Anthropology* 11 (1), 3–10.

Durkheim, E. 1965: *The Elementary Forms of the Religious Life*. New York: Free Press.

Eagleton, T. 2000: *The Idea of Culture*. Oxford: Blackwell.

Evans, T. 1998: "Introduction: Power, Hegemony, and the Universalization of Human Rights" in *Human Rights Fifty Years On: A Reappraisal*, ed. T. Evans. Manchester: Manchester University Press.

Femia, J. 1975: "Hegemony and Consciousness in the Thought of Antonio Gramsci." *Political Studies* 23 (March), 29–48.

Fiorenza, F. S. 2001: "The Challenge of Pluralism and Globalization to Ethical Reflection" in *In Search of Universal Values*, ed. K.-J. Kuschel and D. Mieth. London: SCM Press.

Geertz, C. 1973: *The Interpretation of Cultures*. New York: Basic Books.

Gramsci, A. 1971: *Selections from Prison Notebooks*, ed. Q. Hoare and G. Nowell-Smith. New York: International Publishers.

Grelle, B. 1995: "Hegemony and the 'Universalization' of Moral Ideas: Gramsci's Importance for Comparative Religious Ethics." *Soundings: An Interdisciplinary Journal* 78 (3–4), 519–40.

Gustafson, J. M. 1972: "The Relevance of Historical Understanding" in *Toward a Discipline of Social Ethics*, ed. P. Deats. Boston, MA: Boston University Press.

Harrison, L. E. and Huntington, S. P. (eds.) 2000: *Culture Matters: How Values Shape Human Progress*. New York: Basic Books.

Kelsay, J. and Twiss, S. B. (eds.) 1994: *Religion and Human Rights*. New York: Project on Religion and Human Rights.

Küng, H. and Kuschel, K.-J. 1995: *A Global Ethic: The Declaration of the Parliament of the World's Religions*. New York: Continuum.

Lincoln, B. 2000: "Culture" in *Guide to the Study of Religion*, ed. W. Braun and R. T. McCutcheon, 409–22. London: Cassell.

MacIntyre, A. 1973: *A Short History of Ethics*. New York: Macmillan.

Masuzawa, T. 1998: "Culture" in *Critical Terms for Religious Studies*, ed. M. C. Taylor, 70–93. Chicago: University of Chicago Press.

Okin, S. M. with respondents. 1999: *Is Multiculturalism Bad for Women?* Princeton, NJ: Princeton University Press.

Paden, W. 1992: *Interpreting the Sacred: Ways of Viewing Religion*. Boston, MA: Beacon Press.

Reynolds, F. E. 1979: "Four Modes of Theravāda Action." *Journal of Religious Ethics* 7 (1), 12–26.

Schilbrack, K. 2002: "Teaching Comparative Religious Ethics." *Journal of Religious Ethics* 30 (2), 297–312.

Shweder, R. A. 2000: "Moral Maps, 'First World' Conceits, and the New Evangelists" in *Culture Matters: How Values Shape Human Progress*, ed. L. E. Harrison and S. P. Huntington, 158–76. New York: Basic Books.

Stout, J. 1988: *Ethics After Babel: The Languages of Morals and Their Discontents*. Boston, MA: Beacon Press.

Tanner, K. 1997: *Theories of Culture: A New Agenda for Theology*. Minneapolis, MN: Fortress Press.

Twiss, S. B. and Grelle, B. 1995: "Human Rights and Comparative Religious Ethics: A New Venue." *Annual of the Society of Christian Ethics*, 21–48.

Twiss, S. B and Grelle, B. (eds.) 1998: *Explorations in Global Ethics: Comparative Religious Ethics and Interreligious Dialogue*. Boulder, CO: Westview Press.

Williams, R. 1978: *Marxism and Literature*. Oxford: Oxford University Press.

—— 1981: *Culture*. Glasgow: Fontana.

Yearley, L. H. 1994: "New Religious Virtues and the Study of Religion." University Lecture in Religion, February 10, Arizona State University.

CHAPTER 15

History of Religions

Donald K. Swearer

Exploring Religious Ethics

Previous chapters of this Companion have explored topics in religious traditions, ranging from the metaphysical backing of moral beliefs to the dynamics of text and canon. This chapter examines the place of the history of religions with respect to the work of comparative religious ethics. It is hardly surprising that the development of the study of the history of religions has also attended to matters in ethics. And it is thereby also not surprising that many of the themes that occupy scholarly attention in exploring religious ethics come to light from the perspective of the history of religions.

Among the several contributions that the history of religions makes to the study of comparative religious ethics, two, in particular, stand out. First, as part of a religious system, ethics is informed by the several components that constitute the polychromatic network of a religion; for example, cosmology, soteriology, and ritual (see chapters 13 and 9). Second, the history of religions brings to the work of religious ethics an emphasis on the descriptive historical and contextual, but not at the expense of inductively derived general truths or general ethical patterns (see chapter 12). My examination of these and other contributions of the history of religions to reflection about the nature of religious ethics follows the recent history of the development of the interaction between historians of religions and ethicists. I configure the ongoing process and results of this interaction around the following themes important for comparative reflection: particularism and holism; cosmology and ethical naturalism; narrative ethics and soteriology; history of religions and a global ethic.

The history of religions was one of the midwives assisting at the birth of comparative religious ethics in the 1970s. These beginnings were characterized by a debate between ethicists trained in the methodologies of Western philosophy and social sciences, and historians of religions schooled in the historical traditions (texts, languages, social and institutional histories) of the world's religions. Although neither side was monolithic and the dividing line between the two was fluid and overlapping, the historians of religions challenged the ethicists on the grounds of methodological reductionism and theoretical over-kill, and for imposing Western analytical models and formal structures of moral reasoning onto richly diverse, historically and culturally embedded indigenous religio-ethical systems. The ethicists, in turn, saw the agenda of the historians of religions as promoting a religio-cultural particularism lacking analytical rigor, unable to provide a coherent framework or general structure essential for meaningful normative and comparative work. Analogues to this debate can be found elsewhere in disputes between a communitarian, virtue approach to ethics versus a formal, universalizable structure of moral reasoning, and postcolonial critiques of the imposition of essentializing categories forged in the academic and political cultures of the West on quite disparate cultures.

Historians of religions challenge interpretations of religious ethics that require precise analytical concepts and a primary focus on moral reasoning. We argue for a more holistic approach that includes not only doctrinal texts and seminal philosophical concepts, but also the lived tradition in its greater complexity – its rituals and practices, its popular stories as well as grand narratives, and the cultural ethos in which religious traditions are embedded. Historians are not opposed to conceptual frameworks per se, but question "their degree of precision and specification, their source, and their illuminative powers. Hardened conceptual tools may break as much as they dig out, and inappropriate tools may damage the terrain" (Childress 1979: 4).

Historians of religions consider that their discipline avoids reductive, univocal conceptions of religion/religious ethics or preconceived frames of reference imposed on historically distinctive and dynamic living traditions. Instead, they bring a holistic, comparative-inductive approach to the study of religion that investigates a wide variety of continuities among different systems of belief and practice without reducing them to a single referent (Bianchi 1995: 400). This contextual, historical approach does not depend on or lead to a universal theory. Its interdisciplinary approach results in the construction of a historical, typological, multi-dimensional map of the actual religious terrain. In brief, the history of religions proposes that religious ethics should be mapped within the contextual frameworks of the worldview and ethos of a particular religious tradition. But what does this claim mean in practical terms? The remainder of this chapter proposes to forge a response to this question using recent history of religions' contributions to the field of religious ethics.

Particularism and Holism: The Example of Buddhism

In the 1980s and 1990s Buddhist ethics emerged as a major field of study, not only as part of Buddhist studies but also within the context of the history of religions/religious ethics discussions. Several factors contributed to this development: the provocative interpretation of Theravāda ethics in *Comparative Religious Ethics: A New Method* (Little and Twiss 1978) and the resultant debate between David Little and several historians of religions, in particular, Frank E. Reynolds; the appearance of the digital *Journal of Buddhist Ethics* (JBE) in 1994 and its online conferences; a dramatic increase in published monographs in the area of Buddhist ethics, most notably the work of Damien

Keown, who co-founded JBE with Charles Prebish; and the impact of socially engaged Buddhism on both the development of American Buddhism and Buddhist social ethics.

Until quite recently, the study of Buddhism in the West tended to romanticize the tradition as an esoteric "other," defined it in terms of an other-worldly soteriology, or approached it as a philosophical system constructed on the seminal teachings of suffering (*dukkha*), not-self, emptiness, and nirvāna (see chapter 29). Much that went on in Buddhist societies and cultures was ignored, or perceived as epiphenomenal, or critiqued as an accommodation to uneducated lay folk who lacked the intellect and spiritual dedication of monks. Buddhism, then, was constructed as a two-storey affair: "real" Buddhism was a monastic, soteriological religion; Buddhist ethics was either provisional or essentially assimilated into Buddhist soteriology. Scholars who contributed to this dualistic construction included Max Weber, who represented Buddhism as an other-worldly mysticism type of religion, a shadow that fell on *Comparative Religious Ethics*, characterized by one reviewer as "Weber's progeny, once removed" (Stout 1980).

Metaethically, Little and Twiss (1978) propose that a religious ethic integrates a *religious action guide* and a *moral action guide*. The first is based on the supreme authority ascribed to a religion's cosmology or object of ultimate concern, such as *nirvāna* or God, an authority that resolves life's deepest enigmas (e.g., suffering) (see chapter 1). A moral action guide addresses problems of other-regard, cooperation, and caring for the material welfare of others. In the case of Buddhism, Little and Twiss argue that the ultimate vindicating authority of *nirvāna* as the supreme *dharma*, predicated on the deconstruction of the self (*anātman*), so dominates Theravādin practical reasoning that an ethic of regard for the material welfare of others is problematized and undermined. Consequently, moral action guiding texts that stipulate norms of mutual responsibility, cooperation, and other-regard are judged to be provisional because of Buddhism's "fundamental belief in the ultimate unreality of human persons" (Little and Twiss 1978: 241).

In contrast to models for the study of comparative religious ethics built on the structure of moral reasoning *à la* Little and Twiss or neo-Kantian rationalism (Green 1978), Frank E. Reynolds proposes that the historian of religions' approach to comparative religious ethics should begin with a broad, general understanding of the religions under investigation; then focus specifically on their ethical dimension; identify the central religio-ethical pattern that plays a predominant role in the traditions; investigate the substantive similarities and differences among the ways the common pattern has been articulated in these religious contexts; and compare the ways in which these patterns have functioned in the lives of religious communities (Reynolds 1980). The descriptive picture or map that results from this process challenges rigid distinctions between soteriology and ethics; specifically, in the Buddhist case between a teleological, *nirvānic* ethic and a consequentialist, *karmic* ethic. Reynolds does not obviate such distinctions; instead, he integrates diverse ethical "modalities" into a broader whole bound together by a common religio-ethical pattern. This pattern correlates modes of moral reasoning with multiple cosmologies and different social locations. It situates ethics in relationship to other components of the Buddhist worldview (viz. cosmology, epistemology), modes of activity and practice (viz. meditation, ritual), and sectors of the Buddhist community.

Methodologically, the history of religions approach to the study of ethics is holistic in the sense proposed above. It does not presume to account for the entirety of a religious tradition or construct an "essence" that defines the whole tradition vis-à-vis its "manifestations." Rather, the history of religions maps action guides and ethical discourse within a general picture and a central pattern, but not a general theory. This approach involves an "intensive study of the structure, dynamics and social implications of the normative modes of action which different traditions have, at various times and places, expressed in their teachings and manifested in their community life" (Reynolds 1979: 23). While some Buddhologists attempt to correlate Buddhist ethics with particular Western metaethical theories, such as Aristotelian eudaemonistic ethics (Keown 1991: ch. 8), others argue that Buddhist ethics should not be constructed in terms of a particular theory and that to do so robs a reading of narrative texts, in particular, of their rich particularity as discursive ethical sites (Hallisey 1996). As the preceding discussion indicates, the history of religions may be said to bring the twin perspectives of historical particularism and inductive holism to the enterprise of comparative religious ethics. An investigation of the historical and contextual particularity of religions enables one to derive a general picture or map and a common religio-ethical pattern.

Cosmology and Ethical Naturalism

Historians of religion contend that moral reasoning should not be treated as an isolated system but studied as part of a complex cultural whole that includes not only moral beliefs but also beliefs about reality (see chapters 4 and 5). This view rests on the assumption that how one acts and reflects on the meaning and reasons for one's actions mirrors the larger picture of how one understands the nature of the world (i.e., the cosmology). In this context, the term "cosmology" is broadly construed as a "study of the ways in which cultures and individuals relate their basic notions of the origins of the reality in which they live their lives to the patterns of action that they consider to be . . . worthy of choice" (Lovin and Reynolds 1985: 8). Historians of religions argue that within the scope of religious ethics an account of moral action and moral reason that does not engage the cosmology in which it is set will be restricted; that is, the picture justifying a particular course of action will be incomplete; and, of even greater significance, the symbolic web of meaning that informs moral agency will be lost. For example, it has been argued that the uniqueness of Confucian ethics reflects its embeddedness in a non-dualistic, organismic worldview (Geaney 2000: 467). Furthermore, historians of religion contend that the purview of investigation should not be confined to formal schema of moral reasoning but should include a wide variety of expressive modes, including narratives, doctrinal treatises, legal codes, ritual, and ceremonial patterns (Lovin and Reynolds 1985: 4).

The correlation between the way people identify their moral choices and how they identify and test their beliefs about reality has been characterized as ethical naturalism (see chapter 2). The empirical cast of ethical naturalism challenges both *a priori* and descriptive formal patterns of moral reasoning: "[it] seeks to describe the relationships between worldviews and norms in ways that accurately reflect the tensions and controversies in a community's experience, in ways that reproduce the complexity of a tradition and allow the identification and meaningful comparison of the most crucial elements within it" (Lovin and Reynolds 1985: 30). Ethical naturalists, therefore, affirm ethical pluralism over-against both universalistic formalism and subjective relativism or idealist versus positivist analyses of moralities (Bird 1981: 162). While embracing cultural diversity, ethical naturalism also sees similarities among the limits and possibilities of human experience that make moral judgments and choices intelligible across cultures (Lovin and Reynolds 1992: 273). These similarities emerge inductively from the dialogical practice of comparative religious ethics itself, rather than being imposed as a deep structure or derived as a universal pattern of practical reason. This practical engagement calls for an imaginative act of translation more akin to metaphor than to syllogism, to mimetic performance than to logical argument (Schweiker 1992: 269ff.).

The historian of religions' dialogue with different religio-ethical systems can and has been extended to include systematic analyses of religious ethics, as well. In her descriptive study of Aztec cosmology, for example, Kay Read demonstrates that Aztec myths embody a paradigm of transformative sacrifice that guides all levels of conduct in Aztec society. Charles Reynolds and Ronald Green find Read's analysis of the ways in which Aztec myths validate and vindicate the moral norms of Aztec society a model of what comparative ethics can be if ethicists and historians of religions engage one another in serious dialogue (Reynolds and Green 1986: 147). They suggest a "thick theory" for understanding the ethical significance of cosmogony, a universal feature of religious traditions that would pursue the following questions: how do cosmogonies vindicate basic ethical norms of individual conduct, social institutions, and moral virtue; how do they validate normative ethical standards; how do they guide individuals and groups in the selection of specific ethical principles and rules; how do they help individuals and groups answer the question of why be moral, and how to deal with moral failure; and how do social forces and cultural traditions inform cosmogonies (Reynolds and Green 1986: 146). With these questions, Reynolds and Green are proposing a "conceptual agenda" with the intention of bridging the gap between theory and description in order to enhance both (Reynolds and Green 1986: 147). The issue remains, however, whether such a conceptual agenda with its emphasis on moral reasoning, vindication, and validation does not overly constrain the ethical textures embedded in the broad mythologized and ritualized cosmological frameworks at the core of religious traditions.

Soteriology: Saints and Virtues

I . . . recommend that an hour spent in the company of a Pachomius . . . or a Saint Martin can tell us . . . how to begin to answer the challenge posed by Dietrich Bonhoeffer: "It is becoming clear every day that the most urgent problem besetting our church is this: how can we live the Christian life in the modern world." (Brown 1987: 14)

Saints are models from whom one learns "patterns of life for which no principle or code can serve as an adequate representation" (Hawley 1987: xiv) (see chapter 10). Saints' lives bridge the gap between soteriology and ethics, between social and personal, moral and religious virtues. Saints are exemplary models – both examples of something and examples to someone. They embody the core pattern of a tradition, not in an abstract or theoretical way, but particularized in narratives, modes of behavior, and specific communities. Saints' lives are concrete expressions of a religio-ethical tradition as a whole and the core pattern/value of the tradition. They are not merely examples typifying the whole; rather, they are convincingly the whole, showing the way to a coherent personhood that contrasts markedly with the "world of shards and fallen fragments by which they are surrounded" (Hawley 1987: xv).

For historians of religions, the narrated lives of saints instantiate and thereby mediate moral principles for a community of faith or members of a society. In this sense they provide an alternative to a model of comparative religious ethics that focuses primarily on modes of moral reason. Narrated lives of saints, furthermore, also uniquely integrate religious and moral action guides. They embody a religio-moral perfection that paradoxically reflects but goes beyond the moral systems that govern ordinary morality and cannot be precisely articulated within the confines of practical reason (Hawley 1987: xvi). For example, the Confucian "paradigmatic individual" or *chün-tzu* exemplifies the spirit of *jen* (human heartedness, compassion) without slavish adherence to conventional rules of propriety (Cua 1992: 58). A Mother Theresa embodies the Christian ideal of agapic love that judges the inadequacies and imperfections of the ethics of distributive justice; yet, at the same time, she creates a community dedicated to the equitable treatment of the impoverished poor and, in doing so, is venerated as a source of beneficent succor for devotees from all walks of life for all kinds of reasons. As Hawley observes, saints are perceived not only as exemplars of individual moral perfection or even of an imagined fellowship of faith and morality, but also as living agents of moral transformation and even physical well-being (Hawley 1987: xxi). They serve as models of moral aspiration and inspiration. For the historian of religions, furthermore, the lives of saints offer both a paradigm of exemplary behavior and an approach to the study of comparative religious ethics that challenges the focus of philosophical ethics on moral reasoning.

Narratives of saints' lives serve a holistic function. They integrate the plural ethical modalities within and among religious traditions, and bridge the divide between the rational and affective dimensions of the moral life. As William Barbieri observes of narrative ethics more generally, it broadens the horizons of contemporary ethics beyond its characteristic concern with moral principles and criteria for decision making (Barbieri 1998: 361). Saints' lives have the capacity to convey more about the motivational and aspirational dimension of the moral life, one of the key features of religio-ethical traditions and also of any reasoned consideration of descriptive and normative ethical agendas.

Religions and Global Ethics

Human beings are held to have access to human rights and to be accountable and obligated to live up to them *not* because they are Muslim or Christian or Buddhist or Jewish or Hindu or a member of any particular religious or philosophical tradition (Little 1999: 166).

The ethicists' critique of the particularism and pluralism of the history of religions' approach to comparative religious ethics assumes special cogency in the debates over the prospects of a global ethic, especially with regard to the urgent and pervasive issue of human rights (see chapter 51). Critics of efforts to promote a global ethic, such as the United Nations' Universal Declaration on Human Rights adopted in 1948, include proponents of cultural diversity with views not unlike the historians of religions' claim that religious ethics are historically and culturally embedded, not abstract systems of moral reasoning (Nino 1991: 90). Questions about universal human rights standards have also been raised from the perspective of differing worldviews and cultural traditions; in particular that the UN Declaration frames human rights in terms of a distinctively Western conception of the autonomous self or individualism (see chapter 14).

Historians of religions bring to the discussion of a global ethic a respect for historical and cultural pluralism both within and among traditions, while at the same time rejecting a skeptical moral relativism. We are not positivists; our maps of religion depict generalizable contours and patterns, not simply discrete particulars. Our descriptive, inductive method does not preclude the possibility of normative claims regarding moral competence and moral responsibility, but disagrees with the position that the idea of human rights requires a neutrally formulated normative regimen. Views resonant with the method of the history of religions include Tore Lindholm's (1992) notion of overlapping consensus; Sumner Twiss' (1998) contention that intercultural dialogue can lead to a shared sense of human moral capacity, common vulnerability to suffering and oppression, and analogous moral principles; and John P. Reeder Jr.'s neo-pragmatist proposal regarding concrete universals achieved through the discovery of convergences among moral, valuational, and factual beliefs (Reeder 1993: 194). Historians of religion agree with the neo-pragmatist's position that religio-cultural traditions are not locked into fixed conceptual schemes between which there is no possibility of translation and the compatible view that concrete universals may be extrapolated analogically over a range of moral experiences (Reeder 1993: 200–1). Although the historians of religions' inductive approach values pluralism, we affirm that comparative religious ethics is not merely a descriptive study of diverse moral traditions, but is also a dialogical process to which our discipline brings a distinctive perspective, one fundamentally attuned with William Schweiker's observation regarding comparative ethics:

> The practice of comparative ethics contributes to the enactment of a shared moral universe in which the diverse ways of being human are preserved amid the claims of [shared] responsibilities . . . It reaches its goal when through encountering others in the performative act of interpretation there is some apprehension of the shape, texture, and direction of their lives and our own within a shared space of meaning and responsibility. (Schweiker 1992: 285). (See also chapter "On Religious Ethics")

In a world increasingly fraught with ethnic and religious violence justified politically by religio-moral absolutes, the history of religions' valuation of diversity and plurality, while affirming that all human communities share not only a physical planet but also a moral universe of meaning and responsibility, has more than an academic import. I suggest the contribution of the historian of religions to the future of comparative religious ethics is nothing less than a moral imperative.

Bibliography

Barbieri, W. A., Jr. 1998: "Ethics and the Narrated Life." *Journal of Religious Ethics* 78 (3), 361–86.

Bianchi, U. 1995: "History of Religions" in *Encyclopedia of Religion*, ed. M. Eliade, 399–408. New York: Macmillan.

Bird, F. 1981: "Paradigms and Parameters for the Comparative Study of Religious and Ideological Ethics." *Journal of Religious Ethics* 9 (2), 157–85.

Brown, P. 1987: "The Saint as Exemplar in Late Antiquity" in *Saints and Virtues*, ed. J. S. Hawley, 3–14. Berkeley: University of California Press.

Childress, J. 1979: "Methodological Issues in Comparative Religious Ethics." *Journal of Religious Ethics* 7 (1), 1–10.

Cua, A. S. 1992: "Competence, Concern, and the Role of Paradigmatic Individuals (chün-tzu) in Moral Education." *Philosophy East and West* 42 (1), 49–68.

Geaney, J. 2000: "Chinese Cosmology and Recent Studies in Confucian Ethics: A Review Essay." *Journal of Religious Ethics* 23 (3), 451–70.

Green, R. M. 1978: *Religious Reason: The Rational and Moral Basis of Religious Belief.* New York: Oxford University Press.

Hallisey, C. 1996: "Ethical Particularism in Theravāda Buddhism." *Journal of Religious Ethics* (3).

Hawley, J. S. (ed.) 1987: *Saints and Virtues.* Berkeley: University of California Press.

Keown, D. 1992: *The Nature of Buddhist Ethics.* New York: St. Martin's Press.

Lindholm, T. 1992: "Prospects for Research on the Cultural Legitimacy of Human Rights: The Cases of Liberalism and Marxism" in *Human Rights in Cross-Cultural Perspectives*, ed. A. A. An-Nai'im, 387–426. Philadelphia: University of Pennsylvania Press.

Little, D. 1999: "Rethinking Human Rights: A Review Essay on Religion, Relativism, and Other Matters." *Journal of Religious Ethics* 27 (1), 151–77.

Little, D. and Twiss, S. B. 1978: *Comparative Religious Ethics.* New York: Harper & Row.

Lovin , R. W. and Reynolds, F. E. 1985: *Cosmology and Ethical Order: New Studies in Comparative Ethics.* Chicago: University of Chicago Press.

—— 1992: "Ethical Naturalism and Indigenous Cultures: Introduction." *Journal of Religious Ethics* 20 (2), 267–78.

Nino, C. S. 1991: *The Ethics of Human Rights.* Oxford: Clarendon Press.

Reeder, J. P., Jr. 1993: "Foundations without Foundationalism" in *Prospects for a Common Morality*, ed. G. Outka and J. P. Reeder, Jr. Princeton, NJ: Princeton University Press.

Reynolds, C. and Green, R. 1986: "Cosmogony and the 'Questions of Ethics.'" *Journal of Religious Ethics* 14, 139–56.

Reynolds, F. E. 1979: "Four Modes of Theravāda Action." *Journal of Religious Ethics* 7 (1), 12–27.

—— 1980: "Contrasting Modes of Action: A Comparative Study of Buddhist and Christian Ethics." *History of Religions* 20 (1–2), 128–46.

Schweiker, W. 1992: "The Drama of Interpretation and the Philosophy of Religions: An Essay on Understanding in Comparative Religious Ethics" in *Discourse and Practice*, ed. F. E. Reynolds and D. Tracey. Albany: State University of New York Press.

Stout, J. 1980: "Weber's Progeny, Once Removed." *Religious Studies Review* 6 (4), 288–95.

Twiss, S. B. 1998: "Moral Grounds and Plural Cultures: Interpreting Human Rights in the International Community." *Journal of Religious Ethics* 26 (2), 271–82.

CHAPTER 16
Comparison in Religious Ethics

Sumner B. Twiss

Overview

Religious ethics in the comparative mode represents cross-traditional and cross-cultural ethical inquiry with simultaneous hermeneutical, critical, constructive, and theoretical dimensions (see Twiss and Grelle 2000 and chapter "On Religious Ethics"). The hermeneutical dimension entails interpreting moral and religious cultural systems, thinkers, practices, and patterns of reasoning in social and historical context. The critical dimension involves analyzing the social, political, economic, and institutional influences on these systems, thinkers, practices, and patterns. The constructive dimension requires identifying and developing intercultural moral resources for articulating new self and social understandings as well as practical strategies for advancing human well-being. And the theoretical dimension involves reflecting on systemic issues raised by the preceding dimensions; for example, ethnocentrism, methodological distortion, universalism versus relativism, justification and truth, the role of imagination, and relations among understanding, interpretation, and explanation. As presently understood and practiced, comparative religious ethics embraces methodological pluralism (and complementarity) and accepts the role of the comparative ethicist as a transformative public intellectual. Although some would argue that this field of inquiry is a discipline, others prefer to regard it as an ongoing conversation among scholars of different disciplines united by the aforementioned dimensions (see Stout 1994).

Whether discipline or conversation, comparative religious ethics has a complex history that crosses disciplines and is marked by intellectual controversy over goals, methods, and results. Its emergence as a focused academic subject is often dated to 1978, when three works simultaneously appeared: Green (1978), Hindery (1978), and Little and Twiss (1978). This coincidence was made all the more remarkable by the fact that the authors were working independently of one another and had somewhat different lineages, ranging across and combining social theory, anthropology, history of religions, and philosophical ethics. The coincidence may be explained in part by the desire of religious ethicists to break from the ethnocentric hegemonies of Christian ethics and purely Western philosophical ethics. Despite the apparent watershed year of 1978, it is important to be aware of earlier developments. These are never far from the view of current scholarship and identify certain themes and issues that are still part of the conversation. In lieu of an exhaustive survey of this development, only a few prominent and illustrative figures and landmarks will be cited, along with features of continuing significance.

History

From the period of classical social theory and philosophy, the illustrative landmark figures are Emile Durkheim, Max Weber and Ernst Troeltsch, and Edward Westermarck and L. T. Hobhouse. Durkheim pioneered the idea of developing a positive science of social life. A science of morality should treat moral and religious beliefs and practices as natural phenomena for which were sought the causes, functions, and laws on a *sui generis* social plane (Durkheim 1915). From Durkheim's perspective, the science of morality provided an intellectual basis for guiding enlightened social and political policy. In fact, he played a significant role as a transformative public intellectual during the period of the Third French Republic.

Unlike Durkheim, Weber distinguished between politics and scholarship. He developed a program of value-neutral scientific inquiry into social phenomena. Weber's distinctive methodology of *Verstehen* uncovered the subjective motives of agents – complemented by causal and historical explanation and involving the use of ideal types of rational behavior (Weber 1963). Using this methodology, Weber pioneered sociological inquiry into distinctive types of religious ethical systems within correlated political economies. This was informed by an overarching evolutionary view of rational social development.

Although in significant agreement with Weber's method, Troeltsch crystallized the meaning and challenge of historicism for dealing with the moral and religious diversity and the internal development of supposedly absolute ethical and religious values (Troeltsch 1971). Unlike Weber, Troeltsch was not shy about playing a public intellectual role in German political society, particularly after World War I.

While not trained social scientists, philosophers Westermarck and Hobhouse undertook comparative surveys of moral phenomena all over the world. Their contrasting normative and theoretical conclusions – ethical relativism and moral universalism, respectively – illustrated the challenge of Troeltsch's "crisis of historicism" for the field of ethics (Westermarck 1906; Hobhouse 1916). Both Westermarck and Hobhouse played significant public intellectual roles in, respectively, Finnish and English politics.

The major themes of this first phase of development are: interest in a science of morality with evolutionary overtones; attempts to articulate a method of systematic comparison; awareness of how historicism poses the acute challenge of universality versus relativism in the sphere of ethics; and a tendency to accept the role of public transformative intellectual.

The second phase is marked by anthropological interventions, whether pursued by professional anthropologists or by philosophers guided by such professionals. Two philosophers, Richard Brandt and John Ladd, did limited fieldwork among the Hopi and Navajo, respectively, utilizing Western moral theory (theory types) to expose the logical structure of the reasoning and worldviews of their subjects (Brandt 1954; Ladd 1957). Both were widely read in the ethnographic literature and used informants and professional translators for limited periods of field research. Both used "ideal types" to guide their inquiry and to analyze their results. They regarded their studies as forays into what was called "descriptive ethics," that is, analyzing the moral reasoning of subjective agents from their internal perspective. Yet their work also compared Western patterns of reasoning and justification with those of indigenous peoples. Neither Brandt nor Ladd envisioned himself as a transformative intellectual.

By contrast, the anthropologist Bronislaw Malinowski undertook intensive field studies of the people of Melanesia. Curtailing the use of theoretical ideas and professional informants, he relied on long-term participant observation in order to ascertain how they reasoned and made sense of their world (Malinowski 1948). Malinowski's ethnographic method was influenced by American pragmatism (specifically, William James). He attempted to determine how his subjects' behavior made sense or was reasonable inasmuch as it pragmatically satisfied their basic needs. The total field of data was scrutinized from the perspective of how the data fit holistically and pragmatically in order to form an intelligible world. Malinowski was not interested in comparison per se, or in using ideal types as bridges of comprehension, which might distort the data and do an injustice to the way his subjects actually reasoned.

By way of summary, the main themes of this phase of development are: a contrast between methods of inquiry about moral reasoning (inquiry into its logical structure guided by a descriptive typology versus intensive fieldwork guided only by a non-theoretical pragmatic holism); movement toward explicit systematic comparison versus a suspicion of such comparison; and the apparent demise of the role of the public or transformative intellectual.

The third phase of development begins with the aforementioned watershed books of 1978, followed by intensive scrutiny of their presuppositions, methods, and results. Ronald Green's book was predicated on a theory of moral and religious rationality derived from Kant's moral philosophy (and to a lesser extent John Rawls' theory of justice). This theory was used to probe the structure of reasoning in Judaism, Christianity, and the religions of India (Green 1978).

Roderick Hindery was guided in part by Weber's work on religious ethics, as well as other methodological studies. He used primary sources and history of religions literature to challenge simplistic views of the ethics of Hindu and Buddhist traditions (Hindery 1978).

David Little and Sumner Twiss explicitly adapted Ladd's descriptive ethics – by adding definitions of certain key concepts (morality, law, religion) – to probe the reasoning and justificatory patterns of selected data from three moral traditions: the Navajo, early Christianity, and Theravāda Buddhism. This study was also informed by contemporary ethnological and historical scholarship (Little and Twiss 1978).

The response to some of these works was immediate and sustained. Green was criticized for imposing an *a priori* and ethnocentric account of rationality on religious–moral traditions that distorted their views. Little and Twiss' study was criticized for being overly positivistic and deploying categories and ideal-typical structures of reasoning that were too static and unnuanced to capture the dynamics of reasoning within the complex worldviews in which they are embedded.

In reaction to these criticisms, Robin Lovin and Frank Reynolds published an anthology of essays in 1985 on cosmogonies and ethics that explicitly propounded a Malinowski-like pragmatic holism as the proper way to study texts and phenomena within diverse moral traditions. This continued the suspicion of systematic comparative work in ethics, while opening the possibility that pragmatic holism could be used for non-systematic comparison in the future (Lovin and Reynolds 1985). The majority of essays in their anthology were particularistic studies of limited texts and traditions (considered within themselves), not explicit comparisons across traditions or cultures. The majority of the authors were historians of religions and anthropologists. For this phase as a whole, none of the scholars advocated the role of the comparative ethicist as a transformative intellectual.

A number of trends are remarkable in light of the preceding phases: a continuing interest in a grand theoretical (although not explicitly evolutionary) account of morality across traditions; the continuing use of ideal types (even if challenged) in comparative ethics; and a continuing interest in deploying less systematic and more pragmatic approaches to the subject. In addition, the theme of universality versus relativism carried through many of these works. Green's theory presupposed moral universalism. Little and Twiss' patterns of moral reasoning were portrayed as descriptive universals. Lovin and Reynolds worried about the possible relativistic implications of their pragmatic holism.

Contemporary Situation

In order to fill out the picture of comparative religious ethics and lay the groundwork for looking toward the future, it is important to ferret out certain themes and trends within current work. It is useful to distinguish these themes and trends into two broad categories: (1) internal features of comparative scholarship and (2) substantive focal concerns of that scholarship. *Internal features* include aims, depth of comparison, categories of analysis, methods, social and intellectual location, and variegated sub-traditions. *Focal concerns* refer to the emergence of substantive areas of scholarship which use comparative methods to enrich such fields as moral psychology, history of religions, biomedical ethics, environmental ethics, and political ethics, to mention but a few.

As presently practiced, comparative religious ethics encompasses a number of aims, ranging across enriched cultural moral self-understanding, appreciation of other traditions, enhancement of cross-cultural communication, addressing shared social problems, and systematic theorizing about religion and ethics. While individual scholars may emphasize certain of these aims more than others, all appear to accept the fact that their work is relevant to advancing these aims. There appear to be two types of depth of comparison: implicit and thin, and explicit and robust. The thin type of comparison brings categories of analysis – whether Western-derived or adapted from previous historical and comparative study – to bear on describing, interpreting, and analyzing one tradition, thinker, text, or genre. This analysis is followed by critically revisiting (and possibly revising) the original categories of analysis. More robust comparative studies explicitly compare two different traditions, thinkers, texts, or genres in order to elicit significant similarities and differences between the objects of comparison. Categories of analysis employed in either of these types range across intentionally theory-thin bridge concepts (way of life, notion of agency), more normatively loaded concepts (particular moral norms, a particular notion of rationality, a theory-type such as natural law or virtue theory), and the inductive elicitation of comparable themes from the materials under scrutiny (discursive strategies, elements of worldview, praxis). The methods used by scholars are myriad and range across a number of options; for example, formal–conceptual (using moral theories as sortals), historical–philological (focusing on key normative terms), phenomenological–ethnographic (investigation of lived reality), hermeneutical–dialogical (mutual interrogation of moral worldviews, reasoning, praxis) (Twiss and Grelle 2000). Although these methods are hardly exhaustive, they are legitimate options for inquiry that can be selectively used and combined in the comparative task, depending on the choice of aim and material. The spirit of methodological pluralism and complementarity is now a leitmotif for this field of study.

As scholarship has progressed, and as appropriate in a world characterized by global intercultural communication, transport, and education, non-Western scholars have entered the conversation of comparative religious ethics. They are guided by similar or analogous aims, methods, and categories, although now enriched by indigenous social and intellectual locations. This trend is likely to continue and strengthen, eroding perceptions (or misperceptions) of the hegemony of Western scholarship. This trend, in turn, has surfaced – or at least emphasized – the fact that non-Western traditions embody diverse sub-traditions (an internal moral pluralism) that accounts for the fact that previous scholars have offered seemingly competing readings of non-Western traditions, thinkers, and texts. Monolithic interpretation of these traditions is forever eroded.

Some of the most important work in comparative ethics is now being done by indigenous scholars interested in philosophical and practical issues and the way that their societies and traditions deviate from Western moral reasoning and praxis. This scholarship is complemented by Western scholars equally interested in the reasons for such deviation, as well as being alert to ways that Western reasoning and praxis might have something to learn from non-Western traditions or at least be enriched by them. Illustrative examples of this development range from comparative studies of the self (relevant to moral psychology), to cross-cultural studies of human rights and just war theory (relevant to political ethics), to comparative studies of health, medicine, and healthcare delivery (relevant to biomedical ethics), to cross-cultural studies of ecological thought and practice (relevant to environmental ethics). The list could continue because so many substantive focal concerns are now involved in the comparative enterprise (see Part III).

The fact that comparative inquiry is being integrated into substantive areas reflects a maturation and acceptance of the field by other scholars. It also points to the re-emergence of the role of the comparative ethicist as a public intellectual committed to working with others – locally, nationally, internationally – in the attempt to resolve social problems shared by diverse peoples and traditions (Twiss and Grelle 2000). This development, while welcome, does not gainsay scholars' continuing interests in other more theoretical issues and aims. The fact is perhaps aptly illustrated by continuing dialogue about issues of universality versus relativism, now within the form of arguments and counter-arguments about prospects for a common morality or global ethic (see chapter 49). The parameters, then, for the conversation or discipline that is comparative religious ethics are both expanding in certain respects and reflective of concerns that originated with its emergence.

Future

In order to concretize further the maturity attained by comparative religious ethics and to illustrate directions for future scholarship, it is necessary to note in more detail work now being pursued. As mentioned previously, comparative ethics is now being undertaken in substantive focal areas of concern.

(1) Comparative inquiry into selfhood and moral agency subsumes study of particular topics, such as self-cultivation, the sources of human moral evil, particular virtues, notions of conscience and their analogues, among others. Much of this work constitutes rather thin comparisons between non-Western conceptions of self and related phenomena, on the one hand, and somewhat broadly cast notions of Western metaphysics and virtue theory, on the other (Allen 1997). By contrast, other studies are much thicker and more robust comparisons between particular thinkers or key normative concepts from two different traditions – for example, Mencius and Aquinas, Augustine and Xunzi, *jen* (Confucian humaneness) and *agape* (Christian neighbor-love) (see Yearley 1990). These studies push comparisons in the direction of trying to solve a genuine human problem, such as how to relate reason and emotion, how to overcome moral evil, or how to sustain the project of becoming a good person. This type of robust comparison is especially difficult, since it requires mastery of two different traditions, their languages, and their internal historical development, in addition to using a combination of methods (philological, conceptual, historical) and carefully controlled bridge concepts (person, will, rationality, virtue). Nonetheless, scholars are increasingly trained to undertake such studies, and one can anticipate more such work in the future.

(2) The emergence of social, applied, or practical ethics from the perspective of non-Western moral traditions, while not explicitly comparative, is a phenomenon worthy of note. It portends the general potential for scholars of non-Western and Western traditions to collaborate on seeking answers to shared moral dilemmas cutting across traditional and cultural boundaries. It is simply a fact, for example, that scholars of Buddhism, Confucianism, and Hinduism – whatever their social and intellectual loca-

tion – are probing moral issues concerning medicine and healthcare, ecology, statecraft, business, and human rights (see Keown 2000). Given the processes of globalization, one can easily anticipate an explosion of such work that can only benefit the scope and quality of comparative inquiry in applied ethics.

As one example of how far this general phenomenon has developed, the area of comparative medical ethics and healthcare delivery is represented by not only ground-breaking tradition-focused work (Hinduism, Buddhism, Native-American traditions, Confucianism), but also explicit cross-cultural comparison of, for example, concepts of health and disease, issues of suicide, euthanasia and human experimentation, and patterns and modes of healthcare delivery (see Coward and Ratanakul 1999) (see chapter 53). This work has thus far focused on challenging Western paradigms for handling these concepts and issues, which are often controlled by the influence of the scientific biomedical model. Similarly, there have been challenges to the Western biomedical focus on individual patient autonomy versus other traditions' openness to family and community consultation and decision making. Western healthcare delivery that values high-technology medicine over community-oriented preventive and palliative strategies is also challenged. Again, evidence indicates that this area of comparative ethical inquiry will intensify and become more robust in the future.

(3) One encounters similar developments in the area of ecological and environmental ethics, although with a twist. Disenchanted environmentally minded Western scholars are taking the lead in looking toward non-Western traditions for conceptual and practical resources to mitigate environmental pollution, ecological destruction, species extinction, and depletion of non-renewable energy sources that are exacerbated by modern industrialized economies (see chapter 47). The hope is that comparative study of non-Western moral traditions will yield new ways of conceptualizing a positive regard for nature, as well as correlated practical strategies for reining in energy and resource-hungry Western societies. There is a spate of studies on non-Western traditions focusing on conceptions of nature, ecological balance, appropriate land use, and harmony between humans and other species, among other related topics (see Callicott and Ames 1989). As the environmental crisis constitutes a worldwide problem, one can, again, anticipate increasingly robust comparative work in this area.

(4) Comparative ethics and political theory has been high on the agenda of comparativists for the last two decades. It has been intensified by recent political, military, and terrorist events. Amid claims of an inevitable clash of civilizations, scholars of comparative ethics have been patiently addressing issues of war and statecraft – just war theory and its analogues – and human rights that are increasingly translated into discourse for public consumption and education (see chapter 55). With respect to just war thinking, the comparative work thus far is focused on Islam, Christianity (or Western tradition more broadly), and Buddhism (see Kelsay 1993; Bartholomeusz 2002). In regard to human rights, comparative work has focused on the enlightened retrospective interpretation of myriad non-Western and Western moral and religious traditions in light of their congruence with or deviation from traditions of international law and human rights (see Bloom et al., 1996) (see chapter 51). Increasingly, this work is also taking on a public intellectual dimension in the form of cross-cultural dialogues, both

non-governmental and governmentally sponsored (see Twiss 1996). As human rights atrocities and war continue to plague the peoples of the world, one can confidently predict that this area of comparative ethics will grow in importance.

(5) The final substantive area – search for a common morality – brings us full circle to a perdurable concern of comparative religious ethics since its earliest inception: universality versus relativism. While theoretical in tone, this issue has a very practical moral dimension, since if there is (or can be) a universal, common, or global ethic or morality, a strong groundwork is provided for intercultural moral dialogue and praxis. Comparativists have been working on the prospects for a common morality from a number of angles: deploying diverse philosophical theories (Kantian, Aristotelian) informed by comparative data; forging a practical overlapping normative consensus among diverse moral and political traditions; showing pragmatically that a common set of moral norms is the best way to solve shared problems and advance human well-being (see Outka and Reeder 1993). In addition, this search – which is likely to continue into the foreseeable future – continues to press the theoretical issue about whether comparative ethics can produce generalizable moral knowledge indicating some deep truths about our human moral nature.

Bibliography

Allen, D. (ed.) 1997: *Culture and Self: Philosophical and Religious Perspectives, East and West.* Boulder, CO: Westview Press.

Bartholomeusz, T. J. 2002: *In Defense of Dharma: Just-War Ideology in Buddhist Sri Lanka.* London: Routledge Curzon.

Bloom, I. et al. (eds.) 1996: *Religious Diversity and Human Rights.* New York: Columbia University Press.

Brandt, R. B. 1954: *Hopi Ethics.* Chicago: University of Chicago Press.

Callicott, J. B. and Ames, R. T. (eds.) 1989: *Nature in Asian Traditions of Thought: Essays in Environmental Philosophy.* Albany: State University of New York Press.

Coward, H. and Ratanakul, P. (eds.) 1999: *A Cross-Cultural Dialogue on Health Care Ethics.* Waterloo, Ontario: Wilfrid Laurier University Press.

Durkheim, E. 1915: *The Elementary Forms of the Religious Life,* trans. J. W. Swain. London: George Allen & Unwin.

Green, R. M. 1978: *Religious Reason: The Rational and Moral Basis of Religious Belief.* New York: Oxford University Press.

——1988: *Religion and Moral Reason: A New Method for Comparative Study.* New York: Oxford University Press.

Hindery, R. 1978: *Comparative Ethics in Hindu and Buddhist Traditions.* Delhi: Motilal Banarsidass.

Hobhouse, L. T. 1916: *Morals in Evolution.* New York: Henry Holt.

Kelsay, J. 1993: *Islam and War: A Study in Comparative Ethics.* Louisville, KY: Westminster/John Knox Press.

Keown, D. (ed.) 2000: *Contemporary Buddhist Ethics.* Richmond, Surrey: Curzon Press.

Ladd, J. 1957: *The Structure of a Moral Code: A Philosophical Analysis of Ethical Discourse Applied to the Ethics of the Navaho Indians.* Cambridge, MA: Harvard University Press.

Little, D. and Twiss, S. B. 1978: *Comparative Religious Ethics: A New Method.* San Francisco: Harper & Row.

Lovin, R. W. and Reynolds, F. E. (eds.) 1985: *Cosmogony and Ethical Order: New Studies in Comparative Ethics*. Chicago: University of Chicago Press.

Malinowski, B. 1948: *Magic, Science and Religion and Other Essays*. New York: Free Press.

Outka, G. and Reeder, J. (eds.) 1993: *Prospects for a Common Morality*. Princeton, NJ: Princeton University Press.

Stout, J. 1994: "The Rhetoric of Revolution: Comparative Ethics after Kuhn and Gunneman" in *Religion and Practical Reason: New Essays in the Comparative Philosophy of Religions*, ed. F. E. Reynolds and D. Tracy. New York: State University of New York Press.

Troeltsch, E. 1971 [1929]: *The Absoluteness of Christianity and the History of Religions*, trans. D. Reid. Richmond, VA: John Knox Press.

Twiss, S. B. 1996: "Comparative Ethics and Intercultural Human Rights Dialogues: A Programmatic Inquiry" in *Christian Ethics: Problems and Prospects*, ed. L. S. Cahill and J. F. Childress, 357–78. Cleveland, OH: Pilgrim Press.

Twiss, S. B. and Grelle, B. (eds.) 2000: *Explorations in Global Ethics: Comparative Religious Ethics and Interreligious Dialogue*. Boulder, CO: Westview Press.

Weber, M. 1963 [1922]: *The Sociology of Religion*, trans. E. Fischoff. Boston, MA: Beacon Press.

Westermarck, E. 1906: *Origin and Development of the Moral Ideas*. London: Macmillan.

Yearley, L. H. 1990: *Mencius and Aquinas: Theories of Virtue and Conceptions of Courage*. New York: State University of New York Press.

1   Jewish Ethics

CHAPTER 17

Jewish Ethics?

Hilary Putnam

It would require scholarship on biblical archeology, the Jewish Bible, Second Temple Judaism, rabbinics, Jewish philosophy (from Philo to Levinas), the Jewish movements during and following the Enlightenment, and more besides to write a "comprehensive" account of "Jewish ethics." Instead of attempting the impossible, I shall employ the traditional Jewish teaching method of focusing on a single passage in the Talmud and proceeding from there. The passage is a fanciful description of how God spends his day:

> Rab Judah said in the name of Rab: "The day consists of twelve hours; during the first three hours the Holy One, blessed be He, is occupying Himself with the Torah, during the second three He sits in judgment on the whole world, and when He sees that the world is so guilty as to deserve destruction, He transfers Himself from the seat of Justice to the seat of Mercy; during the third quarter, He feeds the whole world . . . during the fourth quarter He sports with the leviathan, as it is said, There is leviathan, whom Thou hast formed to sport therewith." Said R. Nahman b. Isaac: Yes, He sports with His creatures, but does not laugh at His creatures except on that day. (TB Avodah Zarah 3b)

In this passage, study of the Torah[1] is conceived of as worthy of occupying a quarter of God's day! God does not engage in trivial pursuits. This passage tells us that study is truly a divine activity.

The point of this chapter will be that *this*, the very special value attached to *study*, indeed, the identification of study and discussion of sacred texts (when conducted in the right spirit and in the right way) with the truest human flourishing, is *the* distinctive feature of "Jewish ethics" (see chapters 7 and 18).

But Why Call This "Ethics"?

The reason for calling this "ethics" is that in the Greek tradition (and "ethics" is, after all, a notion we acquired from Greek philosophy), the *central* ethical question was not "what are the right rules of conduct?" (although that was an important question), nor even "what are the several virtues?" but "what should be the supreme aim of a well-lived human life?" (see chapters "On Religious Ethics" and 1). If studying Torah (and expressing one's learning in one's actions), and similarly studying the discussions and controversies which grow out of the study of Torah, and doing all this in the service of God (*l'shem sh'mayim*) as well as the service of humanity, is seen as the inclusive human end for Jews, then it is appropriate to say that *study* – in this inclusive sense – is the Jewish equivalent to the Greek notion of *eudaimonia*.

But the study in question is described as the study of "Torah." And is not this too *particularistic* to count as a notion of universal human flourishing?

I shall say two things in response. First, traditional Judaism did aspire to universality, for it is part of the belief in the eventual coming of the Messiah and a final Redemption which was a vital part of the Jewish religion for at least two millennia that at the end of days all of humanity would be converted to Judaism. And in this Messianic age, everyone will presumably study Torah just as God is pictured as doing in our passage from the Talmud. Secondly, there is a more immediate (and yet complicated) sense in which the study of Torah is part of the ideal flourishing of a gentile life as well as a Jewish one, even prior to Redemption. What makes it a "complicated sense" is that the "Torah" the ideally virtuous gentile studies is *not* the Jewish Torah.

The Gentile's Torah and the Jews' Torah

The Talmud teaches:

> R. Meir used to say, "Whence can we learn that where a gentile occupies himself with the study of Torah he equals [in status] the High Priest? We find it stated: . . . 'which if a man do he shall live in them,' [Leviticus 11:21] it does not say 'priests, Levites and Israelites,' but 'a man,' which shows that even if the gentile occupies himself with the study of the Torah he equals [in status] the High Priest!" – That refers to their own seven laws. (TB Sanhedrin 59a)

The Torah that Rabbi Meir imagined a gentile occupying himself with is, thus, the seven Noachide Laws. The Jewish tradition holds that every human being is a son or daughter of "the covenant of Noah" (see Genesis 9). While Jews are obligated to observe the entire Halakhah, every non-Jew is obliged to obey the (universal, minimal) moral obligations of this Noachide covenant (TB Sanhedrin 56–60). According to the rabbis of the Talmud, a non-Jew who accepts these obligations is a *ger-toshav* (resident foreigner) or even a "semi-convert" (TB Avodah Zarah 64b). The seven Noachide commandments as traditionally enumerated are (Roth and Wigoder 1996 XII: 1190): the prohibition of idolatry, blasphemy, bloodshed, sexual sins, theft, and eating from a living animal, as well as the injunction to establish a legal system (TB Sanhedrin 56a).[2] They are derived from divine commands addressed to Adam (Genesis 2:16) and Noah (see TB Sanhedrin 59b), the ancestors of all humankind.

If the valorization of "study of Torah" is thus universalized, there is still a sense in which Jewish ethics *is* particularistic. There is a special virtue reserved for those who obey the *mitzvah* (commandment) to study because it is commanded to do so (that is, commanded by the halakhah) and not simply because their natural inclination or their religious sensibility leads them to do so. We see this in the Talmudic tractate *Baba Kama* (38a). In the passage I have in mind, Mar ben Rabana has just interpreted a biblical verse by saying: "It only means that even were they [the gentiles] to keep the seven commandments they would receive no reward," and this is immediately objected to (by the anonymous redactor), who cites the passage we just discussed. At this point, someone (presumably Mar ben Rabana, qualifying his original statement) says:

> I mean [in saying that they would receive no reward] that they will receive reward not like those who having been enjoined perform commandments, but like those who not having been enjoined perform good deeds: for R. Hanina has stated: Greater is the reward of those who having been enjoined perform good deeds than of those who not having been enjoined [but merely out of good will] do good deeds. (TB Baba Kama 38a)

What is remarkable to a modern secular ear is the idea that although there is merit in a gentile's studying the principles of universal morality (the gentile "Torah" or Noachide laws), there is *less* merit in this than the Jew's studying the Jew's Torah *because the Jew does it to obey a divine command and does not simply do it of his own free will*. Here we seem to encounter both the familiar (the idea that at least some basic norms are universally valid) and the unfamiliar (being commanded is better than spontaneously doing good)!

The Question of "Legalism"

It is impossible, in this connection, not to face the longstanding controversy between traditional Christianity and traditional Judaism concerning the merit of obeying *mitzvot* (commandments) (see chapters 19, 20, and 22). Ever since St. Paul famously contrasted "the law" which "worketh wrath" (Romans 4:15) and "faith without the deeds of the law" by which we are "justified" (Romans 3:28), Judaism has been denounced as a soullessly legalistic religion (although there has been considerable rethinking of this in the Christian world in the last century). Here is an example of the polemical use of this contrast by a Protestant theologian (a liberal one, noted for his "liberation theology," his feminism, etc.). Robert MacAfee Brown explained that in the time of Ezra and Jeremiah the Jews "developed a way of life based on adherence to a set of rules" (Brown 1985: 248–9). He tells us that by the end of the Old Testament period Jews had "613 different laws or rules," and says: "You are 'good' if you obeyed the rules, and 'bad' if you disregarded them." Brown then asks the rhetorical question "What happens?" and answers as follows:

> It is clear what happens. You become so worried about breaking one of the rules, or one of the rules about rules, or one of the rulings about the rules about one of the rules – that all your time is taken up with a meticulous observance of these details. And the notion of a living relation with God (which is what the law was originally all about) is lost and forgotten. So is the idea of loving your neighbor. Who would dare to do a spontaneous act of

kindness for his neighbor when such an act might violate one of the demands of the law?
(Brown 1985: 249)

Traditional Jews think this is nonsense. For them, the joy of obeying a divine command
and the love of one's neighbor are not incompatible, but mutually supporting parts of
a complex religious way of life. The valorization of doing something virtuous *because*
God commanded us to do it even above doing it simply out of spontaneous good will is a
distinctive feature of the traditional Jewish ethical outlook and so is the love of one's
neighbor.[3]

In response to Brown's claim that in Judaism the notion of a living relation with God
and the idea of loving your neighbor are "lost and forgotten," it should suffice to point
out that in all of its versions, Judaism has always portrayed God as being tremendously
concerned with our morality. At times one's duty to God seems to be identified with
ethical behavior, as when the Bible tells us:

> Will the LORD be pleased with thousands of rams, or with ten thousands of rivers of oil?
> Shall I give my firstborn for my transgression, the fruit of my body for the sin of my soul?
> He has told thee, O man, what is good; and what does the LORD require of thee, but to do
> justly, and to love mercy, and to walk humbly with thy GOD? (Micah 6:7–8)

And in the Talmud, we learn the famous story of Hillel who, when asked by someone
to summarize the whole Torah with utmost brevity ("while standing on one foot"),
replied: "That which is hateful to thee, do not do unto thy neighbor. That is the whole
Torah – the rest is commentary – Go study!" (TB Shabbath 31a).

Indeed, the picture of the traditional Jew living a life of constant worry about breaking one of the rules is a gross caricature. In every religion, people who lead traditional
lives have so internalized not just the "rules," but also attitudes and customs, that following the way of life is what comes naturally. This is not to deny that there are people
who make Judaism or any other religious way of life burdensome and oppressive. That
type is well known. But it is not characteristic of Judaism.

Study, Innovation, and Interpretation

For traditional Jews, there is no conflict between finding joy in carrying out God's commandments and "loving one's fellow creatures." And we are told that the observance
of the commandment to study "surpasses them all" (TB Shabbat 127a). But there is
something important I need to add.

Study, especially of sacred texts, is often associated with traditionalism. But in the
Talmud it is associated *both* with traditionalism and *anti-traditionalism*, and the struggle runs through large stretches of the Talmud (see Fisch 1997; Hartman 1999). In
particular, we find a continual willingness to reinterpret both the Bible and the Mishnah
when they conflict with the rabbis' moral sensibility.

The ways in which the Talmud avoided imposing capital punishments prescribed by
biblical law and even avoided imposing capital punishments prescribed by halakhah

itself illustrates this willingness. For example, Deuteronomy 21:18–21 prescribes that the father and mother of a "stubborn and rebellious son" shall bring him out to the elders of the town and say, "This son of ours is disloyal and defiant; he does not heed us. He is a glutton and a drunkard. Thereupon the men of his town shall stone him to death." The Talmud, through interpretation, restricted the possibility of carrying out the death penalty against such a son to the point where they made it completely impossible in actual practice to carry out this law! (Elon 1994 I: 365).

Similarly, in Deuteronomy 13:13–17, we encounter the law that "If you hear it said" that someone has persuaded the inhabitants of a town in the land of Israel to become idolators, we are to (1) "investigate and inquire and interrogate thoroughly"; and (2) if "the fact is established," we are to "put the inhabitants of the town to the sword" and "burn the town and all its spoil entirely." The sages hedged this law around with restriction after restriction. Thus:

1   " 'If you hear it said of one of your towns.' But not if you are the source yourself." In other words, only if the report comes to your attention unbidden are you to investigate; you are not to investigate on your own initiative. (*Midrash Tannaim*, Deuteronomy, 66)
2   " 'If you hear it said of one of your towns.' But not by one who roams around to eavesdrop." (*Sifrei*, Deuteronomy, Re'eh, sec. 92, 153)
3   "Jerusalem cannot have the status of an idolatrous town, for the Torah says 'your towns' – and Jerusalem was not allocated among the [Israelite] tribes." (TB Baba Kama 82b)
4   "R Eliezer says: Every town that contains even one *mezuzah* cannot have the status of an idolatrous town, since it is written: 'Burn the town and all its spoil entirely.' This, however, is not possible where there is a mezuzah." (TB Sanhedrin 113a, 71a)

As we see from these examples, the words of God are not read as if their meaning were self-evident. Rather, their meaning is expected to emerge from the ongoing and admittedly fallible process of arguing about the text and of finding ever new and additional meanings in it. Study, innovation (*hiddush*), and interpretation are always linked.

This study and interpretation was supposed to be engaged in by every male Jew (alas, the tradition *was* chauvinistic!). Indeed, every Jewish community was obligated to support universal education precisely so that this should be possible. We discussed a negative view of all this study. I wish to close by describing a different view. David Hartman writes:

> The word, then, at the deepest, most fundamental level of Torah culture, embodies the living reality of God. And, contrary to the standard interpretation of Paul's description of mitzvah and Halakhah . . . the phrase that best describes the essence of rabbinic religiosity is not "the burden of the law" but "*simcha shel mitzvah*," the joy of mitzvah. (Hartman 1999: 8)

Two reasons may make this difficult for moderns to grasp. The first is the common assumption that study of religious texts involves unquestioning acceptance of tradition. As we have seen, the rabbis delighted in finding ever-new interpretations of the text. As Hartman describes this:

> Rabbi Akiva read the Bible as an intimate love letter. He read and reread the words; he, so to speak, felt the parchment and examined the handwriting, the shapes of the letters, and the marks on the page, always looking for signs and clues to secret meanings and hidden messages. In modern terminology, the medium became part of the message, conveying the rich and subtle complexity of the divine world. (Hartman 1999: 9–10)

The second reason is our tendency to assume that seeing a text as ambiguous, complex, difficult, must involve seeing it as creating a *distance* between the recipient and the author. But this is not the way the rabbinic tradition experienced matters. If there is a fundamental novelty in rabbinic religiosity, it is that the sages saw figuring out what God means by his words as a form of *intimacy* with God. Judaism is an interpretive tradition, and as Hartman puts it, "In the interpretive tradition, God never abandons you, because His word is always with you" (1999: 11).

Conclusion

In this chapter I have described a unique aspect of the ethical vision of traditional Judaism. That aspect – the valorization of study – is shared by the contemporary Jewish denominational movements, and some trace of it, however attenuated, can be discerned in the thought of most independent Jewish thinkers. That is my justification for calling what I have described "Jewish ethics" and not simply "the ethics of the Talmud."

Notes

1   The oldest stratum of the Talmud is the Mishnah, a corpus of Jewish law (in Hebrew) traditionally held to have been codified by Judah ha-Nasi (ca. 135–ca. 220). The other stratum is the Gemara, a corpus of interpretations of the Mishnah (in Aramaic). The flexible concept "Torah" can mean just the Pentateuch, or the whole Tanakh (the Jewish Bible), or all this plus the "Oral Torah," and the latter can include not just the Talmud but also the exegesis and the legends that have grown up during and after (and in some cases even before) the Talmudic period.

2   The prohibition of idolatry was understood to mean that the gentile does not have to "know God" but must abjure false gods. For references, see the article in *Encyclopedia Judaica* (Roth and Wigoder, 1996: 1189–91) cited in the text. It must also be mentioned that there are indications that in the Tanaitic period (the period during which the Mishnah – the oldest stratum of the Talmud – was composed) there was disagreement on the number and the contents of the Noachide laws. (See the article just cited for references.)

3   I wish to emphasize that in this chapter I am not taking the view (because I don't believe it) that any one form of Judaism is "normative Judaism," although traditional rabbinic Judaism (today known as "Orthodox" Judaism) was the Judaism of the overwhelming majority of Jews for the better part of two millennia, which justifies the attention that we are giving it here.

Bibliography

All references to the Mishnah (M) or Babylonian Talmud (TB) are by tractate and citation. References to the Babylonian Talmud are to the Soncino Press edition (London and Brooklyn, 1962+).

Brown, R. M. 1985: *The Bible Speaks to You*. Philadelphia, PA: Westminster Press.

Elon, M. 1994: *Jewish Law: History, Sources, Principles*. Philadelphia, PA: Jewish Publication Society.

Fisch, M. 1997: *Rational Rabbis: Science and Talmudic Culture*. Bloomington: Indiana University Press.

Hartman, D. 1999: *A Heart of Many Rooms: Celebrating the Many Voices within Judaism*. Woodstock, VT: Jewish Lights.

Roth, C. and Wigoder, G. (eds.) 1996: *Encyclopedia Judaica*. Jerusalem: Keter Publishing House.

CHAPTER 18
Foundations of Jewish Ethics

Ronald M. Green

Any effort to describe the origins and foundations of Jewish ethics faces an immediate problem. If we take "ethics" to mean systematic, reasoned reflection about the norms and values governing human conduct, then the phrase "Jewish ethics" is inadequate to describe the centuries-long Jewish tradition of ethical thought. A focus only on systematic ethical reflection leads one to privilege Jewish philosophical discussions of the medieval and modern periods and ignore the vast corpus of moral instruction found in classical Jewish religious law (*halakhah*).

The lesser place given to systematic ethical reflection in Jewish thought stems from the fact that Judaism developed independently of the two traditions that shaped Western approaches to ethics: the Greco-Roman tradition of moral philosophy, and the Christian tradition of ethical teaching. The philosophers of Greece and Rome imparted to the field of ethics a commitment to the rational analysis and reasoned justification of moral norms in terms of their impact on human well-being. Although Jewish ethics was profoundly influenced by similar concerns, its foundation in revealed law often obscured the human and reasoned processes at work within it.

Christianity, in turn, introduced a series of influential distinctions that were partly shaped by its polemic with Judaism. These include the distinction between law and morality, ritual and morality, inner intention and outer deed, obligation and supererogation, justice and love, communal versus individual accountability, and particular versus universal loyalties. Many of these distinctions are implicitly recognized in Jewish thought. Nevertheless, Jewish ethical teaching typically lacks explicit analysis of ethics in terms of these distinctions. Hence, the effort to understand the bases and development of Jewish ethics must avoid imposing these approaches or categories. Instead, it must develop the body of moral instruction that originates in the Hebrew Bible, continues through the formation of Jewish law in the Talmudic period, and only develops systematic ethical reflection following encounters with Greco-Roman philosophy and Christian ethics in the medieval and early modern periods.

Foundational Texts

The Hebrew Bible or Torah forms the heart of the Jewish ethical tradition (see chapter 7). The multitude of commandments (*mitzvoth*) found in the Pentateuch became the core of Jewish ethical teaching. These were further illuminated by the many narrative and homiletic elements found elsewhere in the Bible, including the book of Genesis, the historical writings, the books of the prophets, and various books of the wisdom tradition (especially Proverbs and Ecclesiastes). Within this vast landscape of moral requirements, ideals, and complex portraits of virtue and vice, we can identify at least two foundational texts that shape Jewish teaching from the start.

Genesis

Genesis establishes a profoundly universalistic motif in Jewish ethics. It does so, first, by locating God's purposes in relation to the history of the human race as a whole, not just the national experience of Israel. This motif reappears elsewhere in the Bible, especially in prophetic writings like Isaiah 2:3 where Israel's mission is presented as educating the entire world to God's nature and lofty moral standards. This universalistic vision, eventually a part of Judaism's messianic expectations, is later imparted to both the Christian and Islamic faiths (see chapters 21 and 25).

For Jewish thought, moral universalism was reinforced by the statement in Genesis 1:27 that "God made man in His own image." While the concept of the "divine image" eventually gave rise to diverse interpretations in Jewish ethical, philosophical, and mystical literature, it was always understood to encompass human beings' ability to understand and heed moral requirements (see chapter 3). Hence, the "divine image" served to ground a Jewish sense of human freedom and moral responsibility. In addition, this text reinforced the Jewish commitment to the dignity and sanctity of each individual human being regardless of the person's social status. Thus, the Mishnah, the compilation of the earliest post-biblical teachings by the sages, points to our shared descent from Adam to affirm that "whoever destroys a single life is deemed by Scripture as if he had destroyed a whole world; and whoever saves a single life is deemed by Scripture as if he had saved a whole world" (M. Sanhedrin 4.5). In the Jewish tradition, this universalistic motif finds expression in divers texts that extend God's compassion beyond the confines of Israel. In one text dealing with the Exodus account, God chastises the angels for celebrating the death of the Egyptian pursuers. "My children are drowning in the sea, and you are singing songs?" (TB Megillah 10b). In other texts, the rabbis generalized this respect for the worth of each person. They condemned conduct that abased or humiliated anyone and they permitted the suspension of any prohibitory law of Torah to spare another person from indignity (see TB Shabbat 81b).

Jewish philosophers have debated whether Judaism possesses a concept of natural law like that found in the Roman Catholic moral tradition. Those who defend the presence of this concept in Jewish thinking have looked to the Genesis narratives and to the related rabbinic concept of the "seven laws of the descendants of Noah" in support of their arguments (see chapter 17). As presented in the Talmud, these norms precede the specific laws of the covenant and are regarded as pertaining to all human beings. They include one positive requirement, the establishment of a judicial system in society, and six prohibitions: against (1) blasphemy; (2) idolatry; (3) the wanton destruction of human life; (4) adultery, incest, homosexuality, and bestiality; (5) robbery; and (6) eating the flesh of a living animal (TB Avodah Zarah 8:4; TB Sanhedrin 56a). Rabbinic speculation on Noachide legislation presumes that all human beings are capable of understanding and respecting the moral norms governing civilized life (Novak 1998). Such "natural law" thinking forms a "precondition" for the very ideas of revelation and covenant that are so central to Jewish ethics.

Although these observations capture an important aspect of Jewish ethical thinking, we must also recognize that some features of Western natural law have no place in Jewish ethical thought. Jewish ethical thinking could never accept the distinction, so closely associated with natural law theory, between norms based on reason and those based on revelation. From a traditional Jewish perspective, both the Noachide laws and any moral norms rationally accessible by human beings are regarded as inseparable from God's creative activity. The revelation of God's moral purposes for humanity begins with creation, continues through the bestowal of norms on all humanity prior to the covenant, and reaches its culmination in the giving of the Law at Sinai.

The Genesis narrative also furnishes Jewish ethics with a specific understanding of human sexuality and human beings' place in the natural order. Like Christian thinkers, Jewish sages utilized the narratives surrounding Adam and Eve to identify heterosexuality, marriage, and family as created goods and morally required patterns of conduct. However, unlike the Christian tradition, Jewish ethics tended not to elaborate these ideas into a veneration of existing patterns in nature or a tendency to biological "vitalism." Jewish thinkers generally permitted the modification of nature in order to improve human life. Thus, despite the conviction that "healing is from God," almost all Jewish thinkers rejected passivity before disease processes and permitted human medical interventions. Although specific forms of male birth control were prohibited as violating a commandment against the "wastage" of semen, broad latitude was given for female contraceptive measures (see Genesis 38:8–10; Feldman 1974). The "unfinished" nature of creation and human beings' creative role in it was signaled by the ritual event of circumcision. The need for this was explained by the rabbis under the principle "Whatever was created in the first six days requires further preparation" (Genesis Rabbah 11.3 in Freedman and Simon 1939; see also Green 1998, 1999). Also important as a basis for resisting biological vitalism and passivity before nature is the extreme sacredness of human life in Jewish teaching and the generally "death averse" sensibility that prevails. In Jewish law, the preservation of life is such a central value that it takes precedence over even the most important ritual requirements, such as Sabbath observance or the annual day of fasting at Yom Kippur.

A final and very important reason for Jewish resistance to biological vitalism is the Genesis-derived understanding of the human being as a psychosomatic unity and the perceived goodness of the material world (see chapter 54). While it is not right to say that Judaism lacks a sense of the dangerous power of human material or sexual desires, the tradition always resisted any kind of dualism that elevated the spiritual aspects of human life and denigrated the corporeal. One Talmudic passage focuses on the "evil impulse" or *yetzer harah*, the indwelling aspect of lust and greed in human nature that drives so much wrongdoing. Noting that God declares each day's creation to be "good," the text asks whether the "evil impulse" is also good. Yes, it replies, for "were it not for that impulse, a man would not build a house, marry a wife, beget children or conduct business affairs" (M. Avot 3:18). It follows from this that the Jewish ethical tradition rejected asceticism as a religious value. This distinctive appreciation of the physical world and embodied existence also explains a host of Jewish practices and beliefs, ranging from the care given the body in funerary rituals through the relatively "this-worldly" messianic hope of restored national existence in the land of Israel.

Exodus and covenant

Despite its sequential priority within the biblical texts, Genesis probably takes second place in terms of its importance for Jewish ethics to the narratives concerning the Exodus and Sinaitic Covenant. Together, these constitute the central "story" of the Jewish ethical tradition (Dorff 2002). Within this corpus, at least four key motifs emerge that profoundly shape subsequent Jewish ethical thought as well as Jewish ways of "doing ethics." We turn now to consider these key motifs.

Key Motifs

Redemption and social justice

The first motif anchors the whole body of Jewish law and commandments in God's redemption of the people from slavery and oppression. The Hebrews agree to obey God not merely because of his awesome power, but because of his demonstrated justice, righteousness, and compassion. This theme, echoed again and again in biblical and later Jewish texts, confounds the simple oppositions introduced by later ethical theory between heteronomy and autonomy, reason and revelation (Green 1988: ch. 4). That God's will, embodied in his commandments, must be obeyed is a cornerstone of all traditional Jewish thinking. But equally important is the conviction that God's will is righteous. Faith and ethics cannot conflict. For Judaism, faith is not merely belief in God but the confidence that, despite any appearances to the contrary, God's will and purposes are righteous.

This redemptive motif also underlies the commitment to social justice that characterizes all expressions of Jewish ethics from the ancient to the modern period. It is not accidental that the Ten Commandments, which begin with the thundering reminder "I am the Lord your God, who brought you out of the land of Egypt, out of the house of bondage" (Exodus 20:2), are followed by an extensive body of legislation requiring compassion for the poor, the sojourner, the widow, and the orphan. Having experienced conditions of marginality and oppression, God's covenanted people are presumed to have special insight into how evil these states are. As a result, they are required to avoid practices that create new suffering for the powerless in their midst. "You shall not wrong a stranger or oppress him, for you were strangers in Egypt. You shall not afflict any widow or orphan"(Exodus 22:21–2).

These themes are not confined to the Exodus narratives, but sweep through the whole tradition. In the Pentateuch they take form in numerous commandments that make provision for the poor. These include the tithing of harvests (Deut. 14:28–29), the right of the poor to gleanings (Lev. 19:10), the cancellation of debts in the Sabbatical year of release (Deut. 15:1–2), and the return of alienated property in the Jubilee year (Lev. 25:9–13). In the prophetic writings, social justice becomes pivotal; the Israelites' failure to observe covenantal requirements pertaining to the poor are the most frequently mentioned cause of God's wrath. Following the Roman War in 70 CE, the center of Jewish communal life moved from the agricultural environment of Israel to the more urban communities of the Diaspora. In these new circumstances, the rabbinic sages elaborated under the headings of "Zedakah" and "Gemilut Hasadim" a new set of rulings and norms designed to express this commitment to social justice. Zedakah included the legally enforced payment of poor taxes, while Gemilut Hasadim encompassed the more open-ended and voluntary obligations of interpersonal charity. So extensive were these requirements that everywhere across the Diaspora, Jewish communities took the form of "a modified welfare city-state, with its special functionaries who collect the compulsory levy and act as trustees for the poor and the needy" (Twersky 1963).

The ethical impulse to law

This conversion of ethical norms into concrete legal (*halakhic*) requirements is the second major motif formative for Jewish ethics found in the Exodus-Covenant narratives. From the start of this tradition, the ethical impulse takes expression as law: concrete, publicly known, authoritative enactments meant to govern the conduct of all members of the community. The core of this legal corpus are the 613 commandments identified in scripture. Beyond this core is a vast and growing penumbra of legislation hinted at and, in a sense authorized by, the biblical text itself. Anticipating the need to apply the numerous covenantal commandments to the ongoing life of the community, Deuteronomy 17 establishes a process whereby controversies and disputes will be brought for decision before the "Levitical priests" and "the judge who is in office in those days." The authority of these officials is final (see chapter 6).

Eventually, this mandate for ongoing judicial interpretation results in a vast body of recorded debates, opinions, and rulings, some of which come to be regarded as parts of an "Oral Torah" revealed to Moses at Sinai. This was viewed as an extended explanation of how the written laws should be executed and followed. Many of these teachings are gathered in the text of the Mishnah (literally, "repetition") produced by the earliest sages (*Tanaim*) who worked during the inter-testamental period. In turn, the Mishnah forms the basis of a further commentary tradition (optimistically called "Gemara" or "completion"). Together with Mishnah, this material was developed from 200 to 500 CE by later generations of rabbinic scholars known as the *Amoraim*. This compilation became the Talmud, which, in its larger and more authoritative Babylonian version, contains 63 tractates (comprising 17 volumes in the Soncino English translation). Although much of the text is *halakhic* in nature, recording important debates and rulings on legal materials, the Talmud also contains substantial *aggadic* (narrative, speculative, and homiletic) material, a portable culture for a people in exile. Since the need for normative reflection and enactment never ends, the *halakhic* tradition continues beyond the Talmud in efforts to codify the accumulated body of norms and in rabbinic rulings and interpretations (*responsa*) elicited in each generation by new circumstances of life.

The impulse to law is partly explained by a major ethical conviction of Jewish faith: that for moral requirements and ideals to be taken seriously, they have to be actively embodied in the life of a community and must be incumbent on every member of the community. While it is good to advocate demanding moral requirements and lofty ideals, these become realities only when their performance is expected of all community members and when their neglect is subject to punishment or censure.

Of course, there is the danger that a law-creating ethic of this sort can become a "monument of inflexible injunctions and prohibitions." There is also the danger that "spontaneity and inwardness in ethical decision may shrivel into a deadening conformity to the book of statutes" (Schulweis 1995: 34). Although these dangers are always present in a law-based system, there are corresponding dangers in leaving ethical matters to individual decision making and abandoning efforts to shape the abiding public norms that govern communal life. Faced with these twin dangers, Jewish ethics opted for the risks of law.

Jewish thinkers tried to moderate this risk by introducing into legal analysis a series of principles that permitted and in some cases required individuals to go beyond the bounds of the law. An example is the principle of *lifnim m'shurat ha-din*, signifying conduct "beyond the line of the law." This involved conduct in which one does more than the law requires or presses one's legal rights less strictly than the law permits. For example, according to rabbinic teaching, a sales contract is not complete until goods have been transferred (TB Baba Metzia 47b; see Lauterbach 1951: 288). This provides a window of time during which a merchant might legally renege on an agreement. Someone who refuses to do this is regarded as acting "beyond the line of the law." In these and other instances the rabbis were prepared to extend the "fence" around the law to encompass forms of supererogatory behavior.

Interpretive autonomy

Superficially regarded, Judaism's reliance on a fixed and revealed set of norms would seem to be the antithesis of moral rationality and practical reasoning (see chapter 5). Not only are the commandments regarded as having their source in God's eternal will, as opposed to human reason, but also, once understood, they must be strictly obeyed without concessions to human needs or inclinations. Despite this appearance of absoluteness, however, Jewish ethics gives enormous scope to human reason through its frank recognition and authorization of the hermeneutic or interpretive task. This feature of the Jewish ethical tradition is also implicit in Deuteronomy 17, where, side by side with the admonition against deviating "to the right hand or the left," the authority for applying the law to current disputes is given to "the judge who is in office in those days." The Talmud reinforced this impulse to judicial interpretation. Pirke Avoth, the "Chapters of the fathers," one of the most ethically explicit texts of the Mishnah, begins with this famous observation:

> Moses received Torah from Sinai and delivered it to Joshua, and Joshua to the elders, and the elders to the prophets and the prophets delivered it to the men of the great synagogue. These said three things: "Be deliberate in judging, raise up many disciples, and make a fence around the Torah." (M. Avoth 1)

Use of the word "fence" here is particularly apt. Within the Jewish tradition, the interpretive judicial task was not usually regarded as one of innovation. Rather, it was protection of the once-given body of divine legislation. However, since a fence necessarily extends beyond the perimeter of what it protects, the interpretive task also became an expansive enterprise (see chapter 7).

Expansion was guided by two fundamental beliefs. One was the conviction that the interpretive enterprise rests inescapably on human reason and human experience. A key text here is Deuteronomy 30:11–12: "this commandment which I command you this day is not too hard for you; neither is it far off. It is not in heaven, that you should say, 'Who will go up for us to heaven, and bring it to us.'" In later Jewish thinking, the principle "it is not in heaven" becomes, negatively, a rejection of any supernatural appeals or charismatic assertions of religious authority. According to the rabbis, God's direct and supernatural communication came to an end in the prophetic period. From that time forward, God's will is instantiated in the revealed law.

Positively, the phrase "it is not in heaven" founds reliance on the rational interpretive rules and "democratic" procedures established over the generations in countless rabbinic debates. Foremost among these is the requirement that final authority in the settlement of all *halakhic* disputes rests with the majority of a community's rabbinic scholars and decisors. In the Talmudic tractate *Baba Metzia* (59b) this teaching finds imaginative expression in the account of a debate about a minor point of ritual law between Rabbi Eliezer and Rabbi Joshua. When Rabbi Eliezer sees that Rabbi Joshua's opinion commands majority assent, he invokes a series of miraculous events to support his own position, a sequence that culminates in a Divine voice from heaven (*bat kol*) asking: "What have you against Rabbi Eliezer? The law is always as he says." In response to this intervention, Rabbi Joshua stands up and declares: "It is not in heaven," reminding God himself of the authority invested in the rabbinic majority. The narrative ends with the report that on that day, God smiled and declared: "My children have defeated me, my children have defeated me."

Paradoxically, this mandate for reasoned interpretation of the law was strengthened by a rabbinic belief that would seem to limit the scope of human moral autonomy: the conviction that the law was complete in its revealed content as this was found in scripture and the received oral law. There was never a question for the rabbis of creating or discovering new laws. Nevertheless, the plenitude of scripture, and the confidence that every word, letter, or punctuation mark was expressive of divine intent, afforded limitless opportunities for morally creative interpretations that could respond to emergent problems and express evolving moral sensibilities.

One of the more famous examples of hermeneutic freedom based on textual literalism is the replacement of the *lex talonis* of Exodus 21:24 ("an eye for an eye") by a requirement of monetary compensation for personal injuries. Drawing on Numbers 35:31 ("You may not accept a ransom for the life of a murderer who is guilty of a capital crime"), the rabbis concluded that this explicit prohibition of monetary compensation in capital cases means that monetary payment applies to all lesser circumstances of personal injury (TB Baba Kama 83b).

Taken together, reliance on reasoned rabbinic decision and the scope of interpretive freedom ensured that the norms emerging from the *halakhic* process would provide continuity with the received tradition while being able to adapt to new circumstances and questions. What emerged was a "quasi-democratic theocracy" in which collective wisdom replaced revelation and continual deliberation about the moral norms governing communal life became a central feature of Jewish identity. Within this context, the contrast between a "heteronomous" revealed law, and an "autonomous" law of reason or conscience, makes no sense (see Ross 1968).

Study and obedience

Above all, deliberation about the law and obedience to it had religious significance (see Walzer et al. 2000). A fourth major motif of Jewish ethics is the profound liturgical and ritual dimension of the *halakhic* enterprise. Once again, the texts recording the Exodus and Covenant events establish this sensibility. There we learn that the commandments do not just order Israel's life and govern social conduct. Their deeper aim is to create a "holy people" that evidences God's nature and purposes in the world. The law is meant to "separate" this people from the profane world and confer upon them the kind of purity and sanctity – holiness – associated with divine things.

A distinctive feature of this tradition is the fact that the central purificatory ritual is the *halakhic* process itself: the ongoing task of achieving higher levels of *halakhic* insight and observance. Things that depart from *halakhah* defile and must be avoided and cleansed because they distance the people from God and impair their role as mediators between God and man, a nation of "holy" priests. The goal is to create a morally and religiously pure community. All members participate in this common effort and share a common destiny. The moral excellences of some enhance the community's stature and invite God's favor, while the failures of even a few blemish the community and alienate God.

This commitment to collective purity also explains the tendency of Jewish religious law to interweave both ritual and moral requirements. The seemingly indiscriminate juxtaposition of profoundly moral injunctions, such as the requirement to "love your neighbor as yourself" (Leviticus 19:18), with rules against making a garment out of two kinds of cloth (Leviticus 19:19), has led to the assumption that Jewish law is only secondarily driven by moral intent, that Judaism is "a religion of pots and pans" (Kellner

1978). This impression is reinforced by repeated insistences that all the commandments are equally mandatory. Thus Pirke Avoth (2:1) admonishes man to be "heedful of a light precept as of a grave one."

The reality of Jewish teaching and practice was otherwise. From the earliest date, sages and rabbis perceived important differences between the commandments enjoining ritual matters and those that related to the human interpersonal realm. They were informed in this by prophetic utterances like Amos' imprecation: "I hate, I despise your feasts; and I take no delight in your solemn assemblies . . . but let justice roll down like waters, and righteousness like an ever-flowing stream" (Amos 5:21–24). This sensibility is carried over into the Talmud and expressed by a consistent permission to subordinate ritual requirements to urgent human needs. Ultimately, the rabbis ruled that any commandment could be disobeyed – except for the three foundational ones prohibiting idolatry, murder, or incest – in order to save a human life (TB Sanhedrin 74a).

There are at least four explanations for this odd pattern of affirming the equal bindingness of all commandments while giving operative priority to the moral ones. First, the rabbis could not formally impose a hierarchy among commandments that are laid down with undifferentiated obligatoriness in the Torah. If choices had to be made in favor of commandments protecting human beings and community life, this was to be done by means of interpretive reasoning rather than by a direct assault on the unity and revealed nature of the law. Second, the rabbis perceived that adhering to any commandment, ritual or moral, required the kind of self-discipline that was necessary for any striving toward moral integrity. Third, some of the commandments had both moral and ritual significance. This was particularly true of those dealing with sexuality. In both the Bible and Talmud, homosexual behavior, bestiality, and forms of incest are viewed not only as morally repugnant, but also as defiling the purity to which the holy people were called (Kirschner 1988). Fourth, obedience to all the commandments, even the most seemingly trivial and irrational, was understood in moral terms as a matter of loyalty. Throughout history, Jews suffered an unending succession of trials and hardships as a consequence of the cultural distinctiveness created by obedience to the law. To abandon that distinctiveness was construed as an act of betrayal of God and one's forbears.

Conclusion

In the medieval period, partly in response to the encounter of Jewish thinkers with other cultural traditions, Jewish treatises specifically devoted to "ethics" first make their appearance. In imitation of Greco-Roman or Christian ideas, many of these dwell on supra-legal norms and ideals, or stress moral self-development and personal virtue. Whether influenced by Aristotle or more closely rooted in Jewish values, however, these discussions do not represent the mainstream of Jewish ethics. Instead, this is found in the tradition of law that extends back to the Bible and forward into the ever-evolving tradition of *halakhic* deliberation.

Within this *halakhic* tradition, detailed laws or rulings governing all areas of life and lofty encouragements to saintly behavior exist side by side. What bound this together was the effort to produce a community that mirrored the perfection of a just and compassionate God. Sometimes, this effort fell short of its mark. But if this happened, it was because the task was so demanding and not because Judaism mistook law for ethics or placed ritual over ethics. Whenever it was necessary, Jewish thinkers showed themselves capable of responsibly and imaginatively ordering ritual, legal, and ethical norms. Nevertheless, they resisted the pressure to make these distinctions and continued to adhere to the Jewish vision of an organic unity of the moral, communal, and religious life.

Bibliography

All references to the Mishnah (M) are by tractate and citation. References to the Babylonian Talmud (TB) are to the edition by I. Epstein (London: Soncino Press, 1938–52).

Dorff, E. N. 2002: *To Do the Right and the Good: A Jewish Approach to Modern Social Ethics.* Philadelphia, PA: Jewish Publication Society.

Feldman, D. M. 1974: *Marital Relations, Birth Control, and Abortion in Jewish Law.* New York: Schocken Books.

Freedman, H. and Simon, M. (eds.) 1939: *Midrash Rabbah.* London: Soncino Press.

Green, R. 1988: *Religion and Moral Reason.* New York: Oxford University Press.

—— 1998: "Jewish Teaching on the Sanctity and Quality of Life" in *Jewish and Catholic Bioethics: An Ecumenical Dialogue*, ed. E. D. Pellegrino and A. I. Faden, 25–42. Washington, DC: Georgetown University Press.

—— 1999: "Religion and Bioethics" in *Notes from a Narrow Ridge*, ed. D. S. Davis and L. Zoloth-Dorfman, 165–81. Frederick, MD: University Publishing.

Kellner, M. M. 1978: "The Structure of Jewish Ethics" in *Contemporary Jewish Ethics*, ed. M. M. Kellner, 3–18. New York: Sanhedrin Press.

Kirschner, R. 1988: "Halakhah and Homosexuality: A Reappraisal." *Judaism* 37 (4), 450–8.

Lauterbach, J. Z. 1951: *Rabbinic Essays.* Cincinnati, OH: Hebrew Union College.

Novak, D. 1998: *Natural Law in Judaism.* Cambridge: Cambridge University Press.

Ross, J. 1968: "Morality and the Law." *Tradition* 10, 5–16.

Schulweis, H. M. 1995: "Judaism: From Either/Or to Both/And" in *Contemporary Jewish Ethics and Morality*, ed. E. N. Dorff and L. E. Newman, 25–37. New York: Oxford University Press.

Twersky, I. 1963: "Some Aspects of the Jewish Attitude Toward the Welfare State." *Tradition* 5 (2), 137–58.

Walzer, M., Lorberbaum, M., Zohar, N., and Lorberbaum, Y. (eds.) 2000: *Authority, Vol. 1: The Jewish Political Tradition.* New Haven, CT: Yale University Press.

CHAPTER 19

Ethics Differentiated from the Law

Shaul Magid

The field of Jewish ethics encompasses the entirety of the Jewish literary tradition, from the Bible to contemporary Jewish thought. However, while ancient and medieval Jewish texts speak of ethics, defined here simply as interhuman relations, it is arguably the case that "Jewish ethics" as a scholarly discipline is an exclusively modern phenomenon. Judaism is built on the foundation of covenant – a reciprocal relationship between God and the Israelite people forged in the desert of Sinai (see chapter 18). The fulcrum of the covenant is a system of mitzvot, commandments the Israelites and their descendants are obliged to guard and fulfill, thereby executing their covenantal relationship to God. In the Bible these mitzvot comprise both ritual and ethical acts without any inherent distinction between divine–human and interhuman commandments. In classical Judaism, the sages of the Talmud distinguish between divine–human and interhuman mitzvot. In the rabbinic mind, however, this distinction did not result in ethics as an independent category of mitzvot. Ethical mitzvot (interhuman commandments) were still viewed within the larger framework of Israel's covenantal relationship to God (divine–human commandments) (see M Yoma 8:9; BT Rosh ha-Shana 18b; Yoma 85b, 86b; cf. Maimonides *Mishneh Torah*, "Laws of Repentance," 2:8, 9).

In the middle ages, Jews began to rethink this distinction in light of exposure to other ethical systems. Moses Maimonides, for example, built his Jewish ethical theory on the golden mean of Aristotle, reread through the lens of classical Jewish sources, but still did not posit ethics as a sovereign realm of Jewish discourse (see *Mishneh Torah*, "Laws on Moral Dispositions," ch. 1). For Maimonides, ethics, even as it is rationally justified and philosophically constructed, is still always intertwined with Israel's covenantal relationship to God, resulting, *inter alia*, in a particularized hierarchy whereby ethics is defined differently between Jew and Jew and Jew and Gentile. While certainly more universal than the rabbis, Maimonides' philosophical ethics still does not break out of the rabbinic model that ties ethics to the divine–human realm (Dan 1986: 13). The question as to the universal nature and implementation of Jewish ethics and the formulation of ethics as independent of, although not in conflict with, human devotion to God (i.e., severing the dependence of interhuman relations to divine–human relations) is thus a product of modernity, specifically as formulated by Jews writing in light of the Enlightenment.

My concern in this chapter is not with the origin of Jewish ethics or how modernity impacts how Jews think (or can think) about ethics (Gibbs 2000). My intention is to question the conventional claim that Jewish ethics, even in modernity, is always framed in terms of its relationship to the law (*halakha*). The claim is that Judaism is reluctant, or perhaps unable, to construct an ethics not born out of, or already encompassed in, the performance of the law. I argue that Hasidism, a late eighteenth-century Jewish pietism built on the foundations of classical Jewish mysticism, disentangles ethics from the law by assuming that the law, while essential, does not and cannot fully cultivate the ethical personality. This chapter thereby explores a twofold "differentiation" in Jewish ethics: (1) the differentiation of Hasidic thought and practice from other forms of Judaism, and (2) the problem of the possibility of differentiating law and ethics in Jewish life.

Jewish Ethics and the Law: Contemporary Views

Traditional Judaism posits that *halakha* is the exclusive vehicle for devotional behavior, its fulfillment being the sum total of covenantal living. This is built on the foundation of the oft-cited rabbinic dictum that "God only dwells within the four ells of the law" (BT Berakhot 8a). In an attempt to address the relationship between ethics and the law, traditional Jewish thought, which is devoted to the all-encompassing nature of *halakha*, focuses on supererogatory behavior as a foundation for discussing Jewish ethics. Jews who advocate supererogation as part of, yet not identical to, *halakha*, argue that the origin of supererogation is rooted in the Bible. The Bible, in its delineation of specific rituals and positive law, also contains various general directives to behave beyond the letter of the law (see Lev. 19:2; Deut. 6:18; and Nahmanides' comment ad. loc.). However, the biblical exegetes who introduce this biblical charge of supererogation are quick to add the caveat that these directives, while more general than the law, are not outside and thus not independent of the law (see Halivni 1978; Sagi 1998: 230–56). One significant challenge to Jewish ethicists, especially those who write from a traditional and philosophical perspective, is how to forge a Jewish ethical system that protects the commandedness of *halakha* (its heteronymous origin, at least as depicted in classical Judaism) while affirming the principle of autonomy and human freedom basic to ethics. For this reason, law (*halakha*), understood as commandment, plays such a prominent role, and is such a serious problem, in any discussion of Jewish ethics (Siegel and Gertel 1977: 124–32). If ethics were completely outside the sphere of commandments (i.e., if there really were an "ethic independent of *halakha*"), how would ethical behavior be tied to the covenant of commandment forged at Sinai, and, more alarmingly, how would Jews protect the commandments from an external ethical critique?

In his seminal essay on Jewish ethics, Aaron Lichtenstein (1978) explores the notion of supererogatory behavior (*lifnim m'shurat ha-din* – beyond the letter of the law) in rabbinic and post-rabbinic legal code literature to determine whether and to what extent supererogation is part of the law. The sources indicate that if supererogation exists independent of the law (i.e., if it is not required or actionable), then the answer to the question as to whether Judaism accepts an ethic outside *halakha* would be affirmative. Lichtenstein's final answer is equivocal (1978: 119). He argues that *lifnim m'shurat hadin* is surely not simply *halakha* (if it were, then it would not be *lifnim* – beyond or inside). However, he continues, the sources indicate that supererogation is also not independent of the law. The rabbinic and post-rabbinic readings of biblical passages that refer to ethical behavior not tied to any specific mitzvah are absorbed into the larger halakhic system, occupying a special status in that system that Lichtenstein seeks to explore. What Lichtenstein accomplishes in acknowledging the need for a segment of the law to be "outside" normative *halakha* (supererogation), but to deny that segment any power to alter the halakhic system, is twofold. First, it tacitly acknowledges that formal law is, by itself, insufficient to produce ethics. Second, it protects the halakhic system from any ethical critique that cannot be justified within tradition. The distinction between law and ethics is maintained, albeit in an attenuated way, while the destabilizing potential to wage an ethical critique against the law is diffused.

This last point is precisely what others find so problematic in Lichtenstein's argument. By tying supererogation so intimately with *halakha*, Lichtenstein prevents the "ethical impulse" the rabbis wanted to cultivate in their readers from scrutinizing the construction of certain dimensions of the *halakha* itself. Eugene Borowitz (1987) argues that the ethical impulse so clearly a part of Rabbinic Judaism is stifled by Lichtenstein's analysis and that, without so much as saying so, the rabbis wanted us to look outside the law in order to strengthen it. Borowitz notes the status of women in Judaism as an example. While he essentially agrees "historically" with those who argue that "the so-called ethical impulse behind the women's issue is a gentile importation into Judaism," the "impulse" to offer supra-legal responses to ethical issues, even those born outside rabbinic discourse, is part of the spirit of Rabbinic Judaism's concept of supererogation (1987: 501; see also Rose 1993: 31–2). On the question as to whether there is an ethic independent of *halakha*, Borowitz claims there is an ethical impulse inside, and thus a part of, the *halakha* that may, at times, require Jews to look outside the *halakha* in order to resolve ethical issues that arise in the *halakha*. This is the case precisely with issues that arise as a result of our confrontation with other cultures and ethical systems.

David Novak takes this discussion in a different direction by stating, "if 'ethics' is defined prima facie as a system of rules governing interhuman relations, then 'Jewish' ethics is identified with Jewish law. It is *Halakha*" (1998: 63). He quickly rejects that identification. For Novak, the difference between ethics and law, and the independence of ethics from law, is that ethics is not about "rules" or "cases" (*halakha*), but about principals that govern how rules are determined. Ethics "is about governance and not just guidance" (1998: 76; see also Dan 1986: 2–5). That is, ethics is a kind of *ta'amei ha-mitzvot* (reasons for the commandments) that determines the meaning of the law but is not determined by it. While *ta'amei ha-mitzvot* only arises from a system of law, it is not bound by the specifics of the law and can offer rationalizations of the commandments that address larger universal claims (see Heinemen 1954; Stern 1998). *Ta'amei ha-mitzvot* consists of two major categories: the historical and the rational. The historical category determines laws (primarily ritual and communal laws) that are exclusive to those who share a particular historical experience (Jews). The rational category determines laws that have no historical basis but result from natural law. This is the category of Jewish ethics. "There can be no idea of natural law in Judaism unless there is an authentic Jewish ethics, part of which is not exclusive to Jews" (Novak 1998: 72).

While establishing a modern category of Jewish ethics through natural law, independent of and even determining the law, Novak laments what he sees as the modern Jewish attempt to conflate ethics with Judaism, making ethics the dominant if not exclusive expression of the Jewish covenantal experience. The destructive nature of the modern conflation of Judaism and ethics is that it destroys the covenant as constituted by tradition, a covenant that has God as the noumenal partner who, through mitzvot, mediates between himself (the ideal) and the real world. In equating Judaism with ethics, God becomes incarnate in the ethical ideal, fully realized and rationally (naturally) determined, leaving no unknowable covenantal partner with whom to relate. While this idea may be aligned with basic tenets of Christianity (incarnation and reconciliation), Novak argues it cannot be born out of Jewish sources (Wyschogrod 1983: 181–2). In this sense, Novak claims that thus far Judaism, traditionally construed, cannot survive the Kantian and post-Kantian critique without rejecting the very premises of that critique, premises that he believes are essentially true. Divine election, and Jewish particularism, cannot be forsaken, even for the sake of a universal ethics (see Sagi 1998: 316–34; Novak 1995: 50–77). However, universal ethics need not be sacrificed in order to maintain halakhic Judaism.

Novak strikes a kind of dialectical synthesis between Lichtenstein and Borowitz by locating Jewish ethics in a universal source (natural law), seemingly independent of *halakha*, yet functioning within the particularistic frame of the covenant (*halakha*). In this way, ethics can indeed criticize the law (Borowitz), but it cannot change the law without the law. That is, it cannot change the law unless that change can be validated and supported by a particularistic covenantal construction (i.e., via classical Jewish texts). This is not because ethics is a species of the law (Lichtenstein), but because Jewish ethics is the particularistic expression of the universal and must be validated through that particularistic lens.

The cases noted thus far typify the range of options in Jewish thought about "ethics" after the classical period. The law either limits (Lichtenstein), serves as the impulse for (Borowitz), or the contextual frame of (Novak), Jewish ethics. In the two Hasidic cases that follow, the question of *halakha* rarely arises. What is at stake is not the law or its performance (which are taken for granted), but a kind of existential disposition necessary to function as an ethical human being, understood in these texts simply as the ability to love another, be it God or the neighbor. The law, while remaining alive and sacred, is surreptitiously problematized in the pietistic and existential imagination of these Hasidic thinkers.

Hasidism: A Short Introduction

Hasidism can be described as a Jewish revivalist movement beginning in the last third of the eighteenth century in the provinces of Poldolia and Volhynia of Eastern Europe (what now constitutes parts of Poland and the Ukraine). Its enigmatic and mysterious founder, Rabbi Israel ben Eliezer, known as the Baal Shem Tov ("Master of the Good Name," 1700–60), used earlier Jewish traditions of kabbalah and medieval pietism as a foundation for a Jewish renewal of religious praxis based on joy (*simha*) and ecstatic devotion. The Baal Shem Tov's charismatic personality and his reputation as a faith healer and miracle worker attracted other Jewish mystics and pietists and even some prominent rabbinic figures to his circle of disciples (see Rosman 1996; Etkes 2000: 54–162). Many of these disciples became the inner circle of the Baal Shem Tov's admirers. After his passing in 1760, some of these figures began to develop pietistic circles of their own, migrating into the cities and environs of Poland, Lithuania, White Russia, Galicia, Hungary, and other parts of Eastern Europe, spreading the Baal Shem Tov's popular and populist message of serving God with joy, challenging the asceticism of earlier pietistic movements and the hierarchical rabbinical class structure that had come to dominate much of the traditional Eastern European Jewish landscape.

One of early Hasidism's great contributions to Jewish life and letters is its construction of a piety not dominated by the neoplatonic division of body–soul and matter–spirit, but on the search for God in the mundane and everyday. This resulted in, among other things, a kind of non-ascetic Jewish piety. While remaining committed to an ultra-traditionalist lifestyle, Hasidism widened the scope of how one can serve God and, in some very significant ways, problematized the rabbinic dictum cited earlier that "God only dwells in the four ells of the law." But like other movements in traditional Judaism, Hasidism does not have a word for ethics. In this sense it faithfully inherits the rabbinic and later pietistic traditions of the past. However, Hasidism understands "ethics" (interhuman relations) as an expression of an internal disposition that *halakha* alone cannot fully cultivate. *Halakha* is defined as the formal set of requirements each Jew is obligated to perform in order to live in a full covenantal relationship with God. While *halakha* may encourage such a disposition of piety – that is, it may have ethics as part of its goal – it does not formally (i.e., legally) require it. Moreover, the fulfillment of *halakha*, even in a supererogatory manner, may not always result in ethical behavior. The disposition that the following Hasidic texts speak of is one of absorbing divinity, allowing it to become so much a part of one's being that one acts in the world as divine and subsequently treats the world (both the individual and the collective) as divine.

R. Menahem Mendel of Vitebsk and incarnational ethics

It has often been said that Jewish ethics is an expression of the divine self/soul who relates to the "other" as a divine image, using the divine attributes of mercy and kindness as models for interhuman relations (BT Shabbat 133b; Sota 14a and Sifre "Torat Cohanim" to Leviticus, "Kedoshim," 86; see also Shapiro 1978: 127; Greenberg 1997: 387ff.). While this is surely supported by a myriad of sources, it is too simplistic a definition for Hasidism. For Hasidism, a Jewish pietism that focuses on the innate divinity of the person, the notion of divine image does not adequately capture its provocative position. R. Menahem Mendel of Vitebsk was a contemporary of the Baal Shem Tov and later became an influential part of the circle of the Maggid of Mezeritch (one of the spiritual heirs of the Baal Shem Tov). He immigrated to Palestine in 1777, living in Safed and Tiberias, where his collected writings and letters were completed. He is considered one of the most prominent figures in the first two generations of Hasidism.

His collected writings, entitled *Pri Ha-'Aretz* (lit. "fruits of the land"), presents a nuanced version of the Jewish idea of humanity's divine image and the part it plays in the expression of ethics (Mendel 1987). The first part of the text addresses the question of preliminaries; that is, what is the existential posture necessary to create the possibility of being overcome by the divine. What is suggested is a stance of absolute impotence, emptying oneself of will to make room for the influx, and subsequent incarnation, of God.

This preliminary state of absolute impotence is required because R. Menahem Mendel holds that the core of one's humanness is the autonomous will that invariably interprets human action as sovereign and severed from God. Human beings, acting as independent volitional agents, will always see their actions as sovereign and independent of God. As a result, humans *qua* human cannot love, because love is divine. God is love and only God can love. And the only object of love is God. Therefore, in order to love, and thus to act ethically, one must become filled with God – one must create the context allowing love (God) to descend and overcome the volitional self. This emerges from a creative rendering of a midrashic passage. In describing the simultaneity of God's transcendence and immanence, the midrash states: "God is the place of the world but the world is not his place" (Genesis Raba 78:9; Pesikta Rabati, 21). One half of this phrase is employed here, in one variant subtly substituting "world" for "humankind." That is, God's true residence in this world is the human being (see Vital 1864: 182d).

To be fully human is to become God-like. For R. Menahem Mendel, this requires the dissolution of volition. This experience of radical indwelling, which I maintain crosses over into incarnation, has two immediate consequences: first, it experientially affirms the human impotence that was merely posited earlier; second, and more importantly, it enables the individual to love.

> This [expression of] love results in connecting him to all creatures (*b'eyi 'olam*) and all human beings after realizing that this love is a love of grace that he did not merit in his own soul (M. Rosh Ha-Shana 1:2; Maimonides, *Mishneh Torah*, "Laws of Sabbatical and Jubilee Years" 13:13; and "Laws of Kings" 8:10). This is because it is impossible to create or merit this divinity. It is the will of God that it is given as a gift. If he gives this gift of love to another, his friend would be similarly inspired. And, his friend would realize that this gift is not from him [but from God]. (Mendel 1987: 121, 122)

This experience of incarnation enables one to love all things because one sees how all things, even those that are evil (i.e., transgressors), share a divine source. The difference between one who loves and transgressors is that the latter have not yet opened themselves up to the experience of "incarnation" (divine indwelling) and still see themselves acting independent of God. One's ability to elevate those souls is equal to one's ability to love, for love, being divine, is that which elevates (elevation here being the act that reunites a thing with its source).

This ability is not procured simply by following the law. In fact, the law presents certain challenges to this ideal because the practitioner can easily err in seeing herself as an autonomous agent.

> This is not the case with one who envisions himself as having the autonomy and strength to study and fulfill the entire Torah. This person is considered as one who hates Jews and "it is as if he has no God" (Babylonian Talmud, Avodah Zara, 17b). He is surely worse than all the transgressors, *like a troubled sea* (Isaiah 57:20) (see BT Sota 8a). This person empowers the demonic forces more than all transgressors and descends to the greatest depths. This individual is a *querulous man* (Proverbs 18:8, 26:22) who *alienates his neighbor* (Proverbs 17:9). He severs the trait of fear, which is the Shekhina (divine presence) from all of life by saying "This is not divine but the work of my hands." Thus Hillel the Sage, who surely was a very humble man, said, "If I ('*ani*) am here everything is here' (BT, Sukkah, 53a). That is, in every place Hillel finds himself, he finds all of humankind – [because he realizes that] he is like one of them and it is only God who is his redeemer. When he ascends, they all ascend with him. (Mendel 1987: 122)

This admonishment of autonomous righteousness is quite stark and uncharacteristically framed around the practitioner of Torah and mitzvot. Why is this righteousness ("fulfilling the entire Torah") worse than transgression, and why is such a person one "who hates Jews" and "one who has no God"?

The basis of these comments is taken from the conventional kabbalistic idea that the demonic is empowered by utilizing the holy (Torah and mitzvot) (see Vital and Agasi 1990: 122–5; Tishby 1984: 28–32). Autonomous righteousness can only be false (and thus demonic) because, as autonomous (i.e., without God), it cannot be based on love. Such a person "hates Jews" because the Torah she lives is an expression of Torah without love, love only being possible through "incarnation." A Torah without love does not result in elevation (of the self or another) but descent ("and [he] descends to the greatest depths"). R. Menahem Mendel seems to be saying that hatred is exclusively a human trait, perhaps subtly invoking Genesis 6:5, whereas only the divine can love. Therefore, in order for humankind to love, it must become divine, or at least be overcome with its own divinity.

Having established an incarnational ethics whereby love is dependent on the realization of one's inner divinity, R. Menahem Mendel turns back to the question of how that posture is cultivated.

> One must [always] contemplate: who do I fear? It is God, who fills all possible worlds, without whom nothing exists. What is the source of my existence? It is God. Where I am destined to go? Toward God. If that is so, what am I? There is no fear except the fear of God's glory. When one achieves this fear he will comprehend that it is also created by God and contains divine effluence, without which it would not exist. If one draws down this fear of God from its lofty place it will become compacted [in human experience] as love because any divine life force that is drawn down and implanted in this world is love. This will evoke love of God, resulting in "the descent of a thread of grace from the source of blessing" (Babylonian Talmud Hagigah 12b). From there, *you will be like a watered garden, like a spring whose waters do not fail* (Isaiah 58:11). (Mendel 1987: 122)

"Who am I?" I am God's residence on earth, which enables me to love others whose divine potential I can also see. This love is the basis of ethics for R. Menahem Mendel because only love creates love, resulting in an interhuman (ethical) world that is really a Divine–divine world. To love is to be (fully) God-like, for only then can the divine in others be recognized. To be God-like is to be full of God and empty of self – it is to be incarnate.

R. Levi Isaac of Berditchev: Ethics and the universalization of the covenant

R. Levi Isaac of Berditchev, a younger contemporary of R. Menahem Mendel, is one of the most celebrated disciples of the Maggid of Mezeritch. His collected teachings, entitled *Kedushat Levi*, remains a popular and important work of the early period of Hasidism. R. Levi Isaac attempts to reframe the relationship between the divine–human and interhuman realm first suggested in the Talmud. In doing so, he argues for an ethics built on the foundation of unity – first the unity of God, and second the unity of humanity (or, at least, the community that recognizes divine unity). The covenant and its ethical expression is an outgrowth of that dual unity. The first unity creates the possibility for the second; the second unity serves as the earthly embodiment of the first. The surprising end to this approach is that the transference from the divine to the collective results in the universalization of the covenant, or the Judaization of humanity.

R. Levi Isaac begins by juxtaposing two seemingly contradictory passages in the Talmud.

> On the rabbinic dictum "[the aspiring convert asked Hillel the Sage] 'Teach me all of the Torah on one foot.' Hillel the Sage responds 'what you would hate another to do to you, do not do to him.'" (TB Shabbat 31a)

> Other rabbinic sages teach that the first commandments *I am the Lord your God* and *Do not have any other gods before me* were both heard from the mouth of God (*m'pi ha-gevurah*) (see TB Makkot 24b; TB Horayot 8a; Exodus Raba 33:7). [This means] the entire Torah is included in them. That is, all its reasons and secret hints are included in the notion of divine unity (*ahdut ha-Shem*) [as expressed in those two commandments]. All the reasons are hinted at [in these two commandments] in order that we recognize them when we bind ourselves and serve the Creator. So it is that all the esoteric teachings teach that all the mitzvot only serve to teach us of the unity of God. (Isaac 1992: 141a/b)

Given the opportunity to "teach the *entire Torah* on one foot," Hillel cites a negative version of "Love your neighbor as yourself" (Leviticus 19:18), one of the standard biblical verses employed to define Jewish ethics (see *Sefer Mitzvot Gedolot* (SM'G), positive commandment no. 9; and *Sefer Ha-Hinukh*, commandment no. 243).

However, R. Levi Isaac continues, we have another talmudic dictum that states that the *entire Torah* was communicated and is embodied in the first two commandments, referring to the doctrine of divine unity (*ahdut ha-Shem*). If this is so, why didn't Hillel cite these two commandments and their interpretation to the aspiring convert? He answers by interpreting the talmudic distinction of divine–human and interhuman mitzvot.

However, it is widely known that the mitzvot of the Torah are divided into two distinct categories. The first category is mitzvot between Israel and their Father in Heaven, such as ritual fringes (*zizit*), phylacteries (*tefillin*), and sacrifices (*korbanot*). The other category is mitzvot that are interhuman, which can be encapsulated in *Love your neighbor as yourself* (Leviticus 19:18), as it says, "Rabbi Akiba says, this [*Love your neighbor . . .*] is the great principle of the Torah" (Palestinian Talmud, Nedarim, p. 30b). We must understand that interhuman mitzvot are included in the principle of divine unity, as we said *I am the Lord Your God*, and *Do not have any other gods . . .* were heard directly from the mouth of God and encompass the entire Torah. (Isaac 1992: 141b)

The foundation of ethics presented here (Hillel's remark) is the result of the transference of the divine unity realized at Sinai to the unity of Israel as one body. When R. Levi Isaac says, "we must understand that interhuman mitzvot are included in the principle of divine unity," he means that the interhuman, as Hillel frames it, is only possible by first realizing divine unity through the first two commandments (Sinai). The consequence of realizing that unity is the realization of the unity of the community as one body. We act ethically toward our neighbor (here, only our Israelite neighbor) because we identify with him or her as part of the unified self that is forged at Sinai (hearing the first two commandments). The covenant with God fostered through the recognition of divine unity is the basis of the covenant with human beings fostered through the realization that any community that recognizes divine unity is "a community that stands as one."

Up to this point R. Levi Isaac supports the normative idea that covenant and divine election underlie the foundation of Jewish ethics. The commandment "love thy neighbor," as interpreted by the rabbis, refers only to the Israelite neighbor and Israel is defined as that collective and their progeny who share, either directly or by proxy, the historical experience of Sinai (*ahdut ha-Shem*). This is necessary as only Israel, who hear the first two commandments, has a notion of the community as a unified body that makes religious ethics possible. From our earlier discussion of different approaches of relating law and ethics, this would support an ethics that exists within and not independent of *halakha*, both born out of a shared experience at Sinai.

However, R. Levi Isaac does not stop here. He is curious about why the rabbinic discussion of Hillel's declaration of Jewish ethics is framed in a conversation with an aspiring convert. Turning from Hillel's answer to the underlying premise of the convert's question, R. Levi Isaac problematizes the idea that election, and thus ethics ("love thy neighbor"), is limited to the original community at Sinai. The aspiring convert wants to know how interhuman relations (ethics) are connected to divine–human relations. He knew that one need not be Jewish to be ethical or to serve God. Being Jewish here is now defined precisely as understanding the dependence of ethics on divine unity (*ahdut ha-shem*). According to R. Levi Isaac's reading, the convert in this talmudic passage serves as a metaphor for those civilizations that did not experience the historical beneficence of the Sinai covenant but desired to understand how ethics relates to depiction of that Sinaitic God.

Hillel's answer is that ethics is born out of a realization of the unity of the human community that emerges out of the Sinaitic revelation (the unity of God). Ethics results from the transference of divine unity to humankind that is born out of a particular collective human experience of God. While Sinai provides this for Israel, the realization of divine unity can also be cultivated in reverse, that is, by first realizing the unity of the human community and, by extension, the unity of God. This seems to be R. Levi Isaac's idea of conversion. Instead of conversion simply being the ability of others to share in the historical covenant of Israel, R. Levi Isaac suggests that conversion, in an expansive sense, is the deconstruction of the particularistic nature of divine election – or, the substitution of the historical for the universal. "Therefore, all the nations (ha-'amim) must become one nation ('am ehad)." This is a creative play on the prophetic declaration that, "in that day, the Lord will be One and His Name will be one" (Zechariah 14:9). Universal recognition of divine unity, and universal religion, is realized by the recognition of the unity of humankind, the place where the historical meets and is subsumed in the universal. "This will result in the transformation of all nations to a nation of God." Becoming one nation through ethics results in the universal realization of divine unity and the completion of the Israelite mission to the world.

That is why Hillel responds to the convert with "love your neighbor" (the universal) and does not bring up the first two commandments (the historical). Those commandments only work for those who heard them directly from God (Israel). For those at Sinai, the experience and completion of divine unity must translate into ethics via the transference of divine unity to the unity of the community. For those not at Sinai, however, the way to that unity begins in ethics, culminating in the transference of humankind's unity to divine unity. When the non-Israelite community realizes this connection, both communities actually meet and become 'am ehad via living the ethical ideal as one community – it is just that they begin from opposite places.

Conclusion

This brief presentation of two examples of Hasidic ethics disentangled from halakha serves as an alternative model to the contemporary discussions of Jewish ethics discussed in the first section of this chapter. R. Menahem Mendel suggests that ethics is an outgrowth of divine love achieved through a kind of incarnation of God into the emptied human vessel. This love serves to elevate all of creation by evoking the divinity in one's neighbor as a recipient of that love, that is, in receiving God's grace. In this case, while the law may indeed serve as an obligatory and necessary component for the Jew, the law does not produce or even cultivate this love – this love is achieved via supra-legal means, through contemplation and the practice of emptying the self of one's ego and will. In R Menahem Mendel's reading, the rabbinic dichotomy between divine–human and interhuman collapses into a "trinitarian" relation. The divine self is completed via incarnation in the individual and, as divine, discovers and relates to the divinity in the other through love. Love of God and love of the neighbor become fused.

In the three contemporary approaches to law and ethics discussed in the first section, ethics was tied very tightly to the mitzvot (halakha), either as part of the system of halakha (Lichtenstein), implied in the spirit of the halakha (Borowitz), or that the halakha, as covenantal expression, was the particularistic frame of ethics (Novak's "postmodern" alternative that presented ethics as natural law and Jewish ethics as part of divine election). R. Menahem Mendel's approach, while not directly addressing these constructions, offers a model of ethics that is, in a significant way, "independent of *halakha*."

R. Levi Isaac's text is more relevant to our modern interpreters, as he directly addresses the rabbinic dichotomy of divine–human and interhuman mitzvot. Instead of simply locating interhuman relations in divine–human relations, something that David Novak claims is fundamental to classical Judaism and largely disappears in modern Jewish ethics, R. Levi Isaac presents interhuman relations for Israel ("love thy neighbor") as an outgrowth of divine–human relations ("I am the Lord your God"), but uses that correlation to construct a universal message of Judaism that, if manifested successfully, deconstructs the particularistic formulation of divine election. The inter-human moves beyond being exclusive to Israel and includes anyone who recognizes the unity of God, even as that unity is achieved through ethics (the universal) and not via Sinai (the historical). For the non-Israelite who did not (and does not) partake in the historical covenant at Sinai, interhuman relations are the source for divine–human relations (i.e., Hillel's answer to the convert). Moreover, the success of this universal message to the convert is that Israel and the rest of humanity forge one world com-munity, all elected because they all recognize the unity of God, each feeling equally obligated to live ethically. While the historical roots of each community may remain distinct (an issue R. Levi Isaac never addresses), the shared recognition of the unity of God creates a universal ethics out of the transference of divine unity to the human community and vice versa. If this is not an ethic "independent of *halakha*" it is surely an ethic that transcends *halakha*, because it applies to those who have no share in the historical roots of the halakhic system.

This chapter does not claim to offer a definitive account of Hasidic ethics. What it claims is that Hasidism, seen through the window of these select texts, offers a vision of ethics disentangled, albeit not severed, from the law. Both examples subtly criticize the notion of the exclusivity of the law as the sum total of Jewish living. Whereas even modern thinkers, in different ways, wed ethics to the law, these Hasidic texts offer an alternative showing how the ethical personality is cultivated and nurtured in Judaism. By disentangling ethics from the law, Hasidism challenges some basic conventions about Judaism, both as envisioned from within and from without. The breakdown of those conventions may provide new ways of thinking comparatively about Jewish ethics as part of the larger discourse in the study of religion.

Bibliography

All references to the Mishnah (M) are by tractate and citation. References to the Babylonian Talmud (TB) are to the edition by I. Epstein (London: Soncino Press, 1938–52). All transla-tions are by the author.

Borowitz, E. 1987: "The Authority of the Ethical Impulse in 'Halakha'" in *Studies in Jewish Phi-losophy: Collected Essays of the Academy for Jewish Philosophy, 1980–1985*, ed. N. M. Samuel-son, 489–505. Lanham, MD: University Press of America.

Dan, J. 1986: *Jewish Mysticism and Jewish Ethics*. Seattle: University of Washington Press.

Etkes, I. 2000: *Ba'al ha-shem: ha-Besht – magyah, mistikah, hanhagah* [Ba'al Hashem: The Besht – Magic, Mysticism, Leadership]. Jerusalem: Merkaz Zalman Shazar le-toldot Yisra'el.

Gibbs, R. 2000: *Why Ethics?: Signs of Responsibilities*. Princeton, NJ: Princeton University Press.

Greenberg, I. 1997: "Seeking the Religious Roots of Pluralism: In the Image of God and Covenant." *Journal of Ecumenical Studies* 34 (3), 387–94.

Halivni, W. 1978: "Can a Religious Law be Immoral" in *Perspectives on Jews and Judaism*, ed. Arthur A. Chiel. New York: Rabbinical Assembly of America.

Heinemen, I. 1954: *Ta'amei ha-Mitzvot b' Sifrut Yisrael*, Vol. 1. Jerusalem: Ha-Mador Ha-Dati.

Isaac, R. Levi. 1992: *Sefer Kedushat Levi ha-Shalem: bi-sheloshah halakim*. Jerusalem: Makhon Kedushat Levi.

Lichtenstein, A. 1978: "Does Jewish Tradition Recognize an Ethic Independent of Halakha?" in *Contemporary Jewish Ethics*, ed. M. M. Kellner, 102–23. New York: Sanhedrin Press.

Mendel, R. M. 1987: *Pri Ha-'Aretz*. Jerusalem: Mesorah Press.

Novak, D. 1995: *The Election of Israel: The Idea of the Chosen People*. Cambridge: Cambridge University Press.

——1998: *Natural Law in Judaism*. Cambridge: Cambridge University Press.

Rose, G. 1993: *Judaism and Modernity: Philosophical Essays*. Oxford: Blackwell.

Rosman, M. J. 1996: *Founder of Hasidism: A Quest for the Historical Ba'al Shem Tov*. Berkeley: University of California Press.

Sagi, A. 1998: *Yahadut: Bein Dat l'Mussar* [Judaism: Between Religion and Morality]. Tel Aviv: Ha-Kibbutz Ha-me'uhad.

Shapiro, D. 1978: "The Doctrine of the Image of God and *Imitatio Dei*" in *Contemporary Jewish Ethics*, ed. M. M. Kellner, 127–61. New York: Sanhedrin Press.

Siegel, S. and Gertel, E. (eds.) 1977: *Conservative Judaism and Jewish Law*. New York: Rabbinical Assembly.

Stern, J. 1998: *Problems and Parables of Law: Maimonides and Nahmanides on Reasons for the Commandments (Ta'amei Ha-Mitzvot)*. Albany: State University of New York Press.

Tishby, I. 1984: *Torat ha-Ra'Veha-Kelipah be-Kabalat ha-Ari* [The Doctrine of Evil and the "Kelippah" in Lurianic Kabbalism]. Jerusalem: Magnes Press.

Vital, R. H. 1864: *'Etz Ha-Da'at Tov*. Zolkiew: n.p.

Vital, R. H. and Agasi, S. A. 1990: *Sha'ar Ha-gilgulim: Hu Ha-Sha'ar Ha-Shemini Mi-Shemonah She'arim*. Jerusalem: Keren hotsa'at sifre rabane Bavel.

Wyschogrod, M. 1983: *The Body of Faith: Judaism as Corporeal Election*. New York: Seabury Press.

CHAPTER 20

From Law to Ethics...
and Back

Nancy Levene

R. Simlai said: Six hundred and thirteen commandments were given to Moses, 365 negative commandments answering to the number of days of the year, and 248 positive commandments answering to the number of a person's members.

Then David came and reduced them to eleven: "Lord, who shall dwell in Your taberna-
cle? Who shall sojourn in Your holy mountain? He that walks uprightly, works righteousness, speaks truth in his heart; has no slander upon his tongue, nor does evil to his fellow,
nor reproaches his neighbor; in whose eyes a vile person is despised, but honors those who
fear the Lord. He swears to his own heart and doesn't change. He does not lend his money
on interest, nor take a bribe against the innocent. He that does these things shall never be
moved." [Ps. 15]

Then came Isaiah, and reduced them to six: "He that walks righteously, and speaks
uprightly, he that despises oppressors, who shakes his hand from bribes, who stops his ear
from hearing about bloodshed, and shuts his eyes so as not to see evil – he shall dwell on
high." [Isa. 33:15–16]

Then came Micah, and reduced them to three: "It has been told you, O man, what is
good, and what the Lord requires of you: only to do justly, and to love mercy, and to walk
humbly before your God." [Mic. 6:8]

Then Isaiah came again, and reduced them to two: "Thus says the Lord: keep justice
and do righteousness." [Isa. 56:1]

Then came Amos, and reduced them to one: "Seek the Lord and live" [Amos 5:4]. Or
one may say, then came Habakkuk, and reduced them to one: "The righteous shall live by
their faith." [Hab. 2:4]

Babylonian Talmud, Makkot 24a

(Trans. excerpted in Borowitz and Schwartz 1999: 222–3)

It is sometimes worthwhile simply to pause over a text such as this one from Makkot,
a talmudic tractate devoted to the judicial procedures concerning false witnesses and
other prohibitions. It provides a striking window into classical Jewish reflection on the
relationship of law and ethics, quite in contrast to what one finds in contemporary
literature, which is beset by such questions as: What do law and ethics have to do with

each other? How should they be related? How can one think about the relationship between them without feeling the pressure of Christian appraisals of the law? Is there an ethics outside of law? A law outside of ethics? Should there be? These questions are in fact only the tip of a rather large iceberg (see Lichtenstein 1978: 222–3; Kellner 1978; Dorff and Newman 1995; Fox 1975; Newman 1995; Gibbs 2000; Goodman 1998; Rose 1993). "What iceberg?" ask the rabbis of Makkot, and in one creative exegetical gesture, bring what seems a perfectly lucid ancient solution to a modern problem. Or is it a modern solution to an ancient problem?

I want to offer a few reflections on this suggestive text before moving to the question of how one might think about contemporary trajectories in Jewish ethics in light of rabbinic reasoning. There will be some interesting cross-pollinations: Judaism, Kant, the rabbis, modernity. It is frequently Kant who gets blamed for bifurcating, for ruining, what the Talmud holds together (law, ethics), and Kant who thus occupies a kind of negative centrality in Jewish thought. Kant, the stranger to Judaism, is the one who makes it so painfully clear why Jews are forever strangers in the modern West. Or so it is usually argued. I want to say something else: that Kant has much more in common with the Hebrew Bible and the Talmud than one might think, and this is to notice at least three curious things: (1) that "modernity" may be a concept that is indigenous to a Judaism that originates in antiquity; (2) that Kant's Enlightenment may be less a threat to Jewish thought than a working out of its central premises; and (3) that the traditional historiography of Judaism that sees modernity as an unwelcome divorce from a medieval world that successfully integrates law and ethics may need to be entirely reversed. I cannot prove these claims in any detail in this chapter, but I want to raise them as food for thought.

An Arrestingly Simple Logic

According to the text quoted above, the commandments given to Moses numbered 613, divided into positive and negative laws – for example, keep the Sabbath with joy in your heart and refrain from work on that day. Here is what we call in English "the law" – those things that are to guide conduct, restrain passion, and promote fellowship and social harmony in the spheres of family, civil society, and polity (with rabbinic interpretations, they ultimately number far more than 613).

What happens next? "Then David came and reduced [*he'emidan*] them to eleven," a trope that is then repeated throughout the remaining five paragraphs. Each successive reduction involves bringing a biblical passage which comments upon the previous one and leads to the next, culminating in the final passage in which there is only one commandment, interpreted variously in Amos and Habakkuk. The effect of the whole is of a seamless commentary on Jewish values, which begins with the law, condenses this law ever more potently into ethical maxims, and then arguably (suggestively, indirectly) reopens law at the end through the notions of "life" and "faith." It is also, not incidentally, a condensation of what Jews call the Tanakh (Bible), containing words of "Torah" (the five books of Moses), "Nevi'im" (prophets), and "Kethubim" (writings, or wisdom literature). Finally, and perhaps most importantly, its words are biblical – the Bible (all three components) being the touchstone for ethical reasoning in Judaism, yet its "composition" is rabbinic ("R. Simlai said") – the rabbis of the Talmud being the preeminent source of law in the tradition.

To be sure, what I am calling "seamless" here is not quite as it seems. The key depends on the interpretation of the word *he'emidan*, to reduce, to found. Reduction implies paring down. But why do that? We are given 613 commandments. Is this too many? Is nine easier to understand? Is six easier than nine? Is ease of understanding even the issue? Reduction has other meanings. To reduce is to concentrate, as in here is the law in its essence. But why essence? Does this help to follow it better? Is it to motivate, or perhaps to explain the law to others?

One might fruitfully trace the entire history of Jewish ethical reasoning through the various avenues opened by this single passage. Taken alone, it has the tone of responding to a general question, such as "how should a person live?" One might deduce, from the source of the compilation and from the surrounding narratives of the revelation on Mount Sinai, that the passage only concerns Jews, but there is otherwise no indication that there is a specific audience intended. On the basis of the passage alone, Moses could be understood to be God's emissary for all persons, and the revealed commandments relevant to all.

This ambiguity is noteworthy, because one well-attested way of distinguishing law from ethics – and indeed what is often at stake in doing so – is to claim that law (or positive law) refers to a particular people, while ethics (or natural law) is universalizable. Hence, to move from law to ethics in this case is to move from Judaism to all the nations, without any clear sense of how to move back. On this reading, what is happening with the reduction is that the yoke of the law given to Moses is instantly relieved by David – law is *translated* into ethics without remainder – and from then on it is a matter of acquiring a list of qualities (uprightness, honesty, integrity, goodheartedness, humility, and so on) rather than obeying a set of prescriptions. Alternatively, one could read the translation as internal to law itself – what is translated is not law *into* ethics, but legal prescriptions into legal norms and maxims. In this latter version, one moves from law as commandment to ethics as one might move from the US Constitution to its Bill of Rights (amendments), a movement of greater generality within a single class. It follows that there would still be a need to ask how one moves back – that is, how one holds together the ultra-general with the ultra-specific – but this is presumably far less strenuous than trying to retrieve the law having moved in a unidirectional flight away from it.

These are two of many interpretations possible, but they do capture a tension that the passage makes no effort to hide (see Novak 1998). It almost seems to dare the reader to take the antinomian way out, declaring that since faith and righteousness are what the commandments *amount to*, they themselves are not necessary. But the passage evinces no particular concern about this conclusion, and it would be left to later rabbis and philosophers to close off this option. On its face, there is no compelling reason to read it in an antinomian way, no reason to agonize about whether ethics goes further than or takes one away from the law, or whether one of them translates or interprets the other out of existence, or into existence, or neither. We have Moses and we have Amos and Habakkuk, and everything in between, and it is all as "R. Simlai said." The law can be reduced to ethics, and, one gets the sense, ethics can be reduced to law (or would one speak of reconstitution here?), and this is as it should be.

But, of course, Jews *have* agonized. One could even say that the history of Jewish ethics just is this agonizing. In part this is due to the proximity of Christianity through the ages, and its claim to "fulfill" the law through ethics (see Gal. 2:16; Rom. 3:31). If Judaism, then, is going to have an "ethics," it cannot be sovereign; it cannot lead away, but must in fact lead back to the law. With the advent of liberal Judaism and the philosophies of the Jewish enlightenment, this defensiveness was turned inward as Jewish defenders of the centrality of law battled those who pushed ethics – in the form of ethical monotheism – to the fore. In all cases there is this palpable anxiety concerning – in the language of our passage – the move from Moses to David, as if the movement is one of stepping off a cliff. Where is one going? How might one get back . . . to the law? For it *is* about law, as even R. Simlai knew – without it, there is no ethics. And it *is*, equally, about ethics, as R. Simlai knew – without it, there is no law. I will come back to this point in due course. Let me turn now to the question of trajectories in Jewish ethics.

The Modern Challenge: Law to Ethics

The greatest challenge of thinking through trajectories in Jewish ethics is confronting the modern history of the term, which has tended to interpret the reduction in our passage literally – as an act of diminution. More precisely, law and ethics have been siphoned off as independently existing entities, with ethics emerging as the prime focus of philosophical energy. From Immanuel Kant, of course, we are bequeathed the notion that a true ethics is one that is independent of any modifier: there can be no "Jewish" ethics, just as there can be no "French" or "left-wing" or "feminist" ethics. From modern Judaism, and especially from Kant's strongest Jewish reader Hermann Cohen, we are bequeathed the contrary notion that ethics must be grounded in its sources, that is, it must emerge out of the reasoning of a people, community, set of texts, and life-world (see Cohen 1995). One hesitates to see this as a distinction between autonomy (independence, universality) and heteronomy (dependence, particularity), since to do so would seem already to grant to Kant the terms of the debate, and thus to privilege the autonomy he privileges, to the distinct disadvantage of Judaism (*pace* Cohen). But for modern readers, unlike for R. Simlai and his cohort, there may be no easy way to avoid the question that Kant raises for us, namely, how is Jewish ethics possible? (See chapter 17.)

The question is not only whether Judaism (or any tradition) can count as generating a foundational ethics if it clings to the communal priority of its own members; the question is also can Judaism provide an ethics that is achievable? As Kant is wont to put it, human beings *ought* to be ethical, therefore they must be able to be (Kant 1960: 55). This simple statement is crucial for Kant because it rules out the classical project of *imitatio Dei*, the imitation of God that, according to the Jewish and Christian Bibles, was to constitute the highest human end. While the Christian story of the life of God in Jesus may have seemingly made this imitation more doable, the injunction comes from God's words to the Israelites in Leviticus 19:2: "You shall be holy [*kadosh*], for I, your God, am holy." Both Jews and Christians have had to struggle with this exhortation, for the narratives in which God acts in both traditions are various, complex, and sometimes contradictory. Kant wanted to do away with the uncertainty of this project altogether, though not with imitation per se. In his model, it is the moral human being I am to imitate in my conduct, and I need look no further for the model than my own heart. Prima facie this would seem to insist that insofar as Judaism has an "ethics," this ethics cannot be (solely) Jewish.

Of course, Kant is not the only thinker to dominate ethical reasoning in the modern world, and certainly the starkness of his ethics, and responses to this starkness, are attested elsewhere in Western philosophy. Indeed, the struggles over what counts as ethical in the West have historically tended to vacillate between satisfying the condition of universality as Kant understood it and attending to the particular details and priorities of a given situation or community – a given ethos (see chapter 15). Yet Kant was enormously influential for modern Jewish philosophy, and more importantly, the particular problem he addressed is one that goes to the heart of the project of "reducing" Jewish ethics (Seeskin 2001). The question is not only the alternation of ethos versus universality. The question is whether Jewish ethics presents another case study in this same alternation, or does it add yet a third condition – the "religious" – that disturbs the relationship between human and human assumed both by ethics rooted in ethos and ethics as universality?

The provisional answer to this question has to be yes: Jewish ethics is religious ethics, and therefore presents to the Kantian position a particular kind of counterview. At the very least, and again, these terms are Kant's, it involves the distinction between rooting the source of obligation in God and conceiving the end of ethics to culminate in God. Kant insisted on the propriety of the second as strongly as he took issue with the first. If God is the source, he reasoned, I am not solely the author of my own moral actions. It is not just that I would be acting morally *for* God but that my ability to act morally would be dependent on a being other than myself (see chapter 19). For Kant, Jewish ethics is not possible because ethics just means independence and independent is the one thing the partners to a covenant with a law-giving God seem not to be (see Seeskin 2001: 233).

The question is, though: Is Kant's question – "How is Jewish ethics possible?" – a Jewish one? Need Jewish ethics respond to a critique that challenges its most foundational terms – that assails its right to reveal a uniquely Jewish contribution to the problems and challenges that beset the achievement of moral aims and conduct? In asking, moreover, whether Kant's question is Jewish – more specifically, whether it can be justified in Jewish terms and/or whether Jews do or should ask it – a second series of questions seems also to come to the fore. What is modern about Jewish ethics? How has modernity impacted ethical reasoning in Judaism and how has Judaism impacted ethical reasoning in modernity? (See chapter 5.) This connection between Kant, Judaism, and modernity was suggested historically by the Jewish philosopher Moses Mendlessohn, whose final Jewish work, *Jerusalem*, contended (in so many words) that Kant's universalism posed no problem at all for Judaism. Jews, like all other rational beings, were able to attain the knowledge of universal truths (such as the moral law) irrespective of tradition, while tradition, in the form of a revealed law, could give sustenance to Jews on their path towards holiness (Mendelssohn 1983: 126–39). In his own way Mendelssohn dismissed the possibility of religious ethics altogether by making religion and ethics part of distinct and irreconcilable conceptual planes.

Contemporary Options?

For Jewish ethics, then, Kant presents a singular challenge, even for those thinkers who *mutatis mutandis* aligned themselves with his worldview. The thinkers most committed to retrieving Jewish ethics from the narrowness of the modern debates initiated by Mendelssohn and Kant have been those who refuse the Kantian question altogether. For Martin Buber and Emmanuel Levinas, the question of the nature of *Jewish* ethics is not even asked. What they both ask is, simply, what is ethical? What does the ethical demand of me now and what will it demand of me tomorrow? Both draw freely on classical Jewish sources, but neither could be said to be reasoning *out of* these sources in the way that Hermann Cohen is. For the Buber of the classic work *I and Thou*, "in the beginning is relation," a "wholeness," he says, in which "persons are still embedded like reliefs without achieving the fully rounded independence of nouns and pronouns. What counts is not these products of analysis and reflection but the genuine original unity, the lived relationship" (Buber 1970: 69–70). Levinas expresses something similar in the dense knots of his *Totality and Infinity* (1961) when he speaks of the ethical (which one accesses as metaphysics) as the foundation of existence: "Metaphysics, transcendence, the welcoming of the other by the same, of the Other by me, is concretely produced as the calling into question of the same by the other, that is, as the ethics that accomplishes the critical essence of knowledge" (1961: 43; see chapter 12, this volume). At the heart of these works is a conception of ethics as "first philosophy," as the groundwork, the primordial place of origin, out of which all human possibility, as well as corruption, emerges (Levinas 1989). Both thinkers also have their "Jewish" works in which they grapple explicitly with concepts like covenant, revelation, tradition, law, and text (see Buber 1967; Levinas 1990a, 1990b, 1994). But their commitment to an ethical refashioning of philosophy is what each most contributes to modern thought. In a curious way, it could be said that in refusing the Kantian question, each is following Kant in his insistence that ethics not be hyphenated. Their Judaism can be seen to impact their thinking in the same way that Kant's Protestant Christianity impacted his, providing simply a vocabulary, a set of values, a vernacular (see chapter 24).

But something plagues these Jewish standpoints (beyond the charge that they are not Jewish enough), as it plagued Kant. The translation of law into ethics – or ethics into law – still sees the ethical as something to be retrieved, something disconnected from the ordinary, even (or precisely) as it is placed at the center of thinking. "When man truly approaches the Other," Levinas writes, "he is uprooted from history" (1961: 52). There is a flavor of overcompensation here, as if "otherness" can coexist with "history" only by (provisionally) banishing it. Like the distinctions between ethics and law, or even Athens and Jerusalem, Greek and Jew, German and Jew, there is the sense that in modernity the terms are straining away from each other at the very moment of contact (see Derrida 2002). The very locution "religious ethics" seems unconsciously to reflect this strain, glossing over these uncomfortable pairs in a breezy hybrid.

When the question is asked how modernity has impacted Judaism and Judaism modernity, it is with these uneasy distinctions that one must wrestle. It is these distinctions that most envelope the Jew in the modern and the modern in the Jew. In the modernity of Mendelssohn and his heirs, these distinctions between Judaism and its others and within Judaism itself become uncoupled and strange, calling not for "reduction" in Rav Simlai's sense but rather for redress, mediation, therapy.

Yet if modernity is a problem for Judaism because law and ethics are seen to have radically distinct spheres, this is surely the flip side of medieval Jewish philosophy and its classical Greek sources, where the thrust was to domesticate dualities in one of two ways: either via Aristotle, according to whom one thing cannot at once be itself and something else, or Plato, according to whom difference is ultimately (from the perspective of the one) illusory. The first asserts that thinking about difference is thinking about contradiction and incommensurability; the second that it is about shadows and appearances. In deducing that Jewish dualities were threatening, modern thinkers were doing nothing less than following out the conceptual trajectory laid down by Maimonides, whose philosophical work displays both the Platonic and the Aristotelian impulses. What emerges from Maimonides is the ultimate identity of a purified ethics and the laws of God, without giving up the notion that they are contradictory kinds of things (1972: 379–80). Indeed, this topos is the Christian medieval anxiety in a nutshell: theology and philosophy can be harmonized only if it is absolutely clear that they are incommensurate. Is it Kant who troubles this Maimonidean serenity? Certainly, the Maimonidean legacy was precisely the circulation of a purified ethics as the *solution* to modern Judaism and its conceptual dilemmas. But in so doing, all modern Judaism did was to conceal the either/or of contradiction or illusion (identity) at the heart of medieval Jewish thinking.

Ethics is made therapeutic, serving to unify the Jew unhappily bifurcated between law and ethics – ethics becomes the standard of both itself and the law. And the modern Jew is conceived as escaping, narrowly, the medieval mindset which would have forced a choice – Jew or modern – only by siphoning off the ethical as an end – or a beginning – in itself. How do we get around the violence ("war") that presents itself through the very "exercise of reason," Levinas asks at the beginning of *Totality and Infinity*? "A primordial and original relation with being is needed" that begins and ends with the face of the particular other, beyond reason (1961: 21–2). This beautifully captures the ambiguity of the move from law to ethics in the passage from Makkot. What it does not reveal as clearly is the way back. For if what the law shows is that in the beginning was ethics, how will ethics itself account for the origin of law? (See chapter 11.)

Ethics and Law

There is a temptation in modern Jewish ethics to conjure an eden, an original, "before the law," from which one would be protected from the constant, unremitting labor – the agon, as Gillian Rose often put it – of lawful resistance: to war, to injustice, to thoughtlessness. We moderns stumble over this eden precisely because it is so foreign to the ordinary terrain we walk on, where the distinctions between law and ethics seem to shift with ground under our feet. This eden is not, though, the fault of Kant, or "modernity," or even Buber and Levinas, who do, to be sure, romanticize the ethical moment. Indeed, what enables Rav Simlai to move (via reduction) from Moses to David is what Judaism *shares* with Kant, over against the Maimonidean (dis)union of ethics and law. For in Rav Simlai, as Kant and his Jewish inheritors, Buber and Levinas, struggle to embody, the insistence seems to be that there can be no bifurcation between law and ethics, just as there can be no identity between them. The one can be reduced to the other precisely because each is only true if contained, reductively, in the other; each can become the other *with remainder . . .* such that there can always be a movement back.

The difference between autonomy and heteronomy is not between ethics and law; the difference is between an ethics that struggles with law (a law that struggles with ethics) and one that seeks to bypass these struggles with recourse to a commanding source. It is possible to see this recourse as at the heart of Judaism; this has certainly been the Jewish argument with Kant, however much he is then rehabilitated. But it is also possible to see that what Kant insisted upon was no different than what Rav Simlai teaches courtesy of David, Isaiah, Micah, Amos, and Habbakuk, namely that commandments must be founded upon righteousness, which lives in and through them, and that righteousness is, above all, law. That those commandments were "given" to Moses makes hardly more difference than the moral law being "given" to humanity from who knows where (Kant 1993). The point in both cases is the same, namely that ethics is sorted out in the law of interpretation and the interpretation of law. One could say that the maxim "the righteous shall live by their faith" is commanded 613 times so that those who miss it the first time can still learn how to live by it.

Contemporary Jews stumble, perhaps, over what Rav Simlai passes over gracefully because unlike him, we have learned to see this struggle as a problem to be concluded. We have learned to feel anxious about whether we have the resources to wage a battle for the ethical in the heart of the struggle between commandment and freedom. It is not that the grace of the rabbis was subsequently broken by modernity. Even Rav Simlai appears to know that the "reduction" involves breakage, if only through the language of *he'emidan.* Perhaps this breakage and its constant repair is from a Jewish perspective the human task *par excellence.* Certainly, it is just as possible to see the rabbis as moderns solving an age-old problem as it is to see them as ancients hauled in to respond to a specifically modern problem. What they see for us, with us, is that ethics cannot be hyphenated, except by the laws (whosoever they happen to be) that are its eternal partner. The question, then, "How is Jewish ethics possible?" is not just Kant's question. It is a question Judaism asks from the beginning; a question that shows us the way back to the law even as it makes the way itself the point.

Bibliography

Borowitz, E. B. and Schwartz, F. W. (eds.) 1999: *The Jewish Moral Virtues.* Philadelphia, PA: Jewish Publication Society.

Buber, M. 1967: "Judaism and Mankind" in *On Judaism*, ed. N. Glatzer. New York: Schocken.

—— 1970: *I and Thou*, trans. W. Kaufmann. New York: Charles Scribner's Sons.

Cohen, H. 1995 [1919]: *The Religion of Reason, Out of the Sources of Judaism*, trans. S. Kaplan. Atlanta, GA: Scholars Press.

Derrida, J. 2002: "Interpretations at War: Kant, the Jew, the German" in *Acts of Religion*, ed. G. Anidjar, 137–88. New York: Routledge.

Dorff, E. N. and Newman, L. E. (eds.) 1995: *Contemporary Jewish Ethics and Morality*. New York: Oxford University Press.

Fox, M. (ed.) 1975: *Modern Jewish Ethics: Theory and Practice*. Columbus: Ohio State University Press.

Gibbs, R. 2000: *Why Ethics? Signs of Responsibility*. Princeton, NJ: Princeton University Press.

Goodman, L. E. 1998: *Human Rights and Human Values*. New York: Oxford University Press.

Kant, I. 1960: *Religion within the Limits of Reason Alone*, trans. T. M. Green and H. H. Hudson. New York: Harper Torchbooks.

—— 1993: *Critique of Practical Reason*, trans. L. W. Beck. New York: Macmillan.

Kellner, M. M. (ed.) 1978: *Contemporary Jewish Ethics*. New York: Sanhedrin Press.

Levinas, E. 1961: *Totality and Infinity, An Essay on Exteriority*, trans. A. Lingis. Pittsburgh, PA: Duquesne University Press.

—— 1989: "Ethics as First Philosophy" in *The Levinas Reader*, ed. S. Hand, 75–87. Cambridge, MA: Blackwell.

—— 1990a: *Difficult Freedom: Essays on Judaism*, trans. S. Hand. Baltimore, MD: Johns Hopkins University Press.

—— 1990b: *Nine Talmudic Readings*, trans. A. Aronowicz. Bloomington: Indiana University Press.

—— 1994: *Beyond the Verse: Talmudic Readings and Lectures*, trans. G. D. Mole. Bloomington: Indiana University Press.

Lichtenstein, A. 1978: "Does Jewish Tradition Recognize an Ethic Independent of Halakha?" in *Contemporary Jewish Ethics*, ed. M. M. Kellner, 102–23. New York: Sanhedrin Press.

Maimonides, M. 1972: "Eight Chapters" in *A Maimonides Reader*, ed. I. Twersky. New York: Behrman House.

Mendelssohn, M. 1983: *Jerusalem, or, On Religious Power and Judaism*, trans. A. Arkush. Hanover, NH: Brandeis University Press.

Newman, L. E. 1995: "Ethics as Law, Law as Religion: Reflections on the Problem of Law and Ethics in Judaism" in *Contemporary Jewish Ethics and Morality*, ed. E. N. Dorff and L. E. Newman, 79–93. New York: Oxford University Press.

Novak, D. 1998: *Natural Law in Judaism*. Cambridge: Cambridge University Press.

Rose, G. 1993: *Judaism and Modernity: Philosophical Essays*. Oxford: Blackwell.

Seeskin, K. 2001: *Autonomy in Jewish Philosophy*. Cambridge: Cambridge University Press.

2 Christian Ethics

CHAPTER 21
Christian Ethics?

Gene Outka

The Question of Appropriateness

Does Western discourse about "ethics" afford an appropriate way to think about the moral life of Christianity? On one highly general but non-trivial level, let us stipulate that "ethics," Christian, Western, and otherwise, is self-conscious inquiry into a human activity as common as cooking or doing sums. This activity is *judging* (e.g., that certain kinds of actions are right or wrong, that certain kinds of character are good or bad). "Ethics" examines everyday normative judgments concerned with human actions, character, and social arrangements; in short, with the "guidance of life." It reflects upon, theorizes about these; it describes, analyzes, and assesses them (see chapters "On Religious Ethics," 1, and 2).

Although the activity is common, two considerations suggest complexity and ambiguity. First, when we consider actual moral judgments across centuries and regions, we find differences, disagreements, and clashes, together with similarities, agreements, and overlaps. Often conflicting judgments are not provisionally held. Adherents within many traditions who are committed to certain judgments do not look tolerantly on the positions of those in the same or other traditions who disagree. Yet their efforts to persuade may fail. Moreover, each tradition may explain disagreements differently.

Second, religious traditions bring distinctive commitments and conflicts, including the multiple "sources" employed in reaching judgments. Christians take two sources as basic to their own identity. One is the Bible, which retains indispensable, non-transferable authority. References to the biblical God may then reverberate in various judgments. The other is tradition, which makes attention to the institutional church also indispensable. With Western thinkers, Christians employ three other sources: practical reason, experience (including emotions and desires), and human learning (in both the sciences and humanities).

Christians bring this combination of sources to every culture in which they find themselves. Yet Western discourse presents peculiar challenges. It offers inquiries exceptional in variety and volume. Christians encounter diverse movements and figures (e.g., Platonic, Aristotelian, Kantian, Hegelian, utilitarian, and feminist). And Christians must make their way among elaborate disputes on all manner of ethical subjects; for example, how to regard distinguishable domains (actions, consequences, virtues, and motives), divergent normative theories (deontological and consequentialist), and rival estimates of status and justification (ethical relativism, ethical objectivism, "universalist" and "particularist" clams about morality) (see chapter 1).

From these preliminaries, we draw out three more determinate ways that Christians address the question of appropriateness.

First, how Christians employ the multiple sources to which they are committed characteristically generates a line of division between what we shall call *intramural* and *extramural* questions. Intramural questions assume that the Bible and tradition retain non-transferable authority for depicting the moral life of Christianity. The questions focus on action guidance within the church, on the manner of life that Christians enjoin on one another. Extramural questions shift attention to surrounding social worlds, including ethical and political standards, theories, and institutional arrangements, various forms of cultural life, and so on. These two sets of questions represent more than a convenient starting point for discussion; they indicate a permanent orientation. Christian ethics as self-conscious inquiry ordinarily distinguishes the two sets, though it includes asking how continuous or discontinuous the intramural and extramural are with one another. Answers to the latter influence estimates of appropriateness (see chapter 17).

Second, many Christians themselves deliberate on whether they may cross the line between intramural and extramural in one significant way. They ask how far they may *vindicate* certain moral insights that arise outside their tradition and incorporate these into a depiction of the moral life that they themselves present as true. Here Christians feel the force of the question of appropriateness from the inside. They take over the question, and articulate certain types of answers to it.

Third, Christians also confront the question of appropriateness when they offer judgments on particular normative topics. One topic serves here as an extended illustration: the ethics of peace and war. We meet a central case where the Christian tradition's self-description is evident, and some of its own continuities of conflict are embodied. We further suggest how the line of division and the question of vindication described above affect the judgments made.

Let us now sketch these three determinate ways more fully.

Intramural and Extramural Questions: Christian Ethics as Self-Conscious Inquiry

First, we face intramural questions about the content of the manner of life displaying Christian convictions. What is discernibly Christian in such a life? Can Christians locate a pattern of discipleship for all centuries, or only changeable patterns for different centuries? If a single pattern perdures, how should we specify it? Does the pattern consist in attitudes and virtues only, or fixed sorts of behavior also? Can we find a key notion or category to which we might always appeal as we carry out the work of specification? How much homogeneity should the church demand in its common life? Are there lifestyles and values that it requires everyone to exemplify and uphold? Is a whole pattern of normative thought implied which we can trace and apply to issues left unaddressed?

Second, we face extramural questions about the moral and political values and institutional arrangements with which surrounding cultures confront the church. If we are in the church, which of these values and arrangements can we positively assimilate? Which may we indifferently leave alone? Which should we resist as incompatible? Should we specify a general strategy for the church's relation to the world? If so, should the strategy be communal withdrawal, qualified participation, or attempted dominance? Should the church proceed rather in a piecemeal or ad hoc way, confronting forms of daily life and various issues one by one?

Intramural questions often correlate with "thick" moralities (rich and detailed, for a particular community); extramural questions often correlate with "thin" moralities (minimal prohibitions of actions found to be destructive of the bonds of any human community). Finally, Christian versions of the contrast between thick and thin often correlate with a distinction between the Christian community, or the "religious–spiritual" government, on the one side, and the civil community, or the "civil–moral" government, on the other side. A shorthand referent is "the doctrine of the Two." This doctrine exerts enormous influence on Western ethics and politics. Insofar as the doctrine of the Two mandates divided loyalties and circumscribes the competence of the civil–moral government, it conflicts with totalizing schemes, both theocratic and secular (e.g., fascism and certain variants of Marxism). According to such schemes, one explicit worldview, one complete way of life, governing a whole society, culture, or civilization, should be singly promulgated, comprehensively preferred, and coercively enforced. To be sure, the doctrine of the Two is hospitable to a view of the church as a thick community (in this regard, the language of "religious–spiritual" should not obscure social and political dimensions). But partly because this thick community excludes a full range of coercive activities ("banning" and "excommunication" may occur, yet these do not rely necessarily on civic policing and "crime control"), it resists mandating a single society that intervenes and enforces coercively, from top to bottom.

How Far Should Christians Vindicate Moral Insights that Arise Outside?

Certain types of answers to this question that Christians give make their several estimates about appropriateness more precise. How many and which insights should be vindicated? Some Christians limit them to the Decalogue as prohibiting actions destructive of the bonds of any community. Other Christians put the question more ambitiously: Should Christians subscribe *qua* Christians to any comprehensive ethical scheme whose intelligibility is established and sustained *independently* of Christian convictions? We can link this question to the matter of "sources." Do some ethical schemes systematically subordinate the first two sources (the Bible and tradition) to a combination of the other three? Western discourse formidably advances a variety of such comprehensive ethical schemes. Practical reason (say) puts the ingredients of an ethical scheme in place and adjudicates. Christians give at least three answers to this ambitious version of the question of appropriateness (Outka 1996).

First, some reject the terms of subordination and deny that any such scheme contains positive insights that Christians should incorporate. Christian ethics depends on comprehensive convictions to which there is no universal epistemic access. It specifies behavioral thickness that is not generalizable to those outside. Between patterns inside and outside, normative discontinuities reign.

Second, some reject the terms of subordination, and are prepared at most to vindicate certain moral insights that arise outside, after they review, modify, and integrate them. Still, Christian ethics depends on comprehensive convictions, and these include a doctrine of creation that presents more than a morally structureless world. Appropriations should always bear the marks of particularist convictions. Christians should not commit themselves to justifying any part of their morality in terms that are wholly available to them before they encounter the Christological paradigm. Between patterns inside and outside, they find complex encounters, where normative continuities and discontinuities both obtain.

Third, some accept the terms of subordination with regard to morality, because what the Christological paradigm discloses is never at odds with what rational persons apprehend morally, when their practical reasoning is in good order. Alan Donagan accepts, for instance, the claim on behalf of a Kantian scheme that morality "does not presuppose the truth of the Christian faith, but is presupposed by it" (Donagan 1993: 54). A similar claim about what Christianity presupposes is sometimes made on behalf of the natural law and the cardinal virtues. To be sure, the Christological paradigm discloses more than this (e.g., about a relation to God). But again, what the paradigm discloses morally is continuous with what persons can apprehend when they do not fail as moral reasoners. When the paradigm tells them something that is morally incompatible with what they tell themselves, this is because they have in fact failed as reasoners, or have been corrupted by erroneous moral theories or deformed cultural practices.

We amplify as we turn to the ethics of peace and war.

The Status of Pacifism and the Just War: Interlocking Judgments

Christians elucidate and defend two stances, "pacifism" and the "just war." (We leave aside notions of the "holy war," or the "crusade," because so many Christians have progressively subjected them to critique, denying them the fixed place that the other two now occupy. See chapter 55.)

Pacifism covers several distinguishable views. Traditional pacifists judge that it is intrinsically wrong to participate *directly* in *killing* in *all* wars. "Abolitionists" dwell on war's palpable evils and believe that we may reasonably hope to eliminate it. "Non-violent resisters" actively oppose evil and seek effective non-violent means to pursue justice. Evangelical Anabaptists and Quakers exemplify pacifist views (Yoder 1992).

Evangelical Anabaptists press normative differences between intramural and extramural ways of life. Regarding the former, they claim that Christians identify a pattern of discipleship for all centuries, not changeable patterns for different centuries. The pattern depends on historically particular events, yet is not itself historically variable. It seeks to imitate Christ, and dwells on specific exhortations such as the Sermon on the Mount and on crucifixion. The New Testament teaches what characteristic attitudes and virtues and fixed sorts of behavior discipleship requires. Pacifism is not only an acceptable stance; it is the only acceptable stance.

Extramural questions receive these replies. We leave the sword alone both in our church life and in our relations to neighbors outside the church, and so witness *consistently*. Whether the church should follow a general strategy of communal withdrawal or qualified participation is a question on which Christian pacifists differ. Quakers discriminate among the uses of force. They accept policing but disallow soldiering. In some measure, they seek "peace through politics." For them, the civil–moral government presents constructive as well as destructive possibilities.

Just war doctrine stems from the Christian tradition as well, though secular sources play important roles too (e.g., the chivalric code of the knightly class and the *jus gentium*). The doctrine's roots go back to Augustine, but its classic form appears at the end of the middle ages. Later, it receives articulation in secular international law (Johnson 1975). It interacts with Western discourse about ethics and politics in extensive ways. Indeed, it serves increasingly in certain societies as a normative point of reference.

We may plot responses to intramural and extramural questions within the Augustinian legacy as follows. Christians identify a pattern of discipleship for all centuries, and appeal not only to the Sermon on the Mount and to the crucifixion, but also to the double love commandment, to justice, and to the Decalogue, among other things. Love for God and love of neighbor predominate. Augustine lauds peace as a richly active condition. Yet to regard pacifism as the only acceptable stance for Christians leaves innocent neighbors at the mercy of the unscrupulous. This prospect offends against care for the needy that Jesus enjoins. Discipleship requires a comprehensive depiction where love rather than non-violence per se integrates its myriad commitments. The depiction further requires that we attend to creation, human sinfulness, and eschatology, together with Christology and ecclesiology.

Extramural questions receive these replies. As we extend care, we meet social worlds where injustice and brutality call for judgments that are both diminishing to weigh and unloving to ignore. One such judgment is that it can be loving for societal representatives to intervene, in order to enforce the prohibition against murder. The estimate is that more, not fewer, benefits accrue from organized efforts of the civil community to restrain unjust coercion by counter-coercion. Such counter-coercion need not be sheerly arbitrary, although it is permanently corruptible. Policing and soldiering as vocations in civil society deserve better than to be condemned or placed outside the sphere of what Christians might do.

These replies to extramural questions lead us neither to equate policing and soldiering nor to separate them entirely. Both are sad necessities. Yet policing is liable to a greater measure of public oversight. To bring soldiering under moral evaluation, we look to the just war doctrine, and uphold both parts of its distinction between *jus ad bellum* (criteria for limiting resort *to* war) and *jus in bello* (criteria governing just conduct *in* war).

Alliance and Misalliance with Ethics

Christian defenders of pacifism and the just war find different points of alliance and misalliance with Western discourse. Christian pacifists sometimes appeal to "all persons of good will" to banish war's horrors. The timbre of these appeals is "universalist." They are justified without necessary recourse to particular beliefs and practices. More frequently, however, Christian pacifists find "particularist" accounts of morality more appropriate. They embrace historically oriented moral philosophy that views traditions and local cultural agreements as not accidental but essential to moral knowledge. They may also invoke "postmodern" critiques of "universalist" moral schemes (see chapter 2). Here they purport to "unmask" legitimations of violence and domination that universalist schemes simultaneously hide from view and perpetuate.

Some Christian defenders of just war seek to address two overlapping audiences, one that is Christian and another that is wider. Their defense stems overall from particularist Christian warrants; for example, the way Augustine in some cases extends charity to a mournful acceptance of force. Yet they also hold that their verdicts do not confront a structureless moral world where every normative appeal is exhaustively subject to historical variation and cultural change. Hence a second audience can come into view. Its members need not formulate just war teachings out of their own resources. But they may find them intelligible following exposure, and come to make them their own.

Other Christian defenders of just war articulate a natural law theory that is "logically independent" of Christian convictions (Finnis 1996). They present the basic tenets of just war as binding on all persons of good will. These tenets map the moral landscape of war for good. Christian convictions that increase awareness are not at odds with what we apprehend morally as rational persons. Teachings on just war are permanently valid, though we must combat moral blindness.

While Christianity is emphatically a world religion, its long history in the West requires continued engagement here as well as elsewhere, and renewed attempts to make the most of interactions already bequeathed. We have seen that no single answer to the question of appropriateness persuades all Christians, but that certain considerations lend structure to their several answers. One is a recurrent line of division between intramural and extramural questions. Another is a series of answers to the question of vindicating moral insights that arise outside the tradition, where the matter of appropriateness is felt from the inside. Still another is where Christians face their own continuities of conflict (e.g., the ethics of peace and war). Christians address this conflict by referring to the line of division, and by choosing parts of Western discourse that ally themselves most closely with what defenders of pacifism and just war each extol. The balance of views canvassed here suggests that for the moral life of Christianity to retain its own identity, Christians should at the end of the day keep their own counsels about everything, including Western discourse.

Bibliography

Donagan, A. 1993: "Common Morality and Kant's Enlightenment Project" in *Prospects for a Common Morality*, ed. G. Outka and J. P. Reeder, 53–72. Princeton, NJ: Princeton University Press.

Finnis, J. 1996: "The Ethics of War and Peace in the Catholic Natural Law Tradition" in *The Ethics of War and Peace: Religious and Secular Perspectives*, ed. T. Nardin, 15–39. Princeton, NJ: Princeton University Press.

Johnson, J. T. 1975: *Ideology, Reason, and the Limitation of War: Religious and Secular Concepts, 1200–1740*. Princeton, NJ: Princeton University Press.

Outka, G. 1996: "The Particularist Turn in Theological and Philosophical Ethics" in *Christian Ethics: Problems and Prospects*, ed. L. S. Cahill and J. F. Childress, 93–118. Cleveland, OH: Pilgrim Press.

Yoder, J. H. 1992: *Nevertheless: The Varieties and Shortcomings of Religious Pacifism*, revd. edn. Scottdale, PA: Herald Press.

CHAPTER 22

Origins of Christian Ethics

Jef Van Gerwen

It may be useful at the outset to clarify a number of issues that are related to early Christian ethics, so that we get a distinct picture of the typical limits and characteristics of the subject.

First, this study is not limited to the moral teaching of Jesus of Nazareth or to New Testament ethics. It covers the debates and texts on Christian morality during the entire period of late antiquity from the first to the fifth century CE. This larger scope opens some interesting perspectives for interpretation, since it does not only focus on the founders of this tradition, but also on the enculturation of Christianity outside its original Jewish setting. Christians gradually integrated elements of Greek, Roman, and other Mediterranean cultures into their ethical codes of conduct as the Christian message spreads far beyond the limits of the Holy Land.

Secondly, ethics for early Christians was a matter of attitudes or habits, rather than just rules and commandments. Although the Jewish Law (especially the Ten Commandments) played a central role in it, Christian morality was primarily based on the practice of a number of virtues, such as love, hope, justice, forgiveness, and patience (see chapter 18). Consequently, it was committed to fight vices such as hate, envy, lust, sloth, and anger. Early Christian ethics resembles more closely other antique schools of ethics, such as Aristotelianism or Stoicism, than our modern Kantian and utilitarian paradigms.

Thirdly, our present knowledge of early Christian ethics is biased because of the selection process to which the primary sources have been subjected throughout history. All the texts of early Christianity (called Patristic literature, or Patrology) have been transmitted to us mostly by monks. These members of religious orders tended to show more interest in the ascetical and mystical aspects of Christian life than in the urban and professional life of married lay Christians. As celibate males living in a patriarchal culture, their gender perspective was one-sided, to say the least. They were often involved in long disputes between heretic and orthodox movements within Christianity, and this may also have led them to exclude or to misrepresent a number of positions on doctrine and ethics.

New Testament Ethics

The ethical teaching of Jesus of Nazareth fits perfectly into the tradition of prophetic and early rabbinical representatives of Jewish ethics. In the line of the prophets, Jesus stresses the importance of the virtues of justice and mercy over the ritualistic ethics of purity and cult offerings that had been developed in the Jewish Law (the books of Leviticus and Deuteronomy). In his interpretation of the Mosaic Law (Matthew 5–7) he focuses on the purity of intention of the agent, rather than on the mere act of trespassing a rule of law. The intentions of his followers are to be trained by the virtues of justice, humility, hope, patience, and forgiveness within the communal setting of the group of disciples. Their primary virtue is love, as God himself is love (1 John 4, 9). Christian love should not be identified with friendship or erotic passion, but rather with hospitality and attention to the needs of neighbors, especially strangers and the poor. This type of solidarity is suggested by the typical Christian term for love, which is charity (Latin: *caritas*; Greek: *agape*).

Jesus' moral teaching demonstrates a tendency towards ascetic radicalism, which was a typical corollary of the prevalent Messianic and eschatological expectations of his day. The Messiah is the "Anointed one," a righteous prophet-king who would restore Israel to its ideal state; "Christ" is the Greek synonym for Messiah. He proposed a radical ethic of pacifism, common property, voluntary celibacy, and renunciation of family ties, in order to prepare oneself for the imminent coming of the Kingdom of God. In doing so, he followed an original course among other Jewish movements, dissociating himself from collaborators with the Roman occupying forces (Sadducees), from armed rebels (Sicarii, Zealots), as well as from more secluded desert communities (Essenes). Similarly, he did not comply with the popular image of the Messiah as a mighty military and religious leader, but rather chose to give a different meaning to Messianism by accepting the role of the humble and suffering servant of God (see Isaiah 53). After his death, when the end of times (and the related Second Coming of Christ) failed to occur as soon as the first generation of Christians had expected, the Christian movement needed to redefine its place in history and in society. This adaptation was already initiated in the New Testament letters of Paul and Peter, in which the believers are admonished to adopt a long-term perspective of the future, and to get settled as citizens and church members.

The New Testament, with its 27 different writings (including Gospels, Acts, Letters, and the book of Revelation), includes a plurality of ethical stances, rather than one uniform position. All New Testament authors, however, agree on the following main issues:

1 All moral commitments depend on a prior acceptance of God's redemptive coming into the world in Jesus of Nazareth. This affirmation of faith offers the foundation for any ethical orientation. As a consequence, ethics is understood as a way of imitating Christ, following the way of Jesus in daily practice.
2 The love of God and the love of neighbors are intimately linked in one commandment, which represents the core of Christian (and Jewish!) ethics (Mark 12:30–31; see chapter 20, this volume).

3   The message of Jesus cannot be limited to a Jewish audience; it has a universal meaning. However, some authors, such as Paul and Luke, move further than others in directing the Christian message to non-Jewish followers.

The writings in the New Testament may present divergent ethical orientations on many other topics. This is the case, for example, with the relationship between faith and good works as a basis for the justification of the believers (the letters of Paul versus the letter of James or the gospel of John), or with the respect that is due to political authorities (Paul's letter to the Romans, ch. 13, versus Revelation, ch. 13).

Each of the four gospels also presents a particular perspective on Jesus' teaching, reflecting its specific social setting. The gospel according to Mark focuses on the ethics of discipleship, stressing the paradox of human fulfillment through a process of self-abnegation (the acceptance of the Cross). Matthew, writing for a community of Jewish Christians, offers the most thorough reinterpretation of the Jewish Law as a code of righteousness. Luke pays attention to the ethics of riches and poverty, and to practices of healing and service to the needy. John's gospel is built on the opposition between the community of brotherly love of the faithful over against the evil nature of the outside world.

Apostolic Fathers

The texts of the New Testament were composed between 50 and 120 CE. As such they reflect the doctrinal and ethical attitudes of the first generations of Christians. Not all early Christian texts of that period were included in the biblical canon. A wide variety of non-biblical sources has been conserved, such as the Apostolic teachings, Gnostic literature, and Apologetics, that provide us with valuable information on the moral life of Christians in the first and second centuries.

Among the collection of Apostolic teachings, a most interesting source for ethical reflection is the Teaching of the Apostles (*Didache*), especially the teaching on the Two Ways (of life and death) that refers to the Sermon on the Mount (Matthew 5–7) and to the lists of virtues in the letters of Paul (e.g., Galatians 5:19–22). The anonymous letter to Diognetus offers an excellent short treatise on Christian lifestyle written for a non-Christian audience. One may find a third type of approach in the Shepherd of Hermas, which represents a more rigoristic doctrine on sin and penance in a rich symbolic ("hermetic" = hard to disclose) language.

The moral teachings of the Apostolic Fathers move between two poles. On the one hand, they contain a faithful commentary to the canonical writings; on the other hand, they incline more or less to the doctrines of Gnosticism and rigorism that exerted a strong influence on the worldview of Greek-speaking Christians during the first two centuries CE. Gnosticism is a religious philosophy that is derived from neoplatonism, a rather popular philosophy in antique Mediterranean society. *Gnosis* means "knowledge," referring to a mystical type of insight into the world of eternal ideas. It is based on a dualistic view of reality: material reality is considered as inferior to the realm of ideas, and so is the human body with regard to the soul. The passions, such as erotic affection, anger or envy, are seen as sources of evil and corruption for the good life. Salvation is possible: a divine seed has been detached from the divine being by one of its aeons (higher spiritual beings, usually identified by Christian Gnostics with Christ as the preexisting Son of God). This spark of light has been introduced into the human body as a living soul, where it is held prisoner. By asceticism and spiritual growth, the soul will be set free and enabled to enter into communion with the divine mystery.

For most of its Christian adherents, the Gnostic movement called for a rigoristic ethics (Greek: *Encratism*, from the word *egkrateia*, temperance or continence), which moved beyond the ethical radicalism of Jesus and his disciples. Instead of an ethics in view of the imminent coming of the Kingdom, a permanent attitude of abstinence from sexual intercourse was considered a superior mode of conduct to married life. The use of cosmetics and the consumption of meat, wine, and other luxury goods are to be avoided, whereas practices of frequent fasting and of frugality are promoted. Many Christians opt for a solitary life in the desert, rather than pursuing their professional activities in an urban setting. As a consequence, a fundamental distinction appears between two classes of believers: the *gnoostikoi* (those who know, who strive after perfection) and the *koine pistis* (the ordinary believers). This distinction was institutionalized in the hierarchical structure of religious orders with the clergy over against the laity. The first group must follow a more radical ethics of the evangelical counsels (poverty or community of goods, celibacy, and obedience to an abbot or bishop); the second group has to obey to the ethics of the mandates (i.e., the Ten Commandments). Gnostic sources include figures such as Marcion, Montanus, Tatian, Basilides, and Valentinus, and non-official gospels (called Apocrypha) such as the gospel of Thomas.

Starting from the second century, Christian intellectuals were also answering anti-Christian critiques coming from political and philosophical circles. The ethical critiques often focused on accusations of atheism, anthropophagy, and promiscuity. The issue of atheism was raised in relation to the official cult of the emperor as a sacred or divine ruler, to which Roman citizens owed a public display of loyalty. Christians were accused of forming a secret society with an attitude of disloyalty to the emperor and to the public order. They believed in one God, and failed to pay respect to the deities of other religions. The other accusations originated in misunderstandings concerning the rituals of the Eucharist and baptism. Outsiders supposed that the "eating of the body of Christ" included some form of cannibalism and human sacrifice, and that the baptism of adult people led to sexual promiscuity or orgiastic excesses. Christian authors such as Justinus Martyr (Apology), Athenagoras (A plea for the Christians), Clement of Alexandria (Christ the Educator; Can Rich Men Be Saved?), Irenaeus (Against Heresies) and Tertullian (Apologeticum; Treatises on Marriage; The Chaplet; Spectacles; On Idolatry) wrote a number of treatises to defend the position of Christians for a non-Christian public. The works of Clement and Origen had a strong influence on subsequent developments, because they were speaking as trained philosophers of the school of Alexandria. Their thoughts on the nature of evil and on anthropology provided the first systematic framework for Christian ethics, finding a third way between the rationalism of classic Platonism and the deterministic views of neoplatonism, with its Manicheistic and Gnostic overtones. They did so in stressing simultaneously the fundamental goodness and transcendence of God, the freedom of human beings (including responsibility for their wrongdoings) and the human need for divine grace.

Tertullian, born in Carthage as the son of a Roman centurion, presents another interesting source for ethics, because he comments on a number of concrete ethical cases, such as the participation of Christians in the public life of the empire, and the apparel of women. Generally speaking, Tertullian defends a rigoristic position. Christians should not bear arms as soldiers in the Roman army; neither should they accept administrative positions in the empire, nor assist in the spectacles of the amphitheater or the theater, because all these public activities are tainted by idolatry and the contempt for human life. Indeed, human sacrifices were not uncommon in theater plays and circus events. Women should show modesty in dress and behavior. Christian marriage is interpreted as an indissoluble and exclusive bond between husband and wife; sexual intercourse is justified for the cause of procreating offspring only, not for the sake of pleasure. On this last point, Christians tended to agree with the Stoic teachings of their era.

The Church Fathers of the Third and Fourth Centuries

The split between the Eastern and Western parts of the Roman empire also led to a growing divergence between the Eastern and Western Latin churches. Active centers of Latin Christianity were found in North Africa (Numidia), Italy, and Gaul; the major centers of Eastern Christianity were situated in Alexandria, Byzantium, Greece, and Cappadocia. During this period Christianity was slowly evolving from a marginal social position as a semi-secret society, prone to persecution, towards an established religious institution. As the social position of Christians is rising, political leaders, including the emperors, start to take an active interest in church organization (e.g., the formulation of the common Symbolum of Faith by the Synods of Nicea (321) and Chalcedon (381), guaranteeing the unity of the church in the empire). In the domain of ethics, Christian positions were moving toward a less radical stand, especially in economic and political matters, as Christians start to take active responsibility in the public domain. This is demonstrated, for example, in the writings of Ambrose (Letters, On the Duties of the Clergy) and Augustine (*The City of God*). Examples of this shift toward an ethics of responsibility are the appearance of the just war theory and the deontology of public office.

With regard to the former issue, Christians had initially been defending a pacifist ethic: the believers could not use violence, and Christian converts had to leave the army (see chapter 21). Gradually, however, Christians started to accept the right to defend oneself against an aggressor, especially in order to protect the weak; later, the right to legitimate self-defense was also accepted. As a result, Christian authors such as Augustine developed a theory of just war (see his Reply to Faustus the Manichean), in which the ethical criteria to start and continue armed struggle were strictly defined. Also in the realm of economic ethics, Christian communities had initially accepted a radical critique of wealth and private property, asking the believers to sell their possessions for the benefit of the poor, and to organize a system of common goods in the local church (see chapter

45). At the end of the second century, Clement of Alexandria had already defended a more pragmatic position, in which the rich could be saved, not by actually distancing themselves from their wealth. Rather, they should manage their property in a spirit of inner detachment for the good of their households and the surrounding community. Eventually, this ethic of responsible management (or stewardship) became the dominant ethic for laypersons. Only monks were supposed to follow the more radical ethic of poverty and sharing of all goods within the monastic community.

These adaptations were stimulated to a great extent by the decline of the Roman empire in the West. As the public administration of the empire was crumbling under the weight of Germanic invasions, the church leaders took over more tasks that belonged to the public domain, ranging from schooling and transportation to public defense and administration. In order to do so, they needed a new type of political and economic ethics, taking into account the conditions of effective government. In the East, however, the Roman empire continued to function for several centuries. As a consequence, the Eastern churches were in a different position. On the one hand, they were used by emperors as an instrument for maintaining the unity of the empire, and are kept under the control of his political power. This led to a regime of "Caesaropapism," in which the emperor imposed himself as the effective head of the church. But on the other hand, several groups of believers, and especially the members of religious orders, maintained a critical distance and autonomy with regard to their political rulers. Such critical attitude can be observed, for example, in the Two Treatises against Julian the Emperor by Gregory of Nazianzus, and in the Twenty-One Homilies on the Statues of John Chrysostom. Other important authors in the Eastern empire are Basilius and Gregory of Nyssa. In the West, next to Ambrose and Augustine, one may consult the works of Lactantius (The Divine Institutes) and Prudentius (The Spiritual Combat) to get a good view on Christian virtue ethics in the fourth century.

In matters of sexual ethics, including marriage and celibacy, Christians changed their positions. The initial ideal to give equal consideration to men and women in Christian communities (cf. Paul's letter to the Galatians 3:28) was abandoned for a more traditional patriarchal conception of gender relations, including a tendency towards misogyny (see chapter 54). Typically, most fourth-century writings on the subject of women address the position of virgins as a model of Christian lifestyle and organization. Virgins and widows represented a socially vulnerable position in a patriarchal society, in need of social protection. By giving a specific status to virgins as a sort of precursor to female religious orders, the early Christians were pursuing a social aim (solidarity) as well as a gender (submission) and an ascetical (abstinence) agenda.

New ethical debates appeared in the context of church discipline. Church leaders (mostly bishops) not only faced persecutions and criticisms coming from outside, but also faced divisions within their churches on matters of doctrine and morality. Countless schisms and heretical movements flourished, as Christianity spread fast over the entire Roman empire (and even outside it, into Ethiopia and the Middle East). The church organization still remained decentralized. Ethical discipline was established gradually, for example through the initiative of Cyprian, bishop of Carthage (The Lapsed, The Unity of the Christian Church) and by Zephirinus and Callistus, bishops of Rome. These bishops argued for a more lenient position against the rigoristic camp on the issue of penance and the forgiveness of sins. The crucial question they faced was the reacceptance into the church of "the fallen brothers and sisters" (i.e., those who had forsaken their faith during persecutions). The rigorists wanted to exclude those defectors permanently, since they had broken their faith commitment. The lenient party argued that Christians had to meet the gospel demand of forgiving sinners, and pleaded for a procedure of public penance (temporary exclusion from the liturgy, public confession) for those who had committed serious sins. Serious sins were considered to be homicide, adultery, and idolatry – the last sin included those who had left the church during persecutions. After fulfilling their penance requirement, they had to be readmitted into the communion of the church. Later, under the influence of the Irish monks, this practice of penance would develop into a ritual of private confession and moral counseling.

The experience of persecutions also led to the recognition of the importance of martyrdom, meaning public witness of the faithful, even if this would imply public execution and a violent death. These martyrs became the objects of public veneration, which evolved later into the popular practice of venerating local saints as role models of Christian life (see chapter 10). The stories of martyrs and church founders provide an important source of narrative Christian ethics, not only in antiquity, but also during the middle ages. Interesting early examples are the *Life of Cyprian*, written by his deacon Pontius, the *Life of Macrina*, written by her brother Gregory of Nyssa, and the *Life of Anthony* by Athanasius of Alexandria.

Conclusion: Trends in Early Christian Ethics

The demarcation line between early Christian ethics and medieval ethics is not a clear one, even if one accepts the fall of the Western Roman empire (476 CE) as a major historical marker. The orientations that had been set in place by the authors of the fourth century continued to influence ethical thought and practice during the subsequent centuries: authors such as Boethius, Cassiodorus, Benedictus, and Isidorus continue to build on the tradition of antique Christianity. The same was true even to a greater extent in the Eastern empire, where the political regime remained intact. Nevertheless, the fourth century represents a clear demarcation line for sociological reasons: during that century, Christianity left behind its marginal status and become a major established religion in the Roman empire. Medieval society would be organized, indeed, around the dyadic structure of the "two kingdoms," one directed toward the pursuit of temporary interests (the state, the empire) and another to eternal values (the church, the pope, and the bishops) (see chapter 21).

If one looks for a synthetic overview of this rather complex period, one should at least consider the following five major factors that have shaped early Christian ethics.

Eschatology and an open-ended future

Christians regularly needed to adapt their views on time and history during this period. They started with the short-term perspective of eschatological literature, expecting the return of Christ and the Kingdom of God to come soon and to introduce the end of the known world. The death and resurrection of Jesus became indeed a symbolic turning point of history, but it did not immediately introduce the end of time or of this world. As a consequence, Christians had to resituate themselves with regard to a long-term and unknown future, learning to deal with the power structures of the present social order. This process ended with Augustine's *City of God*, in which even the fall of the Western Roman empire no longer foretold the end of time, but was accepted as a secular event. This process of reinterpretation relied on the neoplatonic scheme of a dualistic worldview, distinguishing clearly between heaven and earth, and between the heavenly and the earthly city. In the Jewish view of history, these two symbolic spheres had always remained united: the Kingdom of God was a transcendent reality, a gift of grace, but it had to be realized gradually within this world, and not referred to some afterlife outside the realm of human history. In Augustine's view, the distinction had become almost a separation. This reinterpretation also implied a more compromising attitude towards the logic of power and of the secular world. Christians have to avoid absolutizing the importance of the earthly city, but they can deal with it, rather than opting for a principled course of withdrawal.

Radicalism and compromise

This second characteristic flows as a logical conclusion from the previous point. For historical as well as institutional reasons, early Christians came to accept a double strategy of church membership and ethics. On the one hand, they maintained a radical ethics for the clergy and the religious orders, which reflected more directly the ascetical demands of original Christianity as an other-worldly community, based on poverty, celibacy, discipleship, non-violence, and strict obedience to a spiritual leader. On the other hand, they developed an ethics of lay Christians, of soldiers, traders, and married couples, living in households that from an outside perspective could barely be distinguished from non-Christian households. Lay Christians followed an ethics of compromise with the existing world, while holding fast to the Ten Commandments and to the central virtues of love, justice, and forgiveness as beacons for Christian life. This double strategy produced great results in the organization of Christian hospitality, schooling, political order, and economic stewardship. It proved to be better adapted to the use of power and of institutional government than the prophetic ethic of the founders of Christianity. By accepting such adaptations, the church tried to find a middle ground between faithfulness to its origins and the necessity to adapt to the new era. But the tension between the two types of ethics remained present in subsequent church history, and the ethics of compromise would regularly be put to the test by new movements of radical reform (see chapter 24).

Jewish and non-Jewish cultural contexts

The Jewish people inherited a rich tradition of Semitic culture, with its roots in Egyptian and Mesopotamian societies. Christianity emerged within this same environment, but soon had to translate its message into a variety of other cultures, such as Greek, Roman, Celtic, and Germanic settings. This transfer posed a formidable challenge to Christian philosophers, missionaries, and teachers alike, which they met with considerable creativity and inspiration. Nevertheless, some crucial insights of Jewish thought may have been lost in the process, and this had a far reaching effect on the future of Christian doctrine and ethics. The concept of God among the Jews and Greeks, for instance, was not an identical one. Jews tended to stress the intersubjective and intrahistorical qualities of Yahweh, who is a God of a concrete people, the God of Abraham, Isaac, and Jacob. Most Greek philosophers, on the contrary, represented God as an absolute and unchangeable being, functioning as the cornerstone of the universe. Many ethical differences follow from this fundamental distinction. The Greek belief in the eternal existence of the soul may not have the same meaning as the Jewish concept of the resurrection of the body; Greek concepts of virtue (prudence, justice, magnanimity) do not find their counterpart in Jewish virtue ethics, or have different connotations. The Greeks had different ideas on the reality of radical evil, and on the role of the human will and conscience, than those that were implied in the Jewish concepts of freedom, guilt, and redemption. And last but not least, the sexual and gender ethics of the Gnostics, Stoics, and neoplatonists had a long-lasting effect on later Christian morality. Early Christians had no choice but to enculturate their faith in new settings, as they felt called to establish a worldwide, multicultural community of God. By doing so, they also wanted to express the correspondence of their faith with the insights of reason, and the universal significance of their vision. But from time to time, a call would be heard to "return to the (New Testamentic, Jewish) sources" once the enculturation process has gone astray.

Internal pluralism, no uniformity

The early church started as a multiform charismatic movement, not as a well-disciplined institution. Initially, the highest authority resided in the circle of the Twelve Apostles, but divergent attitudes between Greek and Jewish Christians emerged as soon as missionary efforts led to the establishment of various local Christian communities. Faced with an unending series of internal schisms and conflicts, the Christian churches made continuous attempts to maintain a unity of hearts and of faith, based on one canon of scripture, one creed, and on a vast communication network between local churches and their leaders. Nevertheless, efforts to maintain unity often failed, as doctrinal controversies, such as the one between rigorists and lenients, continued to divide the faithful. Also, in liturgical customs and in ethical practice, a great plurality could be observed from the start. Eventually, greater organizational uniformity was established, both under the influence of the bishops of major centers (Rome, Carthage, Byzantium, Alexandria) and because of political pressure by the emperors, who saw in the unity of the Christian church a means to reinforce the unity of the empire.

Ethics of virtue

Early Christians all agreed that morality was a matter of training in the basic virtues, rather than just the application of a universal set of rules or rational principles. These approaches stress the particular features of moral education in a concrete sociohistorical community. Morality depends on the training of character, and seeing and imitating concrete examples, such as Jesus Christ, the saints, or the ordinary faithful. This ethical approach is not contrary to reason. The insights of Greek philosophy and of Roman legal thought were also readily integrated into the Christian tradition. But the moral outlook of early Christians did not depend as exclusively on the role of reason and on the ideal of the self-sufficient individual as was usual within the rationalistic logic of Platonism or late Hellenistic thought.

Bibliography

Those who are able to read Greek and Latin texts may consult an edition of the original sources, such as J. J. Migne, *Patrologiae cursus completus: Series Latina or Series Graeca*, Paris, 1912, or a more recent edition, such as the *Corpus Christianorum of Brepols*, Turnhout, Belgium. Most texts are also available in English translation: *The Ante-Nicene Christian Library*, Edinburgh: T. and T. Clark, 1867; *A Select Library of Nicene and Post-Nicene Fathers of the Christian Church*, New York: Christian Literature Co., 1896; *The Fathers of the Church Series*, New York, 1959, later continued by the Catholic University of America Press, Washington, DC, 1962.

Brown, P. 1988: *The Body and Society: Men, Women, and Sexual Renunciation in Early Christianity*. New York: Columbia University Press.

—— 1995: *Authority and the Sacred: Aspects of Christianization of the Roman World*. Cambridge: Cambridge University Press.

Chadwick, H. 1985: *Early Christian Thought and the Classical Tradition: Studies in Justin, Clement and Origen*. Oxford: Clarendon Press.

—— 1986: *The Early Church*. New York: Dorset.

Di Bernardo, A. 1992: *Encyclopedia of the Early Church*. Institutum Patristicum Augustinianum. Cambridge: James Clarke.

Dihle, A. 1966: "Ethik" in *Reallexikon für Antike und Christentum*, Vol. 6, ed. T. Klausner, 646–796. Stuttgart: Anton Hiersemann.

Forell, G. W. 1979: *History of Christian Ethics*, Vol. 1. Minneapolis, MN: Augsburg Publishing.

Schnackenburg, R. 1965: *The Moral Teaching of the New Testament*. London: Burns and Oates.

CHAPTER 23

Differentiation in Christian Ethics

Vigen Guroian

For the purposes of this chapter, differentiation may be defined as the process of growth and diversification of ethical attitudes and judgments that results from the response of a religion to changing conditions of life. In this sense, differentiation inevitably is an accompaniment of history. Every religion, Christianity included, has a vital interest to ensure that moral beliefs and behaviors are consistent with a complex of convictions, rules, activities, and institutions that comprise the whole of the religion. Thus, differentiation, though it inevitably attends history, is never a neutral thing from the standpoint of a religion. For it can strengthen a religion or weaken it, measured by that religion's internal criteria of orthodoxy and heterodoxy (see chapter 21). Within Christianity, results of differentiation are judged good and creative or deleterious and destructive according to core beliefs about the character of God, nature and grace, human goodness and human sin, and valuations of the course of human history and God's purposes within it.

Though differentiation may be an inevitable concomitant of history, the Christian faith, by affirming divine and human freedom and rejecting fatalism and determinism, is bound to regard differentiation as something that can and ought to be controlled and directed. Of the three major traditions that comprise historic Christianity, Protestantism is decidedly the most "open" to differentiation. Protestantism seems highly fissiparous, producing a continuous stream of new denominations and sects. While this dynamism of Protestantism can reinvigorate ossified forms or help to shed old for new and suppler "skin," it also can weaken legitimate authority and threaten the essential unity of the church. Even the most free-spirited Protestant, who is thoughtful, will agree with more tradition-conscious Orthodox and Roman Catholic co-religionists that differentiation in ethics is almost always a two-edged sword.

This chapter examines differentiation in Christian ethics that has defined the distinctive character of the three great Christian confessions: Orthodoxy, Roman Catholicism, and Protestantism. First, however, it is important to take a look at another kind of differentiation that effects how Christian ethics is understood in relation to the faith as a whole and as an academic discipline. This concerns an ongoing debate, internal to the faith, over whether a distinction should be made between ethics and other dimensions and expressions of the Christian religion, and, if so, how sharply that distinction ought to be drawn.

Differentiation of Ethics and Christian Life in Modern Thought

Since the European Enlightenment there has been a strong impulse within some sectors of Christianity to treat ethics as a subject or discipline separate from other parts of Christian life, such as worship, sacraments, dogma, and pastoral practice. This impulse is closely associated with a debate over the so-called autonomy of ethics. Immanuel Kant defined the terms of this debate with his attempt to demonstrate that universalizable moral judgments are grounded in practical reason and cannot be derived from or verified by religious beliefs and practices. Kant's analysis has heavily influenced modern Protestant ethics and to a lesser degree Roman Catholic ethics. Each in its own fashion has taken up the challenge to give a systematic account of Christian ethics and clearly establish its foundations either in reason, as Kant would have it, or faith, or both.

Until Kant, Protestantism did not strongly distinguish between ethics and theology or moral norms and ecclesial discipline, and ethics has continued to function within Protestant Christianity as a pedagogical tool (Gustafson 1978: 3–4). Much of Protestant ethics has been built upon the dual concepts of law and gospel as elaborated by both Luther (1483–1546) and Calvin (1509–64). Within that vision, biblical law plays a role in Christian ethics insofar as it exposes the fallen and sinful character of human existence and leads the repentant sinner to Christ. Calvin describes a third use of the law as a teacher to spur Christians "to learn what that will of God is which they aspire to follow" (*Institutes* 2.7.12). Both Luther and Calvin agree, however, that the law compels and convicts, whereas the gospel of love is a gift of justification, forgiveness, and salvation. The gospel of love is the good news ("gospel") of the release of sinful humanity from the condemnation of the law that Jesus Christ has accomplished by his own willing and pure sacrifice on the cross and resurrection from the dead. Jesus summed up the ethical heart of the gospel of love as love of God and love of neighbor as oneself and promised that those who live by this double commandment will inherit the Kingdom of God (Mark 12:29–30, 34). Under Kant's influence, Protestant ethicists have endeavored to found this rule in practical reason or the rational will, giving it a formal claim to universality that does not need to be secured in a particular religious vision of the ultimate good.

From early on, Roman Catholic moral theology was closely allied with canon law. The medieval canon lawyers mastered the art of moral casuistry and made it useful to priestly confessors, in whose hands Catholic moral theology was applied to daily living (see chapter 5). Under these conditions, Catholic moral theology assumed a distinctively juridical character tied closely to church order and penitential practices. Thomas Aquinas (ca. 1225–74) expounded a Christian natural law ethics in detail. Aquinas drew from Aristotle (388–322 BCE) for his ethical theory and relied upon St. Augustine (354–430) for theological muscle. The main idea in Catholic natural law theory is that by creating human persons as rational beings God has built into them – into human nature itself – a capacity for discerning the divine law, whether they immediately recognize it as such or not (see Rom. 2:14–15). As propounded by Aquinas, natural law morality is theonomous. It is a mode of participation in the divine law that leads to mystical communion with God. Morality is tied closely to prayer, the sacraments, blessing, and doxology. Over time, however, especially as impacted by the Renaissance and Enlightenment, proponents of natural law commenced upon a project to stand natural law on its own. Similar to the attempts of some modern Protestant ethicists to ground the law of love in a doctrine of man and only secondarily a doctrine of God, some modern Catholic theorists have argued that natural law is a rational standard of morality fixed in human nature. There it obtains an autonomous standing that makes it accessible and knowable for all human beings. This has enabled contemporary Catholic theologians to argue that there is no fundamental difference between Christian ethics and all the rest of human morality (see Curran 1976).

Of the three major traditions of the Christian faith, Eastern Orthodoxy is least drawn to this modern project to ground, or "reground," Christian ethics in reason and/or nature with the goal of a universal morality that transcends religious boundaries. Orthodox theologians and ethicists have judged that these endeavors narrow the meaning and content of Christian ethics and the Christian faith as a whole. Eastern Orthodox writers have hesitated even to speak of Christian ethics as a separate discipline. As Stanley Harakas writes:

> For Orthodox Christianity, doctrine and ethics may be distinguished but they may never be separated. It is only the "division of labor" in which some theologians of the church turn their attention to things, which in the words of St. Athanasios, "make known the word concerning Christ, and the mystery regarding him," on the one hand, while other theologians concern themselves primarily with the Christian teaching, again in the words of St. Athanasios, whose intention is "to point to the correction of habits." (Harakas 1983: 1)

Orthodox theologians, however, are not the only ones that hold this view. Important contemporary Protestant and Roman Catholic theologians and ethicists have argued similarly against the autonomy of ethics and the assimilation of Christian ethics to a "cosmopolitan" ethics that substitutes formal rules and principles for religious teachings and norms.

In the ethics of the Eastern church, morality has to do principally with the goal of faith itself, the restoration of the image of God in human beings and their *theosis* or growth in holiness and god-likeness. Love is the "sacrament" or "medicine" that cures humanity's sinful and mortal condition and the energy that unites persons in communion with God. There is no room in this vision for the autonomy of ethics. Rather, ethics is a peculiarly human mode of apprehending and living the truth of existence. The twin ends of human morality are holiness and immortality. In the human person the ontological "is" posits a moral ought. God has implanted this ought in the human "heart" as an "inner" imperative, a "natural" dynamic principle of life (Guroian 2001: 21–2).

Orthodox Christianity has not elaborated a formal theory of natural law with a hierarchy of divine, natural, and civil law. Nor is the duality of law and gospel the fulcrum of its ethics. It does not draw the sharp distinction between nature and grace that is often entailed in natural law theory and also the law and gospel formula. Rather, the Incarnation demonstrates that the ontological gulf between God and creature may be bridged by love once sin is removed and death is overcome. Redemption is not merely a corrective or remedy for original sin. Just as important, it is the continuance of God's creative and perfecting action in the world. Its aim is that all creatures, but most especially the one whom God has created in his very own image, be drawn into an evermore intimate communion with God's Triune Being.

According to this view, Christian ethics is Christocentric and theocentric. It depends upon conversion (*metanoia*) and faith in the truth of salvation and eternal life revealed fully by God in Jesus Christ. The Christian is made a new creature by baptism, as he or she is transformed and renewed in mind and heart. This is not merely metaphor: it is sacramentally and ontologically real and actual. The Christian yearns for God and his Kingdom. She is moved to deeds of love from the gratitude she has for what God has done for her and for his abundant grace that transforms her from within and assimilates her into the divine life. It is in this sense that Christian ethics is singular if not, in fact, *sui generis*. The ascetic and mystic Pseudo-Macarius (fourth to fifth centuries) sums up this Orthodox stance. He admonishes and corrects Christians of his own day who believe that whatever differences there are between Christians in their belief and behavior and others are merely matters of form or externals. Although "many Christians believe the difference does lie in some eternal sign . . . it is through the renewing of the mind and the tranquility experienced in our thoughts and the love of God and love of heavenly things that every new creation of Christians distinguishes them from the men of this world. For this reason did the Lord come" (Maloney 1992: 64–5, homily 5:4–5).

The modern project to establish the autonomy of ethics – or at least a basis for Christian ethics that ensures it is fully accessible even to non-Christians – reflects a broader concern shared by contemporary religious and secular people alike to identify universal norms of conduct that might be employed to address and negotiate a vast array of moral issues and problems confronting pluralistic modern societies. Such issues and problems include biotechnology, environment, poverty, weaponry, wars of insurgency, and international law. This modern project may be judged foolish or wise from the standpoint of Christian faith. But there is no doubt that it is an instance and example of differentiation in Christian ethics.

Differentiation and the Beginnings of Christian Ethics

The lodestar of all Christian ethics is the person and ministry of Jesus Christ. His story is told by the gospels and explicitly applied to Christian living and the church's mission by the Pauline, Johannine, and other epistles of the New Testament. Early Christianity turns to the entirety of scripture, both Old and New Testaments, as the source of moral guidance and help with judgments and decisions about behavior befitting the saints. Late first and second century apostolic writers, such as the author of the "Didache,"

Clement of Rome, and Ignatius of Antioch, describe a new life in Christ embarked upon through baptism and repentance, nourished by Eucharistic worship, and perfected by the Spirit in the communion of the saints. The book of Acts reports that on Pentecost many to whom Peter preached in Jerusalem were "cut to the heart" and repented, being "baptized . . . in the name of Jesus Christ for the remission of sins" and received "the gift of the Holy Spirit" (Acts 2:37, 39). After their repentance and baptisms these new Christians "devoted themselves to the apostle's teaching and fellowship, the breaking of bread, and the prayers (Acts 2:42). In like manner, St. Paul instructs the Christian community in Rome to "present your bodies as a living sacrifice, holy and acceptable to God, which is your spiritual worship," adding: "Do not be conformed to this world, but be transformed by the renewal of your mind that you may prove what is the will of God, what is good and acceptable and perfect" (Romans 12:1–2).

The early Church Fathers and Mothers conceive of ethics as integral to the whole of the Christian religion. For example, 1 Clement, a late first-century apostolic letter written from Rome to the church of Corinth, assumes that Christian prayer, doxology, and good works are interwoven, framed by the eschatological hope for the full and final advent of the Kingdom of God:

> The good workman receives the bread of this labor with boldness; the lazy and careless cannot look his employer in the face. Therefore we must be prompt in well-doing, for all things are from him [Christ]. For he warns us: "Behold the Lord cometh, and his reward is before his face to pay each according to his work. He exhorts us therefore if we believe on him with our whole heart not to be lazy or careless in every good work." Let our glory-ing and confidence be in him; let us be subject to his will; let us consider the whole multi-tude of his angels, how they stand ready and minister to his will. For the Scripture says, "Ten thousand times ten thousand stood by him, and thousand thousands ministered to him, and they cried Holy, Holy, Holy is the Lord of Sabbaoth, the whole creation is full of thy glory." Therefore, we too must gather together with concord in our conscience and cry earnestly to him, as it were with one mouth, that we may share in his great and glorious promises. (Lake 1998: 1 Clement 34)

The early church did not invent its ethics out of whole cloth or from within a her-metically sealed community. In his parenetic admonitions and advice on right and appropriate Christian conduct, St. Paul sets the pattern and tone for relations with the secular order. He and his immediate followers in the apostolic age are influenced by a variety of "external" sources and pressures. First, they are indebted to the ethical thought of Judaism in the Hebrew scriptures, although they interpret it strictly in light of the Christ event. Second, they seek and find analogies for their ethical reasoning in Stoicism and Platonism. For example, Origen (ca. 185–ca. 254), Gregory of Nyssa (ca. 330–ca. 395), Ambrose of Milan (ca. 339–97), John Chrysostom (ca. 347–407), and Augustine of Hippo (354–430) employ "the early ethical terminology of the philoso-phers but also" assimilate into their Christian ethics "the philosophical ideal of a prac-tice of virtue that led to fellowship with, and likeness to, the Divine" (Norris 1986: 453).

Our contemporary debate about the autonomy of ethics, along with the issue of whether or not there is a singularly distinct or *sui generis* Christian ethics, genuinely would have puzzled these early Christian writers. While the ethics of Christians certainly could overlap with pagan and philosophical ethics, they thought that salvation in Jesus Christ is an objective fact that transforms human ethics just as it transforms human life.

Differentiations in Premodern Christian Ethics

If we apply the concept of differentiation to premodern Christian ethics, what comes immediately into view is, of course, the major division of world Christianity into Eastern and Western, and subsequently Orthodox, Roman Catholic, and Protestant churches. Just as these major divisions of the Christian church reflect real differences in worship and doctrine, so too, as we have begun to see, they express and embody differences of ethical content and vision. Nevertheless, in their classical and magisterial forms, all three of these traditions hold together the relationship of ethics with worship and dogma. This distinguishes the classical phase of differentiation from differentiation that has happened in contemporary Christian ethics. In their classical forms, Eastern Orthodoxy, Roman Catholicism, and Protestantism (Lutheran and Reformed) are quite conscious that Christian ethics originates in baptism – that, in other words, Christian ethics is simply inconceivable apart from conversion and the freely given grace of God – and is oriented toward salvation and eternal life.

The remainder of this chapter explores more deeply this classic differentiation in Christian ethics through an examination of two subjects with which Christians have wrestled from the very start. The first is the nature and purposes of Christian marriage and family and the second is church and state relations. These two issues are connected in at least two important ways. First, both draw upon and ground themselves in the Christian understanding of the human person as a social being created in the image of a triune and personal God. Second, whereas the first concerns the microcosm of Christian life and morality, the latter addresses the macrocosm of church and world. Over time, Orthodox, Roman Catholic, and Protestant responses to these issues have assumed quite different forms from within a broadly shared faith.

Before beginning a discussion of these two issues in which differentiation marks off the three great Christian confessions, another type of differentiation has to be mentioned, although there is not room here to discuss it. In addition to differentiation that follows the threefold division of Orthodox, Catholic, and Protestant, historically there occurs also differentiation that stretches *across* classical confessional boundaries. One example is Luther's redefinition (as I mention below) of marriage that rejects Roman Catholicism's sacramental and contractual interest in that institution, yet draws nearer to the Orthodox vision of marriage as a churchly vocation.

Marriage

Questions about the moral dimensions of marriage arise early in the history of the Christian faith (see chapter 54). For Christianity, the state of marriage presupposes also the valid choice of singleness. St. Paul sets down the terms for a debate in the Patristic era and middle ages over the relative good of each of these ways of life. He favors a life of singleness and continence over the married state (1 Cor. 7:25ff.). A variety of factors influence his opinion. The most noteworthy is Paul's evident expectation that the *parousia* is imminent and that therefore marriage may detract from preparation for that event. Gnosticism and other currents of extreme asceticism deprecating the human body and sexuality, some condemning marriage outright, also challenge the church. Paul is aware of these also and rejects them. Thus, even as he favors singleness, Paul affirms the goodness of the body and the psychosomatic wholeness of the human person (see chapter 54). He therefore commends marriage "in the Lord" as a legitimate way of life for Christians who cannot or do not want to remain single and celibate.

By the middle of the second century, important writers launch a strong defense of marital monogamy as a valid arena for Christian askesis and sanctification. Celibacy and singleness certainly remain serious options, as witnessed by the rapid spread of Christian monasticism from the third century forward. Indeed, the medieval Roman Catholic Church propounds a formal teaching that elevates celibacy above marriage as morally and spiritually superior. It interprets the beatitudes of the Sermon on the Mount as marking off two distinct paths or "tracks" for Christians. For those who choose a "religious" vocation, the beatitudes are strict counsels of perfection, whereas for lay and married persons the beatitudes may be received merely as general precepts for moral guidance. Not until Vatican II (*Gaudium et Spes*, 50) does the Catholic church officially revise this teaching and declare that religious and lay life are equally valuable and honorable paths.

The Eastern church has left undecided which if any form of Christian living is the more perfect or honorable. It never has spoken officially of Christian ethics as on two tracks or as two-tiered. Early, there even arose strong voices in the East who insisted that marriage and not celibate life is the more difficult school of holiness. In the second century, Clement of Alexandria (ca. 150–ca. 215) argues "true manhood is shown . . . by him, I say, who in the midst of his solicitude for his family shows himself inseparable from the love of God and rises superior to every temptation which assails him through children and wife and servants and possessions." He "who has no family is in the most respects untried" (Meyendorff 1984: 95). Some Eastern Patristic writers criticize those in the church who excuse laity from the highest standards of Christian morality and holiness. They argue that this teaching contradicts the Christian doctrine that God proffers salvation to all men and women. St. John Chrysostom states that it is unthinkable and absolutely inconsistent with God's love that the beatitudes do not apply to married people every bit as much as the monk. The beatitudes, he insists, should not be viewed as "spoken to solitaries only." For Christ himself "permitted marriage" and he would not have barred the way for the vast majority of humankind to enter the kingdom of heaven (Chrysostom 1890: 402, homily on Hebrews 7). There are, of course, some in the East, especially among the severe ascetics, who do insist that celibacy is a superior life. Nevertheless, the view of Clement and Chrysostom that marriage is no less high and demanding a vocation as monastic living retains a strong place in the Eastern tradition.

In Western Christianity, Martin Luther breathed new life into this vision of marriage as a high Christian calling. Like Chrysostom, Luther objects to a double-track Christian morality. He argues that this demotes the lives of the vast number of Christians to an inferior status unworthy of God's love or of human freedom and potential. Luther condemns celibacy and monasticism as well as the Catholic teaching of marriage as a sacrament. Protestantism, in general, comes to the view that marriage and its ethical core are summed up as a sacred partnership of male and female entered by *free consent* for the purposes of Christian living and family.

Orthodoxy and Roman Catholicism have continued to teach that marriage is a sacrament that belongs to the church and is in its own right a vehicle of salvation. Despite a rich harvest during medieval times of profound mystical writings on the love of man and woman as metaphor and symbol of the soul's union with God and the church's marriage to Christ, Roman law made a distinct impact on the Catholic Church's interpretation of marriage. Roman legal tradition stipulated that the essence of marriage is in the free consent of the couple. The canon lawyers laid a heavy veneer of contractualism and legalism over the mystical and sacramental vision of marriage as conjugal union in Christ. In the East, the principle of free consent arrived late and never made the impact on its theology of marriage that it did on the Roman Catholic Church. Emphasis remained on the conjugal union as the heart of marriage. For example, in the Greek Orthodox version of the rite of holy matrimony there is no exchange of vows. In other Orthodox churches, these vows are added under Western influence.

In the Roman Catholic Church, a legalistc interpretation of marriage would obscure the deeper theological meaning of marriage as covenant and weaken the ancient ecclesial and soteriological, even eschatological, vision of marriage. In the East, the understanding of marriage as a "small church" and school of the virtues of the heavenly kingdom remained strong. St. John Chrysostom stands out as the great champion of this view of marriage. The goods of marriage are strictly the conjugal love, union, and procreation, in that order. The ultimate end of the sacrament of marriage is to render persons fit to inherit the Kingdom of God. Therefore, marriage requires a self-denying love that secures the union of the husband and wife in mutual self-giving and ensures the good upbringing of children. The crowning of the bride and groom in Orthodox weddings signifies not only that the marriage is a sacrament of the Kingdom but that in holy union the spouses put to death their selfish desires and bravely in humility endure whatever discomforts come along the way. The crowns, therefore, are not just the crowns of a king and queen but also crowns of martyrdom (i.e., a witness to holy and righteous living).

God holds parents responsible for disciplining and educating their children in virtue, not merely to make them good citizens but, first and most important, to make them saints. One's children are not only one's nearest neighbors; also, they are the weak and the vulnerable, deserving of special care. Christian marriage (and family) is a moral calling precisely because it is an ecclesial, soteriological, and eschatological entity. "If we regulate our households [properly] . . . we will also be fit to oversee the Church, for indeed the household is a little Church," Chrysostom insists (Chrysostom 1986: 57, homily 20 on Ephesians).

Virtually everything that the Eastern Christian tradition believes about marriage as a special location of self-sacrificial love and moral perfection may be found in

Protestant and Roman Catholic interpretations of marriage. Protestantism and Roman Catholicism, however, lend to these themes lesser or greater emphases that, in turn, introduce significant variances of meaning and practice. Different ecclesiologies and sacrament theologies account for a large part of this. For instance, the Anglican Church interprets marriage as a sacred covenant between a man and woman, not a sacrament. Nevertheless, Anglicans may speak of marriage as "an image of divine reality" and "divine love." Like other Protestants (and the Roman Catholic Church), however, Anglicans hold that the bride and groom marry each other and that the church merely witnesses to the union. In other words, bride and groom are the ministers (or officiates) of their own wedding. In sharp contrast, the Orthodox tradition states that the church marries the couple and accepts them into its ecclesial body. According to the former interpretation, marriage may be an "image of divine reality" but is not necessarily regarded as an ecclesial entity or a vehicle of salvation. "It does not denigrate marriage to say that it belongs to creation rather than to redemption," states the Anglican theologian Helen Oppenheimer. "It is made, not by prayer, but by the consent of the spouses" (1986: 366–7). One sees, from this example alone, that the marital virtues of self-sacrificial love, fidelity, and mutual assistance, which rank high in all three of the great Christian traditions, obtain significantly different meanings due to differences of ecclesiology and sacramentology.

Politics

The story of the early relations of the Christian church with the Roman empire through Constantine has been told many times (see chapter 48). The sources of the tension between the first-century church and the Roman imperial power were broader and deeper than mere politics. After Pentecost, the church's initial problems with the Roman state were not centered on formal relations, for these did not yet exist. The early Christians certainly bore no inherent objections to secular rule. Jesus did not oppose offering tribute in taxes to the state (Mark 12:17). And St. Paul called for obedience to the secular powers (Rom. 13:1–7), since they are ordained by God to keep order and justice in a sinful world. However, the book of Revelation also graphically depicts the empire as a demonic beast arisen from the abyss ready to consume the saints. This reflects the early Christian conviction that the empire was inherently idolatrous, witnessed by its insistence upon worship of the emperor and its claim to universal and everlasting dominion over the whole human race. The church struggled to gain sufficient freedom and space within this world order so that it might organize openly and pursue its evangelical mission.

The argument often is made that the source of the church's tension with the empire was a world-denying faith accompanied by a radical expectation of the imminent *parousia*. This is not true. The church did not deny the value of this world created by a good and loving God, but it did have a different vision of the world's origin, condition, and destiny than the empire's civil religion. The church believed that this world obtains lasting value strictly through its relationship to God as its creator and redeemer, and the fulfillment of the Kingdom of God. The early church was not anti-world or antiempire: it was pro-Kingdom of God. This put the church at odds with the imperial ideo-logy that identified Rome as the eternal city. Nor was it mere opportunism that moved the church to "accept" the "invitation" by the Emperor Theodosius I in 380 to become the legally established religion of the empire. There was a sincere, though perhaps mis-guided, desire on the part of the church to render a "holy service" for society, to exor-cise the imperial idolatry, and give the world back to its true Lord (Guroian 2001: 145). At the start, the church in the Greek- and Latin-speaking West held a common vision of a unified Christian society in which the two entities of church and state cooperated and essentially joined together to ensure that the commonweal prosper.

Ideologies developed differently, however, as the empire divided politically and geo-graphically, and then ecclesiastically, with Constantinople and Rome issuing mutual anathemas against one another in 1054. The different visions of a *corpus Christianum* are commonly identified as Caesaro-papism in the East and theocracy in the West. Nevertheless, both East and West made two fundamental theological errors in articu-lating their distinct visions. The first was "in thinking that the authority of Christ could be identified with the political *power* of the state." The second was "in considering that the *universality* of the gospel is definable in political terms" (Meyendorff 1978: 143). In the fifth century, Pope Gelasius I articulated the key terminology of the Western theo-cratic idea in his doctrine of the two swords. Christendom, he said, is ruled by two inde-pendent powers, the church represented by the pope and the imperial state by the emperor or king. This idea was used to secure sufficient freedom for the church to enable it to maintain independence from the state. It even opened the opportunity and justifi-cation for the papacy to dominate in a politically weakened empire. Meanwhile, the Byzantine Emperor Justinian I lent classic expression to the East's conception of the Christian empire as a "symphony" of church and state under the rule of the emperor.

Caesaro-papism and theocracy are misleading terms, however. They do not accu-rately describe or contrast the situations that develop in East and West. It makes more sense to identify two deep and differing metaphysical biases: monism in the East and dualism in the West. These two biases, respectively, bear quite different fruits in the organization of empire and relations of church and political order. Eastern monism and Western dualism have theological, ethical, juridical, and institutional dimensions. The West's dualism may be traced back to the language of Pope Leo I's (d. 461) famous tomb on Christology that figured prominently at the fourth Great Ecumenical Council of Chalcedon in 451,wherein he offered a doctrine of two natures in Christ that was suspected in many Eastern locations as scented with the Nestorian error of virtually dividing the One Lord, Jesus Christ, in two: into a human entity and divine entity who were joined but not truly united in one person. Leo may not have committed the Nesto-rian error, but his bias was toward dualism.

In the Latin West, this dualistic bias was not restricted to Christology; it also obtained juridical expression and emphasis, as the church quite deliberately defined itself vis-à-vis the state as a legal entity in order to gain leverage and power over it. The centrifu-gal force of the Protestant Reformation and the later dismemberment of political Christendom into nation-states, however, undercut the imperial church's efforts to maintain its independence and equal (if not superior) legal relationship with the state. These events and processes gave rise, ultimately, to national churches that for a time kept alive the vision of Christendom in their own separate territories. All the same, the national churches fell increasingly under state control and supervision. This is called Erastianism within Protestantism and Josephism (or Febronianism) within Roman Catholicism. The Enlightenment crystallized a process of secularization that was prompted and furthered by the Western dualism, and the churches' influence diminished in virtually all locations. In some instances, as under fascism and communism in the twentieth century, the churches even lost their legal status and freedom to practice the faith openly. Elsewhere in Europe, national churches continued to function under increasing pressures of religious pluralism. In America a system of complete disestablishment came about that resulted in a separation of church and state. It may be that the dualism embraced by the Western churches, both Catholic and Protestant, is no longer sustainable and over the long term will bring about its very negation under a thoroughly autonomous state and a unitary secularism.

The bias toward monism within Orthodox Christianity has borne different fruit. This monism is traceable to the East's emphasis on the hypostatic union of humanity and divinity in Christ and an extension of that dogma to the vision of the *corpus Christianum*. This monistic bias was reflected in the modification made by the Second Council of Constantinople (553) to the Christological formula of Chalcedon. It emphasized the more monophysitically oriented Christological teaching of St. Cyril of Alexandria (d. 444). Thus, the East envisioned Byzantium as a unified Christian society, fully church and fully imperial order, mirroring the doctrine that Jesus Christ is wholly God and wholly human being and still a single indivisible person. A powerful realized eschatology that got joined to this vision made trouble for the church. The resulting utopian ideology did harm to the freedom of the church. The idea that the Kingdom of God was being realized already in the temporal realm permitted the emperor and Byzantine state to dominate over the church.

Yet it is a misconception to interpret this in juridical terms, as the term Caesaropapism invites. There was not an understanding of one juridical entity, the church, subordinated to another juridical entity, the state. The Byzantine idea of symphony conceived of just one subject, not two. The church got defined as a function of the state – not an independent juridical entity, but a sympathetic sacramental organ whose function it was to bring the world increasingly under the rule of Christ and thus make the Kingdom of God present on earth. By accepting this role, the Byzantine church forgot two fundamental perceptions about its relationship to the world that it inherited from the ancient church. First, it forgot that this world is fallen and mortally sick. The church, having said *yes* to the invitation to render the empire holy before God, did not say *no* to the claim that the imperial realm was also the Kingdom of God brought to earth. Second, the church permitted itself to be defined as a hierarchy, with the *authority* of spiritual dogmas and the *power* of sacramental grace, at the awful price of losing sight of its calling as a *free community of faith*, whose presence in the world is also a judgment and limitation upon the inordinate and inevitably corrupt claims to power and authority of all earthly kingdoms (Guroian 2001: 147): "For better or worse, the unity of the Eastern Christian commonwealth was not broken as it was in the West." Byzantium did not shatter into pieces, but fell hard and whole to the alien forces of Islam. Georges Florovsky concludes: "Byzantium collapsed as a Christian kingdom, under the burden of its tremendous claims" (1974: 123–4). Byzantium failed as an experiment in Christian politics, but it left no experience or legacy of the secular and autonomous state in which there exists a plurality of Christian denominations. This helps to explain why, even after the collapse of the Soviet Union and communist regimes in Eastern Europe, there has been little enthusiasm for adopting an American model of separation of church and state and an almost equal unwillingness to give strong legal sanction to religious pluralism.

Differentiations in the Contemporary Scene

The future will tell how church and state issues are worked out in the Orthodox countries of Eastern Europe and the former Soviet Union. But however things turn out, in the interim, the church and state issue may actually take more classic form in these locations than in the West, although the results may differ from legal arrangements in the West. The so-called national Orthodox churches of the East lay much more powerful claim on the imaginations and memory of the people than do the deracinated Christian denominations in America and the highly eviscerated churches of Great Britain and Western Europe. Whereas the immediate danger in Western nations in which Roman Catholics and Protestants predominate is assimilation into a unitary secular society, the danger in the East seems inherently related to Orthodoxy's historically monistic and mystical biases. The national Orthodox churches bethink themselves as representatives of the ethnos and nation and are tempted habitually to imagine that collaboration with state authority and special privileges gained from the state will secure their legitimacy and an influence over the nation. Thoughts of being compromised through such concordats do not come easily to these churches that have thought of themselves as the soul of the nation.

The church and state issue as it is unfolding in the "new" nations of Africa, Latin America, and Asia forms the contemporary horizon of this analysis (see chapter 49). In most African, Latin American, and Asian countries, Christianity is represented predominantly by Roman Catholicism and/or Protestantism and so developments follow patterns of separation of church and state truer to the dualistic and juridical biases described above than in Orthodox lands. Nevertheless, in Africa and Asia, especially, strong forces of nationalism enter the mix in ways that especially invite comparison with events in Eastern Europe and the former Soviet Union. This is a reminder also that differentiation in Christian ethics is not limited to the historic divisions of Orthodox, Roman Catholic, and Protestant, but often crosses boundaries.

Bibliography

Chrysostom, J. 1890: "Homilies on the Hebrews" in *A Select Library of Nicene and Post-Nicene Fathers of the Christian Church*, Vol. 14. New York: Christian Literature Library.
—— 1986: *On Marriage and Family Life*, trans. C. P. Roth and D. Anderson. Crestwood, NY: St. Vladimir's Seminary Press.

—— 1988: *A Comparison Between a King and a Monk/Against the Opponents of Monastic Life*, trans. D. G. Hunter. Lewiston, NY: Edward Mellon Press.

Curran, C. E. 1976: *Catholic Moral Theology in Dialogue*. Notre Dame, IN: University of Notre Dame Press.

Florovsky, G. 1974: *Christianity and Culture, Vol. 2: The Collected Works of Georges Florovsky*. Belmont, MA: Nordland.

Fuchs, J., SJ. 1980: "Is There a Christian Morality?" in *Readings in Moral Theology*, ed. C. Curran and R. McCormick. New York: Paulist Press.

Guroian, V. 2001: *Incarnate Love: Essays in Orthodox Ethics*, 2nd edn. Notre Dame, IN: University of Notre Dame Press.

Gustafson, J. M. 1978: *Protestant and Roman Catholic Ethics: Prospects for Rapprochement*. Chicago: University of Chicago Press.

Harakas, S. S. 1983: *Toward Transfigured Life: The Theoria of Orthodox Ethics*. Minneapolis, MN: Light and Life Publishers.

Lake, K. (trans.) 1998: "The First Epistle of Clement to the Corinthians" in *The Apostolic Fathers*, Vol. 1. Loeb Classic Library 24. Cambridge, MA: Harvard University Press.

Maloney, G. A. (trans.) 1992: *Pseudo-Macarius: The Fifty Spiritual Homilies and the Great Letter*. Mahwah, NJ: Paulist Press.

Meyendorff, J. 1978: *Living Tradition*. Crestwood, NY: St. Vladimir's Seminary Press.

—— 1984: *Marriage: An Orthodox Perspective*. Crestwood, NY: St. Vladimir's Seminary Press.

Norris, R. 1986: "Patristic Ethics" in *The Westminster Dictionary of Christian Ethics*, ed. J. F. Childress and J. Macquarrie. Philadelphia, PA: Westminster Press.

Oppenheimer, H. 1986: "Marriage" in *The Westminster Dictionary of Christian Ethics*, ed. J. F. Childress and J. Macquarrie. Philadelphia, PA: Westminster Press.

CHAPTER 24
Trajectories in Christian Ethics

Jean Porter

During the course of the last century, the field of Christian ethics has been characterized by a bewildering profusion of approaches, methodologies, and concerns. On first inspection, this diversity appears as an embarrassment of riches, too complex to be sorted through. Yet on closer examination, it is given form by the recurrence of certain key motifs, which serve as touchstones for the development of specific theories. These recurrent themes set trajectories of reflection, which provide the Christian moral tradition with much of its coherence. Given the scope of this chapter, I will confine myself to examining three trajectories that have historically been central to Christian moral reflection, and will conclude with a brief look at recent developments. In the modern and contemporary period, I will focus primarily (but not exclusively) on Anglophone authors.

Moral Norms as Divine Commands

The image of God as a lawgiver, and correlatively, an approach to moral norms that construes them as God's commands or laws, is central to the Hebrew Bible (see chapters 17 and 18). Even though later Christian reflection emphasized the contrast between the supposed legalism of the Old Testament and the orientation to grace characterizing the New Testament, more recent biblical scholarship has underscored the fact that God is characterized as a lawgiver in parts of the Christian scriptures as well (Meeks 1993: 119–210). This is what we would expect, since the Jewish and Christian conception of God as both a supreme being and a personal reality lends itself to a perception of morality as a set of divine decrees. Among Christians, this idea was expanded to include dominical commands, that is, the authoritative moral teachings of Jesus, which for many Christians carry divine authority. Given this scriptural orientation, it is scarcely surprising that an approach to moral norms that emphasizes their authoritative status as expressions of God's will emerged very early in Christian moral reflection.

This trajectory continued throughout the Patristic and medieval period. It is particularly evident in the moral thought of Augustine (354–430 CE), who placed great emphasis on the authoritative status of morality, seen as an expression of God's eternal law. Augustine's influence, in turn, helped to guarantee that an emphasis on the authoritative status of morality as an expression of God's will continued to play a central role in Christian thought, at least in the West. In the medieval period, this tendency was re-enforced by a juridical approach to sin and repentance. This approach reflected early medieval practices of penance, which were governed by penitentials in which sins were carefully defined and their appropriate penalties were set out in some detail. Later theological reflections on sin and developments in the practice of private confession led to more sophisticated and humane practices of reconciliation, but this practice continued to reflect a juridical model of sin and repentance throughout the medieval period (and among Roman Catholics, up until the modern period).

Yet it would be misleading to characterize either Patristic or medieval conceptions of morality as versions of a divine command ethics, as that term later came to be understood. Divine command theories are characterized by the fact that they distinguish God's will or authority from other aspects of the divine reality and identify this aspect as the ground of morality, whether as a foundation which grounds and encompasses other sources of morality, or as the sole source of morality which is set over against other putative sources of moral obligation (see chapter 2). Certainly, Christian ethical reflection has always traced morality back to some aspect of God's will, wisdom, or providential love, but until the later middle ages, God's will was not set over against other aspects of the divine reality in such a way as to give rise to a divine command morality in the strict sense. While moral norms were thought to reflect God's will, they were also seen as reflections of God's wisdom or benevolence, insofar as they reflected exigencies of reason or human nature. Medieval theologians did raise the theoretical possibility that moral norms might depend on God's authoritative will alone, but in general they resisted separating this aspect of morality from its rational or naturalistic aspects.

The first theologian to defend a divine command theory of ethics appears to have been Duns Scotus (1266–1308). Scotus claimed that God's will is not bound by any considerations of order or justice, or any rational considerations save the law of non-contradiction, since on his view the will is nobler than the intellect and cannot be constrained by it. Hence, only those laws governing our relationship to God are natural laws in the strict sense, because only these follow by strict necessity from the divine nature. The laws of nature pertaining to our relations with one another are seen as expressions of God's ordained power, but not God's absolute power. That is, God forbids (for example) murder and adultery, but absolutely speaking, God could have commanded otherwise, rendering such actions just and right. Scotus' fellow Franciscan William of Ockham (ca. 1285–1349) took this line of argument one step further, arguing that absolutely speaking, God could even have commanded us to hate God. Similar considerations led both Martin Luther (1483–1546) and John Calvin (1509–64) to affirm that God is the ultimate source of justice and morality. Not only does this mean that moral norms derive from God's will; it also implies that God's actions cannot be evaluated by our standards of justice and consistency.

Similar concerns to preserve God's complete and unconditional priority to, and inde-pendence from, impersonal structures of reason, justice, or even consistency have con-tinued to shape theological ethics up to the present. One of the most influential expressions of this approach was offered by Søren Kierkegaard (1813–55) in *Fear and Trembling*, in which he takes God's command to Abraham to sacrifice Isaac as the start-ing point for raising the possibility of a teleological suspension of the ethical, in which God's direct command may supersede the demands of universal morality. This treatise, one of Kierkegaard's pseudonymous writings, is too complex to be taken as a straight-forward defense of divine command morality, but by raising the possibility that God's command can transcend the ethical universal, it has proven to be an influential source for later divine command moralities.

Probably the most influential statement of a divine command theory of ethics in the twentieth century is that developed by Karl Barth in his *Church Dogmatics* (1957: 509–781). For Barth, any attempt to develop an ethic based on considerations of nature, reasonableness, or the like reflects human rebellion against the sovereignty of God, who confronts the human person with a Word of command that is both heteronomous and absolutely binding. Barth insists on this, not only to uphold the omnipotence of God, but also to uphold God's personal character as one who establishes a relationship of authority and obedience through divine commands. At the same time, through Jesus Christ, God's commands confer liberty, even as they bind us to obedience. God commands us in order to claim us through grace for our ultimate salvation.

Moral Norms as Natural Law

Since classical antiquity, the idea of law has been interpreted in at least two ways, that is, as authoritative command and as intrinsic principle of order (see chapter 11). The first line of interpretation lends itself to a divine command approach to morality; when the latter approach to law is emphasized, we see the emergence of a second central tra-jectory in Christian ethics, namely, the construal of moral norms as a natural law. There have been many forms of natural law morality, including both moralities that stress the intrinsic moral significance of pre-rational natural processes, and those that ground it in the exigencies of reason. What these have in common, however, is a view of moral-ity which grounds it in intrinsic, ordered structures of being, in contrast to approaches that emphasize authoritative will. So understood, the idea of natural law appears to have originated with the Stoics, and we find it expressed near the beginning of the common era by the Roman philosopher Cicero (106–43 BCE).

It might seem that the Hebrew scriptures, with their strong emphasis on God as law-giver, would not lend themselves to a natural law interpretation of morality. However, the psalms and wisdom literature place great weight on God's law as an expression of wisdom, more excellent than the philosophical wisdom of any other nation; even within Deuteronomy, we read that the excellence of God's law will be acknowledged by all the nations of the earth (Deut. 4:6–8). This strain of Hebrew scriptures lends itself to an interpretation of God's law which emphasizes its origins in God's wisdom, and which therefore opens the way to presenting it as an expression of natural law (Barton 1998: 58–76). In the Jewish philosopher Philo (b. ca. 10 BCE), writing roughly a generation after Cicero, we find precisely this interpretation; according to Philo, the Law of Moses represents the law of nature in perfect written form. Similarly, St. Paul's appeals to nature and conscience as a source for moral norms, and as the basis for a law that stands parallel to the Law of Moses for the Gentiles (Rom. 2:14–16), were foundational for later Christian theories of the natural law.

When we turn to the Patristic era, we once again find Augustine playing a decisive role in setting an agenda for later Christian moral thought, at least in the West. We observed above that Augustine placed great emphasis on the authoritative status of law. Yet he also understood law as an intrinsic principle of order, along the lines of classical accounts of the natural law. These two approaches to law came together in his conception of God's Eternal Law, which Augustine understands as an expression of God's ordering wisdom as well as God's authoritative will. In addition, Augustine, together with many other Patristic authors, took the Golden Rule to be the fundamental principle of the natural law inscribed in the conscience of every human person, and the Decalogue to be a summary of its basic precepts.

In the medieval period, the natural law approach came to dominate Christian moral reflection, at least among the scholastic jurists and theologians whose work laid the foundations for so much later work in Christian ethics. The most influential medieval exponent of a natural law approach to ethics is Thomas Aquinas (ca. 1225–74). For Aquinas, the natural law in its primary sense consists of basic, self-evident principles of practical reason (for example, the principle that the good is to be pursued and done and the bad avoided), which are analogous to first principles of speculative reason, such as the law of non-contradiction. In a secondary sense, the natural law consists of precepts ordered around basic human inclinations to live, to reproduce, to seek the truth about God, and the like; Aquinas also endorses the almost unanimous view that the Decalogue offers a summary of the precepts of the natural law. Seen from yet another perspective, the natural law represents the human person's participation in God's eternal law, understood in Augustinian terms, but with a stronger emphasis on the eternal law as an expression of God's wisdom, rather than God's will (Porter 1999: 92–5).

In the modern period, natural law reflection took a new turn. Under the influence of the early modern revolution in mathematical and scientific thought, moral thinkers began to aspire to a theory of the natural law based on deductions from first principles, which theory would have the same perspicuous rational force as a mathematical system such as Euclidean geometry. On this view, distinctively theological claims have no foundational or essential place in a theory of the natural law, although they may serve to confirm, correct, or supplement the moral code generated by moral reasoning. This approach also led to a greater emphasis on the discrete rules that comprise the natural law. This approach to the natural law, in turn, lent itself to the more pronounced emphasis on the natural law as an expression of God's authoritative will, and at this point, the two trajectories, divine command ethics and natural law ethics, began to come together in the work of such theologians as Suarez (Schneewind 1998: 58–78, 118–38).

Luther's radical critique of the idea of salvation through works kept the idea of natural law from taking much hold in Protestant theology, although it continued to play some role in Anglican and Reformed thought. However, versions of the natural law similar to that developed by Suarez continued to be foundational to Catholic moral theology up until the twentieth century. In the years just before and after Vatican II, the idea of an immutable natural law was sharply criticized by Catholic theologians, and these criticisms, together with controversies over questions of sexual ethics after Vatican II, seriously undermined the credibility of the natural law among Catholic theologians.

More recently, there has been a revival of interest in natural law approaches to ethics. One of the most influential contemporary versions is the "new theory of the natural law" (Grisez 1983: 173–274; Finnis 1998: 103–31). On this view, moral laws are derived from an apprehension of certain basic goods, which are known to be such as soon as they are experienced, together with norms of practical reasonableness which determine how we are to relate to these goods. This version of the natural law places great emphasis on its rational character, and allows only a very limited place for the moral significance of pre-rational human nature. However, recent developments in biotechnology, medicine, and ecology have led to a revival of interest in the moral significance of pre- or non-rational nature, among both Protestant and Catholic scholars (Gustafson 1981; Pope 1994). At the same time, a renewed interest in human or natural rights has led to the revival of other strands of the natural law tradition (Nussbaum 2000: 34–110; Tierney 1997: 1–12; Schweiker 1995). Finally, it should be noted that some Protestant scholars have recently argued for an account of moral norms similar to that associated with the natural law, but grounded in explicitly theological principles such as Christian love (Ramsey 1967).

Ideals of Virtue

In recent years, the topic of virtue has received a great deal of attention from Christian ethicists as well as philosophers (see chapter 4). In fact, there are many theologians who argue that, correctly understood, Christian ethics is predominantly or even exclusively an ethic of virtues, rather than an ethic of rules. Yet this would not have been obvious at every point in Christian history.

The virtues as such do not seem to have been a central theme for early Patristic thought, although we do find discussions of the traits of character appropriate to, or contrary to, the Christian life in this period. Augustine offers a reformulation of a Stoic conception of virtue as wisdom, according to which Christian love is the fundamental virtue that other virtues express in specific circumstances. However, the best-known aspect of Augustine's treatment of virtue is his severe critique of classical Roman ideals of virtue, which on his view were at best vitiated by pride and a failure to know and love the true God (Rist 1994: 148–202).

Virtue began to be a central topic for Christian ethics in the medieval period. By the mid-twelfth century, two distinctive approaches to virtue ethics had emerged, exemplified by Peter Abelard (1074–ca. 1142) and Peter Lombard (ca. 1100–60), respectively.

According to Abelard, the virtues are human excellences that can be attained even without grace. They existed among the best of the pagans, and were adequately described in philosophical terms. Lombard, in contrast, understood the virtues in Augustinian terms as expressions of Christian charity, which as such presuppose grace. For most of the later scholastics, however, these alternatives are too stark, and they attempt to synthesize them by developing accounts of the virtues, which allow for them to be understood both as human attainments and as gifts of grace. Typically, the complex character of virtue is spelled out in terms of a distinction between the political virtues, which can be attained through human ability alone and understood in philosophical terms, and theological virtues that presuppose grace and can only be identified through revelation. The former are generally identified with the classical cardinal virtues of prudence, justice, courage and temperance, the latter with the Pauline triad of faith, hope, and love.

We find a different approach to synthesizing these two conceptions of virtue in Aquinas, who offers the most influential scholastic theory of the virtues and their place in the Christian life. In the place of the widely accepted distinction between political and theological virtues, Aquinas introduced a distinction between the acquired virtues, which can be attained through human effort, and the infused virtues, which can only be attained through grace and which correlatively provide the operative principles through which grace becomes an effective principle for action. The acquired virtues include both the traditional cardinal virtues and other traditional virtues that are analyzed as derivative from these four. The infused virtues include the three theological virtues, but they also include infused counterparts to the acquired virtues. These latter resemble their acquired counterparts in some respects, but differ insofar as they are directed towards a distinctive end, that is to say, union with God as opposed to human well-being understood in purely rational terms.

In the early modern period, theologians began to question the suitability of the idea of virtue as a category for Christian moral reflection. One of the most thoroughgoing such critiques was offered by Luther, for whom an emphasis on virtue reflected a more general tendency to attempt to guarantee one's salvation through personal works, in contrast to relying on God's free grace. Yet Luther also insisted that the Christian life is marked by stable dispositions such as joyfulness and a readiness to be of service to others. While he did not speak of these dispositions as virtues, there are clear affinities between this aspect of his thought and virtue ethics, and some contemporary Lutheran theologians have taken the relevant aspects of his thought as a starting point for a distinctively Lutheran virtue ethic (Meilaender 1984: 100–26; Stock 1995).

Catholic thought in the modern period continued to use the traditional language of the cardinal and theological virtues, yet these were increasingly reduced to organizing principles for moral rules, while many of the traditional concerns of virtue ethics were relegated to the study of spirituality or mysticism. Yet during the modern period the idea of virtue continued to play an important role for some Protestant and secular thinkers. The Puritan theologian Jonathan Edwards (1703–58), the greatest American theologian before the twentieth century, devoted a treatise, *On the Nature of True Virtue*, to developing a Christian theory of virtue out of elements of the moral sense theory. True virtue consists in benevolence towards Being in general, and as such it goes beyond natural virtue to take in love for God as supreme Being. Only true virtue can be considered to be an effect and sign of election to salvation. Yet natural virtue is good in itself, and it is not destroyed, but transformed by true virtue (Edwards 1960). Even more significant is the work of Friedrich Schleiermacher (1768–1834). Schleiermacher offers an interpretation of virtue as a capacity to grasp and to act upon the concrete implications of the moral law, which is similar in some respects to the Aristotelian idea of practical wisdom. However, Schleiermacher's overall theology has probably been more important, from the standpoint of contemporary virtue ethics, than his remarks on virtue per se. According to him, all genuine religion is grounded in an awareness of an infinite and eternal source of all finite realities, together with a sense of our absolute dependence on that infinite source. For the Christian, this awareness takes the form of reverence for Christ as the mediator between God and the human person. In our own time, this approach to theology has inspired an ethics of piety or Christian dispositions, among both English speaking and German theologians (see Gerrish 1984; Gustafson 1981, 1984).

During the early part of the twentieth century, virtue was not a major theme among either Catholic or Protestant theologians. Among Catholics, one of the earliest and most influential such attempts to reclaim virtue theory was that of Bernard Häring (1965), who provided a moral theology based on charity, understood as the paradigmatic Christian virtue. Similarly, the Jesuit moral theologian Gerard Gilleman (1959) attempted to retrieve Aquinas' account of charity as the root of the Christian moral and spiritual life, and his fellow Jesuit Karl Rahner (1969) developed an account of love as a fundamental option which lends itself very readily to a virtue-oriented moral theology. More recently, a number of theologians, predominantly but not exclusively Catholics, have turned to Aquinas to provide starting points for a contemporary Christian virtue ethics (Abbà 1983; Cates 1996; Keenan 1992; Porter 1999; Rhonheimer 1994).

Among Protestant theologians, advocates of a return to virtue ethics argue that it provides the best way to understand the distinctive character of discipleship within the Christian community (Hauerwas 1981). The Christian community is rooted in ideals of non-violence and communal solidarity quite different from those which prevail in the dominant culture. Christian ethics should reflect these differences by focusing on the virtues which enable the individual to live in a truly Christian fashion. During the last decades of the twentieth century, there has been a revival of virtue ethics among philosophers (MacIntyre 1984). The trajectory set by reflection on the virtues as well as divine commands and natural law continues to play an important role in Christian moral reflection.

Recent Developments in the Field of Christian Ethics

To a considerable degree, the diversity within the field of Christian ethics has reflected the variety of concerns faced by Christians in the twentieth century. At the beginning of the last century, the plight of workers within an increasingly industrial and global economy gave rise to the social gospel movement, most closely associated today with

Walter Rauschenbusch. His *Christianity and the Social Crisis* (1991) combined search-ing social critique and deep optimism for the possibilities for communal reform and regeneration. Yet this very optimism led to widespread critiques, including most notably Reinhold Niebuhr's widely influential Christian realism, which emphasizes the tension between the ideal of Christian love and the harsh necessity of sustaining justice in a fallen world (see Niebuhr 1941–3) (see chapter 45).

The challenges posed by war and peace continued to be central to Christian ethics throughout the twentieth century, culminating in a widely influential revival of a prin-cipled Christian pacifism (see Yoder 1994; Hauerwas 1981). At the same time, however, beginning in the 1960s, other social issues emerged as central concerns for Christian ethics. This was of course a decade of social ferment and concern for the previously marginalized, including women, historically disadvantaged minorities, and sexual minorities. These concerns shaped Christian ethics in a variety of ways. Around this time, feminist voices began to emerge within Christian ethics (Daly 1973; Ruether 1975; Harrison 1985), while at the same time liberation theology inspired a new atten-tiveness to the concerns of the poor and marginalized around the world (Gutiérrez 1973). In the United States, the liberation paradigm was quickly applied to the situa-tion of African Americans and other marginalized groups (Cone 1969; West 1982). Finally, during the last decades of the past century, scholars in Christian ethics increas-ingly turned their attention to the challenges presented by globalization, the need to defend human rights in a pluralistic world, new possibilities in biomedicine, and the imperative to protect the environment (see chapters 52 and 53).

In addition to the varieties of Christian ethics generated by specific social concerns, this field has also been diversified through the adoption of a variety of theoretical per-spectives and methodological approaches. One of the most influential early works of twentieth-century social ethics, Ernst Troeltsch's *The Social Teaching of the Christian Churches* (1995), fostered an interdisciplinary approach to Christian ethics through its appropriation of sociological theory. This approach continues to provide a starting point for discussions of the interaction between Christian beliefs and the wider society (see Niebuhr 1951). In addition, H. Richard Niebuhr pioneered the appropriation of American pragmatism, which he developed into his own distinctive theory of Christian ethics as a form of responsiveness to, and responsibility in the face of, the divine initia-tive (Niebuhr 1963). This approach has proven to be widely influential. It was devel-oped by James Gustafson (1981, 1984) with serious attention to the constraints of contemporary science and social theory. Still more recently, "responsibility ethics" has been enriched through the appropriation of European hermeneutical theory and dis-course ethics in order to develop a more robust account of what is involved in con-struing a situation from a theistic viewpoint (Schweiker 1995). The "responsibility ethics" approach has also been adopted by some Catholic moral theologians, most notably Charles Curran (1999).

Bibliography

Abbà, G. 1983: *Lex et virtus: studi sull'evoluzione della dottrina morale di san Tommaso d'Aquino.* Rome: Las.

Barth, K. 1957: *Church Dogmatics*, Vol. II.4, trans. and ed. G. W. Bromiley and T. F. Torrance. Edinburgh: T. & T. Clark.

Barton, J. 1998: *Ethics and the Old Testament*. Harrisburg, PA: Trinity Press International.

Cates, D. F. 1996: *Choosing to Feel: Virtue, Friendship and Compassion for Friends*. Notre Dame, IN: University of Notre Dame Press.

Cone, J. H. 1969: *Black Theology and Black Power*. New York: Seabury Press.

Curran, C. E. 1999: *The Catholic Moral Tradition Today: A Synthesis*. Washington, DC: Georgetown University Press.

Daly, M. 1973: *Beyond God the Father: Toward a Philosophy of Women's Liberation*. Boston, MA: Beacon Press.

Edwards, J. 1960 [1765]: *The Nature of True Virtue*. Ann Arbor: University of Michigan Press.

Finnis, J. 1998: *Aquinas: Moral, Political, and Legal Theory*. New York: Oxford University Press.

Gerrish, B. A. 1984: *A Prince of the Church: Schleiermacher and the Beginnings of Modern Theology*. Philadelphia, PA: Fortress Press.

Gilleman, G. 1959: *The Primacy of Charity in Moral Theology*. Westminster, MD: Newman Press.

Grisez, G. G. 1983: *The Way of the Lord Jesus*, Vol. 1. Chicago: Franciscan Herald Press.

Gustafson, J. M. 1981, 1984: *Ethics from a Theocentric Perspective*, 2 vols. Chicago: University of Chicago Press.

Gutiérrez, G. 1973: *A Theology of Liberation: History, Politics, and Salvation*. Maryknoll, NY: Orbis Books.

Häring, B. 1965: *The Law of Christ: Moral Theology for Priests and Laity*. Westminster, MD: Newman Press.

Harrison, B. W. (ed.) 1985: *Making the Connections: Essays in Feminist Social Ethics*. Boston, MA: Beacon Press.

Hauerwas, S. 1981: *The Peaceable Kingdom: A Primer in Christian Ethics*. Notre Dame, IN: University of Notre Dame Press.

Keenan, J. F. 1992: *Goodness and Rightness in Thomas Aquinas's Summa Theologiae*. Washington, DC: Georgetown University Press.

MacIntyre, A. C. 1984: *After Virtue: A Study in Moral Theory*, 2nd edn. Notre Dame, IN: University of Notre Dame Press.

Meeks, W. A. 1993: *The Origins of Christian Morality: The First Two Centuries*. New Haven, CT: Yale University Press.

Meilaender, G. 1984: *The Theory and Practice of Virtue*. Notre Dame, IN: University of Notre Dame Press.

Niebuhr, H. R. 1951: *Christ and Culture*. New York: Harper.

——1963: *The Responsible Self: An Essay in Christian Moral Philosophy*. New York: Harper & Row.

Niebuhr, R. 1941–3: *The Nature and Destiny of Man: A Christian Interpretation*, 2 vols. New York: Charles Scribner's Sons.

Nussbaum, M. C. 2000: *Women and Human Development: The Capabilities Approach*. New York: Cambridge University Press.

Pope, S. J. 1994: *The Evolution of Altruism and the Ordering of Love*. Washington, DC: Georgetown University Press.

Porter, J. 1999: *Natural and Divine Law: Reclaiming the Tradition for Christian Ethics*. Ottawa: Novalis.

Rahner, K. 1969: "Reflections of the Unity of the Love of Neighbor and the Love of God" in *Theological Investigations*, Vol. 6, 231–52. New York: Crossroad.

Ramsey, P. 1967: *Deeds and Rules in Christian Ethics*. New York: Scribner.

Rauschenbusch, W. 1991 [1907]: *Christianity and the Social Crisis*. Louisville, KY: Westminster/John Knox Press.

Rhonheimer, M. 1994: *Praktische Vernuft und Vernunftigkeit der Praxis*. Berlin: Akademie Verlag.

Rist, J. M. 1994: *Augustine: Ancient Thought Baptized*. New York: Cambridge University Press.

Ruether, R. R. 1975: *New Woman, New Earth: Sexist Ideologies and Human Liberation*. New York: Seabury Press.

Schneewind, J. B. 1998: *The Invention of Autonomy: A History of Modern Moral Philosophy*. New York: Cambridge University Press.

Schweiker, W. 1995: *Responsibility and Christian Ethics*. New York: Cambridge University Press.

Stock, K. 1995: *Grundlegung der protestantischen Tugendlehre*. Gutersloh: Chr. Kaiser/Gutersloher Verlagshaus.

Tierney, B. 1997: *The Idea of Natural Rights: Studies on Natural Rights, Natural Law, and Church Law, 1150–1625*. Atlanta, GA: Scholars Press.

Troeltsch, E. 1995: *The Social Teaching of the Christian Churches*, 2 vols. Library of Theological Ethics. Louisville, KY: Westminster/John Knox Press.

West, C. 1982: *Prophecy Deliverance!* Philadelphia, PA: Westminster Press.

Yoder, J. H. 1994: *The Politics of Jesus*. Grand Rapids, MI: Eerdmans Press.

3 Islamic Ethics

CHAPTER 25

Muslim Ethics?

Ebrahim Moosa

The Idea of Ethics in Islam

As part of the Abrahamic tradition, Muslim ethics both resemble and differ from the way ethics is practiced in Judaism and Christianity. Given the geographical breadth of the cultures in which Islam flourished, one cannot ignore the complex crucibles in which Muslim ethics were formed. The genealogy of Muslim ethics can be traced to pre-Islamic Arabia, Islamic Arabia, and Persian, Greek and sūfī (mystical) sources, as well as later influences of an African and Asian provenance. However, the formation of ethics is not a mechanical and instrumental use of cultural resources. It occurs gradually as Muslim communities organically become established within different cultural and social settings.

The discipline of ethics has several synonymous nomenclatures in Muslim culture. It is most often described as the "science of innate dispositions" (*'ilm al-akhlāq*), the "science of comportment or conduct" (*'ilm al-sulūk*) or "science of mysticism" (*'ilm al-taṣawwuf*). From these descriptions it becomes obvious that the emphasis is almost exclusively focused on the formation and cultivation of individual practices. Two terms, rich in semantic signification, shape the debate on ethics: "character" (*khuluq*, pl. *akhlāq*) and "civility" or "etiquette" (*adab*, pl. *ādāb*).

The word *khuluq* has deep roots in Arabic culture and its use is preserved with its early semantic field. The Prophet Muḥammad is described as being given an "extraordinary noble character"(Qur'ān 68:4). The word *khuluq*, say lexicologists, means "religion" (*dīn*), "nature" (*ṭab'*) and "natural disposition" (*sajiyya*), "chivalry" (*muruwwa*) or even "habit" (*'āda*). Essentially, says the Indian encyclopedist Tahānawī (d. ca. 1777), *khuluq* "is a habitus or disposition (*malaka*) with which the spirit produces certain acts spontaneously, without need of reflection, seeing, and pretense." The other key word is *adab*, meaning right conduct or norms of right conduct. A standard definition is:

> Right conduct (*adab*) constitutes the sum of prudential knowledge that shields one from
> all error in speech, acts, and character. It signifies all the Arabic sciences, for they cumu-
> latively promote etiquette. *Adab* is thus a *habitus* or disposition (*malaka*) that protects one
> from disgrace. A perfectly urbane and cultivated person (*adīb*) is one who possesses this
> *habitus*. Therefore it is said: "the way to ultimate reality is through [the practice of] right
> conduct." (Khānzāda 1980: 4)

Any disciplinary practice that results in the cultivation of a virtue is called norms of
right conduct. Ethics is thus the cultivation of this disposition through education and
practice. In fact, the Arabic word *adab* derives from the root signifying a feast, *ma'duba*,
in order to nourish the body; but in its changed morphology it denotes a disciplinary
practice for the nourishment of the mind.

Persian culture had the most significant impact on the development of ethics in subsequent Islamicate cultures. When speaking about disciplining the self (*adab al-nafs*),
early ethicists also meant the ethics of speaking (*adab al-lisān*), as well as the proper attitude in order to internalize the norms one learns in pedagogy (*adab al-dars*), as both
aspects are indispensable components for a complete ethical formation. 'Abd al-Nabī
al-Aḥmadnagrī (d. 1769), also an Indian encyclopedist, describes the discipline of the
self as shielding the limbs and religious symbols from harm. The principle of non-
maleficience, the obligation not to inflict harm intentionally, is a feature of Muslim ethics.

There is a famous report in which 'Ā'isha describes her husband, the Prophet
Muḥammad, as having a character that mirrors the Qur'ān. He is described as the
embodiment of the values of the Qur'ān. In this pithy statement, the linkage between
the Qur'ān and ethical values should not be ignored. The Prophet Muḥammad embodies the virtues proposed in the Qur'ān. *Imitatio* Muḥammadi is an essential part of
Muslim ethical teaching and practice (see chapter 10). In fact, the Qur'ān, addressing
the Prophet Muḥammad, declares: "Indeed you have been endowed with a noble character" (Qur'ān 68:4). Numerous prophetic reports place an extraordinary emphasis on
the need to cultivate good character, *ḥusn al-khuluq*. It appears as if the aesthetic quality
of beauty (*ḥusn*), inherent in good, serves as an antidote to sinful behavior.

Muslim ethics is a responsibility-based ethics, invoking reciprocal rights and duties.
Thus a range of social actors from parents, teachers, and professionals to every individual is an active moral agent. Ethical discourses are part of all the major disciplines
of religious thought, ranging from the teachings of the Qur'ān, the prophetic reports,
juridical literature, theology, and mysticism to philosophy and literature proper.

Historical Trends

The formal discipline of the "science of ethics" takes shape under the rubric of a
philosophical-cum-literary genre with writers like Miskawayh (d. 1030), Abū Ḥayyān
al-Tawḥīdī (d. 1023), and Abū al-Ḥasan al-'Āmirī (d. 992). In political ethics, the work
of Abū al-Ḥasan al-Māwardī (d. 1058), is significant.

Early Muslim pietists like Hārith al-Muḥāsibī (d. 857), 'Alī bin Muḥammad Ibn
Ḥazm (d. 1064), Rāghib al-Isfahānī (d. ca. 1108), and Abū Ḥāmid al-Ghazālī (d. 1111)
combined the disciplining of the self with the observance of ritual and legal obligations,

better known as positive law (*fiqh*). Obedience to the norms derived from revelation (sharī'a) enables the individual to develop an inner disposition that is analogous to the notion of conscience. Readers of ethical treatises are taught how do undertake a personal moral diagnostic on sincerity, how to cultivate virtuous habits and good character.

Law and ethics are inseparable. Two terms, *fiqh* and sharī'a, signify what we would call the law. The sharī'a refers to revealed normative discourses; *fiqh* (literally meaning "discernment") is the interpretation and application of these discourses. Law (*fiqh*) has to meet two ends: the practices must fulfill worldly ends and simultaneously serve as acts of salvation. The founder of the Ḥanafī school of law, Abū Ḥanīfa (d. 767), described *fiqh* as "the soul/self knowing its rights and its duties." In *fiqh* discourse, piety, morality, theology, and law coalesce into a single coherent narrative. Thus Abū Ḥanīfa named a very brief catechism "The Greater Discernment" (*al-fiqh al-akbar*) that included teachings on doctrines, law, and piety.

In the twelfth century, Ghazālī became dissatisfied with the popular and legalistic understanding of *fiqh* that was preoccupied with hairsplitting and arcane debates. True *fiqh*, he argued, meant more than just the law of marriage and divorce, contracts and sales. Issuing authoritative opinions or *juridical responsa* (*fatwā*, pl. *fatāwā*), Ghazālī said, was the least important part of the law. The earliest iteration of *fiqh* meant "the path of salvation in the afterlife." The external law regulating one's actions must be complemented by an inner discernment (*fiqh al-nafs*), said Ghazālī. *Fiqh* should ideally ensure that the practitioner develops a moral consciousness of the divine (*taqwā*).

Individual responsibility is at the center of Muslim ethics. Even if a jurist issues an informed opinion, the lay person is compelled to subject any ruling to the scrutiny of the inner forum of the conscience. The martyred jurist-mystic, 'Ayn al-Quḍāt al-Hamadhānī (d. 1131), approves of expert knowledge and ethical guidance, but insists that it must be "an opinion of the heart" (*fatwā 'l-qalb*). For some ethicists, the heart is the seat of conscience and a more reliable ethical barometer than the jurists' dispassionate reasoning. A report attributed to the Prophet says: "Solicit a response [*fatwā*] from your heart, even though the jurisconsult [*muftī*] had issued an opinion."

Historian 'Abd al-Raḥmān Ibn Khaldūn (d. 1406) points out that in early Islam *fiqh* was a *malaka* which he conceived of as a sociobiological-cum-moral disposition. Corrupted over time, this disposition became predisposed to soulless legalism. The professionalization of the law estranged it from its deeper ethical and moral impulses. It was the mystics who tried to revive ethics in its embodied form with an emphasis on autonomous intuitive cognition or aesthetic sensibility (*dhawq*), cultivated through extensive ascetic practices (*mujāhada*) and exercises in self-examination (*muḥāsaba*).

Theological Presuppositions and Legal Reasoning

Theological reasoning does indeed shape ethical and moral thinking. Competing theological schools of medieval Islam, namely the rational-pietist Mu'tazila and the traditionalist-rational Ash'arī schools, bequeathed rival moral theories. The Mu'tazila promoted a doctrine of ethical objectivism in which reason and revelation were coeval. The Ash'arīs accepted discursive reason, but for them reason was always subject to the authority of revelation. Their position can be described as ethical subjectivism. For the Mu'tazila, reason is capable of deciding if something is good or detestable; the Ash'aris believe that something is good or bad because the divine discourse declares it to be so (see chapter 2). Muslims affiliated to the Sunnī branch of Islam follow the Ash'ari school or other analogous ones, while those affiliated to the Shī'a branch developed their own type of rationality, also borrowing some ideas from the Mu'tazila doctrine.

Modern debates on legal ethics are informed by premodern theological develop-ments. Abū Ishāq al-Shāṭibī (d. 1388), the jurist from Muslim Spain, argued that one can rationally extrapolate the divine intent embedded in the sharī'a discourses. Shāṭibī theorizes a grand scheme of moral philosophy in relation to the law. The objec-tives of the sharī'a, he said, can be listed in terms of a three-tier hierarchical taxonomy of ethical categories or directives: (1) compelling necessity (ḍarūriyāt), (2) needs (ḥājiyāt), and (3) improvements (taḥsīnāt). Under the category of compelling necessity, the divine lawgiver seeks to preserve and safeguard five ethical objectives: religion, life, property, reason, and paternity. Legal interpretations should ensure that the rules and judgments meet the broad rationality of these objectives, especially in areas where there are no prescribed rules. The category of needs urges the ethical–legal subject to seek out flexibility in order to eliminate hardship. The category of improvements promotes aesthetic perfection and ethical refinement to practices. A doctrine that also has broad currency is (4) public interest (maṣlaḥa). The assumption is that public interests are embedded within legal rules; one extreme view even considers public interest to trump the letter of the law. It is generally agreed that rules premised on custom and public interest considerations change with time and place.

Contemporary Approaches

Debates on contextual legal ethics remain muted in circles of traditional scholarship. Reformist and progressive tendencies take contextual ethics seriously. Very few tradi-tionalist jurists – save for some in Iran and individuals elsewhere – are prepared to examine the letter of the law in terms of its ethical and moral imperatives as well as the altered human subjectivities over time produced by social, political, and economic changes. On issues such as the status of women within the family, marriage, and Islamic governance the ideological differences and methodological fault lines between the different Muslim approaches to ethics become apparent. By supplementing the inherited body of ethical knowledge, Muslim ethics can be updated as a discursive tra-dition. Of course, scholars have always debated the extent to which tradition is open to change, transformation, and updating. Mindful of this tension, one can outline some of the main contemporary approaches to Muslim ethics.

Kinds of traditionalism

Traditionalism, or what some people call orthodoxy, is of course a highly differentiated category. *Doctrinaire traditionalism* is predominant in contemporary Islam. Here, the

formalized legal and ethical opinions of past jurists form the canon of normative teachings. This normativity, rooted in the past, is regarded as universally valid and perfect as
inherited from the ancients. To depart from the views of past authorities is only permitted in very limited instances. Furthermore, *fiqh* is not subject to historicization. Doctrinaire traditionalist circles are indeed receptive to ethics and mysticism. The weakness
of this approach, however, lies in a static and idealistic notion of history. Authenticity
lies in the experience and knowledge of the past savants of the tradition. Contemporary experiences do not qualify to influence adaptation and change to the law or ethics.
Knowledge developed in the present is either resisted or reluctantly adopted in order to
supplement or update the inherited corpus of ethical teachings. While rigidity is the
face of traditionalism in the modern period, historically speaking this same tradition
was much more robust and dynamic in its heyday. Versions of doctrinaire traditionalism are prevalent among large sections of Muslims in the Indian subcontinent, Africa,
East and Central Asia, and the Middle East, and cuts across sectarian divisions of Sunni
and Shi`a.

Given the impact of modernity on some Muslim educational institutions in the
Middle East and East Asia, often by means of coercive state-driven reforms, some sectors
of Muslim traditionalism have taken on board elements of modernism in order to constitute neo-traditionalism. Here, both modernity and tradition are viewed as instruments for pragmatic ends. Some critics point out that this approach is deficient in that
it creates a dichotomous universe, effectively advocating the privatization of religion
and also susceptible to the arbitrary use of tradition without a serious and rigorous
knowledge project to sustain it. This neo-traditionalist approach is viewed with some
skepticism by doctrinaire traditionalists for its eclectic and pragmatic mix of theological and legal doctrines derived from various schools.

Critical traditionalism is an emergent trend in Muslim ethics. Intellectuals who lean
towards this ethical orientation view the juridical tradition as a work-in-progress. They
invoke the critical thinkers of the past, historicize the tradition, and adopt contemporary knowledge and experience as part of tradition. Some in this trend identify themselves as progressive or critical Muslim thinkers. A growing number of scholars in the
Muslim world, especially in Iran as well as those living in the Atlantic world, have suc-
ceeded in engaging both the Muslim and Western knowledge traditions. Often, those
identified with critical traditionalism are engaged in new ethical and legal interpretations of the tradition. Here the attempt is to affect a new knowledge synthesis, starting
with traditional Muslim religious sciences in a dialogical engagement with the modern
social sciences and the humanities. Of course, this tradition appreciates the multiple
and diverse identities of Muslims and the self-reflexive nature of their subjectivities.
What sets the progressive or critical approach to tradition apart from other versions
is its concern for the coexistence of the transcendent and the historical dimensions
of a religious tradition. Norms are generated through the dynamic interaction between the transcendent authority and the mediation of human history. Each of these
traditionalist approaches is a hermeneutical tradition and they vary in terms of their
sophistication.

Doctrinaire traditionalists generally do not distinguish between facts and values.
Some modernist influences on certain aspects of traditionalist thought have resulted in

the anachronistic appropriation of values disembodied from practices. Since facts and historical realities continue to change, the challenge for critical traditionalism is to develop a hermeneutic that accounts for differences in practices rather than valorizing change along the lines of social Darwinism or modernist absolutism.

Modernist transcendentalist approaches

The hallmark of the modernist transcendentalist approach is that it is almost exclusively a revelation-centered hermeneutic without engaging with the equally important lived experience of the community (Sunna) as embodied in history. Even though this approach has same faint premodern antecedents, it received a boost in the modern period in the wake of a revolt against orthodox authoritarianism and clerical monopoly of authority. It also partly stems from a failure of nerve to deal with history. Exaggerated skepticism that reports of the Prophet may have been corrupted during their transmission has also undermined the status of historical sources and implicitly eviscerated the historicity of tradition. Thus, there is an almost exclusive reliance on the Qur'ān as the idealized source of norms and a refusal to attach any credibility to history. There has been little attention to the fact that even transcendent values become manifest in competing and diverse formats.

Of course, anchoring an argument on the authority of a divine text can be rhetorically persuasive, but it also predisposes it to modernist absolutism. Ethics in the transcendentalist key plays down differences and insists that the latest iteration of ethics is the most perfect incarnation of the revealed norms. Past communities are implicitly judged as having failed to discover the true norms – only us moderns have grasped it. But this approach does have the advantage of appealing directly to the authority of scripture with the aura of deriving fresh inspiration from the revelation.

A major weakness of this approach is that it presumes that all norms are self-explanatory and literally derived from the revealed sources. It fails to account for the role of the interpreter as co-author of the normative tradition and our changing subjectivity in both the interpretation and practice of ethical traditions. It is a short step from transcendentalism to text-fundamentalism, with its accompanying ethical fundamentalism.

Conclusion

In order to reinvigorate law and ethics, many modern-day Muslim thinkers have sought relief in the doctrines of public interest and the ethical objectives of the law as construed centuries ago. However, these theories are employed in instrumentalist fashion. Contemporary Muslim thinkers have yet to devise a satisfactory ethical theory in which the dialogic of transcendent norms and history are effectively demonstrated. Perhaps the challenge for Muslim ethics is twofold. How does one foster a law and ethics that continuously responds to a dynamic and changing universe? And how do such changing theories and practices retain their sacrosanct character and simultaneously also meet the psychological criteria to serve as salvific practices and performances? It remains to be seen whether the critical traditionalist/progressive approach can address this pertinent issue of ethical theory.

Bibliography

Hourani, G. F. 1971: *Islamic Rationalism: The Ethics of 'Abd al-Jabbar*. Oxford: Clarendon Press.

Hourani, G. F. 1985: *Reason and Tradition in Islamic Ethics*. Cambridge: Cambridge University Press.

Khānzāda, 'Uways Wafā. 1980: *Minhāj al-yaqīn: sharḥ adab al-dunyā wa al-din*. Beirut: Dar al-Kutub al-Ilmiyya.

Lapidus, I. M. 1984: "Knowledge, Virtue, and Action: The Classical Muslim Conception of Adab and the Nature of Religious Fulfillment in Islam" in *Moral Conduct and Authority*, ed. B. D. Metcalf. Berkeley: University of California Press.

Rahman, F. 1985: "Law and Ethics in Islam" in *Ethics in Islam: Ninth Giorgio Levi Della Vida Conference, 1983, in Honor of Fazlur Rahman*, ed. R. Hovannisian. Malibu, CA: Undena Publications.

CHAPTER 26

Origins of Islamic Ethics: Foundations and Constructions

A. Kevin Reinhart

Scope of the Chapter

Islamic ethics is a term that provokes as much as it defines. Do religions have ethics or is the term irreducibly philosophical? And philosophy, as W. C. Smith (1984) has argued, is itself a competing religious tradition. Given that no religious tradition originates in a cultural vacuum, is "origins" a meaningful term?

Here, by "ethics" we mean norms for the moral life, and also second-order reflection on where the sources of moral norms are to be found, as well as how norms are to be derived from them (see chapters 1 and 2). By "origins" we mean Islamic stipulations found particularly in the Qur'ān that shaped Muslims' moral action and reflection. In addition, we will discuss structural features and lacunae in those sources that were decisive in helping to create what we know as Islamic ethics. Finally, we will briefly show how these three helped form Islamic ethics in its early classical form.

In this chapter we distinguish between "Islamic" – religion in the commonsense understanding of the term – and "Islamicate" – other cultural features of the society in which Islam was the dominant cultural force. This means that Islamicate *falsafah*, the tradition derived particularly from the peripatetic tradition of Greek philosophy, will not be considered here. Nor will we discuss the *adab* tradition of cultivated scribal cultural norms (Hodgson 1974 II: 169–96). Rather, it is from the Qur'ān, the Sunnah, the Prophet, and the early community (as remembered and (re)constructed by subsequent Islamic scholarship), and from *kalām* theology, and above all from the sharī'a or legal–moral sciences that we will draw our argument.

Impinging Norms

Historical Islam arose on the cultural fringes of the Eastern Mediterranean world.[1] In the cities of the Eastern Roman empire – Antioch, Beirut, Damascus, Alexandria,

Smyrna, Caesarea, and, of course, Athens and Constantinople – the full range of Roman, Greek, and Christian moral content and technique was freely in play. In the Persian empire the rich body of moral and religious thought was supported and propagated by the state. Non-Orthodox Christian and several varieties of Jewish thought found a home in greater Persia as well.

It is nearly impossible satisfactorily to sort out the extent to which any of these elements might have influenced the pre-Islamic Arabian world, or the Prophet himself. While it is unlikely that, say, Stoic ethics was read in Mecca, it is clear that to some extent all of these traditions formed a sort of *koiné* substrate to the moral and intellectual life of those living in the Eastern Mediterranean region.

Once Islam appears, it shares many structural features of its ethics with the older Near Eastern traditions. Among the things that Muslims shared with Jews and Christians was the belief that membership in a given community gave one a monopoly on truth and therefore salvation. Muslims also shared with them an ethical cosmology (see chapter 13). Time was seen as moving toward a predetermined endpoint at which moral conduct would be eternally rewarded and vice would be punished. These traditions also shared a view of "progressive revelation." God's unfolding providence is manifested in an increasingly precise and detailed set of injunctions – on how to act, and for all to know how God regarded their community and those outside it. At a general level it is hard to say more than this: certain general ideas from other traditions show up in the earliest Islamic ethical understandings. This is hardly surprising when Islam was understood, among other things, as a movement to reform the previous two Near Eastern traditions (see Smith 1963).

Pre-Islamic Arab ethics

It is easier to discern pre-Islamic Arab ethics in the ethics of early Islam. One example is "thanking the benefactor" (*shukr al-mun'im*). Someone who provides a benefaction to someone, particularly the giving or saving of life, has a claim (*ḥaqq*) on the person benefacted. The benefactor is entitled to satisfaction (*riḍā*) and also to "thanksgiving" (*shukr*), that is, the public acknowledgment of the benefaction given to the benefactor. God has given humankind life, and what satisfies him in return is acknowledging his benefaction by moral conduct and observing the cultus (Qur'ān 5:6–7). The Qur'ān takes for granted this relationship of the giver and gifted and it is the basis of God's claim to obedience and observance from humankind. In this manner, a pre-Islamic view of gratitude as a virtue passed into later Islamic society and became part of the social glue that held Islamicate society together (see Mottahedeh 1980). Similarly, Muslim *convivencia* with the People of the Book (Jews and Christians) may be rooted in the pre-Islamic practice of *al-jizyah 'an yadin*. This is a pre-Islamic practice of granting armistice in return for some gesture of subordination (Bravmann 1972: 199ff.). Such a gesture removes the need to defeat or kill an otherwise antagonistic enemy. Muslim disinclination to force conversion in the way Christians and Jews did may be located in this pre-Islamic warfare practice. In other domains, pre-Islamic values may be present in antithesis. Islamic rules of marriage and chastity are understandable seen as reactions against the anarchy of marriage and descent types in the Arabia of the sixth and seventh centuries. Other features of seventh-century Arabia – polygamy, slavery, warfare – are all taken for granted in the Qur'ān, but disciplined, moderated, and re-understood.

Specifying the outside influences on the formative period of Islamic ethics is difficult. We have too little information on the Persian, Jewish, and Christian worlds at that time. Moreover, any one of these could have influenced the pre-Islamic Arab world and then, indirectly, Muslims, rather than directly influencing Islamic morals and the premises that undergird it. For the study of Islamic ethics' origins, we are on firmer ground if we look to what all but the most radically skeptic scholars acknowledge to be the authentically early Islamic text: the Qur'ān.

Qur'ānic Ethics

The Qur'ān is not a work of analytic ethics but a hortatory work that sometimes specifies the good, but more often assumes that humans know it. As the Qur'ān understands it, the central fact of human life is that humans have moral agency (Qur'ān 81; 82:5). The response of humans to the fact of agency is shaped, however, by their temperament.

Human beings are not fallen. The transgression of Adam was not a cosmic event that determined human nature, but the failure of one human being – the Prophet Adam – to obey God. That failure of course had consequences. Adam and his progeny were expelled from the Garden. Yet this was not, as for Christians, the origin of a permanent estrangement from God. In fact, Adam repented and was reconciled with God (Qur'ān 2:31–8). Still, the Qur'ān presents humans as inclined to be obedient to God in difficult times, but indifferent to God's commands when things go well (Qur'ān 17:83). They are hasty, oppressive, and ignorant (Qur'ān 17:11; 13:34; 33:72). Yet they also "love faith" and hate ingratitude, wickedness, and rebellion (Qur'ān 49:7). Humans are God's bondsmen and bondswomen (the meaning of the common phrase "'Abdallāh") and owe God fealty and obedience.

Throughout its pages, the Qur'ān assumes human beings can discern God's claim on them by the use of "reasoning" from signs[2] and "thinking" or "reflection."[3] Muslims are urged to reflect and consider, on the assumption that reflection is a means to moral knowledge. How it is that reflection leads to morality is not clear. Do we possess knowledge that we come to know through reflection, or do the structures of reflection lead us to moral knowledge? Yet the fact remains that the Qur'ān constantly urges its hearers to do good (to parents, orphans, enemies, wives, husbands) without specifying of what the good consists. If humans can know the good, are they free to act upon that knowledge?

Human volition

Theologians and philosophers require consistency, but that is seldom a feature of religious insight and vision, particularly one with a kerygmatic focus like that of the Qur'ān. Islamic theologians became preoccupied quite early (see below) with the question of whether humans lived in a predestinarian world. The Qur'ān keeps two insights bound together that might seem to be in tension but, for its distinctive vision, are not. The first is that, despite the perspicacity of the Islamic summons, humans respond in ways that disappoint. Moral conduct is sometimes outside the boundaries of suasion and intent. To this fact, the Qur'ān responds: "Whom God leads astray, you can find no path for him" (Qur'ān 30:29). "God caused their hearts to go astray. And God does not guide a corrupt people" (Qur'ān 61:5). And, classically, "God leads astray whom He wishes and guides to Himself those who turn to him" (Qur'ān 13:27). Despite exposure to the good, persuasion, and revelation, one has to recognize that there are incomprehensible limits to some human moral actions.

Yet the Qur'ān is nothing if not a call to moral conduct and moral reform. This would make no sense in the absence of an effective human volition. Repeated discussions of justice, the fact that God does not oppress and so others ought not to oppress their fellows, would be incomprehensible unless humans could freely act. "Who wishes, let him have faith; and who wishes, let him reject," says the Qur'ān (18:29). For "God does not charge a soul beyond what it can encompass. He has for it only what it has earned, and against it what it has earned" (Qur'ān 2:286). God's absolute authority is assumed, yet so is humankind's capacity to act, and so, to be held responsible.

Individual and community

Moral responsibility is the individual's. It is he or she who will be judged for acts done and undone. The Qur'ānic imagery of the Last Day focuses on experience – fear, foreboding, gratification, and ease – all sentiments that are experienced individually. There is no sense that mere membership in any community, including the Muslim, is sufficient to guarantee moral behavior and hence a felicitous outcome on the Day of Judgment. At the same time, the Qur'ān envisions a community sharing with Christians and Jews certain values, but sociologically apart from them (Qur'ān 5:51). It is a community constructed by "commanding the good and prohibiting the reprehensible," a community in which Muslims offer "advice" to one another (Qur'ān 7:79; Cook 2000). It is also a community that replaces the tribe and other kinship groups for purposes of marriage and association (Wagner 1977). Within the community, ethical requirements are shaped by roles: fathers and guardians, adult children responsible for parents, wives and mothers, husbands. What is required of one depends in part on what role one has (Qur'ān 2:215; 2:180; 4:36).

Failure to act rightly is described as "going astray," but also as "betrayal," "enmity," and "reneging on one's contract" (Qur'ān 20:121; 49:7; 66:3–4; 2:98). In later Qur'ānic passages (that is, those that come first in the text of the Qur'ān), there is a strong sense that ethical failure (e.g., fornication, lying, rejection of the Prophet and his message) makes the rejecter not just someone astray (ḍāll) but also an ingrate (kāfir) and an enemy of the community and of God (Qur'ān 9:13–14). This perspective revalorizes the relationship between individual and community. It is not surprising that (a) some believed membership in the community guaranteed salvation, and (b) struggles over the issue of what constituted membership in the community and what merited expulsion raged so fiercely in early Islamic history (Hodgson 1974 I: 214–30).

In sum, there is no doubt that pre-Islamic pagan and Islamic Arabs shared values and ethical practices with Christians, Jews, Persians, and others in the Eastern Mediterranean milieu. Yet, given the state of the historiography, it is neither possible nor very interesting to try to determine the non-Arab, non-Islamic "influences" on Islam. With pagan Arab influences, we may be on somewhat firmer ground, though that ground is still mushy from speculation. The Qur'ān gives us good evidence of early Islamic norms, not least because, read carefully, it is sometimes at variance with later Islamic ethics. The Qur'ān represents humans as weak but capable of acting ethically, which it commands them to do. It exhorts Muslims to act virtuously, frequently without specifying what constitutes virtuous practice. It assumes humans can, by revelation, reflection, and intellectation, know the good from the bad. The Qur'ān assumes human agency while recognizing that some seem doomed to act unjustly. Qur'ānic ethics is individualist while recognizing that knowledge can come from a community and is shaped by social and communal identities. What you must do sometimes depends on who you are.

Lacunae and Islamic Ethics

The key to the historical development of Islamic ethics is the structural tension between the appearance of a highly prescriptive tradition and the actual absence of a great deal of ethical prescription. The Qur'ān requires one to act well, and very occasionally specifies in some detail what the good is. More often it simply exhorts the Muslim to do the good without further information. This created the expectation of detailed prescription without satisfying that expectation.

Take, for example, the repeated Qur'ānic injunction to do "good deeds."[4] What constitutes or defines the good act? Ethicists looking for a Golden Rule definition of the good, or a utilitarian definition, or indeed any definition at all will search in vain. Rather, the Qur'ān assumes that its hearers, certainly in the context of the 610–32 CE period of its revelation, would know the good from the not-good. In another passage, Muslims are told to "vie with one another in good works" (khayrāt), but the good works in which one is to compete are assumed to be known (Qur'ān 2:148; 3:114). Indeed, a very common term for the good is al-maʿrūf, literally, "the known." Yet because it is known, it is not specified.

This would seem an argument for a kind of moral intuitionism (see chapter 2). As Islamic ethical thought developed, nevertheless, the very prescriptivism of parts of the Qur'ān text, especially in the chronologically later passages (generally toward the front of the Qur'ānic text), where the details of contracts, of marriage, and divorce are spelled out, sets up an expectation of precise stipulation that is frustrated by such general terms as "the known" and "good works."

The Qur'ān's anticipation of listeners' moral consensus can be accounted for by its rhetorical strategies. Its text is very often an attempt not to innovate, but to recast what the listener already knows. Hence the text is allusive, intertextual. In chapter 12 (sūrat

Yūsuf), the genealogical narrative of Genesis that explains, through the Joseph story, how the Canaanite Hebrews came to be exiled in Egypt, becomes instead a story of prophetic trial and triumph that foreshadows the mission and challenges of Muḥammad. Similarly, the morally corrective passages in the Qur'ān give Arabians a new perspective and new reasons to do the good, which they likewise already know. It is not to ignorance but to heedlessness that the Qur'ān attributes human failings. So the Qur'ān's prescriptivism and moral exhortation are in tension with the lack of actual Qur'ānic textual prescriptions.

At first, the coherence of Arabian society in effect glossed over the gap between pre-scriptivism and prescription, but the transition from the marginal, lightly urbanized, relatively "mechanical" society of early Islamic Arabia to a complex, highly urban society dissolved the shared values that constituted the moral intuition of Arabs. To provide further "moral data," more information to fill the void left by the disappearance of the organic Arab culture, Muslims essentially enlarged the corpus of scripture. Added to the now-standardized Qur'ānic text were anecdotes of norms and practices by exemplary members of the community, eventually almost exclusively of Muḥammad. These anecdotes, called *ḥadīth*, taken as a whole, constituted the Sunnah, the exemplary norms of Muslims. One may see these as the articulation (and often invention) of norms to fill in the gaps created by such vague terms as "the good" or "good deeds." The gaps that provoked amplification through scripture also allowed the insertion of local practices and conventions. The indigenization that resulted was not only geographical and cultural, but also temporal. It was the way in which Islamic practices and values changed over time, a process Muslim jurists recognized in both their theory and their practice (see chapter 7).

Evolution from Qur'ānic to Third-Century Islamic Ethics

Qur'ānic ethics was perhaps initially imperfectly understood and assimilated. It was certainly mixed with conventional norms of pre-Islamic Arabia. These norms, together with the practices of Muḥammad and of enthusiasts for the new religion, constituted Islamic ethics at the Prophet's death. The religious transformation of Islam during the two-year War of Apostasy after the Prophet's death (632–4) and the Liberation (*fatḥ*) of Egypt, Syria, Iraq, and Iran (634–56) must have seen a shift as dramatic as that of Judaism after the destruction of the Temple or Christianity after the conversion of Constantine. During this period the caliphs Abū Bakr, 'Umar, and 'Uthmān reconstituted a fissiparating Islamic entity. They vindicated the truth of the Qur'ānic message by subjugating much of the known world to Muslim Arabs.

Islam was now a free-standing entity. There was no Prophet to consult, nor could the Prophet consult God on behalf of the community. Muslims had to develop a practical moral epistemology, and techniques by which to discern what might be truly Islamic. The tradition preserves some accounts (perhaps authentic because contrary to later orthodoxies) about the abrogation of Prophetic practice by Abū Bakr and 'Umar to reshape Islamic practice according to contemporary conditions (see Motzki 2002). The successes of Abū Bakr in preserving "Islam" and of 'Umar in spreading Muslims, transformed Islam from a local ethnic cult to, eventually, a universal religion.[5]

The success of the "Emigrants" in conquering the Eastern Mediterranean lands and Persia was seen as a confirmation of Islam's truth. History was now twinned with Islam and Islam was understood to be efficacious in the larger world as it had been in the Arabian peninsula. This confirmation of Islam, together with the leisure and power that the Islamicate conquests had brought, led to the development of religious specialists. These were individuals who, by reason of personal piety, expertise, or lineage were believed to have insight into matters Islamic (see chapter 10). Islam's success also gave them a task; namely, to bring human action into line with God's imperatives and so to continue the harmony between God's desires and Muslim action that, so they believed, had led to historical success. These experts elaborated the Qur'ānic and praxic corpus into what became Islamic theology, law, and the ascetic spirituality that eventually was called Sufism. At first these formed three interpenetrating domains: the spiritual–ascetic, the legal–moral, and the theoretical.

Islamic theological ethics was concerned initially with two problems: membership in/leadership of the community, and predestination/moral responsibility. In the moral rigorism of early Islam these issues were inextricably bound together. Did moral failure mean expulsion from the community? Did moral failure disqualify one from leading the community? Was there a moral obligation to overthrow a corrupt leader? If acts were preordained by God as some passages of the Qur'ān suggest, then was moral criticism possible? Was rebellion a defiance of God's providence? (Watt 1973)

In a letter attributed to al-Ḥasan al-Basrī (643–728) for the caliph 'Abd Marwan we see the beginnings of systematic thought about preordination. This develops into the theological position of Human Capacity (qadar), held most famously by the Mu'tazilah theological school. Al-Ḥasan worked through the issue by contextual and common-sense readings of crucial Qur'ānic texts.

> God – He is exalted – has said {If you reject (kufr), God has no need of you, though He is not pleased with the rejection of His bondsmen; and if you acknowledge (shukr) He is pleased therewith for you. (39:7)} Were, "rejection" (kufr) what God decreed (al-qaḍā') and determined (al-qadar), then He would have been pleased with it, as something He occasioned. God does not decree something and then be displeased with it; neither are injustice or oppression any [part] of the decree of God: but His command to do the virtuous ("the recognized" al-ma'rūf), and justice, and good deeds, and to be agreeable to one's kin is His decree.

On this question of human capacity, the response of al-Ḥasan's critics was largely pious slogans and a repudiation of the capacity of logic and precise argumentation to determine religious truth. In addition, ḥadīth were forged condemning the Qadariyyah by name. By the early 930s, scholars like Ibn Kullāb (d. ca. 854) and al-Ash'arī (d. ca. 936) had begun deploying the techniques of formal theology in defense of predestinarian positions. Eventually, for many, it became a matter of dogma that capacity is God's alone. Elaborate metaphysical constructs were created to reconcile predeterminism with human responsibility. Yet, at the level of moral sensibility, it is not clear that this dogma had any impact. Indeed, theology ceased by the twelfth century to be a significant moral science, for Muslims. They seem to have regarded things over which humans reasonably have control to be matters of moral responsibility, and those over which they did not have control to be God's decree.

We can see the early stages of another ethical tendency in a letter to the caliph 'Umar b. 'Abdal 'azīz attributed also to al-Ḥasan. There is little direct engagement with the texts of scripture in the letter, but, rather, a reflective spiritual engagement with its sentiments. This leads al-Ḥasan to an ascetic, world-renouncing perspective that devalued not only the pursuit of wealth but also any esteem for one's time in this world except as preparation for the next. It reveals an epistemology that was the very essence of later Sufism, one that valued contemplation and religious experience as sources of a religious knowledge that informed and paralleled scriptural knowledge.

> Know that reflection prompts to righteousness and acting according to righteousness; remorse over evil prompts to leaving [evil]. What passes away – though it be much – is not the equal of what abides, though seeking it be arduous. Bearing temporary pain followed by long ease is better than hastening to temporary ease that is followed by abiding pain.
>
> [The world] was presented, with its keys and its treasuries, to our Prophet, upon whom be God's blessings and peace. He did not take them, though there would have been no sin in it, but he scorned to accept them, though there was no impediment to doing so: He would not have been diminished a whit in God's sight. But the Prophet knew that God loathed a thing, so the Prophet loathed it; [He] belittled a thing so [the Prophet] belittled it; [God] disparaged a thing so he disparaged it.

These sentiments were not only those of marginal ascetics but were embedded in sermons, books of advice, and countless hortatory works. What is striking is that the devaluation of the world did not mean disengagement from it. The people who wrote and listened to these works participated in politics, married and had children, were employed, and lived in houses. Yet their valuation of these activities was remarkably low.

The continued engagement with the world and suspicion of radical removal from it results from a third ethical trend in early Islam. Islam's legal–moral sciences (called *fiqh*) and its ancillaries were to be the central intellectual discipline of Islam. They were the lens through which Muslims regarded virtuous and vicious acts and the instrument with which they sought to probe, categorize, and understand the good and the reprehensible. The inception of Islamic jurisprudence is seen in a letter plausibly attributed to the caliph 'Umar b. 'Abdal'azīz (r. 717–20), to whom allegedly the letter just quoted was addressed (Ibn 'Abd al-ḥakam and 'Ubayd 1927: 198 [my trans.]; see Reinhart 2001).

> The "religion of God," who sent His Book via Muḥammad, which he sent down to him, is to obey God and follow His command and avoid what He proscribed and observe His Boundaries (*ḥudūdah*)[6] and do His Duties and permit what he permits and forbid what He forbids and acknowledge His right (*ḥaqq*)[7] [to do so] and to judge according to what He has sent down in [the Book]. Whoever follows the guidance of God is well-guided and whoever impedes one from it {Has gone astray from the Path (Q2:108)}.

The task of Muslims, as they early understood it, was to determine what God had forbidden and allowed, to find his boundaries, and do his duties. While in the period of 'Umar b. 'Abdal'azīz these key terms probably had limited meanings, they opened up to the increasingly diverse world in which Muslims found themselves and incited assessment of all that confronted them.

By the time of al-Shāfi'ī (d. 820) less than one hundred years later, Islamic ethics is embedded in a nascent science of Islamic jurisprudence. The result, eventually, is a world which is sacramentalized. No act is of indifferent value: every act is either required, encouraged, permitted, discouraged, or forbidden (Reinhart 1983). Finding God's Duties (*farḍ*) is now a task for specialists with a distinct disciplinary epistemology. The motivation remains piety and apprehension of the Last Day. Yet the system is now on its way to becoming a complex casuistry that can estimate the virtues and vices of every possible human act and some that, if not impossible, are at least improbable (see chapter 5).

Conclusion

Islamic ethics originated in a complex world of various and competing norms – of other religions, Hellenistic reflection, pagan heroics, and debts of honor. The Qur'ān no doubt reflects, and in many cases assumes, the existence of these norms, but refashions them in characteristic ways. As important as what the Qur'ān says, is what it does not say. Those silences were challenges to Muslim scholars in the centuries to come.

Within two centuries, three characteristic approaches to ethics had appeared: a theological, speculative approach; an ascetic–spiritual approach; and a legal praxic-oriented approach. Though the legal approach developed into the "queen of the Islamic sciences," the other two did not disappear. Together, they formed a rich reservoir of possibilities and approaches that subsequent Muslims draw from and elaborate upon.

Notes

My earlier studies in Islamic ethics have profited from guidance by Ronald M. Green, Walter Sinnot-Armstrong, Bernard Gert, and Matthew Bagger.

1   We use this term to refer to the Islam of academic history. It is of course Muslim doctrine that Adam was the first Muslim and that from his time forward some form of Islam – perhaps corrupted but still grounded in Islam's primordial truths – was in the world.
2   The Qur'ān uses verbs from the root '-q-l.; the noun form means "intellect" ('*aql*).
3   Using verbs from the root *f-k-r*, whose nominal form (*fikr*) means "thought" or "reflection."
4   *ṣāliḥah* pl. *ṣaliḥāt*; and in various verbal forms; the root appears 171 times.
5   That it was an ethnic cult at its beginning – at least in Arab understanding – is suggested by Qur'ānic emphasis on the Qur'ān as an Arabic document, and the Prophet as a national and ethnic figure. (Qur'ān 7:157, where references to "illiteracy" should be read instead as "national." See EI2 s.v. *ummī*; Qur'ān 16:103; 26:195.) Moreover, when the Arabs emerged into Syria the testimony of non-Muslims is that these earliest Muslims – describing them-

selves as "Emigrants [in God's way]" – refused access to Islam to non-Arabs (Hoyland 1997: 337–43). Later piety wishes to depict Islam as perfectly formed by the time of the Prophet's death.

6   Later ḥadd (pl. ḥudūd) comes to be a technical term for the five crimes for which there are mandatory punishments (drunkenness, theft, adultery, slander, highway robbery). At 'Umar's time I do not think it had this restricted meaning, but meant rather the bottom-line rules of moral conduct.

7   The word means "truth," "right," but here, also, the claim that someone has on someone or something.

Bibliography

Bravmann, M. M. 1972: *The Spiritual Background of Early Islam: Studies in Ancient Arab Concepts*. Boston, MA: E. J. Brill.

Cook, M. A. 2000: *Commanding Right and Forbidding Wrong in Islamic Thought*. Cambridge: Cambridge University Press.

Hodgson, M. G. S. 1974: *The Venture of Islam: Conscience and History in a World Civilization*, 4 vols. Chicago: University of Chicago Press.

Hoyland, R. G. 1997: *Seeing Islam As Others Saw It: A Survey and Evaluation of Christian, Jewish, and Zoroastrian Writings on Early Islam*. Princeton, NJ: Darwin Press.

Ibn 'Abdalḥakam, A. h. and 'Ubayd, A. h. 1927: Miṣr: Al-Maktabah al-'Arabiyynh.

Mottahedeh, R. 1980: *Loyalty and Leadership in Early Islamic Society*. Princeton, NJ: Princeton University Press.

Motzki, H. 2002: *The Origins of Islamic Jurisprudence: Meccan Fiqh Before the Classical Schools*. Boston, MA: E. J. Brill.

Reinhart, A. K. 1983: "Islamic Law as Islamic Ethics?" *Journal of Religious Ethics* 11, 186–203.

Smith, W. C. 1963: *The Meaning and End of Religion: A New Approach to the Religious Traditions of Mankind*. New York: Macmillan.

——1984: "Philosophia, as One of the Religious Traditions of Humankind: The Greek Legacy in Western Civilization, Viewed by a Comparativist" in *Différences, valeurs, hiérarchie: Textes offerts à Louis Dumont*, ed. J.-C. Galey, 253–79. Paris: Éditions de l'École des Hautes Études en Sciences Sociales.

Wagner, G. 1977: *La Justice dans l'Ancien Testament et le Coran aux niveaux des marriages et des échanges de biens*. Neuchâtel: Éditions de la Baconnière.

Watt, W. M. 1973: *The Formative Period of Islamic Thought*. Edinburgh: Edinburgh University Press.

CHAPTER 27

Islamic Ethics: Differentiations

Abdulaziz Sachedina

This chapter emphasizes an inherent plurality in Islamic ethical discourse. The pluralist nature of Islamic religious discourse is inevitably bolstered by the absence of a religious institution resembling a church and an organized body of experts speaking on behalf of the entire tradition. Muslim theologians-cum-jurists belonging to different schools of thought have maintained a variety of opinions regarding human moral agency, sources of moral cognition and methods of ethical deliberations, and classifications of moral acts as required or recommended, forbidden or reprehensible. This chapter will outline the main schools without going into all the subsequent variations that appeared, sometimes within a single school of ethical thought. Its essential argument is founded upon the variations in hermeneutical strategies pursued by representative Sunnī and Shī'ite theologians, to differentiate between the two main trends of ethical thought that dominate discussions about the ontology of moral action even today: (1) rationalist–objectivist and (2) theistic–subjectivist ethics. These two trends have also been a marked rationalist–traditionalist divide among Muslim scholars. Clearly, theological disputations about human freewill and predestination in relation to God's justice provided the critical evaluation of a moral act and its ascription to a human agent. Accordingly, I shall limit my analysis of differentiations to theological ethical discourse. Philosophical ethics, with its emphasis on purification of the human soul through the perfection of human character, which was taken up by Muslim philosophers and mystics, is beyond the scope of this chapter.

Ethics in the sense of structured moral reasoning is a post-Quranic development that one studies in Muslim theology, rather than in the juridical corpus of the Sharī'a. Some Western studies on Islamic ethics have argued that the essence of Islamic ethics should be sought in the Sharī'a rather than Muslim theology (Reinhart 1983). Yet while the Qur'ān offers normative moral guidance, it also takes seriously the cultural–historical context connected with the application of these norms in assessing moral responsibility. There is recognition of relativity in the matter of application. The Sharī'a integrates only part of the ethical concerns connected with human conscience or intuitive ethical knowledge in its legal ordinances (Fakhry 1994a). As demonstrated below, Islamic legal theory recognizes an overlap between legal and ethical action guides without pronouncing the resolution as more than what the Sacred Lawgiver wishes humans to know, namely, moral and religious duties whose performance guarantees salvation and reward in the Hereafter (see chapter 5).

Theological Debates Arising from the Qur'ān

Islamic theological debates were shaped by the question of human agency and divine providence. These early debates had their genesis in the determination of the responsibility for the sinful behavior of those who were in power. Did they act as God's free agents or were their acts predetermined by God's overpowering will? To be sure, the Qur'ān suggested a multifaceted correlation between divine predetermination and human responsibility. Inasmuch as human beings are free agents, they can reject God's guidance, although, because of their innate disposition (*fiṭra*) prompting or even urging them subtly to believe in God, they cannot find any valid excuse for this rejection. When human beings choose to reject this guidance, God denies further guidance to them (Qur'ān 16:104). This denial of guidance clearly pertains to the guidance that would lead to the procurement of the desirable end, not to the initial moral guidance that is engraved in the hearts of all human beings, in the form of an innate disposition, to guide them toward the good end.

Significantly, it is at this point that theological differences among Muslim scholars become striking. These differences are rooted in two conflicting conceptions of human responsibility in the procurement of divine justice. The scripture-based discussions on human ethical responsibility were dominated by the proponents of the two major schools of Sunnī Muslim dialectical theology: Mu'tazilite and Ash'arite. Shī'ite Muslim theology shared its ethical epistemology with Mu'tazilites.

The basic Mu'tazilite thesis is that human beings, having been endowed with an innate capacity to know right and wrong, and having been endowed with free will, are responsible for their actions before a just God. Furthermore, good and evil are rational categories that can be known by intuitive reason, independent of revelation. God created the human intellect in such a way that, if unhindered by social traditions and conventions, it is capable of perceiving good and evil objectively. This is a corollary of their main thesis that God's justice depends on the objective knowledge of good and evil, as determined by reason, whether the Lawgiver pronounces it so or not. Without such objective ethical knowledge, and in the absence of any contact with a prophet or sacred scriptures, no human being can be held accountable for his or her deeds. In other words, Mu'tazilites maintained a form of rationalist objectivism (see Hourani 1971) that was further elaborated by guidance through revelation.

The Mu'tazilite standpoint was challenged by Ash'arites who rejected the idea of natural reason as an autonomous source of religious–moral guidance. They maintained that good and evil are as God commanded them in the scripture. It is presumptuous to judge God's action. For Mu'tazilites, Ash'arites argue, there is no way, within the bounds of ordinary logic, to explain the relationship of God's power to human actions. It is more realistic to maintain that everything that happens is the result of God's will, without explanation or justification.

However, Ash'arites distinguished between the actions of responsible human beings and actions attributed to natural laws. Human responsibility is not the result of free choice; rather, God alone creates all actions directly. How does a human being become accountable for his or her actions? This was the source of moral quandary. If human acts are predetermined by God's will, then what is the purpose of the Day of Judgment and the final reward or punishment? Ash'arites introduced the doctrine of "voluntary acquisition" to answer this question. In some actions, they maintained, a special quality of voluntary acquisition was superadded by God's will, thereby making the individual a voluntary agent and responsible for his or her action. Human responsibility is the result of God's will known through the revelation (the Qur'ān and the Tradition, ascribed to the Prophet). This attitude of Ash'arites to ethical knowledge is theistic subjectivism. All ethical values are dependent upon determinations of God's will expressed in the form of revelation, which is both eternal and immutable.

Both these theological standpoints were based on the interpretation of Quranic passages. On the one hand, the Qur'ān contains passages that would support the Mu'tazilite position, which emphasized the complete responsibility in responding to the call of both natural guidance and guidance through revelation. On the other hand, it has passages that could support the Ash'arite viewpoint, which upheld the omnipotence of God, and hence denied humans any role in responding to divine guidance (Rāzī 1938). The Qur'ān allows for both human volition and divine will in the matter of accepting or rejecting faith that entailed the responsibility for procuring justice on earth.

The Nature of Islamic Ethical Discourse

When one considers the normative sources for standards of conduct and character it becomes obvious that besides scriptural sources, Muslim scholars recognized the value of decisions derived from specific human conditions as an equally valid source for social ethics (see chapter 1). Early on, the theologian–jurists conceded that the scriptural sources could not easily cover every situation that might arise, especially when Muslim political rule required rules for urban life, commerce, and government in advanced countries. How exactly was the intellectual endeavor to be directed to discover the rationale ('illa) behind certain paradigm rulings provided in God's commandments, in order to formulate principles for future decisions?

The question had important implications for the administrators who were faced with the practical necessity to make justifiable legal rulings. There was a fear of reason in deriving the details of law. The fear was based on the presumption that if independent human reason could judge what is right and wrong, it could rule on what God could rightly prescribe for humans. It was admitted that although the details of the revealed law can be known through reason and aid human beings in cultivating the moral life, human intelligence was unable to discover what the reason for a particular law is, let alone demonstrate the truth of a particular assertion of the divine commandment. The

divine commandments to which one must adhere if one is to achieve a specific end prescribed in the revealed law are not objectively accessible to human reason. Judgments
of reason were arbitrary, as demonstrated by the fact of their contradicting each other,
and reflected the personal desire of the legal expert.

One problem, then, was resolving the substantive role of reason in understanding
the implicit rationale of a paradigm case and elaborating the juridical–ethical dimension of revelation as it relates to the conduct of human affairs in public and private
spheres. Another problem was situating credible religious authority empowered to
provide validation to the ethical–legal reasoning associated with the philosophy behind
legal rulings. On the one hand, following the lead of Sunnī jurists like Shāfiʿī (d. 820)
and Aḥmad b. Ḥanbal (d. 855), Sunnī Islam located that authority in revelation. These
scholars maintained the Sunni doctrines expounded by the predominant Ashʿari Sunni
theologians. Among these doctrines was the one that maintained one could work out
an entire system of Islamic law based on juridical elaboration of the scriptural sources.
On the other hand, following the line of thought maintained by the Shīʿite Imams,
Shīʿite Islam located that authority in the rightful successors of the Prophet. The Shīʿite
Imams maintained there was an ongoing revelatory guidance available in the exposi-
tory ability of human reason in comprehending the divine revelation. It is exemplified
by the solutions offered by the Shīʿite leadership.

In general, Muslim theologian–jurists paid more attention to God's creation than
God's nature per se. In addition, they discussed human beings' relation to God as the
Creator, Lawgiver, and Judge. They were also interested in understanding the extent of
God's power and human free will as it affected the search for a right prescription for
human behavior. In view of the absence of the institutionalized religious body that
could provide the necessary validation of legal–moral decisions, the problem of determining the Sacred Lawgiver's intent behind juridical–ethical rulings was not an easy
task. The intellectual activity related to Islamic juridical–ethical tradition can be
summed up as the attempt to relate specific moral–legal rulings to the divine purposes
expressed in the form of norms and rules in revelation. Given the incomplete state of
knowledge about present circumstances and future contingencies, the jurists proceeded
to make ethical judgments with a cautious attitude on the basis of what seemed most
likely to be the case. Such ethical judgments were normally appended with a clear, pious
statement that the ruling lacked certainty. Only God was knowledgeable about the true
state of affairs.[1]

In due course, jurists were able to identify two methods for understanding the justification behind a legal–ethical decision. Sometimes the rationale was derived directly
from the explicit statements of the Qurʾān and the Tradition that set forth the purpose
of legislation. At other times, human reason discovered the relationship between the
ruling and the rationale. The jurists admitted and determined the substantive role of
human reasoning in making valid legal or moral decisions. Moreover, human reason's
role depended upon the jurists' comprehension of the nature of ethical knowledge and
the means by which humans can access information about good and evil. In other
words, it depended upon the way the human act was defined in terms of human ethical
discernment about good and evil and the relation of the human act to God's will.
Any advocacy of reason as a substantive rather than formal source for procuring

moral–legal verdicts required authorization derived from revelation. All the jurist–theologians, whether Sunnī or Shīʿite, maintained that without the endorsement of revelation reason could not become an independent source of moral–legal decisions.

This attitude towards reason has its roots in the belief that God's knowledge of the circumstances and of the consequences in any situation of ethical dilemma is exhaustive and infallible. The revealed sources had provided the underlying rationale for some moral–legal rulings when declaring them obligatory or prohibited. Yet, on a number of issues, juridical rulings were expressed simply as God's commands that had to be obeyed without knowing the reasons behind them. For instance, the rationale behind the duty of seeking medical treatment is to avoid grave and irremediable harm to oneself, whereas the reason for the prohibition on taking human life is the sanctity of life as declared by the revelation. The commandments were simply part of God's prerogative as the Creator to demand unquestioning obedience. To act in a manner contrary to divine commands is to act immorally and unlawfully. The major issue in legal thought, then, was related to defining the admissibility and the parameters of human reasoning as a substantive source for legal–moral decisions.

Rationalist and Traditionalist Ethical Reasoning in the Revelation

The use of "rationalist" and "traditionalist" in this section conforms to the general identification of the two major trends in Islamic theological–ethical discourse above. Based on their cautious attitude toward reason as a substantive source for ethical–legal judgments, Muʿtazilites and Shīʿites fall into the rationalist group. In contrast, due to their emphasis on revelation, especially the Tradition, Ashʿarites fall into the traditionalist group. The process of formulating the methodology for deriving sound ethical–legal decisions was undertaken with a clear view of providing principles and rules for deriving predictable judgments in all matters of interpersonal relationships. Central to this discussion was the analytical treatment of the twin concepts of justice (usually defined as "putting something in its appropriate place") and obligation (sometimes defined as "promulgation of divine command and prohibition"). The concept of justice provided a theoretical stance on the question of human obedience to divine commands and the extent of human capacity in carrying out moral–religious obligations. The concept of obligation defined the nature of divine command and provided deontological grounds for complying with it. The commandments have reasons of their own that can be explained in terms of the function they fulfill for the good of humankind.

Gradually, these two responses emerged to meet the pressing need of providing consistent and authentic guidance in the matter of social ethics. Some prominent jurists of the tenth and eleventh centuries maintained that in deciding questions on which there was no specific guidance available from the normative sources of Islamic law and ethics, judges and lawyers had to make rational judgments independent of revelation. This was certainly the case when the law did not provide for peculiar situations. This was, obviously, the rationalist group. Other jurists disapproved of this rational method as not adequately anchored in the normative sources. They insisted that no legal or moral judgment was valid if not based on the revelation. There was no way for human-ity to know the meaning of justice outside the divine revelation. In fact, the tradition-alists contended, justice is nothing but carrying out the requirements of the revealed law. The revealed law, the Sharī'a, provided the scales for justice in all those actions that were declared morally and legally obligatory. Eventually, the traditionalist thesis became the standard view held by the majority of Sunnī Muslims. Some Sunnī and the majority of the Shī'ite Muslims, on the other hand, maintained the rationalist thesis with some adjustment in conformity to their doctrine about the supreme religious authority of the Imam (see Hourani 1971; Fakhry 1994a, 1994b).

This cautious and even negative evaluation of reason in traditionalist ethics had a parallel in the systematization of juridical theory among Muslim jurists. The ethical–legal problem-resolving device was in search of a fundamental principle that could function as a template for the formulation of emerging ethical–legal decisions. The expansion of Muslim political rule beyond Arabia raised questions about the appli-cation of the rulings provided by the revelation. The jurists were quick to realize that such absolute application without considering the specific social and cultural context of these rulings was not without problems. After all, the rulings provided by the revelation emphasized specific human conditions related to custom, everyday human behavior, and ordinary language used to convey moral precepts and attitudes to life in Arabian society. Even when the moral law is wholly promulgated through divine legis-lation in the form of the Qur'ān and the Tradition, such a law is objective because of the diversity that can be observed among human beings.

Very early on scholars of jurisprudence were led to distinguish between duties to God (ritual duties) and duties to fellow human beings (social transactions). Ritual duties were not conditioned by specific human conditions, and hence were absolutely binding. Social transactions were necessarily conditioned by human existence in specific social and political contexts, and hence adjustable to the needs of time. It was in the latter sphere of interpersonal relations that the jurists needed to provide fresh rulings gener-ated by changing conditions. The entire area of social ethics in Islam falls thereby under the social transaction sections of jurisprudence. However, authoritative decisions in matters of social ethics could not be derived without first determining the nature of human acts under obligation. The divine command, understood in terms of reli-gious–moral obligation, provided the entire ethical code of conduct and a teleological view of humankind and the world. Violation of divine command, as Muslim jurists taught, is immoral on the grounds that it interferes with the pursuit of perfection that would guarantee salvation in the Hereafter. Ultimately, human salvation is directly con-nected with human conduct, that is, the subject matter of legal–theological ethics.

Every category of act, whether classified as incumbent, recommended, permitted, disapproved, or forbidden in the Sharī'a, is founded upon explicit or implicit rules in the Qur'ān or the Tradition. Thus, Sharī'a, as a religious–ethical system, is theoretically able to discover the divine judgment on every category of human act in the area of "ritual duties" and "social transactions." However, Sharī'a also investigates the revela-tory sources, and the consensus of the learned, for their admission as evidence in deducing fresh cases occurring in different contexts. This part of juridical studies is con-cerned with legal principles or jurisprudence. Islamic jurisprudence is an inquiry into the principles of normative ethical judgments on external human acts. The philosophical aspects of ethics of action are concerned with fundamental questions about whether intellect on its own can rule things necessary, good, or evil (see Madkur 1960).

Categorizing Necessary, Good, and Evil Acts

To understand the impact of moral epistemology as worked out by the rationalist and traditionalist scholars, we need to see the way obligation or duty is defined and applied in practice. The derivation of ethical judgments (obligatory, recommended, and so on) is related to the ontology of good and evil in human acts. Ultimately, any valuation of divine or human acts is dependent upon the way relevant categories are constructed in theology first and then in law.

In Islamic ethics the categories of value terms resemble the categories of the Sharī'a law, but their definition depends on the way human agency is perceived doctrinally. Among Ash'arite Sunnī jurists all the Sharī'a categories (obligatory, recommended, permitted, disapproved, and forbidden) are defined in relation to actual divine command and prohibition, the rewards and punishments by God in the next life. In contrast, among Mu'tazilite Sunnī and Shī'ite jurists, legal–ethical categories are defined in terms of their relation to whether action is possible from the agent as a result of his power to do it or as a part of his nature that is predetermined by God.

The Ash'arī ethics roots ethical values in the commands and prohibitions of God. This was the divine command theory of ethics. An obligatory act is that which is commanded, and a prohibited act is that which is evil. The rules governing an ethical judgment are neither in the acts themselves nor in their properties. They are grounded in what God commands or prohibits. The ontological reference of an evil act is God's prohibition and not reason's intuitive judgment (Ghazzālī 1904–7: 56–7). In contrast, Mu'tazilite ethics asserted that a command or prohibition, even by God, to do something is insufficient to make the act itself obligatory or evil. The obligatoriness or evilness is characteristic of the act as such. The ontological reference is either to an act's essence or category or to the circumstantial mode of its occurrence. The agent is regarded morally responsible for the act as he or she caused it to come into being simply, or as knowingly and intentionally caused it to occur in a particular way. Hence, these characteristics have to be indicated by words other than just command or prohibition. Accordingly, the command or prohibition should read: "Do it, *because* it is obligatory," and "Don't do it, *because* it is evil." The commands and prohibitions that are admittedly part of the Sharī'a possess ethical properties of their own over and above being commanded and forbidden by God (Ṭūsī 1980).

Muslim jurists define "necessary" or "prudentially necessary" in terms of the juridical category of the obligatory act from the standpoint of the self-interest of the agent.[2] An act is necessary when it is obligatory for the agent to do it if he or she is to avoid harm. It is also prudential because the act serves the practical interest of the agent. Expected harm in this life may be recognized by intellect; whereas expected harm in the next life is known only by revelation.[3] The ethical character of this concept becomes evident when one considers the objective–subjective aspects of a necessary act. An act's objective aspect is determined by the facts of the world other than the opinion of some judge or observer. This sense, this type of ethical knowledge is autonomous and self-validating, having been established by reason as necessary. On the other hand, an act's subjective aspect is determined by the opinion of some judge or observer. Reason does not determine anything morally or religiously necessary, nor are goodness and badness generic or essential qualities of action that can be known through reason. Rather, divine command and prohibition determines an act as good or bad, respectively.

The Mu'tazilite rationalist definition of "necessary" looks at the relations of praise and blame to the agent for the act. Accordingly, "necessary" as applied to an act is that for whose omission the agent deserves blame (Muẓaffar 1966: 24). For instance, when a person suffers pain because of donating a kidney, the two steps of donating a kidney and suffering of pain are connected by a relation of praise. At the same time, while the two steps are empirical facts, the relation of praise that the donor "deserves" is not so in any obvious way. "Deserving praise" suggests the appropriateness of the two successive events. This appropriateness is objective because "deserves" introduces a fact, which is truly or falsely predicated regardless of anyone's opinions. This was the doctrine firmly held by the Shī'ite legal–ethical theorists. The Ash'arites, conversely, denied that an obligatory act was an attribute of certain types of act in itself. God's commanding of certain types of acts was itself the essential characteristic that made them obligatory.

The Ash'arites denied the Mu'tazilite thesis that an obligatory act had an ontological reference in human reason on the basis of the observed fact that there was a disagreement among prudent and intelligent persons regarding the obligatoriness of particular acts under varying circumstances. This observation-based rejection served as the fundamental characteristic of theistic subjectivism or voluntarism among the Sunnī jurist–theologians – more particularly, by the Sunnī law schools of Shāfi'ī and Ibn Ḥanbal. For them, an obligatory act is that for which there is a threat of punishment. A forbidden act is one whose omission is necessary, as prescribed by the revealed law.

It is important to note that the Qur'ān distinguishes objective ethical concepts from God's acts of commanding and forbidding. Thus, when it says "be forward in good works," the category of "good works" is clearly founded on a universally recognizable moral good. It was only through the development of Islamic jurisprudence, and more specifically the legal categories of the Sharī'a, that good was defined in terms of commanded and evil in terms of prohibition. Gradually, the Sharī'a categories, such as acts of disobedience, were widened in application. They came to replace the original ethical terms like "abominable" and "detested," giving rise to ethical voluntarism (theistic subjectivism). This theory, as discussed above, equates the objective ethical categories of good and evil with God's commanding and forbidding, respectively.

The thrust of the Ash'arite argument about an obligatory act is that the conditions that control what is obligatory in the actual world are created by the will of God. These conditions include human nature, which is completely predestined, and the human's natural ends, which are enforced by superior forces. God determines and commands the necessary acts for the natural ends of humanity. Moreover, God imposes sanctions for disobeying God's commands, which renders performance of these acts necessary if one wants to avoid God's punishment. There is no attribute that renders acts necessary for humans to perform in their own interest, other than that they are commanded by God. Accordingly, "necessary" means "necessary because God commands it" and because it is related in an essential way to the long-term interest of the agent.

The Mu'tazilites contended that certain acts of God are necessary for God because of the benefit they confer on God's creatures. For example, God must send prophets in order to inform human beings of the conditions of life to come and prepare them to do what is fundamentally right. As humans are obligated to do what is right and obligatory, so is God obligated to reward them for doing what is right and for fulfilling their moral obligations (Frank 1983: 206ff.). In contrast, the Ash'arites did not regard as necessary that which benefits others, since there is no benefit to God in benefiting others. Since it is impossible to explain God's command in terms of any purpose or end, no reason or purpose can be evoked to explain voluntary conformity to God's command. The ultimate moral perfection of a human being is simply to obey without any expectation of reward in the next life.

Ḥasan, in general meaning "agreeable" or "fitting to an end," although translated as "good" is broader than the English "good." In relation to acts, good is "that for which the agent does not deserve blame" (Ṭūsī 1980: 207). The end or purpose of undertaking a good act may be that of the agent, other persons, or of the agent in one respect or one time, but not others. Thus, good is relative to the end specified, and what is good for John may not be so for Jack, or even for one of them in different respects or times. Thus, an irreligious person may call adultery "good" because he approves of it (Ghazzālī 1916: 100). The technical meaning of good is "whatever is fitting for any end in this life." However, the Ash'arites have adopted the second technical meaning, namely, what is fitting only for the ends of the *next life*. The ends and the means are determined and assigned to everyone by revelation. Good can be extended to cover anything that agents are permitted to do (Ibn Muṭahhar al-Ḥillī [n.d.]: 185). The Mu'tazilites, on the other hand, define good with reference to acts "for the performance of which the agent does not deserve blame."

Qabīḥ, "evil," is in many ways symmetrical with, though diametrically opposed to, good in its various meanings. Generally, the Ash'arites view evil as whatever is repugnant or inappropriate to an end, with attention to its relative rather than absolute character. But the evilness of an act is determined by divine command and not by its inherent nature that merits blame when committed (Asadābādī 1942: 9). These definitions of good and evil resemble that of "necessary." Instead of referring to what it is necessary to do for this life or the Hereafter, as in necessary, good refers simply to what is serviceable to an end, evil to what hinders attainment of an end.

Mu'tazilite belief in the autonomy of the human intellect to discern good and evil led them to object that the meaning of good in common usage is not restricted to what promotes an end, nor the meaning of evil to what hinders attainment of an end. People perform some acts on their intrinsic merits, when they cannot possibly foresee any advantage to themselves. Likewise, they avoid other acts as evil even when they can see no disadvantage to themselves. As an instance of intrinsic good sought, someone gives help and comfort to a dying person with no expectation of reward; she does it simply because it is good to help others in distress. As an instance of intrinsic evil avoided, a physician without belief in religion, and thus in no fear of punishment in the Hereafter, refuses to help a terminally ill patient to commit suicide, even under threat of execution for his refusal. Such a physician regards suicide as evil, not merely in relation to ends, but as evil in itself.

The Ash'arite belief that good and evil have no objective value offered rebuttals of these instances. They explained that the first instance could have been motivated by natural sympathy between human beings, by love of praise, or by the association of ideas which leads one to do in an abnormal situation what would serve an end in a normal one. In the case of a woman helping others in distress, one can detect a motivation based on the expectation that the patient would live and show gratitude. The second instance was explained by the agent's love of praise for not succumbing to the pressure, or by association of ideas (i.e., taking a life, however indirectly through physician-assisted suicide, is normally followed by harmful consequences). Ash'arites looked for self-interested or emotional causes for the acts mentioned, in order to avoid admitting attributes of good and evil intrinsic to the acts and acceptable or unacceptable to the rational mind regardless of personal ends. Their view of ethics is based on extrinsic relations of acts to good and evil. An act is good when it promotes human ends; moreover, it does so not by direct instrumental causation but because God has decided upon rewards for certain acts and punishment for others.

Such a view is coherent with the occasionalist theory of God's relation to the world (Hourani 1985: 143). According to this theory, all activity or development in the world is the result of God's irreversible and inscrutable decrees. A necessary connection between natural events or entities is incompatible with God's lordship or sovereignty. Part of this theory is the belief in God's command being good because it leads humans to attain their final reward. The end of an individual is the attainment of happiness, and happiness is to be found overwhelmingly in the next life. This is known from revelation. The primary means to this end are of two kinds: external acts of obedience to the revealed rules of conduct and internal cultivation of the virtues of the soul. External acts are helpful both because obedience is rewarded directly for its own sake and because these acts contribute to the acquisition of virtues. The inner state of the heart is more important than any external acts in the eyes of God and more conducive to reward. Yet none of the relations just described is causal. Acts do not cause virtues; they do not cause rewards in the next life. Even virtues do not cause rewards. In all cases, God through his grace bestows the rewards or moral progress. Again, God is the only cause and is under no obligation. Religious enlightenment consists largely in understanding these revealed truths. The secondary means are principally knowledge and motivation. These are necessary for the effectiveness of the primary means to happiness. The mission of the prophets is designed to provide these aids, for scripture gives guidance and inspiration, both to acts of obedience and to the virtues. Finally, the Muslim community, when it is working properly, sustains the individual in various ways through its organization and leaders.

Corresponding to the primary and secondary means to happiness are two practical sciences: jurisprudence, which sets forth the principles to derive laws from the scriptural sources, and virtue ethics, which guides the formation of an agent's moral and spiritual character. Sunnī jurisprudence was founded upon the theory of ethical voluntarism. The core of the theory was that the value terms applied to action, such as "necessary," "good," and "evil," have no meanings in themselves. Accordingly, their application to action cannot be known by human reason. These categories acquire ethical meaning only when related to the commands and prohibitions in revelation. Knowledge about their application can be acquired exclusively by studying the revelatory sources. The opponents were, again, the Mu'tazilites and the Shī'ites with their objectivist rationalism. The objectivist position was the commonsense understanding of ethical terms in all or most cultures and languages. Most people think that when they describe someone as "just," "wicked," and so on, they are describing a real quality of that person (however hard to analyze), not merely some relation of obedience or disobedience to a social group or even to God (see chapter 2). The presumption is that a common ethical language is being used, understood clearly and in the same way by the speaker and the addressed parties. Such a language could not depend on their prior acceptance of the particular scripture being delivered by the speaker. Mu'tazilite rationalism allows revelation an indispensable supplement position in determining important truths that reason unaided could not have discovered.

From the beginnings of Islamic theology Quranic references to the overwhelming power of God could not admit that human beings could ever determine on their own, without aid from scripture, what was right and what was wrong in the world, still less what was obligatory for God to do or not to do with his creation. The traditionalists naturally felt this way, since the Mu'tazilite claim undermined the utility of their collections of the traditions that were used as paradigm cases for moral–legal deliberations. More substantially, the Sunnī schools of law were inclined in this direction until voluntarism as a theory of jurisprudence was worked out with the most thoroughgoing logic by Shāfi'ī. Shāfi'ī insisted that the entire legal–ethical system could be derived from the revelation, that is, the Qur'ān and the Tradition, without resorting to reason in the form of "sound opinion" of a jurist. On the side of theology, voluntarism with its theistic subjectivism found a champion in Ash'arī (873–935) and his successors. In the sphere of ethics, the conservative spokesmen of Islam, who referred to themselves as "the people of tradition and the community," continued to react against Mu'tazilite rationalism. The main reason is probably that the Mu'tazilite theory was the only articulate theory that could be set in contrast to the prevailing trend of Islamic thought on ethics in theological and juristic circles.

Concluding Remarks

Mu'tazilites and Shī'ites avoid teleology by defining an act deontologically in terms of its character without reference to consequences. Although the main terms of their ethics affirmed the human ability rationally to know which acts are good and which evil, and to attain practical certainty about the means to ends, they explain "necessary," "good," and "evil" not entirely in relation to ends. "Necessary" as an attribute of acts is defined as "that for the omission of which the agent deserves blame," "evil" as "that for doing of which the agent deserves blame," and so on. The blame can be known by any person of sound reason, as in cases of suicide and infanticide, without reference to consequences. This sharp turn from teleology to deontology in Muʿtazilite ethical theory was probably marked by the new prominence of obligation in Islamic legal–ethical thinking.

The prominence of obligation in revelation is underscored by the requirements of the Sharīʿa, the sacred law. These duties, as the Sharīʿa explains, must be performed by virtue of a contractual agreement between God and humanity. As God's creatures, human beings must serve divine purposes by obeying God's commands. In return for this obedience God promises rewards. Hence, judged on the basis of divine scales of justice provided in the Sharīʿa, every human will receive what he or she deserves (Frank 1983). In such a contractual relation between God as the benefactor and human as the servant, obligation occupies a central role. The Muʿtazilites and the Shīʿites, thus, did not explain obligation wholly in terms of the interest of the subject and its good consequences. Rather, they were concerned to show the essence of a deontological perspective in ethics. Actions become obligatory because of the characteristic of "obligatoriness" in them (i.e., fidelity to promises, truthfulness, and justice).

Their central position on ethics is that a human being of sound mind can know in an immediate intuition that certain acts are good or evil prior to and without the aid of scripture. Ethical predicates refer to objectively real attributes and characteristics of actions they describe. However, ethical judgment should not be based merely on prima facie values of actions. Before arriving at a final decision, different aspects of an act should first be appraised separately, then these aspects should be weighed against each other to deduce an overall judgment. This process will lead to varying conclusions due to the varying circumstances of an act's occurrence. Ethical deliberations in certain classes of act, despite having an invariable value character, do not necessarily lend themselves to the derivation of a clear-cut final judgment. Still, it is in principle possible to derive from these absolute characteristics of a moral act a set of universal rules such that one can know the ethical value of any act in any given situation by reflecting upon the objective facts of value.

Some Sunnī Ashʿarite theologians did not deny the feature of objectivity in Muʿtazilite ethical concepts. They concentrated instead on opposing the partial and inessential feature of absoluteness in some of the rules. The main thrust of their attack is that ethical rules are grounded neither in the acts themselves nor in their rationally accessible properties. In other words, in moral cognition they turned attention to relativism versus absolutism, whereas for Muʿtazilites the issue was one of subjectivism versus objectivism. While some acts are essentially good or evil and agreed on by all people of sound mind without regard to relative conditions, Ashʿarites insisted that there could be relativistic definitions of good, evil, and so on.

This debate about moral epistemology remains contested by both Sunnī and Shīʿite scholars in their contemporary discussions about the modern project of searching for universal and absolute moral values, independent of revelation. Such a universal and autonomous claim is difficult to sustain without due emphasis on intuitive human reasoning in knowing good and evil objectively. Hence, it remains unacceptable to the majority of Sunnī jurist–theologians today. This rejection has led to epistemological crisis in juridical–ethical deliberations in matters that are beyond the scope of traditional jurisprudence. In fact, a majority of the issues related to social ethics in Muslim societies worldwide remains unresolved because of the conservative spirit that permeates juridical–ethical studies in the seminaries. Recent scholarship to resolve this crisis (mostly undertaken by modern educated Muslims) is considered a dissident, secularist approach to social ethics in Muslim societies. Undoubtedly, nothing less than the reinstatement of reason as a substantive partner of revelation will bring back the Quranic ethical discourse to the center stage of religious revival among Muslims.

Notes

1   The usual practice among Muslim jurists is to end their judicial opinion (*fatwā*) with a statement *allāh ʿālim*, that is, "God knows best," indicating that the opinion was given on the basis of what seemed most likely to be the case, rather than claiming that this was an absolute and unrebuttable opinion, which could be derived only from the Qur'ān and the Traditions.

2   There is much disagreement among theologian–jurists in the matter of the definition of *wājib*. The difficulty stems from the way an act is attributed to the agent. Those who regard a human act to be the result of human free will define it as an act whose omission deserves punishment. The term "deserves" imputes the responsibility of the omitted act entirely to the agent. On the other hand, those who regard a human act to be the result of the divine will define the *wājib* act as the one decreed by God, for the omission of which the agent is legally (*shar'an*) censured. For these and other theological views and their analysis, see al-Juwaynī, al-Imām al-Ḥaramayn Abū al-Maʿālī ʿAbd al-Malik b. ʿAbd Allāh, *al-Burhān fī uṣūl al-fiqh* (Cairo: Dār al-Anār, 1400 AH/1976), Vol. 1, pp. 308–10. For the Muʿtazilite and Shīʿite views and objections, see Ṭūsī (1980: 203ff.).

3   Muslims in general believe that a true understanding of any matter related to the faith in the Hereafter is impossible without divine revelation. If we are to understand anything related to God, God himself must tell us. God tells people who he is by speaking through the prophets. His words are recorded in the books of the prophets, that is, the scriptures. Hence, in understanding God and his plans for humanity, we must rely on the Qur'ān as God's revelation to humanity. As for the impending harm in the Hereafter for those who disobey God, this is known through the Qur'ān.

Bibliography

Asadābādī, ʿAbd al-Jabbār ibn Aḥmad. 1942 [1361]: *al-Mughnī fī abwāb al-tawḥīd wa al-ʿadl*, Vol. 6, Part 1. Cairo: al-Miṣriyya al-ʿAmma.

Fakhry, M. 1994a: *Ethical Theories in Islam*. Leiden: E. J. Brill.

——1994b: "The Muʿtazilite View of Man" in *Philosophy, Dogma and the Impact of Greek Thought in Islam*, 107–21. Altershot: Variorium.

Frank, R. M. 1983: "Moral Obligation in Classical Muslim Theology." *Journal of Religious Ethics* 11 (2), 204–23.

Ghazzālī, Muḥammad ibn Muḥammad. 1904–7: *Kitāb al-Mustaṣfā min ʿilm al-uṣūl*, Vol. 1. Cairo: Bulāq.

——1916 [1334]: *Iḥyā' ʿulūm al-dīn*, Vol. 1. Cairo: Mu'assasa Al-Halabī.

Hourani, G. F. 1971: *Islamic Rationalism: The Ethics of ʿAbd al-Jabbār*. Oxford: Clarendon Press.

——1985: *Reason and Tradition in Islamic Ethics*. New York: Cambridge University Press.

Ibn Manẓūr, Muḥammad ibn Mukrim. 1955–6: *Lisān al-'arab*, Vol. 13. Beirut: Dār Ṣādir.

Ibn Muṭahhar al-Ḥillī, al-Hasan ibn Yūsuf. [n.d.]: *Kashf al-murād fī sharḥ tajrīd al-ī'tiqād.* Mashhad: Kitāb-furūshī Ja'farī.

Imām al-Ḥaramayn al-Juwaynī, 'Abd al-Malik ibn 'Abd Allāh. 1976 [1400 AH]: *al-Burhān fī uṣūl al-fiqh*, Vol. 1. Cairo: Dār al-Anār.

Madkur, M. S. 1960: *Mabāḥith al-ḥukm 'inda al-uṣūliyyīn*, Vol. 1. Cairo: Dār al-Nahḍa al-'Arabiyya.

Muẓaffar, Muḥammad Riḍā. 1966: *Uṣūl al-fiqh*, Vol. 2. Najaf: Dār al-Nu'mān.

Marmura, M. E. 1969: "Ghazzālī On Ethical Premises." *Philosophical Forum* (New Series), 1, 393–403.

Rāzī, Fakhr al-Dīn Muḥammad ibn 'Umar. 1938: *Tafsīr kabīr*, Vol. 1. Cairo: Matba'a Al-Bahiyya Al-Miṣriyya.

Reinhart, A. K. 1983: "Islamic Law as Islamic Ethics." *Journal of Religious Ethics* 11 (2), 186–203.

Ṭūsī, Muḥammad ibn al-Ḥasan. 1980 [1358 Sh]: *Tamhīd al-uṣūl dar 'ilm-i kalām-i islām* [being translation of the commentary on al-Sharīf al-Murtaḍā's section on theology in *Jumal al-'ilm wa al-amal*, tran. 'Abd al-Muḥsin Mishkāt al-Dīnī]. Tehran: Anjuman Islāmī Ḥikmat va Falsafī Tihrān.

Wansbrough, J. 1978: *The Sectarian Milieu: Content and Composition of Islamic Salvation History.* Oxford: Clarendon Press.

Wensinck, A. J. 1965: *Muslim Creed*. London: Luzac.

CHAPTER 28

Muslim Ethical Trajectories in the Contemporary Period

Frederick Mathewson Denny

The Ethical Landscape of Islam

The ethical landscape of Islam and Muslims is a combination of mostly traditional legal, ritual, sociocultural, political, and rational customs, practices, preferences, and attitudes. Although formal ethical discourses flourished in classical Islamic philosophy, they did not inform the majority of Muslims about morality. They exhibited a brilliant ongoing intellectual tradition that occurred at elite levels. Muslims have generally depended on the Qur'ān, Islam's revealed scripture, and the Ḥadīth, the reports of the Prophet Muḥammad's words and acts, for their moral and ethical guidance. The Qur'ān

> is not a book of abstract ethics, but neither is it the legal document that Muslim lawyers have made it out to be. It is a work of moral admonition through and through . . . If values and principles were to be derived from the entire Qur'ān, it would be possible to build an ethical system that would be genuinely Quranic. (Rahman 1985: 8–9; see Fakhry 1994)

Historically, the Islamic imperium intervened with the great conquests and a system of law evolved. Although nominally based on the Qur'ān and, increasingly, the Prophet Muḥammad's Sunna (the record of his teachings and example), it extended way beyond those sources in the interests of a complex state administrative and juridical apparatus. The early legists tended to derive their legal and ethical principles from extra-Quranic, general principles of equity and justice, which were difficult to apply in non-arbitrary ways. However, the principles also gave the imperial rulers great scope for a "state-made law that claimed to be sanctioned by Sharī'a law" (Rahman 1985: 9). The early rulers seemed to have no illusions about their choice, so that the Qur'ān would thenceforth function as a rectitude guide, certainly, but not as the actual juristic basis of legislation. In spite of that, the Qur'ān was and continues to be of profound importance in individual, personal, and group morality apart from formal legal determinations.

The modern era has produced many Muslim thinkers and movements desiring to "go back to the Qur'ān" in a general quest for the community's authentic, original faith and order in a manner reminiscent of the *sola scriptura* doctrine of the Protestant Reformation in Europe. The partnership of scripture and tradition has been at least as powerful a process in Islamic legal and political history as in Roman Catholicism, with the major difference being the former's emphasis on worldly governance and law rather than the maintenance of a clerical hierarchy with a sacramental–penitential system of dispensing or withholding grace to adherents.

The classical sources of Islamic jurisprudence, at least in the majority Sunni tradition, have been Qur'ānic revelation, Prophetic Sunna as preserved in the ḥadīth literature, analogical reasoning (known as *qiyās*), and legal consensus, or *ijmā'*. Although the Qur'ān is the supreme authority, closely followed by the Prophet's Sunna, analogical reasoning and consensus exerted great influence in defining, interpreting, and applying (or not) the contents of the two basic sources of teaching. Add to this the problem that so many of the ḥadīhs attributed to the Prophet were either outright forgeries or extremely weak as to provenance. This has been known since the science of ḥadīth came into being in order to evaluate and certify or dismiss candidate texts for the heritage of the Sunna in its literary form.

The Qur'ān itself declares "in the Messenger of Allāh you have a beautiful pattern of conduct" (Qur'ān 33:21). "Believe in Allāh and His Messenger, the unlettered Prophet" (Qur'ān 7:158). Such passages raised Muḥammad to a level such that his own charisma was perceived as having revelatory power, even though he did not claim such for himself. As the generations passed in the establishment of Islamic legal, political, and military sovereignty that was propagated through an extensive civilization, so too did the influence and prestige of Muḥammad, whether in law, spirituality, ethics, or popular piety. The range of material contained in the hundreds of thousands of ḥadīth reports that eventually accumulated is vastly wider and more detailed than the contents of the Qur'ān. They reflect not so much the life and teaching of a morally upright religious visionary and reformer from the traditional tribally ruled regions of Mecca and Medina, as the complex and diverse problems and attempted remedies of a multicultural empire on a civilization-building development path. In time, Muslim political authority and religious–legal institutions extended from Arabia and the Fertile Crescent to the Atlantic in the west, India and Central Asia in the east, as well as far north and south. The figure of the Prophet Muḥammad assumed symbolic and mythical qualities far beyond the ways in which the early Muslim community regarded their revered spiritual and political hero.

In a manner similar to the ways modern Christian thought has distinguished the Jesus of history from the Christ of faith, so also Muslims have raised Muḥammad to a nearly supernatural level in popular piety. If many Christians are stirred to ask themselves when in need of moral advice, "What would Jesus do?" many more Muslims would raise a parallel query and even repair to their ḥadīth sources to discover what in fact the Prophet, as the perfect example for humankind, is reported to have done or said. Muḥammad continues perhaps to be the most frequently consulted source for practical and ethical questions that Muslims need to address.

Islam teaches that humankind is equipped with a sound constitution, called *fitra*. Although Adam and Eve sinned, God later forgave them, and by no means did they introduce a universal disability of original sin as a condition requiring redemption. Muslims are fully aware of the challenges and uncertainties of the moral life, which they believe is humankind's responsibility as servants of God. Humans are free agents under a just God; but on the Last Day, God holds them accountable for a moral and faith-centered justification of their deeds. In today's complex and closely connected world, Muslims are struggling to sustain their traditional faith and values while seeking ways to cope with the problems, perceived threats, and paradoxes of modernity, secularism, and interreligious relations. This chapter focuses on three evolving ethical trajectories among Muslims today: human rights, Muslim women's rights, and progressivist initiatives in a tradition largely dominated by patriarchalist, fundamentalist, and cultural relativist attitudes, habits, and institutions.

Islam and Human Rights

Human rights are one of the most active contexts for practical ethical discourse among Muslims in the current era of globalization (see chapter 51). It is often observed by Muslims that under Islam humans have no rights, only duties. One of the characterizations of a true Muslim is *'abd*, a "servant" or "slave" in relation to God. The best name that a parent can bestow upon a child, according to tradition, is 'Abd Allah, "Servant of Allah," or 'Abd al-Rahman, "Servant of the All-Merciful." The same Arabic root produces *'ibāda*, "service" in the sense of worship services. Like the Christian notion of *opus Dei*, "the work of God," and the Jewish *avodah* (a Semitic cognate of *'ibāda*), there is a strong sense of work, of labor in the service of God (cf. liturgy, "the work of the people"). Although the Qur'ān describes the Muslim as God's "slave," it also bestows the title and privilege of being God's caliph (from Arb. *Khalīfa*) or vicegerent on earth. Humankind has a very broad scope in which to act. But there are no freedoms, let alone rights, for Muslims, apart from obligations.

There does not appear to be any basis in traditional, orthodox/orthoprax Islam – the dominant form today in this age of fundamentalist activism – for human rights in the modern Western sense, based on the individual person in a secular setting. There are, to be sure, legal rights for certain classes of persons within the Islamic system. Majid Khadduri, a leading specialist on justice in Islam (from Iraq, originally, but not a Muslim himself), has listed five important rights of Muslims. The rights are those "that Islam had recognized in the past and those which Muslim states have accepted after the United Nations Declaration of Human Rights was issued" (Khadduri 1984: 235–7; see Arzt 1990). They are (1) dignity and brotherhood; (2) equality among members of the (Muslim) community regardless of race, color, and class [but not sex]; (3) respect for the honor, reputation, and family of each individual; (4) the right of each individual to be "presumed innocent until proven guilty according to law" (Article 11 of UDHR); and (5) individual freedom [in some sense, but this is a debated matter].

Concerning rights in comparison with obligations, one contemporary Muslim international relations specialist has written:

Human rights exist only in relation to human obligations. Individuals possess certain obligations toward God, fellow humans, and nature, all of which are defined by the Shariah. When individuals meet these obligations they acquire certain rights and freedoms which are again prescribed by the Shariah. Those who do not accept these obligations have no rights, and any claims of freedom that they make upon society lack justification. (Said 1979: 92)

The differences between Islam and the West on the issue of human freedom are emphasized in Islam's position of viewing freedom as belonging to the community rather than the "anarchy of liberal individualism." Far from being opposed to the quest for workable global human rights standards and norms, "the concept of human rights must incorporate Islamic and other Third World traditions or it will continue to provoke irreconcilable quarrels" (Said 1979: 93, 96). The author has characterized the dominant Muslim view of the matter. It is a view strongly shaped by cultural relativism rather than the acceptance of universal values in a pluralistic, global context. There is clearly an urgent need for the development of mediating discourses, both heuristic and applied, in order to alleviate both cultural relativism and a widely perceived non-Muslim, secular mindset that does not respect religion in general, and particularly Islam.

Islam has always valued the collective community more than the individual person and views the latter as subordinate to the former. Individualism, in the modern Western sense and as related to human rights, is rejected by most Muslims. Bassam Tibi, an Arab Muslim scholar, writes that "rights are entitlements and are different from duties. In Islam, Muslims, as believers, have duties/*farā'id* vis-à-vis the community/*umma*, but no individual rights in the sense of entitlements" (1994: 289). Tibi asserts a radical transformation in Islam will be necessary to endorse human rights for individuals. He sees Muslim efforts at defining human rights as biased in favor of the rights of Muslims, "in the meaning of the duties of believers," and questionable in their commitment to freedom of religion. "In their schemes Islamic authors provide a concept devoid of the substance of individual human rights." Cultural modernity, not cultural relativism, is what Tibi prescribes.

There are several notable initiatives among Muslims to specify human rights in response to the Universal Declaration of Human Rights of 1948. Yet these can be disquieting concerning protections for freedom of religion. This area is perhaps the most sensitive one from the Islamic standpoint. Islamic law prohibits conversion away from the religion and views it as a capital offense. Moreover, Islam views itself as the primordial religion of humankind, the "religion of unspoiled nature," according to Article 10 of the 1990 Cairo Declaration on Human Rights in Islam (1993: 6). Although Islamic legal prosecution of apostasy is as rare as it is unpleasant, it has some staunch proponents in extremist Muslim fundamentalism. A trend has developed whereby zealous Muslims declare a fellow Muslim to be an apostate and thus consider it lawful to take the accused's life. One Egyptian Muslim, Shaykh Muḥammad al-Ghazālī, who is widely regarded as "*the Islamic authority on human rights . . .* issued a *Fatwā* (religious decree) in which he authorizes killing every Muslim who publicly subscribes to suspending the *sharī'a*" (Tibi 1994: 290, n. 49; Tibi's emphasis). That decree was later used by Algerian fundamentalist fanatics to justify the killing of intellectuals.

Muslim discourses in recent years have sometimes skirted the concept of rights and instead focused on the basic "dignity" of human beings.

> All human beings form one family whose members are united by submission to God and descent from Adam. All men are equal in terms of *basic human dignity* and *basic obligations and responsibilities*, without any discrimination on the grounds of race, color, language, sex, religious belief, political affiliation, social status or other considerations. True faith is the guarantee for enhancing such dignity along the path to human perfection. (Cairo Declaration 1993: 3–4, Art. 1a; emphasis added)

Rights are abundantly referred to in the Cairo Declaration, but in every case they are linked to the Sharīʿa (i.e., God's revealed way for humankind) as the context for their interpretation and application. Regarding freedom of thought: "Everyone shall have the right to express his opinion freely in such manner as would not be contrary to the *principles of the Sharīʿah*" (10, Art. 22a; emphasis added). Or, regarding political participation: "Everyone shall have the right to participate, directly or indirectly, in the administration of his country's public affairs. He shall also have the right to assume public office *in accordance with the provisions of the Sharīʿah*" (10: Art. 23b; emphasis added). A final article states: "All the rights and freedoms stipulated in this Declaration are subject to the Islamic Sharīʿah" (10: Art. 24). The Cairo Declaration's preface affirms "fundamental rights and universal freedoms . . . are an integral part of the Islamic religion . . . [amounting to] binding divine commandment" (3). However, "relying on the sharīʿa to limit or dilute human rights means that the rights that are established under international law are being qualified by standards that are not recognized in international law as legitimate bases for curtailing rights" (Mayer 1998: 66).

The production of human rights declarations by international Muslim bodies is due, in part, to the perceived need for Muslim countries and organizations to get on board a global discourse in a manner that does not surrender their interests (see chapter 49). Such activity in Muslim contexts also indicates a serious interest in universal human rights. In some cases there would be no declarations at all were it not for the language of Sharīʿa referral cited above in several articles of the Cairo Declaration. The whole question of what the Sharīʿa's authority, scope, and application will be in the future is somewhat open nowadays, in light of modernist reforming thought and Muslim feminist discourses. The politics of human rights, for Muslims, whether as an internal process requiring proper regard for the Sharīʿa in the framing of declarations, or in universal terms where religion does not dictate – although it may agree – is a delicate, complex matter. How will Muslim majority countries provide for protection of human rights for all if the Islamic declarations they ratify leave non-Muslims and Muslim women under the ultimate regulative authority of Sharīʿa law?

Muslim Women's Rights

Modern Muslim feminist reformers bent on changing the traditional patriarchal character of Islamic jurisprudence and male chauvinist cultural attitudes and practices

have called for a return to the Qur'ān. They see in the revealed text a much more balanced sex and gender discourse than in the later, developed legal system that relied
heavily on prophetic ḥadīth of all sorts, as well as a male dominated cultural tradition
of legal and ethical priorities. In other words, they view the traditionally prevailing
patriarchalism as a repressive form of cultural relativism. There are significant feminist
developments in Muslim countries today, although they have nothing like the power
and range of such developments in the West. One problem is the perception among
traditionalist Muslims – and their number is enormous – that feminist discourses in
Islamic contexts amount to an invasion of godless Western ideas that will corrupt Islam
and the Muslims. Muslim feminists have a rough road ahead in relation to such
accusations (see Webb 2000).

A prominent Muslim feminist activist–scholar, Riffat Hassan, originally of Pakistan
but now on the faculty of the University of Louisville, takes a position typical of pious
Muslims who harbor suspicions concerning Western sincerity about human rights.
Hassan is somewhat skeptical about universal human rights, but keeps her mind open
to the possibility. She feels that the Universal Declaration of Human Rights' failure to
acknowledge religion as in any way a source of human rights is a "critical flaw"
(Hassan 1996: 365). She also frankly acknowledges the failings and errors in the
Islamic legal and theological traditions of the past that continue to haunt and hinder
Muslims today. Hassan attributes these failings to patriarchalism in a manner paralleled by Jewish and Christian feminist discourses. The original, pure source of Islam –
by which she means the Qur'ān – is free of patriarchalism. The cumulative tradition of
theology, law, and custom has been utterly dominated by males of a patriarchal men-
tality. Hassan discerns a number of human rights guaranteed by the Qur'ān: Right to
Life (6:151); Right to Respect (17:70); Right to Justice (5:8); Right to Freedom, including of religion (3:79); Right to Privacy (24:27–8, 58); Right to Protection from Slander,
Backbiting, and Ridicule (49:11–12); Right to Acquire Knowledge (96:1–5); Right to
Leave One's Homeland Under Oppressive Conditions (4:97–100); Right to Develop
One's Aesthetic Sensibilities and Enjoy the Bounties Created by God (7:32); Right to
Sustenance (11:6); Right to Work (4:32); Right to "The Good Life" (2:229; 5:1; 17:34
et al.), and others (371–80).

Hassan acknowledges that the rights she finds in the Qur'ān are not routinely
honored by Muslims. She seeks to return to the Qur'ān as the primary authority for
Muslims in all dimensions of life. This approach she shares with most Muslim feminists.
They see in the Qur'ān the last best hope for change and improvement for women and
all Muslims, as well. She laments the loss of freedoms that women in early Muslim times
enjoyed. Hassan goes on to list egregious violations of women's human rights: murder
of women by their husbands (e.g., in Pakistan) defended as "honor killings"; the expressions of sadness and disappointment at the birth of a daughter rather than a son; the
marrying off of minor girls, often to much older males; the often extreme difficulty of
divorce for women; the requirement that divorced women give up their sons at age 7
and their daughters at age 12 (generally); the extreme anxiety and fear caused by
the constant threat of divorce; discrimination in inheritance; the putting away of
women in veils and shrouds and behind "locked doors on the pretext of protecting their
chastity, forgetting that according to the Qur'ān confinement to their homes was not a

normal way of life for chaste women but a punishment for 'unchastity' " (Hassan 1996: 363).

Riffat Hassan is a courageous woman who is faithful to her religion to the point of fighting for the restoration of what she believes to be its fundamental ethical principles, free of cultural relativism, particularly regarding human rights for all. It is question-able how free she would be to express herself in her native Pakistan. But her words and writings make their way across the globe, as she is an oft-quoted thinker.

If substantial numbers of Muslims returned to the Qur'ān's admittedly more bal-anced and egalitarian teachings on relations between the sexes and their more nearly equal roles in public life, the conditions for women could substantially improve. But some thinkers who sympathize with Muslim feminists express reservations about the possibility of purely Quranically based reform, because the juristic traditions are so entrenched and authoritative. Clearly, the question of women's rights remains a press-ing trajectory in Islamic thought and life.

From Fundamentalist to Progressivist Muslim Ethical Trajectories

This chapter has not included a survey of conservative, let alone fundamentalist, Muslim thinking on ethics or theology in the contemporary era. If it had, such influ-ential figures as Hasan al-Bannā' (d. 1949), the founder of the Muslim Brotherhood; the Egyptian literary scholar and extremist fundamentalist reformer Sayyid Qutb (d. 1966); the Pakistani journalist Mawlana Abu-l-A'la al-Mawdudi (d. 1979); and the charismatic Iranian Shi'ite revolutionary leader Ayatollah Khomeini (d. 1989), among others, would have been included. Sayyid Qutb, for example, characterized most of con-temporary humanity, Muslim and non-Muslim alike, as steeped in *jāhiliyyah*, the "igno-rant barbarism" that had plagued pre-Islamic Arabia before the coming of Islam. Qutb's views, particularly as disseminated in his polemical tract *Milestones*, continue to inspire and motivate a broad range of Muslim activists and movements, including their most extreme and violent fringes. Qutb called for a revival of Islam by having a "vanguard . . . set out with this determination [of bringing total submission to Allāh] and then keep going, marching through the vast ocean of *jāhiliyyah* which encompasses the entire world" (Qutb 1990: 8–9). His words were prophetic. Sayyid Qutb has arguably been the most forceful articulator of extremist political Islam of the past half century.

Progressive and modernist thinkers in Islamic religious, ethical, and cultural dis-course have also appeared, although they have attracted widespread media attention only recently. One of the leading exponents of what many Muslims increasingly prefer to characterize as a progressivist (rather than "modernist" or "liberal") approach to understanding Islamic religion and behavior is the Iranian philosopher and scientist Abdolkarim Soroush. He has sparked considerable controversy in his country through his criticism of a government run by clergy. He is a graduate of a respected theological school and qualified to belong to Iran's clerical guild. Soroush was also a staunch sup-porter of the Iranian Islamic revolution of the late 1970s. Later, he came to view the rule of Iran by mullahs as an inherent Islamic conflict of interest on ethical grounds.

He has been writing and lecturing for some years on ethics, freedom, reason's role in responsible Islamic life, tolerance, governance, doctrine, and virtue. His views, expressed without apology for the criticism they engender, are attracting significant numbers of thoughtful Muslims who feel that their religion has for some time now been hijacked by extremists, terrorists, Wahhabi fundamentalists, and, in his native Iran, power hungry clerical government leaders and their minions.

Soroush alarms Muslim conservatives, particularly those who would subject all human rights to Sharī'a standards. He claims:

> A religion that is oblivious to human rights (including the need of humanity for freedom and justice) is not tenable in the modern world. In other words, religion needs to be right not only logically, but also ethically . . . Simply put, we cannot evade rational, moral, and extra-religious principles and reasoning about human rights, myopically focusing on nothing but the primary texts and maxims of religion in formulating our jurisprudential edicts. (Soroush 2000: 128)

The final remark clearly sets Soroush apart from the conservative, scripturalist legal and ethical discourses that dominate Muslim religious ideologies today, whether in the Sunni or Shi'ite worlds. Soroush's respectable following in Iran may come as a surprise to Westerners. It is a welcome trend in a nation that wants to participate in the larger world and half of whose population was not born when the revolution occurred.

Soroush views ethics as the "groundwork of religion and life" and thus inherently "delightful." He sees a

> kind of sanctity in ethics that places it above analysis, experimentation, and reduction . . . Ethics seems to entail its own "indeterminacy" theorem. As the accuracy of one side increases, the generality of the other decreases. This lack of determinacy is the enigma of enigmas. It reveals not only that ethics is not an exact science but also that it will never be. Even if we follow the lead of the Mu'tazilite school of thought in designating good and evil as natural and objective categories, deriving ought from is, and establishing commonsensical moral maxims as self-evident, *a priori* precepts devoid of cultural relativity and contingency, we still have failed to shed even a sliver of light on the problem of the "indeterminacy" of morality or on the nature of rights, justice, fairness, power, and freedom. (Soroush 2000: 105ff.)

The Mu'tazilite rationalist theologians of the golden age of Islamic civilization in Baghdad called themselves the "People of Justice and [divine] Unity." They dominated the Abbasid caliphal court of al-Ma'mūn (d. 833) in the ninth century and headed an inquisition (*miḥna*) in defense of their doctrinal views that lasted for fifteen years (833–48). In a manner that would be imitated by other theologians in later centuries, including Christians such as Thomas Aquinas, the Mu'tazilites averred that God can be known through reason (see chapter 24). Where the Mu'tazilites exercised a rationalism unique to their movement was in ethical discourse (see Gimaret 1992). Reason alone enables humans to determine what is good or evil. The Qur'ān confirms what reason dictates, in many cases, but it also provides guidance on what humankind's obligations are under God. The duties of prayer, almsgiving, and so forth are indeed clearly commanded and regulated by the revealed text. There is a great deal of flexibility by which humans may determine ethically sound alternatives among the countless ambiguous and indeterminate choices that arise in life beyond ritual obligations.

Soroush operates in the general framework of ethical discourse that the Mu'tazilites developed in classical times. The Shi'ites have, in fact, continued to cultivate Mu'tazilite-style theological and ethical discourses. Soroush's rational basis as a Shi'ite thinker is not out of the ordinary. But his independence and boldness go far beyond academicism and addressing traditional theological and moral topics. He is not interested in Mu'tazilism per se, but in what Mu'tazilites and other rationally committed believers, whether Muslim or not, have been about wherever they may be found. He insists that one "may not employ reason to attest to the truth of one's opinions, without leaving the door open to its fault-finding critique. The attempt to enjoy the sweet affirmation of reason without tasting its bitter reproach is pure self-delusion" (Soroush 2000: 154).

In his essay "Tolerance and Governance: A Discourse on Religion and Democracy," Soroush argues that only free, democratic societies can provide the environment for the full exercise of reason in a synergistic relationship to faith. Here he is evidently referring to totalitarian Muslim nations and societies. "Religious despotism is most intransigent because a religious despot views his rule not only as his right but as his duty. Only a religious democracy that secures and shelters faith can be secure and sheltered from self-righteous and anti-religious rule" (Soroush 2000: 154; see also Vakilli 2002).

Conclusion

This chapter has charted trajectories in Islamic ethics from fundamentalist to progressive, and through debates about human rights, cultural relativism, and feminism in Islam. These trajectories are obvious forces in the current world. Yet we should conclude this discussion by pointing to an important insight. Soroush contends that much of what is awry in contemporary Islamic theological, ethical, social, and political discourse relates to the mistaken sense that being a Muslim essentially means adopting and defending a particular identity.

> I think one of the greatest theoretical plagues of the Islamic world, in general, is that people are gradually coming to understand Islam as an identity rather than a truth . . . So, I believe that the Islam of identity should yield to the Islam of truth. The latter can coexist with other truths; the former, however, is, by its very nature, belligerent and bellicose. It is the Islam of war, not the Islam of peace. Two identities would fight each other, while two truths would cooperate. (Soroush 2000: 24)

Were Abdolkarim Soroush simply an academic voice speaking from the ivory tower, his views would perhaps be noticed, but essentially disregarded, by most Muslims. The fact that he is also a Muslim public intellectual, however controversial, in Iran and beyond in the Islamic world, suggests that progressivist Islamic theological and ethical discourses are on a rising trajectory.

Bibliography

Arzt, D. 1990: "The Application of International Human Rights Law in Islamic States." *Human Rights Quarterly* 20, 202–30.

Brockopp, J. E. (ed.) 2003: *Islamic Ethics of Life: Abortion, War, and Euthanasia.* Columbia: University of South Carolina Press.

Cairo Declaration on Human Rights in Islam [adopted by the Organization of the Islamic Conference in 1990]. United Nations General Assembly. A/CONF.157/PC/62/Add.18, June 9, 1993. Submitted to the World Conference on Human Rights. Preparatory Committee. Fourth Session. Geneva, April 19–May 7, 1993. Item 5 on the provisional agenda. Annex to RES. No. 49/19-P. New York: United Nations.

Fakhry, M. 1994: *Philosophy, Dogma, and the Impact of Greek Thought in Islam.* Brookfield, VT: Variorum.

Gimaret, D. 1992: "Mu'tazila" in *Encyclopaedia of Islam,* Vol. 7, Fasc. 127: 783–93. Leiden: E. J. Brill.

Hassan, R. 1996: "Rights of Women Within Islamic Communities" in *Religious Human Rights in Global Perspective,* ed. J. Witte, Jr. and J. D. van der Vyver, 361–86. Amsterdam: Kluwer Law International.

Khadduri, M. 1984: *The Islamic Concept of Justice.* Baltimore, MD: Johns Hopkins University Press, appendix "Human Rights in Islam" 233–9.

Mayer, A. E. 1998: *Islam and Human Rights: Tradition and Politics,* 3rd edn. Boulder, CO: Westview Press.

Qutb, S. 1990: *Milestones.* Indianapolis, IN: American Trust Publications.

Rahman, F. 1985: "Law and Ethics in Islam" in *Ethics in Islam, Ninth Giorgio Levi Della Vida Biennial Conference,* ed. R. G. Hovannisian, 3–15. Malibu, CA: Undena Publications.

Safi, O. (ed.) 2003: *Progressive Muslims: On Justice, Gender, and Pluralism.* Oxford: Oneworld.

Said, A. A. 1979: "Human Rights in Islamic Perspectives" in *Human Rights: Cultural and Ideological Perspectives,* ed. A. Pollis and P. Schwab, 86–100. New York: Praeger.

Soroush, A. 2000: *Reason, Freedom, and Democracy in Islam: Essential Writings of Abdolkarim Soroush,* ed. M. Sadri and A. Sadri. New York: Oxford University Press.

Tibi, B. 1994: "Islamic Law/Sharī'a, Human Rights, Universal Morality and International Relations." *Human Rights Quarterly* 16, 277–99.

Vakilli, V. 2002: "Abdolkarim Soroush and Critical Discourse in Iran" in *Makers of Contemporary Islam,* ed. J. L. Esposito and J. O. Voll, 150–76. New York: Oxford University Press.

Webb, G. (ed.) 2000: *Windows of Faith: Muslim Women Scholar–Activists in North America.* Syracuse, NY: Syracuse University Press.

4   Buddhist Ethics

CHAPTER 29

Buddhist Ethics?

John Ross Carter

Situation Prior to System

Ethics, as a discipline in Western philosophy, is a second order reflection on morals (see "On Religious Ethics"). "Buddhist ethics" would refer to a second order reflection on issues of morality, which issues have to do with first order questions and circumstances. Yet first order questions arise from a kind of *zero level* of intuitive awareness, that is, an immediate apprehension of the circumstance of a particular moral case, and one's response mindful of living well, of religious living. The zero level is intuitive awareness, the starting point for subsequent reflection. It is more non-reflective or less deliberate than first order questions about what to do.

A quest for an understanding of this zero level of intuitive awareness is basic to any adequate account of what might be called Buddhist ethics. I will return to the notion of zero level later by introducing two important contributions made by Theravāda Buddhists – a profound notion of awareness and a complementary sense of self-censure together with a corporate sense of mutual respect – and a contribution from Jōdo-Shinshū involving salvific awareness and a sense of indebtedness. Scholars have drawn attention to "systems building" in ethical considerations within the philosophical heritage of the West. Such systems building might appear, on the one hand, to comprehend a disparate subject, covering centuries and cultures. On the other hand, finding a conceptual system of sorts might be the result of projecting a pattern, a network, schematized grid, upon the subject. The point of a persuasive ethical theory is its applicability in providing rational norms for ethical decision making to an evermore inclusive group of people. And the cogency of the rational system is that it provides for commonality in moral discourses relevant for all moral agents regardless of soteriological orientations, ultimates, or engagement with transcendence.

Buddhists have developed systems, too, but of a different order. Any heritage presented to posterity as a path to enlightenment will have its guideposts. A tradition perpetuated through chanted texts in verse and prose will tend to develop mnemonic systems. And in a large textual tradition considered basic for determining the intention of the Buddha, commentarial and exegetical systems for structuring the teachings variously will arise. One thinks of the impressive Abhidhamma literature (see chapter 7). One of the oldest continuing religious institutions known to us today, the Sangha, would be expected to have developed systems of rules and regulations for appropriate and supportive communal religious living. So, Buddhists are not unfamiliar with systems. But these systems were built and maintained in order to indicate a life pattern proclaimed to be soteriologically efficacious. They have been formulated and maintained in order to provide orientation for one's response in becoming engaged with transcendence. Generally, throughout Buddhist history, the systems that have appeared are founded on a fundamental affirmation: the human mind, having become freed from confusion infused by ego assertion, can achieve clarity in perception and knowledge of proper action, entirely attuned to what is fitting, and grounded on the abiding presence of salvific truth.

All of the above suggests the need for an approach, even perspective, that would lead one to consider Buddhist ethics without searching for a general normatively governing first principle or a systematic rational theory. How might one do so? We might look to virtuous persons as models for how to live. A person who seeks to pattern his or her life either directly upon, or by analogy with, persons whose virtue is determined by the cumulative experience and wisdom of the tradition, can provide us with an example of how that tradition coheres, how manners become supportive, and how analogy can be morally instructive. And we learn this without reflecting on a coherent general system of ethics. But when we turn to a study of persons living in another religious tradition, in another culture, or in another time, we become aware, quickly, that an enormous shifting complex of ideas, habits, customs, outlooks, orientations, manners, local histories, and the like, confront us. How does one spot in another person a virtuous quality worthy of emulation?

"Virtue ethics" stemming from Aristotle and his notion of *eudaimon*, which has rightly become interpreted as "human flourishing" rather than "happiness" and is best understood to mean "becoming genuinely human," did not hinge on rational argumentation deduced from a system, but was the result of watching and observing, learning from a virtuous person. If Aristotle had known Sanskrit, surely he would have utilized, in this context, *kalyāṇamitra*.[1] The constructive and supportive assistance provided for one by another person of noble bearing is also communicated in the Theravāda tradition by a standard compound, "voice of another" (*parataghosa*), a timely and well warranted word which helps one to live well (Hardy 1962: 8). There is something of a pattern here, of course, a kind of system, but in a secondary sense. Articulating the position requires systematic construction. Living it requires sensitive receptivity, engaged attentiveness, awareness of what one might call the moral moment, as well as awareness of what one can become. This, in the case of Aristotle and in the Buddhist, too, is at the foundation of the religious life.[2]

From among many strands in this magnificent Buddhist tradition I will consider two that are rarely addressed together: the Theravāda and the Jōdo-Shinshū. There is a theoretical model that arises from this consideration that best fits Buddhist thought and practice, the individual components of which are not entirely unknown in current discussions of ethics in the West. We can call this an *intuitional particularistic virtue ethic.* The "particularism" involved in this account reflects the inadequate applicability of uniform rationalistic "systems" and maintains the distinctiveness of moral situations. The "intuitional" addition indicates attention to that zero level mentioned above. The "virtue ethic" component suggests a commitment to cultivate an enhanced character.

Awareness

Intuitional particularism is not merely subjective in the sense of originating from an individual's whimsical opinion or off-hand reaction. It is generated by and grounded in a much broader context of salvific truth: dharma/dhamma in its highest and most comprehensive sense. We can now trace this kind of intuitional particularistic virtue ethic in two traditions.

Theravāda

The Theravāda tradition has preserved a magnificent account of a salvific transformation involving a cluster of interrelated concepts concerning one's coming to know, to understand, to realize, to perceive, to "come upon," to attain, to awaken, to be aware, to have discriminative knowledge, to apprehend.[3] And there is that great salvific realization translated roughly as "salvific insight-wisdom" in both the customary (*lokiyapaññā*) and world-transcending (*lokuttarapaññā*) dimensions. We have here an *intuitional particularism* that is grounded in a soteriological worldview: be aware of the way things have come to be. One reads, in the Chapter on Awareness (*appamāda-vaggo*) of the *Dhammapada*, "The path to the Deathless is awareness; Unawareness, the path of death . . . Having known this distinctly, Those who are wise in awareness, Rejoice in awareness" (*Dhammapada*, vv. 21–22). The Commentary (*Dhammapadaṭṭhakathā*) provides a significant gloss, "'Awareness [*appamādo*]' Now this [awareness] illumines a massive meaning, spans a massive content; for the entire Word of the Buddha included in the three *piṭakas* taken up and given articulation, boils down to the word 'awareness' only." And, further, the Commentary says, "Now this [awareness] is in essence 'not being bereft of mindfulness [*sati*]'; it is [just another] name for constantly occurring mindfulness [*niccam upaṭṭihitāya satiyā*]" (pp. 109–110). "The Old Commentary of the *Dhammapada* (with Glossary)" (*Dhammapada pūrāṇa sannaya granthipada [vivaraṇa sahita]* fourteenth century), adds, "Awareness, which is 'not being bereft of mindfulness,' with regard to the sphere of qualities of good conduct, is the fundamental cause for all wholesome dharmas and for the benefit of oneself and the benefit of others, pertaining to this world and the next" (p. 431).

This focus on awareness or mindfulness (*appamāda* and *sati*) reflects a dimension of the dynamic core of Theravāda Buddhist thought. It is entirely applicable to human activities ranging from social interaction to quiet meditation, from resolving conflicts between persons to calming the flurry of one's mental activities. Given a moral situation demanding a response, being aware of what has been done and is going on, both generally and particularly, responding in a way that is beneficial for one and for others, and also understanding the causal sequences that have given rise to this or that particular situation, puts one in a position to reflect with insight on the proper course of action. This reflection is not in a conceptual vacuum, devoid of supportive or informative structures provided by a particular cultural context. It is not uninfluenced by the wisdom of a cumulative religious tradition and the example of persons of noble bearing. The importance of the reliability of cognitive processes is emphasized by the prevalence of the key Pali terms already noted. One is not cut adrift, as it were, or left to one's own wits to come up with an appropriate response in a given circumstance.

Closely associated with this notion of awareness (*appamāda*) or mindfulness (*sati*) and providing a central dimension of human self-understanding at the core of Buddhist sensitivities about how to act, arising from the zero level, are notions which are considered "two truly supportive qualities that are guardians of the world" (*dve dhammā lokapālakā*). The two are a sense of "shame" (*hiri*) and a sense of "blame" (*ottappa*). The "shame" in this case has to do with modesty based on a natural valuing of oneself, one's basic sense of self-worth, even respect for oneself (*attagārava*). One would refrain from what is detrimental (*pāpa*) because such behavior is embarrassing, leads to one's being ashamed, is self-incriminating, is simply that which one would not bring oneself to do. The sense of "blame" arises from an awareness of others, a valuing of others, respecting others (*paragārava*) in the sense that their opinions matter. Both of these dimensions, personal-and-also-social, alive dynamically, cooperate in leading one not to do what is detrimental (Warren 1950: ch. 4, para. 142, p. 393).

So one discerns "ethical" parameters, if not quite a formal systematic pattern. One notes the importance of recognizing interdependency (*paṭiccasamuppāda*) and the life setting which is impermanent (*anicca*), awry (*dukkha*), without enduring substantiality (*anattā*). Knowing what persons have done for one (*kataññu*) is an important variable. The perception of how matters have come to be as they are (*yathābhutañāna*) and thinking carefully about the given circumstance (*yonisomanasikāra*) provide sure foundations for acting with insight. Appropriating the admirable dispositions (*brahmavihāra*) of friendliness (*mettā*), compassion (*karuṇā*), sympathetic joy (*muditā*), and equanimity (*upekkhā*) which have arisen in the contemplative life, one contributes to one's own quality of life and benefits others. And these parameters, as well as the paradigms provided by noble persons (*kalyaṇamitta*), are available for one in the context of cultural mores and manners, of one's own sense of what is personally and socially appropriate (*hiri* and *ottappa*). Uppermost and foundational for all of this are unobtrusive awareness (*appamāda*) and mindfulness (*sati*). Insofar as one's actions are in accord with those parameters, one acts morally. The response is intuitive *within* the scope of these parameters. Combining some or all of these parameters with the almost limitless particular circumstances that might arise leads to a multiplicity of possibilities and a variety of analytic interpretations. Yet an act is right to the degree that it is in accord with dharma/dhamma in the deepest and widest and highest sense: from what is fitting, as culturally determined, to what is righteous, in the sense of just, and to what is explicitly taught in the religious tradition, to salvific truth.

Jōdo-Shinshū

We turn now to Jōdo-Shinshū, in Japan, and Shinran (1173–1262). It should be kept in mind that this movement is, so to speak, on the other side of China from India and the Theravāda. The Buddhist cumulative tradition moved from North India, through Central Asia, through China, with all the associated vicissitudes of history, cultural inter-impingements, and creative intellectual responses, and subsequently into Japan's cultural matrix. It did so centuries before Shinran was enabled to grace humanity with profound insights.

Jōdo-Shinshū notions might be more adequately understood in light of parallel Theravāda ideas. For example, there is the great Jōdo-Shinshū term *shinjin*, which the majority of English-writing interpreters have unhappily translated as "faith." The term actually means the arising of a pure, genuine, authentic heart/mind. It is the mind of Amida Buddha given to one in a salvific instance when the utterance of praise for Amida (*nembutsu*) arises without any calculation (*hakarai*) whatsoever in a person of faith. The soteriological force of this notion seems entirely similar to what Theravāda Buddhists have known in "world-transcending insight-wisdom" (*lokuttarapaññā*) upon the arising of the soteriological path (*magga*) (Carter 1987). Shinran urged that one avoid calculation (*hakarai*), wondering all the while whether such was possible. Surely, he maintained, overcoming calculation could not be the result of one's own deliberate effort. We always have some ulterior motive, some subtle self-oriented agenda determining our actions. So, of course, the arising of *shinjin* is not the immediate result of *our* actions. A Theravāda Buddhist might begin to understand the qualities of a person who lives and acts without "calculation," in a manner the older tradition knew as without "self-estimation" (*mana*).

Shinjin, an awareness suggestive of zero-level immediate consciousness, is a very difficult notion to try to put into ethical analysis. But inferring that the notion is much too subjective to provide a basis for understanding the way things are would be amiss. Nothing is more personal, it seems, than *shinjin*; yet because *shinjin* is the mind of Amida Buddha, nothing is more expressive of the truth of the way things really are. Persons in whom *shinjin* has not arisen would turn again to the notion of analogy for a procedure by means of which to determine how to act well. The presence of *shinjin* yields a quality of character entirely admirable and symbolizes a spontaneity of compassion in the life of a person completely consonant with the order of compassionate reality in the world. Acting in consonance with this personal quality and salvific reality is moral.

Another near zero-level category among Jōdo-Shinshū Buddhists is *button*. It means standing in a relationship of indebtedness to Amida Buddha and also to Shakyamuni Buddha for what has been done for one by them (compare *kataññu*). The sense of indebtedness, communicated in the notion of *on*, is also at the core of Japanese sensibilities about what is involved in human relationships. There are other key terms indicating contextuality of interpretation of one's life setting in particular circumstances: that one has taken refuge (*kimyō*, *kie*; compare the Theravāda notion of *saraṇa*), that one has entrusted one's life (*tanomu*, *makaseru*) to compassionate reality, and that one is capable of authentically understanding, really hearing, the salvific efficacy in the order of reality, metaphorically communicated as the call of Amida. All of these notions are integral in the key concept of *shinjin*. In Japan the Buddhist tradition has not forgotten the twin dimensions of becoming engaged with the fundamentally real and of humanity at its comprehensive best; of wisdom (*hannya* and also *chie*, compare *prajñā*, *paññā*) and compassion (*jihi*, compare *karuṇā*).

In What Sense "Buddhist Ethics"?

Where does this bring us in our consideration of "Buddhist ethics"? There appears to be no clear-cut system gaining prominence. Within the cumulative tradition one can infer a deontological (from the Greek, *déon*, what is necessary, proper, right) scheme, that is, acting in accord with what is fitting, proper, and right, acting from a sense of duty. One surely could so interpret actions in light of dharma/dhamma, that is, acting both from and in accord with dharma/dhamma. This deontological dimension can be seen in the monastic community and the commitment to obey rules of the discipline (*vinaya*). One can also readily find themes that indicate a teleological structure, a focus on the consequences of one's actions (*kammavipāka/kammaphala*) or in the soteriological efficacy of dharma/dhamma yielding to the arising of Nirvāṇa/Nibbāna. In a given circumstance, a Buddhist might well lean toward one or the other of these orientations in determining how to act, or might find his or her motivation arising from varying degrees of awareness of these orientations. Further, the quality of cultivating virtue, becoming fully human, is also present for Buddhists as a framework for moral action. One is to act in such a way as to become a virtuous person imaged by the paradigm of the Buddha, leading saintly figures of the past, and persons of virtuous quality living today (*kalyāṇamitra*). All these orientations (duties, consequences, awareness, and paradigms of virtue) can be present at the moment of decision, and each to varying degrees. And there can be occasions, surely, when these categories of ethical analysis do not clearly arise.

It is at this point that terms addressing the importance of being aware, of having the capacity of analyzing the situation at hand, lead one to insist on the significance of *intuitional particularism* in "Buddhist ethics." The emphasis placed on understanding the particular context, how it has come to be, in what sense it has arisen with ramifications for other issues, not in subjective isolationism but in the supportive context of a person engaged with a received tradition, enables one to explore moral responses without subscribing to a normative general theory or system, to respond to the particular case with moral integrity. Key in a consideration of Buddhist ethics is a recognition of the priority of a person's capacity to apprehend the given situation, the causal processes giving rise to a particular circumstance, and, simultaneously, to sense a grounding in a received tradition, both religious and cultural. This *capacity* and this *sense* do not at all bind the person into a scheme or system or theoretical rubric primarily so that he or she can know how to act in a morally praiseworthy way, but to enable that person to live freely and well as a genuine human being, that is, to live religiously.

Comparative religious ethics needs somehow to move to an understanding of a zero level as the ground from which persons begin their reflection on responses in circumstances that can then be considered moral. Care must be taken not to separate a study of ethics from an understanding of religious living. When we focus on categories developed in an intellectual heritage not arising from the religious worldview of the persons whose actions are being considered, we run the risk of developing systems while not understanding persons. Stated more strongly, "ethics" itself must begin with awareness of the forces from which it arises, the lives of religious persons.

The zero level, the area of presuppositions, assumptions, and basic frames of reference, is the level at which one would want to work. At that level, Buddhists offer a view of humanity that is at ease with an intuitional response to the wisdom of the cumulative religious tradition and the cultural context at large. One finds an ideal orientation to living well that is founded on awareness and leads to the formation of persons. This clarifies the importance of intuitional particularism in describing Buddhist ethics. But our focus on the zero level has also led us further – and deeper – to foundational thinking about who we are as moral human beings. Some thinkers stress human freedom and the importance of autonomy in decision making as the crucial foundation of ethics. We have seen how Buddhists propose a foundation for moral action – awareness – that allows for the exercise of freedom, even the necessity for autonomy, but that offers an orientation in which autonomy is neither primary nor an end in itself. A decision-making orientation that seeks rational and defensible foundations for ethical choices seems to stress the formation of systems. When awareness is foundational, emphasis is placed on the formation of the person, and hence our emphasis on the presence of a component of virtue ethics. In the former case, the check on human behavior is rational consistency. In the latter case, a pointer is provided by the wisdom of tradition and the example of noble persons.

Persons have averred, remarkably, that when one is truly aware, when awareness or mindfulness fully arises, one *will* act well. From this point of view, one acts best when one acts with the wisdom and compassion that reflect reality, when one does not calculate or engage in the kind of self-estimation that centripetally focuses on ego-centeredness, when one acts with awareness of propriety and of what is fitting in community, when one avoids "clinging to views" (*diṭṭhupādāna*), or seeking defensible rationales, or being driven by adherence to a system of thought (see chapter 2). Awareness is foundational and dynamic. The fundamental affirmation is not primarily that human beings are autonomous. Rather, human beings are capable of this awareness, ever immediate, ever in process.

Notes

1   A person of impressively alluring qualities, such as having faith, being well-learned, generous, virtuous, and wise, who becomes one's friend, leading one into an enhanced quality of life through rebuke, or admonition, or instruction while consistently maintaining the quality of being a marvelous exemplar.
2   The Japanese have distinguished *dōtoku*, "morality, morals," better "virtue" or "excellence" (*toku*) of the way (*dō* [cf. *tao/dao*]), and *rinri*, "ethics, morals, a code of conduct." The

former is religious; the latter, more recent, more like current Anglo-American notions of "ethics."

3 Consider our terms above: *yonisomanasikāra*, *yathābhutañāna*, and also *avabujati*, *avabodha*, *avabodhati*, *avagacchati*, *adhigacchati*, *vijānati*, *bujjhati*; indeed, *buddha*, *bodhi*, *appamāda*, and *sati*, to mention but a few.

Bibliography

A Buddhist Manual of Psychological Ethics . . . entitled Dhamma-sangaṇī. 1974 [1900]: London: Pali Text Society, distributed by Routledge & Kegan Paul.

Carter, J. R. 1987: "The Arising of *Magga* and *Shinjin*." *The Pure Land* (New Series), 3, 95–106.

Carter, J. R. and Palihawadana, M. 1998: *Dhammapada.* New York: Oxford University Press.

Davids, C. A. F. R. (ed.) 1920: *The Visuddhi-magga of Buddhaghosa.* London: Pali Text Society, Humphrey Milford.

Davids, T. W. R. and Stede, W. (eds.) 1966 [1921–5]: *The Pali Text Society's Pali–English Dictionary.* London: Luzac.

Hardy, E. (ed.) 1962 [1902]: *The Netti-pakaraṇa.* London: Pali Text Society and Luzac.

Nyanaponika (ed.) 1972: *Buddhist Dictionary.* Colombo: Frewin.

Pe Maung Tin (trans.) 1958 [1920]: *The Expositor (Atthasālinī) Buddhaghosa's Commentary on the Dhammasangaṇī,* ed. and revd. R. Davids. London: Pali Text Society and Luzac.

Warren, H. C. (1950): *Visuddhimagga of Buddhaghosācariya,* revd. D. Kosambi. Cambridge, MA: Harvard University Press.

CHAPTER 30

Origins of Buddhist Ethics

Damien Keown

Buddhism was founded in northeast India by Siddhārtha Gautama (ca. 490–ca. 410 BCE), who gained enlightenment at the age of 35 and was thereafter known by the honorific title of Buddha ("awakened one"). Buddhism spread rapidly from India to other parts of Asia, but this chapter is concerned only with the first few centuries of Buddhism in India, a period extending down to about 250 BCE. The form of Buddhism which most resembles this early period is Theravāda Buddhism, which is today predominant in South Asia, particularly in Sri Lanka, Burma, and Thailand. The Theravāda school regards itself as the orthodox custodian of the Buddha's teachings preserved intact from ancient times.

In Buddhism there is no central authority on matters of doctrine and ethics (see chapter 6). The order of monks (*sangha*) instituted by the Buddha is regarded by most Buddhists as the legitimate interpreter of the Buddha's teachings. Although there are national organizations there is no one body which represents the many different monastic communities worldwide. The question of whether a common moral core can be found among the diverse Buddhist schools of Asia is a question upon which scholars are presently divided. Buddhists of all schools, however, seek the same goal – nirvāna – a state of spiritual and moral perfection which it is claimed can be attained by any human being who lives in accordance with Buddhist teachings.

Buddhism does not believe in a Supreme Being or creator god and its precepts and ethical teachings are seen not as divine commands, but as rational principles which, if followed, will promote the welfare of oneself and others. It may therefore be regarded as a form of virtue ethics sharing many features with Aristotle's notion of the good life being one devoted to the cultivation of virtue and culminating in a condition of happiness or flourishing (*eudaimonia*) (see Keown 2001) (see chapters 1 and 4).

Origins

In one sense the origin of Buddhist moral teachings is easy to define. In common with all other beliefs and practices characterized as "Buddhist," they stem from the oral teachings of a single historical individual, Siddhārtha Gautama. According to the traditional accounts of his life, Siddhārtha, the Buddha-to-be, was a prince who renounced his kingdom at the age of 29 to become a religious mendicant. His quest was for a solution to the suffering (*dukkha*) inherent in human life, and six years after leaving home, at the age of 35, he declared that he had attained the goal of spiritual awakening known as nirvāna. From that time he devoted the remaining 35 years of his life to traveling around the towns and villages of northeast India disseminating his teachings. A large mendicant community grew up around him, and semi-permanent residences in the form of monastic institutions (*vihāras*) became established. The Buddha died at the age of 80, and appointed no successor, stating that his followers should rely on his teachings as their guide. Without their leader, the Buddha's follow-ers did not remain united for long, and in the centuries following the Buddha's death many sects and schools arose. Several of these preserved their own records of the Buddha's teachings, such that variant canons came into being (see chapter 7). The only one of these canons to have survived intact is the canon of the Theravāda school, com-posed in the Pali language and known accordingly as the Pali canon. This canon was originally transmitted orally, but was reduced to writing around 70 BCE in Sri Lanka.

The Pali canon consists of three divisions, the most important of which contains the Discourses (*sutta*) of the Buddha. The second is the Monastic Rule (*vinaya*), which is a code of behavior for those who have taken monastic vows. It is likely that this reached its final form about a century after the Buddha's enlightenment, or around 350 BCE. The third division, the Scholastic Treatises (*abhidhamma*), contains material of interest for ethics, mainly from a psychological perspective, although its relevance is sometimes disguised by a terse analytical style. This is the latest portion of the canon and can be dated to approximately 250 BCE. The discussion of ethics in this chapter is based pri-marily upon the material contained in the first division of this canon, the Discourses.

The Indian Religious Background

Although stemming from a single historical individual, Buddhist moral teachings were not formulated in a vacuum. The Buddha lived towards the end of the Vedic period, the name given to the first phase of Indian religion, encompassing the period of a thou-sand years or so down to 500 BCE (see chapter 34). At this time the prevailing religious orthodoxy was brahmanism, the ancestor of what is commonly known in the West as Hinduism. The brahmanical phase of Vedic religion takes its name from the dominance enjoyed by the brahman or hereditary priestly caste. It was characterized by the per-formance of lavish and complex rituals, often sponsored by the king or wealthy patrons. In parallel with this, however, other less formal and more individualistic religious prac-tices – notably those involving ascetic and yogic techniques – were being explored. Further influences on Buddhism came by way of unorthodox religious movements such as Jainism, and the teachings of numerous itinerant philosophers (*samaṇas*), including skeptics, determinists, and nihilists, many of whom denied the reality of moral choice. Such teachings were criticized by the Buddha, believing as he did in free will and holding that individuals inevitably suffer the consequences of their moral acts.

Dharma

A concept of fundamental importance deriving from the pan-Indian pre-Buddhist heritage is dharma. The word has many meanings and nuances, but the underlying idea is of a universal law which determines both the material and moral evolution of the universe. Every aspect of life is regulated by dharma: the physical laws which regulate the rising of the sun, the succession of the seasons, the movement of the constellations; and also the moral laws which regulate the operation of karma or moral retribution (see below), define what is right and wrong, and determine the duties and responsibilities of every member of society. By extension, dharma also means the corpus of Buddhist teachings (since they are thought to be grounded in the nature of things), the practice of the Buddhist Path, and the spiritual realization made possible by the practice of the Path. Living in accordance with dharma and implementing its requirements is said to lead to happiness, fulfillment, and salvation; neglecting or transgressing against it is said to lead to endless suffering in the cycle of rebirth (*saṃsāra*) (see chapter 2).

Dharma is neither caused by nor under the control of a supreme being. Even the gods (who may be thought of as akin to the angels of Christianity) are subject to its laws. Dharma may be translated as "natural law," a term which captures both its important meanings, namely as the principle of order and regularity seen in the behavior of natural phenomena, and also the idea of a universal moral law whose requirements have been discovered (not invented) by enlightened beings such as the Buddha. In Buddhist thought morality is woven into the very fabric of reality and moral goodness is seen as a natural quality which must be progressively cultivated by each individual if he or she is to achieve the *summum bonum* of nirvāna. In the Buddhist view, ethics and metaphysics dovetail to form a single whole, and morality forms part of the structure of things in a way that cannot be accounted for by ethical theories such as subjectivism, relativism, or consequentialism (see chapter 12).

Karma

Common to Buddhism and all major Indian traditions is the belief in karma, the doctrine that moral actions inevitably have repercussions on the one who performs them. Moral action is a unique class of action in that it has two distinctive effects: first, it is soteriologically transformative and modifies the spiritual status of the one who performs it; and second, it determines the good and bad fortune which a person experiences in life. Although a number of the Buddha's contemporaries denied that moral action in itself had any intrinsic significance, the Buddha rejected this idea and emphasized that the moral life was integral to the quest for salvation. The saints of early Buddhism display the highest standards of moral conduct in their lives, as did the Buddha himself, and the goal of nirvāna is inconceivable for one whose behavior is not morally perfect.

Rebirth

Closely associated with the doctrine of karma is belief in rebirth. In terms of this belief, which appears in the later Vedic period several centuries before the Buddha, the higher forms of life (such as gods, human beings, and animals) migrate from one existence to another in accordance with their moral behavior in each existence. Good conduct is rewarded by rebirth in more auspicious circumstances. The long course of an individual existence might be visualized as an upwards or downwards spiral extending over eons of time. The fact that the same living being might appear at one time as a human being and at another as an animal means that Buddhism is much more ready than Western traditions to accord moral status to non-human life forms (see chapter 47).

In this formative period Buddhism thus refined its moral teachings by including and rejecting elements from both the orthodox and unorthodox branches of Indian religion. Continuity with the orthodox tradition can be seen in the common notion of a cosmic moral order (dharma) and belief in moral retribution and rebirth (karma). A new direction was taken by (1) the rejection of animal sacrifice, which was contrary to the ideal of non-violence or respect for life (*ahiṃsā*) emphasized in Buddhism and other non-orthodox traditions (especially Jainism); (2) Buddhism's rejection of the complex and pervasive web of brahmanical ritual which it regarded as stultifying and mechanical; and (3) the Buddha's dislike of the caste system, which he saw as elevating birth over personal moral integrity. These factors establish the broad parameters within which early Buddhist ethical teachings were developed.

Early Texts on Ethics

In the Discourses (the first of the three divisions of the Pali canon), the Buddha's moral teachings are set out in a straightforward way. The Buddha is reported as teaching (S.v.353f), for example, that you should not inflict on another what you yourself find unpleasant (the Buddhist version of the "Golden Rule"); that wrong actions are those which intend harm to any being; that one should repay the kindness of beings who in the past may have been relatives or friends (S.ii.189f); and that one should be mindful at all times of the effect one's actions might have on others. The style is a cross between the Christian gospels and the Socratic dialogues. Parables and metaphors are often used to get the point across. Ethical themes appear repeatedly throughout the Discourses, yet certain Discourses are particularly significant for their moral content. The *Discourse on Brahmā's Net* (*Brahmajāla Sutta*) contains long lists of moral precepts and points of etiquette, and may be regarded as the source of many subsequent preceptual codes. Part of this discourse takes the form of a eulogy of the Buddha's conduct in which individual aspects of his behavior are assembled into lists which collectively define the conduct of a perfect mendicant, and by extension that of the perfect human being.

A text which accords well with the Western belief in individualism is the *Kālāma Sutta* (A.i.188). The Buddha counsels against accepting doctrines purely on the authority of tradition. Each individual is advised to consider carefully what he hears and test it against his own experience, not being afraid to reject any teachings found deficient in practice. We can imagine the Buddha doing the same thing, founding the new religion of Buddhism as a result of his rejection of the rigidity of brahmanical orthodoxy. It should not be thought, however, that the Buddha is commending a "free for all' approach to ethics or promoting autonomy to the position of supreme moral principle. On the contrary, it is clear he believes that all who reflect rightly will come to the very same conclusions about right and wrong. The Buddha is not here saying "Make your own truth" but "Make the truth your own" (Collins, quoted in Gombrich 1987: 72).

The *Discourse to Sigāla* (*Sigālaka Sutta*) is of special importance for lay ethics, and is often described as a Monastic Rule for householders. This text explains the duties of a lay householder towards six groups of people: parents, teachers, wives and children, friends, employees and servants, and religious practitioners. Important for its emphasis on the cultivation of a loving attitude (*mettā*) is the *Discourse on Loving-kindness* (*Metta Sutta*). There is also a very popular and well-known Buddhist text known as the *Dhammapada* which in a single verse sums up the whole of Buddhism. This verse reads: "To avoid all evil, to cultivate good, and to purify one's mind – this is the teaching of the Buddhas" (*Dhammapada* v.183). This verse makes clear the central place of morality in Buddhism. Buddhist teachings are essentially about living a virtuous life and purifying one's mind, by which is meant developing the intellectual virtue of understanding. Another early text, the *Sonadanda Sutta*, similarly compares morality and wisdom to two hands that wash one another, indicating that these two qualities go together and are indispensable in the quest for enlightenment.

Basic Themes

The Four Noble Truths

As well as giving general moral guidance of this kind, the Buddha formulated doctrine systematically in four propositions known as the Four Noble Truths:

1 Suffering (*dukkha*) is inherent in life.
2 Suffering is caused by craving (*tanhā*).
3 There can be an end to suffering (this is the state known as nirvāna).
4 The way to attain nirvāna is through a structured plan of life known as the Noble Eightfold Path.

The Four Noble Truths are sometimes compared to the diagnosis and remedy provided by a physician. The first step is to diagnose the condition; the next is to investigate the causes of the complaint; the third step is to determine whether a cure is available; and fourth and finally comes the question of deciding on the appropriate treatment. Sometimes medical treatment just involves taking a pill, but increasingly physicians are becoming aware that many of the problems from which their patients suffer cannot be cured by repeated prescriptions. They are due more to lifestyle problems than anything else. In these cases the cure involves the patient taking action to change his way of life; for example, by taking more exercise, avoiding stressful situations, giving up smoking, making changes to his diet, and so forth. This is the kind of lifestyle change required by the Fourth Noble Truth. It does not offer a quick fix or instant cure, but calls upon people to live well, in the sense of leading a saner, more moderate and balanced life. This approach to life is what is known in Buddhism as the Middle Way.

The Middle Way

The Middle Way (which only superficially resembles Aristotle's Doctrine of the Mean) is essentially the principle of neither too much, nor too little. Neither total indulgence on the one hand, nor complete abstinence on the other. This principle derives from the Buddha's own experience in his life, first as a pampered prince, and later, as a homeless mendicant practicing austerities in the forest for six years. Neither of these extremes worked. He eventually renounced them in favor of a more moderate and balanced way of life. Once he did this he attained enlightenment. This *via media* is given specific content in the Fourth Noble Truth.

The Fourth Noble Truth shows the way to happiness, fulfillment, and human flourishing in the form of a path with eight components, known as the Noble Eightfold Path. The eight factors of the Path are:

1 Right View (*sammā-diṭṭhi*)
2 Right Resolve (*sammā-sankappa*)
3 Right Speech (*sammā-vācā*)
4 Right Action (*sammā-kammanta*)
5 Right Livelihood (*sammā-ājīva*)
6 Right Effort (*sammā-vāyāma*)
7 Right Mindfulness (*sammā-sati*)
8 Right Meditation (*sammā-samādhi*)

Right View means first the acceptance of Buddhist teachings and later their experiential confirmation. Right Resolve means making a serious commitment to developing right attitudes. Right Speech means telling the truth and speaking in a thoughtful and sensitive way at the appropriate time. Right Action means abstaining from wrongful bodily behavior such as killing, stealing, inappropriate sexual conduct, telling lies, and taking alcohol or drugs. Right Livelihood means not engaging in an occupation which causes harm to others. Right Effort means gaining control of one's thoughts and cultivating positive and wholesome states of mind. Right Meditation means developing deep levels of mental calm through various techniques which concentrate the mind and integrate the personality.

The eight factors of the path fall into three categories: Morality (*Sīla*), Meditation (*Samādhi*), and Wisdom (*Paññā*). The first two items (Right View and Right Resolve) promote Wisdom. The last three (Right Effort, Right Mindfulness, and Right Meditation) cultivate mental calm. The middle three (Right Speech, Right Action, and Right Livelihood) ensure correct moral conduct. This threefold categorization gives us a quick sense of the shape of the "good life" from a Buddhist perspective. It tells us that the life of virtue involves personal development in these three areas. First, one must be moral and live in accordance with Buddhist ethical precepts. A moral person, according to Buddhism, will be calm, confident, trustworthy, and open, with nothing to fear and without guilty secrets to hide. This condition is conducive to the next phase of the path which is Meditation. Buddhists see meditation as a technique which can be harnessed to accelerate spiritual progress. It has the effect of changing moral sentiments, for example by making one more compassionate and sensitive to the needs of others, and also of concentrating the mind. The final area for development is the faculty of understanding, usually translated as "wisdom." This involves a deep and penetrating insight into the true nature of the human condition, into human nature and its potential for fulfillment in the state of nirvāna.

Precepts

Morality (*Sīla*) in the Eightfold Path and elsewhere includes the notion of things to be done, and things to be avoided. The things to be avoided are enumerated in various lists of precepts, of which there are five main sets:

1   The Five Precepts (*pañca-sīla*)
2   The Eight Precepts (*aṭṭhaṅga-sīla*)
3   The Ten Precepts (*dasa-sīla*)
4   The Ten Good Paths of Action (*dasa-kusala-kamma-patha*)
5   The Monastic Disciplinary Code (*pātimokkha*)

The best known of these codes is the Five Precepts for laymen. The Five Precepts, mentioned earlier as the fourth component of the Noble Eightfold Path, prohibit (1) killing, (2) stealing, (3) sexual immorality, (4) lying, and (5) taking intoxicants. The nucleus of Buddhist morality may be found in the first four (which Buddhism shares with Jainism). These are then supplemented by more rigorous precepts according to the status of the practitioner or to suit particular ceremonial occasions. The precept against taking intoxicants, for example, is thought to be particularly applicable to layfolk, and the Eight and Ten precepts, which supplement the basic five with additional restrictions such as on the time when meals may be taken (as well as requiring complete abstention from sexual relations), are commonly adopted as additional commitments on holy days (*uposatha*). The Monastic Disciplinary Code (*pātimokkha*) is a set of 227 rules (the exact number varies between schools) which set out in detail the regulations governing the monastic life of monks. Nuns were obliged to follow a greater number of rules, reflecting the Buddha's initial reluctance to allow women to be ordained.

The various formulations of precepts may be regarded as a combination of moral precepts with additional practices designed to cultivate restraint and self-discipline. The large number of monastic rules requires vigilance and mindfulness at all times, as well as ensuring standardization and conformity within monastic communities. Disputes and disagreements are thereby kept to a minimum and the Order presents itself as a moral microcosm for the world at large. Early Buddhist society was conceived of as an integrated fourfold group comprising monks (*bhikkhu*), nuns (*bhikkhunī*), and pious laymen (*upāsaka*) and laywomen (*upāsikā*). The lay and monastic "wings" of this community ideally serve one another: the laity provide material support to the monastics (*bhikkhu-sangha*), and the latter in return provide religious teachings and guidance (see Chakravarti 1987).

Virtues

Although the precepts are of great importance in Buddhist morality, there is more to the Buddhist moral life than following rules. Rules must also be followed for the right reasons and with the correct motivation. It is here that the role of the virtues becomes important. Buddhist morality as a whole may be likened to a coin with two faces: on one side are the precepts and on the other the virtues. The precepts, in fact, may be thought of simply as a list of things which a virtuous person will never do.

Early sources emphasize the importance of cultivating correct dispositions and habits so that moral conduct is the natural and spontaneous manifestation of internalized and properly integrated beliefs and values, rather than simple conformity to external rules. Many formulations of the precepts make this perfectly clear. The precept against taking life, for example, is sometimes found in the following form: "Laying aside the club and the sword he dwells compassionate and kind to all living things" (D.i.4). Abstention from taking life is the natural result of a compassionate identification with living things. It is a constraint imposed contrary to natural inclination. To arrive at such an integrated state is not easy, and involves a profound transformation of an intellectual and moral kind. To observe the first precept perfectly requires a profound understanding of the metaphysical relationship between living things coupled with an unswerving disposition of universal benevolence and compassion. Few people are capable of either of these things. Yet by respecting the precept they habituate themselves to the condition of one who is, and in so doing take a step closer to enlightenment.

The virtues, as Aristotle points out, are about what is difficult for people. The task of the virtues is to counteract negative dispositions (or vices) such as pride and selfishness. The lengthy lists of virtues and vices which appear in later literature are extrapolated from a key cluster of three virtues and their opposing vices. The three Buddhist Cardinal Virtues are Unselfishness (*alobha*), Benevolence (*adosa*), and Understanding (*amoha*). Benevolence is an attitude of good will to all living creatures. Unselfishness means the absence of that selfish desire which taints all moral behavior by allocating a privileged status to one's own needs. Understanding is knowledge of human nature and human good as expressed in basic doctrines such as the Four Noble Truths.

Meditation

As we have seen, meditation (*Samādhi*) is the second component of the Eightfold Path, and it plays an important role in the cultivation of the virtues. Of particular importance is a group of four meditational dispositions known as the four Sublime States (*Brahmā-vihāra*): Love (*mettā*), Compassion (*karuṇā*), Gladness for Others (*muditā*), and Equanimity (*upekkhā*). Detailed guidance is provided in Buddhist literature as to the way in which these dispositions can be cultivated and deepened. In the cultivation of love, for instance, after first of all developing positive feelings towards oneself, the disposition is slowly extended in an ever-increasing circle of friends and relations, the local community, and finally the world at large. Through this practice the mind becomes free of anger, hostility, and resentment and other negative traits which are common sources of immoral action.

The same method of practice is applied to the second and third Sublime States. Compassion is directed towards all who are experiencing misfortune, with the aspiration that their suffering may soon cease. Gladness is for those in good fortune with the wish that their good fortune should remain and increase. When the first three have been developed, the practice of equanimity can begin. The importance of equanimity is that it ensures that none of the other dispositions are allowed to predominate. There is a danger for the moral life in allowing any disposition, however virtuous in itself, to become dominant. It is sometimes claimed, for example, that so long as one acts with a compassionate motive no wrong can be done. This is not the Buddhist view. The role of equanimity is to ensure that moral judgments are not distorted by an imbalance between dispositions leading to an overemphasis on any one of them.

Nirvāna

As noted, the aim of all Buddhists is to attain nirvāna. There are different views as to what nirvāna means. The tradition recognizes two kinds of nirvāna: (1) the kind attained in the course of a lifetime and (2) the kind attained by an enlightened person at death. In this discussion we are concerned only with the former.

There has been a tendency to understand nirvāna primarily in intellectual terms as the gaining of mystical knowledge. On this view it has sometimes been thought that in the experience of awakening (*bodhi*) an enlightened being "transcends" moral values and passes "beyond good and evil." It can be seen from the Buddha's conduct, however, that he personally did no such thing, nor did he anywhere express the view that it would be appropriate for others to do so. The only sense in which the Buddha passed "beyond good and evil" was in not having to pause to deliberate between them: he instinctively knew the right course. Nevertheless, the well-known Parable of the Raft (M.i.134f) is often read as supporting the view that morality is of a temporary and provisional nature. It is supposedly a "means to an end" and something ultimately to be discarded like a raft after one has crossed the stream.

This overly intellectualized view of nirvāna results from misunderstanding the relationship between the three components of the Eightfold Path – Morality, Meditation, and Wisdom – and seeing the Path to Enlightenment as a kind of ladder or staircase that one ascends step by step. The problem with the ladder metaphor is that it implies that as one makes progress towards nirvāna, the lower rungs are passed over and left behind. Certain parts of the Path are deemed higher and therefore more important than others. In fact, this is not the case. There is no point at which morality is left behind. On the contrary, one becomes increasingly moral the closer one comes to nirvāna. It is more helpful to picture Morality, Meditation, and Wisdom as forming three sides of a triangle, wherein each side is connected to the others. The three together brace and mutually support one another. This conveys better the sense that morality forms an intrinsic part of the architecture of the enlightened consciousness. If the Buddhist understanding of nirvāna incorporates moral perfection in the way suggested, ethics becomes integral to the final goal. Understood in this way, nirvāna as *summum bonum* is an inclusive final end. The path that leads to it is nothing other than the gradual cultivation and manifestation of the virtues which constitute the end.

Summary

We may summarize the key features of Buddhist ethics in the earliest period as follows:

1 The arrival of Buddhism is characterized by both continuity and change. Buddhism takes from brahmanism the concepts of dharma and karma, but rejects ritual sacrifice and the caste system.
2 The Buddha taught a humanistic ethics emphasizing non-violence (*ahiṃsā*), benevolence, and the search for self-perfection (nirvāna) in the three areas of Morality (*Sīla*), Meditation (*Samādhi*), and Wisdom (*Paññā*).
3 Moderation in the form of the concept of the Middle Way becomes an important action-guiding principle.
4 Buddhism has no central authority competent to pronounce on moral issues. Individuals must decide for themselves after consulting the scriptures, seeking the advice of teachers, and meditating on all aspects of the matter in question. However, the precepts are at all times to be respected.

Bibliography

Chakravarti, U. 1987. *The Social Dimensions of Early Buddhism*. Delhi: Oxford University Press.
Gombrich, R. F. 1987. *Theravāda Buddhism: A Social History from Ancient Benares to Modern Colombo*. London: Routledge & Kegan Paul.
Harvey, P. 2000. *An Introduction to Buddhist Ethics*. Cambridge: Cambridge University Press.
Kalupahana, D. J. 1995. *Ethics in Early Buddhism*. Honolulu: University of Hawai'i Press.

Keown, D. 1996. *Buddhism: A Very Short Introduction*. Oxford: Oxford University Press.

—— 2000. *Contemporary Buddhist Ethics*. London: Curzon Press.

—— 2001. *The Nature of Buddhist Ethics*. Basingstoke: Palgrave.

McDermott, J. P. 1980. "Karma and Rebirth in Early Buddhism" in *Karma and Rebirth in Classical Indian Traditions*, ed. W. O'Flaherty. Berkeley: University of California Press.

Reynolds, F. E. and R. Campany, R. 1987. "Buddhist Ethics" in *The Encyclopedia of Religion*, Vol. 2, ed. M. Eliade, 498–504. New York: Macmillan.

CHAPTER 31

Cultural Differentiation in Buddhist Ethics

Thomas P. Kasulis

This chapter explores differentiations in "Buddhist ethics." In using the term "Buddhist ethics," we are speaking of the ethics not of *Buddhism*, but of *Buddhists*. It is not as if Buddhism were an abstract entity transcending both culture and the people who identify themselves as Buddhist. Without Buddhist people, there would be no Buddhism, not to mention Buddhist ethics. This idea – that there are no "religions," only "religious peoples" – may seem obvious, but its implications are critical for understanding both the nature of religious ethics in general and the character of Buddhist ethics in particular. Seldom (if ever) is ethics the domain of religion alone. Buddhism is part, but only part, of the ethical lives of people from radically different cultures, languages, and ethnicities. The dynamic between cultural identity and religious identity in the Buddhist moral agent is the main concern of this chapter (see chapter 14).

Given the premise that persons negotiate both their religious and cultural identities in developing their ethical positions, three corollaries will affect our ensuing discussion. First, moral agency, however much it might be imbued with religious or cultural ideologies, always lies in human choice. People – not "-isms" – decide not only *whether* to live a life religiously or ethically, but also *how* to do so within the parameters of tradition. Second, in analyzing Buddhists rather than Buddhism, it is obvious that Buddhist ethics is articulated in a multitude of languages today, not just the "canonical" languages of ancient Buddhist texts: Sanskrit, Pali, Tibetan, and Chinese. The "Buddhist tradition" is more than what Buddhism was in the past. Tradition involves a way of living in the present with attention to the way the religious life has been lived previously. In such an understanding, tradition is always being lived and negotiated in the *present*. The third corollary relates to what makes a person a "Buddhist." For simplicity's sake, we can stipulate that people are "Buddhist" when they say without deception, at least in some contexts, "I am a Buddhist." Yet, being a Buddhist is never *exhaustive* of anyone's self-attributed identity. In other contexts, those same people might identify themselves differently: "I am Chinese" or "I am Sinhalese"; "I am a woman" or "I am a man"; "I am a teacher" or "I am a carpenter"; and so forth. Those cultural identities are lived out alongside Buddhist identities. And they often interact in influencing the character of Buddhist ethics in any local context.

Our analysis of Buddhist ethics across traditions proceeds in two stages. First, we will consider a general orientation Buddhism brings to the understanding of self and agency that differs from common Western assumptions, and therefore needs special treatment if we are to understand Buddhist ethics on its own terms (see chapter 3). The second stage of our analysis will consider some cultural differences in how Buddhist ethics has been conceived and practiced over time in four global regions. Such a sampling, however limited, will shed some light on the variety in Buddhist ethics and how that variety might have a bearing on the project of comparative ethics.

Buddhism on Self and Agency

Allowing for some cultural variations, all Buddhist traditions accept the basic tenet of "no-I" (*anātman*). The doctrine originated, as the name suggests, in opposition to a traditional Indian (Hindu) idea of *ātman*. The latter holds that behind the ordinary world – the world of change and diversity (*māyā*) – lies the true ground of reality: eternal, distinctionless, and absolute (*brahman*). This *brahman* was often identified with the true self, a persisting, changeless soul (*ātman*) that is never the object of experience, but makes experience possible ("that which sees but is never seen" or "that which knows but is never known," and so forth) (see Kasulis 1997). The crucial point for ethics is how the Buddhist view differs not only from Hindu assumptions, but from many modern Western assumptions as well.

Perhaps the easiest way to distinguish the Buddhist model of self from the dominant Western one is to discuss the two in terms of an "intimacy" model built on internal relations, as contrasted with an "external integrity" model built on external relations. An external integrity orientation understands moral agency in terms of how the self autonomously forms external relations to "others," whether the others are people or things. (See figure 31.1, wherein *a* is the self and *b–i* various "others.") Such ethical systems commonly develop rules or principles for how "I" should develop the external relational ties (the *R*s in the diagram). External integrity orientations often universalize those principles, generalizing how *R* should be constituted regardless of who the self or other may be: the situation's uniqueness is subordinated to the nature of the relation. For example, an ethics might state "I" should treat the "others" as if I were they. Because of its tendency to universalize, external integrity requires respect for the "rights" of others.

Buddhism, in contrast, favors intimacy over such external integrity by analyzing the self as internally related to others: others are *inherently* part of me. I do not connect with them by forging ethical relations. Ethics derives from my understanding the relations that are *already* part of me (see figure 31.2). Because I (the *a* in the diagram) am internally connected with others, there is no principle or rule necessary for connecting with them.

Buddhism takes the intimacy orientation further. According to the *anātman* doctrine, there is *no* aspect of "I" (not even the unshaded small part preserved in figure 31.2)

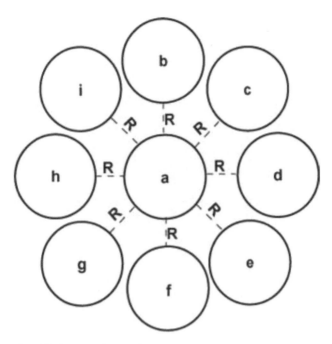

Figure 31.1 The self of external integrity

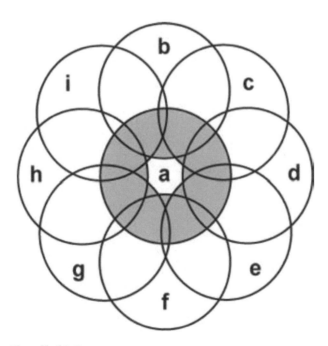

Figure 31.2 The self of intimacy

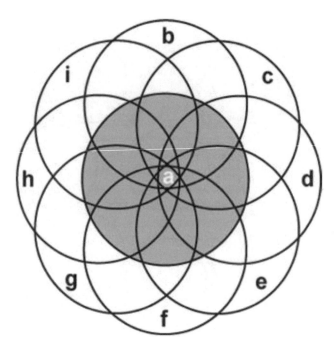

Figure 31.3   The Buddhist self

that is not conditioned or not interconnected with at least something else (see figure 31.3). My "self" is completely interdependent and in no way independent. "I" do not exist, even theoretically, as an isolated agent choosing my connections to the world (as both figures 31.1 and 32.2 allow). Ethics for Buddhism is not a matter of establishing external relations, but instead of recognizing inherent interrelations. This difference leads to a distinctive interpretation of agency.

In an external integrity orientation, the agent autonomously formulates and performs relations with others. To be moral, the agent must analyze the circumstances (a factual or "is" determination) and make a response according to some value (a normative or "ought" decision). That normative decision may be made in various ways and may involve, to cite three common options, a calculus of benefits and harms (as in utilitarianism), an imaginative act of putting oneself in the other's shoes (as in the Golden Rule), or a more legalistic analysis of applying a general rule of goodness or fairness to the particular case (as in Kant's categorical imperative).

The idea of agency derived from Buddhism's not-I theory is less intuitive to many modern Westerners. In the Buddhist model, what is to be known and what ought to be done are much less sharply distinguished. For Buddhists, knowing the other and knowing myself are not fully discrete activities. If I know who I truly am (an "is" issue), I will realize my interdependent relations with others as they "should" be (an "ought" issue). That is, I will articulate myself as part of an interdependent responsive system, instead of as an independent agent creating moral connections with others.

Let us summarize these two contrasting ideas of agency. The external integrity orientation says I am moral when I transcend myself by tempering self-interest, whereas Buddhist's intimacy orientation says I am moral when I am most truly my self. The two positions are not as opposed as they might at first seem, however. For external integrity, the self is independent of circumstances and stands alone and independent. In effect, without forming any external relations, the self is just an isolated "I," an "ego." Moral responsibility transcends this ego, taking one beyond the individual to the collective. Through moral education I can learn to form relations making me "more than myself" or becoming capable of "thinking about something or someone other than myself." In contrast, the Buddhist model starts with a view of self that is *anātman*, a no-I. This no-I must be fathomed for moral responsiveness to arise. To know and be myself – in the fullest Buddhist sense – is to recognize the interdependencies constituting all I am.

Because of the difference in how "self" is understood, Buddhist moral education is aimed not at getting beyond self-interest, but at delving more deeply into oneself. As the thirteenth-century Japanese Zen Master Dōgen expressed it:

> To learn by modeling yourself after the way of the buddhas is to learn by modeling yourself after yourself. To learn by modeling yourself after yourself is to forget yourself. To forget yourself is to be authenticated by all phenomena. (From *Shōbōgenzō*, *"Genjōkoan"*)

Dōgen suggests the Buddhist acts as a moral agent by being responsive within the conflux of conditioning factors. Importantly, some of those phenomena are cultural. To be yourself and to be a morally responsive agent, you must recognize that you are inherently part of a cultural system. This takes us into the issue of cultural difference. How do the specifics of cultural conditions affect Buddhist ethical thinking and behavior?

Cultural Variety in Buddhist Ethics

For the comparative purposes of this chapter, we will look at four geographical areas in relation to the development of Buddhist ethics: India (especially as home to early Buddhism), Southeast Asia (as the center of Theravāda Buddhism), Northeast Asia (especially Chinese and Japanese Mahāyāna Buddhism), and the United States (especially the communities with membership drawing mainly from people without ethnic ties to Buddhist cultures). With such a broad sweep, we will have little opportunity for detailed analysis, but our focus is to compare and contrast the interplay between Buddhist and cultural identities in the way Buddhist ethical issues have been addressed.

Since we will be analyzing the role of cultural conditions in the formation of Buddhist ethics, let us begin with how Buddhists generally understand the relation between conditionedness and ethics. With the dominance of the external integrity view of agency in the modern West, the tendency there is to think of conditions as external factors operating on the self: "*I* am conditioned by my culture or society," for example. The main Western question is whether there is any autonomous aspect of the self *not* so conditioned (hence, the debate between behavioral determinism and freedom of choice). This set of issues is quite alien to Buddhism, wherein conditions are understood to be *within* the system of interrelations defining me. Hence, conditioning is both self-conditioning and being conditioned by surrounding factors.

As an analogy, think of an athlete in training (see chapter 4). To succeed, the athlete must be willing to be conditioned (must be "coachable") and must have a coach who can create the right environment for learning. Similarly, Buddhist moral training involves an openness to changing one's own negative habits in response to the mentor's guidance. It is significant that the normative term in early Buddhism literally means "skillful" (*kuśala*) rather than "good." Buddhist moral development is, then, a matter of retraining that deepens one's awareness of interdependence and conditionedness. Then the improvement of conditions may be directly either inwardly or outwardly. For example, suppose I am in a noisy environment where I find it difficult to concentrate. It would be "skillful" for me either (a) to train myself to focus better or (b) to change the environment so it is not as noisy. If I do either, the environment becomes less distracting. From the Buddhist standpoint, one can become more skillful (more "moral") by transforming either one's psychological or one's environmental conditions. In this light, let us turn to how Buddhists in different cultural contexts developed variations in ethics.

Buddhist ethics in India

For its personal training methods, Indian Buddhism borrowed extensively from (Hindu-related) practices prominent in the culture 25 centuries ago: meditation, dietary control, abstention from harming others, control of sexual activity, avoidance of intoxicants, and so forth. There were two key areas in which Buddhists diverged, however.

First, Buddhists generally rejected the common Upanishadic idea that reality is illusory (*māyā*). For Buddhism, the human predicament derives from delusion, not illusion. Reality shows itself as it is (Buddhists designated it with terms like "suchness" or "thatness"), but unenlightened persons add to that appearance delusions arising from their desires for how they would prefer reality to be (something unchanging belonging to an eternal "me"). Buddhism consequently reconstrued the purpose of religious praxis from seeing *through* or *beyond* the world of flux, to seeing *into* it without the addition of any delusional projections about permanence. The Buddhist strategy for discovering the true nature of self and things was, therefore, to examine coolly the arising and decaying of phenomena. Only then can one discover there is no entity free from flux. Rather than emphasizing meditative practices leading to trance experiences of oneness, early Buddhist meditation emphasized attentiveness to processes of change (the flow of one's own breathing, the visualization of bodily decay, the awareness of the psychological patterns supporting ideas of "mine" or "ego," etc.). The goal was an introspective sensitivity to the formation of attachments and a therapeutic for eradicating the cravings behind them. The therapeutic was originally formulated in terms of the Noble Eightfold Path and involved the effort to reprogram the three domains of human activity: thought, word, and deed. From this standpoint, personal ethics amounted to the reform of one's own character, the deprogramming of unskillful, delusional tendencies in behavior or attitude. If one could eradicate ego-centered desire, morality (in the Western sense as defined above) would take care of itself.

The second divergence from common Indian assumptions of the era relates to social ethics. By the Buddha's time, Indian society increasingly exemplified a social stratification according to caste or class (see chapter 35). The society supported a hierarchical system in which an elite brahmanic or priestly caste had oversight of both scholarship and religious ritual. People were born into their castes and social mobility was very limited or impossible. As suggested by texts like the *Bhagavad Gītā* it was assumed that the dharma (at this point primarily meaning moral or social "duty") varied according to caste and gender. Because of their belief in karma and rebirth, Indians assumed that a person was born into a caste because of proclivities carried over from previous lifetimes. Social improvement was often construed as living this lifetime properly and being reborn into a higher caste in one's next lifetime.

Indian Buddhism rejected the caste system. In developing its theory of praxis, the early Buddhists maintained that since the causes of delusion are the same in everyone, the praxis to eliminate them should be essentially the same as well. Class and gender should not matter. Yet the early Buddhists recognized that the conditions leading to delusions are not only fixed within personal habitualized psychological patterns of behavior, but also reinforced in institutionalized forms throughout society. Thus, social conditions have to be addressed as well.

The early Buddhists responded not by trying to change Indian society as much as by trying to form an alternative, utopian community within India. Thus was born Buddhist monasticism. Monks and nuns had separate communities. (They were separate, but not really equal – patriarchal cultural assumptions still subordinated the order of nuns to that of monks.) Many monastics remained itinerant (following the tradition of holy seekers in pre-Buddhist India), but the long monsoon seasons were a time for even them to live together in larger communities. Eventually, some of these became centers of study as well as meditative practice. As a society separate from secular laws, the monastic communities developed their own system of moral guidelines and internal laws. This added a layer of social behavior and sanctions that went beyond the basic precepts and guidelines for personal training contained in such formulations as the Noble Eightfold Path. Within the monasteries and nunneries, one could follow a strict regimen for self-examination and training aimed at eliminating ego-centered attitudes and behavior.

As Buddhism grew in popularity, the role of the laity needed clarification. The monastic centers typically depended on local villagers for material support and the question arose about the responsibility of religious orders toward those lay patrons. Different models developed in India as Buddhist clergy assumed an increasing role in educating and training the laity in the fundamentals of doctrine and practice. The two major branches of Buddhism that emerged – Theravāda and Mahāyāna – had somewhat different approaches to the clergy–laity interface. Those differences sometimes affected the tenor of Buddhist ethics in different locales. Since the Theravāda traditions tended to dominate in Southeast Asia and the Mahāyāna in Northeast Asia, we discuss those differences within those cultural contexts. Before leaving the discussion of India, though, one further development is noteworthy. It is an example of a Buddhist social ethic at work in modern times.

Buddhism became a major religious presence in India (to the point of becoming the state religion under King Aśoka in the third century BCE). Yet it eventually died out after the incursion of Islam in the early centuries of the second millennium CE. Buddhism has enjoyed a small revival since India's independence in 1947, however. In particular, many Dalit ("untouchables" in the classical Hindu caste system) converted to Buddhism. The major figure in this movement was himself a Dalit, Bhimrao Ramji Ambedkar, an Indian government leader and attorney with doctorates from both Columbia University and the University of London. Ambedkar believed that to improve the plight of the Dalit, two kinds of changes were needed. First, the legal system had to prohibit all forms of discrimination against them. Under his legal and legislative leadership, that was accomplished rather soon after national independence. He came to realize by the mid-1950s, however, that a psychological problem remained. The Dalit needed to develop a sense of self-esteem, something difficult to do as long as they identified themselves vis-à-vis the traditional Hindu caste system. So, he converted to Buddhism and led a movement resulting in the conversion of millions of others. This exemplifies a typically Buddhist analysis of the link between spirituality and social action.

Theravāda Buddhist ethics in Southeast Asia

With the exception of Vietnam, which was influenced more by Buddhism from China, the Southeast Asian countries (including Sri Lanka) were introduced to Buddhism via India, starting mainly around the time of the Indian Buddhist King Aśoka. Most Buddhist doctrines and institutional monastic structures found in India were carried over into these other countries and developed further there within the eventually dominant Theravāda branch of Buddhism. In terms of personal moral development, the goal was, once again, disengaging the habitual responses arising from desire and egocentrism. The needed therapeutic was considered so extensive, however, that it would take a multitude of lifetimes before one could complete the program. Until then one had to settle for gradual karmic progress from one lifetime to the next. Given this belief, it was assumed that those who come into this world with proclivities leading them to pursue the monastic life were more advanced on the path than those who chose a layperson's life. (Since the institutions for nuns eventually died out, this also meant that women could not become monastics and that, by definition, no woman could be as spiritually advanced as a male monk.) This system of beliefs resulted in a rather sharp bifurcation between monks and laity corresponding to a different set of behavioral norms for the two groups.

As compared with East Asian Mahāyāna clergy, the monks from Theravāda countries take upon themselves a more restrictive rule of life (strict celibacy, a dietary restriction forbidding eating after noontime, a vow of complete poverty). Monks leave their families and become monastics in hopes of making best use of their excellent conditions within this rebirth. The underlying goal of their precepts, rules, and vows is to bring about detachment – the proof of *anātman* and the prelude to nirvāna. The monks depend on the generosity of the laypeople for their sustenance and the laity's charity brings them merit toward their own future rebirths. In gratitude, the monks take care of the laypeople's basic spiritual needs: preaching the basic doctrines of the Buddha, performing rituals in the villages, and supervising lay retreats during the monsoon season (even the king of Thailand has participated in such retreats). The purpose is to influence society by aiding in the spiritual development of the laity. Although laypersons may lack the monks' opportunity to develop to their fullest spiritually, they can begin to understand the nature of desire or attachment and thereby make progress. Although no one but an enlightened being can be perfectly "moral" or "skillful," the Theravādin assumption is that by creating the right kind of interdependencies between monks and laity, both groups will grow spiritually and set the basis for a moral society.

In practice the dual-layered social structure runs the peril of becoming elitist in a way comparable to the caste system Buddhism originally rejected. The Theravādin institutions may reinforce patriarchy (women by birth *must* be laypersons because there is no longer a monastic option) and the idea that the majority of society's members (the laity) should do physical labor so that the minority (the clergy) do not have to. The emphasis on detachment, understandable within the Buddhist account of the dangers of desire, can also disconnect the monks from the plight of the disadvantaged. Detachment can become a way of ignoring social interdependencies. In the past few decades, responding in part to the change in conditions brought by the influence of communism, Christianity, and the Buddhist conversions of the Dalit in India, a new social ethic called "Engaged Buddhism" has developed in Theravāda countries. Clergy and laity cooperate in programs to help the needy in society and to preserve the natural environment. As an example of the latter, Thai monks sometimes "ordain" trees in the rainforest as fellow monks (see chapter 47). Because killing a monk is one of the most heinous offenses in Buddhism, the hope is that this ritual action will cause the timber workers to desist and the rainforest will be spared.

In one sense, Engaged Buddhism is a new modality for social action in Southeast Asia. Yet its rationale is consistent with the ancient principle that Buddhists – clergy and laity alike – need to change external as well as psychological conditions that arise from and support unskillful patterns of behavior.

East Asian Buddhist ethics

Buddhism's rival in China was not Hinduism, but Confucianism and Daoism (see chapter 40). The two indigenous Chinese religions emphasized harmony as the primary spiritual value. Confucianism tended to focus most on social harmony and Daoism on harmony with nature. Neither held to a theory of rebirth or the karmic carry-over from one lifetime to the next. Nor was there in China a religious-based caste system determined by birth. Chinese Confucianism did advocate a kind of social hierarchy, but it was based in the basic relations such as parent–child, elder–younger, and ruler–subject. Furthermore, elite positions in the government bureaucracy were, at least in theory, related not to aristocratic birth, but to performance in a civil service exam. When

Buddhism entered China there was no immediate need to change the social order or pose an alternative to the status quo as there had been vis-à-vis India's caste system. The assumption was that a social system conditioned by Confucian values need not obstruct skillful Buddhist praxis on the personal level. Even the monastic establishments in East Asia were not as separated from the secular communities as they had been in India. East Asian Buddhist institutions often openly sought imperial support and monks sometimes served as court officials.

Given these conditions, it is not surprising that Mahāyāna Buddhism took hold most firmly in China and in the surrounding regions like Korea, Japan, and Vietnam. The differences between Mahāyāna and Theravāda are numerous, but here the focus is only on the relevance to ethics. In this regard, three contrasts are most important. First, Mahāyāna deemphasizes the sharp distinction between clergy and laity. According to most Mahāyāna schools, every person – clergy or laity, male or female, educated or uneducated – has the capacity to become fully enlightened in this lifetime. Second, following on the idea that reality appears as it is without illusion, Mahāyānists emphasized that the only difference between the real world and the delusional world is how we look at it. Ignorance arises not from being tricked by false appearances, but from making distorting human projections. Therefore, reasoned the Mahāyānists, the ordinary world (samsāra) and the world of enlightenment (nirvāna) are fundamentally the same. Whereas the early and Theravāda Buddhist formulations understood enlightenment as the movement from samsāra to nirvāna, the Mahāyānists claimed there was no place to go to or to move from. For East Asians, steeped in Confucian and Daoist ideas, it was reassuring that Mahāyāna Buddhism presented an ideal of enlightenment that could be lived in the world of ordinary social and natural phenomena.

Third, Mahāyāna Buddhism emphasizes a more collective, rather than individual, understanding of the process of enlightenment. Along with a (somewhat less stringent) set of vows and precepts resembling those used by Theravāda monks and laity, the Mahāyānists added a new one, giving it special prominence – the bodhisattva vow. This vow promises to put the ultimate spiritual progress of others ahead of one's own. One will not allow oneself to achieve full enlightenment until everyone else is also ready to do so. In contrast with Theravādins, Mahāyānists envision a situation in which people achieve full enlightenment not one by one over many eons, but rather all at once at some future moment. In this respect, the external conditions supporting delusion took on a special focus in Mahāyāna Buddhism. The traditional Mahāyāna formulation is that the wisdom of enlightenment cannot be separated from the compassion of enlightenment. To know the anguish of others is to feel that anguish as one's own. Alternatively, to have wisdom is to engage, not escape, the suffering of ordinary existence. Here we see a clear application of the Buddhist notion of agency based in internal relations.

Given Confucian and Daoist cultural influences, the Chinese Buddhists understood the samsāra–nirvāna dynamic as a call to use compassion and wisdom to harmonize ordinary and enlightened activity. The Indian Buddhist assumption was that impermanence is the nature of reality and because it runs counter to our desires for permanence, we delude ourselves into thinking of it as other than it is. The Buddha's message was understood to be the resigned acceptance of that impermanence through the elimination of all attachments. The East Asian Buddhist understanding was different. The

East Asians (reflecting Confucian and Daoist assumptions) generally understood the Buddha's message as not being detached from the world of flux, but instead as being in *harmony* with it (see chapter 2). In fact, in Japan, the idea of "impermanence" (*mujō*) assumed a positive aesthetic value as the *appreciation* of evanescence. According to this interpretation, the sadness at, say, the passing of the short-lived cherry blossoms was considered an enlightened sensitivity as long as it was not accompanied by a *desire* for permanence, a wish that the cherry blossoms would never die.

Because the East Asian Buddhist goal was now to be more fully in touch with the world, enlightenment came to be viewed as living fully in the everyday. The East Asian Buddhists placed special emphasis on Mahāyāna metaphors for seeing the whole in the individual thing ("all worlds in one moment of thought"; "each jewel at each nexus in Indra's net of reality reflects every other"). This blended with an indigenous valorization of spontaneity and naturalness associated mainly with Daoism. In the development of personal ethics, the shift was away from detachment to "openness" (the Mahāyāna Buddhist idea of "emptiness" as filtered through the Daoist emphasis on "non-being" as the source of being). Ethically, this meant an emphasis on responsiveness rather than following fixed rules of behavior. The Mahāyāna precepts tended more toward a minimal set of self-imposed restrictions that would generate the compassion–wisdom necessary to change how one sees and behaves in the world.

Following the Mahāyānist inclination, East Asian Buddhists generally assumed no significant spiritual difference between monastics and laity. All people are inherently enlightened insofar as saṃsāra is nirvāna. The problem is that people do not realize this fact and act accordingly. The vows and precepts for clergy and laity were quite close (outside special rules related to harmonious living within monastic confines). Although the monastic communities still looked to the laity and the court for patronage and support, they became more self-sufficient than their Southeast Asian counterparts. The goal of Buddhism remained the same – the realization of *anātman* – but in East Asia this tended to be glossed as a harmonization with the impermanent world, instead of a cool detachment from it.

Many forms of East Asian Buddhism (Zen being the clearest example) thereby developed a situational approach to ethics. Because saṃsāra and nirvāna were considered indistinguishable on some level, the emphasis became not so much what one did or did not do, but *how* one did it. The same act done by one person in one situation might be "unskillful," but by another in a different situation "skillful." The "heart-and-mind" of the agent is the determining factor. In a famous Zen story the master finds his disciples squabbling over the ownership of a cat. So he challenges the students in a Zen dialogue. Dismayed at their response, he kills the cat to shock his students out of their petty possessiveness. By ordinary Buddhist standards, the master's action would be criticized as harming a sentient being. In this case, however, the Zen tradition focuses on the master's enlightened intent. Given such examples, it is not surprising that even the martial arts sometimes flourished within the confines of East Asian Buddhist temples. In Japan especially, any activity – arranging flowers, wielding a sword, shooting an arrow, writing calligraphically, or preparing and serving tea – could be a way to show one's harmony with the world as it is and engaging it with a "buddha mind-heart." To sum up this contrast: whereas early and Theravāda Buddhism often saw a close connection between ethics and epistemology, in many cases East Asian Buddhism related ethics to aesthetics instead.

Because of its emphasis on compassion, a socially "engaged Buddhism" has appeared within the Mahāyāna East Asian tradition at various points in its history. During the 1960s many Vietnamese monks actively opposed the war. Some even self-immolated themselves as a form of protest. The act of suicide was understood to have negative karmic effects on their personal rebirths. Yet the monks believed the social conditions for spiritual development were so endangered by warfare that they made the sacrifice as an expression of their bodhisattva vow. In China during the sixth and seventh centuries, the Third Period School of Buddhism developed a treasury of funds to help the needy. In seventh-century Japan one of the first major temples, Shitennō-ji, included a public hospital as part of its complex. In the early ninth century Kūkai's temple in Kyoto operated a public school for children of all classes, girls as well as boys.

In recent decades, however, there has been criticism in East Asia about the actual practices of Mahāyāna Buddhism, especially in light of the new social conscience developing around the Engaged Buddhism movement. In Japan, for example, there is an originally scholarly movement called "Critical Buddhism." The Critical Buddhists note that despite the emphasis on compassion in Mahāyāna Buddhism, its overall record of social ethics has been quite poor. They criticize the Mahāyāna perspective as heretical because it places its moral emphasis on *how* something is done instead of *what* is done. They also claim that in saying that the world-as-it-is is already nirvāna (or that everyone is already somehow enlightened), Mahāyāna Buddhists have tolerated the status quo even when including conditions of social injustice. The Critical Buddhism movement in Japan is in some ways also a response to what is happening in our fourth region for this study: contemporary North America.

Buddhist ethics in the United States

Buddhist communities in the United States can be divided into two groups that have had (at least until recently) relatively little interaction with each other. The first group originated from Asian immigrants who came to the United States from Buddhist countries. One such group is the Buddhist Churches of America, established on the west coast of North America about a century ago by Shin Buddhist immigrants from Japan. In general, the immigrational groups brought Buddhism to the United States as part of their members' ethnic identities. They became for the most part cultural–religious enclaves within a pluralistic American society, reflecting the general range of educational and class backgrounds as other US ethnic groups. In this respect they functioned much like European immigrants such as Russian Americans who brought Russian Orthodox Christianity to the United States. The immigrant Asian Buddhists did little to convert Americans of different ethnicities.

The second kind of American Buddhist, our primary focus in this discussion, originated with Americans of non-Asian ancestry who "converted" to Buddhism. Typically, the groups coalesced around a Buddhist missionary teacher. The most popular of these groups belong to the Zen, Theravāda, and Tibetan traditions. The members come from a diversity of ethnic backgrounds. We can call these groups "adoptive" rather than "immigrational." Two striking characteristics of the adoptive Buddhist groups are relevant to the development of American Buddhist ethics. First, because of their educational background and the way they (or their parents) first encountered Buddhism, they often have a comparative religious perspective. Aware of the strong tradition of social ethics in the Abrahamic religious traditions dominant in US culture, they have looked for a parallel in Buddhism. Often disappointed in their search, the question arose for them of "how can our Buddhist perspective inform our moral position vis-à-vis the social and environmental issues of today?" In many cases, they brought this question to their teachers from Asia, and, in so doing, stirred within them a heightened urgency to answer the same question. For example, American Zen communities (with the support of American adoptive Zen Buddhists like the poet Gary Snyder) built on the Japanese religio-aesthetic views of nature to foster ecological concerns. In turn, some ideas and projects from American Zen Buddhism began to influence Zen Buddhist scholars and teachers in Japan. This process resulted in the founding of centers for environmental studies within some Zen Buddhist universities. Meanwhile, Engaged Buddhist practices from Asia (in part influenced by issues of modernization, including an awareness of Christian and communist ideals of social justice and responsibility) became a focus for scholarship and ethical thinking among Buddhists in the United States. Because so many issues of social and environmental ethics are global in nature and because of the rapid exchange of information through technology, this cross-fertilization across Buddhist communities is becoming the rule rather than the exception.

This brings us to the second striking feature related to Buddhist ethics in the United States. Buddhism's identity as a single religion with global manifestations was in part a construction by the West. Two centuries ago, for example, Buddhists in Thailand felt no strong connection to Buddhists in, say, Japan. It was partly the nineteenth-century Westerners' attempt to understand Buddhism that led to the historical and philological studies revealing how the various Buddhist traditions evolved out of each other. Only since the mid-twentieth century do we find pan-Buddhist associations such as the World Fellowship of Buddhists and the World Buddhist Sangha Council. In the United States, though, collaboration among adoptive Buddhist groups (unlike immigrational groups, at least until recently) has occurred on a regular basis for some time. The assumption seems to be that since all the groups are "Buddhist," they share basic values. This is perhaps more obvious to the adoptive rather than immigrational Buddhists because their Buddhism is not as intermixed with ethnic and cultural differences. This situation encourages within the United States the possible development of a generic Buddhist ethics, one that crosses the lines among the varied traditions.

An interesting result of this generic Buddhist ethic arising within the United States is that it interfaces with American cultural expectations about what religious ethics or social ethics is supposed to accomplish. As suggested earlier, those expectations often derive more from an external integrity orientation that uses concepts like "autonomy," "rights," "moral responsibility," and so forth. For the most part Buddhism has historically used concepts derived more from a cultural orientation of intimacy, however. Will American Buddhist ethics successfully formulate Buddhism anew, using external integrity terms? Or will it try to change the dominant American conceptual map of ethics by shifting it to an intimacy orientation in tune with classical Buddhist terminology? American Buddhists have multiple identities – they are both Buddhist and American. How they negotiate that dual identity will be a new chapter in the interface between culture and Buddhist ethics.

Buddhist Ethics as the Ethics of Buddhists

In summarizing, it is tempting to think of Buddhism as adapting its ethics to local cultural conditions, maintaining along the way certain core values. This phrasing is not, however, a particularly *Buddhist* one. The wording reifies and essentializes "Buddhism" into a discrete system that adapts to its external environment. It makes Buddhism seem an independent agent, as if Buddhism were acted upon by culture and responds to it in return. Such an interpretation makes the relation between culture and Buddhism external rather than internal.

As suggested at the outset, Buddhists not Buddhism are what differ from one culture to the next. This is not because Buddhists are the effects of their social, cultural, and physical conditions, but rather because they *are* those conditions. Yet those conditions do not constitute some mindless mechanism. Rather, the interdependent processes are more like a conscious self-regulating, even self-healing system. The Buddha's Four Noble Truths were formulated in the medical progression of symptom, diagnosis, prognosis, therapy. He apparently understood his message as a kind of self-awareness leading to self-healing. Let us pursue this analogy between Buddhism and medicine a bit further.

Medical research suggests that the self-healing processes of the human body work best if the person is sensitive to somatic experience. If a person thinks about a particular part of the body, for example, the blood flow and temperature of that area shifts slightly. This can aid healing. The interdependent somatic processes signal injury or malfunction through tingling, pain, burning, itching, and so forth. If people are aware of these signals, they can respond to them while the problems are mild. If they repress or ignore the information, however, the conditions will often worsen. Where is the agency here? It is the body, but the body as including self-consciousness. The more the whole body (including the mind) is self-aware, the better it self-heals.

Let us apply this medical analogy to the Buddhist person as a system of interdependent, self-aware, and self-regulating processes. Viewed in this light, the point of Buddhist ethics is to make one more self-aware and self-responsive – more "skillful." Buddhists try to be aware of the "signals" of distress indicating the need for healing. Some may seem internal (the persistence of attachments, the desire for permanence, the preservation of a sense of ego) and some may seem external (the problems inherent in the caste system, economic inequality, gender prejudice, ecological degeneration). By being alert to the signals, the complex of conditions has a better chance to heal itself. To heighten this sensitivity, Buddhists have developed various techniques of praxis, principles of self-discipline, and reminders for how to keep the spiritual therapy on track.

Spiritual illnesses arise within certain conditions: cultural, social, personal, physical. Like physical illnesses, though, they often differ from one locale to another. So we should not expect Sri Lankan Buddhism to be any more like Mongolian Buddhism than we would expect Sri Lankan medicine to be like Mongolian medicine. The conditions are different and so different therapies develop. If we focus on the difference in the illness, we will find great variety. But if we focus on the goal of health, the differences tend to disappear. If in India Buddhist therapy connected more with epistemology and in Japan more with aesthetics, we can see those as different therapeutic strategies to treat the distress signals of different environments. But the goal of the therapies – the basic insight of self, world, and "skillful" agency – remains basically consistent across the variations.

Bibliography

Fu, C. W.-h. and Wawrytko, S. A. (eds.) 1991: *Buddhist Ethics and Modern Society: An International Symposium*. New York: Greenwood Press.

Harvey, P. 2000: *An Introduction to Buddhist Ethics: Foundations, Values, and Issues*. New York: Cambridge University Press.

Hubbard, J. and Swanson, P. L. (eds.) 1997: *Pruning the Bodhi Tree: The Storm over Critical Buddhism*. Honolulu: University of Hawai'i Press.

Kalupahana, D. 1995: *Ethics in Early Buddhism*. Honolulu: University of Hawai'i Press.

Kasulis, T. P. 1997: "The Buddhist Concept of Self" in *A Companion to World Philosophies*, ed. E. Deutsch and R. Bontekoe, 400–9. Oxford: Blackwell.

——2002: *Intimacy or Integrity: Philosophy and Cultural Difference*. Honolulu: University of Hawai'i Press.

Keown, D. 1992: *The Nature of Buddhist Ethics*. New York: St. Martin's Press.

Keown, D. and Prebish, C. S. 1994–: *Journal of Buddhist Ethics* (online journal). Available from http://jbe.gold.ac.uk.

King, W. L. 1964: *In the Hope of Nibbana: An Essay on Theravāda Buddhist Ethics*. LaSalle, IL: Open Court.

Sizemore, R. F. and Swearer, D. (eds.) 1990: *Ethics, Wealth, and Salvation: A Study in Buddhist Social Ethics*. Columbia: University of South Carolina Press.

Tucker, M. E. and Williams, D. R. (eds.) 1997: *Buddhism and Ecology: The Interconnection of Dharma and Deeds*. Cambridge, MA: Harvard University Center for the Study of World Religions.

CHAPTER 32

Buddhist Ethics: Trajectories

Charles Hallisey

Varied Trajectories

Over the past centuries, Buddhists have both been caught in and embraced the global processes of colonialism, modernity, and globalization (see chapter 49). Each of these processes has changed how Buddhists apprehend the world. As a result, each has left a profound imprint on Buddhist moral experience, values, and practice. Moreover, each process sets in motion relatively novel trajectories that continue to shape Buddhist moral thought and practice, from metaethics to normative ethics to applied ethics (see chapter 1). A critical appreciation of the generative presence of these trajectories is essential to any understanding of modern Buddhist ethics as a form of religious ethics. Put differently, these generative forces provoke new and different conceptions of "ethics" and human persons from traditional Buddhist ethics. They also enable thinkers to reclaim aspects of past teaching in novel ways. A range of responses to these large-scale dynamics has given rise to versions of ethics now seen in the Buddhist world. Understanding these responses is the subject of this chapter.

Some of these new trajectories are relatively easy to spot. They are the result of Buddhist encounters with ideas and values whose origins lie historically outside of the Buddhist world. This is the case with Buddhist acceptance of the modern concept of historicity and the notion of human rights. It is also true of Buddhist responses to contemporary challenges that are without precedent in history, as is the case with global environmental degradation. Other new trajectories are harder to perceive. These are shaped by shared assumptions and institutions that broadly structure otherwise diverse understandings of human life and our place in the world: assumptions of historicity, culture, and society; institutions like courts, state-supported education, and markets.

These trajectories come together to form what are seemingly ethical creoles in which the moral vocabulary may be Buddhist but the ethical syntax stems from the increasingly common habitus of the modern world. Conversely, the moral vocabulary of an "ethical creole" may be modern but the ethical syntax stems from traditional Buddhist values and practices. Prawet Wasi, a Thai Buddhist activist, gives an example of the first kind of ethical creole. Buddhism, he insists, must have a centrally visible role in development. The traditional Buddhist notions of *sīla* (self-discipline of behavior through morality), *samādhi* (the cultivation of mental self-discipline in meditation), and *paññā* (a wise understanding of the nature of human nature and the world) are central to human development. Yet on closer examination his understanding of perfect development is inflected more by middle-class and urban values than by the Buddhist ideas and ideals found in Thai villages, the ostensible object of national development (van Esterik 2000: 81). Payutto, a Thai monk and among the most significant contemporary Buddhist thinkers, gives an example of the second kind of ethical creole. His reflections on political and social freedom, celebrated in Thailand as much as anywhere else in the world, are embedded in a moral framework that culminates in a freedom from oneself, from one's own desires and ignorance. This freedom from oneself is, for Payutto, nirvāna, the *summum bonum* of Buddhism. Nirvāna, as ultimate freedom, is the standard by which all other instances of human freedom are to be judged. Unlike much modern Western ethics, where freedom is a given *sine qua non* of morality, freedom here is a condition to be striven for. "The process by which to achieve freedom (and peace and happiness) is called development (*bhāvanā*) [a traditional Buddhist term for meditation and other forms of mental culture], and in Buddhism, as far as man is concerned, development is synonymous with education (*sikkhā*) [a traditional Buddhist term for training in discipline, particularly used for monastic precepts]" (Payutto 1990: 37).

This chapter explores the "trajectories" in Buddhist ethics attentive to the complex interaction of these large-scale processes and mindful of the emergence of ethical creoles in varied contexts. It is important to grasp just how "modern" current Buddhist ethics has become. Hopefully, in this way, something of the vitality as well as the moral challenges facing "Buddhists" around the world will become evident.

Large-Scale Processes

When we try to bring large-scale processes like colonialism, modernity, and globalization into view and consider their significance for the understanding of modern Buddhist ethics, it is critical to avoid the common tendency to delimit their presence only to particular spheres of thought and practice in particular times and places (see chapter 49). The importance of avoiding this tendency can be illustrated by considering, first, the continuing impact of colonialism on Buddhist ethics.

Colonialism

Colonialism affected the whole world – colonizers, colonized, and those who were neither – not just in different ways, but in unequal ways as well. Even those communities that were outside any specific colonial political economy were shaped by colonialism's way of ordering the world and its justification of that world order by emphasizing human difference and structures of value based on that difference.

Modern colonialism cannot be delimited to a period that is now firmly in the past. Its values, possibilities, and constraints continue to shape the moral thought and practice of all humans, even while the political economy of colonialism has overtly given way to a world order constituted with the foundational notion of the nation. All of these generalizations apply to every part of the Buddhist world, from Central Asia to Southeast Asia to East Asia, just as much as they apply to any other part of the world.

Of course, for some Buddhists who were colonized, like those in Sri Lanka and Cambodia, the general legacy of colonialism makes them part of the "third world." But Buddhists were not only colonized. Some Buddhists colonized others (like the Japanese in Korea), some were "independent" (like the Thai) throughout the colonial period, and these have their own specific legacies of colonialism just as much as those Buddhist communities which were colonized. Whatever their colonial status historically, Buddhist communities all share a common heritage from colonialism. The various modes in which contemporary Buddhists apprehend themselves as *Buddhist* generally stem from the global processes of colonialism that began in the sixteenth century. Indeed, some argue persuasively that the very notion of Buddhism is primarily a colonial product. It goes without saying that Buddhists did have a range of indigenous terms for self-ascription in precolonial times. Yet the cultural syntax that ordered human difference in colonial times was vastly different from anything before and left an indelible mark on all Buddhist terms of self-ascription.

It is only in the colonial period that Buddhists became capable of distinguishing themselves from other humans using the categories of culture and religion. Neither the modern notion of culture nor religion was known in precolonial Asia. One aspect of this colonial legacy that makes "religion" one of the primary ways of "othering" humans is the still-common impulse to define Buddhism by what makes it *different* from other religions rather than by what constitutes Buddhism. Students of religion too often assume that difference itself is the key rationale for the study of anything Buddhist. They are on the lookout for what is uniquely "Buddhist." This is an academic issue, but it is not only that. The colonial assumptions of human difference remain a key element of nationalisms in the postcolonial world. "The most powerful as well as the most creative results of the nationalist imagination in Asia and Africa are posited not on an identity, but rather on a *difference* with the 'modular' forms of the national society propagated by the modern West" (Chatterjee 1993: 5). Religion loomed large in Asian nationalisms precisely because "the European criticism of Indian [or Chinese or Khmer, or whatever] tradition as barbaric had focused to a large extent on religious beliefs and practices, especially those relating to the treatment of women" (Chatterjee 1993: 9).

Colonialism, modernity, and globalization are big words with even bigger referents. The large-scale processes named by these terms appear increasingly complex as they are investigated more concretely and theorized more adequately (see chapter "On Religious Ethics"). They seem to elude adequate definition. Only the simplest delineation can be stipulated for each of these processes. The definitions provided must necessarily be suggestive and open-ended. Moreover, these delineations are focused on the topics of morality and ethics, understanding the distinction between the two to be that between first and second order phenomena. "Ethics" is thinking and talking about the values, ideas, and practices of morality.

Modernity

Modernity occupies the central place among the three, since colonialism and global-ization are defined in conjunction to modernity. Although our understanding of the origins, history, and future of modernity is becoming increasingly open to doubt and tentativeness, the general contours of modernity remain sufficiently conventionalized. By "modernity" is meant a theoretical vision of human nature determined by a con-stellation of ideas about the individual as a free and discrete agent who, in cooperation with others, is able to transcend the constraints of inherited conditions (especially "culture," "society," and "religion") and is able to construct new "life-worlds" of meaning and well-being.

This constellation of ideas is everywhere apparent in the Buddhist world today. One sees them clearly even in the references to Prawet Wasi and Payutto above. We can also see them in the comments of Daisaku Ikeda, president of Soka Gakkai International, a new Buddhist movement that emerged in postwar Japan, about anecdotes from the biographies of the Buddha. These anecdotes "illustrate an important point in Bud-dhism, the fact that it does not seek to create any fixed image of the ideal man or demand that everyone attempt to conform to one particular stereotype. Rather it encourages its adherents, while embracing a certain sense of mission, to give full play to their individual abilities and characteristics" (Ikeda 1996: 97).

In modernity, a human being is a self-creating and self-governing individual, and this gives ethics a special pride of place in modernity's vision of a person. Ethics was the primal site of human freedom: a person chooses to be responsible for the kind of life she chooses to lead; a "moral agent" takes responsibility for guiding and regulating her own behavior. Everywhere in the contemporary Buddhist world there is a routine acceptance of modernity's vision of the human, and especially its vision of the impor-tance of ethics. Comparison with the Buddhist past makes this clear, especially in so far as major strands of premodern Buddhist ethics often included starkly probative visions of human capacities: ignorant and riven with desires, we can never be other than beings of "blind passion and karmic evil" (a self-ascription of Shinran's, the great Pure Land thinker from thirteenth-century Japan). On this more classical vision, human beings are constitutionally incapable of constructing life-worlds of meaning and well-being for themselves. The "modern" idea about persons and moral agents, arising out of a large-scale process, is then the condition for the kind of ethical creole seen in the words of Ikeda and others, as well as the very importance of "ethics" in contemporary Buddhist thought and practice.

The inflections of modernity in contemporary Buddhist ethics are partially obscured by the legacy of colonialism. This obscuration occurs in many ways, but generally all to the same effect. Buddhism is posited as apart from the modern, making the manner in which Buddhists articulate a modern ethics more problematic. For example, Prawet Wasi's advocacy of development is an acceptance of the universal vision of modernity that leaves the Thai Buddhist community outside modernity. "Development" is the process by which men and women in certain communities become capable of the ethical self-creation and self-regulation so central to modernity's vision of the moral agent. When Buddhism is constructed as apart from the modern, then the Buddhist past, with all of its ethical and cultural resources, must be measured by the standards of modernity and sometimes transcended en route to the modern. This is seen in the contemporary Tibetan poet Dhondup Gyal's poem, "Waterfall of Youth":

> The thousand brilliant accomplishments of the past
>   cannot serve today's purpose,
> yesterday's salty water cannot quench today's thirsts,
>   the withered body of history is lifeless
>   without the soul of today,
> the pulse of progress will not beat,
> the blood of progress will not flow. (Gyal 2000)

Communities which are "not yet modern" were defined as such in the world-ordering vision of colonialism as part of its justification of the inevitability of colonial regimes and their beneficence in initiating the processes of technological, social, and cultural development.

Colonial critiques of Buddhist communities were often couched in moral terms. These were deeply felt – they stung – and their force was often internalized, sometimes emerging in advocacy for new forms of morality among Buddhists. The early twentieth-century Sri Lankan Buddhist activist Anagarika Dharmapala wrote a handbook of moral behavior for Buddhist laypeople that became quite popular and influential. Actually, it was a condemnation of what was accepted in the moral communities of rural Buddhists in colonial Sri Lanka.

> In some instances [in Dharmapala's handbook] Western norms are directly advocated as, for example, eating with fork and spoon and using toilet paper before water during ablutions . . . Some points do not conflict with tradition, but by and large Protestant and Western norms have been assimilated as pure and ideal Buddhist norms. Sociologically viewed, Dharmapala's social reform provided a value system to a new class, an emerging bourgeoisie. In many non-Western nations, nineteenth-century Western values, generally Victorian, have been assimilated into the fabric of indigenous bourgeois society . . .
>
>   The Sri Lanka case is especially striking since the new value system was articulated into a powerful ethic of this-worldly asceticism. (Gombrich and Obeyesekere 1988: 12)

The example of Dharmapala makes it clear that colonialism's manner of establishing differences among communities changed the way in which Buddhists imagined themselves. This is true to the degree that they were always aware of the condemnatory gaze of Europeans. Buddhist life-worlds and moral communities have been created since the time of colonialism by Buddhists and non-Buddhists as they encountered each other in contexts of critique, governance, and resistance.

One important trajectory of modern Buddhist thought stemming from colonialism is deeply defensive. It is part of an inherited response to colonial accusations of the inherent inadequacy of Buddhist thought, practice, and experience in the context of modernity. The shadow of this defensiveness is pervasive, and helps one to understand many features of contemporary Buddhist ethics, such as the routine contrast between

Buddhist ethics and vaguely theistic ethics. This contrast is obviously apologetic. It is a way of aligning Buddhist ethics more closely with the secular ethics of the modern West and thereby making Buddhist ethics less susceptible to anticipated criticism of "religion."

This apologetic can be seen in comments by Payutto. One should note especially the claims for systematic rationality, heroic autonomy, freedom, objectivity, and universality in Buddhist ethics. All of these ideas are cardinal features of the self-understanding of modernity, and they are supposedly absent in theistic forms of ethics. Payutto's comments clearly resonate with standard critiques, and also the oversights, of theistically grounded ethics made by European Enlightenment thinkers.

> The moral code of Buddhism must be understood as a rational, integrated system of ethics so that the Buddhist practitioner can correctly proceed along the Path. In general, the code of ethics for theistic religions amounts to divine commandments or expressions of divine purpose, which are all separate and different . . . Sīla, or the Buddhist system of ethics, is a universal set of objective principles established in accordance with natural truths . . . Good and bad, right and wrong, blame and blamelessness all exist; you must be willing to accept these for what they are depending on your actions. You must be brave enough to accept that you are right or wrong according to the facts present, not according to your own inclinations.

There are several good things about the commandments of theistic religions. And yet problems remain that render theistic ethics untenable in the contemporary world.

> The determination of what is right and wrong, true and untrue has been clearly designated so that if a person believes and is loyal, the positive results of proper behavior are quick and effective. But a problem subsequently arises: in a rationalistic and positivistic age, what can be done to maintain people's beliefs in these commandments? And in the long run, how will people adhering to different faiths be able to live together? And if belief depends on loyalty to commandments, how will people achieve the freedom necessary to attain true wisdom? (Payutto 1995: 249–50)

Colonialism set in motion a dynamic set of images of communities and cultures and thereby helped to spread the "modern" vision of the human. These were used by individuals to establish their own identity as members of a community (e.g. "I am Thai, and as such, I am a free man, because Thailand was never colonized"). The conjunction of modern ideas and colonial processes helps to back "creole" moral identities that characterize much of contemporary Buddhist ethics as "different" than Western religious ethics, but also surprisingly compatible with "modern" ethics.

Globalization

Globalization, the accelerated flow of goods, peoples, images, and ideologies through circuits of economic and cultural interdependence, has intensified the dynamism of the colonial system of images. It has also generated new images that circulate in advertising, tourism, and university classrooms. In other words, globalization has intensified the impact of the "gaze of others," knowledge through images, setting in motion a "process of doubling" in the Buddhist world (Lopez 1998: 200). This process of doubling builds on but goes beyond the assimilation of European moral values and practices in the colonial world. It is a process of internal self-critique fostered not by defensiveness towards the anticipated critiques of non-Buddhists. Here, self-critique is fostered by measuring oneself against an image of "Buddhism," an image that is free-floating and thus apparently true. So, for example, "young lay Tibetans growing up in India . . . criticize Tibetan monks for not living up to the image of Tibetan Buddhism they have read about in English" (Lopez 1998: 201). The process of doubling does not only occur with images created by non-Buddhists, as one might be inclined to suppose from this Tibetan instance. We see in Thailand and Japan, for example, shifting presentations of images for local consumption that claim to find and display the essence of Thainess (*khwampen Thai*) or Japaneseness (*Nihonji*) (see van Esterik 2000; Morris 2000; Ivy 1995).

The process of doubling is particularly powerful in Buddhist morality and ethics. Globalization consistently spreads an image of Buddhism as a religion grounded in compassion, one which is "above all a religion of reason dedicated to bringing an end to suffering. [A religion which] is strongly ethical and is devoted to non-violence, and as such is a vehicle for social reform" (Lopez 1998: 185). In Buddhist communities shaped by globalization, ethics inevitably becomes second order reflection on Buddhist morality as mediated by these images, not on the values and moral practices of actual Buddhist communities. Common aspects of Buddhist moral life that remain outside these images, such as relations between teachers and students, relations between parents and children, sorcery, and exorcism are thus frequently omitted from consideration in contemporary Buddhist ethics. In this way, globalization continues modern and colonial processes with greater scope, spread, and speed, thereby shaping trajectories in contemporary Buddhist ethics.

The sets of images about particular Buddhist communities (e.g., Thailand as "the land of smiles," victimized Tibet), about Buddhism in general (e.g., an advertisement that promises that "you can reach business nirvāna" if you use a certain computer program), and about modern ethical ideas (e.g., human rights) that circulate globally are far more fluid and malleable than those systems of ideas, values, and practices that are generally denoted with notions of culture or systematic religious thought. The significance of these sets of images cannot be overemphasized for any understanding of contemporary Buddhist ethics. Accounts of contemporary Buddhist ethics that turn only to culture or systematic thought cannot adequately account for the cacophony of contemporary Buddhist ethical discourse. It is a cacophony because statements are sometimes made in particular ways more to gain the sympathetic attention of those far away, much like the placards in English that can be routinely seen on television reports of demonstrations in places like Beijing or Baghdad, than as an articulation of a systematic and stable ethical position.

Vincanne Adams has noted this in accounts of imprisonment and torture made by Tibetan nuns in a film by Ellen Bruno, *Satya: A Prayer for the Enemy*:

Heard by activists outside of Tibet, these accounts [of imprisonment and torture] are interpreted as utterances of suffering, not simply of the sort that can bring spiritual salvation,
but of the sort that can bring about a political revolution. Suffering in this latter sense is
about creating a space of shared meaning between Buddhist and non-Buddhist, Tibetan
and Tibetan refugee, Tibetan and foreign activist, Tibetan refugee and foreign activist. Suffering has to be made into something that for non-Tibetans and Tibetans alike can transform the religious into the political by the fact that it results from a presumed universally
shared understanding. Suffering is asked to speak in the language of the one who is perceived as being able to alleviate it. Thus the nuns respond to the Western filmmaker, and
in their voices we perceive both something that is produced by the Western gaze and some
things that may be contrary to it. (Adams 2002: 389)

What "is produced by the Western gaze" and what "may be contrary to it" are equally
Buddhist in contemporary Buddhist ethics, even if they are not equally Buddhist in
terms of the history of Buddhist ethical thought. It is also important to take note of the
ethical resonance of the notion of suffering. *Dukkha* (suffering, dis-ease, dissatisfaction)
is a generative element in the Buddhist moral vision. Finally, it is important to take note
of the site of moral discourse. Bruno's film was made for viewing in non-Tibetan communities. All of this is related to the impact of global processes on Buddhist ethics. This
takes one deeper into the kind of "creole ethics" presently found among contemporary
Buddhist communities and thinkers and thereby clarifies the important changes that
virtually define various trajectories in "Buddhist ethics."

Defining Changes

One of the biggest changes in contemporary Buddhist ethics is the shift to new sites for
the production of moral and ethical discourse. In the premodern Buddhist world, ethics
was a product of monastic culture. It bore the imprint of the particular disciplinary and
pedagogical practices that structured monastic life in different Buddhist communities.
Like other areas of intellectual life, ethical thought was pursued and embedded in social
patterns organized around person-to-person relationships of spiritual guidance with
particular teachers (see chapters 8, 9, and 10). The practices of devotion and respect
that displayed these relationships contextualized and organized a thinker's relationship
with the intellectual and systematic content of the *dharma*, including ethics.

In the modern world, the site of ethics is no longer exclusively monastic. Ethics are
taught and studied in state-sponsored schools and universities, disseminated in books,
newspapers, and pamphlets, and in the mission statements of NGOs. This expansion of
the sites in which Buddhist ethics are encountered and appropriated has introduced
a marked ethical change. The mechanisms of print culture encourage an experience
of horizontal anonymity between individuals, on the model of the experience of
citizens of a nation, rather than the more personalized but more hierarchical
dependence that is typical of premodern relationships between monastic teachers and
students. In short, the practices of modern print culture require and reinforce the

"modern" ethical understanding of a person as an autonomous and capable individual agent. And this shapes, as we have seen, trajectories in contemporary Buddhism about the very subject of ethical discourse and the importance of "ethics" in Buddhist life.

Aside from shifts in how to understand the human person, there is one other change that helps to define the ethics of contemporary Buddhism. It is a shift in the "cosmological" frameworks for understanding the status of moral practices. In general, contemporary Buddhist ethics has made a turn to embracing a thin form of moral realism that is more foundational than what was seen in premodern Buddhist ethics (see chapter 2). In the latter, the cosmological framework for morality was located in the structures of *karma* and rebirth (see chapter 13). These structures were "real" in a significant way. It was generally thought that denial of *karma* and its fruits in various realms of rebirth (heavens, titans, humans, animals, ghosts, and hells) would put one outside the Buddhist fold. Insofar as the structures of rebirth could be said to represent "real" features of the world, premodern Buddhist ethics represented a form of moral realism. Yet this kind of moral realism was both more robust and more tempered than presently found. That was due to the importance in traditional Buddhist thought of the common notion of "two truths." One angle of vision on the world represents the way things really are, an ultimate truth. The other offers conventional truth, based on practical efficacy and shared assumptions between the users of accepted categories of thought, discourse, and evaluation. For example, a person from the perspective of ultimate truth is insubstantial and impermanent, best described as an aggregate of impersonal elements and forces. This "person" is profoundly unlike the modern Western idea. And yet, a person from the perspective of conventional truth is a discrete entity that exists and acts in space and across time. This "person" is much more like the modern vision of a moral agent. The difference between the two perspectives on a "person" is close to the difference between saying "I am hungry" (which would be a conventional description) and "There is an abundance of acids irritating the lining of the stomach" (a description from the perspective of ultimate truth). Both statements describe the same state of affairs, yet they can warrant very different ethical judgments. In premodern Buddhist thought, "morality" and "ethics" in the modern sense, along with a modern vision of persons, were within the realm of conventional truth. It was explicitly denied that moral claims could be persuasive or even understandable if expressed in ultimate rather than conventional terms (see chapter 3).

Not surprisingly, accounts of rebirth in various realms, while the very stuff of premodern Buddhist ethics, were vulnerable to modern critiques of religion. They represented a bid for a robust but tempered moral realism that could not be sustained in the face of scientific accounts of the world. Buddhist ethics were quickly "demythologized" in response to these critiques of Buddhist cosmology. The bid for moral realism was now made by a turn to accounts of the world that use the categories of ultimate truth. This had the effect of truncating the Buddhist vision while seemingly extending its insights into the modern world. In particular, the concept of "co-dependent origination" was made to sustain a "realistic" ethics. Traditionally, this doctrine was used in relatively limited ways to explain the presence of a person in time and space using strictly impersonal categories. In contemporary Buddhism it has assumed "seemingly magnetic" powers that affect all areas of Buddhist ethics (Keown 2000: 78, n. 46).

For example, the Dalai Lama makes it clear in his *Ethics for the New Millennium* that the moral realism of co-dependent origination gives a prudential moral imperative. It is in our own interests to be moral and this moral realism gives guidance on how we should live.

> When we come to see that everything we perceive and experience arises as a result of an indefinite series of interrelated causes and conditions, our whole perspective changes. We begin to see that the universe we inhabit can be understood in terms of a living organism where each cell works in balanced cooperation with every other cell to sustain the whole. If then, just one of these cells is harmed, as when disease strikes, that balance is harmed and there is danger to the whole. This, in turn, suggests, that our individual well-being is intimately connected both with that of all others and with the environment within which we live . . . Such an understanding of reality as suggested by this concept of dependent origination also presents us with a significant challenge. It presents us to see things and events less in terms of black and white and more in terms of complex interlinking of relationships, which are hard to pin down. (Dalai Lama 1999: 4)

The change in cosmological outlook, and so the kind of moral realism endorsed, when linked to shifts in ideas about persons arising within new sites of moral discourse, goes a long way in helping us understand trajectories in Buddhist ethics. It enables us to see the possibility of Buddhists constructing differing creole identities that continue and yet also revise traditional Buddhist beliefs, practices, and outlooks.

Realism and Situationalism

We see in the comments of the Dalai Lama a final feature of contemporary Buddhist ethics, at once traditional and also modern. The principles of normative ethics are theoretically obvious (they include the well-being of others in relationship with oneself), but they are particularly hard to discern in practical terms. The (ultimate) nature of the human and natural world makes it impossible to specify particular moral norms that would be universally applicable in all instances. Interestingly enough, the moral realism of traditional Buddhist metaethics as the real backing for a contemporary ethics yields an acceptance of situational ethics in the area of normative ethics. It reduplicates in a novel way some of the same insights as the classical "two truths." And, further, this move also allows contemporary Buddhist ethicists to accept the insights of historical and cultural relativism in describing morality without rejecting the objectivity and universalism of moral realism as seen in the Buddha's teachings. In this respect, we see Buddhist ethicists finding a way to allow for moral disagreements without insisting that one point of view must be wrong, as is often the case in ethical positions that are morally realistic. We also see how a classical tradition can locate within its own resources means to respond to the large-scale processes now shaping human life on this planet.

Bibliography

Adams, V. 2002: "Politicized Bodies and Human Rights in Tibet" in *The Anthropology of Globalization Reader*, ed. J. X. Inda and R. Rosaldo. Malden, MA: Blackwell.

Chatterjee, P. 1993: *The Nation and Its Fragments*. Princeton, NJ: Princeton University Press.

Dalai Lama. 1999: *Ethics for the New Millennium*. New York: Penguin Putnam.

Gombrich, R. and Obeyesekere, G. 1988: *Buddhism Transformed*. Princeton, NJ: Princeton University Press.

Gyal, D. 2000: "The Waterfall of Youth," trans. T Shakya, in *Manoa* 12, 2.

Ikeda, D. 1996: *The Living Buddha*. New York: Weatherhill.

Ivy, M. 1995: *Discourses of the Vanishing: Modernity, Phantasm, Japan*. Chicago: University of Chicago Press.

Keown, D. 2000: "Buddhism and Human Rights" in *Contemporary Buddhist Ethics*, ed. D. Keown. London: Curzon Press.

Lopez, D. 1998: *Prisoners of Shangri-La*. Chicago: University of Chicago Press.

Morris, R. 2000: *In the Place of Origins: Modernity and its Mediums in Northern Thailand*. Durham, NC: Duke University Press.

Payutto, Venerable Prayudh. 1990: *Freedom, Individual and Social*. Bangkok: Buddhadhamma Foundation.

——1995: *Buddhadhamma*. Albany: State University of New York Press.

van Esterik, P. 2000: *Materializing Thailand*. New York: Berg.

5 Indian/Hindu Ethics

CHAPTER 33

Hindu Ethics?

Roy W. Perrett

Is There Hindu Moral Theory?

Is there such a thing as Hindu ethics? Is the category of ethics appropriate to the moral thought of the Hindu religious tradition? Obviously enough, the answers to these questions depend very much on what we mean by "ethics" (see chapter 1). One very broad characterization might be something like this: ethics is a set of substantive proposals concerning how to live, how to act, or what sort of person to be. In this sense there certainly is Hindu ethics, with a large variety of texts in Sanskrit and other Indian languages setting forth various such proposals (see, Holdrege 1991).

But ethics is also often taken to be a branch of philosophy, and hence a body of the-oretical discourse centrally concerned with analysis and justification. There certainly exists a highly articulated Hindu philosophical tradition, but is there Hindu ethics in the philosophical sense of that term (i.e., a body of developed moral theory)? The answer is not so clear, for although classical Indian philosophy is incredibly rich in rigorous and extended discussions of topics in epistemology, logics, and metaphysics, comparable discussions in philosophical ethics do not abound. Hence, too, the relative paucity of extended contemporary studies of Hindu moral philosophy (see Maitra 1956; Hiriyanna 1975; Perrett 1998).

Some have seen this lacuna in the otherwise enormous Indian philosophical litera-ture as implying that "morality, its origins and its expression in various commands and interdictions, was taken too much for granted to be discussed" (Hopkins 1924: 88). But this is not quite right. The classical Indian philosophers obviously had a great deal to say about ethics insofar as they vigorously discussed topics like the ends of life and the relation of virtuous action to those ends.

Others have suggested the gap in the literature does not point to the Indians' indif-ference to ethics, but just to their indifference to ethical theory of a certain universal-istic sort. Max Weber's views have been influential in this connection:

There was no universally valid ethic, but only a strict status compartmentalization of private and social ethic, disregarding the few absolute and general ritualistic prohibitions (particularly the killing of cows). This was of great moment. The doctrine of *karma* deduced from the principle of compensation for previous deeds of the world, not only explained the caste organization but the rank order of divine, human and animal beings of all degrees. Hence it provided for the coexistence of different ethical codes for different status groups which not only differed widely but were often in sharp conflict . . . [Men] were as unlike as man and animal. (Weber 1958: 144)

More recently, A. K. Ramanujan has often been cited as claiming such particularism to be a characteristic "Indian way of thinking":

One has only to read Manu after a bit of Kant to be struck by the former's extraordinary lack of universality. He seems to have no clear notion of a universal *human* nature from which one can deduce ethical decrees like "Man shall not kill," or "Man shall not tell an untruth." One is aware of no notion of a "state," no unitary law of all men . . . To be moral, for Manu, is to particularize . . . I think cultures (may be said to) have overall tendencies . . . to *idealize*, and think in terms of, either the context-free or the context-sensitive kind of rules . . . In cultures like India's, the context-sensitive kind of rule is the preferred formulation. (Ramanujan 1989: 45–7)

All of this might too hastily suggest a picture of Hindu ethics as a variety of anti-theoretical particularism, prefiguring certain trends in contemporary Western ethics (see chapter 2). On such a view, the absence of a developed Hindu moral theory not only fails to show that there is no Hindu ethics, but it may very well also show that the Hindu ethicists deliberately eschewed universalistic theory because they better understood the radically particularistic nature of ethics than have most Western ethicists.

Such a picture of Hindu ethics as particularistic anti-theory, however, is unconvincing. First, if the Indian philosophers really were anti-theorists about ethics, this clearly had nothing to do with any principled general objection to the construction of universalistic philosophical theories: witness the growth of the intricate edifice of classical Indian epistemological theory (*pramāṇavāda*). Second, the classical Hindu ethicists did recognize the existence of some kinds of universal moral rules: the *dharmaśāstrins* explicitly distinguished the particular duties of one's caste and stage in life (*varṇāśrama-dharma*) from the universal duties (*sādhāraṇa-dharma*) incumbent on all, regardless of age or occupation. Third, the classification of Hindu ethics as particularist unhappily saddles Hindu moral philosophers with the problem of how to make coherent the often inconsistent deliverances of commonsense moral judgments on particular cases – especially since in other domains Indian philosophers have been just as reluctant to accept contradictions as have their Western counterparts.

A third position is that Hindu thinking on *dharma* does indeed provide a moral theory, but one of a uniquely pluralistic sort:

Part of it is a theory of moral rules, part of it a theory of virtues, another part communitarian, and added to all these, there is a layer of Kantian-like duty for duty's sake subserving a transcendent goal of *mokṣa*, where ethics transcends itself. (Mohanty 2000: 122)

There are difficulties, however, with this way of representing Hindu moral theory. First, it can all too readily be taken to suggest that Hindu moral theory is just an uneasy – and probably unstable – patchwork of parts of various more familiar Western moral theories. Second, it is exegetically implausible to represent the corpus of Indian writings on ethics, scattered over a variety of sources and genres, as constituting a single synthetic moral theory.

Is there a better picture of Hindu ethics available, one that does justice to its special theoretical character while also acknowledging the relative thinness of the moral theory actually developed by the Indians – its thinness, that is, when compared to paradigms like Western moral theory or classical Indian *pramāṇavāda?* I think so, but providing it requires the use of a rather different map of the territory of ethics than that which has become the standard one.

Two Maps of Ethics

A familiar Western map of ethics divides the territory up into two basic approaches: non-normative and normative (see chapters 1 and 2). Non-normative approaches, on the one hand, include both descriptive ethics and metaethics. Metaethical theories are either cognitivist or non-cognitivist. Cognitivist theories are either naturalist or non-naturalist. Normative approaches, on the other hand, divide into normative ethics and applied ethics. Normative ethics then divides into teleological and deontological theories. The main teleological theories are egoism, consequentialism (including utilitarianism), and virtue ethics.

Such a map would not have the currency it does if it failed to capture any of the territory. Hence, it is at least prima facie embarrassing to find that there exists nothing identifiable as Hindu ethics which can be located comfortably on this map. Nor is it enough just to plead that Hindu ethics is *sui generis*, for then we still need to supply a better map of the territory of ethics: one on which Hindu ethics can be located, together with all the other theories already captured on the standard map. Fortunately for the cause of Hindu ethics, however, some recent work in Western moral theory not only supports the claim that the standard map of ethics is inadequate as a complete representation of the logical space of the possible theories, but also offers a more promising rival map (see Kagan 1992, 1998; Donagan 1977) (see chapter "On Religious Ethics").

First, the rival map suggests that the distinction between metaethics, normative ethics, and applied ethics is arguably better understood as roughly marking positions on a continuum, rather than sharp lines of division. Just as we cannot articulate substantive moral claims in applied ethics without reference to the sorts of more fundamental claims about the content of morality traditionally counted as part of normative ethics, so too we cannot articulate these more fundamental normative claims without reference to second order claims about the very nature of morality. Metaethics and normative ethics, then, are not as independent of each other as is often claimed.

Second, the new map of ethics suggests that when we consider the structure of normative ethics it is fruitful to distinguish between normative *factors* and normative *foundations*. For example, when considering a particular act, we typically seek to articulate both the various factors relevant to determining the moral status of that act and the foundational devices that generate and explain the favored list of normatively relevant factors.

A normative factor is one relevant to determining moral status and most moral theorists favor admitting a variety of them – including outcomes, constraints, special obligations, options, and so on. More controversial is exactly how these various factors interact and how they are to be weighted relative to each other in the event of conflict. To get a grip on the notion of a normative factor, imagine a situation where I take a boat to rescue someone who is drowning. Clearly, saving a life is a good outcome and this factor is relevant to the moral evaluation of my deed. But many think this may not be the only morally relevant factor here. Suppose, for instance, the boat belongs to someone else and so to rescue the drowning person I have to steal the boat. Should someone else's property rights constrain my rescue attempt? Or suppose the drowning person is my daughter. Do I then have a special obligation, stronger than my obligation to save a stranger? And so on. In both Western and Indian ethics there are a number of alternative theories about the morally relevant factors and their interaction.

The foundational theories are supposed to help us with these issues by offering mechanisms that purport to generate and thus explain the list of normatively relevant factors. Of course, some ethicists are *non-foundationalists*, holding that there is no further explanation possible at the foundational level of the normative factors and their interaction principles. *Foundationalists*, on the other hand, deny this and offer competing theories that seek to justify their choice of a factoral list. (Note, however, that the ethical foundationalist is not necessarily committed to the thesis that the foundational level theories are *epistemically* prior to, or more basic than, the factoral level theories. Epistemically speaking, it might well be that neither level is more fundamental than the other.)

Foundational theories may be either teleological or deontological. Teleological theories explain the significance of the factors in terms of their significance for the good, either the individual good or the overall good. Examples of such teleological foundational theories include egoism, virtue ethics, and consequentialism. Deontological theories deny that the ultimate basis of ethics lies in terms of some central good or goods, except for that agreement they differ about the details of their positive foundational accounts. Examples of deontological foundational theories include contractarianism, universalizability theory, ideal observer theory, and reflection theories.

It is important to realize that the choice of a theory about the morally relevant factors can be relatively independent of the choice of a foundational theory. This point is not always well appreciated. Two people might well agree, for instance, about the list of normative factors, but disagree about the correct foundational theory. Whereas it is too often assumed that a foundational theory uniquely generates a particular list of factors, in fact two rival foundational theories might well generate the same list of factors. For example, admitting the moral relevance of factors in addition to outcomes does not preclude all of these factors being given a purely consequentialist explanation at the foundational level. On the other hand, two people might well agree on the correctness of a given foundational theory and yet disagree about which factors are generated by that theory. For example, many consequentialists have too hastily assumed that consequentialism as a foundational theory commits us to the (relatively unpopular) view that outcomes are the only morally relevant factors. But in fact one can quite consistently be a consequentialist at the foundational level without being a consequentialist at the factoral level.

The distinction between theories of normative factors and foundational theories, then, fruitfully enriches the logical space that ethical theories occupy: there are far more theoretical possibilities than has usually been thought. But there are still two further foundational issues a complete normative theory has to address.

The first issue is the problem of whether to embrace *monism* or *pluralism* at the foundational level. A pluralist at the factoral level holds that more than one normative factor has weight in its own right. This does not, however, preclude there being a single foundational theory that justifies and explains this plurality of factors. Someone who believes there is such a single foundational theory is a foundational monist. In contrast, a pluralist at the foundational level holds that the different factors are grounded in different foundational devices.

There are two ways this might be done. One is right to insist that that there is an ultimate and irreducible pluralism at the foundations of normative ethics. The other is a bit more exotic: a foundational pluralism which also admits of the possibility of *multilayering*. The idea here is that there may be at a deeper foundational level still some single foundational theory that grounds and explains the plurality of more superficial foundational theories. There are many structural possibilities along these lines that are still to be explored fully. For example, egoism might be invoked to support contractarianism, which in turn might generate the factoral level; or the ideal observer might support universalizability. Nor is there any obvious reason why we must stop with a single deeper foundational layer: perhaps the multilayering goes much deeper than that. Indeed, using this notion of multilayering, perhaps we can combine elements of both monism and pluralism at the foundational level and construct a foundational theory which has several layers containing more than one component account, with pluralism at one level grounded in monism at a deeper level. The theoretical possibilities in this area are surely much richer than has usually been appreciated.

Second, a complete foundational theory needs to address the issue of *evaluative focal points*. Rival theories in normative ethics have often disagreed as to what kinds of objects provide the *primary* evaluative focal point. Thus the familiar debate between act- and rule-consequentialists: are acts to be the primary evaluative focal point, with rules evaluated in a secondary or derivative way, or should it be the other way around. But acts and rules do not exhaust the list of plausible primary evaluative focal points. Other possibilities include motives, institutions, norms, character traits, and intentions. Taking each of these we can construct a variant of any given foundational approach. The choice of focal point will then significantly influence what is generated at the factoral level. Once again, ethicists have done relatively little independent investigation of the evaluative focal points, as opposed to promoting rival foundational theories which already incorporate choices about focal points. An exception is recent work by virtue theorists, where significant intramural differences of opinion at the foundational and factoral levels have not been able to obscure a fundamental point of agreement: that it is virtues, rather than acts or rules, that ought to be our primary evaluative focal point.

To sum up then. On this new map of ethics we can think of normative ethics as having two major levels: the foundational and the factoral. At the foundational level we can then further subdivide the concerns of ethical theory into two: the choice of foundational devices and the choice of focal points. Taken together, these latter two generate the favored list of normative factors. Ideally, a complete moral theory will include all three components and give an account of their interconnections. It will also take a stand on the foundational monism/pluralism issue (see chapter 14).

Implications

Suppose that a complete moral theory ought to include all of these components. Is there such a fully developed Hindu moral theory? The answer is clear: there exists no credible Indian candidate for such an exalted role. But equally there is no credible Western candidate for such an exalted role. Even the most fully articulated Western moral theories fail to address all of the ethical territory represented on the new map of ethics. Of course, some Western moral theorists have explored some parts of that territory in considerably more systematic detail than have any of their Indian counterparts: this is what gave rise to the impression that there was no Hindu moral theory. But arguably most Western ethical theories effectively confine themselves to less than the three areas a complete theory is supposed to discuss.

Thinking of the usual standard Western normative theories as incomplete moral theories from which there is nevertheless something to be learned helps us to understand better the limits and achievements of Hindu moral theory. It is not that the Hindus have developed a uniquely pluralistic, synthetic moral theory, scattered over a variety of sources and genres. Rather, what the Hindu moralists have done is much like what their Western counterparts have done: they have investigated different regions of the moral map, with their different sorts of normative investigations often proceeding independently of one another, and they have managed at best to develop only significantly incomplete normative theories (notwithstanding the interest of these fragments).

Of course, sometimes the Indian theories happen to be weak in precisely the areas that the Western theories are strongest: hence the Western valorization of Western foundational theory and metaethics. In reality the Hindu moral theorists have done some very good work centered on factoral and focal issues: see, for instance, the rich discussions of the normative factors, foci, and their interactions to be found in the *dharmaśāstra* and *arthaśāstra* texts, or in the epic narratives of the *Mahābhārata* and *Rāmāyaṇa* (see chapter 7). Moreover, in some areas the Hindus have arguably done pioneering work as yet unmatched by their Western counterparts: for instance, whereas the issue of multilayered foundational pluralism has been largely unexplored in Western ethics, the Hindu discussions of the nature of the *puruṣārthas* and their relationships to one another are remarkably suggestive in this respect.

On this theoretical map of the territory of ethics, much of the fine-grained detail has yet to be filled in. Using this map, however, we can successfully capture what both Western and Hindu ethicists have done and what they have as yet failed to do. In other words, we have an attractive representation of ethics which allows us to view both Western and Indian moral philosophers as importantly engaged in common activity aimed at the same regulative goal: contributing to the construction of an ideally complete moral theory. In this sense, then, there most definitely is Hindu ethics.

Bibliography

Donagan, A. 1977: *The Theory of Morality*. Chicago: University of Chicago Press.

Hiriyanna, M. 1975: *Indian Conception of Values*. Mysore: Kavyalaya Publishers.

Holdrege, B. 1991: "Hindu Ethics" in *A Bibliographic Guide to the Comparative Study of Religious Ethics*, ed. J. Carman and M. Juergensmeyer. New York: Cambridge University Press.

Hopkins, E. W. 1924: *Ethics of India*. New Haven, CT: Yale University Press.

Kagan, S. 1992: "The Structure of Normative Ethics." *Philosophical Perspectives* 6, 223–42.

——1998: *Normative Ethics*. Boulder, CO: Westview Press.

Maitra, S. K. 1956: *The Ethics of the Hindus*, 2nd edn. Calcutta: Calcutta University Press.

Mohanty, J. N. 2000: *Classical Indian Philosophy*. Lanham, MD: Rowman & Littlefield

Perrett, R. W. 1998: *Hindu Ethics: A Philosophical Study*. Honolulu: University of Hawai'i Press.

Ramanujan, A. K. 1989: "Is There an Indian Way of Thinking? An Informal Essay." *Contributions to Indian Sociology* (New Series) 23, 41–58.

Weber, M. 1958: *The Religion of India*. New York: Free Press.

CHAPTER 34
Origins of Hindu Ethics

Anne E. Monius

Focusing on the classical model of the ideal human life as it emerges from the texts of Hinduism's religious elites by the turn of the common era, this chapter examines the origins and fundamentals of Hindu ethics, phrased here as the inquiry into the nature of dharma, a moral, social, and cosmological "order" that lies at the heart of traditional Hindu thinking about the moral life. In the complex of Hindu religious traditions that tend to emphasize orthopraxy over orthodoxy, where "what a Hindu does in relation to his or her social standing and context is far more important than what a Hindu thinks" (Flood 1994: 69), dharma suggests something other than an ethics of general and abstract principle, of rationally derived universal law and application.

The Ritual Beginnings

For those accustomed to the Euro-American discipline of moral philosophy, the effort to understand Hindu ethics begins in an unlikely place: with the sacrificial ritual traditions of the most ancient and authoritative of Hindu texts, the Vedas (see chapter 9). The Vedas, literally texts of "knowledge," combine myth, poetry, and sacrificial injunction. They are complex and voluminous works whose oral composition spans more than a millennium, from the hymns of the Rig Veda, composed perhaps in the second millennium BCE, to the more speculative sections known as the Upaniṣads, datable roughly to the eighth through sixth centuries BCE. Hindu tradition assumes the Vedas to be eternal and authorless (see chapter 7). It refers to the entire textual corpus as śruti, "that which has been heard": truths about the nature of reality received by great sages of a far distant age. Composed in a religious language known as Sanskrit (literally "perfected" language), the Vedas have remained, until the advent of modern Euro-American Indology, the provenance of a class of religious specialists known as the brahmans. Recognition of the supreme authority of the Vedas has served as one of the strongest measures of Hindu identity in the great diversity of Indian religiosity.

The Vedas – and all texts to be considered in this chapter on origins – represent only the perspectives of an elite priestly class. The voices of women, the lowest social classes, and other marginal groups are largely silent until the modern period. Although the full practice of Vedic sacrifice survives only in a few isolated communities in modern India, and generations of non-brahmans and non-Hindus have arisen to challenge the brahmanic model of the ideal human life, the traditions of moral inquiry to be discussed below remain central to all Hindu moral reflection to the present day.

In the Vedic world of *yajña*, "sacrifice," performed by brahmans for their wealthy patrons, dharma, derived from a verbal root meaning "to uphold," significantly occurs most often in the plural. Found more than sixty times in the Rig Veda alone, dharma and its derivatives signal ritual acts properly performed by brahman virtuosos to rejuvenate and reinvigorate universal order. Correctly enacted sacrificial rites are critical to the well-being of the cosmos, for the world is not an independent or objective reality. Universal order is *constructed* by the ritual performance (Halbfass 1988: 314–16). As the "Hymn to the Primeval Man" (Rig Veda X.90) demonstrates, dharmas as rites of sacrifice serve to create and order the entire world, from the heavens above to the very fabric of Hindu society: the social classes or castes, elsewhere termed *varṇas* or "colors":

> The Primeval Man had a thousand heads, a thousand eyes, a thousand feet . . .
> When the gods performed a sacrifice with the Primeval Man as the oblation,
>> spring was the clarified butter, summer the fuel, and autumn the offering . . .
> From that sacrifice, offered entirely, the drops of clarified butter came together;
>> [that] made all the animals: those of the air, those of the forest, and those of
>> the village . . .
> His mouth was the brahman; his arms made the ruler;
>> that which was his thigh was the merchant; the servant was born from his
>> feet . . .
>> With [this] sacrifice, the gods sacrificed to the sacrifice; these were the first
>>> sacrificial acts [dharmas] . . .

As these primordial rites of sacrifice first constitute cosmic order, so, in turn, must the members of the priestly caste maintain that order: "these were the first sacrificial acts [dharmas]" to be enacted again and again by the priestly community.

The vision of the moral life that emerges from the large and complex body of the Vedas is thus highly performative, tied to the structured ritual actions of the sacrifices that fashion and maintain the world. The human being's moral challenge – particularly that of the brahman male – is to conform to one's place in that tightly woven, hierarchical world (see chapter 2). To find one's place and so conform to the obligations and rhythms of the planets, the forces of nature, the world of animals and plants, and the intricate web of society is to participate actively in an aesthetic whole, enacting the sacrifice that both sustains that whole and ties one to a specific position therein. In the Vedic conception of dharma, the "intermeshing of natural and normative is taken for granted" (Chatterjee 1986: 178). The proper ordering of the universe and human society emerges both from the raw stuff of the world itself (the body of the Primeval Man) and from the human ritual activity that shapes and sustains that matter. To be moral, to act rightly, is to realize actively one's place in the ritually constituted cosmos.

The cult of ritual sacrifice dominated by brahman officiants no longer survives apart from a few isolated instances, and perhaps has not existed in any significant way since the demise of royal patronage by powerful medieval Hindu kings. Yet these most ancient views on dharma remain central to later developments in Hindu ethics. In the voluminous Vedic texts that incorporate many centuries of gradual change in practice and thought, dharma also emerges as an important term in the singular. If the plural signifies the multiplicity of ritual acts necessary to constructing and maintaining universal order, the more abstract singular term implies the result of such ritually creative activity, the established norm to which the individual should conform to the best of his ability: the brahman to perform sacrifice; the warrior to rule; the merchant to trade and till the soil; the servant class to labor wherever necessary. While dharma as a "totality of binding norms" (Halbfass 1988: 314) becomes increasingly the focus of ethical inquiry, the creative activity of the ritual is never fully lost in Hindu understandings of the term. Dharma is not a natural law or objective truth but the result of human activities, denoting a "reciprocity" between cosmogony and ethics, human action and natural events (Halbfass 1988: 318). Just as the ritual-performative aspects of Vedic dharma remain constant, so, too, does the notion of multiple dharmas. In the classic model of ideal human behavior discussed below, dharma is constituted by an emphatically plural set of behavioral codes (see chapter 4). While moral order is singular and cosmic, its constituent parts are plural and particular.

An Alternative Vedic Ethics of Withdrawal and Transcendence

Before turning directly to the development of the classic orthodox model of Hindu dharma, brief mention of diversity within the Vedic tradition itself must first be made. There exists within the Vedic corpus, in the latter portions known collectively as the Upaniṣads, a rejection of ritual that will be taken seriously by all brahmanical moral theorists to come. Where this turn from ritual to more philosophical speculation on the nature of reality originates is unclear. Whatever their source, the teachings of the Upaniṣads discard the world of ritual in favor of a new goal: mokṣa, literally "release," an ultimate freedom from a vision of human life in which the soul suffers endless rebirths and redeaths (termed saṃsāra). Mokṣa is to be achieved, according to the Upaniṣads, not by the performance of highly patterned ritual activities, but by withdrawing from the world of ritual, and from the world of human activity in general, to contemplate the true nature of self and world through meditation. "For dangerous are these boats of sacrifice . . . / The foolish who praise [them as] the highest / indeed go again to old age and death" (Muṇḍaka Upaniṣad 1.2.7).

This vision of the human condition mired in the miseries of endless reincarnation demands a reworking of a number of earlier Vedic concepts, stripping them of their original ritual connotations and imbuing each with a new sensibility. One such lexical transformation lies in the redefinition of karma. While karma (from a verb meaning "to do"), in the ritual injunctions of the Vedas, refers to the performance of the ritual act, karma acquires a more abstract, ethicized set of meanings in the Upaniṣads, signaling not just action but the ongoing, cumulative moral fruits of that action across many lifetimes. Reconceived as the ethical repercussions of human deeds, karma guides the human soul through its succession of rebirths: "As one does, as one conducts oneself, thus he becomes . . . One becomes virtuous through virtuous action, wicked by wrong action" (*Bṛhadāraṇyaka Upaniṣad* 4.4.5). Since it is karmic activity that keeps human beings trapped in the realm of rebirth, the path to liberation lies in the complete cessation of all such activity, accompanied by meditative austerities meant to generate the Upaniṣadic equivalent of the heat of the sacrificial fire, *tapas*, an internal "heat" that is powerfully transformative. The quest for liberating knowledge replaces sacrificial ritual as the central activity of human beings. It lies not in the realm of the gods or the heavens, but in the experiential awareness of the underlying ontological unity of the world, expressed in terms of the identity of Self (Ātman) and highest Reality (Brahman).

The moral life is to be found in the pursuit of the knowledge of Brahman and Ātman, superseding the life of ritual performance embraced in other parts of the scriptural corpus. The paradigmatic life of the sage – restrained in activity, detached from sensory participation in the world, meditating on an object of knowledge that lies beyond the human capacities for language and description – embraces an ethics of restraint and austerity. As the *Kaṭha Upaniṣad* (3.3.9) declares:

> Know that the Self is the owner of a chariot, and the body is the chariot itself;
> > know that reason is the charioteer and that mind, indeed, is the reins . . .
> The man whose charioteer is discernment and who reins in his mind,
> > he reaches the end of [his] journey . . .

The Upaniṣadic focus on the individual's quest for liberating knowledge of the ultimate identity of Self and Reality survives in the form envisioned by the ancients no more than do the sacrificial traditions embraced by the more ritually oriented portions of the Vedic corpus. Yet, like the performative ethics described above, this ethics of renunciation and transcendence plays a critical role in all Hindu formulations of the ideal life. It is the intertwining of these two Vedic moral visions – that of ritual activity and that of renunciation – that generates the most powerful and enduring orthodox Hindu model of the ideal human life.

An Ethics of Human Particularity

The two models of human behavior outlined in the Vedas do not remain forever at odds. Among the earliest layers of brahmanic commentary on the Vedas, the *Dharmasūtras*, literally "Short Texts on the Nature of Dharma," focus on the ideal life of the priestly householder, one in which "the ritual, the moral, and the social constitute . . . a continuum" (Olivelle 1999: xxxviii). Citing the ritual injunctions of the Vedas as the primary source of dharma, the *sūtra* literature applies the performance of public rituals to the everyday activities of the brahman householder. While the texts repeatedly sing the praises of the householder, the possibility also exists of living one's life in service to the guru or teacher of Vedic tradition, in forest retreat, or in the state of full renunciation (see Olivelle 1993). There also emerges from the *sūtras* a clear vision of distinct pursuits suitable to human life, the *puruṣārthas* or "goals of man." These include not only dharma or moral behavior but also *artha*, the pursuit of wealth and power, and *kāma*, literally "lust," the pursuit of the pleasures of love and family (later authors will add *mokṣa* as a fourth and final goal of human life).

The *sūtra* literature expresses a vision of the moral life firmly rooted in the brahman householder's ritual activities directed toward the gods, the ancestors, and the cosmos writ large. Yet here dharma also begins to grow into a vision of the moral life that is both performative and intentional, an ethic of worldly works and inner cultivation of a particular frame of mind and heart. Dharma implies not only ritual propriety, but also morality in a wider sense, the cultivation of virtues deemed generally beneficial.

The older Vedic notion of rites done for worldly – or even universal – gain is super-seded in the *sūtras* by a focus on cultivating proper intention, proper frame of mind, while at work in the world as a brahman householder. As Āpastamba notes, "Let him not follow the Laws for the sake of worldly benefits, for then the Laws produce no fruit at harvest time" (1.20.1–2, in Olivelle 1999: 31). While dharma remains rooted in the ultimate authority of the Vedas, Āpastamba and other *sūtra* authors also cite com-mentaries on the Vedas (*smṛti*, literally "that which is remembered"), the conduct of those learned in the Vedas, and accepted custom. The uncertainty of dharma, the dif-ficulties in determining the proper path of conduct for the brahman male householder amid the messiness of human life, obviously weigh heavily on the minds of the *sūtra* authors as each struggles to discern a wider system of human ethics amid a contested array of opinions and customs.

These *sūtra* themes are consolidated and elaborated upon in the large body of impor-tant texts known as *Dharmaśāstras*, extended treatises on the nature of moral life. The most important of these in Hindu history is the *Manusmṛti* or *Mānavadharmaśāstra*, often translated into English as "The Laws of Manu" (Doniger and Smith 1991). Manu attempts to claim a certain universality absent in the individual *sūtras* that remain tied to specific Vedic schools and to expand the themes outlined above to include not only rules of conduct (*ācāra*) and expiatory rites (*prāyaścitta*) but the administration of law, both criminal and civil (*vyavahāra*). Attributed to a figure, Manu, about whom nothing is known, and datable roughly to the turn of the common era or earlier (Doniger and Smith 1991: xvii), the Laws of Manu are comprised of 2,685 Sanskrit metrical verses, composed by and for the members of the brahman priestly elite. The focus of the text lies in constructing an all-encompassing model for human moral behavior: *varṇāśra-madharma*, literally an "ethics of life stage and social caste," a moral vision based on innate differences among human beings. Beginning with large metaphysical claims about the authority of his vision of dharma, Manu then focuses on the specific duties and obligations of the three upper or "twice-born" castes, with occasional references to lower social groups, including women. Particular attention is paid to the conduct-ing of life-cycle rituals known as the *saṃskāras*, rites of transformation meant to create and shape the moral human being. The four life choices of the male Brahmin found in the *sūtra* literature, now significantly rearranged as successive life "stages" (*āśrama*), organize the central portion of the text. Manu then moves on to discuss the duties of kings and the administration of justice.

The Laws of Manu consist of long and often mind-numbing lists of prohibitions and exhortations to eat certain foods, mix with certain people, and avoid all others. Such lists, to the modern Western eye, seem random, confusing, and completely confining. Consider, for example, what Manu has to say about urination:

> He should not urinate on a path, on ashes, in a cowshed, on ploughed [land],
>> in water, on a funeral pyre, and not on a mountain . . .
> He should never discharge urine or feces
>> while facing the wind, fire, a priest, the sun, or water . . .
> In the daytime he should discharge urine and feces facing north,
>> at night facing south, and during morning and evening twilight as during the
>> day.
> [Urination] on fire, at the sun, or at the moon . . . destroys [one's] intelligence (4.45–52)

Despite such impossible lists of rules, the Laws of Manu also betray a quintessentially realistic view of human fallibility. In the context above, Manu recognizes that one cannot always control the circumstances of nature's call. As in nearly every situation, he provides an escape clause of sorts, a statement about the possibilities of violating all the carefully articulated laws "in extremity" (*āpad*): "The twice-born [male], when fearing injury, should do it facing whichever way, / whether it be in shade or darkness, at night or during the day" (4.51). Manu also builds on the rites of expiation outlined in the earlier *Dharmasūtra* literature, allowing for the ritual correction of any mistakes.

Keeping in mind these escape clauses of expiatory rite and extremity, we now turn to the central focus of Manu's work. The model of *varṇāśramadharma*, the morality of social class and life-stage, brings together those two competing Vedic visions of morality: the life of active ritual participation in, no less construction of, the world and that of complete renunciation of ritual and society. The model of *varṇāśramadharma* rests on the assumption of qualitative human difference, of particularities of substance, space, time, and circumstance. In Manu's world of class and life-stage, there can be no concept of universal human nature or rights; Manu refers repeatedly to the innate tendencies and activities of each social class. The hallmark of social and moral order for Manu lies in the ever-vigilant separation of distinct groups of people and earthly things. There is a general appreciation in the *Laws of Manu* for universal values such as non-injury to living beings (*ahiṃsā*): "non-injury, truth, not stealing, purity, and control of the senses . . . is the concise dharma of the four classes" (10.63). Yet the substance of ethical discussion focuses on the particular duties of those specifically located in the social and universal order. Dharma is sensitive to context: "to be moral, for Manu, is to particularize" (Ramanujan 1989: 45).

The particularities of human nature, as well as the moral codes of behavior that govern each, are arranged not horizontally in the dharma of caste and life-stage, but vertically. In this text written by and for brahman priests, the brahmans enjoy the pre-eminent position over the warrior, the merchant, and the servant. This hierarchy of particularity and the separation among peoples and things is marked in Manu by what he terms "purity" (*śuddha*) and "impurity" or "pollution" (*aśuddha*). These are almost substantive qualities that are contagious, transmitted through contact or close proximity. All things in the world possess a purity factor that is both fixed and relative. Brahmans are pure, warriors less so, merchants even less so. Yet what is polluting for the brahman – a particular food, contact with a particular person – might be quite purifying for the lowly servant. The priestly caste's presence at the apex of the social order is due to its collective purity. The bulk of Manu's text aims to maintain that very purity from the polluting dangers of the world and of other social classes that surround the brahman. Purity is not an entirely natural state, however. It is carefully constructed and maintained through a lifetime of ritual observances. The brahman's capacity for purification rests in Manu's cosmogony, in the fact that priests issue forth from the mouth, the purest part of the Primeval Man who gave birth to the universe (1.92–94). Manu's rites of expiation are essentially rites of purification, cleansing the self of moral "dirt" accrued through contact with the substantively/ethically "unclean."

Yet this ethics of particularity, of difference and hierarchy, does not necessarily imply inter-class hatred or distrust. Manu's treatment of women is a good case in point. On the one hand, women of any class are dangerously impure and polluting, largely because their bodies are prone to excreting more polluting liquids than their male counterparts. Women are also dangerous to the brahman male in search of sensual restraint. Due to the dangers they pose to men seeking lives of self-control, women must never be allowed independence of thought or circumstance: "[Her] father protects [her] in childhood; [her] husband protects [her] in youth; / and [her] son protects [her] in old age" (9.3). Yet, for all the sexual dangers women pose, the horrifying impurity of their menses and the bodily excretions of childbirth, Manu is also constant in his exhortations to respect and honor women for their invaluable place in the order of the world. Although women are barred from Vedic recitation, for example, their presence is deemed critical to the success of any ritual performance: "Where women are honored, there the gods rejoice; / but where they are not honored, there all rituals are without fruit" (3.56).

In addition to the particularities of substance that govern the dharma of *varṇa* or social class, dharma is also shaped by qualities of time. In the largest, most universal of senses, the Hindu cosmos endlessly cycles through four great ages that tend toward moral entropy. In the first, dharma as order both moral and cosmic stands complete; *adharma*, disorder, is entirely unknown. Through each successive stage, dharma grows increasingly diminished (Manu 1.79–86). The dharmic duties of men are different in each age, and human beings now live in the most morally decrepit of eras, when perfect morality, perfect sacrifice, perfect anything is utterly impossible. Not only is dharma difficult to discern, but, even when located in this most amoral and blackest of cosmic eras, it can be but partially revealed.

The individual – at least of the three upper or "twice-born" classes – is also subject to temporal particularity. The stages of one's life demand that different moral codes be followed. In a brilliant interpretive move that weaves together the world-embracing and world-renouncing strands of Vedic thought, Manu presents the ideal human life as one of four discrete stages or *āśramas*. An upper-class male's life ideally begins with the stage of celibate studenthood, serving his teacher while learning the Vedic texts and traditions of ritual performance. Following mastery of the Vedas, the student ritually departs from his teacher, marries, and enters into what remains for Manu the most important of the life-stages. The householder actively performs Vedic rites and meets his three debts to the Vedic sages, the deities, and the ancestors. In the life of the brahman householder, one pursues the first three of the human goals: dharma, power, and sensual happiness. This emphasis on the life of the actively engaged householder, accounting for the bulk of Manu's text, implies a moral vision focused not only on acting correctly but also on living well, in the bosom of family, prosperity, and meaningful daily activity.

After the priestly householder has fulfilled his ritual and reproductive debts to ancestors, gods, and sages, he may turn over all his property to his sons and retreat from the world. There, "alone, he should contemplate continually in solitude on what is beneficial to the Self; / for alone, [so] contemplating, he approaches the highest good" (Manu 4.258). By making the life of ritual dharma a prerequisite for pursuit of the fourth human goal of ultimate liberation, Manu incorporates the Upaniṣadic quest for mokṣa into the final two stages of human life: the forest-dweller who gradually withdraws from society and severs all social ties, and the full renunciant who single-mindedly pursues self-knowledge. By realizing the ultimate identity of Self and Reality, Manu writes, "he who sees the Self in all living beings through the Self / achieves equanimity toward all and approaches Reality, the highest step" (12.125). The call for the householder to engage actively in his world, maintaining the course of the planets and the order of society through ritual performance, becomes repugnant to the man who seeks release in the final stages of his life. The dharma of a single man at one point in his life utterly contradicts his dharma at another.

Manu's incorporation of the Upaniṣadic call to reject the life of ritual activity that earlier portions of the Vedas enjoin does not stop with his arrangement of the āśramas or life stages. The Laws of Manu also use the Upaniṣadic language of tapas or "inner heat" generated by self-restraint and austerities to describe the attitude with which a priestly householder ought to approach Vedic recitation and rite. An ethic of self-restraint and sensory control should guide the priestly householder, long before he heads for the forest in search of spiritual liberation. Inner heat, sustained through single-minded focus upon the Vedas, ensures both the success of the rites and placement on the path to liberation.

While the Laws of Manu attend consistently to the karmic principles of future reward or debt based on the moral seeds sown in this life, emphasis is repeatedly placed on the cultivation of proper moral attitude while carrying out the behaviors appropriate to one's particular place in space and time. The necessity of seeking to do what is right – even if failing to fulfill each and every rule of conduct – seems, in fact, to govern much of what Manu has to say about dharma. The virtues of self-restraint, sensory control, and concern for the well-being of others constitute the good intentions necessary for the life of ritual and meditative contemplation to bear its desired fruit. In a cosmic age in which dharma is broken, the intention to act according to social position and life-stage serves as a moral compass point by which all behavior should be guided.

According to Manu's model of *varṇāśramadharma* and its ethics of particularity, the moral life lies first of all in realizing the specifics of one's existence in terms of social class and life-stage and of the innate capabilities and tendencies that each implies, as well as one's place vis-à-vis specific qualities of space and time. One must act in accordance with moral and cosmic order, pursuing and preserving a state of purity as far as is humanly possible, performing rituals if one is a priest, ruling wisely if one is a king, and so on. Yet this "acting in accordance" is difficult to determine, much less maintain, in the face of ever-changing human and natural circumstances. The measure of a man's moral aptitude lies in his ability to maneuver productively in the complex web of human relationships that constitute the social order and in the ever-changing facets of the cosmos that constitute the universal order. In the often tangled mess that is human life, the struggle lies in meeting the demands of one's own position, rather than attempting to live according to another's (Manu 10.97). Important throughout is the cultivation of moral intention. Most significant is the intention to act in preservation of the social/human order, for even dharma remains subservient to preserving the intricate web of relations that constitute human society: "[one should abandon] even dharma if it ends in unhappiness and causes people anger" (Manu 4.176). This ethics of particularity is, on the one hand, fixed. The brahman priest should not do the work of the servant, at least not while the sun is shining, peace reigns in the land, and there exists no circumstance in extremity. On the other hand, it is also thoroughly relational, thoroughly flexible, speaking to the particularities of space, time, and specific context. When those particularities are not clear, one must, at the very least, intend to do that which conforms to the overall cosmic, social, and moral order.

The Standard Moral Vision

Since the Laws of Manu assume such a humble assessment of human capabilities, providing so many escape clauses of exception and extreme possibility, the question must be raised as to whether or not the text is actually meant to be read as prescriptive code. Why provide such lengthy and confining rules of behavior if, in fact, intention is what really matters? Why does Manu acknowledge that no one can actually live fully in accordance with his moral vision? For all their length and tediousness, Manu's lists simply do not cover all possible human situations on any single topic. What, for example, counts as "in extremity"? What if a man truly believes his life to be in danger, but realizes only after urinating in an inappropriate place that he mistook a menacing shadow for a homicidal maniac? Must he do an expiatory rite to cleanse himself? The text's many nods to the sheer impossibility of living up to the exact letter of the law perhaps suggest that Manu is not meant to be read as prescriptive code. Rather, it is a study in pattern, in conditioning the brahman student to see the world in a certain way: as a universe defined by innate human differences, as a cosmos in which the substance of those differences is easily transferred and must be avoided, a world in which every activity, particularly the performance of Vedic rites, must be done by the proper persons in accordance with the proper alignment of the planets, in the proper season, and at the proper time of day. For while the Vedas may serve as the ultimate source of the moral life for Manu, dharma can also be learned from the lowest of people, including women, children, and servants (2.239). Rather than creating a literal code to be enforced by the letter, Manu throughout suggests a spirit of the law in which one trains oneself to see the patterns of moral order in the world. One is to realize the webs of connection among people and cosmos and to act accordingly, even in extremity. Less precepts to be memorized than intricate series of patterns and relationships to be internalized, Manu's text envisions a morally mature human being who ultimately requires no behavioral code to feel the fragile moral order that surrounds him and to respond to life, appropriately and creatively, in order to sustain that order.

Resources for Challenge and Change

Manu's model of *varṇāśramadharma*, with its focus on human situatedness, rapidly becomes the standard moral vision for upper-caste orthodox Hinduism. In this model of the ideal human life tightly woven into the fabric of a cosmic order perpetuated by the ritual performances of a priestly class, there would seem to be little tolerance for challenge or change from within. Those who arise to question or undermine this vision hail primarily from castes other than the brahman: the Buddha and Jina Mahāvīra, for example, both remembered by their respective communities as members of the warrior or ruling caste; the epic *Mahābhārata*, whose warrior-oriented ethos challenges at every turn the efficacy of Vedic ritualism in the current cosmic age of moral darkness; and the saints of the *bhakti* or devotional traditions, many from among the lowest social classes, whose poetry reorients the moral cosmos around a personal and loving deity who demands but single-minded devotion from his followers.

Even the devotional orientation of the great medieval saints – that so clearly attempts to steer human activity away from both ritual performance and Manu's commitment to human particularity toward an ideal life of selfless devotion and service – bears witness to the enduring influence of the classical *varṇāśramadharma* model. The exemplary lives of the great north Indian saints both champion love for the lord and its attendant virtues and "accomplish . . . the ends of dharma" (Hawley 1987: 69). Dharma, even Manu's model of caste and life-stage, is "not ultimately abandoned but transformed" (68). In overturning brahmanic norms, the narratives of Hindu devotional hagiography are stories of everything turning out all right in the end, of kings acting royally, of merchants engaging prosperously in business, of brahmans performing their rituals. Yet all of this is accomplished with new or transformed intentions focused on serving a personal and accessible lord. Indeed, the very rite at the heart of Hindu devotional life – *pūjā*, ritual offerings to an image of the deity – "simultaneously replaces the *yajña* while it incorporates within itself many rites from the Vedic sacrifice" (Smith 1998: 214). From the eschewing of purity as a moral ideal by the medieval practitioners of tantra and the championing of a single intention of worth (love for a personal lord) by the great poet-saints, to the political activism of the lowest social classes in modern India, *varṇāśramadharma* – embraced, despised, or modified – provides the cornerstone for all subsequent Hindu thinking about the nature of the moral life.

Bibliography

Bandhu, V. (ed.) 1965: *Ṛgveda with the Padapāṭha and the Available Portions of the Bhāṣyas by Skandasvamin and Udgītha, the Vyākhyā by Veṅkaṭa-Mādhava and Mudgala's Vṛtti Based on Sāyaṇabhāṣya*. V. V. Research Institute Publication, No. 353, Vol. 7. Hoshiarpur: Vishveshvaranand Vedic Research Institute.

Chatterjee, M. 1986: "The Concept of Dharma" in *Facts and Values: Philosophical Reflections from Western and Non-Western Perspectives*, ed. M. C. Doeser and J. N. Kraay, 177–87. Boston, MA: Martinus Nijhoff.

Doniger, W. (trans.) 1981: *The Rig Veda: An Anthology*. New York: Penguin Books.

Doniger, W. and Smith, B. K. (trans.) 1991: *The Laws of Manu*. New York: Penguin Books.

Dumont, L. 1980: *Homo Hierarchicus: The Caste System and Its Implications*. Chicago: University of Chicago Press.

Flood, G. D. 1994: "Hinduism" in *Making Moral Decisions*, ed. J. Holm with J. Bowker, 68–94. New York: Pinter.

Halbfass, W. (ed.) 1988: *India and Europe: An Essay in Understanding*. Albany: State University of New York Press.

Hawley, J. S. 1987: "Morality Beyond Morality in the Lives of Three Hindu Saints" in *Saints and Virtues*, ed. J. S. Hawley, 51–72. Berkeley: University of California Press.

Holdrege, B. A. 1991: "Hindu Ethics" in *A Bibliographic Guide to the Comparative Study of Ethics*, ed. J. Carman and M. Jeurgensmeyer, 12–69. New York: Cambridge University Press.

Kunhan Raja, C. (ed.) 1984 [1935–6]: *Daśopaniṣads with the Commentary of Śrī Upaniṣadbrahmayogin*, Vol. 2, revd. A. A. Ramanathan. Adyar Library Series, No. 15. Adyar, Madras: Adyar Library and Research Centre.

Manu 1887: *Mānava Dharma-śāstra: The Code of Manu*, ed. J. Jolly. London: Trübner.

Olivelle, P. 1993: *The Āśrama System: The History and Hermeneutics of a Religious Institution*. New York: Oxford University Press.

——(trans.) 1996: *The Upaniṣads*. New York: Oxford University Press.

——(trans.) 1999: *Dharmasūtras: The Law Codes of Āpastamba, Gautama, Baudhāyana, and Vasiṣṭha*. New York: Oxford University Press.

Perrett, R. W. 1998: *Hindu Ethics: A Philosophical Study*. Society for Asian and Comparative Philosophy, Monograph 17. Honolulu: University of Hawai'i Press.

Ramanujan, A. K. 1989: "Is There an Indian Way of Thinking? An Informal Essay." *Contributions to Indian Sociology* 23 (1), 41–58.

Smith, B. K. 1998: *Reflections on Resemblance, Ritual, and Religion*. Delhi: Motilal Banarsidass.

CHAPTER 35

Differentiations in Hindu Ethics

Maria Heim

In its three millennia of recorded history, South Asian civilization has produced diverse traditions of ethical reflection. Perhaps more than the other world religions considered in this volume, Hinduism presents a rich plurality of moral and religious systems. Hinduism itself can hardly be said to be a single religion. The term "Hinduism" embraces several interlocking yet distinctive religions. These in turn have developed divergent responses to questions of human nature and the moral life. In addition, dialogue with non-Hindu traditions, in premodern times Buddhism and Jainism, and, more recently, Islam and the modern West, has stimulated Hindu modes of moral discourse and their range of concerns. An accurate portrait of Hindu ethics, then, keeps the complexity and divergences ever in view, even while it delineates patterns and continuities where they emerge.

Indians did not devote a single branch of philosophical thought to what is called ethics. Instead, they incorporated moral considerations into various philosophical, literary, and theological genres in Sanskrit and the vernaculars. The chief sources of moral reflection from the Sanskrit intellectual traditions are brahmanical, that is, texts composed by and reflecting the ideologies of, the elite classes of literati learned in Sanskrit and in Vedic revelation. Of particular importance for morality is a branch of prescriptive brahmanical knowledge called Dharmaśāstra. Hindus have also employed literature – folktales, epic narratives, and poetry – to pose moral inquiry and as itself a means to stimulate moral response. Narratives create a shared moral past and cultural terrain. They explore the morality of social obligation, not through rules and categories like Dharmaśāstra discourse, but through life stories of particular epic figures. In addition, Indian literati have much to offer on how they understand literature's capacity for stimulating the moral imagination. Finally, religious treatises which seek soteriological aims through either renunciation or theistic devotion offer a range of perspectives on the relationship between spiritual attainments and moral duty. This chapter explores these diverse forms of moral discourse found in the Indian context.

Normative Discourse

At one time far distant in human memory the natural and moral order (dharma) of the world stood firmly and securely like a bull planted on four legs (see chapter 13). Over time, as the gradual decadence and decay in the cosmic order set in, dharma was reduced to standing on three legs, and then, precariously, on two. We now find ourselves in an era, called the Dark Age, where dharma teeters on one leg only and threatens to topple.

Dharma

These vast cosmic eras in which dharma is brought down foot by foot provide the backdrop for the drama of human moral activity and reflection. Moral activity becomes rarer and more difficult to accomplish, yet ever more urgent and necessary to sustain and uphold the cosmic order. Moral reflection is oriented towards the past; moral knowledge was established and complete in previous eras and so moral inquiry takes the form of preservation and recovery of that distant knowledge.

Since dharma is a natural order, sources whereby humans come to know about it, and thus learn to reflect upon how human beings should act, do not necessarily include reason. Dharma is not described as the *rational* ordering of human or natural affairs, but rather simply as the way things are. While reason is not denigrated as a useful tool for intellectual work in this tradition, it is preempted by the authority of revelation and memory as sources for learning about dharma. Revelation and memory are vested in the textual tradition, in particular, in a genre of textual knowledge known as *śāstra*. *Śāstra*, according to the eighth-century Mīmāṃsā theorist, Kumārilabhaṭṭa, is "that which teaches people what they should and should not do" (see Pollock 1985: 501). Broadly conceived, *śāstra* includes revelation (the Vedas) and recollections and inferences, derived from revelation, about human conduct. *Śāstras* codify nearly every branch of learning and human practice, from the mores of statecraft to the regulations of ritual activity. The *śāstra* that concerns moral behavior is called Dharmaśāstra.

While Dharmaśāstra articulates the rules and customs governing human social conventions, including law and religious practices, our concern is the category that regulates moral behavior (*ācāra*). The term *ācāra* means right conduct, customs, and conventions. The conflation of custom or convention with moral practice is consistent with the tradition's orientation to the past as a source of moral guidance. Customs are conservative and are thought to enshrine practices established when dharma was more secure in the world. One knows correct *ācāra* by three sources, in descending order of authority: revelation, texts composed by the learned who have inferred what is not explicitly stated in revelation, and the practices of learned people (see chapter 7). The best guides for right behavior are passed down from previous generations and the correct customs carry weight in large part because of their antiquity. Sometimes personal conscience is admitted as a further source of dharma, though it carries the least authority (Manu 2.6). Reason does not secure moral guidance except when it is employed to discern what to do when moral codes in the ancient texts appear to conflict.

Just as dharma is not evenly spread out over time, it also varies from place to place. Hindus are sensitive to the geography of moral difference. Morality's close link to custom, and the variation of local customs, suggest both tolerance for differentiation as well as classifying and ranking places, customs, and peoples. Traditionally, the heartland of India, between the Himalayas and the Vindhya mountains "where the black antelope ranges by nature," is the country in which dharma is most fully established. One should endeavor to live there (Manu 2.21–3).

Dharma's structural unevenness in space and time resists the application of categorical or universal laws. That is not to say that there are no attempts to delineate general duties or virtues common to all good people. Rather, it means that most normative deliberations on dharma are highly particularist in forming principles or regulations for behavior. While modern Western ethical systems often presume and emphasize human sameness and equality as the very foundations for ethical reasoning and justice, the brahmanical traditions assume that what is morally relevant about human beings resides in their differences. Human beings differ from one another in a variety of ways, most of which are considered relevant for understanding their moral responsibilities. Since no single homogenous moral subject is presumed, establishing moral codes is not conceived to be a quest for universal principles or laws to govern human behavior in all times and all places (see chapters 1 and 3).

In what ways are human beings different from one another? How are these differences morally relevant? Human beings vary with regard to their locations within the social order. Since the social order is highly differentiated, moral obligations are also highly differentiated, contextual, and particularized. Since morality is not easily separated from social structure, moral obligations coincide with the fulfillment of social roles and expectations. Moreover, the social structure is conceived to be just, with one's place within the hierarchy determined by previous moral actions via the mechanisms of karma. All moral actions have consequences that will be reaped in either this life or a future life, determining one's future condition. Not only does past moral action determine one's location in the social order, but also where one fits determines a large part of present moral obligation. As a result, brahmanical moral discourse aims to establish the nature of different human social roles and the duties incumbent upon them with regard to their place in the natural order of things.

Nevertheless, sometimes lists are formulated to name virtues of common appeal that can cut across human difference. The Dharmaśāstra authority Yājñavalkya lists nine duties common to all: non-violence, truth, refraining from theft, purity, control of senses, generosity, self-control, compassion, and patience (1.122). Manu says that non-violence, honesty, abjuring theft, purification, and restraint of the senses are the duties shared in common by all social classes (10.63). In the third century BCE the great emperor King Aśoka inscribed in stone throughout his empire these universal virtues: compassion, liberality, truth, purity, gentleness, peace, joyousness, saintliness, and self-control (Kane 1974 V: 10). The *Mahābhārata* also lists freedom from anger, truthfulness, sharing one's wealth, forbearance, procreation only with one's own wife, purity, absence of enmity, straight-forwardness, and maintaining one's dependents (12.60 in Roy 1955: 134–5).

Apart from such general attempts to describe virtues with widespread application, the bulk of this discourse recognizes that dharma "has many doors" and is concerned with specific duties and obligations for the different classes in society (*Mahābhārata* 12.174 in Roy 1955: 1). To encapsulate the range of duties of the social body composed of individuals in different roles, brahmanical authors articulated the ideological system of *varṇāśramadharma*, the duties of social class and stage of life. Each social class – the elite priestly class (brahman), kings and warriors (*kṣatriya*), commoners (*vaiśya*), and servants (*śūdra*) – has particular duties prescribed for it, specific to its function and stature in the social order. In addition, the course of human life is regulated by duties prescribed for each stage of it: studentship, householder life, retirement, and final renunciation. Distinctions between the sexes are also significant. The *śāstras* generally assume a male moral subject and delineate a special class of duties enjoined for women (*strīdharma*).

This tidy conception of the ideal social body was conceived and glorified by brahmanical elites as the proper way for human beings to uphold the natural order of dharma. The dharma of social class and stage of life provides each individual with his or her own duties (*svadharma*). Morality resides in conforming to the mandates of one's station and function in the social body. This is not an ideology that prizes social mobility or individual autonomy. Straying from one's own duties (*svadharma*) is censured. Brahmanical ideology depicts a moral agent that is not autonomous and unmediated by social norms, but rather is constituted by them.

Despite the śāstric impulse to regulate nearly every aspect of human activity, there remains within Dharmaśāstra ideology a nod to local custom and difference. This results in a curious blend of authoritarianism and flexibility. The Dharmaśāstra writers are sometimes inclined to recognize and even defer to the law of the land or the family, enjoining adherence to family or local customs where śāstric norms conflict or when their application is unclear. An early Dharmasūtra author, Āpastamba, acknowledges the weight of local custom, which is often known and preserved best by the women in the family. He prescribes that in some cases people should understand from women what laws to follow (2.15.9; 2.29.11, 15, in Olivelle 1999: 59, 72–3).

Although some Dharmaśāstric discourse prescribes social rules and customs with little apparent critique and reflection, there are topics and treatises within this genre that evince second order reflection on moral behavior. Such discourses do not merely pattern moral behavior. They stand back from prescribed social practices and theorize them. One example is the development of Dharmaśāstra attention to the ethics of giving (*dāna*), a social practice that comes to be highly articulated and systematized in the medieval commentaries and compendia (*dāna-nibandhas*). These comprise extensive books given over to the rules and values of gift giving, with sustained scrutiny of the virtues and qualities of the donor and the recipient, and the etiquette of the face-to-face hospitality encounter. In some of their discussions, the authors shift from expounding duties to analyzing motivations and intentions. In these discourses, the authors set forth their social practices as objects for reflection and analysis.

That giving should come to be a chief category of moral investigation is entirely consistent with the advance of the Dark Age. In each of the four eras of time, a single duty is emphasized: in the first eon of perfection humans practiced *meditation* as the highest virtue, followed by the pursuit of *knowledge* in the next eon, then *sacrifice*, and now, in the last age, *gift giving*. It is significant that in the last and most decadent time we turn to social relationships and exchanges, rather than individual religious pursuits, to preserve what remains of the moral order in the world.

Human nature

The mandates of *svadharma* – one's own particular duty – though binding in terms of the constraints of gender, social class, and age, are not conceived to be arbitrarily imposed from without. Through karma one is born into a station of life to which one is by nature suited. Previous action, or karma, not only creates consequences and effects that will be experienced in future lives, but it also determines one's present character. It is not only the conditions in which moral subjects act that are highly particularist and differentiated, but also human nature itself. No one enters the world as a "blank slate"; the character of one's present nature is the result of activities performed and dispositions developed in previous births.

While many of the earliest Vedic ritual texts and later Mīmāṃsā expositions of them were concerned less with internal disposition than with correct external ritual form, the Upaniṣads turned to questions of character in their interpretation of the workings of karma. Here, karma is not simply ritual action resulting in future benefit, but rather moral activity that conditions one's future nature. The logic of action and rebirth is that "like produces like," as the following passage suggests:

> Now, people here whose behavior is pleasant can expect to enter a pleasant womb, like that of a woman of the Brahmin, the Kṣatriya, or the Vaiśya class. But people of foul behavior can expect to enter a foul womb, like that of a dog, a pig, or an outcaste woman. (*Chāndogya Upaniṣad* 5.10.7, in Olivelle 1996: 142)

Injunctions that require one to perform one's own duty rather than another's appeal not only to the dictates of maintaining social order with everyone in his or her place. They also appeal to convictions about the formation of human nature and character across births.

Hindu thinkers have much to contribute to reflections about how moral and ritual activity is related to internal disposition (see chapter 9). For some, moral action is generated out of human nature or disposition. The *Mahābhārata* says "all propensities for action that exist in the universe may be seen to flow from the very natures of the creatures (to which they inhere)" (12.179, in Roy 1955: 16). One ancient schema for classifying human nature depicts three psychic and moral conditions which drive all activity in the material world. These qualities are *sattva* (goodness, purity, brightness, intelligence), *rajas* (passion, lust, anger, activity), and *tamas* (darkness, inertia, gloom, ignorance). Each is present in everything and everyone, but in different and changing proportions. Human beings can be characterized by which of these three qualities predominates in their characters and actions. The elements that make up moral disposition and character are deeply rooted yet constantly changing and developing. The means of developing correct moral behavior is cultivating certain internal states and natures (see chapter 4).

In other conceptions quite the reverse is true. Action is considered to be prior to character and human nature. Sometimes moral behavior is simply conflated with conformity to rules and any internal dimension in correct behavior is irrelevant. A Mīmāṃsā definition of dharma is simply "rule-boundedness" (*PūrMīmSū*.1.1.2, in Pollock 1985: 511). Concerned with external form, much Mīmāṃsā ritual discourse prescribes the following of rules rather than the development of virtue. In this view, dharma is exhaustively described by human activity, without reference to character or disposition.

Other reflections on ritual practice see external adherence to rules as conducive to the development of inner virtue. Theories of karma assume that human nature is pliable and unfixed. One is always in a state of becoming rather than being, and action itself generates disposition. Theoretical reflections on the ritual sacraments or *saṃskāras* (life-cycle rites such as birth ceremonies, investiture with the sacred thread, marriage rites, etc.) are a further instance where external ritual is thought to cultivate internal transformation. The *saṃskāras* are said to be actions and rites which "impart fitness." Fitness arises from the removal of moral taints and by the generation of new virtues (Śabara's commentary on Jaimini III.1.3 in Kane 1974 V: 190–1). Bringing a person into fitness or eligibility is a moral transformation. The more advanced *saṃskāras* introduce a person to new relationships with self and others, with new responsibilities and statuses. Additionally, the *saṃskāras* are thought to be external actions that leave an imprint or trace on the memory and personality that develops character and disposition. Here, *saṃskāra*, like karma, is conceived to be external action that molds internal moral character through patterning and habit. This movement from the gross to the subtle finds expression in multiple traditions of Indian thought. Purification and self-mastery often begin with bodily actions and advance to inner and subjective states once the outer forms are disciplined.

The Contributions of Narrative

Where Hindus have used Dharmaśāstra texts to delineate the ideal moral life framed within the context of given social roles, they have often turned to literature to test and challenge the limits of such roles. The great epics of India, the *Mahābhārata* and the *Rāmāyaṇa*, study social and political life within embedded contexts of collective memory and history. In an intriguing way they reaffirm brahmanical norms while providing the contexts and opportunities for critiquing them.

The *Mahābhārata* presents itself as the story that tells all stories and all that can be known: "what is found here may be found somewhere else, but what is not found here is found nowhere" (1.56.34, in van Buitenen 1973 I: xxiii). Indeed, the sheer bulk of the text gives initial credence to this assertion. The *Mahābhārata* is perhaps the longest book from the ancient world, and its contents range considerably beyond its frame story concerning the ancient dynasty of the Bhāratas. The epic tells the story of the great fratricidal war between the Pāṇḍavas and the Kauravas. Along the way it also incorporates other stories, as well as entire books given over to moral, philosophical, and religious instruction, including the Bhagavad Gītā and long chapters on Dharmaśāstra.

The claim that the text exhaustively describes what human beings can know is more than a statement about its length and comprehensiveness. It is also a claim that sees in these stories and in the instruction given by its characters an inheritance, a repository of cultural memory and precedent. The epics furnish the historical memory that situates Hindus in the world and provides an awareness of themselves as moral agents against a moral background. The epics provide a moral compass by showing where others have walked before, and suggest a further instance of deriving a moral present from the memory of a moral past. Describing itself as "brimming with wisdom" (1.2.33, in van Buitenen 1973 I: 33), the *Mahābhārata* says "no story is found on earth that does not rest on this epic – nobody endures without living off its food" (1.2.240, in van Buitenen 1973 I: 43). This story to end all stories is the very nourishment of human endurance.

At the same time, the text's claim to its own exhaustiveness of knowledge is authoritarian, refusing to allow outside critique, reason, or new knowledge to enter into the great questions and answers it raises about the human condition. Such an assertion, like other brahmanical claims to all-encompassing authority, elevates the text's own status and import in the world by its claims to completing what can be known. Despite the potential of narrative to explore moral dilemmas in greater complexity than normative discourse, the epics still anchor moral knowledge on events and norms from the past.

Within its own parameters, however, the *Mahābhārata* does provide the resources to critique nearly every social norm and value it considers. It depicts a cast of heroes, who, in the critical moments of the epic, are faced with moral conundrums where duties conflict and the right course is unclear. Such moments portray widely held cultural presuppositions as well as conscious moral choices. Dharma is tested at every turn. The apocalyptic ending of the epic in which the Pāṇḍava brothers are victorious, but nearly the entire world has been destroyed in battle, preserves the tensions in righteous victory to the very end.

Perhaps nowhere are the ambiguities regarding social roles more perplexing than in the tragic circumstances concerning the figure of Karṇa. The elder brother of the Pāṇḍavas, Karṇa is conceived out of wedlock and abandoned at birth, and is thus deprived of his noble status and kinship. He befriends and allies himself with the Pāṇḍavas' enemy, Duryodhana, who fights an arrogant, unrighteous, and ultimately unsuccessful war at great cost to all involved. Even upon learning of his true birth, Karṇa rejects the social status of which he was originally deprived and refuses to join the Pāṇḍavas. He honors the genuine and constant bonds of affection and loyalty offered to him by his low caste adopted family and Duryodhana. He is aware he will ultimately battle his brothers and fail. His death is the result of a dishonorable breach in the rules of warfare, when he is struck by Arjuna while unarmed. Though he is not entirely blameless, Karṇa is nevertheless a deeply sympathetic character. He has been wronged by strict social codes that privilege status and birth. His character posits an ethics of friendship that may slip past the grasp of the social roles and rules of dharma.

Of equal importance as this literature's capacity to pose and wrestle with moral dilemmas is its capacity to refine and cultivate those who come to know it in ways that are morally significant. The epics describe how knowledge of them creates moral agency. By incorporating the very telling of its story into the narrative as the bard Vaiśaṃpāyana, prompted and queried by Janamejaya, relates the tale, we learn the effect of the story on the reader. Janamejaya repeatedly pleads for more of the story to unfold, for he "cannot hear enough of the great deeds of the ancient" (1.56.4, in van Buitenen 1973 I: 129). He interrogates the bard on the intricacies of dharma. Moreover, the text specifies the nature of the audience's reaction to the story: "sons become obedient and servants compliant, the evil done with body, words, or thought vanishes at once for a man who listens to it . . . if a man in his ignorance chances to do evil in his day, it will vanish as soon as he has heard the story of the *Mahābhārata*" (1.56.23–30, in van Buitenen 1973 I: 130). The text attributes to itself moral agency and efficacy in its capacity to shape and refine human moral sensibilities.

The *Rāmāyaṇa* describes itself as born of sorrow. Its author Vālmīki witnessed a pair of birds in love shot down with a hunter's arrow and blurted out the world's first verse, thereby giving birth to the first poem. The *Rāmāyaṇa*, and by extension all literature, is the product and the producer of sensitivity in human beings. That its origins arise from a witness to violence and injustice is significant in terms of its deliberations on morality. It is itself formulated out of a response to unrighteousness. The *Rāmāyaṇa* describes the effect it in turn should have on its hearers. Rāma's story "confers righteousness, worldly prosperity and delight on the reader . . . [it] does not degrade the mind and grants release from sorrow, that story which charms the heart" (1.3, in Shastri 1952 I: 12).

The *Rāmāyaṇa* is the tale of the wrongful exclusion from succession to kingship and the exile of Rāma, followed by the kidnapping of his wife Sītā, and the eventual restoration of both. Along the way it offers sustained examination of the conditions of social life: the nature of righteous kingship; the complexities of social and sexual relationships; and the role and place of violence in the social and political order. The characters of the epic are considerably less conflicted than those in the *Mahābhārata*. They are held up as paradigms of model behavior. Rāma is less of a hero in the Greek sense – that is, engaged in valiant and noble efforts despite facing certain defeat – than an ideal to be emulated. He is the righteous king whose convictions about proper conduct remain unruffled despite the many forces attempting to undermine him.

Rāma's only possible fault may be an overweening preoccupation with his honor and public opinion about him. This in turn is revealing about what is important. A large part of moral duty is fulfilling the expectations of one's social role without invoking censure and disapproval of others. Rāma is constantly aware that the eyes of the world are upon him. This "most truthful of men" offers reflections on his role of exemplifying dharma to others by not disobeying his father's command to go into exile. Implicit in Rāma's fixation with honor and shame is a sense that the moral order of the world rests on him, and on his capacity to attract the esteem and emulation of the world. This is cast in terms of selflessness. The world needs an icon of correct dharma to esteem and revere. The other characters in the story are no less paradigmatic in exemplifying models of behavior. They provide examples in two capacities: models appropriate to their particular social locations, as well as models of esteem and reverence for Rāma. Sītā provides a model of a faithful and loyal wife, Lakṣmaṇa, of dutiful brotherly affection and loyalty, and Hanumān, of unwavering service and devotion. Throughout the epic is the overarching theme that moral duty consists in "obedience and the suppression of the individual will" which is realized in part through recognition and esteem for honored others (Pollock 1986: 33).

Narratives are understood in this tradition as communicating not just erudition and the wisdom of past lore, nor simply as providing the models for virtuous behavior, but also allowing for intimacy and association with noble people critical for moral development. The *Rāmcaritmānas*, a Hindi telling of the *Rāmāyaṇa*, claims that hearing its tale provides association with the virtuous. It is only through association with holy men that human aspirations may be realized: "Through contact with the virtuous even the wicked get reformed, just as base metal is transmuted by the touch of the philosopher's stone" (Tulsidas 1976: 21–2) (see chapter 10). The text also sees itself as bringing one closer to God by celebrating the exploits of Lord Rāma, who is considered an incarnation of the great god Viṣṇu. Exalting virtuous people and God fosters devotion and humility, which the text sees as producing pious and worthy persons. Hindus from all ages have cherished stories of saints and gurus, of holy men and women, and of gods and goddesses, that bring them into contact with what is noble and good. Recognition and reverence of virtues in others is the mark of a cultivated and moral person.

In addition to the epics, other stories serve as sources of moral reflection and allow for inquiry that tends in a different direction than the epics' concern with the fulfillment of social roles. Popular collections of folktales such as the *Pañcatantra* and the *Hitopadeśa* are regarded as morally edifying stories full of practical wisdom for everyday life. In addition to offering general good counsel, these collections of mostly animal fables allow for a particular mode of moral reflection not always possible in stories and reflections about human beings. Animal stories can be free of the usual human social categories and hierarchies. Consideration of character and virtue can be carried out independently of the determining factors of class, caste, and social location that mark human social structures. Animal tales require their audience to divert the moral imagination away from social roles to consider generic moral virtues. Such stories can explore the intricacies of friendship, loyalty, and wise policy without correlating them to fixed social roles. Intriguingly, it is in a world of greedy jackals, clever monkeys, prudent mice, fickle crows, and courageous lions that the baseness and the nobility of human character may be most fully explored.

Morality and Religious Practice

Hindu traditions recognize four distinct values or goals of human life: love and physical pleasure (*kāma*), the acquisition of material well-being (*artha*), morality and the good (*dharma*), and spiritual liberation (*mokṣa*). Hindu thinkers have differed over the precise relationship of these different aims, especially when they conflict with one another. However, they tend to agree that each aim is a distinct and legitimate human end valued for its own good, rather than a means to something else.

Some interpreters of Indian ethics have identified what they regard as a tension between the last two aims, dharma and *mokṣa*, which distinguish between moral claims and spiritual aspirations. In this view, the ultimate spiritual aim of *mokṣa*, which by definition transcends the saṃsāric world of moral consequence and karma, is regarded as so beyond our realm of ordinary experience and its duties that it is seen to bear little relationship to them. If *mokṣa* utterly transcends the social world of worldly obligations it may appear to have nothing to do with ethics (see chapter 31). In this view, ultimate spiritual aims radically relativize or trivialize moral codes. Another charge against some forms of Indian spirituality is that they would seem to articulate antisocial as well as potentially antinomian tendencies. The pursuit of human perfection pursued by renouncers – in which one is to leave behind home and hearth and take up the life of a wandering mendicant free of all social ties – does not seem to describe a morally significant life lived with and for others.

These critiques can be investigated further in terms of the different forms of Hindu spiritual practices. The tradition of introspective discipline and self-mastery (*yoga*) articulated in Patañjali's *Yoga-sūtra* describes eight stages of the religious path of the spiritual seeker (*yogin*). The eight stages are: moral principles, religious observances, posture, breath control, withdrawal of the senses, concentration, meditation, and pure contemplation. The path begins with moral practices (*yama*), which Patañjali defines as five "universal moral principles, unrestricted by conditions of birth, place, time, or circumstance": non-violence, truthfulness, abjuration of stealing, celibacy, and lack of greed (2.31, 35–9, in Miller 1998: 53–4). In this schema, the foundation of religious discipline and the contemplative life is moral practice. Far from being opposed to the spiritual life, moral practice is conceived as a necessary prerequisite for it. It is noteworthy that the term for moral practice, *yama*, also means self-control. Moral practice can best be seen as contiguous with the yogic life of discipline, because morality is itself viewed as a kind of self-restraint. Reigning in one's damaging effect upon others by curbing one's capacity for harm, deceit, theft, sexual activity, and avarice is part of what it means to gain mastery of self. Care of the self is necessarily morally significant, since through self-mastery the moral life is made possible. The discipline of renunciation requires the examination of the interior life which includes purifying moral disposition.

We might also consider the aims of the discipline and try to conceive of what the fully realized and self-controlled individual would be like. Patañjali says that perfect discipline (*samyama*) results in extraordinary cognitive abilities that include sensitivity to and knowledge of others' thoughts. One can hear "the cries of all creatures" (3.17, 19, in Miller 1998: 64). Among other strengths and powers, the *yogin* gains the strengths of discipline of friendship, compassion, joy, and impartiality (3.23). Moral heroism is the effect of self-mastery and discipline. When perfected, it leads the practitioner out of self toward a new and heightened sensitivity to others.

Theistic systems of religious practice also attempt to meet the charge of antinomianism in a variety of creative ways. The theistic system developed in the religious classic the Bhagavad Gītā articulates a novel approach to moral issues. Competing religious movements articulate compelling doctrines of retreat from social and moral activity in favor of a life lived for spiritual attainments alone. The Bhagavad Gītā attempts to buttress moral duty in the world by framing the individual human life within a larger divine plan.

The teachings of the Bhagavad Gītā emerge as a response to one of the most famous war protests ever registered. The hero Arjuna refuses to do battle against his kinsmen in the great war of the *Mahābhārata*. Arjuna, a *kṣatriya* or warrior, is required by duty to fight in battle. He balks, however, at the prospect of killing his family and teachers in what has climaxed in a devastating fratricidal war. He questions the ultimate value of dutiful action that requires such bloodshed. In response, the Bhagavad Gītā argues that human action is unavoidable. The proper response is to divest one's self of personal agency and desire for reward by dedicating one's action to God. The divine plan is glimpsed in a theophany in which Lord Kṛṣṇa displays at once both his impersonal supremacy as well as his personal intimacy with human life. The fulfillment of moral duties, including the violence of righteous warfare, is to be interpreted as sacrificed and surrendered to the service of God (see chapter 55). The Bhagavad Gītā affirms the different duties imposed on the fourfold class system, which require Arjuna to uphold the moral order by vanquishing those who threaten justice and righteousness. True moral conduct is the performance of one's particular dharma, done without personal desire for ends and dedicated to God.

The Bhagavad Gītā articulates various complementary but distinct paths of spiritual and moral practice. These are appropriate to different human capacities and natures, which are, again, an acknowledgment of differentiation in the moral life. The text describes three paths: the path of correct social and ritual action (*karmayoga*), the path of discriminating wisdom (*jñānayoga*), and the path of devotion to God (*bhaktiyoga*). The merits of these differing but complementary approaches to religious and ethical perfection are elaborated in great detail in the Bhagavad Gītā, providing later commentators with material rich with interpretive possibilities for their own theological systems.

The best known and successful of later commentators are the eighth-century Śankara and the eleventh-century Rāmānuja. Both thinkers developed theistic religions that have had great influence on Indian religiosity since. They emerged from their readings of the Bhagavad Gītā, the Upaniṣads, and other scriptures with very different interpretations of the value and nature of the moral life. Śankara's emphasis is on union with the divine as a result of cultivating spiritual knowledge and insight. Ultimate spiritual liberation (*mokṣa*) is the realization that the individual human soul is not different from the ultimate reality, Brahman, the ground of all existence and the goal of all experience. The human condition is analyzed in terms of cognitive error, that is, failure to realize this unity. Correct knowledge (*jñāna*) is the only way to obtain absolute freedom that realizing this unity yields. This absolute freedom is beyond moral distinctions of good and evil. Śankara's thought explicitly denies that moral practice is sufficient for *mokṣa* – since *mokṣa* is unconditioned, it cannot be brought about by actions. One realizes it through understanding the true nature of the self's relationship to the divine. Morality is something one transcends in perfect wisdom, though once one has obtained *mokṣa* one is free of selfishness and corruption.

The eleventh-century theologian Rāmānuja took a very different approach to the question of morality. Rāmānuja agreed with Śankara that ultimately there is no distinction between absolute Brahman and the human soul. Yet, in the context of ethics, Brahman is best understood as the eminent and sinless ruler or controller of creation. The proper human response to divine transcendence is reverence, devotion, and self-surrender. Human beings best display their reverence for God by devotion and the performance of religious and moral obligations.

Many of the *bhakti* or devotional traditions, with their single-minded faithfulness to God and emphasis on grace, though not altogether amoral systems, cannot be seen as privileging either moral duty or ethical reflection. They draw from passages in the Bhagavad Gītā which emphasize devotion to God above all else. In this interpretation, while the Bhagavad Gītā endorses dharma by making it an instrument for spiritual pursuits, in the end it suggests that love of God is all that matters. This profoundly theistic turn affirms the importance of moral action, but still holds out for the final preeminence of pure love of God. The humdrum world of everyday social intercourse pales in comparison to the yearning for God. In addition, the doctrine of divine grace in some of these traditions undermines the importance of works and the human capacity for moral and spiritual effort (Ramanujan 1973: 30–1).

While devotional traditions generally were not engaged in systematic exploration of moral action, nor with reforming the injustices of brahmanical ideology, some of them did offer a critique of and alternative to brahmanical claims to predominance. With the religious value of pure and heartfelt devotion to God regarded as the chief axis of value, social norms based on ritual purity, Vedic and śāstric learning, and caste regulations could be dismissed or trivialized. The *Basava Purāṇa*, a twelfth-century religious text of the Vīraśaivas, a cult devoted to Lord Śiva, ridicules uppity brahmans. It states that "ten million brahmans, even if they were scholars in the Vedas, *purāṇas*, and *śāstras*, would not be equal to a single devotee" (*Basava Purāṇa* in Rao 1990: 235). The Vaiṣṇavas also subverted brahmanical systems of value by making devotion to God the primary consideration of religious and social status, though they did not entirely nor consistently dismantle rules pertaining to *varṇāśramadharma*.

Though sometimes critical of duty and works, the devotional poets also expound an ethic of love and care for fellow creatures. Basavaṇṇa explicitly links religion to ethics in asking, "where is religion without loving-kindness?" (Ramanujan 1973: 54). A later nineteenth-century reformer, Bankim Chandra Chatterji, explicitly conflates devotion to God with love of humankind and allows for no distinction between them (Chatterji 1977: 138). In addition, some of the medieval *bhakti* poets find in their love for God a profound humility, which they link to a gentleness and concern for God's creatures. One saint's poem reads:

> Knowing one's lowliness
> in every word;
> the spray of insects in the air
> in every gesture of the hand;
> things living, things moving
> come sprung from the earth
> under every footfall;
> and when holding a plant
> or joining it to another
> or in the letting it go
> to be all mercy
> to be light
> as a dusting brush
> of peacock feathers:

such moving, such awareness
is love that makes us one
with the Lord
Dasarēśwara
(translated from the Kannada by Ramanujan 1973: 54–5)

Religious sentiment is paired with tenderness and moral sensitivity. This heightened awareness of the condition of other creatures might be compared with the advanced *yogin*'s capacity to hear "the cries of all creatures." The devotee attains such moral sensitivity through submissiveness and devotion to God, while the *yogin* reaches it through self-mastery and discipline.

Conclusion

In Hindu thought, normative discourses pattern or condition moral behavior, inscribing the natural moral order on persons and behavior. The rules of Dharmaśāstra provide not only detailed specifications on how to live. They also communicate that the social and natural world is rule governed, and that each person has duties and obligations within it. Yet even as Hindus have acknowledged the constraints of the dharmic order, they have also sought ways to glimpse human moral capacity independently of it. The epic poet sets out to test the very limits and foundations of dharma. The *yogin* embarks on a quest of self-discovery by renouncing social norms. The religious devotee seeks out alternative axes of value to replace brahmanical structures of purity.

Moral discourses in India not only dictate and theorize moral practice, but they also contribute to moral agency. Hindus find themselves living in a storied world, where narratives link them to past moral ideals. We find in these narratives not only practical moral instruction, but also the means to expand and stimulate the moral imagination. Literature – epic, folk, or poetic – cultivates moral persons by prefiguring the moral imagination in multiple ways: either by providing models of ideal behavior within the social structure, or by suggesting exemplary behavior outside of it. One of Hinduism's key contributions to the study of religious ethics is its recognition of the capacity of literary language to stimulate sensitivity and refine those who come into contact with it.

Bibliography

Chatterji, B. C. 1977: *Essentials of Dharma*, trans. M. Ghose. Calcutta: Sribhumi.
Doniger, W. and Smith, B. K. (trans.) 1991: *The Laws of Manu*. New York: Penguin Books.
Gharpure, J. R. (ed.) 1914: *Yājñavalkyasmṛti with commentary Mitākṣarā*. Bombay: Ghapure.
Goldman, R. (trans.) 1984: *The Rāmāyaṇa of Vālmīki, Vol. I: Bālakāṇḍa*. Princeton, NJ: Princeton University Press.
Kane, P. V. 1930–74: *History of Dharmaśāstra*, Vols. 1–5. Poona: Bhandarkar Oriental Research Institute.
Hutchens, F. G. 1985: *Animal Fables of India: Narayana's Hitopadesha*. West Franklin, NH: Amarta Press.

Miller, B. S. (trans.) 1986: *The Bhagavad Gītā: Kṛṣṇa's Counsel in Time of War*. New York: Bantam Books.

——(trans.) 1998: *Yoga: Discipline of Freedom, the Yoga-sūtra attributed to Patañjali*. Berkeley: University of California Press.

Olivelle, P. (trans.) 1996: *The Upaniṣads*. New York: Oxford University Press.

——(trans.) 1997: *Pañcatantra: The Book of India's Folk Wisdom*. Oxford: Oxford University Press.

——(trans.) 1999: *Dharmasūtras: The Law Codes of Āpastamba, Gautama, Baudhāyana, and Vasiṣṭha*. New York: Oxford University Press.

Pollock, S. (trans.) 1985: "The Theory of Practice and the Practice of Theory in Indian Intellectual History." *Journal of the American Oriental Society* 105 (3), 499–519.

——(trans.) 1986, 1991: *The Rāmāyaṇa of Vālmīki*, Vols. 2–3: *Ayodhyākāṇḍa and Araṇyakāṇḍa*. Princeton, NJ: Princeton University Press.

Ramanujan, A. K. 1973: *Speaking of Śiva*. London: Penguin Books.

Rao, V. N. (trans.). 1990: *Śiva's Warriors*. Princeton, NJ: Princeton University Press.

Roy, P. C. (trans.) 1955: *Śāntiparva of the Mahābhārata*, Vols. 8–9. Calcutta: Oriental Publishing.

Shastri, H. P. (trans.) 1952: *The Ramayana of Valmiki*, Vols. 1–2. London: Shanti Sadan.

Tulsidas 1976: *Srī Rāmacharitamānasa*. Gorakhpur: Gita Press.

van Buitenen, J. A. B. (trans.) 1973–8: *The Mahābhārata*, Books 1–5. Chicago: University of Chicago Press.

CHAPTER 36
Trajectories of Hindu Ethics

Joseph Prabhu

It is impossible within one chapter to cover a 5,000-year tradition in any depth. In this context it is also unnecessary given the accompanying chapters that describe and analyze features of Hindu ethics. What follows is a set of commentarial remarks on four aspects of this tradition: (1) the ambiguity of a *Hindu* ethics, (2) whether there is a Hindu *ethics*, (3) the tension between tradition and modernity in the Indian context generally and in Gandhi's ethics in particular, and (4) the prospects and challenges facing Hindu ethics in the future. One of the purposes herein is to highlight what is distinctive about Hindu ethics and also what it shares with other religio-cultural traditions.

The Ambiguity of *Hindu* Ethics

The term "Hindu" does not unproblematically pick out a singular religion in the modern Western sense of the term, signifying homogeneity of belief or creed under the aegis of some controlling authority. There is no such homogeneity or controlling authority in the Hindu case (see chapter 34). For much of its history, "Hindu" was as much a cultural as a religious designation. Even such a self-consciously secular individual as Jawaharlal Nehru, India's first prime minister, or an avowed atheist like J. N. Mohanty, the prominent Indian philosopher, consider(ed) themselves Hindus in a cultural sense.

The term closest in the Hindu system to religion is "dharma," which connotes a variety of different things falling under the broad rubric of a way of life. Dharma, however, carries different connotations than the term religion, something examined below. Consider the example of the medieval Indian poet Kabir, who regarded himself and was regarded by others as both Muslim and Hindu. Likewise, there are many Christians in India today who call themselves Hindu-Christian. Multiple religious belonging is not seen as a problem. "In premodern India . . . the term 'Hindu' . . . was essentially a racial, cultural expression and Buddhists, Sikhs, Jains, and those we refer to as Hindus now, all shared the same multifaceted ethnicity of the subcontinent. They perceived themselves as all belonging to the same extended cultural family" (Lipner 1998: 14–15). "Hinduism" and "Hindu" in the modern sense were largely Western creations, the legacy of British colonialism. It was part of the political and intellectual project of providing for administrative and other purposes a homogeneity and a rigid classification which were quite foreign to the spirit of this family of culturally similar traditions. Hinduism evolved as a fluid and open ended reality which was free to seek truth in, and to adapt to, different circumstances, all the while maintaining a continuity, but not a sameness, with the past.

What counts as Hindu today is a product of interactions among groups who now would be classified as non-Hindu. This indicates a philosophical difference between India and the West which has ethical repercussions. The Western logical imagination from Aristotle onwards articulates identity in terms of difference, whereas premodern India, as often as not, saw identity in terms of continuity rather than difference and in terms of adaptation rather than differentiation. Hence the relative ease with which Hindu figures like Gandhi or Ramakrishna were able to identify themselves with "non-Hindu" faiths. Their example points to the non-dogmatic temper of the Hindu sensibility at its best, open to truth wherever it is to be found, and tolerant, indeed receptive to, differences.

Unfortunately, that is not the whole story. Quite often tolerance changed to inclusiveness or assimilation and often to hostility, as the fate of Buddhism, which was essentially driven out from the country of its birth, attests. The famous *Advaita* philosopher Śaṃkara, for example, often called a crypto-Buddhist, displayed features of an "anxiety of influence" in seeking to denigrate and vanquish his Buddhist opponents. Nor is this just an academic question. Hindus who for centuries were happy to operate with porous boundaries and to move freely across them, have in recent times sought to politicize their religion. Some have called this development the "Westernization" of Hinduism, as it has tried to codify its beliefs and practices and to exclude those who fall outside essentialist definitions. Present day Hinduism displays an intolerance and a separatism strikingly at odds with an earlier pluralism and open mindedness. When writing on Hindu ethics, it is appropriate to ask which Hinduism we are considering, because as already indicated, there are shifts of tone as between premodern and modern Hinduism.

In order to sketch current "trajectories," the next section will focus on the background of classical brahmanic Hinduism. There were many challenges to Brahman authority, both within the mainstream and on the margins. The sway of Sanskritic brahman culture was such, however, that even the challenges had to be articulated within its framework. At the same time, this framework accommodated an extraordinary internal heterogeneity of beliefs and practices held together by some unifying concepts.

Is There a Hindu *Ethics?*

There is an apparent paradox at the heart of Hindu ethics. On the one hand, it is claimed that ethics was not a prominent branch of Indian thought. Bimal Matilal, one of India's most eminent philosophers, complained:

Certainly, there exists a lacuna in the tradition of Indian philosophy. Professional philosophers of India over the last two thousand years have been consistently concerned with the
problems of logic and epistemology, metaphysics and soteriology, and sometimes they have
made very important contributions to the global heritage of philosophy. But, except [for]
some cursory comments and some insightful observations, the professional philosophers
of India very seldom discussed what we call moral philosophy today. (Matilal 1999: 21)

On the other hand, much of the Indian philosophical tradition has a definite value
orientation and is centrally concerned with the practical ideals of *dharma* (morality
loosely defined), and *mokṣa* (spiritual liberation), and with spelling out how other
values stand in relation to them. One of the distinguishing features of Indian thought
is this strong practical emphasis. Theory exists for the sake, and as part, of practice. At
this level, there is much written not only about values but also about conflicts and
dilemmas and the challenges of practical wisdom.

The appearance of paradox depends on a hidden assumption. Much of Western
moral philosophy is preoccupied with the search for universal moral principles, which
can serve as the legitimizing ground for moral belief and actions. In that sense of
the term, there is perhaps an absence of "ethics" in Indian thought. But is that the
normative sense of the concept? As is well known, this abstract theoretical conceptualization of ethics has recently come under fire (see chapters 1 and 2). With the
rehabilitation of virtue theory, the emphasis in current literature seems to have shifted
to descriptive analyses of human excellences and action (see chapter 4). This change
in Western moral philosophy sits well with the Indian situation. A large part of Indian
thought deals with an elaborate articulation of different values and human ends or
goals designed primarily to guide the individual along a path of spiritual liberation.
There is also a codified system of social duties and obligations nuanced according to
class, caste, and the stages of a life-cycle (*varṇāshrama dharmas*).

The concept in Western ethics that might from a theoretical perspective best capture
the spirit, if not the letter, of Indian moral reflection would be Hegel's notion of
Sittlichkeit. Sittlichkeit refers to the actual set of norms, duties, values, and goods that a
community valorizes. It also includes the habits, practices, laws, and customs that constitute the ethical life of a society and that actualize these values and norms. All these
sustain and in turn have to be sustained by an ongoing community. In the Hindu tradition, dharma constitutes the handed-down rules of morality and practice that provide
the content of social ethics. These are grounded in custom and convention, no further
moral justification being deemed necessary because they have met the pragmatic test
of "workability."

There is, however, a feature of Hindu ethics that distinguishes it even from this
strand of Western moral theory. There is a close kinship between humans and other
manifestations of nature in Hindu ethics. The scope of human responsibility extends
not only to other humans, but also to the whole cosmos. Thus, the *Bṛhadāraṇyaka
Upaniṣad* says: "This Atman [breath or vital essence] is the same in the ant, the same
in the gnat, the same in the elephant, the same in these three worlds, the same in the
universe" (1, 3, 22). This range of ethical reference is mirrored in the crucial term of
Hindu moral discourse, namely the idea of *dharma*, as it figures in classical discussion.
Dharma is the fixed position of duty and of right, in the sense of what is proper and

normative. It is not restricted to personal ethics, but also designates religious observance and secular law, prescribing the individual's social and legal standing within the
wider domains of community, caste, class, and station. Expanding its range even
further, *dharma* connotes a cosmic contract to which the individual is bound, both
in the sense that she derives support from it (Sanskrit, *dhar*) and the corresponding
obligation to support it. This, as universal order, assigns to each entity, personal or
impersonal, its specific place in the cosmic, social, and personal orders.

This notion of *dharma* is at once metaphysical and ethical. The problem becomes
what the precise connection is between the two. It would be incorrect to suggest that
the ethical is deduced from the metaphysical. The logic is rather one of analogy and
isomorphism, with custom and tradition playing the mediating role of providing the
specific rights and duties attached to the individual. They are obviously able to play this
mediating role more easily in a closed and highly structured setting rather than in a
mobile, fluid, and pluralistic society. This fact will form one of the trajectories of Hindu
ethics explored below.

Importantly, *dharma* is only one of four human ends discussed in the classical view,
which might be said to have intrinsic value. The others are *artha*, or material interests,
kāma, pleasure and emotional fulfillment, and *mokṣa*, or spiritual liberation. Even
though *artha* and *kāma* have ethical dimensions, conceptually they belong to the fields
of political economy (*artha*) and aesthetics and psychology (*kāma*), and so fall outside
the scope of our discussion. What is of interest for ethics is the connection between
dharma and *mokṣa*. While it is generally agreed that the ideal of *mokṣa* trumps the
claims of *dharma*, the exact relationship between the two ideals and the validity of
dharma when seen from the perspective of *mokṣa* have been subjects of debate. On the
one hand, *dharma* is seen as a means to the attainment of *mokṣa*, but from the perspective of *mokṣa*, *dharma* with its rigid clan/caste/family structure is often regarded
as an obstacle to *mokṣa*. Orthodoxy often held that *dharma* had absolute validity even
for the person who had attained *mokṣa*; but there were – and are – many influential
views that question this assertion. After all, *mokṣa* is a state of consciousness conse-
quent upon the knowledge of the true nature of things, while *dharma* belongs to the
realm of action and will. Put otherwise, *dharma* upholds the established social–ethical
order, whereas *mokṣa* is "release" from this order in order to achieve self-realization, a
free spiritual individuality that transcends the "ethical" realm.

This has given rise to the common, and somewhat tedious, Western reproach of
the purported amorality and the alleged life-negating quality of Hindu spirituality
(Schweitzer 1955). Even long-time students of Indian religions like R. C. Zaehner, analyzing the ritual murders of Charles Manson and his followers, argue that the killings
may well have derived their moral justification from the teachings of the Upaniṣads,
according to which the enlightened individual lives "beyond good and evil" and
transcends the conventional morality of right and wrong (Zaehner 1974: 97–8). This
interpretation is based on a strange mistranslation of the relevant Upaniṣadic texts
(see Lipner 1998). It is, however, a sufficiently widespread view to warrant rebuttal.

First, the very definition of the enlightened sage is one who has developmentally
advanced beyond his empirical self and its interests, and is established in a "transcendental" wisdom. To ascribe egoistic acts like murder to such an individual is to misun-

derstand what enlightenment means and entails. Second, while *dharma* strictly speaking is neither a necessary nor a sufficient means for *moksha*, in actual fact, *dharma* is often presupposed as a condition for *moksha*. Even though *moksha* lies beyond *dharma* the means of achieving both are not vastly different. In the *Bhagavad Gītā*, one of the central ethical texts of the tradition, Arjuna, the protagonist, is instructed in the path of *dharma* as a precondition for enlightenment. The *Bhagavad Gītā* attempts to synthesize two moral ideals, the outer one of social obligation and the inner one of renunciation and detachment. It is made clear to Arjuna that this goal of renunciation *in*, but not *of*, action requires, among other disciplines, that of *karma yoga*, the path of selfless service. Third, there are texts that challenge this harmonizing interpretation, like Śaṃkara's *Advaita Vedānta*. Yet nowhere is it suggested that the enlightened person can disregard everyday morality with impunity. Spiritual liberation is a progression beyond, not a regression from, the strictures of dharma.

Nonetheless, viewing morality from this developmental perspective results in a shift of meaning and emphasis compared to some Western understandings of the term (see chapter 56). The life-cycle is seen as progressing through four stages, each with its appropriate code of conduct. Studentship (*brahmacarya*) requires habits of studiousness, sobriety, and reverence for one's teachers; the householder (*gṛhastha*) stage entails the responsibilities of marriage, family, career, money, and power; the forest-dweller (*vānaprastha*) stage brings with it a gradual withdrawal from worldly pursuits and interests; while finally the stage of renunciation (*saṃnyāsa*) calls for complete withdrawal from society so as to have freedom for spiritual contemplation. To these social stations and their duties are fused the four life goals mentioned earlier. At each stage of life there is a basis in custom and convention for one's responsibilities. Individuals operate on the basis of a moral appropriateness that seems fitting in the circumstances. This is not "situation ethics" calling for ad hoc responses. Rather, the understanding of "morality" is subtly different. It is neither the application of abstract moral rules, nor the invocation of general principles that is deemed important (see chapter 5). More vital is the unfolding journey of self-realization and the demands which this journey imposes at each stage. There is a close relation between ethics and religion in the Hindu tradition. Still, there is no doubt that questions of "ultimacy" and of spiritual liberation relativize morality and render it ultimately subordinate to spiritual goals.

The Dialogue of Tradition and Modernity: The Case of Gandhi

This chapter has emphasized so far the classical moral tradition articulated in the long interval from the Vedas (before 1500 BCE) to the working out of philosophical systems and commentaries on scriptures culminating with the dualist *Vedantin* Madhva in the fourteenth century CE. What comes after that period are the Moghul and British invasions. These caused great disruptions in Hindu thought, at least in its philosophical aspects, until the modern period heralded by Rammohan Roy and the Bengal Renaissance in the early nineteenth century. As this is not a historical inquiry, what will be perhaps of greatest interest is how modern Hindu thinkers received and appropriated their traditions (see chapter 35).

Much of classical moral thought took shape within a highly structured and traditional society, where custom and convention, though by no means static, were able to specify moral roles and responsibilities. Modernity, with its scientific temper, technological innovation, economic and social mobility, and democratic ethos, issues a quite different set of moral demands. The question arises how well the traditions are able to adapt to modern conditions. Custom, by definition, remains local and defies universal application. In a modern society like India's, with more than a billion people, it should not be surprising that forces besides custom take on the role of moral arbiters. Increasingly, constitutional, legal, and parliamentary debates assume greater importance than social conventions and habits. It is important in this light to distinguish between orthodoxy and tradition. Orthodoxy hypostatizes tradition rendering it static and unchanging, whereas tradition, from its very etymology, suggests that which is carried forward, as it seeks to preserve significations and create new meanings in changed circumstances. The real issue for ethics outside the strictures of orthodoxy is, then, that tradition and modernity, ideally speaking, are caught up in an ongoing dialogue, each challenging and questioning the other.

In recent Indian religious ethics, the most consequential dialogue of tradition and modernity was conducted by Gandhi (see chapter 6). Two considerations motivate the focus on Gandhi. First, without any question Gandhi is the modern Indian who has most caught the world's imagination. His ethics of non-violence, though not particularly original in its theoretical underpinnings, is striking in its practical applications. It represents the most significant development of Hindu ethics in the twentieth century. Second, his successes and failures point to some of the challenges now facing Hindu ethics in the twenty-first century, as noted below.

Gandhi is a moralist through and through and yet it is difficult to write philosophically about his ethics (Prabhu 2001, 2004). This is because Gandhi is concerned with practice rather than with theory or abstract thought, and such philosophy as he used was meant to reveal its "truth" in the crucible of experience. Hence the subtitle of his *Autobiography*: "the story of my experiments in truth." The truth of concepts, values, and ideals is fulfilled only in practice. Prior to that practical fulfillment they remain spectral and abstract. Furthermore, Gandhi's ethics are inextricably tied up with his religion, which itself is unconventional. Though an avowed Hindu, he was a Hindu in a philosophical rather than a sectarian sense. There was much Hindu ritual and practice that he subjected to critique. His religion could be described as the life of the self attempting to realize itself as Self, thus achieving *mokṣa* or spiritual liberation. *Karmayogi* that he was, self-realization had to be expressed through work in the world and the details of daily life rather than through renunciation of the world. Gandhi's own ethics have a decidedly spiritual cast, but because he takes pains to express them in a neutral philosophical manner, he intends them to have general validity. When he switches from affirming that God is Truth to saying that Truth is God, his rationale is that the latter is a more general statement which has resonance even for unbelievers. This is a testament to Gandhi's innate sense of tolerance and inclusiveness, in that he believes that his ideals of truth and non-violence are accessible even to those who do not share his religious metaphysics.

Truth for Gandhi is not merely, or even primarily, the property of statements. He does not deny the importance of factual truth or the correspondence between propositions and states of affairs in the world that either confirm or refute them. Rather, his multi-faceted notion of truth emphasizes ontological, moral, and existential aspects. Ontologically, *satya* is derived from *Sat*, the self-existent essence, both the Is and the Ought of reality. It was this derivation that led Gandhi often to say, "Nothing exists in reality except Truth, everything else is illusion." Beyond the illusory temporal flux of phenomena lies the eternal Truth, what Gandhi also called Absolute Truth. We humans, with our finite capacities, can have access however only to relative truth, an assertion Gandhi uses to justify epistemological humility and tolerance. All our perceptions of truth are inevitably partial and therefore claims of cognitive absoluteness are unwarranted and dangerous.

While the ontological aspect of truth points to a more objective notion, the moral and existential aspects move in the direction of a more subjective dimension, the deeply personal intuition of truth which can be experienced only through action. "Gandhi could not regard truth either as solely the object of reason or as simply the product of human decision. For him . . . truth is nothing less than the splendor of reality and cannot be gained without an understanding of the Eternal Law of Nature, but when it is perceived and seized it must be acted upon" (Iyer 1973: 154). Truth for Gandhi found its fullest expression in the field of politics, which in accordance with his moral outlook he regarded as the arena for doing good on the largest possible scale. The idea used to encapsulate this moral conception of politics was *satyāgraha*. This was conceived as a practical experiment to introduce truth and non-violence into the political field. Gandhi adopted this idea early in his political career when he chose *satyāgraha* as the name for his resistance movement against the repressive South African government. Gandhi wrote, "Truth [*satya*] implies love and firmness [*agraha*] and therefore serves as a synonym for force. I thus began to call the Indian movement *satyāgraha*, that is to say, the force which is born of truth and love of non-violence" (Gandhi 1938: 172).

The forceful and activist character of *satyāgraha* should correct a common misperception, namely, that it denotes a passivity of resistance, a mere turning of the other cheek. Although Gandhi insisted that violence be met with love and understanding, the non-violent means chosen should not obscure the powerful end of establishing justice and truth. He is on record as saying that if the choice were between the passive acceptance of injustice and violent resistance to it, he would choose the latter. He was convinced, however, that non-violent resistance was superior to both alternatives.

Satyāgraha begins with reasoning with one's opponent or adversary in an attempt to arrive at a just solution, recognizing that no party has a monopoly on the truth, or is wholly in the right. The purpose is to work out a rational compromise that will be agreeable to both sides. It is only when such processes of reasoning, persuasion, and compromise have been tried and have proved unsuccessful that one adopts the direct action techniques of *satyāgraha*. *Satyāgraha* involves performing actions such as non-cooperation (strikes, boycotts, lockouts, fasts); civil disobedience (non-payment of taxes, disregard of specific laws or injunctions); publicizing one's cause through marches, rallies, picketing, and other forms of peaceful protest; and constructive programs (low-cost housing, education, health facilities, cooperative banks for the poor). A big part of non-violent resistance is *tapas* or the willingness to suffer for one's cause. "It is the assumption of *satyāgraha* that when reasoning fails to move the head, the argument of suffering by the *satyāgrahis* helps move the heart of the oppressor or opponent. Self-suffering, moreover, is the truth-serving alternative to the truth-denying method of inflicting violence on others" (Pantham 1987: 292–310). Contained in this idea of *satyāgraha* is the question of means and ends. Gandhi disagrees with the common political idea that the ends justify the means. To the contrary, he held that immoral means taint and distort potentially good ends and to that extent he placed at least as much, if not more, emphasis on the means, which he described as ends in actions. "The means may be likened to a seed, the end to a tree; and there is just the same inviolable connection between the means and the end as there is between the seed and the tree" (Gandhi 1956–94, X: 431).

The forceful and activist character of *satyāgraha* leads naturally to the idea of non-violence. Gandhi invokes the Jain precept of *ahiṃsā*, or not causing deliberate injury or harm to any being. He takes the precept beyond its merely negative formulation to mean the largest love, the greatest charity. "If I am a follower of *ahiṃsā*, I must love my enemy or a stranger as I would love my wrong-doing father or son. This *ahiṃsā* necessarily includes truth and fearlessness" (Gandhi 1916, in Iyer 1973: 180). *Ahiṃsā* is the deployment of moral force to persuade one's opponent or adversary. It differs from violence in that it respects the autonomy and dignity of the other, whereas violence does not. *Ahiṃsā* differs from violence in the perpetual willingness to dialogue and negotiate with the other and, as far as is consistent with rightness, to come to a compromise. Given that one's grasp of the truth is at best partial, it is imperative to see and appreciate the truth in the position of the other and to try and achieve a higher or dialectical reconciliation of conflicting ends. This negotiated compromise has the opposite effect of violence, which involves vanquishing and putting down one's opponent that inevitably sets up a cycle of resentment, ill will, and further violence. The search for truth becomes a shared quest based on epistemological humility and mutual respect, notwithstanding the differences that still remain after the effort at understanding.

Gandhi was not so naive as to think that such moral persuasion would come easily. He was aware that people who exercise power over others are not likely to give it up without some pressure being exerted. All the means of *satyāgraha* should then be adopted as a way of morally coercing one's opponent to negotiate. It is true that coercion is being exerted, but it is a coercion that still respects the moral agency and dignity of the other, not least by the willingness to undergo self-suffering. The strategy presupposes that the opponent does have a minimal openness to such moral appeal, a trait that Gandhi was willing to grant to most people. However, he also recognized that there are madmen and tyrants, rapists and aggressors who would not fall within that category. In those extreme cases Gandhi was willing to use physical force for the purpose of self-defense. For example, he sanctioned the use of military force to drive back the Pakistani Army in what he considered to be the invasion of Kashmir in 1947–8.

The three concepts discussed, *satya*, *satyāgraha*, and *ahiṃsā*, might give some idea of the texture of Gandhi's ethical thought. The ideas of truth and non-violence are certainly to be found in the Jain, Buddhist, and Hindu traditions, but there is a difference between Gandhi's conceptualization of these ideas and traditional ones. The high standards of moral and spiritual discipline that Gandhi invokes were traditionally part of the *sādhana* of monks and saints, but decidedly not of people in political life. To the contrary, political thinkers like Manu and Kautilya sanctioned the use of physical force both for self-defense and for purposes of political order. Gandhi, by contrast, considerably softens the traditional dualism between religion and politics. Instead, he attempts to forge a non-dual relationship between the two, where religion, seen as reverence for and service to Life, necessarily leads to politics, the arena for the greatest potential public service. Politics in turn is saved from power mongering and the conflict of factional interests by the moral purification involved in religion at its best. It is important to distinguish Gandhi's highly moral notions of religion and politics from the ideological conceptions of them all too common in our time. Certainly, the rise of religious fundamentalism and right-wing religious groups would make any peace-loving person nervous about the marriage of religion and politics. It should be clear, however, that the moral checks and balances that Gandhi exercised over religion and politics purified both domains and offered the world a different and more noble conception of them that we have yet to live out.

These principles of Gandhi represent only one aspect of his ethics – his ethics of love. Love, for Gandhi, was not a simple sentimental matter, or just a benevolence towards all, demanding as that ethic might be. Love in the full sense incorporates justice, treating people fairly, if not always equally. It was these elements of love and truth, on the one hand, and justice and fairness on the other, that constitute his comprehensive philosophy of peace. What warrants its claim to comprehensiveness is that it tackles overt and structural violence, the violence that is all too visible, and the more subtle and less visible violence contained in unjust practices and institutions. Peace, for Gandhi, was not simply a narrowly conceived moral and spiritual matter. It encompassed a holistic way of life that includes economic and social concerns.

As early as 1909 Gandhi wrote *Hind Swarāj*, a book that was in many ways the foundation for his subsequent thinking. In it he criticizes the Western path of modernization as unstable and alienating. It is materialistic, exploitative of nature and human beings, unrestrained, and lacking a sense of direction of moral purpose. The key factor responsible for this state of affairs is the conception of human beings and of human nature that underlies it. Instead of seeing humans as essentially moral and spiritual beings, Western modernity regards them fundamentally as consumers driven by greed and self-indulgence (see chapter 45). The goal of the modern economic system is endlessly to produce goods in response to the ever-increasing demand of consumers, continually driven and inflamed by advertising. Modernity confuses material production for progress, restlessness for vitality, acceleration for efficiency, and consumer satisfaction for an improved quality of life.

From his critique of Western modernity, we can infer the character of Gandhi's alternative modernity in dialogue with tradition. It is based on a picture of human beings as moral, spiritual, and culturally creative. From this basic conception of human nature, Gandhi derives some regulative principles that should govern a good society. First, it should be informed by a reverence for life. Because human beings are not the masters or owners, but are instead the caretakers and trustees of creation, they should organize their affairs in such a way that they respect nature's integrity, diversity, and rhythm, and adjust their demands accordingly. Second, because human beings are interdependent, a sound social system should discourage all forms of exploitation, domination, and inequality, and instead promote the values of love, truthfulness, co-operation, and solidarity. Third, because human beings are creative and spiritual in nature, a good society should encourage them to develop these capacities, and in particular, their capacity for *swarāj* (moral self-rule). When Gandhi applied these principles to the social and economic spheres, the ideas he emphasized are those of decentralization, regional development, local self-sufficiency, and the creation of a technology adapted to the needs and resources of a particular area and to the creativity of people. He insisted that economic growth should proceed in harmony with nature and between people, even if such growth is slower and more gradual than that brought about by heavy industry and high technology. Gandhi had nothing against wealth or productivity as such. His point was that the production of wealth should be regulated by a set of moral values rather than being an end in itself.

Gandhi's critique of modernity by no means implied a complete rejection of modernization. He greatly valued the scientific temper of modernity and its emphasis on investigation and experimentation. Gandhi also valued the spirit of the Enlightenment with its valorization of independence, critical thinking, and moral autonomy. Conversely, there were many aspects of his tradition that Gandhi criticized, from caste and untouchability to the oppression of women. By the same token, modernity for Gandhi did not imply a wholesale rejection of tradition and an embrace of the new for its own sake. Rather, he sought to assimilate the best of tradition and modernity, as measured by his own evolving standards. To that extent, we can justify Gandhi's vision as being in tune with the spirit of openness and independence of thought betokened by modernity.

The Prospects and Challenges Facing Hindu Ethics

Gandhi was assassinated by a fellow Hindu – a rabid nationalist who feared that he was betraying Hinduism – in 1948. The dialogue that he initiated between tradition and modernity is one that has continued since his time. India today, as a full-fledged nation-state, grapples internally with a range of ethical problems, from questions of distributive justice and minority rights to a uniform civil code for the diverse social and religious groups. At the same time, operating within the community of nations, and being the largest democracy in the world, it is faced with its share of transnational challenges, from the impact of globalization and global ecology to problems of war and peace (see chapter 49).

In meeting these challenges, Hinduism has a rich ethical tradition to draw on, with moral ideas that are complex enough to allow for reinterpretation in new settings. These resources for contemporary trajectories in ethics are rooted in the past forms of thought noted above. Consider a few examples. The idea of dharma, with its cosmic, holistic, and ecologically sensitive perspectives, provides a counter-weight to the possessive individualism, acquisitiveness, and nature-dominating features of modern and postmodern society. The ethic of the *Bhagavad Gītā* of doing one's duty selflessly and with inner-detachment is one that has wide resonance. Gandhi's ethic of non-violence has long attracted the attention of groups in civil society working for peace, human rights, transnational distributive justice, and ecological harmony. In an age of globalization, it is heartening to read the praise of a renowned scholar of comparative legal systems: "The genius of India . . . is peaceful coexistence between groups, creative co-prosperity. India has harnessed the concepts of religion not to *activity*, nor to a meditative and self-absorbed *stagnation*, but to the creative co-prosperity of groups each recognizing the other's right to contribute to the whole. A balance of forces is still needed and because it favors it, Hinduism still dominates" (Derrett, in Smith 2003: 202).

However, any dispassionate student of Hindu ethics will readily admit that there are urgent tasks ahead that any use of traditional resources must address. The future trajectories of Hindu ethics will be along the lines of these urgent tasks. In this way, contemporary Hindu ethics will enact in its own way the dialogue of tradition and modernity.

First, in relation to the paradox about Hindu ethics isolated above, it still remains true that the lacuna of a *systematic ethics*, though often remarked on, has still not been filled or even adequately addressed (but see Bilimoria, Prabhu, and Sharma, 2004; Gupta 2002; Perrett 1998). Granted the distinctive features of Hindu ethics, there still remains a puzzle as to the paucity of good accounts of the subject that meet modern canons of rigor and thoroughness. The few that do exist are largely descriptive treatments detailing the ethical features of various philosophical systems and texts, but displaying relatively little analytical acumen (Hopkins 1924; Dasgupta 1965; Jhingran 1989). If one considers another tradition quite different from the West – the Chinese, for example – one would have to concede that studies of Indian ethics fare poorly in comparison (see chapter 37). It is possible that as scholars face the challenges of contemporary moral problems more resolutely, they will also examine the traditions more carefully.

Beyond this academic trajectory, however, there is a set of practical ethical challenges that India faces. One challenge surrounds *toleration and pluralism*. The peaceful coexistence of many different beliefs, practices, and institutions within Hinduism, and its tolerant attitude towards non-Hindu traditions, has been a hallmark from earliest times. There is at least a threefold basis for this tolerance: religious, philosophical, and psychological. The Vedic maxim "Truth is one, though sages call it by different names" (*ekam sat viprā bahudhā vadanti*) captures the pervasive sense of religious pluralism that Hinduism often espouses. The Jain doctrine of *Anekāntavāda*, the many-sidedness of truth, referring to the perspectival quality of truth in general, signals the philosophical open-mindedness and rejection of dogma of Hinduism at its best. Psychologically, the idea of karma (moral cause and effect), together with the recognition of differences in personality, social station, aptitude, etc., points towards a latitude of lifestyle and conduct. While there are indeed basic moral rules and norms (*sādhāraṇadharmas*), these get applied differently to caste and one's stage of life (*varṇāshramadharmas*). This tolerance has gone together with a general disposition in favor of non-violence. It is both wrong and wrong-headed to coerce someone into agreement with one's particular moral standards, because that involves a violation of her or his moral integrity. This is a relativistic position, but one (a systematic ethics would show) that stops well short of a self-defeating relativism. There *are* appropriate standards which can be justified, but the appropriateness is nuanced according to caste, class, stage of life, etc.

All this is theoretical and like many theoretical pronouncements does not always translate into practice. Indian Muslims and Christians, in recent times, have tested the limits of Hindu tolerance, and one cannot say that the results have been encouraging. Hindu–Muslim and Hindu–Christian tensions, alas, are now fairly common and on the rise. This is a complex topic and the many causes of this development cannot be explored. Suffice it so say that there is fault on all sides; suffice it also to say that many Hindus regret the chauvinism and fundamentalism that seem to be conspicuous features of their religion today. It is important for the future of Hindu ethics to distinguish the pluralism and genuine tolerance of Gandhi and Ramakrishna from inclusivism, which has often been mistaken for them. Inclusivism is the position in which one's particular tradition is taken to represent the final or ultimate truth, and other traditions are seen either as aspects of, or stages leading up to, such final truth. It easily absorbs or assimilates or subordinates other traditions. The difference between pluralism and inclusivism comes at the point where they deal with difference. Where inclusivism tends to neutralize difference and reduce it to the same, pluralism either celebrates difference as part of the infinite plenitude of being, or when differences harden into oppositions and celebration is not possible, tries to live with such oppositions. Some, but by no means all, of Hindu tolerance has been of this inclusivist kind. Even that is an improvement on the exclusivism and marked intolerance that recent Hindu fundamentalism often displays. But the question of *toleration* requires more reflection.

If religious violence points to a dimming of the great ideals of tolerance and spiritual unity that once animated India, there is another area of ethics which has never been strongly addressed. This is the theme of *social justice* treated systematically in ethics; its relative absence in the literature is a troubling lacuna in the tradition. While the classical tradition espoused the idea of impartiality (Doniger and Smith 1991), this is counterbalanced by the belief of inequality among castes and between genders. The caste system was not always the hierarchical and inegalitarian institution it has become. At its inception, it was a functional system based on a division of labor, talent, and disposition and one could argue that it may not then have been prima facie unjust. That argument cannot be sustained today. It is impossible to examine here the details of something as complicated as the caste system. Caste poses serious questions for the democracy and egalitarianism that post-independence India has espoused. In this egalitarian ethos, all sorts of oppressed groups, from tribal peoples and "untouchables" to women and landless laborers, demand justice in a system that has not adequately thematized it.

The problem generally expressed is how to fashion a just social order out of a hierarchical system that embodies inequalities of rank, status, and power. Gandhi thought he could retain the caste system by interpreting it as a functional order expressing differentiation, though not necessarily inequality. In this judgment, he was naive at best, and self-deluded at worst. B. R. Ambedkar, the father of the Indian constitution and an "untouchable" himself, in his exchange with Gandhi exposed the latter's wishful thinking. Ambedkar organized a mass conversion of his fellow "untouchables" to Buddhism as a mark of protest against Hindu caste oppression (Zelliott 1996). It is not surprising that the burden of trying to meet some of these demands for social justice has fallen disproportionately on the law courts without much ethical reflection to draw on (Larson 2002). Here, too, the lack of a *systematic ethical reflection* is linked to grave practical matters.

This selective treatment highlights a few of the challenges that Hindu ethics faces in the future: to develop *modes of moral reflection*, to clarify features of *toleration*, and to address basic issues of *social justice*. Modern India has opted for a democratic and egalitarian society. While it has a rich ethical legacy to draw on, it nevertheless faces a daunting task as it seeks to revise its hierarchical social system and the beliefs that support it to meet these urgent demands.

Bibliography

Bilimoria, P., Prabhu, J., and Sharma, A. (eds.) 2004: *Indian Ethics: Classical Traditions and Contemporary Challenges*. London: Ashgate Press.

Dasgupta, S. 1965: *Development of Moral Philosophy in India*. New York: Frederick Ungar.

Doniger, W. and Smith, B. K. (trans.) 1991: *The Laws of Manu*. New York: Penguin Books.

Gandhi, M. K. 1938: *Satyagraha in South Africa*, trans. V. G. Desai. Madras: S. Ganesa.

—— 1956–94: *The Collected Works of Mahatma Gandhi*, 90 vols. New Delhi: Publications Division.

Gupta, B. (ed.) 2002: *Ethical Questions: East and West*. Lanham, MD: Rowman and Littlefield.

Hopkins, E. W. 1924: *Ethics of India*. New Haven, CT: Yale University Press.

Iyer, R. 1973: *The Moral and Political Thought of Mahatma Gandhi*. Oxford: Oxford University Press.

Jhingran, S. 1989: *Aspects of Hindu Morality*. Delhi: Motilal Banarsidass.

Larson, G. 2002: *Religion and Personal Law in Secular India: A Call to Judgment*. Bloomington: Indiana University Press.

Lipner, J. 1998: *The Hindus*. London: Routledge.

Matilal, B. 1999: "Moral Dilemmas: Insights from Indian Epics" in *Collected Papers*, Vol. 1. Delhi: Oxford University Press.

Pantham, T. 1987. "Habermas's Practical Discourse and Gandhi's *Satyagraha*" in *Political Discourse: Explorations in Indian and Western Thought*, ed. B. Parekh and T. Pantham. London: Ashgate Press.

Perrett, R. 1998: *Hindu Ethics: A Philosophical Study*. Honolulu: University of Hawai'i Press.

Prabhu, J. 2001: "Gandhi: Visionary for a Globalized World." *ReVision* 24, 1.

—— 2004: "Gandhi, Empire, and a Culture of Peace" in *Indian Ethics: Classical Traditions and Contemporary Challenges*, ed. P. Bilimoria, J. Prabhu, and A. Sharma. London: Ashgate Press.

Schweitzer, A. 1955: *Indian Thought and Its Development*. Boston, MA: Beacon Press.

Smith, D. 2003: *Hinduism and Modernity*. Oxford: Blackwell.

Zaehner, R. C. 1974: *Our Savage God*. London: Collins.

Zelliott, E. 1996: *From Untouchable to Dalit: Essays on the Ambedkar Movement*. New Delhi: Manohar Publishers.

6 Chinese Ethics

CHAPTER 37

Chinese Ethics?

Eske Møllgaard

The main concern of traditional Chinese thinkers has been what we call ethics, and not epistemology, logic, or theology, to name a few other important European interests. For a Western reader, the rich field of Chinese ethical thought is difficult to approach. The discourse of "ethics" does not easily map onto the Chinese tradition (see chapter 1). First, the field of knowledge was structured differently in China than in the West. Second, we must consider the question of the difference in conceptual schemes between Western and Chinese thought. The third difficulty is the pervasive authoritarianism in the Chinese tradition (see chapter 6). This is particularly important to highlight when Chinese thought is read within a Western liberal and postmodern context.

Fields of Knowledge

The fields of knowledge in traditional China are not divided according to the familiar Western academic disciplines: ethics, politics, history, literature, and so on. Tradition-ally, Chinese learning was divided into the "six arts" (*liuyi*): *shu* (history), *shi* (poetry), *yi* (changes), *li* (ritual), the *chunqiu* (the Spring and Autumn Annals), and *yue* (music). During the Han dynasty (206 BCE – 220 CE) this division was codified in the study of the *Five Classics* (*wujing*): *Book of History, Book of Poetry, Book of Changes, Book of Rites, Spring and Autumn Annals* (a *Book of Music* either never existed or was lost). It may be tempting to take the Chinese categories roughly to correspond to what we call history, poetry, metaphysics, and the socio-ethical domain. But in translating the Chinese terms we find no strict equivalencies: *shu* (history) does not historicize in the way modern history does; *shi* (poetry) is not poetic in the way of modern poetry; the book on *yi* (*changes*) is concerned with divination of changes rather than with our familiar meta-physics of being; and the *li* (rituals) cover the whole field of civilized behavior from bowing to an elder to conducting animal sacrifices.

The point to grasp is that in traditional China the ethical is not a separate category but pervades all the fields of knowledge. Traditional Chinese "learning" (*xue*) has no separate discipline of ethics. To be sure, the works of the early "Masters" (*zi*) and later the "collected works" (*wenji*) of scholar-officials have much to say about "humanity and righteousness" (*renyi*) and "moral conduct" (*dexing*). There are also works that catalogue and explain ethical terms, yet no philosophical ethics is found in traditional China. (The Mohists made a beginning, but their theories had no impact on the tradition.) There never was in China an Aristotle, who defined practical wisdom in relation to scientific knowledge, craft knowledge, and sagely wisdom. It was only with the encounter with the West that the Chinese came to see ethics as a separate domain and coined terms for it: *lunlixue* or *daodexue*. What we call "Chinese ethics" is therefore an object constructed according to the logic of Western science.

The tradition of Chinese ethics does not have our familiar landmarks, in particular the division between ancient and modern ethics. Chinese ethics may seem at once premodern and postmodern, or it may impress us, as Confucius did Elias Canetti, as being thoroughly modern. But if we do not find in traditional China a theory of moral autonomy, we have in the various traditional Chinese schools of thought not only a great deal of moralism but also more importantly an invaluable range of ethics not as theory but as spiritual exercise. Like in ancient philosophy in the West, we find in the Chinese tradition examples of ways of forming oneself as an ethical subject that are of universal significance. In the Greek tradition the ideal is the philosopher who is a lover of wisdom but does not possess wisdom, and is a true lover precisely because the consummation is denied. In China the ideal is the sage, who embodies wisdom – at the price, perhaps, of giving up the *eros* of the philosopher (expressed in irony, dialectics, speculative propositions, and so on). Most Chinese schools of thought justify themselves by referring back to "sages" (*shengren*) of the past and the "sage knowledge" (*shengzhi*) they possessed (see chapter 2). Most schools promote a particular "way" (*dao*) of "learning to become a sage" (*shengxue*), and in many of the schools the politico-ethical ideal culminates in the "sage king" (*shengwang*).

This dominance of the figure of the sage in the Chinese tradition poses difficulties for the Western interpreter. In the modern West the image of the sage has lost its force and has become largely irrelevant for speculative thought. By default, Western interpreters treat Chinese thinkers as "philosophers." But for the Chinese the point is to *embody* wisdom, not to contemplate it. Here we may be tempted to say that the Chinese value practice rather than theory (see chapter 4). But this reversal of the Western valuation remains inscribed in the Western dichotomy; it does not quite capture what is at stake in Chinese thought. Perhaps we should say that for the ancient Chinese, practice was theoretical (or metaphysical) – as if one could see with the hand.

In regard to religious ethics, it is decisive that whereas the philosopher is situated somewhere in-between human opinion and human wisdom, the sage is situated somewhere in-between human wisdom and the divine. The Confucian sage is closer to the wise human being; the Daoist sage is closer to the divine. It appears that in China the ethical and the religious are split between the two indigenous traditions: Confucianism and Daoism. Everyone agrees that Confucianism has an ethics, but it is controversial if Confucianism is a religion. The prestigious Chinese Academy of Social Sciences, for instance, does not include Confucianism among the World Religions. On the other hand, everyone agrees that Daoism is a religion, but many scholars, in traditional China as well as in the modern West, emphatically deny that Daoism has any ethics at all. (By "Daoism" I mean the *Laozi* and the *Zhuangzi* and not later Daoist schools and movements, which had strict ethical codes.) Concerted efforts have been made to present Confucianism as a religion. But it may not be before the profoundly ethical nature of early Daoist thought is brought to view that we are in a position to assess China's most important contribution to religious ethics.

Conceptual Schemes

The view that Chinese thought relies on conceptual schemes that are radically different from those of Western thought has a long history in sinology. Most recently, it has been claimed the Chinese have no concepts of rationality, causal thinking, objective truth, dialectics, and definition. It is said that Europe and China rely on opposed valuations. Whereas Europeans value being, individuality, freedom, and rights, the Chinese value becoming, relation, spontaneity, and rites. Not long ago the conceptual difference now claimed for China would have relegated Chinese ethics to the most dense substantiality without any development towards autonomy. In the present postmodern climate of Western philosophy, Chinese ethics is seen rather as an aesthetic expression liberated from all foundationalism. Yet this construction and comparison of conceptual schemes comes at the price of interpretive reductionism. The very moment we establish the difference *between* the two traditions, we homogenize differences *within* each of the traditions. Chinese thinkers are now merely representatives of underlying linguistic and conceptual formations, and the same holds true for the Western interpreter. The result of this operation is that all unique (existential) features disappear (see chapter 14).

Against this reductionism we should emphasize that the other, just like the self, is always also an other (a stranger) to itself, and precisely this provides the possibility for mutual understanding between different cultures. Consider a well-known but underappreciated fact of translation. We know that our best translation is not adequate, but we do not know exactly what it is we know in knowing this. For instance, we know that the English word "humanity" does not quite cover the meaning of the Chinese *ren*, but we do not know *precisely* what it is we know when we know this (if we did, the deficiency could easily be remedied). But Confucius himself was not really sure what the word *ren* meant. For him, too, the word had an uncanny excess of meaning that he could not express. Just like the modern translator, Confucius knows that he does not know the full meaning of the word, but he does not know precisely what he knows in knowing this. It is from the meeting of these two lacks of understanding (Confucius' and ours) that the universal emerges (Žižek 1997: 49–50).

The differences in conceptual schemes are important, but most often it is not conceptual differences but a certain chinoiserie that prevents the Western reader from seeing what is at stake in Chinese ethics. This has led to the prevalent view that Chinese ethics is a kind of aestheticism. According to F. S. C. Northrop, for instance, Chinese ethics has to do with "warm, vivid, personal experiences filled with aesthetic content, such as the crunching of bamboo sprouts between one's teeth, the enjoyment of the flavor of sharks' fins, or the quiet aesthetic intuition of the fragrance and flavor of a cup of tea" (Saussy 2002: 105). This aesthetic interpretation of Chinese ethics is also found in recent postmodern celebrations of Chinese thought. The claim is that because the Chinese sage is not hampered by universal rules, he correctly assesses the ethical flavor of a particular situation – much like a connoisseur appreciates a bowl of sharks' fins soup. This may be a pleasant view, but the real substance of Chinese ethics lies elsewhere: in authoritarianism and strategic thinking.

Authoritarianism

Kinship and bureaucracy are the two fundamental factors of traditional Chinese culture. Society was viewed in terms of the hierarchical structure of the family, and there was a continuum reaching from the family to the scholar-officials (the "father–mother official"), all the way to the earthly emperor (the "son of Heaven") and further into the realm of ancestors and divine bureaucrats that serve the Jade Emperor in Heaven. This continuum may seem to preclude any notion of transcendence, but the power invested in the king (or the emperor) is the one transcending power in China. Whereas everyone in the continuum of hierarchical relations had to bend to their superior (and so lost their moral autonomy), the king was the only one who in principle could act without any regard for such strictures.

This king's transcendent power was absolutely necessary to maintain the traditional system. The power that circulated in the continuum of hierarchical relationships was not bound by a transcending principle (such as God or justice), but was maintained rather through constant strategic manipulation. The ideal (and the ideology) was that the system of hierarchical relations could be strategically manipulated in such a way that it functioned harmoniously as second nature. On two occasions, the intervention of a power that transcends the system was necessary. First, the power that circulates within the system cannot itself found the system. Therefore, at the founding of a new dynasty, the "mandate of Heaven" (*tianming*) had to intervene. The system had to be recharged, as it were, by investing the new ruler with transcendent power. Second, once the system is operating there is always the danger that it may crash. The harmony may be so seriously disturbed that it cannot be restored by strategic manipulation. Again, in this state of exception, to borrow Carl Schmitt's term, the transcending power must intervene, and the one who rules over the exception is the king.

In early China the philosophers and the kings compete over the right to rule over the exception. Competition with the ruler for command of the state is the distinguishing characteristic of the early Chinese schools. The early Chinese "Masters" (*zi*) (Mozi, Mengzi, Hanfeizi, Xunzi, etc.), says Mark Edward Lewis (1999: ch. 2), create in their texts "parallel realities" or "an imaginary counterstate" to the actually existing polity (see chapter 7). In this imaginary realm the Master or the sage (who himself was a textual creation) is put in a position that parallels that of the king in the actual polity. In this way the king and the sage (or, rather, the Master as the sage's representative) are in competition with each other, yet they are also identified in the figure of the sage-king, or the ruler who embodies the "wisdom" (*zhi*) provided by the Master.

If Greek philosophy originated in the competition between citizens and friends and implies a certain equality, the Chinese Masters competed with the king for a power that produces a fundamental split between the ruler (the regulator) and the ruled (the regulated). The Masters claim that they possess a higher order strategic competence: a flexible wisdom that transcends the set responses of particular skills and arts. The philosophical schools present themselves, says Lewis, "as exponents of a generalist, regulatory intelligence comparable to that of the monarch, in contrast to the particular, technical skills of other text-based traditions" (1999: 96). It is precisely as regulators of regulation that the sage and the king coincide. Both are exceptional in that they can act without regard to the strictures that hold for everyone else in the continuum of hierarchical relations. This is well illustrated, for instance, in the idea that Confucius transcends the dichotomy between what is "allowable" (*ke*) and "not allowable" (*buke*) and simply "falls in with what is right" (*yizhi yubi*). This type of sagely "wisdom" (*zhi*) has been compared to Western forms of practical wisdom (*phronesis* or *prudentia*), or to a kind of aesthetic perception (see chapter 5). It is should be understood in terms of the attempt to put oneself in the exceptional position of ruling over the exception, and so control the entire system of hierarchical relations.

In their own imaginary textual world, the Masters may have won the competition with the kings. In the real world, of course, the kings and emperors remained in power. They did, however, adopt a combination of Confucian moralism and Legalist authoritarianism as state ideology. The exercise of state power in China consists in distributing rewards (honor and favors) and punishments (mutilation and death) in a strategic balancing of powers, where the center of power remains obscure or "empty," that is to say, in no particular position and therefore impossible to attack. Confucian "sage knowledge" (*shengzi*) provided important ideological support for this particular configuration of power, which proved to be one of the most enduring in human history. It is remarkable that the ancient Chinese not only developed a bureaucratic form of government that is comparable to that of modern Europe, but also conceived of a totalitarian regime that in its intention is similar to the totalitarian states of the twentieth century. The first Western counterpart to this concept of power may be Bentham's panopticon, sometimes seen as characteristic of modernity. But, as François Jullien points out, in China it had already been invented in antiquity, "and not simply on the cautious, modest scale of a prison but on a scale that controlled the whole of humanity" (1995: 57).

The profoundly authoritarian character of Chinese culture had decisive consequences for Chinese ethics and religious ethics in particular. If state power, the exceptional power to rule over the exception, is sacrilized as the "empty" space beyond any determination, then it can tolerate no competition. Any claim to a competing transcendence must be immediately suppressed. This explains why the Chinese state and its scholar-officials viewed religion with such suspicion and fear. In traditional China it was the responsibility of the county magistrate to collect taxes, employ clerks, sheriffs, and jailers, give lectures on morality, and make offerings at the officially recognized temples. But the magistrate also "kept close watch over all religious activities, especially those involving voluntary organizations of people outside the family and locality groups, whose actions might threaten the sovereignty and religious prerogative of the state" (Teiser 1999: 115). Many have wondered why the present regime in Beijing so brutally suppresses the Falun gong religious movement, not to mention the incarceration, torture, and murder of so many Buddhists and Christians. The response seems out of proportion to the threat. But the regime in Beijing is well aware that the foundation of its power – which is entirely traditional – can tolerate no competition. As a transcendent power, state power must remain one and undivided. This notion of power is the main impediment for China's transition to modernity. One may expect that the most pressing concern of Chinese scholars today would be to formulate an ethics that, unlike the traditional ethics, is not inextricably bound to the notion of a transcendent (sacred) state power.

Bibliography

Jullien, F. 1995: *The Propensity of Things: Toward a History of Efficacy in China*, trans. J. Lloyd. New York: Zone Books.

Lewis, M. E. 1999: *Writing and Authority in Early China*. Albany: State University of New York Press.

Saussy, H. 2002: "No Time Like the Present: The Category of Contemporaneity in Chinese Studies" in *Great Walls of Discourse and Other Adventures in Cultural China*. Harvard East Asian Monographs 212. Cambridge, MA: Harvard University Press.

Teiser, S. F. 1999: "Religions of China in Practice" in *Asian Religions in Practice*, ed. D. S. Lopez, Jr. and S. Donald. Princeton, NJ: Princeton University Press.

Žižek, S. 1997: "The Abyss of Freedom" in *The Abyss of Freedom/Ages of the World*. Ann Arbor: University of Michigan Press.

CHAPTER 38

Origins of Chinese Ethics

Philip J. Ivanhoe

Any account of the "origin of ethics" will be to some degree speculative, for it attempts to explain not only what we know about the written records of another time and place, but also to reconstruct what the authors of these texts were trying to achieve by writing them. For ethics is the attempt to explain oneself to others, to offer a story that one believes other reasonable people will take as in some sense justifying why one acts, believes, and feels as one does (see chapter 5). In this brief account of the origin of Chinese ethics, I will introduce some of the religious and philosophical concepts and orientations that informed the early development of Chinese thought. I will begin with material from the Bronze Age culture of the twelfth century BCE, and then focus on what many regard as the "classic period" of Chinese philosophy, roughly the period between the sixth and third centuries BCE.

The Bronze Age and Early Chinese Ethics

The rulers of twelfth-century BCE China, the latter part of a period known as the Shang Dynasty, relied upon divination to consult a variety of spirits concerning what actions and policies they should pursue (see chapter 44). One method involved the use of shell and bone. Questions would be posed to various ancestral and nature spirits and specially prepared shells or bones would then be cracked by applying the tip of some type of hot implement. The resulting fissures would then be "read" by a diviner – often the king himself – and an answer to the inquiry determined. The questions and often the responses as well would then be carved onto the bone or shell and stored away, perhaps for future reference.

Oracular divination of this period was an important feature of Chinese society, for it enabled the ruling elite to discern and influence events in the spirit world. The early Chinese thought that spirits in general were quite capricious, often hostile or at best indifferent to human well-being. Oracular consultation and sacrifice were ways to understand and influence the powerful spirits who were thought to control many important events, both on the personal and larger social and political levels. Ancestral spirits were especially important in this regard as they retained some of the concern for their posterity that they felt while alive. Hence they were important allies for their living descendants.

The goal of divination was to understand and influence the spiritual world in order to comprehend and control events in the human realm. Successful divination required two primary abilities. On the one hand, the diviner needed to be a master of and be aided by those who could prepare and conduct the physical acts which constituted the divination. Regardless of the type of divination being performed, special *technical* skills and knowledge were needed simply to move through the process. On the other hand, the diviner also needed to be a certain kind of person and to have a certain *character* in order for the divination to succeed. Among other things, he needed to show the proper reverence for the spirits whose aid he sought. Even the most technically flawless divination or sacrifice would prove ineffective if the person performing it was not properly oriented and attuned to the spiritual world. Only a properly sensitive diviner could discern the true meaning of the cracks produced on shell and bone. These three features of early oracular practice – its general goal of understanding "Heaven" in order to facilitate human well-being and the combination of technical knowledge and personal character needed for success – played critical roles in the development of Chinese ethics.

In certain oracular inscriptions, we encounter early forms of a Chinese character which in the modern Mandarin dialect is pronounced *de* ("virtue") (see chapter 4). In these early Shang contexts, *de* was a kind of power which accrued to and resided within an individual who had acted favorably toward a spirit or another person. The favor shown could be some common act of kindness or in the case of a spirit the proper presentation of an appropriate sacrificial offering. It was believed that the recipients of such favorable treatment would feel a psychic debt toward their benefactor and this feeling would, in turn, engender a desire to "respond to" or "repay" the kindness. In this early period, the notion of *de* is almost always found in contexts concerning rulers and had the sense of that virtue particular to a good ruler. A king with "royal virtue" had the endorsement of ancestral spirits, and such support was thought necessary for him to gain and maintain his rule.

With the emergence of a new ruling line, known as the Zhou Dynasty, around the eleventh century BCE, the notion of "virtue" began to change, particularly in regard to the person of the king. A king's ability to rule and the legitimacy of his rule came to be seen as something he could earn or forfeit. An improper ruler, one who neglected his ritual duties, dissipated his *de*, which in turn led to the collapse of his rule. Such a king would lose *tianming* ("Heaven's Mandate") to rule. A ruler who was scrupulous in his conduct, preserved and could even augment his personal power. Rulers were thought to have a role-specific obligation to "take reverential care of" their virtue. They did this primarily by paying strict attention to their ritual obligations as king. These obligations were numerous and varied but underlying them all was the idea that the king must put the good of the people before the satisfaction of his personal desires. At times, the king might even be called upon to put himself at risk in order to benefit his people. A king who failed to revere his virtue, by indulging personal desires at the expense of his royal obligations, would dissipate his virtue and weaken his rule.

The fall of the Western Zhou, in 771 BCE, is traditionally explained in terms of the last king's lack of virtue. It seems that King Yu was deeply enamored of his concubine Bao Si and indulged himself by amusing her. Bao Si was fond of having the king light the series of beacon fires that were supposed to be used to summon his vassals from surrounding territories in times of attack. Even though there was no danger of attack, King Yu would have the fires lit for her amusement. Vassals would gather their forces and rush to the capital, only to find that it was a false alarm. After a number of such false alarms, they stopped coming and hence were not there when the real attack came and toppled his regime.

The story illustrates the belief that self-indulgence weakens the power of a ruler and that eventually this will result in the loss of Heaven's Mandate to rule. Political failure was strongly correlated with moral decay and the latter was understood primarily in terms of sacrificing proper role-specific duties by indulging personal pleasure and advantage. The duties incumbent upon a good king – one who reveres his Heavenly virtue – were for the most part defined by a set of ceremonies and social practices known collectively as the *li* ("rites"). These included high religious ceremonies of state, the regular administration of the government, personal deportment and behavior, and what we would call matters of etiquette. Since everything the ruler did contributed, in some small measure, to the character of his virtue, almost everything he did took on great significance. One sees how the trajectory of this style of thinking leads to a concern with self-cultivation, namely, the attempt, through concerted effort and reflection, to transform one's basic inclinations and dispositions.

Along with and to some extent as consequences of these changes in the concept of "virtue," two related shifts in the Chinese religious and philosophical paradigm were important for the emerging ethical consciousness. First, an appeal to kinship was no longer seen as sufficient grounds to legitimate one's rule. Heaven's Mandate was no longer simply viewed as a hereditary right or a question of fate. The right to rule was thought to depend upon the ritual propriety of the ruler. Second, what mattered in cases of ritual propriety was not simply acting or behaving in a certain way; more important was acting out of proper motivations. One had to perform one's ritual obligations with the appropriate feelings and these were defined largely in terms of self-restraint and other-regarding, ethical qualities.

One can see in this constellation of concerns the influence of the "general goal" and "two primary abilities" needed for divination that were described above. A good king sought to serve and gain the favor of Heaven in order to control important events in the human realm. In order to do this, he needed to master an impressive body of technical knowledge concerning the rites, while at the same time working to cultivate the personal character required to carry them out effectively.

The Classic Period of Chinese Philosophy

Kongzi (551–479 BCE) or "Confucius" and his early followers preserved all three of these central features of early Chinese oracular culture and in this respect they show a conservative tendency. However, they also transformed these ideas into more distinctively ethical concepts. For example, while they believed that properly performed ritual actions had the power to influence events in the world, they tended to believe that this occurred as a result of the force of the ethical example that a practitioner displayed rather than as a manifestation of spiritual powers. In the case of Xunzi (310–219 BCE), a sophisticated and influential follower of Kongzi's teachings, there is an explicit rejection of magical understandings of ritual. He argues for the critical importance of ritual, but in terms that a modern sociologist could easily embrace.

The Confucians are distinctive among early Chinese philosophers for the great emphasis they placed upon rituals and culture in general. They believed that the influence one receives through the practice of certain rituals and the appreciation of certain cultural pursuits such as archery, charioteering, poetry, and music were necessary for the development of moral character. In this set of beliefs, we hear clear echoes of the two "primary abilities" discussed above. In order to realize the Confucian ideal, one needed to master a substantial body of technical knowledge regarding the rites, while at the same time learning how to perform them with the attitudes and sensibilities needed for efficacious performance. While remarkably influential throughout later Chinese history, this characteristically Confucian approach to ethics was rejected by two important competitors: the Mohists and Daoists.

While Mozi (ca. 480–390 BCE) and his followers sought to understand Heaven and control the spirits in order to benefit human beings, they explicitly rejected and ridiculed the Confucian concern with ritual and culture in general and the related emphasis on self-cultivation. Mohists rejected the need for ritual and culture because they did not believe these things in fact helped to shape people's character. They saw Confucian ritual and advocacy of culture as a wasteful extravagance which served as a source of oppression for the common people.

Mohists also strenuously objected to the way that Confucians tended to deemphasize overt faith in and direct appeal to Heaven and the spirits. In contrast, they advocated a literal belief in spirits as the agents of Heaven who regularly acted in the world to ensure that Heaven's will was obeyed. They also believed that certain well-formed arguments proved the truth of their teachings and would convince anyone who was able to follow their arguments to adopt their beliefs. For example, they argued that Heaven cares for and seeks to benefit the people and shows no favorites, supporting only those who are righteous. Those who want to follow Heaven should therefore directly emulate these qualities and act toward all with "impartial care." These and other Mohist teachings gave rise to a kind of state-centered consequentialism. They believed that if people rejected Confucian teachings regarding the importance of ritual and cultural pursuits, as well as the central importance of familial ties, and instead acted with impartial care to increase the basic common goods of wealth, population, and order within the state, everyone would be better off.

Daoist texts such as the *Daodejing*, purportedly the work of the legendary Laozi, and *Zhuangzi*, the "Inner Chapters" of which at least seem to express the views of a historical individual named Zhuangzi, date from the fourth to third centuries BCE. Both texts emphasize the need to follow *tian* ("Heaven") and develop *de* ("virtue"), but understand these ideals in distinctive ways. The *Daodejing* offers a vision of a pristine and innocent stage of human existence, when people enjoyed simple yet satisfying lives in a primitive village-based utopia. Such conditions offered people a way to preserve and strengthen their natural "virtue," "power," or "vitality." They also offered an opportunity to live in peace and harmony, avoiding the dire consequences that are described as the inevitable consequence of more "developed" societies.

The *Daodejing* offers a mystical teaching that purportedly enables one to pre-reflectively understand and move in harmony with natural, Heavenly patterns and processes, thereby avoiding harm and attaining various benefits. In this way, it preserves the "goal" of early oracular approaches. However, it strenuously denies the efficacy or value of ritual and high culture. The *Daodejing* claims instead that such pursuits obscure and deform one's original *de*. The text describes a form of self-cultivation, but one that is designed to pare away and eliminate cultural embellishment and return one to a spontaneous, natural state of understanding and action.

The *Zhuangzi* also seeks to find a way to live in harmony with Heaven or Nature. It is distinctive among the texts discussed in that it does not link the ethical vision it advocates with any particular social or political philosophy. Rather than insisting on the need to reform or reconstitute society, the author describes a way to live in the social world but not be fettered and ruined by it. The *Zhuangzi* notes the importance of *de* ("virtue"). The Confucians tended to regard virtue as a power to attract people and inspire them to greater ethical heights. Zhuangzi sees it as an ability to put others at ease and help relieve them of the debilitating posturing that is seen as characteristic of normal human society. Like the *Daodejing* and the Mohists, Zhuangzi holds ritual and culture as sources of a great deal of human deceit, hypocrisy, and suffering. However, unlike the Mohists, who place great faith in reason, these Daoist thinkers believe that human nature is fundamentally benign and simply needs to be liberated from social practices and norms. Like the *Daodejing*, the *Zhuangzi* advocates a form of self-cultivation that aims at eliminating the pernicious effects of socialization. The author advocates practices like "fasting the heart and mind" and "sitting in forgetfulness" as ways to return to the natural state that is his ideal. Zhuangzi is unique among the thinkers discussed above in explicitly arguing that our natural, authentic state of being is compatible with a wide variety of equally good and proper human lives. He is more than a pluralist; he is ethically promiscuous. He believes that the remarkable variety of good lives the Way engenders offers a valuable lesson. It can make us aware of the vast, open-ended diversity of good lives and help us avoid the common failing of taking our particular point of view as the definitive standard for what is good.

Early Chinese concerns about the power of the spiritual world and the need to understand and control it played a central role in the development of Chinese ethics. Later thinkers retained these concerns and worked to devise ways to comprehend and tap into Heavenly powers, to flow along with the stream of Heaven. In significant contrast to the Mohists, Confucians as well as Daoists of the classical period tended to naturalize earlier, explicitly anthropocentric conceptions of Heaven and the spirits. Yet all three of these schools sought to understand and accord with the Heavenly in a way that would enable human beings to avoid harm and to flourish.

The thinkers we have discussed offered different views about the need for and relationship between the "technical knowledge" and "personal character" that were described as the "primary abilities" for successful divination. Confucians insisted on the importance of both and saw the ethical life as arising from the reflective interplay of ritual, traditional culture, and personal character. Mohists rejected the need for self-cultivation and the value of tradition. They advocated a more rational understanding of the nature and function of both the Heavenly and human realms. Daoists were opposed to Confucian ritual and tradition as well as Mohist rationality. They believed in a spontaneous, pre-reflective style of understanding and action.

The Mohist school died out around the time of the Qin unification in 221 BCE and their demise saw the end of explicitly rational approaches to ethics in China. Confucianism and Daoism continued to flourish and mutually influence one another and were joined by Buddhism, which arrived in China sometime during the first century CE, to constitute the three "Great Traditions" of later Chinese culture (see chapter 29).

Subsequent Developments

Throughout the subsequent course of Chinese history, Confucian, Daoist, and Buddhist thinkers continued to elaborate new variations on the ancient themes. The aim of understanding and tapping into the power of Heaven remained a central concern, especially for Confucians and Daoists. The interplay between the mastery of technical knowledge and the cultivation of personal character proved to be a productive tension for thinkers in all three traditions. It can be seen at work across a range of very different cultural activities. This is one reason why ethical concerns often are not sharply distinguished from other cultural practices within the Chinese tradition. Whether one was consulting the *Yijing*, compiling a history, writing calligraphy, composing a poem, or producing a painting, one was relying on the mastery of technical knowledge that enabled one to cultivate and to express one's personal character. Many of the debates between these three traditions and within each of them about the nature and practice of ethics turned on the relative importance of technical knowledge – often conceived of primarily in terms of traditional methods and standards – versus personal character – often described in terms of innate intuitions or spontaneous tendencies. Regardless of the value attached to these related concerns, they were aimed at cultivating an understanding of Heaven or Nature that would enable human beings to avoid harm and fare well. In this, we see the distinctive orientation of Chinese ethics.

Bibliography

Chang, K. C. 1980: *Shang Civilization*. New Haven, CT: Yale University Press.
Csikszentmihalyi, M. and Ivanhoe, P. J. (eds.) 1999: *Religious and Philosophical Aspects of the Laozi*. Albany: State University of New York Press.
Graham, A. C. 1978: *Later Mohist Logic, Ethics and Science*. Hong Kong: Chinese University Press.
—— 1989: *Disputers of the Tao*. LaSalle, IL: Open Court Press.
Ivanhoe, P. J. 2000: *Confucian Moral Self Cultivation*. Indianapolis, IN: Hackett Publishing.
Keightley, D. N. (ed.) 1983: *The Origins of Chinese Civilization*. Berkeley: University of California Press.

Kjellberg, P. and Ivanhoe, P. J. (eds.) 1996: *Essays on Skepticism, Relativism and Ethics in the Zhuangzi*. Albany: State University of New York Press.

Kline, T. C. III. 2003: *Ritual and Religion in the Xunzi*. New York: Seven Bridges Press.

Schwartz, B. I. 1985: *The World of Thought in Ancient China*. Cambridge, MA: Belknap Press.

Van Norden, B. W. (ed.) 2000: *Confucius and the Analects: New Essays*. New York: Oxford University Press.

CHAPTER 39

Differentiations in Chinese Ethics

Mark Csikszentmihalyi

"Learning from moral models" is what China's President Jiang Zemin prescribed to combat materialism and corruption in a July 2001 speech promoting a combination of law and morality. In doing so, Jiang was continuing a longstanding practice of redesigning socialism to make it compatible with the structures of traditional Chinese ethics. At the height of the Cultural Revolution, when Confucius was criticized as a reactionary who upheld the ideals of a slave society, his model was replaced by "the untroubled image of Mao as the fountainhead of all morality, standing high above all laws and institutions." Ethical behavior was promoted by broadly publicizing the exemplary behaviors of socialist paragons "capable of heroic acts of self-transcendence" and who drew their inspiration from Mao himself (Schwartz 1970: 168). Viewed against the backdrop of traditional China, accommodations to Marx, Lenin, and the ideology of the "market" are the latest in a series of variations resulting from internal conflicts and encounters with foreign religious traditions (see chapter 5). While grounded in a set of canonical texts, and in a set of virtues and the mythic figures that exemplify these virtues, Chinese traditions have constantly varied the elements of these sets in response to such external challenges (see chapter 10).

This chapter will proceed chronologically through the major stages in the development of China's ethical and political traditions. The subjects of the sections that follow are:

1   The three major strands of ethical thinking that were woven together by the historical figure of Kongzi (Kong Qiu, i.e., Confucius), traditionally said to have lived from 551 to 479 BCE.
2   The legacy of Kongzi, his disciples, and the two major Warring States period works that developed systematic accounts of human nature based on the example of Kongzi.
3   Responses to the different traditions labeled as "Daoism" (i.e., Taoism): a naturalization of ethics into a unified theory of the cosmos under the rubric of Way (*Dao*)

in the synthetic atmosphere of the early imperial period, and, on the popular level, the developing role of superhuman entities as arbiters of morality and fate in organized Daoism.

4   The response to Buddhism in the Six Dynasties and Tang periods, as well as its influence on canon formation in the Song Dynasty.

5   The development of scholasticism in the "Study of Principle" (*Lixue*) school associated with Zhu Xi and the "Study of Mind" (*Xinxue*) school associated with Liu Jiuyuan and Wang Yangming in the late imperial period from the Song through the Qing dynasties.

The encounter with the West led to attempts at fusion with non-Chinese traditions and transformed ethical thinking in significant ways while preserving important structures of ethical learning and behavior. Throughout, special attention will be paid to the interplay between the three earliest strands of ethics that were combined to form Kongzi's model of self-cultivation of the virtues.

Three Strands of Ethical Thinking Before Kongzi

The view that Kongzi was "the fountainhead of all morality" in China is not only an artifact of the tradition of moral paragons, but runs counter to the words attributed to Kongzi in the *Analects* (*Lunyu*): "I am a transmitter, not a creator" (7.1). Kongzi's avowed project was not specifically ethical, but rather the recreation of the cultural patterns of the Zhou (trad. 1027–221 BCE): "If there was someone who would make use of me, could I not make a Zhou in the East?" (17.5). Kongzi is not simply being modest: his didactic use of the Zhou *Classic of Odes* (*Shijing*, hereafter *Odes*) and elements of its ritual code are only the most explicit instances of his appropriation of Zhou cultural standards. In particular, three strands of ethical thought appear to have been well developed prior to Kongzi: a political morality, a ritual blueprint for society, and a theory of self-formation based in part on internalizing classic texts. Their common recourse to the ancient sage kings was perhaps the most significant shared characteristic of the three strands prior to their being woven together by the *Analects* and by subsequent attempts to synthesize the heritage of the moral models of the past.

The assertion that Kongzi's religious ethics was in part *political* risks obscuring the more important point that, at least until the time of the early empire in the third century BCE, ruling authority had always been both political and religious. The clearest illustration of this identity was the concept of "Heaven's Mandate" (*tianming*), the fulcrum of many of the proclamations that make up the *Classic of Documents* (*Shujing*, hereafter *Documents*), also known as the *Books of the Predecessors* (*Shangshu*). Heaven's Mandate was the command issued to the Zhou founders, King Wen and King Wu, to overthrow the last corrupt ruler of the Shang in the eleventh century BCE. More generally, it refers to an endorsement by divine authority that both good rulers and virtuous rebels received. Although often viewed as a heterogeneous set of historical works, the texts in the earliest stratum of the *Documents* are orations that repeatedly champion the political authority of the speakers, justifying events such as the Zhou conquest of the Shang and the forced move of the Shang capital to Anyang. These early chapters, thought to date to the reign of Wen's son King Cheng of Zhou, illustrate the way in which the ruler's link with Heaven was the source of his personal morality and of his political authority. The "Announcement of Kang" (*Kanggao*) illustrates the way in which morality and authority are granted by Heaven, albeit conditionally. The tension in the *Documents* between a picture of the ruler as simply a conduit for the divine and the volitional ruler subject to Heaven's sanction becomes an important theme in later discussions of the "mandate" (*ming*), a term that came to connote a limited concept of "fate" in the context of individual lives (see chapter 6). These narratives of political justification, first centered on the Zhou, were later retold about sage rulers of greater and greater antiquity, whose privileged connection with Heaven was identified as the source of their morality.

A separate set of standards of behavior grew out of the multiple contexts of Zhou *ritual performance* (see chapter 9). In areas of intense ritual attention such as sacrifice and funerals, normative attitudes and behaviors were abstracted into general ritual scripts, and then into virtues whose cultivation signaled an acceptance of those roles. Both the *Odes* and the *Documents* preserve early Zhou liturgical formulas that illuminate the degree to which gesture, expression, and appearance were seen as both formative and expressive of ethical dispositions. The *Rituals of Zhou* (*Zhouli*), *Ceremonials and Rituals* (*Yili*), and *Records of Ritual* (*Liji*), three compendia that purported to reconstruct the ritual system of the Zhou, contain elaborate descriptions of the proper attitudes of reverence in sacrifice and grief in mourning. A quotation of Kongzi preserved in the early third century BCE *Mengzi* (Master Meng) explains how when a king dies, the exemplary crown prince's face turns a deep inky black. Other mourners are reassured by this proof of his heartfelt reaction: "When it comes time for the burial, people come from all directions to see it. The devastation on his countenance and the sorrow of his crying (leave) the mourners greatly satisfied."

In writings that post-date Kongzi, a view developed that saw ritual participation as both process and end of self-cultivation practice. In the fourth and third centuries BCE, theorists went to great lengths to explain mechanisms behind the correlation between external signs (e.g., demeanor, gait, and bearing) in ritual contexts, and the internal virtues that they evidenced. Just as the sage kings exemplified an ideal political morality, they were also associated with the construction of the ideal ritual framework.

Bound with these two strands of ethics was a third grounded in a *pedagogical method* based on the interpretation of sacred texts (see chapter 7). While it is difficult to reconstruct the social context of the early transmission of the *Odes* and *Documents*, archeological evidence supports the conclusion that sophisticated exegesis of early texts was a central aspect of the early community associated with Kongzi. In the *Analects* and in excavated texts like the late fourth-century "Kongzi discusses the *Odes*" (*kongzi shilum* among the tomb texts purchased by the Shanghai Museum in 1994), Kongzi offers didactic readings of ancient texts, and twice praises a disciple by saying: "only with you can I discuss the *Odes*!" (*Analects* 1.16 and 3.8). The hermeneutic assumption of exegetes was that the classics expressed the aims (*zhi*) of the early sage kings. As one commentary held, "the *Odes* articulate aims," and so the study and performance of their compositions provided direct religious inspiration. Teaching the proper understanding of these texts led to the development of distinctive modes of exegesis and was a central means of the transmission of the tradition (Van Zoeren 1991). In the second century BCE the Five Classics (*Wujing*, including the *Classic of Changes* – *Yijing* – and *Spring and Autumn* – *Chunqiu* – in addition to the *Odes*, *Documents*, and *Ritual*) became the curriculum associated with the imperial civil service examinations. This began the long process of state sponsorship and institutionalization of their interpretation. In contrast to the other two strands, the actual practice of interpreting the message of the sage kings was attached much more immediately to a fixed set of texts.

These three strands were interwoven from a very early time. For example, the performance of mantic arts by the Zhou rulers as a means of divining Heaven's Mandate was a ritual event that demanded the proper attitude of awe, and which was then memorialized in the *Documents*. However, in context, these three strands appear to have often been separate in terms of social practice, specific sources of authority, and the texts they generated. What they shared was their common perception that they were all part of the bequest of the sage kings of the past.

The Legacy of Kongzi

The diverse teachings of the sage kings were systematized in writings that have come to be identified with the pivotal figure of Kongzi. One of the most controversial scholarly questions today is when that identification began to be made. Chinese writing is usually thought to have originated with official records of communication with the divine inscribed on media of divination, inscriptions commemorating noble individuals or events inscribed on sumptuary vessels, and records of the speeches and edicts of early rulers. Even in the case of new genres of the kinds identified with Kongzi, archeology reveals that texts rarely circulated with authorship explicitly identified. The biographies of the putative authors of many early Chinese texts appear to be little more than later projections of voices found in the texts themselves. Despite centuries of attempts to discover the authentic Kongzi, this problem and a related one imperils any claim to authoritative biography: there are too many texts and so too many possible Kongzis to definitively select one as authoritative.

Despite the lack of an authoritative biography, there are common tropes and concerns in many of the earliest attributed materials. Descriptions of Kongzi differ from that of the celebrated sage kings in one major detail: Kongzi, despite his intention to revive the ritual and political system of Zhou, was unable to attain the political influence to do so. The earliest biography of Kongzi, dating to the *Grand Scribe's Records* (*Shiji*) at the end of the second century BCE, narrates his life as a circuit of feudal states during which Kongzi was by turns slandered, overlooked, or treated in a ritually improper way. Though he occupied minor offices, he suffered the fate that the age never recognized his talents. As a result, narratives about Kongzi's deeds were less important than his recorded advice to rulers and disciples aspiring to hold official positions.

Several canonical sources draw from a body of diverse sayings and anecdotes written on bamboo slips and circulated in the late Spring and Autumn and Warring States periods, but do so based on different principles of selection. The *Transmission of Zuo*

(*Zuozhuan*), a commentary to the terse chronicle *Spring and Autumn*, transmits quotations that are loosely concerned with historical episodes, issues of fate and contingency, and, occasionally, a form of historically informed observation that resembles the reading of omens. The *Analects* (*Lunyu*, literally "Considered discussions"), by contrast, appears to have been assembled in the early imperial period, probably in the second century BCE. The conversations in the work represent the sage's advice to rulers and disciples. They are concerned with self-cultivation practices that result in reliable stewardship of state or office. Early imperial collections like the *Records of Ritual* and the *Lineage sayings of Kongzi* (*Kongzi jiayu*) preserve large amounts of Kongzi's recorded speech, but are generally more diverse and thought to mix material from Kongzi's time, Warring States period inventions, and genealogies and prophecies from the early dynastic period.

It is the *Analects* that has long been the basis for the later reception of Kongzi's ethics. The work as a whole incorporates all three strands outlined above into an ideal of moral perfection based on the internalization of a set of behaviors designed to qualify one for the performance of official duties. The process of self-transformation in the *Analects* focuses on developing benevolence (*ren*), righteousness (*yi*), wisdom (*zhi*), and trustworthiness (*xin*). *Benevolence* entails acting with awareness of the personhood of others, entailing both kindness and compassion. *Righteousness* is an obligation to act fairly, especially in official contexts. *Wisdom* is often discussed in the context of discerning the character of others or evaluating the appropriateness of actions in particular circumstances. *Trustworthiness* is acting in a manner consistent with one's words.

In the system of the *Analects*, ethical action was also role-specific. Self-transformation consisted of locating oneself correctly with respect to one's family through filial piety (*xiao*) and to one's community through ritual propriety (*li*). Speech and demeanor proper to one's status in the family and society were not seen as "surface" requirements, but as transparent and spontaneous signs of developed ethical dispositions. The *Records of Ritual* make this connection: "This is the same reason that the gentleman is ashamed of wearing suitable clothes but having the incorrect deportment, of having the correct deportment but saying the wrong things, of saying the right things but lacking the appropriate virtue, of having the appropriate virtue but lacking the proper action." The progression from dress to ethical action is not a matter of etiquette. It confirms that the actor understands the way in which clothing, deportment, speech, virtue, and action are all inextricably linked, and mutually entail each other. Besides this central place of ritual self-cultivation, the *Analects* also champions the position that Heaven's Mandate, as testified to in the *Odes* and the *Documents*, had been granted to the ancient sage kings on account of their virtue.

In the centuries after Kongzi's death, changes in society led to modifications in his system. One third-century BCE source, *Master Fei of Han* (*Han Feizi*), records that after Kongzi's death, his disciples split into eight factions, each of which emphasized different aspects of Kongzi's message. The fragmentation that was to have the most influence on the tradition dates to a third-century BCE debate on human nature. While there is no question that the major synthesis of the three strands of ethics had already occurred by the time of the fourth and third century BCE writers Mengzi (Meng Ke or Mencius, ca. 380–ca. 290 BCE) and Xunzi (Xun Qing or Hsün Tzu, ca. 310–ca. 238

BCE), they extended the legacy of Kongzi in ways that made the synthesis ethically robust. Both figures are known through the texts that bear their names, the 14-chapter *Mengzi* and the 32-chapter *Xunzi*.

The *Mengzi* argues that within each person's mind are incipient bases of the virtues. These were the "minds" of compassion (*ceyin*), shame (*xiu'wu*), yielding (*cirang*), and right and wrong (*shifei*). These "sprouts" (*duan*) of moral reactions are already present in the inner mind, and may be nurtured to become the four virtues of benevolence, righteousness, ritual propriety, and wisdom, respectively. The *Mengzi* does not really argue that human nature is good, but instead that the mind has dispositions to goodness, which need to be developed through reflection and practice (Ivanhoe 2002). The *Mengzi*'s picture is an innatist one. The moral education of Kongzi was held to be the best way of developing moral dispositions that were inherent in human physiology.

The contents of the *Xunzi* are extremely diverse, but the chapters thought to be authentically the work of Xunzi are generally concerned with ritual and music as a means to transform individuals, and thereby society. A famous catechism in its first chapter, *Quanxue* (Encouraging Learning), outlines the central role of a course of training: "In terms of its process, [learning] begins with reciting the classics and ends with reading the rites. In terms of its significance, [learning] begins with being a candidate for office, and it ends with being a sage." The reason one studies ritual is that it allows one to cultivate the virtues, which is an indirect means to promoting social order. The *Lilun* (Discussion of Ritual) chapter emphasizes how rituals and obligations (*li* and *yi*) were developed by the sage kings to "nourish the people's desires and satisfy their needs." In the *Xunzi*, society is an expression of the sages' desire for order, the only sense in which moral tendencies might be considered "innate" (Wong 2000).

The connection between ritual's radical reshaping of a person in the *Xunzi* and the development of incipient "sprouts" through reflection on the *Odes* and *Documents* in the *Mengzi* also illustrates how the program of ethical training favored in each text is consistent with its implicit moral psychology. The *Xunzi*'s focus is not on innate dispositions as in the *Mengzi*, but rather on external influences. Proper training conditions a person to have a certain set of reactions to external stimuli, in effect transforming the individual's basic nature and the affective dispositions that guide his or her reactions. The *Xunzi* explicitly and implicitly attacks the *Mengzi* and indicts the notion that anything inherent in the body will aid the process of training.

To some extent, these developments of the synthesis associated with Kongzi may be seen as a redifferentiation of the tradition in response to changes in society in the Warring States period. Li Zehou (1986) has argued that the changes in social structure allowed the *Mengzi* to go further than *Analects* in separating noble status from virtue, and promoting moral self-restraint. Hou Wailu (1947) wrote that the late third century's integration of law and ritual, as well as attempts at synthesizing diverse modes of knowledge under the rubric of the "Way," are all clear influences on the *Xunzi*. The competing pictures of human nature in these two texts, then, have been read as variations on Kongzi's synthesis resulting from contrasting social conditions. The unification of the Chinese empire in the third and second centuries BCE exerted another type of influence on these ethical traditions, one in which the "Way" played the major role.

Ethics and the Way in the Early Empire

Both the *Mengzi* and *Xunzi* continued to be read after the consolidation of the empire in the third century BCE, yet the major transformation of ethics was a result of its integration with other discourses. The Qin (221–206 BCE) and Han (206 BCE–220 CE) dynasties established a precedent for many of the structures that are now identified as essential characteristics of Chinese society. Despite its brevity, Qin structures of imperial control and its methods for unifying diverse groups were adopted by the Han. It was the sustained and unified empire of the Han that established the pattern for everything from political institutions to historical writing throughout later dynastic history. From the perspective of religion and philosophy, the introduction of Buddhism in the first century CE and the formation of organized Daoism in the late second century CE exerted profound effects on the legacy of Kongzi. The systematization of theories of natural cycles based on *yinyang* dualism, the physics of the five phases (*wuxing*, i.e., water, wood, fire, earth, and metal), and other classifications of phenomena became the basis for the growth of a plethora of technical disciplines in areas from divination to astronomy to medicine.

The political consolidation of the early empire set the tone for an attempt to integrate regional traditions and specializations that had hitherto been differentiated. The Han synthetic impulse extended to ethics, and many Han texts integrated the diverse influences on Kongzi's thinking into other frameworks, such as theories of natural cycles. In the first century BCE *Elder Dai's Records of Ritual* (*DaDai Liji*), attributed to Dai De, the ritual and obligations central to *Xunzi*'s picture of ethics are likened to the alternation of the five phases according to the seasons: "That the pattern changes is because ritual is like the five phases and obligation is like the four seasons." The fact that ritual forms depend on one's obligations reflects the progress of the five phases according to the four seasons. Often, these correlations had the effect of erasing the remaining distinctiveness of the early strands of ethics explored above. An example is the recently excavated Han commentary on a pre-imperial work on ethics called the *Five Kinds of Action* (*Wuxing*). The anonymous commentary explains a verse from the *Odes* about King Wen of Zhou's reception of the mandate from Heaven by paraphrasing the *Xunzi*'s account of the origins of ritual, thereby homogenizing all three strands of thinking identified above. What both these uses of the earlier writer Xunzi have in common is that they put less emphasis on the role of the sage kings in cultural creation. Instead, they imply that ritual patterns were incipient in the natural order and provide for the possibility that the patterns may change.

The increasing importance of concepts of natural order and change in the Han synthesis reflects the influence of fourth and third century works like the *Laozi* and *Zhuangzi*, often identified with Daoism or as the canonical texts of "philosophical" Daoism. These works in general rejected the ethics of virtue in favor of a call to return to the spontaneous reactions characteristic of one's original nature (*xing*). The normative or originary picture of a world in which everything follows its nature is expressed using the concept of an overarching Dao (Way), which was then picked up in the Han as a universal framework on which a synthesis of disparate ideals could be built.

The Way was used to similar purposes in the second and third centuries CE by a set of healers who combined medical and shamanistic practices with the rhetoric of the *Laozi* to create the social organization of the *tianshi* (Celestial Masters). As Qing Xitai (1988) has argued, the notion of an automatic reward for good and bad actions found in the earliest strata of the Celestial Masters tradition has much in common with the consequentialist mechanisms of the fourth century BCE *Mozi*, yet because the celestial masters used the same emblem of the Way, they are today also labeled as Daoist. An emphasis on the aid of salvific divinities, perhaps in part a response to the arrival of the forerunners of Buddhism in China, may also have led to an increasing emphasis on the role of a semi-divine Kongzi in the newly unified ethical systems. His chronicle *Spring and Autumn* acquired commentaries that read it as an encoded manual for rulership. The Han historical work *Shiji* (Grand Scribe's Records) traced the project of classical exegesis to the initial efforts of Kongzi, whose birth was accompanied by auspicious portents. Finally, the Kong family's maintenance of ritual traditions at the birthplace of Kongzi in Qufu (in modern Shandong province) became the model for the later imperial system of Kongzi temple sacrifice. In the synthetic atmosphere of the Han, the malleability of Kongzi's biography was used as a resource for unifying the diverse strands of pre-imperial ethical thought.

The Influence of Buddhism in the Six Dynasties and Tang

The Six Dynasties period (222–589 CE) was a pivot in the history of Chinese religions in that it marked the period in which the "three teachings" (*sanjiao*) of Confucianism, Daoism, and Buddhism became self-conscious traditions. The common suffix *jiao*, which meant "teaching" and later came to be used for "religion," identified them for the first time as being of the same kind, so engaged in similar projects, and potentially in competition. Imperially sponsored debates between the adherents of two or three of the "three teachings" made clear the degree to which they could be, for the first time, viewed as mutually exclusive systems of belief.

The Six Dynasties period saw a resurgence of interest in the classics *Laozi* and *Zhuangzi*, and figures like Wang Bi (226–49 CE) and Guo Xiang (d. 312 CE) read such "Daoist" works alongside works attributed to Kongzi. They also applied terms deriving from the former texts, such as "naturalness" (*ziran*), to the understanding of the latter. Guo Xiang, in his commentary to the *Zhuangzi*, explains how a person who has stripped him or herself of the artificial trappings of morality would have no use for praise of the sage kings: "condemnation and glorification both arise from insufficiency, so those of ultimate sufficiency forget good and evil, and dispense with death and life. They become one with change and transformation, and in their vastness nothing is not proper". This challenge to the ethics of virtue was answered by figures like Fan Ning (339–401 CE), who specifically criticized Wang Bi for allowing "benevolence and righteousness [to] sink into darkness."

Criticisms of Daoism, however, were tempered by the fact that some of its notions were useful in anti-Buddhist polemics. The close relationship between Buddhist cosmology and ethics meant that in order to rebut the Buddhist eschatological framework, writers had to enlist aspects of indigenous cosmology that were better developed in Daoist texts (see chapter 30). In the Six Dynasties period, Liu Jun (462–521 CE) echoed the argument of Dai Kui (330–95 CE) that natural endowments of pneumas and unpredictable environmental influences all had determining effects on people's lives in a way that had nothing to do with notions of karma. In refuting Buddhist cosmology, Liu Jun expanded the notion of the "mandate of Heaven" to resemble the *Zhuangzi*'s notion of "naturalness."

In the newly centralized China of the Tang Dynasty (618–906 CE), Buddhist and Daoist institutions developed and received official support, and Confucianism adopted some of their models of lineage and transmission. In particular, the notions of *Daotong* (transmission of the Way) and *Zhengtong* (transmission of good governance) developed as an attempt to define both a Confucian orthodoxy and orthopraxy that might be distinguished from doctrines and practices that had been "polluted" by Buddhism and Daoism. Official support for Confucianism was exemplified by Emperor Taizong's commission of Yan Shigu (581–645 CE) to annotate the Five Classics. Anti-Daoist and anti-Buddhist writings rebutted the challenges of these traditions to Confucian ethics on a fundamentally different basis than the challenges to Buddhist cosmology of the Six Dynasties period.

The task of defining an authoritative "transmission of the Way" was a central element of the nascent Confucian revival of the Tang. Because the transmission was traced to pre-Buddhist China, this definition was part of an effort to legitimate Confucian traditions. Han Yu (768–824 CE), an influential and iconoclastic Tang essayist, traced the transmission of the Way from the ancient sage kings, to the rulers of the Zhou dynasty, to Kongzi and then to Mengzi. The loss of the transmission roughly coincided with the arrival of Buddhism in China. The biography of Han Yu in the *New History of the Tang* (*Xin Tangshu*) draws a comparison between Han's critiques of Buddhism and Daoism and Mengzi's earlier criticisms of the figures Yang Zhu and Mozi, implicitly identifying Han Yu as the next figure in the line of the Daotong or Daoxue (Learning of the Way). Han Yu attacked Buddhism on a number of counts. Foremost was a genealogical argument: Buddhist traditions did not derive from the Way of the ancient sage kings of China, and as a result lacked the proper connection between knowledge and action. At the same time, Han Yu was also implying that Han and Six Dynasties exegetes had also lost the Way. In so doing he was attempting to refocus the Confucian enterprise back to the Warring States concern with moral rulership and social engagement.

Han Yu's contemporary Li Ao (d. ca. 844 CE) promoted a model of self-cultivation based on a concept of "returning to one's nature" (*fuxing*) that had strong overtones of the Tiantai Buddhist conception of the recovery of the "original mind" (*benxin*). For Li, the goal of Confucian practice is not simply the development of cultivated ethical dispositions. It is also to clear away desires in order to attain a sagely ideal that was described with many of the same terms used to characterize Buddhist enlightenment. While the Confucian emphasis on social engagement was held up as a major factor that differentiated it from Buddhism, Confucian writers also began to reread their tradition to recover its idealist aspects and resuscitate its moral psychology.

In the Tang and the Song Dynasties, in part in response to such needs, the Confucian canon was gradually redefined. Those elements of indigenous traditions that could rebut Buddhist notions of the mind and enlightenment were preferentially revived. The establishment of the "Four Books" (*sishu*) in the Song Dynasty was actually the result of changes that had been underway for centuries. At that time, the *Analects* was raised to canonical status along with the *Mengzi* and two chapters of the *Record of Ritual: Great Learning* (*Daxue*) and the *Doctrine of the Mean* (*Zhongyong*). The *Mengzi*'s place in the canon may be traced back at least to Han Yu's contention that Mengzi was the last classical representative of the Transmission of the Way. One reason the *Mengzi*, *Great Learning*, and *Doctrine of the Mean* were especially appealing in the post-Buddhist context was their development of moral psychology and of links between that psychology and a cosmology that included the magnetic power of *cheng* (sincerity) and the quasi-divine conception of the *sheng* (sage). These texts furnished a basis for constructing models of transcendence compatible with the goal of returning to an original "nature" unclouded by desires.

"Study of Principle" and "Study of Mind" in the Later Empire

The late imperial revival of the legacy of Kongzi bifurcated into two competing traditions in the Song (960–1279), Yuan (1280–1367), and Ming (1368–1643) dynasties. Both offered solutions to the problem of how to reconcile traditional practice and the imperative to social engagement with the reemergent psychologistic and idealist orientation represented in the newly elevated "Four Books." The solutions of the "Study of Principle" (*lixue*) school associated with Zhu Xi (Zhu Yuanhui, 1130–1200) were critiqued by Lu Jiuyuan (Lu Xiangshan, 1139–93) and later by Wang Yangming (born Wang Shouren, or Wang Bo'an, 1472–1529). The latter critiques developed into another tradition, sometimes called "Study of the Mind" (*xinxue*).

The early "Study of Principle" school structured its theory of moral knowledge on a view of the cosmos based on the dualism between *li* "principle" and *qi* "matter" (see chapter 13). The cosmological basis of this school is often traced back to Zhou Dunyi's (Zhou Maoshu, 1017–73) "Explanation of the Diagram of the Supreme Ultimate" (*Taijitu shuo*), which combines the symbolic scheme of the *Classic of Changes* with the moral language of the "Four Books." Zhou Dunyi's "supreme ultimate" (*taiji*) imbues all things, both animate and inanimate, but is expressed in its purest state in the nature of human beings. The basic disposition to good found in the *Mengzi* is no longer an aspect of the physiological model of incipient "sprouts" of virtue, but a reflection of the purity of this cosmic principle contained in human nature, identified with the sage's quality of sincerity. The brothers Cheng Hao (Cheng Mingdao, 1032–85) and Cheng Yi (Cheng Yichuan, 1033–1107), who exerted a major influence on the views of Zhu Xi, developed and elevated the notion of human nature to subsume allied notions of fate, mind, affective dispositions, the Way, and Heaven. Cheng Yi held that morality inheres in the aspect of one's nature that is an expression of the natural pattern of principle, but is obscured by the *qi* of one's material nature. "Settling one's nature" (*ding xing*) and cultivating an attitude of reverence refines the neutral *qi* in the mind, making it possible to discover principle. In this way, the dualism between *li* and *qi* became the cosmological background to a new understanding of self-cultivation as the search for a transcendent order permeating the universe.

Zhu Xi's influence as a religious systematizer and a commentator on the "Four Books" exerted a defining influence on the "Study of Principle" school. His views became a reference point for future argumentation in ethical traditions. At the heart of the "Study of Principle" (also called the Cheng-Zhu school) was Zhu Xi's systematic application of the Cheng's notion of principle to his scholarly reformation of prior doctrine and practice. For this reason, some writers have applied terms like "rationalist" or "metaphysical" to what has been called Zhu Xi's "Neo-Confucian" position. It is true that human nature became entrained with a conception of principle that transcended not only the individual but also the category of human beings in general. Indeed, Zhu Xi wrote that jackals and otters carried out sacrifices, while tigers and wolves cared for their young, citing this as proof that animals could also penetrate principle. At the same time, Zhu's early exposure to Chan Buddhism translated into an appreciation of the role of institutions and practice in the maintenance of traditions, and the study of the classics was at the core of his self-cultivation practice.

Zhu Xi's synthesis centered on transcendent principle, and was tied to a program of cultivation practice directed to gaining access to that principle. Since ritual, the virtues, and social hierarchies were all expressions of this incipient pattern, Zhu Xi was able to resynthesize the strands of early Chinese ethics in a way that more closely matched the needs of a post-Buddhist age. The mind was the vehicle for understanding "principle," but this was not accomplished in isolation because principle was embodied in the works of the sages and worthies of the past. To properly engage these works, a program that combined quiet sitting (*qingzuo*) to clarify the mind and a particular method of studying the classics with was developed. Zhu Xi adopted Cheng Yi's application of the phrase "penetrating things" (*gewu*) from the *Great Learning* to his hermeneutical method. He meant to foster a resonance between the principle in the interpreter's mind and the principle of the things being interpreted. This method of mutual activation was a crucial aspect of Zhu Xi's self-cultivation program. It had the effect of restoring the ethical status of exegesis by making interpretation an active process integral to becoming a moral person.

The "Study of Mind" (*Xinxue*) school became a formal rival of the "Study of Principle" school, especially following the explicit criticism of Zhu Xi's understanding of "penetrating things" by Wang Yangming in the early Ming Dynasty. Some early Song writers, such as Zhang Zai (Zhang Hengju, 1020–77) and to some extent even Cheng Hao, conceptualized the apprehension of principle as largely a matter of intuition. It was Zhu Xi's contemporary Lu Jiuyuan who argued that principle was discernable in the mind, and as such practice needed to be organized around the realization that, in Lu's words: "The universe and my mind are identical." Harkening back to the physiological arguments of the *Mengzi*, Lu saw the structure of the mind as being universal, and therefore held that the principle that ran through the works of the sages and worthies of the past was accessible in one's own mind.

Wang Yangming, the other major figure in the "Study of Mind" school (also called the Lu-Wang school), extended Lu's position by criticizing Zhu Xi for artificially dividing the mind and principle. Wang Yangming's critique of "Study of Principle" revolves around his view of the necessary relationship between knowledge and action, and of the inferiority of "ordinary knowledge" gained through study to experiential knowledge connected with daily action. Wang Yangming's fame rests on his reputation for swift action in his official career, and on his related emphasis on accessing an intuitive level of understanding. This has led some to label his thought "idealist." Wang adopts the phrase "true knowledge" (*liangzhi*) from the *Mengzi*, where it is explained as "the things a person knows without having to reflect" (*suo bulu er shi*), such as parental love and respect for elders. He used it to explain the way in which knowledge of principle is incipient in the mind.

While both the "Study of Principle" and the "Study of the Mind" criticized Buddhism, both their views on the mind and on specific meditative practices clearly owed much to Buddhist traditions. Lu Jiuyuan explicitly criticized Zhu Xi as advocating Chan Buddhism, yet was also criticized by Zhu Xi's disciple Chen Chun (Chen Anqing, 1159–1223) for "sitting in silence all day, during which time even a slight idea is taken as a sign of enlightenment, and said to be an authentic secret that had not been transmitted from the time of the ancient sages." Wang Yangming also directly criticized Buddhist practitioners for their detachment from the world. Nevertheless, modern scholars have compared his view that moral knowledge depends on clearing away the dust of the desires to reveal the mind's inherent moral principles to Chan Buddhist notions of the "original mind." Liu Zongzhou (Liu Qidong, 1578–1645), a revisionist "Study of the Mind" scholar, acknowledged the nature of the mutual influence when he wrote that Zhu Xi "was affected by Chan but then repudiated Chan," Liu Jiuyuan "interacted with Chan but then shunned Chan," and Wang Yangming "resembled Chan but then condemned Chan."

The institutional aspects of Confucian writing in later imperial China reflect the importance of orthodoxy in its concern with the "transmission of the Way." Zhu Xi's redefinition of that transmission included the early Confucians connected with the composition of the "Four Books." He located the Late Imperial resumption of the transmission with Zhou Dunyi and the Cheng brothers. Zhu Xi's own commentaries became orthodox parts of the civil service examination system at the start of the fourteenth century. This happened despite the fact that one area in which both the "Study of Principle" and the "Study of the Mind" schools agreed was in their criticism of the examination system as encouraging people to pursue Confucian training out of a desire for self-advancement.

Conclusion

Transformations of Chinese ethics resulting from the encounter with the West may be seen in the rather syncretic moral works of the Qing (1644–1911). In the work of revisionists like Kang Youwei (1858–1927), the portrait of Confucius as a social reformer was part of an effort not only to change the corrupt system of Manchu rule, but also exert a unifying effect in the manner that Christianity was perceived to have done in the West. A more critical attitude toward many aspects of traditional culture was taken by the 1919 May Fourth Movement, an attempt to reform the post-imperial Republican government. When the 1949 Communist Revolution established the People's Republic of China, the locus of new Confucian thinking and scholarship moved to Taiwan, Hong Kong, and the Chinese diaspora. The destruction of the connection between the state, the performance of Confucian ritual, and the mastery of traditional texts significantly changed the nature of the modern tradition. This has effectively shifted the locus of its transmission from the imperial government to the international university.

Because Kongzi's vision of ethical self-transformation was intended to make a person worthy of stewardship, it was predicated on a particular model of familial and social relations. For this reason, ethics in the contemporary Chinese family is still predicated on preserving a connection between particular social institutions and personal morality. Perhaps this best explains why, while the understanding of both individual virtues and the optimal means of cultivating them changed significantly in response to factors like the arrival of Buddhism and changes in society, the goal of emulating a set of moral exemplars by developing ethical dispositions has remained constant.

Bibliography

Cady, L. 1939: *The Philosophy of Lu Hsiang-shan*. Taibei: Pacific Cultural Foundation.

Chaffee, J. 1995: *The Thorny Gates of Learning in Sung China*. Albany: State University of New York Press.

Csikszentmihalyi, M. 2001: "Confucius" in *The Rivers of Paradise*, ed. D. N. Freedman and M. J. McClymond, 233–308. Grand Rapids, MI: Eerdmans.

Gardner, D. K. 1986: *Chu Hsi and the Ta-hsüeh: Neo-Confucian Reflection on the Confucian Canon*. Cambridge, MA: Harvard Council on East Asian Studies.

Graham, A. C. 1989: *Disputers of the Tao: Philosophical Argument in Ancient China*. La Salle, IL: Open Court.

Henderson, J. B. 1991: *Scripture, Canon, and Commentary*. Princeton, NJ: Princeton University Press.

Hou, W. 1947: *Zhongguo sixiang tongshi*. Shanghai: Xinzhi shudian.

Ivanhoe, P. J. 2002: *Ethics in the Confucian Tradition*. Indianapolis, IN: Hackett.

Knoblock, J. 1988–94: *Xunzi: A Translation and Study of the Complete Works*, 3 vols. Stanford, CA: Stanford University Press.

Li Zehou. 1986: *Zhongguo gudai sixiang shi lun*. Beijing: Renmin chubanshe.

Ng, O.-C. 2001: *Cheng-Zhu Confucianism in the Early Qing*. Albany: State University of New York Press.

Nylan, M. 2001: *The Five "Confucian" Classics*. New Haven, CT: Yale University Press.

Qing, X. 1988: *Zhongguo Daojiao shi*. Chengdu: Sichuan renmin.

Schwartz, B. 1970: "The Reign of Virtue: Some Broad Perspectives on Leader and Party in the

Cultural Revolution" in *Party Leadership and Revolutionary Power in China*, ed. J. W. Lewis. Cambridge: Cambridge University Press.

Van Zoeren, S. 1991: *Poetry and Personality*. Stanford, CA: Stanford University Press.

Wong, D. B. 2000: "Xunzi on Moral Motivation" in *Virtue, Nature, and Moral Agency in the Xunzi*, ed. T. C. Kline and P. J. Ivanhoe, 135–54. Indianapolis, IN: Hackett.

CHAPTER 40

Trajectories of Chinese Religious Ethics

Mark Berkson

The Chinese traditions that date from the classical period (ca. sixth to second centuries BCE) – most prominently the *Rujia* ("The School of the Scholars," or "Confucianism") and *Daojia* ("Philosophical Daoism," exemplified in the *Daodejing* and *Zhuangzi*) – as well as the organized Daoist religious traditions (*Daojiao*) that date from the late Han (second to third centuries CE), establish a number of essential themes, terms, and concepts that have remained significant to the present. These give Chinese religious ethics a certain coherence, albeit a remarkably plural one with numerous tensions. To this set of indigenous traditions is added Indian Buddhism around the beginning of the common era, which constitutes the first major outside cultural and religious influence on China (see chapter 31). Throughout China's history there has been only one example of foreign influence that rivals the Buddhist, namely the modern encounter with "the West." This encounter – far more violent, both literally and metaphorically, than the Indian Buddhist – shook China's foundations. It threatened China's political and cultural integrity and posed a major intellectual challenge to the inheritors of its religious traditions. The ways in which Chinese thinkers drew on the resources of and/or critiqued Confucianism, Daoism, and Buddhism in response to the challenges of the West constitutes one of the most significant aspects of modern and contemporary Chinese thought. These efforts have resulted in the development of distinctive forms of Chinese religious ethics characterized by an engagement with Western philosophy, democracy, economics, technology, natural sciences, and more recently, ecology, feminism, and postmodern thought. This chapter considers common themes and current trajectories in Chinese ethics.

Common Threads

While "Chinese religious ethics" contains multiple traditions that differ from each other in significant ways, there is also a discernible set of ethical concerns, concepts, and orientations shared by the indigenous traditions and those that are "sinicized," such as Chinese Buddhism of the Tang Dynasty (618–907) and beyond. These themes include the following:

1   A prominent role for "nature" in the ethical framework. This includes the Confucian concern with the cultivation/realization of human nature; the Daoist emphasis on following the natural Dao; and the Buddhist focus on realizing Buddha Nature.
2   A "this-worldly" emphasis focusing on practical considerations of how to live well, how to become a "good" or "true" person. There is not the kind of emphasis on the next world or afterlife that there is in Christianity and Islam, particularly among the indigenous Chinese traditions.
3   An emphasis on self-cultivation and a belief in human perfectibility. The goal is the achievement of sagehood, a possibility for any human being.
4   Syncretism and pluralism, seen in both thinkers who are deeply informed by multiple traditions, and in organizations and movements that bring together many traditions.
5   A notion of order and harmony as the highest goods, involving both an inner harmony within each human being (e.g., between mind and body) and, ultimately, a harmonization of heaven, earth, and humanity.

The Challenge of the West and Modernity

The unprecedented shock that China received in the mid-nineteenth to early-twentieth centuries came from the West both in the form of political–military challenges and new intellectual currents. Beginning in the 1840s, Chinese military defeats resulted in a loss of territory and the imposition of unequal treaties, producing feelings of humiliation and powerlessness in many Chinese. On the intellectual front, works of Western thought were becoming increasingly available in China.

Chinese intellectuals focused on the question of how China should adapt to meet these challenges while retaining its own identity in the process. One prominent response came in the form of the "Self-Strengthening Movement." It argued that China did not need to change institutions or philosophical foundations, but needed only to master Western arts like shipbuilding and weaponmaking in order to repel the "barbarians" and protect Chinese civilization.

Other thinkers, such as Kang Youwei (1858–1927), believed that China did need to make institutional changes, but that this could be done in an entirely Confucian manner. Rather than looking to a past Golden Age, Kang looked to a future utopia characterized by the Confucian virtue of *ren* (benevolence), egalitarianism (including equality of women), and universalism.

Some Chinese thinkers advocated the more radical goal of replacing traditional Chinese culture. One of the leading critics of Confucianism was Chen Duxiu (1879–1942), a founder of the Chinese Communist Party, who argued that Chinese ethics is the "ethics of a feudal age" and sharply attacked Confucianism for its patriarchy. Despite the harsh criticism often directed at Confucianism by communists, it is clear that Chinese communist ethics was influenced by Confucian thought. For example, Liu Shaoqi, a chief theoretician of the Chinese Communist Party, wrote "The Self-Cultivation of a Party Member" (the very title employs a Confucian theme), which emphasized the Confucian practice of moral self-reflection in party members.

Another radical critic of traditional Chinese thought was Hu Shi (1891–1962). Hu embraced American pragmatism, rationalism, and science, and was a harsh critic of Buddhism and Confucianism. Hu admired the restless striving toward advancement found in the West and argued that China's "culture of contentment" was an obstacle to progress.

Varieties of New Confucianism

The Confucian thinkers of the nineteenth century and beyond are often characterized as constituting the "Third Epoch" of Confucianism. The first was the classical period of the late Zhou, during which the foundations of the tradition were laid; the second was the "Neo-Confucianism" that arose from Confucian thinkers' engagement with Buddhist thought. The Third Epoch, known as "Contemporary Neo-Confucianism" or, more commonly, "New Confucianism," is characterized by the response to, and integration with, Western thought through the critical examination and creative renewal of the tradition.

The thinkers of this period, often working in Taiwan and Hong Kong, emphasize the "religious" or "spiritual" dimension of Confucianism grounded in a cosmic source (*tian*, "Heaven") that is both transcendent and immanent. The vision has been described as "anthropocosmic," centered on humanity, but not in an "anthropocentric" way. It recognizes the micro/macrocosm interconnection and correspondence between the human and heavenly realms. The metaphysics is grounded in the notion of a single, integrated cosmos, one ultimate reality that embraces and harmonizes all individuals (see chapter 12). This Way can be found within the individual human heart-mind (*xin*). Embodying the Way (*Dao*) is equivalent to revealing and manifesting the moral heart-mind, the heavenly endowment within each of us. The essential nature of this heart-mind (and thus the moral cosmos) is *ren*, the overarching Confucian virtue of "benevolence" or "humanity."

Most New Confucians have advocated a form of idealism and intuitionism, particularly as articulated by the Neo-Confucian Wang Yangming (1472–1529) and the Consciousness-Only (*Yogācāra*, *Weishi*) school of Mahāyāna Buddhism. Most also exhibit a tendency toward creating syncretistic systems that combine Western and Chinese thought and feature a systematic moral metaphysics.

One feature of New Confucianism that has emerged largely as a result of the encounter with Western thought is an increased emphasis on equality (including political, economic, and gender equality) and a corresponding critique of Confucianism's traditional hierarchical worldview. In general, New Confucians have seen the value of democracy, science, human rights, and the importance of critical reason. They also caution against the excesses to which some Western ideas tend (e.g., rationalism, scientism). They want to present a reformed and revitalized tradition that they believe will be seen as at least equal to Western thought, and amenable to fruitful harmonization with it.

Xiong Shili and his students

There are debates over the point at which a coherent "New Confucian" school coalesced and who belongs in its ranks. One common picture emphasizes the lineage of philosopher Xiong Shili and his students, "second generation" members Xu Fuguan, Tang Junyi, and Mou Zongsan. Xiong Shili (1885–1968) brought together Neo-Confucian and Buddhist thought with *Yi Jing* cosmology and Western influences, such as science and nationalism. Xiong's emphasis was on unity, and he criticized the separations of *li* (principle) and *qi* (psychophysical energy), tranquility and activity, and substance and function. All of these dualities are merely different aspects of the same reality, the "Great Ultimate," which is a fundamental unity underlying all individual things. He employed the common Buddhist metaphor of water and waves to describe a pervasive ultimate reality that gives rise to individual instantiations that are not ultimately separable from it. Human beings can apprehend this reality with intuition, through which we "awaken to our original nature," which is *ren*. Echoing earlier Neo-Confucians, he wrote: "A man of *ren* forms one body with all things." Xiong advocated a balance of activity and quietude, a full participation in social life grounded in the pure, unchanging moral mind. Xiong emphasized an aphoristic formulation which was then picked up by later New Confucians: "Sage Within, King Without." This illustrates how realizing the moral self leads to social and political action.

Xu Fuguan (1903–82) was the least interested in metaphysical speculation among the disciples of Xiong. He emphasized the practical dimension. One of his contributions was the positing of a "sense of anxiety" as a central feature of Chinese culture. Unlike the notion of existential *angst*, original sin, or *dukkha*, Xu's notion is a fully moral one. It describes the feeling of responsibility toward the world, arising from our conscience, that leads us to want to cultivate our moral selves and improve the world. Sages are those people who are true to their own nature by overcoming selfish desires and allowing the inner moral reality to manifest itself in virtuous action. For Xu and the others, Confucian ethics is deeply political. He argued that not only is Confucianism compatible with democracy (the people are seen as "heaven's representatives"), but that "democracy can obtain a more supreme ground from the revival of the Confucian spirit, and Confucianism can complete its actual objective structure through the establishment of a democratic polity."

The two other well-known students of Xiong, Tang Junyi (1909–78) and Mou Zongsan (1909–95), both constructed elaborate metaphysical systems to ground their ethics. Mou wrote that the trajectory of Chinese thought, unlike Western thought with its origins in Greek natural philosophy, had its origins in moral sage kings and always maintained ethics at the center. Mou's ethics takes the moral subject as a starting point, seeing intellectual/moral intuition as the foundation for systematic philosophy. He focused on "concern consciousness," a sense of worry and concern for other people and the world that is a source for the developing moral consciousness. Mou was profoundly influenced by Kant, whose distinction of noumena and phenomena played a central role in Mou's thought. Mou argued that we have two kinds of intuition: a sensible intuition that allows for the apprehension of worldly phenomena, and an intellectual intuition that enables us to grasp the noumenal. He believed that the intellectual/moral consciousness is rational, and that to follow it is to realize our nature. This results in happiness, the *summum bonum* understood as a fully moral achievement. The mind is "the transcendental foundation of moral behavior and is itself absolutely and infinitely universal."

The third generation and beyond

Contemporary New Confucians are often called the "Third Generation" and share many characteristics with their predecessors. The best known among the contemporary New Confucians is Tu Weiming, who teaches at Harvard University. His work sympathetically presents the Confucian vision to a Western audience and contributes to its interpretation, reform, and modern application through commentaries and philosophical work. Tu advocates Confucian dialogue not only with other religions and Western philosophy, but also with psychoanalysis and Marxism (a departure from the strong anti-Marxist stances of most earlier New Confucians).

Tu's prominence is one example of the lively development of Chinese thought in the West. An aspect of this trend is the growing involvement of non-Chinese scholars in both the interpretation of Chinese thought (Confucian, Daoist, and Buddhist) and active participation in constructive daological work. There are even "schools" of Chinese thought developing in the West. The most famous is the "Boston Confucians" that includes Chinese scholars living in the area and American thinkers such as Robert Cummings Neville and John Berthrong, who bring in Christian and Western philosophical perspectives to their Confucianism. Understood broadly, "Boston Confucians" can apply to all Confucians living in the West whose goal, in Neville's words, is "bringing Confucian philosophy into the world philosophic conversation." A related phenomenon is the growing presence of people who see themselves as having a "multiple religious identity." Some members of the Boston Confucian school, for example, have a deep commitment to the values and worldviews of both Confucianism and Christianity, making them "Confucian Christians."

Another significant trend is the recent development of New Confucianism in mainland China and a growing dialogue between mainland and overseas Chinese. In the decades that followed the Communist Revolution, the Marxist–Maoist orthodoxy, enforced by the coercive power of the state, virtually silenced other forms of thought. After the ascension of Deng Xiaoping and the significant, though unpredictable, opening and reform that has occurred since, Chinese religious and philosophical traditions have enjoyed something of a renaissance. Conferences on Confucian thought have been held in China, volumes published, and a "China Confucius Foundation" established. One notable voice has been that of Fang Keli. He describes communism, liberalism, and New Confucianism as the three major streams of Chinese thought, all of which must work together for the modernization of China.

Global Confucian philosophy

Three of the main areas in which the increasingly global Confucian philosophy is participating are ecology, feminism, and human rights. Thinkers representing Chinese traditions have pointed out that the Western "Enlightenment Mentality," while producing many admirable achievements, has also led to serious crises. One of the most severe crises is environmental (see chapter 47). Some thinkers suggest that the anthropocentrism that characterizes much of the Abrahamic faiths' attitude toward the rest of creation has been at least partly responsible for the current problems. Chinese thinkers propose that the "anthropocosmic" Chinese view might provide a better foundation for a sustainable environmentalism. China's "naturalistic cosmology" is grounded in a notion of the Dao as the natural pattern underlying all things. It is characterized by an emphasis on the interdependence of all things and an underlying psychophysical foundation of *qi*. Confucian thinkers point out that this "continuity of being," and the possibility of attaining a harmonious triad of Heaven, Earth, and Humanity, make Confucianism a good candidate for contributing vital perspectives to the environmental movement.

Many modern Chinese thinkers have taken seriously the challenge of feminist critique and have attempted to respond with reinterpretation and reform (see chapter 54). Confucianism's patriarchal history might make it an unlikely candidate in terms of usability for feminist projects. Yet some scholars argue that if one strips Confucianism of its androcentrism and patriarchy, there are valuable resources for feminist thought. Confucianism emphasizes a nature that is shared by all human beings and the possibility of any human being, male or female, achieving sagehood. The primary Confucian virtue of *ren* has been compared with the feminist ethic of care. The relational Confucian self has been understood as somewhat analogous to a feminist conception of the self. Resources for a "Confucian feminism" (which might differ from, and thereby serve as a critical lens on, Western feminism) have been drawn from both classical Confucians as well as later thinkers such as the Ming Dynasty radical thinker Li Zhi (1527–1602). He believed that women, like men, can fully realize themselves through self-cultivation if their lives are not unfairly restricted.

Finally, there is a robust discourse occurring regarding Confucianism and human rights, with scholars representing a wide range of positions (see chapter 51). Some have argued that "rights" is a concept conceived in the West and therefore inextricably tied to its culture and philosophical positions (e.g., a particular notion of the autonomous individual as rights-bearer and a law-based society). Rather than speak of Chinese "rights," we should look at Chinese "rites." This provides an ethical alternative that should be explored by the West as a supplement to the discourse of rights. On the other end of the spectrum are those who argue that rights are universal, whether or not any particular culture recognizes them or has an indigenous notion of them. Some scholars point to the embrace of human rights notions by Chinese students and intellectuals during the uprising of June 1989 as evidence of their universal applicability. There are also scholars who argue that, while traditional China had no concept or term for "rights," such a notion was implicit in Chinese ethics. There are many thinkers who are now working on ways to bring together Chinese "concept clusters" (to use Henry Rosemont's term) involving virtues, the relational self, and role-specific obligations with Western clusters involving rights and the autonomous individual. The idea is to mutually enrich both and create a more "international philosophical language."

Developments in Daoist and Buddhist Ethics

Throughout history, Confucians have criticized Daoist and Buddhist quietude and detachment, particularly the Daoist notion of "non-action" and avoidance of political service, and Buddhist monasticism and emphasis on sitting meditation or simple chanting. The criticisms are somewhat unfair, as there are well-developed ethical dimensions in both Daoism and Buddhism. There is also some truth to that characterization when applied to certain forms of the two traditions. This has led modern Daoists and Buddhists to work on developing more socially engaged forms of their traditions.

Daoism

"Daoism" has been used to refer to both the philosophical–daological traditions represented most commonly by the *Daodejing* and the *Zhuangzi*, and the multiple "religious"/liturgical traditions that originated in the Han Dynasty. One area in which an increasing number of Daoist thinkers and scholars are working is ecological thought. Some scholars caution against the tendency to think of Laozi and Zhuangzi as allies in environmentalism (particularly because of the dimension of non-action and non-interference in these texts, which would undermine the activist orientation that most environmentalists endorse). However, many believe that the worldview informed by "philosophical Daoism" provides a way of thinking about and acting toward the non-human natural realm that produces a harmonious and mutually beneficial relationship. The Dao is understood as the natural pattern that underlies all living things, and is described as a creative, nurturing force. The texts caution about interference with its processes and over-reliance on human intelligence. They advocate a way of acting that is fully in accordance with the movement of the Dao (*wu wei*, "effortless action"), rather than self-conscious striving. This would produce a tendency to "let Nature be," so that the Dao will act as harmonizer of all things. Harmonization occurs when each thing acts *ziran*, in accordance with what is "so of itself" without artificial impositions. While there is what might be called an "ethic" involving harmonization, the guidance of nature, and the undermining of selfishness and rationalism, there is not the sense of a "moral cosmos" in the Confucian sense. The cosmos is generally seen as amoral (e.g., not characterized by benevolence) and yet harmonization with it, living in accordance with its way, can be seen as the *summum bonum* (see chapter 2). Daoism does not share the Confucian belief that human beings occupy a higher place than other natural beings in the order of things. Daoism holds that the very things that set human beings apart (e.g., the mind's making of distinctions and creation of categories) bring about our downfall.

Daoist "religious" traditions also provide valuable resources for ethics. From the beginning, moral codes were an essential component of Daoist communities. Many Daoists posit a link between moral action and one's spiritual and physical states (immoral action can produce illness, and can be healed through rituals of expiation). Virtue has been connected with longevity or immortality, and Daoist sages are seen as having perfected moral qualities (see chapter 10). Altruism and compassion are common features of the sages featured in the Daoist religious traditions such as *Tianshi* (Celestial Masters), *Lingbao* (Numinous Talisman), and *Quanzhen* (Complete Perfection). Much of what can be described as "Daoist self-cultivation" involves the elimination of selfish desires to achieve harmony with the Dao.

There are two main existing Daoist religious traditions – *Zhengyi* ("Orthodox Unity") and *Quanzhen*. Members of these traditions have increasingly become involved in environmental action. For example, Zhang Jiyu, the 65th descendant of Zhang Daoling, considered to be the founding figure of religious Daoism, has written about ecological consciousness from a Daoist perspective and publicly calls upon Daoists to put these views into practice. He writes: "We shall spread the ecological teachings of Daoism, lead all Daoist followers to abide in the teachings of self-so or non-action . . . and preserve and protect the harmonious relationship of all things with Nature . . . We shall continue the Daoist ecological tradition by planting trees and cultivating forests."

Daoist resources have also been applied to recent work on feminism. Historically, the Daoist religious communities have featured women in leadership roles and as sages to an extent not found in the other Chinese religious traditions. For example, there are Daoist nuns in contemporary Taiwan who lead temples, and they are committed to Daoism's engagement with the modern world, particularly through environmental action. The philosophical texts, with their emphasis on either the need to harmoniously balance the *yin* (female) and *yang* (male) energies, or the primacy of the *yin* (which, seen as "yielding," "non-competitive," and "soft," has the power to ultimately overcome the "hard"), are seen as having much to offer contemporary feminists. Some feminists, who articulate a view grounded in nature, focus on the descriptions of the Dao as fertile, nurturing, and characterized by "feminine" values. Others who have a more "cultural constructivist position," emphasize the theme, found in both the *Daodejing* and the *Zhuangzi*, of the artificiality of all dualities and the complementarity and mutual dependence of all apparent opposites, including male–female.

Buddhism

While Buddhist scholarship was eclipsed by Neo-Confucian developments during the late imperial period, Buddhism in China enjoyed a revival in the late nineteenth and early twentieth centuries. However, along with the other religions, it fared very poorly from 1949 to the 1980s in mainland China, with its nadir during the Cultural

Revolution. Since the 1980s, fortunes have improved in mainland China. In addition, a dramatic Buddhist revival occurred in Taiwan following the establishment of the Nationalist government in 1949.

The best-known figure of the Buddhist revival is the abbot Tai Xu (1889–1947). Beginning in the 1920s, he started a reform movement that advocated social involvement and an approach to education that taught secular subjects in addition to Buddhist studies. Tai Xu believed that the Buddhist emphasis on universal compassion could help bring together the various ethnic groups that make up the Chinese population and thereby strengthen China. The movement connects an emphasis on the revival of monastic life with social engagement, including a central role for the monasteries in helping the poor.

Engaged Buddhists see liberation from *dukkha* (suffering, unsatisfactoriness) as something that can occur not only at the level of the individual practitioner, but also at the social, political, economic, and environmental levels. The very notion of interdependence shows that these levels cannot be separated. Engaged Buddhism often makes use of notions such as interdependence and mutual interpenetration (a theme with powerful ecological applications), no-self, Buddha Nature (a nature shared by all beings), and skillful means to ground the ethical praxis. The bodhisattva ideal, a selfless commitment to work within this world in order to relieve the suffering of others, occupies a prominent place in this religious ethics.

A noteworthy feature of the Buddhist revival in Taiwan is the prominent role of women, who constitute the majority among the thousands of monastics ordained after 1949. One example is the Buddhist nun Ven. Zheng Yan, the founder of Taiwan's largest charitable association. The foundation supports hospitals and free clinics, education and environmental protection, among other things, and Zheng Yan calls on people to "wash the earth clean and purify people's hearts." The ethical commitments are connected with a metaphysical picture. She believes that when people awaken to their original nature, the result will be a spontaneous manifestation of love for all sentient beings. When acted upon, that love produces "a Pure Land of peace and joy."

Fo Guang Shan, another significant movement, was founded by Master Xing Yun. His personal experience of war and poverty moved him to focus on social action (including the founding of medical clinics, orphanages, wildlife preserves, and educational institutions). The group, which advocates the equality of men and women, has an international scope (supporting development efforts in different parts of the world) and has been involved in intrafaith (bringing forms of Buddhism together) and interfaith dialogue.

Over the last few decades, Buddhists, more than the members of any other Asian religious tradition, have engaged in interfaith dialogue with other traditions, particularly Christians and Jews. There has been an increase in people with "dual religious citizenship" who might call themselves "Zen Christians" or "Buddhist Jews." Models of pluralism, syncretism, and multiple religious identity have long existed in much of East Asia. They are beginning to take shape increasingly in the West.

One frequently addressed theoretical issue is the relationship of ethics (often represented by the notion of *śīla* – moral practice in accordance with the precepts, including no harming, lying, stealing, abusing intoxicants or sexual misconduct) and soteriology. Nirvāna is sometimes portrayed as beyond ordinary moral distinctions and therefore transcending ethics. There is a division between those who believe that ethics is a preliminary step to be left behind upon enlightenment, and those who believe that an enlightened Buddha is one who manifests ethical perfection (e.g., the full realization of the Bodhisattva perfections) and thus is never "beyond good and evil." To what degree *upāya*, or skillful means aimed at liberation, can lead to a suspension of the ethical is also the subject of debate.

Popular Religion

There are countless examples of syncretic religious groups or societies in China that have flourished for periods of time. The best-known contemporary Chinese movement, Falun Gong, is a synthesis of Daoist and Buddhist elements. It involves notions of enlightenment and physical and spiritual power that can be achieved through the psychophysical exercises of *qigong*. The group has become well known in light of the crackdown by the Chinese government. Their practice involves exercises that combine movement, breath work, and meditation. Falun Gong, as with other modern syncretic groups, has an ethical dimension, focusing on three main virtues: truth (*zhen*), goodness (*shan*), and forbearance (*ren*). The assumption is that moral cultivation must accompany the physical and contemplative exercises in order for one to achieve enlightenment. Through dedication to the practice, individuals become happy and a harmonious social environment results.

Popular Chinese religious practice focuses on earthly, life-affirming values such as happiness, longevity, and wealth (these goods being represented by deities who can help people achieve them). While much of popular religion does have an element of *quid pro quo* ethics involving gods, ghosts, and ancestors, it also serves as a source of moral education. Like China's elite daological traditions, popular religion is highly syncretic. Popular ethics is characterized by the strong role of ancestors, filial piety, education, and virtue cultivation from Confucianism. It is also informed by notions of karma and hell regions derived from Buddhism. It can be difficult to disentangle the pervasive influence of Daoist religion from that of general "folk religion" in the overall lives of most Chinese people. Chinese deities, for example, combine a bureaucratic model often seen in Daoism (with representation at the home, local, and "imperial" levels) with Buddhas and Bodhisattvas, numerous ghosts and popular gods (such as Mazu), and ancestors. These beings are to be worshipped, revered, propitiated, or petitioned as appropriate. If the deity is treated properly and not angered, one will avoid harm or enjoy benefits. Many Chinese believe that one is watched by a range of deities, both within the body (a Daoist contribution) and without. The deities keep records and decide on rewards and punishments, with consequences for one's lifespan and afterlife existence. Beyond this results-oriented relationship, people express attitudes and feelings such as gratitude, piety, and awe, through ritual, chanting, praying, etc. The "moods and motivations" connected with religious belief and practice certainly have an impact in the ethical sphere.

Conclusion

The Chinese religions' approaches to syncretism and harmonization, along with their "this-worldly" emphasis on nature, interdependence, self-cultivation, and the achievement of sagehood, make them good dialogue partners for the Abrahamic traditions and valuable participants in the global ethical conversation. Having had a profound influence on the East Asian cultural sphere for around two millennia, Chinese religious ethics has now begun to have an impact on the rest of the world. The future trajectory of Chinese religious ethics will likely involve an increasingly global character, a continuation of interfaith dialogue, and philosophical and social engagement with the vital issues of our time, such as ecology, feminism, human rights, and religious pluralism.

Developments in Chinese religious ethics over the last two centuries illustrate both the continuity provided by the core concepts and values that have characterized the Chinese traditions since the classical period, and also the transformations that have occurred as the traditions responded to the confrontations with the West and modernity. Chinese and non-Chinese thinkers alike will continue to apply, develop, and transform the rich ethical resources of China's religious traditions.

Bibliography

Bresciani, U. 2001: *Reinventing Confucianism: The New Confucian Movement*. Taipei: Ricci Institute for Chinese Studies.

Cheng, C.-Y. and Bunnin, N. (ed.) 2002: *Contemporary Chinese Philosophy*. Cambridge, MA: Blackwell.

De Bary, W. T. and Weiming, T. 1998: *Confucianism and Human Rights*. New York: Columbia University Press.

Giraradot, N. J., Miller, J., and Xiaogan, L. 2001: *Daoism and Ecology: Ways Within a Cosmic Landscape*. Cambridge, MA: Harvard University Press.

Li, C. (ed.) 2000: *The Sage and the Second Sex*. Chicago: Open Court.

Tucker, M. E. and Williams, D. R. 1997: *Buddhism and Ecology: The Interconnection of Dharma and Deeds*. Cambridge, MA: Harvard University Press.

CHAPTER 41

African Ethics?

Barry Hallen

Controversial Paradigms

Western scholars have tended to use the word "morality" rather than "ethics" when discussing values in the African context (Beidelman 1993). The presumed reasons for this may be hypothesized as follows. First, the articulated systematic thinking underlying these societies' moral codes is minimal, and so it is better not to obscure this point by associating stipulated forms of moral behavior with the name of a discipline, "ethics", that is defined primarily by articulated systematic thinking and the reasoned principles it produces (see chapters "On Religious Ethics", 1, and 2). Secondly, morality in the African context is practically oriented, in that its primary task is to inculcate and regulate behavior that is socially acceptable or unacceptable.

African intellectuals and scholars have protested vigorously about such studies (Gbadegesin 1991; Gyekye 1995; Wiredu 1996), which falsely portray African societies as communities where individuals mindlessly submit to moral values (characterized as "traditions") that are inherited from the distant past, that continue to be enforced virtually unchanged in the present, and that will be passed on to future generations in an uncritical manner because their ultimate justification is itself an appeal to tradition. "We believe these things are right (or wrong) because this is what we inherited from the forefathers" (see chapter 6).

One of the earliest and still influential publications on this subject by an African scholar is John Mbiti's *African Religions and Philosophy*. Note the plural and singular forms, respectively, of the nouns that constitute the title. This might be taken to imply that, depending upon the particular African culture, the relationship between religion and philosophy can vary. This would mean that, although there is a common philosophical core to all of Africa's cultures (a point now subject to controversy), there are a variety of religions ("native," "traditional" religions) that may or may not impinge upon that philosophy. "Traditional religions are not universal: they are tribal or national. Each religion is bound and limited to the people among whom it has evolved"

(Mbiti 1970: 5). As far as morality is concerned, this would mean that there are cultures in Africa in which moral values derive directly from a divine source (Idowu 1962), as well as cultures in which the linkage between the religious and the ethical is less significant. "There are other societies in which people do not feel that they can offend against God . . . that God has no influence on people's moral values" (Mbiti 1970: 270). The latter would apply to a culture in which the ultimate justification for morality is humanistic – these are the chosen values because they are deemed most likely to secure human happiness – a viewpoint about which there will be a good deal more to say in what follows (Wiredu and Gyekye 1992: 193–8).

The more controversial implication of the title is that there is a single set of philosophical (including ethical) principles that underlie all of Africa's cultures. Whether Mbiti's divergent views on religion and philosophy in the African context would themselves remain consistent becomes a point worthy of consideration, insofar as the same ethical/moral principles and values would be held common to all of Africa regardless of whether they had a divine or secular origin. Mbiti eventually comes down in a fairly one-sided manner on behalf of the divine. "Most African peoples accept or acknowledge God as the final guardian of law and order and of the moral and ethical codes" (1970: 269). He affirms that religion permeates virtually every aspect of African life, as well as viewing African society as an organic whole (he prefers the term "corporate") whereby individual immorality is also communal immorality is also divine immorality.

One unfortunate consequence of this paradigm has been to reaffirm the portrayal of African societies as places where the individual moral consciousness ("Regardless of what my community says is right, what ought I do in this situation?" – MacIntyre 1967: 84–109) was denied in an uncompromising manner. Africa again is presented as an ethical environment where behavior and compliance with rules is the praiseworthy norm, and the role of the individual consciousness in determining or evaluating "traditional" norms inherited from some virtually mythical past is of no real consequence. "Therefore, the essence of African morality is that it is more 'societary' than 'spiritual'; it is a morality of 'conduct' rather than a morality of 'being.' This is what one might call 'dynamic ethics' . . . for it defines what a person *does* rather than what he *is*" (Mbiti 1970: 279).

Divinely Inspired or Humanistic Ethics?

In what follows, interest will center upon the debate among philosophers of Africa as to whether a variety of ethical principles and moral values that may be taken as truly indigenous to Africa's cultures are directly divinely inspired and sanctioned or are more properly seen as of secular origin in societies that are best typed as humanitarian in orientation. One noteworthy consequence of this debate has been the reinstatement of articulated, reasoned ethical principles as intrinsic to the justification of more specific moral values in these societies (Wiredu and Gyekye 1992: 198). Another is that the importance of moral judgments made by the individual in determining and affirming what is or is not ethical in a particular situation has been reasserted (Hallen 2000). These findings have been achieved via the research of a new generation of African scholars, as well as via a vigorous critique of Western views of how thought must be expressed in order to qualify as genuinely philosophical, and thereby ethical, in character.

Though knowledge in cultures that are significantly oral may be expressed in different forms than is conventional in the paradigmatically literate West, this does not mean the character of thought underlying those forms is different (e.g., emotive and pre-reflective rather than reasoned and critical). Myth, poetry, song, verse, proverb, and story, as well as such philosophical staples as language usage and discursive ideas (social or individual), can also be used to express viewpoints that are of theoretical (as well as practical) significance.

Certainly, most Africans have never felt deficient in this regard and were taken aback to find themselves being characterized as such. It was primarily Western scholars, associating such forms or expressions of thought with relatively underdeveloped powers of ratiocination, who persevered in drawing this conclusion. But it is philosophers familiar with the intellectual contexts and content of both Western and African cultures who are challenging it as ethnocentric and insisting that the boundaries of philosophy must be redrawn if it too is not to be labeled the "traditional" beliefs of just one other "tribe" – those of the so-called "West." This need not mean that orthodox philosophical approaches such as analytic philosophy (Hallen 2002), phenomenology/hermeneutics (Serequeberhan 1994), or Marxism (Fashina 1989) become irrelevant to the African ethical context. Rather, with the appropriate adaptations made to facilitate their working within that cultural context, they too may continue to provide insights of genuine value.

In order to place in historical context the claim that ethical principles and moral values in indigenous African cultures can be of secular origin, and therefore may be best characterized as humanitarian, it is important to recall that initially (Western) scholars and missionaries did not even consider this a possibility. The vocabulary that associated the religious with the moral was demeaning, to say the least – emphasizing such terms as "fetishes," "idols," "rituals," "taboos," "juju," "cults," "witchcraft," etc. – all involving exotic beliefs about various "forces," "spirits," or "deities" characterized as "pagan" and unenlightened by comparison with truly "world" religions like Christianity and Islam. (There are a number of published studies that detail how Christianity and Islam are themselves being indigenized – transformed – so as to suit the African context: e.g., Peel 2000.) The image of "tribes" of "natives" bowing down to "fetishes" that were associated with rigidly enforced moral absolutes ("traditions") was more compatible with the portrayal of societies that had been characterized as "primitive" (precursor to the supposedly less offensive "traditional"). This is why, in what follows, more attention will be devoted to recent secular, humanistic renderings of ethics in specific African cultures. Although, to do justice to the relation between indigenous religions and moral values, it will also be necessary to examine the arguments of those new generations of African scholars and intellectuals in this respect as well.

Contemporary Positions

A growing number of contemporary African philosophers maintain that the relationship between religion and morality in Africa's indigenous cultures has been misrepresented by claims about the supposed permeation of religion into all facets of African life. The Ghanaian philosopher Kwasi Wiredu aims to counter this by maintaining: "African conceptions of morals would seem to be of a humanistic orientation" (Wiredu and Gyekye 1992: 194). Wiredu suggests this hypothesis may be confirmed via studies of the basis for morality in individual African societies. To practice what he is "preaching," Wiredu himself has published numerous studies of morality in his native Akan culture.

In what follows, interest will center on Wiredu's writings, as well as those of his Ghanaian colleague, the philosopher Kwame Gyekye. The case they make for the secular basis of morality in Akan culture is compelling. It arises from five specific points:

1   "The remarkable fact that there is no such thing as an institutional religion in Akan culture" (Wiredu and Gyekye 1992: 194). The idea that the cosmos has been created by God with various deities and quasi-physical forces within it is a given. But their primary relevance to human beings is that these deities and forces can be used for personal and/or utilitarian ends if correctly addressed and respected. The motive for doing so is primarily to achieve some form of practical end. The idea of "worshiping" such beings because of their intrinsic holiness is foreign. On the other hand, an attitude of "unconditional reverence and absolute trust" (1992: 195) is extended to the Supreme Being (or God). This is conjoined with the belief that *so* perfect a Being is not in need of worship – in fact might not even welcome it – and therefore remains somehow distant from the created world (Gyekye 1995: 196).

2   The humanitarian origins and focus of morality (in Africa generally) are further justified and explained by Gyekye because of the absence of a prophetic religious tradition:

> The doctrinal system of a religion *revealed* by God to a single person, the founder, invariably includes elaborate prescriptions to guide the ethical life of the people who can accept and practice that religion. A coherent system of ethics can be founded upon such divinely revealed commands . . . It is clear, however, that traditional African religion cannot be said to be a religion whose doctrines were embodied in a revelation. (Gyekye 1995: 206)

3   Given points (1) and (2), the basis for morality must derive directly from humanity. It is human beings who are left to devise systems of values ("all value is derived from human interests"). Furthermore, an essential motivating factor is the consensus that "human fellowship is the most important of human needs" (Wiredu and Gyekye 1992: 194). The good is what is regarded as promoting human interests as defined by human beings themselves.

4   The primary source of moral instruction is the family. "Nor, relatedly, are any such institutions ["institutionalized" religion as a source of moral values] felt to be necessary for the dissemination of moral education or the reinforcement of the will to virtue. The theater of moral upbringing is the home, at parents' feet and within range of kinsmen's inputs. The mechanism is precept, example and correction" (Wiredu and Gyekye 1992: 195).

5   All of the above points mean that religion in Akan society is said to be "purely personal, being just a tenet of an individual's voluntary metaphysic, devoid of social entanglements" (Wiredu and Gyekye 1992: 195).

What becomes of interest are the specific values espoused by such a culture to flesh out what is said to be its basic humanitarian orientation, and what are said to be the ethical principles that underlie and justify those more specific values. The fundamental ethical principles underlying the more specific moral values distinctive of Akan society and culture are two: (1) an obverse form of the Golden Rule: "Do not unto others what you would not they do unto you" (Wiredu and Gyekye 1992: 198) and its corollary (2) individual interest cannot and therefore should not be divorced from communal well-being. "In Akan moral thought the sole criterion of goodness is the welfare or well-being of the community" (Gyekye 1995: 132).

The specific values derived from these principles are "kindness," "generosity," "faithfulness," "honesty," "truthfulness," "compassion," "hospitality," and whatever "brings peace, happiness, dignity and respect" (Gyekye 1995: 132). All of these are said to promote *social* well-being. This should not be taken to mean that an individual's personal interests become totally subordinate to those of the community. Communal and individual interests are balanced so that self-interest encompasses the welfare of the community along with that of the individual (Gbadegesin 1991: 64).

Sanctions play an essential role in the *constitution* of morality in Akan society. But these sanctions, as well, are primarily social insofar as they involve the diminution of an individual's integrity and thereby personhood if, for example, self-interest becomes a motive that has negative consequences for communal well-being. Gyekye ridicules Western philosophers who tout the individual's moral "reason" as the sole basis for doing what one "ought" as unrealistic and impractical. It takes a social context and socially imposed sanctions for morality to become a real force on purely practical grounds (1995: 139–41) (see chapter 3).

The revised role of religion in this overall humanitarian ethical and moral schema is said to be supportive rather than foundational. In certain situations religious beliefs serve as reinforcement for moral behavior that, on logically independent humanitarian grounds, is considered improper. Both Gyekye and the Nigerian philosopher Segun Gbadegesin (1991: 67–78) regard the function of religion in this regard as pragmatic – it can serve as a further, though less direct or powerful, incentive for the individual to be moral. "It may appear puzzling that the practical aspects of a morality whose principles are not grounded in religion should [also] be animated by religion; yet this position does not involve any logical inconsistency" (Gyekye 1995: 141).

The individual person has a self-conscious sense of what is right and wrong (or conscience) in addition to these relatively external sanctions. Indeed, the role of individual moral judgments, and therefore responsibility for one's actions, are another foundational element of Akan ethics and morality. The connection between this individual moral sense and the communal is made explicit when Gyekye argues it "is not innate to man, but [is] something acquired through socialization, through habituation, through moral experience" (Gyekye 1995: 143).

A final dimension to the ethical in the Akan context is the importance attached to "character." When one is said to have a good character, one is awarded the status of being a "good person," which means that one can then be depended upon consciously to try to do the right thing in any situation. This is determined primarily on the basis of behavior and therefore socially, but such behavior is of course thought to arise from individualized and self-conscious intentions.

Among the Yoruba people in Nigeria a good character appears to have epistemological consequences as well, in that such individuals are regarded as reliable sources of information generally. If being good also involves being honest about what one truly knows (or does not know), then ethical values also involve epistemological virtues (Hallen 2000). Among the Yoruba this conjunction of the ethical with the epistemological is further reinforced by the involvement of the aesthetic, in that a person who has a moral character that can be depended upon is also said to embody the highest form of beauty. In other words, the individual who is said to have a good character embodies the highest paradigm of the beautiful, with physical beauty, by comparison, coming in a distant second (Hallen 2000).

Conclusion

Does the emphasis upon being practically relevant diminish a moral system's theoretical integrity? Does the fact that moral precepts must be seen to work in practice – to produce results that benefit both the individual and society – transform theory into dogma, precept into command? The response that seems to be coming from philosophers in and of Africa is a resounding "no." The point of the ethical and the moral *is* to make a difference in people's lives. This need not mean that the importance of the underlying ethical principles is diminished. What it does indicate is that the process of deriving specific moral values from those principles that promote a moral society (and individual character) is of no less importance to their justification.

Bibliography

Beidelman, T. O. 1993: *Moral Imagination in Kaguru Modes of Thought*. Washington, DC: Smithsonian Institution Press.

Fashina, O. 1989: "Frantz Fanon and the Ethical Justification of Anti-Colonial Violence." *Social Theory and Practice* 15, 2, 179–212.

Gbadegesin, S. 1991: *African Philosophy*. New York: Peter Lang.

Gyekye, K. 1995: *An Essay on African Philosophical Thought*, revd. edn. Philadelphia, PA: Temple University Press.

——1996: *African Cultural Values*. Philadelphia, PA: Sankofa Publishing.

Hallen, B. 2000: *The Good, the Bad, and the Beautiful: Discourse About Values in Yoruba Culture*. Bloomington: Indiana University Press.

——2002: *A Short History of African Philosophy*. Bloomington: Indiana University Press.

Idowu, E. B. 1962: *Olodumare: God in Yoruba Belief*. London: Longman.

MacIntyre, A. 1967: *A Short History of Ethics*. London: Routledge & Kegan Paul.

Mbiti, J. 1970: *African Religions and Philosophy*. Garden City, NY: Doubleday.

Peel. J. D. Y. 2000: *Religious Encounter and the Making of the Yoruba*. Bloomington: Indiana University Press.

Serequeberhan, T. 1994: *The Hermeneutics of African Philosophy*. New York: Routledge.

Wiredu, K. 1996: "Custom and Morality: A Comparative Analysis of Some African and Western Conceptions of Morals," in *Cultural Universals and Particulars: An African Perspective.* Bloomington: Indiana University Press.

Wiredu, K. and Gyekye, K. (eds.) 1992: *Person and Community: Ghanaian Philosophical Studies, I.* Washington, DC: Council for Research in Values and Philosophy and UNESCO.

CHAPTER 42

Origins of African Ethics

Segun Gbadegesin

What is African Religion?

John Mbiti's *African Religions and Philosophy* is arguably the vehicle that conveys many Westerners to the corridors of African traditional religion. It is as controversial as it is famous for some of its claims. Two of those claims have been subjected to vicious attacks by African scholars: (1) his assertion that traditional Africans have no concept of future time and (2) his claim that Africans are in all things religious (Mbiti 1989: 1).

While these claims are controversial, they do not define Mbiti's seminal contribution to African traditional religions. Indeed, there are two other claims or assertions by Mbiti that appear to me to strike at the core of African traditional religions. Unfortunately, Mbiti himself seems to have underplayed their significance or indeed may have had a negative attitude toward them. One of them (found in the same volume) is that "because traditional religions permeate all the departments of life, there is no formal distinction between the sacred and the secular, between the religious and the non-religious, between the spiritual and the material areas of life (Mbiti 1989: 2). The second is found in Mbiti's *Introduction to African Religions*, where he claims that African religions "evolved slowly through many centuries, as people responded to the situations of their life and reflected upon their experiences" (Mbiti 1991: 14; see also Masolo 1994).

Both of these claims define the core of African traditional religions. First, religion in traditional Africa is the outcome of reflection on life's circumstances, the vagaries of nature, the inexplicable splendor of the universe, the blue sky, the rugged mountains, and the deep ocean. The loneliness of humans in the midst of these wonders could be perplexing. A religious attitude is the response of the traditional African. The response of the traditional African is one of reverence and devotion, but one that is motivated by the well-being of the human. Thus, for the traditional African contemplating the universe, there is an "apprehension, awareness, or conviction of the existence of a supreme being, or more widely, of supernatural powers or influences controlling one's own, humanity's or nature's destiny," and thus religion, as Webster's dictionary defines it. Yet this manifestation of religion on the African landscape is not an abstract idea. It is purposeful; it is utilitarian. In traditional Africa, humanity is not made for religion, religion is made for humanity.

The Akan attitude to the gods is typical of most African cultures. Kwame Gyekye (1995: 137) has observed that a deity that fails to fulfill a promise would be censured and abandoned by the people. And Busia notes that "the gods are treated with respect if they deliver the goods, and with contempt if they fail . . . Attitudes to . . . [the gods] depend upon their success, and vary from healthy respect to sneering contempt" (1954: 197).

The other claim makes sense in the light of the foregoing. If religion has an instrumental role, if the gods are valued for what they can deliver, then there can be no unbridgeable gulf between the sacred and the secular. Consider the case of the worker in the field. The effectiveness of the gods in his life must be felt in terms of how well his crops do, how safe he is from the wild. He would be much inclined to do his own part, make the necessary supplications to the gods, and expect the logical results. The demarcation between work and religion is eliminated and the secular and the sacred merge. But if there is no unique sacred space, can we still speak of "religion"?

One implication of this feature of religion in traditional Africa should not escape us: the gods are subject to human evaluation and assessment. This does not suggest any possibility of escape from religion as such. With the uncertainties of the stormy world around, one needs a safe anchor. One needs to shop around to identify a god that might provide that safe anchor. This does not mean that one can escape the need for a safe anchor. The religious shoreline has numerous anchors as well as the tools for choosing one. In the case of the Yoruba, the tool is Orunmila, the god of wisdom or divination. A new baby born into the world today needs to have a divination in respect to her destiny, including the god to which she would be devoted. This god will afford her protection and provision. But since it is also believed that uncertainties mark the life of humans, the expectation and advice is that an oracle should be consulted. In this case, it may well be that the baby-become-teenager needs a new or additional god for maximum protection and provision. Changing gods or having additional gods does not entail escape from religion. It is the fulfillment of religion.

The features of African traditional religion just discussed are not exhaustive, but they are the most relevant to this chapter, which is mainly a discussion of the origins of ethical thought in traditional religions. To this I now move with a transitional thought. Masolo complains of African scholars (Mulago, Bahoken, and Mbiti) who "have been eager to demonstrate that African religious concepts could be explained in terms of Greek metaphysics" and then argues that their demonstration "has not been convincing. There is nothing which proves that the idea of unity is superior to that of multiplicity or pluralism, or that monotheism is superior to or develops from polytheism" (Masolo 1994: 122). I agree with this observation. However, Masolo also notes that while it is frequently stated that Africans are notoriously religious, the loose intertwining of religion with nearly all aspects of lives could be a weakness responsible for the demise of the traditional religions. "There may be attempts," he notes, "to drag religion unnecessarily into situations requiring simple practical approaches" (Masolo 1994: 123).

The problem with this way of looking at the matter is that it takes away with the left hand the recognition of the uniqueness of African traditional religions that has previously been offered by the right hand. Scholars do not impose uniqueness on traditional African religions; rather, it is due to the conception of the worldly nature of religion by traditional Africans themselves. It is the original contribution of traditional Africans to religious theory and practice. Religion is not separable from life because it is part of life and it is for life as we live it; it is *this-worldly*. Religion is to benefit human and communal life; hence the conception of the other world in the image of this world. Religion has to be constantly there, even at beer parties, as Mbiti notes. It is not unusual that many of the rules and prohibitions of Christianity – monogamy, for instance – rightly or wrongly, are not part of the core of African traditional religion. There are prudential injunctions on matters of relationship, including monogamy and polygamy. Orunmila, the Yoruba god of wisdom, counsels his devotees against polygamous relationships simply on account of its internal problems. Religion functions for the well-being of the people. So does morality.

The phenomena of morality comprise moral beliefs, rules, principles, and problems (see chapters 1 and 2). The purpose of a "morality" is the furtherance of a harmonious relationship within a particular society, the control and enhancement of its other institutions and individuals, the protection of its land and its individual members, and as a result of success in that area, the survival of that society as an entity. If this is the case, all societies certainly have the incentive to develop a vibrant moral institution for the promotion of their communal existence and individual enhancement. They may adopt different strategies and/or develop different emphases. For some, the moral institution will emerge through the instrumentality of the state. For others, religion and spirituality may be the catalyst that shapes and confirms morality.

The Moral Outlook of African Religious Traditions

We should begin by addressing the question: What is morality to traditional Africans? What purpose does it serve? How do they relate to it? Indeed, how do they come about the idea of a moral institution? Like other cultural traditions, morality comes into play in African cultures as a system of rules and practices for the purpose of maintaining the social order and enhancing the individual's process of self-actualization. These two goals are not exclusive. The enhancement of the self-actualization of individuals is an important means of maintaining the social order. A community with self-respecting individuals will have no problem maintaining its social order. Conversely, maintaining the social order is an important means of enhancing the self-actualization of individuals. A community that succeeds in maintaining its social order is one in which individual members can have the peace of mind and an atmosphere conducive to the realization of their full potentials. This is the way that traditional African societies understand the matter. This is what the process of socialization is about. It is also the main goal of moral education (see chapter 3).

How does religion come into this picture? Is there a specific set of values and morals that come out of religion and serve as ingredients in the moral menu of traditional Africans? In *Introduction to African Religions*, Mbiti discusses the parts of African religion. These include beliefs, practices, ceremonies and festivals, religious objects and places, values and morals, and religious officials and leaders (Mbiti 1991: 11–13). These are what Bolaji Idowu also refers to as the structure of African religion. We may gain a good understanding of African religion if we focus on these features or structure.

If morals and values are a part of traditional religion, in what sense should we understand this? What does it mean to discuss values and morals as part of African religion? It could mean any or all of the following: (1) religion gives birth to societal morals and values; (2) religion shapes morals and values; (3) religion serves as an enforcer of societal morals and values; (4) religion is a source or origin of some specific morals and values. Now, it is fair to say that of these possible interpretations of the claim, Mbiti has the broadest sympathy for (1), which is all-inclusive. What is the claim and what is its support?

According to Mbiti, morality comes from God to Africans. He attributes this verdict to the belief of African peoples themselves. "It is believed by African peoples that God gave moral order to people so that they might live happily and in harmony with one another. Through the moral order, customs and institutions have arisen in all societies to safeguard the life of the individual and the community of which he is part" (Mbiti 1991: 41). This statement may be interpreted in various ways, two of which are crucial. First, it could mean simply that the moral order – the order that exists in the African moral realm – is ordained by God. So God brought the moral institution into being at the same time that God created the African universe. In this case, it would not have mattered what humans did, the moral order would be there to manifest itself and the morality that it represents.

There is a second and more adequate interpretation. Traditional Africans believe that God gives the moral sense to each person, and they use the moral sense to fashion the moral order and its structure. The moral sense includes the sense of right and wrong, the sense of decency, the sense of fittingness, appropriateness, beauty and ugliness, the sense of straightness and crookedness, etc. Understood in this way, the moral sense is contextual, spatial, and temporal. For what is appropriate in one context, in one community, may be inappropriate in another. It is not appropriate to use water recklessly in the desert region, but such a rule is unnecessary in the rain forest. It is the moral sense that helps to discern this distinction. Human beings create the moral order through the use of the moral sense given to them by God. This is the case with traditional Africans.

The foregoing position does not, by itself, suggest a severance of all connections between religion and morality. This seems clear if we focus on the other three interpretations that we have identified. First, it is true that religion shapes morality. If in fact traditional Africans believe that they receive their moral sense from God, this is a crucial way in which religion shapes morality. Second, however, the various contents of our moral norms are also influenced and shaped by religion. To see that this is the case, we only need to compare Christianity and its impact on the African moral realm with traditional religions. In traditional Yoruba religion, as in many African religions, the gods are strict with regard to punishment for particular moral infractions. Adultery, for instance, is punishable by a huge fine and forms of restitution to the aggrieved family. This is not the case in Christianity. In Yoruba religion, it is believed that whoever swears on the altar of Sango, the god of thunder and justice, and breaks his or her oath, will be punished with death. Though Christians swear on the Bible to assure others of their fidelity, there is no belief that any empirical consequences would follow should they renege on their promise (see chapter 22). In this sense, religion shapes the morals and values of the people, and traditional African religion is no exception.

It also seems clear, third, that religion serves as an enforcer of morals and values. Many African religions have little or no conception of a heaven where punishment is given to bad or evil people. What they have is worse, namely the belief that punishment will be given here on earth towards the end of a person's life. Such punishment may include total reversal of fortune. Since no one knows what the future holds, there is a terrifying thought that one may go from an extreme of fortune to one of misfortune. Therefore, there is an interest in pleasing the gods to avoid that kind of fate.

There are certain morals and values that are specifically religious in origin and content. They come out of religious beliefs and practices and they are mobilized for the purpose of observance and advancement of religious practices. These are found in the injunctions of particular gods through their priests for their devotees. The purposes of this class of moral injunctions are ostensibly devotional, but in reality, they are utilitarian. For instance, the devotees of Obatala, the Yoruba god of creation, are enjoined to refrain from alcohol. The purpose is supposedly devotional and referential, to make them clean and sober before the god. But it is also utilitarian and one variant of the myth of Obatala supports this interpretation. According to the Yoruba cosmogony, Obatala was the divinity that Olodumare, the Yoruba supreme being, sent to create the earth. But as he was descending from heaven, he saw a group of palm trees and he helped himself to some of its juice. He got drunk and slept it off. Olodumare had to send Oduduwa, the progenitor of the Yoruba, to finish the job. Thus, Oduduwa took the glory for creating the earth and Obatala never forgot the embarrassment. So he instructed his devotees to avoid alcohol. The devotees, in turn, understand this as a taboo, for the simple reason that it is so enjoined by the divinity they serve. It is a norm of behavior that is clearly religious in origin. This does not mean that a secular rationale may not be found for the norm. Indeed, from the story behind it, the injunction itself has its origin in the embarrassing experience of the divinity after his consumption of alcohol. Therefore, there are both religious (injunction of a divinity) as well as secular (avoidance of embarrassment) reasons for the devotees of Obatala to follow the norm thus enjoined by the divinity (see Idowu 1962).

There are norms of behavior that traditional Africans have come to accept as regular norms without raising any question about their origin. What is crucial for them is that these norms and moral codes have been effective in the furtherance of their communal lives and have served as important guiding lights in their daily lives. Indeed, a significant aspect of the moral outlook of a number of traditional Africans is that it does not really matter to them what is the source of the norms they live by. The communal nature of their lives ensures that they accept the norms that work for the survival and prosperity of their community.

The foregoing point deserves a modification. We must distinguish between the traditional thinkers, that is, the philosophical sages on the one hand, and the priests and practitioners of traditional religion on the other. The first group looks further and deeper to identify the rationale for moral injunctions in the secular world, in terms of the consequences for human beings, though, in a minority, their existence in traditional societies cannot be doubted (Oruka 1990). The second group, the practitioners of traditional religion, is guided by the pronouncements of the gods through the priests and priestesses. They abide by the injunctions because they want to please the gods. For them, the moral norms are the injunctions of the divinities, and are thus religious norms, just as the natural is the spiritual. Their position or attitude is not significantly different than the Christian priest/parishioner in terms of where authority resides in matters of morality (see chapter 6).

Significantly, because of the structure of traditional society, and in particular the continuity between the spiritual and the natural, this group gets enlarged insofar as the traditional political authority is its extension. The traditional ruler is the chief priest of all the religions and therefore religious, moral, and political authority are rolled up in one. When our topic is the origin of African religious traditions and their moral outlook, this group (more than the philosophical sage) has pride of place. I will conclude by identifying some examples of the moral outlooks that are characteristic of African religious traditions as seen from the vantage point of priests and practitioners.

The Essence of an African Moral Outlook

One of the enduring features of African religious traditions is the emphasis placed on good character. The development of good character is the focus of the various religions and processes of informal education. There is recognition of good character as a prerequisite for social harmony and justice, which are the mandate of the divinities on earth. The key to religious devotion in the context of the utilitarian interpretation of religion is the character of each person. The Yoruba people summarize this in a sentence, *iwa l'esin*, or "character is religion." All there is to religious devotion and sacrifice is good character. If you claim to be a devout believer and you do not demonstrate the qualities of body and mind that even non-believers possess, your claim is empty. For the African religious tradition, a person's character is her amulet and it is her character that will judge her in the end. Therefore, one must have good character.

The Yoruba word for character is *iwa. Iwa*, however, has a second meaning, which is "existence." Thus we have *iwa* as character and *iwa* as existence. It has been suggested that the former is a derivative of the latter. *Iwa* as existence is primary in the sense that without existence, we cannot talk of character (Abimbola 1975a: 389–420). But we may talk of the character of a person's existence. This is just a different way of talking about the person's character, which may affect for better or for worse his or her existence. A person with bad character will spoil the means to good fortune. In this sense, *iwa* means the totality of the person's being, including habits of right conduct, right attitude, and right emotions at the right time. We can now isolate the component of *iwa* to conclude this account of African moral outlooks.

Truthfulness

In the African religious traditions, truthfulness, as a component of *iwa*, is an important injunction of the divinities. The Yoruba Ifa oracle instructs devotees of Orunmila (the divinity of wisdom) always to tell the truth because it is those who are truthful that the divinities will promote and bless. Many religious traditions have ways of detecting lying and deceit, and there are instant punishments for such waywardness. In the Yoruba tradition, Sango, the divinity of justice, is summoned whenever there is a suspicion of wayward dealings, and the culprit is punished along with his or her household.

Industry

All divinities of the African pantheon are shining examples of industry. Many of the myths of creation depict the divinities as engaged in one activity or the other. They may clear the bush that leads from heaven to the earth; they may plant the first seeds on earth; they may be skilled hunters. The value of work is the theme of many religious poems. Thus, Yoruba children learn from the cradle a poem that sings the praise of work as a means to avoid poverty. Work is taken seriously as a moral requirement because people who do not work cannot carry out their responsibilities to their families and are likely to become parasites on communal resources.

Moderation

Moderation in food, drink, and bodily pleasure is an important component of character that African religions emphasize. Lack of moderation may result in squandering of resources. It may lead to weakness of the body, mind, and spirit. It may lead to loss of dignity. This is one reason, noted before, that the arch divinity Obatala prohibits devotees from indulgence in alcoholic beverages.

Generosity

The generous person is appreciated by the gods, according to African religious traditions. It is incumbent on devotees of many of the religions to make provision for those in need, no matter how small their own fortunes may be. There is a sense in which sacrifice is understood as a lesson in generosity. When a divination oracle instructs a supplicant to offer a sacrifice of palm oil or used clothes, the idea behind this is to make provision for those in need so that the divinities may look favorably on one and provide for one's specific needs.

Patience

In the Yoruba religious tradition, patience (*suru*) is depicted as the son of Olodumare (supreme being) and father of *iwa* (character). They say "patience, the father or lord of character" (*suru baba iwa*). A person with patience has all she needs for good character. A patient person would have no cause to be immoderate, or to be lazy, or to be dishonest, or to insult the elders. A patient person will not run before she is ready to walk. The story is told of how Orunmila, the divinity of wisdom, lacked patience. His wife was Iwa. She was a dutiful wife, but she had some defects. Orunmila could not stand these defects and he maltreated his wife until she left him. Orunmila had to look for her all over the earth without success. Then after some sacrifice, Esu, the trickster god, led him to where Iwa was in the world beyond. But Iwa refused to go back with Orunmila to the world. Here in this story, the priests depict their own divinity as lacking some important character trait, and because of this, the divinity suffered the consequence, the loss of his precious wife, Iwa. If a divinity could thus suffer for lack of such a trait, the reasoning is that humans should watch out.

Respect for elders

In traditional African cultures old age is held in esteem. With experience of life comes wisdom, which is necessary to avoid falling into the same mistake. Therefore, even if an elder is poor in material wealth, he or she will be rich in wisdom. It is said that if a young one has as many cloth outfits as an old person, there can be no comparison to their stock of rags. Having lived longer, that is, the older person must have more rags. It is therefore incumbent on a young one to respect the elder in order to tap his or her wisdom. Since one expects to grow old too, and since one good turn deserves another, one ought to respect elders so one may be respected in one's old age. Furthermore, there is a strong belief that elders have a mystic power that clings to their spoken word. One would not want to be on the receiving end of a curse from the elders, and surely this may be the case if one shows disrespect to them. Here is another moral injunction that is sanctioned by religion but which has a this-worldly justification.

Respect for community

The community is the source of a person's being in the African understanding. Religion itself is a collective endowment of the community. The particular divinities are communal divinities in the sense that the majority of them are identified with certain peculiarities of the community: its mountains, its rivers, its weather, etc. The community gives existence and validation to religion. The young child is born into the community and is brought up as a community member. He or she experiences the ups and downs of the community and grows up seeing him or herself as nothing outside of the community. This is the meaning of the saying credited to traditional Africa: I am because we are. In this context, the religious injunction of respect for the community only reinforces the recognition of the community's role in one's life. In concrete terms, the injunction requires a devotee to refrain from polluting the land through acts of murder, adulterous relationships, defacement of and defecation on community altars and landscape, and violent acts of robbery. Respect for the gods of the community and for the rules and procedures of the community are religious injunctions that individuals have incentives to obey if they think of the community's role in their own origin, growth, and prosperity.

Conclusion

I have argued that the moral outlook of African religions is essentially this-worldly. Its emphasis is on the promotion of harmonious relationships within communities with a view to enhancing the self-actualization of individual human beings. The specific moral injunctions from the divinities and the supreme being are meant to serve this same purpose. In the final analysis, character is religion, and it is on one's character that one is judged. There is no escape from such judgment at the end of life by appeal to the saving grace of "God." There is reward and punishment in this world and at the end of life for whatever a person does, and there is no intercession from anyone, human or divine.

Bibliography

Abimbola, K. (n.d.) *Spirituality and Applied Ethics: An African Perspective*.
——1994: "God and Evil." *Philosophy Now* 8, 23–5.
Abimbola, W. 1975a: "Iwapele: The Concept of Good Character in Ifa Literary Corpus" in *Yoruba Oral Tradition: Poetry in Music, Dance and Drama*, ed. W. Abimbola, 389–420. Ile-Ife: Department of African Languages and Literature.
——1975b: "The Yoruba Concept of Human Personality" in *La Notion de personne en Afrique Noire*. Paris: Centre National de la Recherche Scientifique.
——1975c: *Sixteen Great Poems of Ifa*. UNESCO.
——1976: *Ifa: An Exposition of Ifa Literary Corpus*. Ibadan: Oxford University Press.
Appiah, A. K. 1992: *In My Father's House: African in the Philosophy of Culture*. New York: Oxford University Press.
Busia, K. A. 1954: *The Ashanti of the Gold Coast*, ed. D. Forde. Oxford: Oxford University Press.
Gbadegesin, S. 1991: *African Philosophy: Traditional Yoruba Philosophy and Contemporary African Realities*. New York: Peter Lang.
Gyekye, K. 1987: *African Philosophical Thought: The Akan Conceptual Scheme*, revd. edn. Philadelphia, PA: Temple University Press.
——1995: *An Essay on African Philosophical Thought*. Philadelphia, PA: Temple University Press.
Idowu, E. B. 1962: *Olodumare: God In Yoruba Belief*. Ikeja, Nigeria: Longman.

Lucas, J. O. 1948: *The Religion of the Yorubas*. Lagos: CMS Bookshop.

Masolo, D. A. 1994: *African Philosophy in Search of Identity*. Bloomington: Indiana University Press.

Mbiti, J. S. 1989: *African Religions and Philosophy*. London: Heinemann.

—— 1991: *Introduction to African Religions*. London: Heinemann.

Mudimbe, V. Y. 1998: *The Invention of Africa: Gnosis, Philosophy, and the Order of Knowledge*. Bloomington: Indiana University Press.

Oruka, O. 1990: *Sage Philosophy: Indigenous Thinkers and Modern Debate on African Philosophy*. Leiden: E. J. Brill.

Wiredu, K. 1998: "The Moral Foundations of an African Culture" in *The African Philosophy Reader*, ed. P. H. Coetzce and A. P. J. Roux. New York: Routledge.

Zahan, D. 1979: *The Religion, Spirituality, and Thought of Traditional Africa*, trans. K. Ezra and L. M. Martin. Chicago: University of Chicago Press.

CHAPTER 43

Differentiations in African Ethics

Bénézet Bujo

This chapter considers the historical aspect of African traditions' origins and the differences among them. From the outset, we must state, together with most African scientists, that it is inappropriate to talk in the plural about ethics or religion in sub-Saharan Africa. Except for a few non-African researchers and scientists, most tend to agree on the unity of religion – and ethics – in Black Africa (Mulago 1965, 1980; Magesa 1998; Mugambi 2001: 7–26; Mbiti 1996). Mugambi notes a great affinity of religious thought throughout all of Africa. This pronounced affinity led the first Western researchers to believe that the only possibility was that Africans had copied their religious conceptions from the Jewish people (see, for instance, research on the Masai in Merker 1910; Hollis 1969). Mugambi rightly refuses to accept this thesis. The differences we can observe among African religions do not concern the substance of the African conception itself, but the way that conception is translated and put into practice (costumes, rites, etc.). It is inappropriate to look for the kind of divergence in African religion we find, for instance, within the various Christian denominations (Catholicism, Protestantism, Orthodoxy) or the various Buddhist, Muslim, and other traditions. The African conception centers on life. Life articulates itself thanks to and through the community of the living, the dead, and the not-yet born, and it never forgets to refer to God, the actual foundation of this three-dimensional community.

To begin with, we will examine the foundation of African ethics before dealing with the problem of the invention and the articulation of norms. We will conclude our journey by showing, based on a few examples, the relevance of African ethics in the modern world.

The Foundation of African Ethics

In order to understand the ethical conception and articulation in Black Africa, we must apply ourselves to its main anthropological basis. Many theologians and philosophers, as well as ethnologists of all tendencies, have already made this kind of study. However, it seems that until now no one has undertaken any systematic elaboration of its ethics. The emphasis of our study lies in systematic ethical reflection (see chapters "On Religious Ethics" and 1).

The three-dimensional community

If, in moral conduct, African thought puts a special emphasis on interhuman relations, this does by no means obliterate God or exclude the role of God in morality. In the traditional African conception, God is an unquestioned postulate, even though God is rarely mentioned. One knows once and for all that God is first and that without God nothing comes about and nothing survives. Myths, legends, tales, etc. evidence that God is not absent from the individual's life. Many African names incorporate without ambiguity God's action. The most obvious examples are in Rwanda and Burundi, where theophorous names are particularly frequent: Habyarimana, Nzeimana, Ndikumana, etc.

By way of illustration, *Imana* indicates God and *Habyarimana* means "God alone begets." When given to a child, this name signifies that life originates in God alone, not in human strength. Similarly, among the Bahema of Congo-Kinshasa, there are children called "Byaruhanga," which means "God's property." This name may be given to a child born after its parents had come to believe they would be deprived of the blessing of children; but precisely at that moment God intervened (Bujo 1992: 19; 1998a: 75). The idea of God as the originator of life and thus of everything humans do is so fundamental that among the traditional Banyarwanda and the Barundi parents will never go to bed in the evening without leaving a little water in a jug. This water is commonly called "Utuzi tw'Imana," "God-Imana's little water." God creates life at night, and after this work of creation, God washes God's hands in this water specially set aside (Mulago 1965: 109–10).

Most of the time in everyday life African morality takes place without necessary and constant mention of God, though God is by no means absent. African ethics concentrates its attention in a very special fashion on the individual and the community (see chapter 41). Africans know that humans are indebted to God for all their undertakings and that, by attempting to articulate their morality within an interpersonal relation with fellow humans and the cosmos as a whole, they ultimately praise the same God (Bujo 2001: 1–71). Insofar as one promotes life in this world, one does God's will as one's ancestors have handed it down to one. The tradition received from them is that to please God and the ancestors is to take into account the three-dimensional community: the living, the dead, and the not-yet born. This community with its threefold dimension constitutes the anthropological foundation of ethics as a whole. According to this conception, the community, unlike society, is an organic whole. It is not based on some kind of contract, but it is a bond rooted in a covenant. This covenant generally implements a reality grounded either in a natural or symbolic common origin. This alludes to the fact that beyond the "natural" blood relation it is possible in Africa to become a member of a family or a community by acts other than birth. For instance, a blood pact does not necessarily mean the material exchange of blood, but it can also take on symbolic forms.

Beyond this last consideration, however, it must be strongly emphasized that, in general, African tradition does not forget the common origin of all humans, which precisely grounds a common membership. Consequently, there is the obligation to see every person as a member of a universal human community in which every individual moves and attempts to be moral. This is what the Baluba of Kasayi in Congo-Kinshasa bring to light through their expression "Muntu-wa-Bende-wa-Mulopo," which means "Human from Bende from God." In others words, every human being comes from Bende, who comes from God. *Bende* here becomes synonymous with the common origin of humans and of the cosmos, an origin that makes sense only with reference to God (Tshiamalenga-Ntumba 1995). The consequence of this affirmation is that the community based on this kind of thinking is not only three-dimensional but four-dimensional as well, since it includes God as ultimate foundation.

However, let us underscore once more that in its everyday life African morality does not thematize this dimension one can call "theandric": its full attention goes to the community of the living, the dead, and the not-yet-born, as if God did not exist (*etsi Deus non daretur!*). The foundation of the morality in this "tripartite" community does not have as its starting point a Cartesian or Kantian philosophical concept. Reason with its *cogito ergo sum* is not what defines human beings and their moral action. Interpersonal relations shape the three-dimensional community as well as the individual and constitute as such a base for ethics itself. The Cartesian principle *cogito ergo sum* falters. Another principle supplants it right away: *cognatus sum, ergo sumus*, because I am related to the others, not only I, but also we, together, exist. The individual as a human being is not a monad but exists in openness to the other.

Beside the three-dimensional community, in daily terrestrial life human beings as persons can only live within a bipolarity implying a tri-polarity. In other words, masculinity necessarily relates to femininity, and both imply in turn a third dimension, the child. The human being, as human, is whole only as man and woman summoned by the child, who is the representative of the world of the not-yet born and at the same time the messenger of the community of the ancestors. Here to some extent is the relevance of the African conception for determining concrete norms; we will come back to this issue in the last part of the chapter. For now, we must underscore another important dimension in African anthropology, namely the problem of the relation between humans and the cosmos.

Cosmic unity or the human as a relation to the surrounding world

In African religion and ethics, everything in the world is intimately connected (see chapter 13). For this reason, humans and the rest of creation have a dialectic relation. All the elements in the universe imply each other and interlock. One cannot touch one of them without causing the whole to vibrate. Humans are not only part of the cosmos, but they are also the summary of its totality, so to speak. "At the same time earth and sky, spirits and cosmic forces, past, present, and future, the human really is a miniature version of the universe, a microcosm within the macrocosm" (Mveng 1985: 12). In Black Africa humans belong at the same time to the world of the living, the dead, and the not-yet born. They can identify with spirits, animals, plants, minerals. They know that between them and the cosmos there is a vital flux making up the solidarity of creation as a whole and ultimately connecting them to the supreme being, God, the source of all life.

Thus, in the traditional rites and in African medicine, one cannot simply talk of symbolic acts (see chapter 9). They are much more about an encounter between life and life: on the one hand, human life, and, on the other, "cosmic" life (plants, minerals, etc.). In this encounter, humans attempt to decipher and to master the tension opposing life and death. If they wish to secure life's victory over death, they must secure allies in the cosmos and identify their opponents. In this sense, for instance, the cosmic elements used in traditional medicine, even if they are minerals, dry wood, animal bones, etc., are not impersonal or inanimate realities. They contain and convey life to the one who utilizes them (Mveng 1985: 11–13). The transmission of vital energy, however, does not only concern the strictly medicinal realm; it is also about nature as a whole in relation to the abundance of life in all its ramifications. This explains the respect the African manifests towards earth, plants, water, etc.

As an illustration, there is a widespread practice in Africa concerning sacred trees. The Bahema of Congo-Kinshasa, for example, have the practice of the *ficus*, which they plant on the tomb of the head of the family. This tree is sacred and represents the one who is buried there. Its branches symbolize the deceased's many descendants. Thus, it represents the life of the family in the African sense. Consequently, it is strictly forbidden to desecrate the tree by cutting it down or by removing any of its branches, twigs, and leaves (Bujo 1996a: 77ff.).

There are many more examples of the importance of certain trees in the lives of African peoples. People's attitudes towards these trees prompt them to cultivate respect towards nature and to strengthen their vital ties with it. Such respect is not limited to one category of trees alone, as such trees are only the representatives of the cosmos in general. For a casual observer, this is primitive, irrational thought that perhaps goes against modernity and development, since for the Western rationalist world the cosmos no longer contains any secret and mystery. Those, however, attempting to penetrate African culture will marvel at its ancestral wisdom. The life–death tension is predominant in the world, and cosmic nature is a companion one has to associate with in order for life to triumph over death.

With this in mind, we must now tackle the issue of the invention and the articulation of ethical norms (see chapter 2).

Elaboration and Articulation of Norms

Since community is of the utmost importance for African moral action, the elaboration of norms and their application can only unfold within the community's frame (see chapter 5). In what follows, we will not be able to present at full length the way ethical norms come into being and unfold in Africa. We will be content to indicate what we take to be essential in order to understand moral action in Africa. To do so, we will begin with *palaver* (the African traditional council dealing with community matters) as an institution where norms are born and brought to bear. We will then examine the relation between communal action and personal life. This will imply a brief presentation of the concepts of person, freedom, and individual conscience.

Palaver as the locus where norms are born

In order to understand palaver's role, one has to keep in mind the function of words in African communities. The word is powerful, and it contains highly explosive elements in Black Africa. A word can be medicine just as it can be poison; it has a life-giving power just as it is capable of bringing forth death. Words are something drinkable or edible; one chews and digests them. Badly chewed and digested, they can destroy the individual and a whole community, whereas in the opposite case they bring life (Bujo 1996a: 25ff.).

In this context, palaver functions as a time during which people reexamine the chewing and digestion of received words. First, there is therapeutic palaver, which is a dialogue between the traditional healer and the patient or his or her circle. As noted, the community is a collection of relations where everything holds and influences everything else. Therapeutic palaver aims at detecting the causes of illness or malaise in general, based on the articulation of the relations experienced in the community. Thus, therapy will not consist in administering medicines without taking into account the patient's life context, but the aim will be to return life to him or her above all by recreating a collection of more life-nurturing relations. To do so, the sick person, the doctor, and the community as a whole must hold a palaver where one manages together to digest the badly chewed and undigested bad words in order to deprive them of their deadly venom and to give them vital and life-nurturing force. The administered medicines will be able to take effect only after good relations are restored.

Besides this therapeutic palaver, one ought to mention, second, family palaver, where people deal behind closed doors with the problems pertaining to the family in the African sense, that is, in its threefold dimension of the living, the dead, and the not-yet born. This form of palaver, just like the one concerning "supra-family" and administrative life (we will talk about this later) can be irenic or antagonistic depending on whether it deals with non-contentious or contentious cases (Bidima 1997: 10). Family palaver is the foremost place where domestic ethics elaborates, grounds, reinforces, and develops. Family palaver covers a wide variety of topics because it seeks to contribute to the growth of the life of the extended family in all its dimensions. The problems it deals with can therefore be about sharing property, reflecting on which attitude to adopt in view of the future, appointing or removing a person responsible for a given area, tackling family feuds of all kinds – the list could go on endlessly. Even apart from contentious cases, family palaver aims at helping to maintain or restore healthy and harmonious relations within the community. In other words, it is about bringing together again the antagonists where there is strife in order for them to learn to listen to each other, and thus it is about managing to develop a new lifestyle where people are ready to support each other in the harshness of life.

Seen from this perspective, palaver also takes on the role of therapeutic and medicinal authority besides its ethical function: while it concerns itself with establishing or abolishing or strengthening ethical norms, palaver takes the individual in his or her dimension of totality and attends to his or her moral and physical health. No wonder, therefore, that most palavers, even the ones that are not related to family, end with a celebration of reconciliation around a meal, for instance, where everybody finds their way back to the initial fellowship.

If a family palaver fails to solve a problem, particularly in the case of a feud, the community can appeal to an extra-family or even an administrative palaver. This palaver is not just a kind of appeals court dealing only with cases beyond family authority. The supra-family and administrative palaver also takes up totally new cases concerning the good beyond isolated families. This palaver has a more political character and even applies to several clan communities. Here, too, we are not dealing exclusively with antagonistic palavers but also irenic palavers, as defined above.

While the traditional doctor (male or female healer) and the family's sage (the elder in general) are in charge, respectively, of therapeutic and family palavers, the situation is different with extra-family and administrative palavers. Here, the chief or the king, but also a member of the counsel of elders, can be the one who is in charge of the session when the palaver takes place. It is important to underline that at no time is the person who presides over the palaver allowed to be arrogant and authoritarian so as to humiliate or silence participants, male and female. On the contrary, he or she has to be attentive and ready to listen to everyone in order to discover the sapiential aspect of what they have to say. "Sapiential" also means that a palaver's discourse uses poetic language, symbolism, proverbs, parables, stories, etc. What takes place in a palaver refers to life's existential foundations, which these various kinds of language must translate.

One cannot help noticing a well-known difference from Western styles of argument. We have already seen how the African conception differs from Cartesian philosophy and its *cogito ergo sum*. It is *cognatus sum, ergo sumus* that is decisive in African ethics: "I am related, therefore we are." This ultimately means that African ethics is not based on the concept of Western natural or moral law, but in the framework of the community. The community is actually the place where norms take shape. In all of this, life in its widest sense is what functions as the hinge for the elaboration of ethical norms. Everything that contributes to maintaining, strengthening, and perfecting individual as well as communal life is good and right. Whether it is an ethical judgment on property, marriage, or sexuality, etc., palaver will determine if it is appropriate for life in abundance for all.

It is interesting to note the differences in argumentation that lead to the grounding and securing of norms in comparison with certain Western models. If, as an example, we take the discourse ethics of Habermas (1983: 99), anyone able to express themselves and to act is entitled to participate in the discussion. In discourse ethics, one can only have a discussion with people able to argue at a rational level. Concerning, for instance, the interests of children and of the generation to come (one can also add the dead and the cosmos), one could argue only in an advocative fashion, that is, speak on behalf of those unable to "reason." African ethics based on palaver follows another procedure because it is not conditioned by rational argumentation so defined. If among Ghana's Ashanti the rule is to exclude no one from palaver, this goes beyond the rule applying to discourse ethics. Even if discourse ethics talks of the unlimited communication community, in fact it is about a community of individuals endowed with intellectual capacities and able to speak (Ndjimbi-Tshiende 1992: 247). By contrast, the rule of the Ashanti (a rule similar to those of several other African ethnic groups) really embraces everybody, including the handicapped, even if they cannot express themselves at the level of language. They can, however, communicate and make themselves understood through symbolic actions and gestures, for instance. Such actions and gestures are of no importance for discourse ethics, whereas they can be decisive for palaver.

Another difference from discourse ethics concerns palaver's religious dimension. God and the world of the ancestors are an integral part of palaver, whereas the argumentation of discourse ethics excludes them. Integrating God and the world of the ancestors does not deprive the palaver's participants of their ability to be critical, but reason must not be turned into an instrument of oppression and omnipotence. In a world where the life–death tension prevails, truth can only be analyzed in an existential and sapiential manner; rational malice cannot manipulate it. Along the same lines, not only God and the ancestors are actively involved in palaver, but people also go so far as to include in it the cosmos as a whole. The Ashanti explicitly state that government agents and any behavior in the community must be consistent with the law of nature as well as with the ancestors. In palaver, one has to ensure that this rule is observed (Ndjimbi-Tshiende 1992: 246–7). For the Ashanti and for Black African communities in general, humans are really the synthesis of the whole universe (Mveng 1979: 234).

In addition, discourse ethics is content with grounding ethical norms, keeping them at the "formal" level without caring about their concrete application. In other words, it is more concerned with macro-ethical problems, and it is vague about micro-ethical questions that deal precisely with the applicability of "formal" principles to concrete cases of daily moral action (Bujo 1993: 33). By contrast, African ethics does not stay at the level of formal principles, but is concerned at the same time with the applicability and the application of the norms proposed in the course of palaver.

The dimension of sin is another characteristic radically setting apart palaver from discourse ethics. In an ethics where religious matters, God, and the ancestors play a predominant role, it is normal to ask about interpersonal relations involving faults, sin, and sanction. One will easily understand, therefore, that particularly antagonistic palaver will usually end with a celebration of reconciliation between all the members. This is often the case with therapeutic palavers, too. In fact, the medicines the traditional doctor administers can only demonstrate their efficiency and restore health if there are good relationships and harmony in the patient's community. Diseases often arise from tensions of all kinds between a community's members, who eat up each other's vital energy. Reconciliation contributes in a decisive way to restoring health to the sick and, by way of prophylactic measures, preventing other ills among still-healthy members (Bujo 1996b: 9–25).

So far, we have described only one type of Western ethics, namely discourse ethics. Another kind, however, is closer to African ethics. It is called communitarianism. Even though communitarianism is represented by several trends, it is nevertheless possible to bring out their common characteristics. Overall, communitarianism strongly opposes the kind of individualism that liberalism advocates. The criticism of liberalism by communitarianism's major representatives is that it has an atomistic conception of the individual: it does not place individuals in their original communities, that is, the context of their life environments (Reese-Schäfer 1994). An individual without ties to other humans, however, does not exist; this determines every human's way of thinking and moral behavior. One of the important consequences of this thesis is that one cannot formulate abstract ethical principles applicable to all humans of all nations and at all times. There is no *single* ethics; rather, there are several, according to the different communities that exist. Unlike discourse ethics, communitarianism emphasizes the ethics of "the good" (*bonum, euzèn*), which does not stay at a purely formal level, but tries to fill ethical principles with substantial content capable of orienting active subjects' daily lives.

If we compare communitarianism with African ethics, we find commonalities but also differences. Both models underscore the contextuality of the individual, who is always to be understood based on the community in which he or she lives and acts. Communitarianism and African ethics also merge with respect to *bonum*: they do not expound it only at the level of principle and without giving it a content applicable in concrete life. In Africa, this *bonum* revolves around the fullness of life.

These commonalities, however, do not erase important differences. Even if both models talk of community, one gets the impression that for communitarians the concept does not sufficiently set itself apart from that of society. Community is more organic than society, and society has a composite and artificial character because it proceeds from the will of individuals seeking a unity.

Western anthropology leaves a fundamental mark on communitarian thinking. It is true that communitarians strongly oppose the atomization of the individual and that they stress the bond between individual and community. Nevertheless, if one compares their conception of community with the African conception, it appears that, as far as moral action is concerned, the individual, though bound to environment and group, is not bound in his or her personal decisions to the extent of referring to his or her community. In other words, the community can shape the individual, but it does not accompany them in their personal dealings: ultimately, decisions belong to the private sphere, in which the community must not meddle. By contrast, in African ethics community is so important that one goes so far as to involve its deceased members in a decision to be made: this is not a passive attitude but, rather, an *active* participation of the whole community which must help the individual before, during, and after a decision in order to put it into practice – always as a community.

At the same time, the communal character of African ethics does not necessarily turn it into a kind of fiction and dogmatism but provides leeway for innovations and creativity: traditions that no longer encourage abundant life must be abolished and new ones must replace them. That is what palaver is all about. In addition, African communitarianism knows how to avoid ethnocentric paralysis in the sense that the various communities are not shut off from each other, they are not atomized entities, but they remain open to other cultural approaches and spheres. The best illustration of this is the *luba* conception of Kasayi in the Democratic Republic of Congo, but it is easily applicable to other ethnic groups. As mentioned above, for the Baluba, every person is a "Muntu-wa-Bende-Wa-Mulopo," a "human being from Bende who himself is from God." Therefore, every human is from God and entitled to respect no matter his or her clan, ethnicity, or nation.

With regard to ethical questions, this means that norms have a universal character while remaining plural. Every human as an individual is required to encourage the abundance of life, but also to take into account each community's characteristics and realities. This is precisely what African ethics attempts to do by using palaver in order to secure norms and put them into practice. This ethics, which has a sapiential character, cannot be confined to a narrow focus on particularity. By dealing with confined, contextual, and singular cases, it knows how to find rules with a universal dimension. The predominant approach does not consist in moving down from the universal to the particular. It is just the opposite. The universal is thus the result of a concrete and particular experience. In studying African proverbs, for instance, one realizes that what a sentence puts into words is the result of several concrete experiences which ultimately make it possible to reach generalizations applicable to everyone.

Although African ethics has some characteristics in common with Western models such as natural law ethics, discourse ethics, and communitarianism, it clearly differs from them in other respects. Above all, its relational character, in all its aspects – notably God, the spirits, the world of the living, the dead, and the not-yet born, and even the cosmos as a whole – gives it its own originality.

However, another question arises. If community shapes so much of African ethics and if every decision and every implementation cannot take place without it, to what extent can one still talk of individual responsibility?

The concepts of person and freedom

It is not uncommon to hear criticism of the influence that the group exerts on the individual. Some consider it to be inadmissible oppression that runs counter to human rights because of its failure to respect individual freedom (see chapter 51).

Undoubtedly, unfortunate and deplorable events have tarnished African tradition. However, this tradition's ideal should not be confused with such breaches, which must ultimately be corrected in the light of the ideal itself. Again, African morality is essentially based on interpersonal relationships. This means that there is no atomized activity removed from other humans who constitute a life community even beyond death. In this context, it is impossible to talk of freedom in the sense in which modern Western philosophy conceives it. Western philosophy sees the essence of freedom in each individual's highly personal self-determination. This is the whole issue of Kantian morality and its keen sense of autonomy. This is also the central topic concerning individual conscience in Roman Catholic morality based on natural law. It is, finally, the whole concern of human rights activists who want to protect individuals from the tyranny of groups.

As for Black African ethics, since the individual can only exist within the "us," it is impossible for them to fulfill their potential outside, beside, or against the community. In order to understand this conception, one must examine the notion of person in Africa. This notion is based neither on the philosophy of being (*naturae rationalis individua substantia*) nor on cognition (*cogito ergo sum*), but on a process that unfolds through the interdependence between the individual and the community, which comprises not only the dead and the not-yet born but also the cosmos and God itself (Bujo 2001: 85–9).

This is what the principle of "cognatio" (*cognatus sum, ergo sumus*) expresses. What is peculiar to this principle is that the reality it expresses does not depend on the community's consent or recognition in relation to the individual. It is something so existential and so fundamental that *not* abiding by it can only lead to the destruction of the individual and the community. The interdependence of both parties concerns more than the biological continuity and the spiritual heritage that relate us to each other or one generation to another. In the Black African conception, it is especially important to stress the uninterrupted interaction between all of a community's members (alive, dead, and not-yet born). Thus, to be called a "person" does not require an ontological membership but an active participation, not in the Western sense of "performance" but in the sense of mutual, interpersonal relations ("being-with"). In other words, individuals become persons provided and to the extent that they do not isolate themselves in their actions, but act together with all the community's members.

Participation in this common life is so essential that even the dead depend on it for safeguarding the growth of their being as a person. Becoming a person is thus a continuous and perpetual process, which does not end at death. Personal identity in the beyond depends on ties to the earthly community and to the one still to come; it increases to the extent that from the beyond one lives in interaction and in harmony with the members of the three-dimensional community. If we look at it close up, this conception also explains the veneration for ancestors in Black Africa. Even if they can no longer suffer or die biologically, they continue to have certain human needs, such as hunger, thirst, love, the sense of justice, peace, etc. They can be worry-free in all this only if the community of the living does not forget them or cause them any harm.

In addition, in order to ensure happiness forever, continuity in the descendents has to be secured. For this reason, the not-yet born occupy an important place in the community. The ancestors make it their business to watch over this continuity and to provide the living with everything necessary for their well-being. In case the ancestors forget, the living will remind them and complain about it, if necessary, by threatening not to bring them food or drink (Nsuka 1970: 264). A prosperous progeny is indisputably one of the conditions ensuring the well-being of all. Thus, one cannot ignore the not-yet born; they already deserve to be called "persons" because, even before they take shape, they embody the living and the dead in such a way that they are the future and carry everybody's hopes.

The articulation of community and individual must be seen as a chance for achieving and completing individual freedom. In Africa, if one cannot fulfill oneself as a person outside the community, individual freedom is possible only through participation in the community's life within "being-with-the-others": my freedom as an individual can only be real and total if I free the community at the same time. In the same way, the community as a whole can enjoy true freedom only if it frees me as an individual. Strong and abundant life for all is possible only in this continual interaction. Seen from this angle, African freedom is never conceived to be something that opposes the individual to the community. The golden rule, rather, is *the individual with the community so that all are with all*. In Western societies, one tends to see too much of the negative side of freedom, in the sense of freeing oneself from obstacles that prevent self-fulfillment. Freedom cannot only consist in *being free from*, but it is also *being free for* and *being free with*. This "being for and with" gives a further dimension to freedom, since it implies sharing life with all.

It is obvious that in a community where the individual must never exercise self-determination without taking into account other members, questions concerning individual conscience will not pose themselves as they do in Western morality. For some Western thinkers, the individual conscience is the ultimate decision-making authority and one must respect it unconditionally. In Africa, on the contrary, the issue of individual conscience has to be discussed in relation to palaver, which is the place and the authority where the community reexamines the words hidden in each person's heart. These chewed and digested words must resurface in order to be ruminated collectively, so that they can prove their innocence. Even if chewed and swallowed, one does not know if the words have also been digested. If it is not the case, they could, if uttered rashly, destroy the community instead of putting it together. For this reason, it is palaver's task to control them and accept them only if they are able to give life abundantly. Ultimately, these tried and sifted words constitute the individual conscience. This conscience is the result of a process based on the ancestors' and the elders' experience, yet regularly subjected to a new examination.

The ancestors' words and deeds, the norms they set, are made available to the current generation so that it has life and continues to look after the deceased, and also so that it prepares the future of the not-yet born. In order to have a clear conscience, it is not enough to know the ancestors' words and deeds, or the norms they set, and to apply this knowledge following a private decision. The community's regular evaluation becomes, so to speak, the norm, "normalizing" individual conscience. If this is the case, the individual conscience is not the highest court of appeal for moral decisions; rather, communal conscience, above all, measures and determines the individual conscience.

This conception of communal conscience is of immense importance because in the end it excludes the fundamentalism, based on privately internalized principles, whereby everyone can make their own decisions and commit acts which can go so far as to be seriously detrimental to the common good. Individual freedom that is not integrated into the community is a bomb that can explode at any time and cause tremendous damage. Based on the above example of conscience, individual freedom does not necessarily lead to personal fulfillment. It also contains a certain amount of tyranny against the community. Communal freedom, by contrast, if it is used in a controlled way, is a necessary safeguard against tyranny in the world.

The Relevance of African Ethics

In what sense is African tradition still of interest in the modern world? Is it a bygone tradition lost in the mists of time? On the contrary, African ethics is of interest to the modern world in at least three areas related to the three-sided community: the practice of human rights, questions concerning the elderly, and issues relating to abortion and euthanasia. In what follows we will not go into the details of these complex debates. Our presentation will be limited to very basic information (see Bujo 1998b: 36–53; 1993: 17–25).

Human rights

The above reflections must make us attentive to another understanding of human rights (see chapter 51). The Western interpretation, which begins with the individual, seems to have little impact on the African anthropological conception. Indeed, for Africans, it cannot be about absolutizing the individual's rights while neglecting the community dimension. Any right deserves to be called a right only to the extent that it does not lose sight of the common good. One of the typical examples is the right to private property. In Africa, the property of the individual belongs at the same time to the community as a whole. It falls to the same individual to manage it well for the general good. In this connection, it is interesting to observe that in many African communities the notion of poverty is somewhat different from that in the Euro-American world. In Africa, the goal is not to possess things but to form relationships. One is not poor because one possesses nothing material, but true poverty consists in having no human relations, after having lost one's parents or other family members, for example. Even with regard to material things, the point is not to "possess" them in the Western sense but to have relationships with them. Certain African languages where the verb "to have" is missing express precisely that. So, in Swahili, one talks about "kuwa na" (to be with). It is the same thing in Lingala, which says "kuzala na" (to be with). This relationship to material things primarily aims at promoting human relations. One sees how the right to private property in Africa must first focus on the community without neglecting the individual. Children's right to education calls for a similar argument. Children do not only belong to the parents in the Euro-American sense, but also to the whole clan community. The right to education must therefore involve this community as a whole and not limit itself to the parents alone. When in modern Africa one talks of human rights violations, it is absolutely necessary to take into account the context as we have just described it.

Issues concerning the elderly

In modern society, particularly in the West, young people no longer seem to be interested in the elderly other than as a burden to get rid of. Advertising praises eternal youth. As everything centers on profitability, the elderly are relegated to oblivion and anonymity, since they prove unable to perform as society requires.

The value of African tradition could usefully be reasserted here. In Africa the elderly are treated with great respect, and by virtue of their long experience are considered a source of wisdom. Even if they are no longer able to generate or bear biological life, they continue to strengthen and increase the life of the whole community through their great wisdom. When one talks of teaching through experience, it is not at all about transmitting technological knowledge, for instance, because younger people can be experts on this. The experience African tradition talks about is at a more existential level; this experience is what provides technology itself with its soul, so that it is not know-how devoid of wisdom. A technology devoid of wisdom is dehumanizing and leads to death. From the African point of view, a society that dispenses with the experience of the elderly ruins itself because it will not be able to identify the forces of life and death in the cosmos. Even supposing that an old person is mentally frail and unable to benefit others with their experiences, this does not degrade them to the level of a "negligible quantity." In Africa, everybody knows they are carried by the elders, even by those elders who are now invalids. We have life in its various manifestations thanks to them. Even if they can no longer hand down their wisdom to us, it is our duty to demonstrate our gratitude and to share with them our presence in order to increase their vital force on their painful path to the ancestors.

Issues concerning abortion and euthanasia

The subject of the elderly closely relates to discussions about the beginning and end of life (see chapter 53). Stormy debates on the status of the embryo reveal many divergent opinions on the determination of the precise moment one can begin to talk of a *person*. The various arguments often hinge on the determination of symptoms indicating cognitive potentialities and other identifiable human performances. In this sense, one talks of the appearance of the "large brain," which is supposed to be a sign that the embryo has evolved towards an "autonomous" human being.

In the African tradition, it would be futile to look for such a debate. If interpersonal relations make up the person, it is appropriate to determine on this basis whether or not the embryo enjoys the status of an individual human person. For a traditional African, there is no doubt that a fetus or an embryo is steeped in interpersonal relations. He or she belongs to the world of the not-yet born and is fully integrated into the community of the living and the dead. The fetus or the embryo lives and is encompassed within the love of the visible and invisible community. He or she is the hope of the living and of the dead, who survive in him or her, not only on the biological level, but also as he or she enriches the community in every way to increase life in the broad sense of the word. In other words, the fetus or the embryo, still incapable of providing services, is the ancestors' messenger, and he or she connects them with their descendents still on earth. Seen from this point of view, there is a continuous interaction between the living, the dead, and the not-yet born, and this too constitutes the embryo as a person whose life must absolutely be respected.

In close relation to this issue is the case of the dying. The discussion which dominates the Western scene as far as euthanasia is concerned does not exist in this form in most of the African traditions. In Black Africa, caring for the dying is crucial. "Caring consists in staying in living touch with the dying person and in conveying to him or her the feeling that he or she is still someone even in this condition, where his or her physical strength abandons him or her," and that he or she keeps developing as a person through his or her pain (Bujo 2002: 19). Dying persons restore their being as a person through interpersonal relations with those caring for them, but in turn, the sick and the dying help the people around them to become aware of their own personality, with its highs and its lows. Thus, through the way they accept their suffering, the sick and dying contribute to the edification of the living, whose personality grows, too. Thus, a dying person's sickness and last days are a chance for everybody, the sick and the dying and those caring for them, to enrich each other and to become even more conscious of their respective identities.

If one refers to this African conception, euthanasia as it is understood in the West, far from protecting human rights, in fact violates them because it annihilates a person's identity. In its original meaning, euthanasia should consist in helping the dying to feel accepted by his or her family circle, as the African tradition tries hard to do.

Conclusion

Our study is only an overview, which by no means claims to exhaust the ethical questions in Black Africa. From what has been said, however, it appears that African ethics has its own logic, which deserves to be respected in intercultural and interreligious dialogue. At a time when the world centers on globalization, denying African culture its identity and wanting to level it to a monoculture or a global ethos, are a kind of neocolonialism, African ethics aims to promote life in abundance. This is possible only if one respects diversity within cultures. Far from being an impoverishment, diversity is an unprecedented chance and treasure, whereas globalization is a cultural cloning seeking to impose a monoculture, which can only be dictatorial and oppressive. By contrast, the world will be able to enhance life and find peace only if we respect the plurality of the cultures in dialogue with each other.

Acknowledgment

The author acknowledges with gratitude the translation of this chapter by Philippe Eberhard.

Bibliography

Bidima, J.-G. 1997: *La Palabre: une juridiction de la parole*. Paris: Michalon.
Bujo, B. 1992: *African Theology in Its Social Context*. Maryknoll, NY: Orbis Books.
——1993: *Die ethische Dimension der Gemeinschaft: Das afrikanische Modell im Nord-Süd-Dialog*. Freiburg: Universitätsverlag.
——1996a: *Dieu devient homme en Afrique noire: méditations sur l'Incarnation*. Kinshasa: Paulines.

——1996b: "Krankheit und Gemeinschaft aus negro-afrikanischer Sicht" in *Heilende Gemein-schaft?: Von der sozialen Dimension der Gesundheit*, ed. G. Koch and J. Pretscher. Würzburg: Echter.

——1998a: *African Christian Morality at the Age of Inculturation*. Nairobi: Paulines.

——1998b: "Welches Weltethos begründet die Menschenrechte?" *Jahrbuch für Christliche Sozial-wissenschaften* 39, 36–53.

——2001: *Foundations of an African Ethic: Beyond the Universal Claims of Western Morality*. New York: Crossroad.

——2002: "Tradition africaine et questions bioéthiques." *Eglise d'Afrique. Revue d'Etudes et d'Expériences Chrétiennes* 3, 17–25.

Habermas, J. 1983: *Moralbewusstsein und kommunikatives Handeln*. Frankfurt am Main: Suhrkamp.

Hollis, A. C. S. 1969: *The Masai: Their Language and Folklore*. Oxford: Clarendon Press.

Magesa, L. 1998: *African Religion: The Moral Traditions of Abundant Life*. Nairobi: Paulines.

Mbiti, J. S. 1996: *Introduction to African Religion*. Nairobi: East African Educational Publishers.

Merker, M. 1910: *Die Masai: Ethnographische Monographie eines ostafrikanischen Semitenvolkes*. Berlin: D. Reimer.

Mugambi, J. 2001: "Africa and the Old Testament" in *Interpreting the Old Testament in Africa*, ed. M. N. Getui, K. Holter, and V. Zinkuratire. Nairobi: Acton Publishers.

Mulago, V. 1965: *Un Visage africain du christianisme. L'union vitale bantu face à l'unité vitale ecclésiale*. Paris: Présence africaine.

——1980: *La Religion traditionnelle des Bantu et leur vision du monde*. Kinshasa: Faculté de théolo-gie catholique.

Mveng, E. 1979: "Essai d'anthropologie négro-africaine." *Bulletin de Théologie Africaine* 1, 229–39.

——1985: *L'Afrique dans l'Eglise: paroles d'un croyant*. Paris: Editions L'Harmattan.

Ndjimbi-Tshiende, O. 1992: *Réciprocité-coopération et le systeme palabrique africain: tradition et herméneutique dans les théories du développement de la conscience morale chez Piaget, Kohlberg et Habermas*. St. Ottilien: EOS Verlag.

Nsuka, Y. 1970: "Une Prière d'invocation kongo." *Cahiers des Religions Africaines* 258–64.

Reese-Schäfer, W. 1994: *Was ist Kommunitarismus?* Frankfurt am Main: Campus Verlag.

Tshiamalenga-Ntumba, M. 1995: "Afrikanische Philosophie. Zum originären Vertrauen des afrikanischen Menschen" in *Eglise et droits de la société africaine*, ed. A. Mutombo-Mwana and E. R. Mbaya Mbujimayi, 109–20. Mbuji-Mayi: Editions CILOWA.

CHAPTER 44

Trajectories in African Ethics

Laura Grillo

When confronted with conflicting demands, inexplicable contradictions threatening
the integrity of one's worldview, or faced with the moral uncertainty that contradictions elicit, recourse must be made to moral deliberation in which one's actions are consciously evaluated and determined by principles and priorities (see chapter 5). West
African religions offer such a discipline in the form of divination, a process that invites
reflection on personal actions and their consequences, and consideration of their place
within the dynamic patterns of cosmos, not just as a backdrop of human action, but
as an integral and determinative part of it (see chapter 10).

West African Divination: Moral Philosophy and
Ethical Enterprise

By common definition, divination is a technique used to determine the future and to
make authoritative pronouncements about it. In the context of West African religious
traditions, this is not its primary objective. Rather than merely projecting the future,
divination inquires about the significance of the present. Its aim is not prediction, but
diagnosis. Divination is sought at moments of crisis, when a person becomes acutely
aware of a disjunction between an ideal model of reality and the experience of human
existence, when what "is" does not conform to what "ought" to be. Clients come to
diviners when confronted with the disquieting experiences of disease, conflict, and
inexplicable misfortune to ask, "Why me? Why now?" The divinatory inquiry never
yields an unambiguous answer, but presents its finding in the form of another puzzle –
a cryptic message encoded in the cast of the diviner's accoutrements (sticks, shells,
seeds, bones). Its interpretation draws the client into a reflection about the self in relation to others and to one's own hidden desires. The divinatory consultation invariably
culminates in a prescription for a sacrifice, that aims at reestablishing a dynamic equi-
librium among individual, society, and cosmos.

West African religions are not concerned with salvation but are focused on health, fecundity, and power – the forces that sustain life and community. These are the values that constitute "the good." The purpose of a divinatory consultation is to root out the source of suffering and alleviate it, restoring social harmony and physical health. These are understood to be mutually dependent and sustained by the ancestors, the guardians of the moral order.

Divination is therefore at the core of a coherent religious system and operates as a pivotal institution. It brings ultimate meaning to bear on the troubling events and circumstances of its clients' everyday lives. Its techniques subject seemingly random experiences to the framework of cosmic order elucidated in myths, and show them to be the reiterated patterns of precedent established by ancestors and culture heroes. For example, in the practice of Ifa, the renowned Yoruba divinatory system, the diviner (*Babalaow* or "father of secrets") recites a verse (*odù*) correlating with the pattern cast by a random throw of cowrie shells. These verses relate how, at the founding of the world, the divinities or other mythic persona resolved dilemmas similar to those facing the client. The sacrifices they performed then become the clients' prescriptions for action in the present. Divination demonstrates that the archetypical actions effected by the primordial forebears still reverberate in the microcosm of the created world and echo in the lives of contemporary humanity. It is premised on the notion that "every concrete being is implicated within the whole [cosmic] system [and it is divination's] reading of the signs that defines this system" (Bastide 1973: 34). Divination is first and foremost a highly pragmatic enterprise. It addresses the immediate and pressing concerns of actual life crises and decisions.

Like ethics, divination addresses the interface between a system of values and the contingencies of experience to which it must be applied. The work of divination is not about articulating the principles and propositions of a moral philosophy, but rather about applying discrimination and discernment to concrete moral problems. Participation in divination and the practice of ethics alike require more than mere conformity to cultural standards of good and evil, right and wrong. Both call for a deliberation of the subtler question of how to apply principles in support of the right and good to the exigencies of everyday existence, and how to adjudicate experience in light of these ideals.

In what follows I first present two well-known cases of West African divination. Arguing that these ritual practices epitomize ethical engagement, I will underscore how divinatory participation demonstrates two key aspects of ethical agency: *responsiveness* (to the immediate contingency of experience and the human beings involved) and *responsibility* (to critical values about good and evil and to social commitments to forge a personal destiny in keeping with these values). To consult a diviner, a deliberate action that invokes personal deliberation on one's most heartfelt desires, hidden motives, personal accountability, choices, and their ramifications, is to practice ethics. The ambiguity of power – spiritual as well as mundane – makes deliberate ethical agency all the more necessary. This inquiry will allow us to trace current trajectories, showing divination to be a vital strategy for coping and for asserting moral purpose.

Dogon of Mali: Responsiveness to Cosmic Dynamic

Dogon divination is generically called "divination by the Fox" and includes the reading of actual fox tracks left across a divining table that has been traced in the sand. The origin of this practice is reflected in Dogon myths (see chapter 13).

According to Dogon cosmogony, Amma's first attempt to create the world failed (Griaule and Dieterlen 1965; Pelton 1980). The elements remained stagnant and sterile. Amma set them into motion by emitting the vibration of his first word. This churned the elements within the cosmic egg to form the original pairs of twin primordial beings. But the world as we know it was created in response to the restless determination of Ogo, one of these beings. The impatient Ogo broke away prematurely from the cosmic egg (or womb), tearing away a piece of the placenta which he scratched and stretched to form the earth. Next, he stole some primordial grain which he used to attempt to create a fecund world of his own making. When this failed and without his intended twin partner, Ogo attempted intercourse with a mound of this placenta-earth, but still failed to produce fecundity. At every turn Amma intervened to thwart Ogo's rebellious efforts. The havoc that Ogo sewed upon the intended cosmic order nevertheless gave shape to the world. Rather than destroying the mutated universe, Amma repossessed the new creation by consecrating it through sacrifice. Then, to ensure the ongoing manipulation of the cosmic elements and the earth's fecundity, Amma created human beings.

In creating men, Amma began with the formation of the clavicle. Its resemblance to a hoe alludes to their purpose on earth – to work the fields and cultivate grain. Agricultural labor recreates the original generative act, Amma's stirring of the first elements. Ultimately, to punish the ever-subversive Ogo, Amma reduced him to the abased form of the fox, Yurugu. But in a last magnanimous gesture, Amma granted Ogo the favor of serving humanity as the bearer of divinatory pronouncement. Because the cunning and duplicitous Ogo-Yurugu, as the mediator of divinatory "speech," retains an important measure of generative power, it is said that he "stole speech" from Amma. Just as Ogo tore and stretched the cosmic placenta to create the earth, the Dogon diviner etches into sand the table of signs, called *kala*, literally meaning "torn." The table represents the world and each person's situation in it. Once the tracks of a fox's pawprints are found traced across these tables, the divinatory interpretation begins. So Ogo, the trickster, is the inaugurator of divination and in the form of Yurugu the fox, is its herald.

From this mythology about the mutually dependent origins of cosmos and divination, we see that Dogon divination cannot provide a simple code for behavior, since its founding mediator is the unpredictable trickster. And precisely because this mythology does not represent a totalizing view of cosmos as fixed and determined by a High God, Dogon divination does not offer a vision of a preordained order either. Instead, from its very inception and by its practice, Dogon divination recognizes that the cosmos is characterized by change, by inexplicable ruptures of order. Full of moral vagaries and indisputable transgression (such as Ogo's incestuous relations with his placenta/Earth-Mother), the myths offer no overt prescription for moral action, nor even a didactic warning against the violation of norms. Instead, the repercussions of Ogo's behavior are extended into the present through divination.

The fact that divination is mediated through the unreliable and deceitful Fox can be interpreted as an implied commentary on humanity's precarious situation within a world of constant permutation. Actually, the anomalous figure of this trickster may be considered an ideal foil for provoking moral reasoning. Through his play with boundaries and mischievous exploration and transmutation of reality, tricksters comment on all forms of social and cosmic order, including moral order. For this reason, Dogon divination does not offer a facile solution to a client's problems, but an opportunity to puzzle out choices and their possible ramifications.

In seeking signs and guidance from within the phenomenal world, Dogon divination is responsive to the symbolic coherence within creation as well as to the creator from whom it is indivisible, for Dogon myth makes clear that Amma *is* the cosmic egg and the vibration from which all creation derives. Moreover, the mythology points to the ongoing *responsibility* human beings bear as determining agents of Amma's dynamic world. It suggests that without the deliberate, ongoing manipulation of the elements, the earth would remain as stagnant and sterile as Amma's earlier, failed attempt at creation. From this view, human beings are charged with an ethical duty of cosmic proportion. Both cosmic and social well-being depend on the fulfillment of their duty in sustaining the fruitfulness of its patterns and rhythms. Therefore, divination can be understood as an ethical act, for the working harmony of the cosmos ultimately rests on a vigilant participation in the dynamics set in motion at the primordium.

I have characterized Dogon divination as evincing *responsiveness* to the coherence of a cosmos, underscoring that this natural world is a milieu in which human action figures significantly as a force that sustains its creative dynamic and therefore "the good." In the discussion of Yoruba divination that follows, we focus on the active engagement of *responsibility*, and divination as the means of negotiating moral identity and forging ethical agency.

Yoruba of Nigeria: Negotiating Moral Identity and Ethical Agency

The ancestors feature prominently in traditional African religions as the guardians of moral order. They ensure conformity to standards of social behavior and enforce moral obligations by inflicting misfortune or suffering upon living kin who transgress these norms. While troublesome and sometimes even serious, such affliction is not considered an "evil," but chastisement aimed at correcting immoral behavior. It is through divination that the specific wishes of the ancestors can be discerned, and it is through the sacrifice prescribed by divination that they are appeased: "Yoruba religious practice depends on two factors, descent and divination. In combination they produce a very fluid religious system" (Drewal and Drewal 1983: 247). Interestingly, the ancestors are not concerned with ethics in the sense of personal virtue. The moral order is a responsibility that humans bear for the proper functioning of the whole, but adherence to the good does not ensure personal reward but life itself. Moral problems are posed less as a choice between good and evil than an alternative between life and death (Thomas 1982: 141).

Where the natural order is viewed as a moral order, events cannot be considered to occur at random. They happen in order to promote an ethical purpose and the distribution of rewards and punishments. Further, from such a perspective, all circumstances and experiences are morally significant (Shweder 1991: 157). However, it does not appear that there is *always* such a clear-cut correlation between moral rectitude and the facts of life in West African systems of thought. Not all suffering and misfortune can be ascribed to the neglect of duty or the sanctions of the ancestors. There is also an acknowledgment of scandalously unjust reversals of fortune in which the cause is not a moral failing of the sufferer. One explanation offered is a bad prenatal destiny, a choice for which the person is not truly deemed accountable but must nevertheless struggle. However, when projects fail despite all efforts and precautions or when health inexplicably shrivels, such meaningless suffering – the essence of evil – is traced to the malevolence of witches. The concept of "witch" in West African traditions is a complex one. People identified as witches are often those who display anti-social sentiments such as anger or jealousy, or whose behavior conveys that they are too self-sufficient: they are reclusive, arrogant, or ungenerous. Not only is it possible that the wicked may prosper, but indeed, inordinate prosperity is suspect as an indication of witchcraft! The source of evil is located in the human world, and lurks in the heart of the hidden person (Marwick 1987: 424). It is diviners who can identify the witch plaguing a client and who, on occasion, may cause the accused culprit to confess and relent. Diviners and witches are often represented as opposites and agonists: witches operate in darkness and secrecy, diviners practice by day in public places; witches veil their activities and obscure their power, the diviner is to serve as a medium of revelation so that the invisible can be given form for all to see; witches intercede to cause sickness and impede success, diviners intervene to diagnose illness or the cause of misfortune, prescribe remedy and protection, and promote the flourishing of destiny.

A closer look at how people use the term "witch" and conceive of witchcraft reveals that in fact an opposition between "diviner" as a force of "good" and "witch" as source of "evil" is too simplistic. Most traditional African societies hold to the belief that certain people are able to use supernatural means for their own ends. Their power is great, but ambiguous. It can be used for good or evil, to protect or destroy life. Yoruba tradition maintains that life-sustaining "power" (*ase*) is an ambivalent force. Its ambivalent nature requires that it be harnessed by culture for the greater good (cf. Drewal and Drewal 1983). So witches derive their power from the same supreme creator god who invests the entire cosmos with its creative impulse. Witches choose to exercise it for evil (see Abimbola 1977).

Many interpreters of African cultures offer a socially pragmatic basis for belief in witchcraft, emphasizing the frustration and aggression that arises within the restricting conditions of a "closed society," one that relies on harmonious relations. Fear of accusation and its repercussions ensures that standards of appropriate moral conduct are scrupulously maintained. However, the ramifications of both accusations and confessions of witchcraft belie this explanation. Rather than serving to alleviate hostilities, the identification of a witch usually increases social tension. Adherence to beliefs in witchcraft actually undermines moral behavior, since it encourages subterfuge and suspicion about others. Belief in witchcraft, in other words, entails a moral system that acknowledges the existence of moral ambiguity and the ambivalent and hidden quality of personal motives, and calls for a process that will attend to these more complex problems.

Because power is ambiguous, the potential for witchcraft is understood to be innate and unconscious. The election of divination as a means of confronting one's hidden motives is an ethical act, for it ensures the proper and responsible direction of personal destiny. The Yoruba recognize that evil intentions are not readily apparent but belong to that occult dimension of the human being to which only divination offers access. "God forgot to split the feet of a duck, and a crane uses its leg as a tail; but no one can recognize the footprints of a cruel man" (Clarke 1939: 249). Divination is a means to explore otherwise unexamined motives and hidden dynamics that reveals one's moral "footprint." Moreover, divination strengthens that inner core of deliberate intention that provides protection as well as moral resolve. Abimbola represents the Yoruba approach in this way: "When a person is troubled by the àjé (witches), he is encouraged to call on his own orí [literally, "head," the seat of the self and personal destiny revealed through divination] which he chose for himself shortly before he left òrun (heaven) for the earth" (Abimbola 1977: 82). Sacrifices are made to the orí to promote the flourishing of destiny, for the type of orí chosen before birth – the very nature of one's destiny – remains unknowable, a mystery that can only be guessed at the end of one's life (Abimbola 1973: 87). It is left to each person to make every attempt to enhance the full potential of his or her allotted destiny through wise choices and proper action; and for this, divination is an essential guide.

Every divinatory inquiry entails an implicit awareness of the competing interests of the public persona and the inner self. The tension between individual and collective, inner and outer self is an ethical dilemma, and while it can never be finally resolved, the ongoing permutations in the dynamic can be negotiated. While clients of divination may come with personal decisions and seemingly private ills, the process necessarily calls upon clients to "formulate and continually revise their moral identity," that is, one established in concert with that of the community, both social and spiritual (Johnson 1993: 126). In order to resolve a dilemma, divination situates the individual within the nexus of relations.

In calling upon the client's sense of responsibility to self and other, divination radically contests a view of a moral person as essentially an atomistic, rational ego, applying universal principles or absolute mandates uniformly. Divination involves an ongoing negotiation between individual and society, and rests on the assumption that no absolute moral law is universally viable. Furthermore, it undercuts the view that "traditional" societies enforce a univocal decree of requirement for action.

Trajectories for West African Ethics

In the context of West African traditions, divination is the core of a pragmatic religious system. In the ethnically heterogeneous context of the city, though, diviners and their clients do not necessarily share a common ethnic origin. Here, divination cannot rely on standard conventions to make its practices coherent and persuasive. There is no common mythic model upon which experience can be predicated and the ritual cannot necessarily exploit a common symbolic lexicon.

Nevertheless, in the West African metropolis of Abidjan (Côte d'Ivoire), amid skyscrapers and traffic jams, diviners are, in fact, very present, strategically placed on street corners and in marketplaces, or operating in recessed courtyards and consulting rooms off bustling streets. Clients come with their most pressing concerns, confident in the efficacy of divinatory techniques to cast their misfortune into manageable terms. The lively presence of divination in Abidjan (as in other West African cities) is an indication that such ritual is not a thing of the past but vividly relevant in the contemporary scene. Extracted from the traditional milieu, does urban divinatory practice still operate as an ethical system in which responsibility and responsiveness are critical components?

The indigenous population of Côte d'Ivoire is comprised of over 60 distinct ethnic peoples. In addition, the long-term political stability and relative economic prosperity drew immigrants and refugees from all over West Africa. The techniques of urban divination are as varied as the many ethnic neighborhoods that comprise Abidjan. While traditional practices flourish, signs advertising clairvoyants and "consultants" who use palmistry, astrology, or tarot also lure the urban clientele. The impressive array of alternative divinatory techniques being practiced in Abidjan strikingly represents the kaleidoscopic quality of religiosity in this city in creative flux and recombination. The prevalence of divination in Abidjan reflects the urban plight even as it provides clients with a means of addressing the acute distress that a modern metropolis engenders. Clients are compelled to seek out divination in light of the social dysfunction of "underdevelopment" and the alienation of the city. Urban diviners are often themselves economic refugees, no longer functioning as ritual specialists in the service of community, but as paid professionals who cater to a clientele of individuals. The promising talents of diviners advertised on billboards are presented like other commodities on the market. The practices reflect the capitalist and individualistic milieu in which they now operate.

These trends do not mean, however, that the ritual process has undergone degeneration to the degree that it no longer holds value as an ethical enterprise. While there is no effort on the part of diviners or their clientele to appeal to an entire, cohesive tradition, urban divination is genuinely grounded in its traditional techniques, and these have always been innovative and adaptive. Even the most consistent of divinatory systems, such as Ifa which requires that every diviner undergo rigorous training and ritual initiation before being admitted into the coterie of specialists, has always included innovation. For example, Ifa diviners invent new *odù*, interpretive verses associated with the ideograms cast by the random fall of kola nuts (William 1966: 408–21). This seems to defy the common assertion that the verses constitute a fixed canon of the Yoruba divinatory technique. Moreover, many traditional divinatory forms exist in which there is no systematic interpretation of signs. Diviners readily admit that even among those who use identical techniques there is no consensus about the meaning of the patterns cast, and that the rules of interpretation are few. What is consistent and authentic in both traditional and urban contexts is the appeal to the practice of divination itself and to the underlying premises that support it.

Contemporary clients continue to perceive a need for protection and release from the tyranny of invisible forces, for even in the city there persists the conviction that, along with the empirically demonstrable facts of underdevelopment, it is the elusive powers of spirits, witches, and spells that undermine life. Divination provides a sense of empowerment by enabling the client to consider the crisis at hand from the overarching vantage point of cosmic dynamics. It allows the client to envision possibilities for control and relief to problems that might otherwise remain beyond the purview of his or her ability to act (see Jackson 1989). As Guedou Joseph, a practitioner of Fa from Benin put it, "God says, 'get up and lift your heavy load and I will help you load it onto your head' [where it can be carried]. When you make sacrifice you lift your burden, and God places it on your head."

Urban divination offers clients a critical alternative to Western, materialist appraisals of the problems of modernity that plague them. Rather than capitulating to the economic rhetoric of development theory to explain the inevitability of the paucity of jobs, the lack of access to adequate healthcare, corruption, bureaucratic mismanagement, and other facts of daily existence, urban West Africans turn to divination as an explanatory frame. It asserts that circumstance must be interpreted in terms of less tangible realities and that destiny must be negotiated accordingly (see van Binsbergen 1995). The potent appeal of urban divination is that it revivifies underlying precepts and values, even as it asserts an alternative interpretation of the miseries that plague the typical inhabitant of the city.

In the urban sphere ancestors play a significantly reduced role. They are neither the source of divinatory messages nor recipients of propitiatory offerings. Rather, it is personal spirits, more anonymous and nebulous, who intercede in the negotiation of destiny. Urban divinatory prescriptions are more individual and therapeutic than political. For example, rather than being asked to sacrifice a goat in a public ritual and distribute meat to relatives involved in a dispute, a client might be asked to wash her face in milk, and leave a kola nut at a crossroad. Furthermore, urban diviners repeatedly assert that a client makes sacrifices not to appease either personal spirits or ancestors, but rather to empower his or her own soul or spiritual double. At first glance, this adjustment seems to reflect adaptation to the anonymous urban situation, where moral precepts can no longer be sustained by adherence to traditional values or community life. However, it is ultimately no different from the Yoruba appeal to one's own *orí*, or "head," as the seat of personal destiny that must be propitiated in order to properly unfold. Divinatory sacrifice is so pervasive that beggars install themselves at busy crossroads where they are certain to secure daily alms. Reinforced by mutual good will, sacrifice elicits a visible acknowledgment of a trans-ethnic African identity. It binds the hybrid population into a visibly coherent moral community.

By validating the reality of essential common postulates like witchcraft as the source of evil and the corrective power of sacrifice, divination has contributed to a popular sense of transnational affiliation across political boundaries. These "traditional" notions are increasingly becoming the hallmarks of a "new amalgam" identity which is clearly being forged today among urban West Africans from various countries, who readily assert that there is no difference among them (Jules-Rosette 1979: 226). This new sense of identity does not fall back on the largely bankrupt notion of citizenship that has had little to offer contemporary Africans whose nations are rife with civil wars, on a continent where the extent of refugee migration lends new meaning to the term

"African Diaspora." The highly visible and vital practices of urban divination rely on a worldview that transcends ethnic boundaries and reinforce an ethos that binds and sustains community. Divination redefines problems in terms of a familiar interpretive framework and transcribes the dynamics of power into idioms that have currency across West Africa. Drawing on this overarching schema, urban divination represents a vital link to the indigenous religious world of meaning even as it shapes contemporary social reality.

In the urban situation every instance of divination is a deliberate undertaking, for it is the client who decides to initiate an inquiry. The client retains a large measure of control over the entire ritual process, from the choice of a diviner to participation in the interpretation of the signs, including the decision whether to accord it any authority at all. No prescription is enforced. It is up to the client whether to perform the recommended sacrifice, or to ignore the prescription and perhaps consult yet another diviner. Thus, divination calls for a constant appraisal of the choices and ramifications of action open to its participants. At the same time it provides for the kind of deliberation and decision making that give principled direction to action. Ultimately, however, divination recommends the individual to the community through sacrifice. In this way the divinatory process straddles the stereotypical thought/action dichotomy in an important way. Its ritual is not an unreflected exercise of repetition, and its foundational beliefs are not unquestioned. Instead, through divination, belief is exercised and practice is deliberated.

In the alienating context of contemporary urban life, where the negotiation of daily existence is increasingly difficult and unpredictable, divination is perhaps more critical than ever as a mechanism by which a sense of communal identity and moral purpose can be asserted, and a sense of personal agency is grasped and affirmed. This makes it easy to predict that divination will certainly continue to assert itself as a critical component of urban life and a vital affirmation of what may be considered a distinctively West African ethic.

Bibliography

Abimbola, W. 1973: "The Yoruba Concept of Human Personality" in *La Notion de personne en Afrique Noire*, ed. G. Dieterlen, 73–89. Paris: Éditions du Centre National de la Recherche Scientifique.

——1977: *Ifa Divination Poetry*. New York: Nok.

Bascom, W. 1966: "Odu Ifa: The Names of the Signs." *Africa* 30 (4), 408–21.

——1980: *Sixteen Cowries: Yoruba Divination from Africa to the New World*. Bloomington: Indiana University Press.

Bastide, R. 1973: "Le Principe d'individuation (contribution à une philosophie africaine)" in *La Notion de personne en Afrique Noire*, ed. G. Dieterlen, 33–43. Paris: Éditions du Centre National de la Recherche Scientifique.

Clarke, J. D. 1939: "Ifa Divination." *Journal of the Royal Anthropological Institute* 69, 235–56.

Drewal, H. J. and Drewal, M. T. 1983: *Gelede: Art and Female Power Among the Yoruba*. Bloomington: Indiana University Press.

Geertz, C. 1983: *Local Knowledge: Further Essays in Interpretive Anthropology.* New York: Basic Books.

Griaule, M. and Dieterlen, G. 1965: *Le Renard pâle, part i, "La Creation du monde."* Vol. 1, *Le Mythe cosmogpnique.* Paris: Université de Paris. Travaux et mémoires de l'Institut d'ethnologie.

Grillo, L. S. 1989: "Dogon Divination as an Ethic of Nature." *Journal of Religious Ethics* 20, 309–30.

Jackson, M. 1978: "An Approach to Kuranko Divination." *Human Relations* 31 (2), 117–38.

—— 1989: "Paths Toward a Clearing: Radical Empiricism and Ethnographic Inquiry" in *African Systems of Thought*, ed. C. S. Bird and I. Karp. Bloomington: Indiana University Press.

Johnson, M. 1993: *Moral Imagination: Implications of Cognitive Science for Ethics.* Chicago: University of Chicago Press.

Jules-Rosette, B. (ed.) 1979: *The New Religions of Africa.* Norwood, NJ: Ablex Publishing.

Marwick, M. G. 1987: "Witchcraft: African Witchcraft" in *The Encyclopedia of Religion*, ed. M. Eliade et al. New York: Macmillan.

Mendonsa, E. L. 1982: *The Politics of Divination: A Processual View of Reactions to Illness and Deviance Among the Sisala of Northern Ghana.* Berkeley: University of California Press.

Pelton, R. D. 1980: *The Trickster in West Africa: A Study of Mythic Irony and Sacred Delight.* Berkeley: University of California Press.

Shweder, R. A. 1991: *Thinking Through Cultures: Expeditions in Cultural Psychology.* Cambridge, MA: Harvard University Press.

Thomas, L.-V. 1982: *La Mort Africaine: idéologie funéraire en Afrique Noire.* Paris: Payot.

van Binsbergen, W. 1995: "Four Tablet Divination as Trans-Regional Medical Technology in Southern Africa." *Journal of Religion in Africa* 25, 114–40.

PART III
Moral Issues

1   Systems

CHAPTER 45

Economics

Max L. Stackhouse

Throughout history, religion has been related to economic life. While every religion has its own constituting framework of moral meaning, religious ideals are modulated by their contextual applications when they encounter other possibilities of thought and worship or find it necessary to address new situations. Although anthropological understandings in the past tended to see each culture as a self-contained system with its own religion, code of conduct, social institutions, and economic strategies, broader studies suggest that cultures change by outside influences, most rapidly when economic and technical exchanges make old ways obsolete and religion legitimates new possibilities. How these change, and whether innovation is tolerated, resisted, or embraced, has to do with the inner character of the religion. Each religion will tend to see some changes as fundamentally immoral, and others as compatible with core values. Such factors indicate whether a society is stable and adaptable, or in decline and ready for collapse or conversion.

The Old Silk Road

Ancient examples of such changes can be found in recent studies of the Old Silk Road. Along its several branches and paths, early interchanges anticipated what we now identify as globalization. Intercultural and interreligious exchanges were facilitated by expansive economic trade that had episodic parallels in Africa and Pre-Columbian America. After the domestication of the camel in Asia, many trade routes developed among previously isolated regions – none more extensive and exemplary for our questions than the routes from the Mediterranean Sea, across Central Asia to China, with lesser extensions by sea to Korea and Japan in the East, to India and Arabia to the South, and into Europe and North Africa in the West. Along these routes, Jewish and Zoroastrian (and, after Alexander, Hellenistic) traders found their way east and Chinese traders found their way west. They met Hindu and Buddhist as well as animist tribal traditions along the routes. Each established enclaves along the way, but they usually represented traditions that were ethnically bound – Hebrew, Persian, Greek, Han, or Indo-Aryan. The exchange of religious and philosophical ideas led to some highly syncretistic spiritualities, but little changed the basic ethos. Still, patterns of "fair dealing" and "not stealing" were sufficiently recognized by all to sustain the exchanges and justly punish violators.

The economic practices of India and of China, legitimated by quite stable religious and ethical systems with differentiated trading and craft classes, are in certain ways similar and in other ways quite different (see chapters 34 and 38). Both formed agricultural, feudal-peasant societies. The hierarchical structure of India was based on the dominance of the brahminic priests, supported by a vast array of local and regional maharajas and princes who, together with the brahmans, enforced quite strict caste distinctions on the ethnically pluralistic, endogamous population. Each caste and princely state had, in fact, subdivisions, each with its own deities and each with an assigned role in the economy – a pattern applied to outcaste peoples as well. This massive complexity fixed groups in their status and functions and even dramatic religious and political incursions – as when the Moguls or British arrived – were largely absorbed into the system.

The imperial structure of China, by contrast, had an integrated political regime supported by a subordinate Mandarin literati who both administered the regional offices of the emperor and propagated an ethic of virtue, duty, and obedience to patriarchal–imperial authority at every level of the society, from the emperor to the family. This unified structure was often less in harmony with nature and heaven than classic theory imagined, but it entailed the consequence that a change of dynasty could change a frightening amount. Stability demanded social as well as cosmic harmony. Centralized authority also allowed greater control of dissent, of the land (as massive irrigation projects or defense walls reveal), and of technology and trade, the fruits of which were enjoyed by elites. The people worked hard, consumed little, and depended on emperors, literati, and local patriarchs to establish the fabric of duties and live in learned leisure.

When the proselytizing religions arose – first Buddhists, then Christians, and later Muslims – they sent missionaries to non-converted regions along the Silk Road. Buddhists bore Indian ideas to the East and West; Christians took the Gospel and Greco-Roman ideas to the East. A rather ample tolerance seems to have been the rule, and each had success in tribal areas where religion served as a link to the wider world. But both Buddhists and Christians of that period were monastic. They thought that the exemplary life required the renunciation of wealth, of politics, and indeed of marriage. Thus, they had little effect on economic ethics except in presenting a basic alternative to it.

When Islam spread along the road, it established a new hegemony from Istanbul to central Asia, with links to the Arab world. And it brought quite another model of religion and economic life. For one thing, Muḥammed, the prophet of Islam, was himself a caravan trader. The lore of the tradition and the laws in the Qur'ān and the Sharī'a reflected an ethos congenial to trade. For another, Muḥammed was a warrior, and there was as little doubt about the spreading of the faith, and economic opportunity for believers, by conquest as there was about the morality of trade. A theocratic political economy given to trade was seen as morally and spiritually quite legitimate.

This attitude differed from the Hindu and Confucian traditions, and, for that matter, most Greek, Roman, and medieval Christian traditions. Although all of these had a place for tradesmen and merchants in society, these activities were not held in high esteem. Not only were they always trying to make a profit, which made them at least appear to be greedy, they also did not stay at home in settled moral systems and often acted immorally on the road – or were thought to. They did not produce as did the settled peasants, they did not provide defense from invaders as did rulers, and they did not cultivate the spiritual, moral, or intellectual virtues to keep the sacred traditions as did the priests and literati.

Still, the ancient Silk Road provided a set of complex channels by which the world became more closely bound together. Arts and technologies, pieties and philosophies, myths and worldviews were more widely disseminated, as goods, money, and produce became increasingly accessible. Many of the crafts and spiritual practices of Asia passed into the West and were adapted to new conditions. Time-keeping devices, gun power, printing techniques, and navigational instruments were adopted by the legacies of Greek philosophy, Roman law, and Hebrew prophecy in reformed Christian theologies, generating a new complex, dynamic civilization on the Occidental end of that road. These, and confrontations with Islam which also was spreading to the West, jarred primitive Europe out of its lethargic feudalism and gradually prompted new religious, ethical, and social changes that we now call Reformation, Renaissance, and the Age of Exploration. The result was a new relationship between economics and religious ethics.

These changes induced a second period of proto-globalization. When the technology of transport changed from caravan to clipper ships, and the new burst of religious zeal invited the faithful to advance world-transforming convictions, entrepreneurs and missionaries took to the seas. There are many causes of these developments, including a rising nationalism in Europe, a development that generated the "Wars of Religion" contained only by the "Peace of Westphalia." But if nations could not expand the range of their rule at home, they could send merchants and missionaries abroad. To protect their investments from expropriation and their faiths from attack, soldiers were soon to follow.

Modern Developments

Of course, indigenous rulers and elders resisted. Still, resentments could no more contain the hunger for goods carried in both directions by traders than control the religio-cultural insights taken abroad or brought home by missionaries. This second period of proto-globalization served the Industrial Revolution, and it, in turn, altered both the religio-cultural and the techno-economic life in much of the world. This is the period of "modernization" – a process that, in many places, is still very much underway and among some peoples is just getting started.

In modernity, however, much of economic activity and theory seemed to be entirely cut off from religious and ethical norms, at least in traditional terms. Many see modern economic developments as entirely secular. In this context two great modern hypotheses about the relation of economics and religion in modernity were developed. These hypotheses were developed respectively by Karl Marx and Max Weber. The long geo-economic war between statist "socialism" and libertarian "capitalism," both usually understood in nineteenth-century terms and neither ever fully made actual, has resolved into a democratic capitalism with some welfare provisions for the very poor and moral qualms for the rest about living in a consumerist society.

Both efforts to understand modern economic systems see them as developments that surpassed traditional and feudal economies in ways that disrupted older communities, alienated workers from traditional relationships, and formed new classes in society. But one view opposes these developments. It generated not only several romantic communitarian movements, but also efforts to form a scientific economics that superseded all traces of tradition, religion, or idealistic moralism. Monumental efforts were made to construct an economic system beyond capitalism, using modes of central planning that would bring liberation, equality, and a new solidarity. Today, these efforts seem universally to have collapsed, but their impact on thought and political policy around the world should not be underestimated. Many religious leaders think about the relationship of religious ethics and economic life in precisely these terms.

What has been increasingly argued, however, is a contrary view that capitalism brings more freedom and works better in producing and distributing goods and services. Further, it is increasingly doubted that capitalism creates the polarization of the classes. The best evidence indicates that it in fact tends to create larger and more inclusive middle classes, even if it also involves greater temporary gaps between those at the top of the economic bell-shaped curve and those newly included at the bottom of that curve. Thus, more poor people seek to migrate to capitalist lands and out of socialist ones. Moreover, most theories today hold that economies work best in a constitutional democracy that also regulates business activities so as to constrain fraud, exploitation, and corruption. They recognize the necessity of legally controlled market exchange and the wisdom of encouraging multiple corporations in it. Indeed, the number of corporations per 100,000 people is a key indicator of economic well-being – an argument for wide access to incorporation procedures and against monopolies by state or industrial collusion.

To be sure, cultures where people are not encouraged to form or sustain viable corporations are left behind economically and become most vulnerable. Some scholars argue that the habits of mind, traditions of trust and trustworthiness, and skills in forming and managing viable institutions for cooperative ventures in modern complex societies depend historically on religious orientations that encourage participation in organizations distinct from state and patriarchal domination. Thus, marginal groups find not only spiritual consolation and moral guidance, but also networks of contacts and the resources of social capital by active participation in church, mosque, or temple. If these are vibrant, the social order becomes more favorable to both religious and corporate development, and to economic well-being.

Two Great Hypotheses

Still, the persistence of the two great hypotheses forces us to inquire further into the nature and character of ethics and religion in relation to economic life. The first hypothesis, associated with Marx, was actually explored long ago by materialist philosophers both in the West and the East. It is, ironically, held in new forms today by some procapitalist economists who link their theory to evolutionary psychology in a fresh version of social Darwinism. This view holds that human motivations are obviously and decisively material interests, that the control of the means of production determines the basic contours of economic life, and that the fittest will and should survive. Religion, in this view, is a survival strategy of earlier stages of evolution that today is propagated by interested parties and blindly inhaled by the branches of the population who remain backward – a kind of opiate for the intellectually incompetent. This view finds forceful contemporary expression, ironically, in the socialist-rooted "world systems theories" of Immanuel M. Wallerstein and the polemics of David C. Korten, as well as capitalist-oriented Nobel Prize winners Gary Becker and, in part, Amartya Sen. In none of these does religion play a role in shaping economic life.

The second hypothesis is associated with the legacy of Max Weber. He claims that the religious convictions of people are among the primary factors that not only influence personal character and behavior, but also the destiny and prosperity of peoples and nations. This view acknowledges, of course, that humans have strong economic interests; but it also holds that humans have ideal interests, ever sensing that there is more to life than material motivations and the struggle to gain control of the means to satisfy them. Indeed, that "more" shapes and selects between various possible interests as well as the kinds of means that are developed to meet these two kinds of interests. This "more" is given historical expression in religion which shapes the moral life and forms civil society in ways that are determinative for human flourishing. Because work is seen as a calling from God, some religious orientations predispose people to develop disciplined personal habits to form corporations to create wealth for the commonwealth, to seek more efficient means of production through technology, and to develop universalistic principles of morality that can regulate open societies.

In this second perspective, religion and religious ethics are not seen essentially as the byproducts of exploitative myth-making, but can best be seen as primary factors in the social dynamics of history. The question, then, is what kind and quality of religion best meets the tests of social justice and civilizational effectiveness. In some ways it appears that some religions encourage, and some inhibit, economic productivity accordingly as they promote the cultivation of trust, the rationalization of the economy, the formation of pluralistic social organizations, the honoring of human rights, and the rewarding of risk and technological innovation. Moreover, advocates of this view argue that modern capitalist societies are not, as some say, more acquisitive than traditional ones, but argue instead that they are in fact rooted in the constraint of immediate desires and interests, the postponement of gratification, and a cultivation of long-term, even trans-historical spiritual and moral concerns that are taken as guides to business life.

Versions of this view today are held by such social scientists as David Landes, Peter Berger, Lawrence Harrison, and Roland Robertson.

Ironically, the chief theorists of these two hypotheses shared one major assumption for most of the past century. They believed that the rational study of these phenomena would, over time, bring increased secularization in all areas of society (see chapter 49). More recently, many have reversed that expectation as, in fact, the world's cultures have not secularized. If anything, the religions have adopted and adapted aspects of contemporary technology and social organization, altered the ways in which particular groups control the means of production, and modulated parts of their own traditions to appropriate selectively aspects of socialism and increasingly of capitalism. In the meantime, they continue to generate habits of personal discipline and economic rationalization, complex modes of social organization outside the family and the state, and more universalistic views of moral and positive law. The most interesting fact in this regard, however, is that the criteria by which peoples are making this selection are based on the convergence of practical results and the resurgent, often conservative religious consciousness. Not only is Christianity experiencing what some call a new "great awakening" in the Americas, and in parts of Africa and Asia; but renewal is also seen in the other great, historic religions – Islam, Hinduism, parts of Buddhism and, in some ways, Confucianism. They are all expanding rapidly, reforming their traditions, and generating fresh religiously driven ethical approaches to contemporary issues – and in the process modifying their economic ethic in a procapitalist way. So, most remarkably, is Maoism, the last great representative of a thoroughly secular religion!

Current Challenges?

When one looks at matters historically and cross-culturally, we can say that the second hypothesis has basically displaced the first one – or better, has incorporated aspects of the first one into the second's more holistic view. Indeed, one can find a rather massive resurgence of efforts to make the connection between religion and economics. Not only have Catholic encyclicals and Protestant statements been issued by official church bodies in the last two decades, business practitioners are also seeking to connect their faith to practical business life, often without the aid of clergy whom they sometimes see as mired in obsolete socialist prejudices.

However, economic life is presently based in increasingly common standards of accounting, management, finance, marketing, communication technology, and the treatment of workers – standards not universally observed. More complex economic systems leave spaces for new criminal activities internal to high profile corporations, and new normative guides as well as regulative means are being developed to inhibit the new forms of corruption. These factors invite the various religious and cultural traditions of ethics to press in a common direction, even if other motifs from these traditions seek to preserve distinctive contours for their host societies.

Yet the infrastructure of something approximating a global civilization is on the virtual horizon, and a critical question is what patterns of ethics will guide it. Although some are still left out of the new levels of productivity and wealth, and perils to ecological sustainability are obvious, quick solutions are not available. Issues of property rights, particularly of intellectual property, become decisive, for those without access to the resources that developed new technologies and modes of production cannot possibly develop alternatives on their own, and thus they fall further behind. Moreover, the great growth of international corporations and financial institutions displaces traditional political means of economic constraint while international law and legal institutions, even if developing rapidly, are too weak to solve fundamental issues.

We can summarize our situation briefly this way:

1 Every civilization requires a common morality to flourish – a basic definition of right and wrong and a fundamental sense of the good to be sought, tied to personal virtues and real contexts, and no such basic morality has ever become pervasive in a civilization without a religious basis.
2 The basic morality that has produced modern, Western culture and has been the mother of globalizing technology, communication, economic productivity, democratic politics, and corporate organization, is rooted in the Christian theological tradition – particularly as it has drawn on and tried to integrate Hebraic, Greco-Roman, and later Enlightenment resources.
3 It is not certain whether this heritage can today develop a generous religious ethic able to engage the world religions and philosophies and, with them, provide the key guidelines of justice and responsibility for a global era without turning to imperial, hierocratic, theocratic, or neocolonial patterns of authoritarianism.

To offer faithful, creative, and simultaneously philosophically, scientifically, and theologically coherent proposals on such issues is a key task of religious ethics today if it is to face the realities of contemporary economic life. It will have to offer a more comprehensive vision of civilizational ethics than even the best historic moments of tolerance and trade, the best studies of business ethics, and the best discussions of capitalism, socialism, and social policy have yet generated.

Bibliography

Berger, P. 1984: *The Capitalist Revolution*. New York: Basic Books.
——1999: *The Desecularization of the World*. Grand Rapids, MI: William Eerdmans.
Dumont, L. 1970: *Homo Hierarchicus*. Chicago: University of Chicago Press.
Foltz, R. C. 1999: *Religions of the Silk Road: Overland Trade and Cultural Exchange from Antiquity to the Fifteenth Century*. New York: St. Martin's Press.
Fukuyama, F. 1995: *Trust: The Social Virtues and the Creation of Prosperity*. New York: Free Press.
Harrison, L. E. and Huntington, S. P. 2000: *Culture Matters: How Values Shape Human Progress*. New York: Basic Books.
Korten, D. C. 1995: *When Corporations Rule the World*. West Hartford, CT: Kumarian Press.
Krueger, D. A., et al. 1997: *The Business Corporation and Productive Justice*. Nashville, TN: Abingdon Press.
Landes, D. S. 1998: *The Wealth and Poverty of Nations: Why Some are So Rich and Some So Poor*. New York: W. W. Norton.

Nelson, R. H. 2001: *Economics as Religion: From Samuelson to Chicago and Beyond*. University Park: Pennsylvania State University Press.

Robertson, R. 1992: *Globalization: Social Theory and Global Culture*. London: Sage.

Sen, A. K. 1999: *Development as Freedom*. New York: Anchor Books.

Stackhouse, M. L., McCann, D. P., Roels, S. J., and Williams, P. N. (eds.) 1994: *On Good Business: Classical and Contemporary Resources on Religion and Economic Life*. Grand Rapids, MI: William Eerdmans.

Stackhouse, M. L., Paris, P. J., Browning, D. S., and Obenchain, D. B. (eds.) 2000–4: *God and Globalization*, 4 vols. Harrisburg, PA: Trinity Press International.

CHAPTER 46

Technology

Gerald P. McKenny

What is Technology?

What challenges does technology pose to religious ethics? The very question points to our contemporary historical and cultural situation. Technology poses the challenge to religious ethics, not vice versa; religious ethics must answer for itself – prove its legitimacy or its efficacy – in the face of technology. But what is technology? And how has it come to place religious ethics in the position of the addressee of a challenge?

In its precise sense "technology" refers not to every human-made device or process, or to the history or theory of such devices and processes, but rather to a complex phenomenon created by the union of scientific knowledge with what were once called the "useful arts," the "mechanic arts," or simply "art." Historians of technology often trace this union to the nineteenth century, when the systematic deployment of scientific knowledge in the service of technical invention and innovation began (see Marx 1997; White 1967). By contrast, many philosophers of technology argue that early modern science is already implicitly technological by virtue of the way it orders nature (see Arendt 1958; Gehlen 1980; Heidegger 1977; Jonas 1974). But regardless of when it began, technology is the product of this union of science and "art."

Technology, then, belongs to the modern world with its profound effects on traditional patterns of thought and conduct, authority and community, meaning and identity. Hans Jonas summed up the problem of technology for ethics in two observations. First, whole regions of existence that for premodern moral evaluation simply formed the unalterable background of the moral life, are now susceptible to deliberate human action and thus subject to ethical evaluation. Second, traditional moral evaluation presupposed the constancy or repetition of conditions subject to ethical judgment and choice. Modern technology, by contrast, overwhelms our established moral categories with problems and situations that are wholly unprecedented (Jonas 1984). In these respects technology seems not only to confirm but also to be paradigmatic of the self-understanding of modernity as a radical break from tradition. So understood, technology poses a considerable challenge to religious ethics, for it requires an altogether new kind of ethics, one that is discontinuous with traditional, including religious, forms of ethics.

Technologies and Technology

We can distinguish between the challenge posed to religious ethics by particular technologies and the challenge posed by technology as such. In an obvious sense, technology consists of the devices and processes that arise from the union of science and art: the new software program, the new prosthetic device, the new method of inserting genes into plants, the new spy plane, the new satellite communications system, and so forth. Here, ethical reflection on technology attempts to inscribe new technologies, or technological progress in a certain field, into an existing framework of natural or religious law or a set of religious beliefs.

Two things can be said of the voluminous literature on religious investigations into particular technologies like these. First, this literature refutes the claim that technology renders traditional forms of religious ethics obsolete. It is impossible to give an account of Jewish and Christian ethics in the past century without treating their extensive engagements with technologies, especially in the domains of medicine, sexuality, and war. It is true that these technologies often required significant extensions and reformulation of existing norms in these traditions. A good example is the impact of aerial bombing and mechanical respiration on the principle of double effect in Roman Catholic natural law thinking. But as that example indicates, technological novelties, unprecedented though they were, did not prevent traditions of religious ethics from dealing with them from out of their own resources. The mere existence of new technologies does not appear to render moral traditions or even the norms that comprise them obsolete.

Second, this literature is overwhelmingly Jewish and Christian. One reason for this is the nature of ethical reflection in these two traditions. In both traditions ethical norms are formulated in a context of textual learning, and a principal (though by no means the only) means of transmission of these norms is by public instruction and proclamation by recognized authorities (see chapters 7 and 5). The casuistic and prophetic genres of ethics that have emerged in such contexts fit well into (and help to form) the discursive spaces in which technologies are typically debated and evaluated. Scholars of other religious traditions are now attempting to invent similar forms of argument on particular technologies (see Keown 1995; Nakasone 2000). However, it is not yet clear whether the insights of these traditions are best expressed in these dominant Western genres or whether instead such attempts deprive us of the challenge of a different way of addressing these technologies.

One could object that traditions of religious ethics accomplish the inscription of new technologies into their traditions only by ignoring technology as such or by treating the latter in a comparatively trivial sense. The case of Jewish and Christian analyses of human gene therapy is instructive (see McKenny 2000, 2002). These analyses show

how gene therapy is analogous to conventional medical interventions and thus justifiable in principle, subject to the same conditions that govern other biomedical interventions. These conditions include informed consent, an acceptable risk–benefit ratio, justice in access to and allocation of treatment and research and in prioritizing gene therapy relative to other biomedical interventions, and so forth. Many Christian analyses rule out or express reservations over gene therapy research that involves non-therapeutic risks to embryos, while official Roman Catholic analyses also reject methods of gene therapy that would involve illicit forms of reproduction. Finally, there is often an effort to identify a limit to gene therapy – a characteristic or set of characteristics that should be off limits to genetic intervention.

It is striking how little reflection on technology as such occurs in these analyses. There is some reflection on technology as a form of human participation in the divine work of creation or as an anticipation of redemption in Christian analyses, or as a way of participating in the task of *tikkun olam*, healing or restoring a broken world, in Jewish analyses. Less positively, in some (mostly Protestant) analyses technology is said to objectify human beings or reduce them to their constituent parts and to involve a potentially problematic control over nature – a central theme in treatments of biotechnology from a Buddhist perspective (see Barnhart 2000; Loy 2000). However, the nature of technology is left unexamined or is only superficially examined in these analyses. As a result, it is unclear whether and how technology can play the role, be it positive or negative, assigned to it. While these analyses prove that religious traditions can meet challenges posed by particular technologies, they do not prove that these traditions can meet the challenge posed by technology as such.

When we move beyond the devices and processes, the particular technologies, to consider technology as such we are faced anew with the claim that technology requires a new kind of ethics, one that is discontinuous with the ethics of religious and other traditions. But what does it mean to consider technology as such? Let us begin with Martin Heidegger's understanding of technology as the culmination of Western metaphysics, with its emphases on efficient causality and on the calculability of natural forces (see Heidegger 1977). Here "technology as such" refers to the disclosure of nature as "standing reserve" in which natural energies are unlocked, stored up, and distributed, and to the human subject as orderer of the standing reserve who stands in peril of being taken (and taking himself) as standing reserve, unreceptive to other ways in which nature might disclose itself. Two facets of this interpretation are especially significant: the notion of nature as standing reserve, and the recognition that technology is recursive – that it folds back on the subject such that the orderer of the standing reserve is also ordered as standing reserve. However, Heidegger's formulations belong to the machine age of technology, in which, as Arendt observes, nature is still used as it is given, however radically technology transforms it. This is the case with Heidegger's paradigmatic technology, the hydroelectric plant, and with his claim that technology discloses human beings as human resources. By contrast the kind of technology that occupied acute observers in the second half of the twentieth century (Arendt 1958; Gehlen 1980; Jonas 1984) does not work on nature as given but, as Arendt again observes, radically remakes nature (Arendt 1958: 147–51). The technological remaking of the external world in turn involves a much more radical recursivity. In Jonas' terms, "*Homo faber* is turning upon himself and gets ready to make over the maker of all the rest" (Jonas 1984: 18).

Theses About Technology

It is technology as the radical remaking of nature (including the human) that has posed the challenge to religious ethics since the mid-twentieth century. Ethical evaluation of technology since then has typically rested on three theses about technology, all of which are relevant to the question of whether we are in need of a radically different kind of ethics. These three theses, however, are all questionable in light of recent developments in biotechnology and information technology. To question these theses is to suggest that the need for a new ethics is exaggerated.

The uniqueness thesis

Modern technology is often thought to involve a kind of rationality (e.g., instrumental rationality) that is distinct from other kinds of rationality, or a kind of action (e.g., making) that is distinct from other kinds of action (e.g., doing). One result is that ethical rationality and action are often thought to be entirely distinct from technological rationality and action. For example, Karl-Otto Apel and Jürgen Habermas sharply distinguish ethical or communicative rationality from instrumental rationality (Apel 1979, 1984; Habermas 1970, 1984). Following Max Weber, they describe a modern context in which value-free instrumental (i.e., technological and strategic) rationality is complemented by pre-rational convention (i.e., the contract) or decision. They worry that if rationality is value-free and value is pre-rational, there can be no rational validation of disputed ethical norms. Their respective solutions involve formulating a non-instrumental ethical rationality based on the conditions for the possibility of the discursive validation of disputed norms. What concerns us here is the assumption that technological rationality, which selects means to defined goals, is thoroughly distinct from ethical or communicative rationality. Similarly, Arendt and Jonas, focusing on action rather than rationality, sharply distinguish ethics and technology by appropriating Aristotle's distinction between doing (*praxis*) and making (*poiesis*). All of these theorists write in the shadow of what they see as a progressive displacement of other kinds of rationality and action by technological rationality and action. The ethical itself is threatened by technology.

The sharp distinction between technology and ethics can now be challenged from both sides. On the one hand, some technologies are not merely more effective means to a given end, and thus purely instrumental, but also play a significant role in forming ends. For example, selective serotonin reuptake inhibitors (SSRIs) were developed and marketed for treatment of clinical depression but soon became a popular way to alter personality (Kramer 1993). The point is not simply that an unintended goal emerged, but rather that SSRIs opened up a whole new kind of self-forming practice. Biomedical technologies help determine which aspects of ourselves – our personalities, bodies, capacities, and performances – we attend to in our self-forming practices; stimulate and direct desires for self-alteration; form our desires into deliberate projects; and bring certain features of ourselves and our activities to our attention while suppressing others. Technology in such instances is not merely a means to an end but also projects new ends, reshapes existing ends, orients us to both new and existing ends, and reorders priorities among ends. Similarly, networked computing is not merely a more effective way for people to communicate with each other but is also a self- (and other-) forming practice in which users create anonymous and pseudonymous personae and evolve new forms of linked community. Of course, technological and ethical *rationality* remain distinct in these cases. However, these cases indicate that technological means are related to ends in ways other than the efficacy aimed at in technological rationality. Where such relations occur, ethical rationality must take account of technology as a kind of pre-rational ethical self-formation.

On the other hand, we can also understand ethics as a kind of technology, at least by analogy. Pierre Hadot and Michel Foucault have drawn attention to ethical activity as a technique or set of techniques of self-formation (see Hadot 1995: 81–144; Foucault 1985: 25–32; 1997: 223–51). The end of ethical activity (*praxis*) is not simply to act well; it is also to make something distinct from the activity itself (*poiesis*). As with technology, the self and its relations to others are a work, the product of deliberate fashioning through cognitive and disciplinary practices.

These comparisons do not suggest that technology and ethics are the same. Technology is concerned with means, however complex their relation to ends. Only ethics critically evaluates proposed ends and deliberates over what rightly pertains to an end. However, despite these differences technology sometimes operates as a kind of ethical self-formation and some kinds of ethical action are analogous to technology. This is sufficient to call into question the uniqueness claim.

The inevitability thesis

Technological progress is often thought to be inevitable. According to one theory, technological inevitability occurs through the force of biological need. Marx and Engels describe a process by which the activity and instruments used to satisfy the initial human need to meet the conditions of material life themselves become needs demanding satisfaction (presumably by additional activities and instruments) (Marx and Engels 1970: 48ff.). For Gehlen, technology expresses an instinctual human need to render the environment stable (1980: 16–19). According to another theory, technological inevitability is a kind of metaphysical force. Jonas, for example, describes the irreversibility, cumulativity, irresistibility, and self-perpetuating character of technological practice and decries the "automatic utopianism" which it forces on us even apart from our desires (1984: 7, 21, 127ff., 140ff., 203). Where these inevitabilist terms prevail, ethical discourse on technology oscillates between a wistful near-resignation in the face of a totalizing force and a determination to gain control over the latter (resignation and control being perhaps the two principal ethical modalities of the West). Criticism of the notion of the inevitability of technology is now prevalent among historians of technology (see Winner 1997). However, it was Heidegger who, in rejection of the inevitability thesis, pointed out what may be its most significant problem, namely that the desire or effort to gain control over technology, the will to mastery over it, is itself technological (1977: 5, 32).

Together, the uniqueness and inevitability theses amount to a kind of autonomy theory which represents technology as a force that ethics must address from outside. The task of ethical reflection is to articulate a distinct form of rationality and action and to deploy the latter in an effort to limit or control technology, which by its nature expands into all domains of life, crowding out other forms of rationality and action. If this autonomy theory is true, technology does not merely pose new problems for ethics, it threatens the domain of ethical discourse and practice itself. To question the autonomy theory is in part to suggest the possibility of an ethical discourse that treats technology, in at least some of its forms, as integrally involved, for good or for ill, in the identification and pursuit of real or apparent human goods. This possibility is explored in the concluding section of this chapter.

The replacement thesis

Twentieth-century ethical evaluation of technology often holds that, left to itself, technology steadily encroaches on and eventually replaces human activities and capacities or even human nature itself. While the uniqueness and inevitability theses can be applied equally to the machine age, the replacement thesis captures what is most distinctive of the post-machine era of technology. In its simplest form the thesis was stated by Hermann Schmidt, for whom technology progresses from the tool, in which physical and intellectual energy must still be supplied by the human subject, to the machine, in which physical energy is objectified but intellectual energy continues to be supplied by the human subject, to the automaton, in which both physical and intellectual energy are objectified (Schmidt 1953; quoted in Gehlen 1980: 19ff.).

Schmidt's formulation is an oversimplification but this narrative of progressive replacement of the natural by the artificial which then, in the form of the automaton, becomes a quasi-nature of its own characterizes reflection on post-machine era technology. For Gehlen (1980), technology is the progressive replacement of the organic by the artificial, beginning with the tool as a substitute for the organ and culminating in cybernetics, in which the basic principle of human action is transferred into the automaton. Arendt traces a progression from a tool-machine stage in which natural materials and forces are channeled into the artifice to a machine-automaton stage in which humans create nature-like processes, as in automated production. Arendt also shows how the understanding of nature in terms of cosmic rather than terrestrial processes in seventeenth-century physics culminated in the technological transformation of terrestrial reality by cosmic forces in twentieth-century physics. Technology, she argues, progressively alienates human beings from the earth (i.e., from the terrestrial processes that bind humans to other organisms), an alienation that culminates in biotechnology, which makes human life itself artificial (Arendt 1958: 2, 4ff., 147–51, 268ff.). Jonas, too, describes technology as the progressive replacement of the natural by the artificial and the artificial as itself a kind of nature with its own necessity – an automaton. Two decades later, he finds us on the threshold of the future foreseen by Arendt, in which the effort to remake external nature is already extending to the human. Not surprisingly, behavior control and genetic engineering, both of which portend the automaton, are two of the technologies Jonas singles out for attention (1984: 10, 17–21).

It is not only philosophers of technology but also its more reflective practitioners who hold the replacement thesis. Marvin Minsky, a central figure in artificial intelligence (AI), articulating what appears to be a widely shared desideratum in the AI community (or at least in the MIT Media Lab), promises a future of "virtual" minds capable of thinking and feeling as humans do, followed by a transformation of our "real" human minds into artifices that operate in the same way and possess the same (superior) capabilities as the "virtual" minds (Minsky 1997: 1125–6). Minsky's utopia is well in the future, but implantable computer chips that replace or create memory, sensory, or reasoning functions are already on the horizon; some prosthetic versions already exist (Maguire and McGee 1999). Similarly, molecular biologists envision a future of artificial chromosomes, though it is unclear whether these will replace or only supplement natural chromosomes, while embryologists anticipate a future of artificial wombs.

If technology is replacing human characteristics then despite the urgency it imposes – at stake is nothing less than the future of human nature and activity – it makes the ethical task remarkably clear. The task is (1) to determine which characteristics cannot be replaced without destroying human nature itself; and (2) to establish why human nature, so understood, should not be destroyed. It is, in short, to come up with a normative conception of the human.

Three things may be said of attempts at this task. First, such attempts are common in treatments of biotechnology in Jewish and Christian ethics, especially efforts to specify human characteristics that should never be subject to genetic engineering. Second, even some secular writers concede that religiously grounded normative conceptions of the human offer a direct path to ruling out biotechnological developments that risk replacing the human. Yet these secular writers also assert the irrelevance of religious conceptions to public debates. However, their arguments for the irrelevance of these attempts are open to criticism. For example, Jonas insists that the category of the sacred has been thoroughly effaced by modern science and technology (1984: 23). This claim is questionable in itself, but Jonas concedes that his own biologically informed philosophical conception of the human is also ruled out of court under the rules of modern thought. If he is willing to challenge these rules on behalf of his philosophical conception, why is he so quick to urge these same rules against religious conceptions? Francis Fukuyama argues that religious conceptions are persuasive only to those who accept their premises. Yet his conception of the human relies on a biological–philosophical theory of emergent properties which, of course, will be persuasive only to those who accept its controversial premises (Fukuyama 2002: 88–91, 160–71). It is not clear, then, that religious conceptions of the human are at any disadvantage relative to secular conceptions.

Third, nearly all normative conceptions of the human identify the normatively human with characteristics (e.g., rationality, purposive action, emotional capacities) that will be threatened with replacement only if technology takes extreme forms. In their focus on the limit (i.e., on what cannot be lost without losing our humanity), these conceptions leave everything this side of the limit to preference satisfaction. The problem is that if technology moves in directions that do not involve the replacement of human characteristics but rather complex interactions between nature and artifice, then the replacement thesis is false, and these conceptions of the normatively human will fail to guide us in the use of technology this side of the limit.

How sound, then, is the replacement thesis? First, the effectiveness of many technological interventions depends on cooperation with human activity. Since most human traits are not solely determined by genetic factors this will certainly be the case for the vast majority of genetic interventions, especially in the case of complex traits. A genetic intervention capable of enhancing cognitive capacities such as memory or intelligence will almost certainly not replace human activity. One will still have to study a foreign language despite the comparative ease in memorizing vocabulary and declensions, and one will still have to read the differential equations textbook. It is therefore inaccurate to speak of such interventions as replacing human activity. Second, many technological interventions do not replace or eliminate traits but suppress or enhance them for a certain temporal duration and/or allow for a certain degree of control over their expression. This is the case, for example, with most pharmacological interventions. A hypothetical drug operating directly on biochemical processes to suppress a feeling of fear clearly bypasses the kinds of human activity by which a Stoic adept engages in cognitive therapy to convince himself that fear is irrational, or by which a Thai Buddhist forest monk cultivates through meditation a habit of suppressing fear in the face of animal predators and malevolent spirits. But the fear has not gone away; given the proper stimulus it will reappear once the drug has worn off. Even if one keeps taking the drug the capacity for fear is still present – perhaps even more so than in the cases of the Stoic or the forest monk, who may no longer have to take direct action to suppress it. Once again, these technological interventions do not replace or destroy a human characteristic.

Third, consider a likely forthcoming technology such as implantable brain chips, which may impart cognitive and perceptual information and capacities more or less wholesale and more or less permanently. Here the replacement thesis seems clearly to apply. Or does it? There is no way of knowing yet how such technologies, if developed and implemented, would be used. But it is not obvious that they would be used in a way that would constitute a clear case of replacement. It is possible that they will complement and supplement rather than replace existing cognitive and perceptual capacities and functions. Nor is this merely a theoretical possibility. In her study of users of networked computing technologies, Sherry Turkle (1995) found that "virtual" online identities did not replace "real" identities. Rather, complex interactions occurred in which, for example, virtual identities were used to work through conflicts in real identities.

Should contemporary technology develop along the lines suggested in these examples rather than along the lines of the replacement thesis, it would mark a significant break with the kind of technology described by many philosophers. While still exhibiting the fundamental characteristics of post-machine technology (remaking and reflexivity), technology would result not in the replacement of nature with the artifice, but in a complex hybridization of nature and artifice, of the organic and the digital. The paradigmatic technology would be not the automaton but the cyborg. Cyborg technologies would challenge religious ethics not at the limits, where something characteristically human must be preserved against the steady replacement of the natural with the artificial, but at every point, where not the human as such but the nature and meaning of human activities, performances, and practices is at stake.

The Ethical Task

What challenges does technology pose for religious ethics? Contrary to the most significant theorists of this post-machine era, technology does not confront religious ethics as an autonomous "other" against which religious ethics must deploy radically alternative forms of rationality and action while building fire walls around certain human characteristics. Nor is there any reason to conclude that post-machine era technology demands a radically new kind of ethics. The challenge is of a different order. Like religious traditions themselves, the technology of the post-machine era is deeply involved in the remaking of human beings (see chapter 52). This means that technology now confronts religious ethics as a potential rival or partner in ethical self-formation, as that which may distort or may assist the cognitive and disciplinary practices by which religious traditions form us. Rather than protecting against the onslaught of a force that threatens to engulf the ethical and the human as such, the challenge for religious ethics may increasingly be to determine what place, if any, technological alteration of human capacities, performances, and character might have in the ethical self-formation practiced in a religious tradition. This would involve two kinds of religious ethical inquiry: critical inquiry to determine how technological means orient us to ends and shape the meanings of activities, and deliberative inquiry to determine whether and how these technological means promote or detract from the orientations and meanings that are normative in a religious tradition. Should these critical and deliberative inquiries flourish in religious ethics, the challenge technology poses to religious ethics will be met by a challenge posed by religious ethics to technology.

Bibliography

Apel, K.-O. 1979: "Types of Rationality Today" in *Rationality Today*, ed. T. Garaets, 307–40. Ottawa: University of Ottawa Press.
——1984: *Understanding and Explanation: A Transcendental–Pragmatic Perspective*. Cambridge, MA: MIT Press.
Arendt, H. 1958: *The Human Condition*. Chicago: University of Chicago Press.
Barnhart, M. 2000: "Nature, Nurture, and No-Self: Bioengineering and Buddhist Values." *Journal of Buddhist Ethics* 7: 126–44.
Foucault, M. 1985: *The Use of Pleasure*, trans. R. Hurley. Vol. 2 of *The History of Sexuality*. New York: Random House.

—— 1997: "Technologies of the Self" in *Ethics*, ed. P. Rabinow, 223–51. Vol. 1 of *The Essential Writings of Michel Foucault*. New York: New Press

Fukuyama, F. 2002: *Our Posthuman Future: Consequences of the Biotechnology Revolution*. New York: Farrer, Straus, & Giroux.

Gehlen, A. 1980: "Man and Technique" in *Man in the Age of Technology*, trans. P. Lipscomb, 1–23. New York: Columbia University Press.

Habermas, J. 1970: "Technology and Science as 'Ideology' " in *Toward a Rational Society*, 81–122. Boston, MA: Beacon Press.

—— 1984: *Reason and the Rationalization of Society*, trans. T. McCarthy. Vol. 1 of *The Theory of Communicative Action*. Boston, MA: Beacon Press.

Hadot, P. 1995: *Philosophy as a Way of Life: Spiritual Exercises from Socrates to Foucault*, ed. A. I. Davidson. Oxford: Blackwell.

Heidegger, M. 1977: "The Question Concerning Technology" in *The Question Concerning Technology and Other Essays*, trans. W. Lovitt. New York: Harper & Row.

Jonas, H. 1974: "Seventeenth Century and After: The Meaning of the Scientific and Technological Revolution" in *Philosophical Essays: From Ancient Creed to Technological Man*, 45–80. Chicago: University of Chicago Press.

—— 1984: *The Imperative of Responsibility*. Chicago: University of Chicago Press.

Keown, D. 1995: *Buddhism and Bioethics*. New York: St. Martin's Press.

Kramer, P. D. 1993: *Listening to Prozac*. New York: Penguin Books.

Loy, D. 2000: "Remaking Ourselves: A Buddhist Perspective on Biotechnology" in *Made Not Born*, ed. S. Casey, 48–59. San Francisco: Sierra Club Books.

McKenny, G. P. 2000: "Gene Therapy, Ethics, Religious Perspectives" in *Encyclopedia of Ethical, Legal, and Policy Issues in Biotechnology*, ed. T. J. Murray and M. J. Mehlman, 300–11. New York: John Wiley & Sons.

—— 2002: "Religion and Gene Therapy: The End of One Debate, the Beginning of Another" in *A Companion to Genethics*, ed. J. Burley and J. Harris, 287–301. Oxford: Blackwell.

Maguire, G. Q., Jr. and McGee, E. M. 1999: "Implantable Brain Chips: Time for Debate." *Hastings Center Report* 29 (1), 7–13.

Marx, K. and Engels, F. 1970: *The German Ideology: Part One with Selections from Parts Two and Three and Supplementary Texts*, ed. C. J. Arthur. New York: International Publishers.

Marx, L. 1997: "Technology: The Emergence of a Hazardous Concept." *Social Research* 64 (3), 965–88.

Minsky, M. 1997: "Technology and Culture." *Social Research* 64 (3), 1119–26.

Nakasone, R. 2000: "Religious Views on Biotechnology: Buddhism" in *Encyclopedia of Ethical, Legal, and Policy Issues in Biotechnology*, ed. T. J. Murray and M. J. Mehlman, 914–24. New York: John Wiley & Sons.

Schmidt, H. 1953: "Die Entwicklung der Technik als Phase der Wandlung des Menschen." *Zeitschrift des Vereins der deutschen Ingenieure* (March).

Turkle, S. 1995: *Life on the Screen: Identity in the Age of the Internet*. New York: Simon & Schuster.

White, L., Jr. 1967: "The Historical Roots of our Ecologic Crisis." *Science* 155, 1203–7.

Winner, L. 1997: "Technology Today: Utopia or Dystopia." *Social Research* 64 (3), 989–1017.

CHAPTER 47
Ecology

William French

The first hint of gray appears over the river as birds begin to call from the far shore. Water buffalos stir in an alley by the temple, but the dogs sleep on. Doors open, and devout Hindus make their way to Benares's riverside *ghats*, down the steps and into the Ganges's waters to bathe and pray. Far to the north the sun's rays strike the peaks of the Himalayas, then the snowfields and glaciers below. Warming begins the day's melt that feeds the headwaters of the Ganges and the Yamuna, the other great sacred river of northern India. These rivers, in turn, sustain India's great northern agricultural plains.

Dawn's sweep across the planet begins a great ecological drama each day as plants, grasses, and plankton – the primary producers of the earth's ecosystems – harness sunlight through photosynthesis to produce the foundations of the planetary food chains. The ecological sciences remind us that the global ecosystem is a vast superpower upon whose outpouring of energy all human communities, national economies, and living species depend. In the last century, however, surging growth in human numbers and powers of production along with globally rising expectations for higher consumption have come to pose significant threats to many long-stable natural ecosystems and the species that these ecosystems sustain. No previous generation has faced the array of ecological concerns that now command attention: habitat destruction, global warming, aquifer overuse, deforestation and erosion, species endangerment and extinction, air and water pollution, acid precipitation, and nuclear waste. Some biologists warn that the synergy between habitat disruption and climate change may well usher in the sixth extinction spasm in Earth's long history, the first for which humanity bears responsibility.

Religious people have begun to identify elements of their religious traditions that might help support the promotion of ecological concern and responsible action. Religious traditions sustain value commitments that often stand in stark contrast to the pro-growth and consumption-centered ethos that dominates governmental and economic agendas around the world. For this reason growing numbers of environmentalists are coming to view the world's religious communities as potentially important partners for mobilizing a global effort to protect the earth's ecosystems. But for the world's religious communities to live up to their ecological potential, they must overcome parts of their heritages that undercut ecological care and concern. This chapter examines Christian and Hindu resources for developing an ecological ethic, as well as elements in these traditions that hinder this effort.

Christianity

Christianity shares with Judaism and Islam a common set of core beliefs stressing the transcendence and sovereignty of God, the goodness of God's creation, and the primacy of the human over the rest of creation (see chapter 22). All three traditions hold that God has granted humanity "dominion" over the rest of nature. Creation is understood as fundamentally good, but generally not, in itself, sacred. Humanity enjoys rights to use animals, plants, and the rest of nature, but in return humans owe nature certain duties of care.

The ethical core of all three traditions came to emphasize an intense concern for human life and value. Down through their histories, the stress on human primacy was balanced by an understanding that humanity remains part of the broader order of God's creation. The rise of modern science, however, enshrined a new mechanistic picture of nature that sharpened a sense of humanity's separation from, and superiority to, the rest of nature. Christian theologians came to understand history, culture, and language as the best frames for understanding the distinctiveness of human life and experience. These came to receive far more emphasis than the traditional picture of humanity as part of the community of God's creation. As the stress on creation waned, the traditional ethic of dominion with its notion of stewardship duties tended to give way to an ethic justifying an unrestrained domination of nature.

With rising public concern about ecological degradation, Protestant, Catholic, and Orthodox Christians have sought to reemphasize the doctrine of creation and to reflect on God's and humanity's relatedness to the natural world. Stung by Lynn White's famous critique in 1967 of Christianity as the most anthropocentric and ecologically unfriendly of all religions, many Christians today are trying to recover a sense of nature's holiness so as to help inspire a greater commitment of care for the earth. Protestants gain inspiration by reexamining the stress on the ordering of creation found in the writings of such giants as John Calvin and Jonathan Edwards, while Orthodox thinkers turn to Maximus the Confessor, Gregory of Nyssa, and other Patristic Fathers for insight. Like the Orthodox, many Catholics are recovering a sacramental understanding of the natural world and turning to the legacy of creation-oriented thinkers like Francis of Assisi and Hildegard of Bingen for inspiration. Some Catholics find Thomas Aquinas's stress on the order of creation and his emphasis on the priority of the "common good" as helpful for thinking through our current ecological responsibilities. In the last two decades many Catholic bishops' conferences in a number of countries have promulgated pastoral letters on a range of ecological concerns even as Pope John Paul II has commented on the seriousness of ecological problems.

Many Christians accept the need to recover the ethic of dominion with its affirmation of stewardship duties of care owed to the rest of nature. There are two distinct schools of stewardship thinking. Some espouse a human-centered stewardship ethic that accepts the traditional primacy accorded to human life and value. According to this view, the problem is not anthropocentrism but our failure to incorporate an eco-logical understanding about humanity's dependency on nature into our accounting of human well-being and self-interest. If sufficiently informed by ecological data, tradi-tional anthropocentrism, it is argued, can easily sustain a robust agenda of environ-mental protection (Derr 1996: 17–47). Others espouse a creation-centered stewardship ethic that condemns anthropocentrism for its exclusive moral concentration on the value of the human and its reductionistic assessment of the rest of nature as a field of objects or resources for human use. In the creation-centered view, animals, plants, and ecosystems must be recognized as "ends in themselves" possessing dignity and intrin-sic value independent of their usefulness to humans (see chapter 1).

Some thinkers worry that the stewardship tradition, even in its creation-centered variant, places too much emphasis on human superiority and agency. They affirm an ecocentric ethic that embraces a more egalitarian view of humanity and the rest of nature as members of a common earth community. However, the stewardship approach has important strengths and can be articulated so as to stand guard against arrogance. Today humanity, for better or worse, is, in fact, the dominant force shaping the destiny of many ecosystems around the world. The creation-centered stewardship approach rightly emphasizes the powers of human agency that differentiate us from the rest of nature. It also acknowledges the heavy responsibility that humanity now bears for restraining human practices that promote ecological degradation.

A number of Christian thinkers and activists find the notions of "animal rights" and "biotic rights" drawn from current debates in environmental ethics helpful for empha-sizing the intrinsic value of non-human living beings and our obligations of care owed to them. Increasing numbers of Christians are considering vegetarianism out of a desire to reduce the suffering of animals caused by the factory farming system and to mitigate the often heavy ecological toll that expanding cattle herds and pig farms entail (Linzey 1994: 3–27, 125–37). Many believe that the intrinsic value and "rights" of all living things must be recognized even as we must acknowledge gradations of value existing across the range of living species due to markedly differing levels of capacities for experience, consciousness, and agency. Many reject anthropocentric ethics as deeply flawed, but accept that in forced-choice cases the life of a human or a primate may appropriately be given moral priority over that of "lower" animals (see Nash 1991: 181–3).

Many thinkers now are trying to ecologize the traditional Christian emphases on love and justice. The ethical stress on "love of the neighbor" has long been understood to push for direct concern and care beyond the narrow confines of self-concern or concern for one's family or group to all human beings, especially those in need. Today, increasing numbers of Christians believe that neighbor love requires an ecologically broadened sense of community with an widely expanded recognition of those "neigh-bors" who deserve our concern and care. Our neighbors, in this view, are not just humans of this generation, but animals, plants, and future human and non-human generations (see chapter 24).

Many Christians with a commitment to social justice worry that the emerging environmental movement might pull attention away from the needs of the poor and oppressed. However, most social activists have come to see that ecological damage tends to hit the poor and oppressed hardest, even as environmentalists have come to articulate more clearly a concern for human communities as well as for the natural world. In the 1970s and 1980s the National Council of Churches and the World Council of Churches began to call for "eco-justice" to underscore the strong link between environmental sustainability and social justice (Hessel 1992). Eco-justice expands the range of the application of justice by considering obligations to future human and non-human generations.

Christian feminists and liberation thinkers have made important contributions by stressing linkages between social injustice and ecological degradation. Many feminists argue that sexism and anthropocentrism draw mutual support from a historically entrenched set of hierarchical value rankings that justify the domination of women and of the natural world itself. Many Christian feminists call for an "ecofeminism" that affirms both the full humanity of women and the intrinsic value of all of creation. Likewise, liberation theologians in Latin America, Africa, India, and the Philippines are now incorporating a concern for ecological well-being into their social and political analysis.

At the grassroots level an impressive number of Christian organizations around the world are now committed to promoting ecological sustainability. The National Religious Partnership for the Environment, the North American Coalition for Christianity and Ecology, and the Evangelical Environmental Network are among a host of religious organizations in North America dedicated to promoting ecological responsibility. In Australia, Catholic Earthcare works for ecological protection, while in the Philippines Colomban priests and nuns have been active in promoting sustainable development and resisting deforestation. In Africa, the Association of African Earthkeeping Churches is made up of 150 churches who have joined to fight forest clearing and habitat destruction. A rich array of similar ecologically oriented Christian organizations exists throughout Europe, Latin America and in parts of Asia.

Hinduism

Western scholars once tended to understand Hinduism as essentially other-worldly in orientation. More recently a number of Indian scholars have portrayed Hinduism as essentially eco-friendly due to its affirmation of the divine presence in the world and the preponderance of devotional (*bhakti*) rituals and practices involving plants, natural elements – water, earth, fire – and animals. Both depictions oversimplify (see chapter 34). Clearly, the traditional Hindu emphasis on *dharma* and the tradition's numerous devotional practices offer elements that *can* support the development of a potent Hindu ecological ethic. However, Hinduism's stress on *mokṣa*, spiritual liberation, continues to pull attention away from the embodied world and its material problems. Furthermore, although rituals may employ natural elements or honor holy trees, plants, or locales, and certain passages in sacred scriptures may refer to the sacredness of embodied reality, we should not assume that such practices and texts necessarily relate to ecological concerns or promote a sense of ecological responsibility (Narayanan 2001: 202, 188).

Clearly, some values present in Hinduism are quite compatible with an ecological ethical agenda. An emphasis on *ahiṃsā* or non-violence, for example, has ancient roots in South Asia and has influenced the development of Hindu sensibilities. Even though vegetarianism is strictly prescribed only for brahmans, ascetics, pilgrims, or residents of sacred cities or regions, Hinduism sustains a general respect for vegetarianism that is lacking in most cultures around the world. Hindu belief in reincarnation grounds an understanding of the self that is strikingly different from the stress on the individual prominent in contemporary Western cultures. Reincarnation understands the self as existing in a fluid medium of life across countless modes and forms of being and existence, including animals. Hindus generally consider human life to be superior to animal life, but the greater suffering of animals can inspire compassion instead of arrogance or callousness. While Hinduism embraces diverse understandings of *karma*, most share the view that actions that purposefully cause others harm bring negative consequences for oneself (see chapter 35). This religious sensitivity to the chain of cause and effect can be directly ecologized to promote an ethical concern to anticipate the chain of effects from current actions and to seek to restrain practices that threaten future environmental degradation (Dwivedi 2000: 14–16; Coward 1998: 41–5).

Other traditional Hindu ideals and values offer potential support for ecological concern. The Upanisads, one of the oldest layers of Hindu scripture, emphasize the existence of an ultimate reality, Brahmā, that underlies and infuses all that exists. Spiritual disciplines described in these texts promote the discovery that at one's core lies a spiritual essence or soul, Atman, and that Atman and Brahmā are one. Self-realization means becoming aware that the true "self" is coextensive with the entire universe of being. This monistic vision places a "potential curb on the desire to oppress, manipulate, or dominate other beings" (Kinsley 1995: 63). Others note parallels between the Hindu emphasis on dharmic order and environmentalists' stress on the need to promote ecological sustainability. Some point in particular to Hindu scriptures that condemn the needless cutting of flowers, plants, and twigs, the harming or destroying of animals, or the polluting of rivers as evidence of a traditional linkage between notions of dharma and care for the natural world.

Vishnu is especially associated with maintaining dharmic order, and the Vaishnava tradition affirms a story rich with ecological implications. Viṣṇu is said to have saved the world when it was dragged beneath the ocean by a demon. Viṣṇu assumed the form of a great boar, battled the demon, and killed it. He then dove to the bottom of the ocean, raised the earth up in his tusks, and laid it out as it is today. Some hold that Vishnu's devotees today must act as Viṣṇu did to save the earth (Mumme 1998: 154). Indeed, all across India, the earth is revered as a mother goddess, known variously as Bhū Devī, Bhumi, Prithvi, Vasudha, Vasundhara, and Avni.

Hindus believe that India constitutes a "sacred geography," with a profusion of sacred sites that are said to manifest the presence of the divine in the embodied world. Across India reverence is given to numerous locales, including cities, forests, and mountains. Certain natural places and cities, like Benares, are said to be *tirthas*, sacred fords or "crossings," where the Divine "crosses over" into the world. Some sites are revered as *dhams*, special divine abodes rendered sacred long ago by the actions of deities or by the contemplative energy of ascetic sages. Major *dhams* lie in India's north, south, east, and west, marking the entire land as sacred (Eck 1998: 63, 65).

Many rivers, like the Ganges, the Yamuna, and the Narmada, are revered as goddesses, but that does not stop cities, towns, and factories from daily dumping raw sewage and industrial waste into these sacred waters. A number of religiously based organizations have taken real leadership roles in addressing the problems of water pollution and the lack of sewage treatment. In 1982 in Benares, for example, Veer Bhadra Mishra, a *mahant* (a religious and administrative head) of one of Benares's major temples, the Sankat Mocan Temple, joined with others to launch the Clean Ganges Campaign. This effort helped inspire Rajiv Gandhi, India's prime minister, in 1986 to develop the Ganga Action Plan to initiate sewage treatment and pollution prevention along the length of the great river.

Hinduism likewise has historically affirmed the need for forest and tree protection. The Laws of Manu condemned the cutting of trees and a number of sources emphasize that one of the important duties of kings is to protect the forests. Today, a number of efforts draw inspiration from this heritage of tree protection. In Rajasthan, for example, one can visit villages of the Bishnois people and see how they continue to protect wildlife and trees in keeping with the religious tenets that their founder set down five centuries ago (Dwivedi 2000: 16–17). Likewise, in South India, the administration of the Venkateswara ("Lord of Venkata Hills") Temple at Tirumala-Tirupati has embarked on a sustained effort to help educate people about the ecological benefits of planting and protecting trees. This temple is the most visited and richest temple in India and its educational efforts are widely noticed.

But India's most famous forest protection effort surely is the Chipko Movement, begun in Uttarakhand, a Himalayan district. Community groups in 1977 began to fight for their traditional rights of forest usage and to resist large-scale lumbering projects. Inspired by a Gandhian activist, they adopted a stance of non-violent resistance and employed the tactic of hugging trees to protect them from lumbermen's axes and saws. Chipko means to "hug" or "embrace." Success spread their message and the movement spread across the region. Chipko efforts eventually forced the government to enact a moratorium on large-scale lumbering even as the movement came to promote appropriate development and to resist the construction of a huge hydroelectric dam at Tehri (see Guha 1991).

Sunderlal Bahuguna, one of Chipko's leaders, connects the dangers of deforestation to an ancient story. In it the goddess Ganges tells that her fall from heaven will bring a pounding flood and massive destruction. Shiva prevents this by breaking the falling rush of water by catching it in the matted locks of his hair. Shiva's action turns destructive floods into life-giving currents. Bahuguna and others believe the forests of Himalaya are Shiva's locks, slowing monsoon rain and snowmelt runoff, and thereby preventing flooding and securing valleys and villages. Deforestation, Bahuguna warns, cuts Shiva's locks and ensures the destructive floods about which the ancient story gave warning (James 2000: 519–20).

While Hinduism's rich array of devotional practices and its emphasis on *dharma* clearly offer resources for inspiring care for the natural world, certain Hindu beliefs and practices tend to block a widespread emphasis on ecological responsibility. Three such obstacles are apparent. First, the stress on *mokṣa* in various streams of Hindu philosophy sustains an other-worldly orientation that holds the affairs of this world, such as ecological degradation, as ultimately unimportant. Second, while the reverence for the Earth Goddess, Bhū Devī/Prithvi, is inspiring, she is outranked in the Hindu pantheon by Sri/Lakshmi, the first wife of Viṣṇu and the Goddess of wealth and good fortune. In Hinduism, as Vasudha Narayanan puts it: "The Earth Goddess faces some very stiff competition" (2001: 198). Like Christianity, Hinduism has many popular beliefs that encourage the pursuit of wealth and acquisition, not simple living, frugality, or conservation. Third, many assume that Hinduism's affirmation that parts of nature are sacred predisposes Hindus toward an ecological ethic. But it is far from clear that a sacralized understanding of nature by itself necessarily leads to such an ethical stance. The popular emphasis on the very greatness of the Earth Goddess, Bhu Devi, or India's various river goddesses actually often appears to undercut a sense of responsibility for pollution control or environmental protection. As ecologists insist the rivers are vulnerable, polluted, and in need of human help, many Hindus respond that the rivers are divinely powerful, able to absorb and destroy all pollution, and that it is we humans who need the help of the sacred rivers (see Nagarajan 1998: 285–6). While environmental groups along the Ganges and Yamuna rivers try to promote concern for the physical cleanliness of the waters as an act of religious respect, many Hindus continue to see little relation between religious and environmentalist concerns (see Alley 2000: 357–9, 379–81).

Conclusion

While many Christians try to recover a sense of the sacredness of nature, Hindu practice reminds us that an affirmation of nature's sacredness does not necessarily promote a sense of ecological responsibility. Hinduism's best potential for developing a vital ecological ethics appears to lie in linking ecologists' analyses about ecosystem degradation to the tradition's nature-oriented devotional practices and its emphasis on sustaining the dharmic order. Christianity's main resource for ecological ethics appears to be the expansion of the requirements of love and justice expressed in an ethics of stewardship. While the critique of anthropocentrism is well founded, it is important to acknowledge that anthropocentric ethical appeal, when informed by ecological data, has in fact been a main force in the passage of environmentally oriented legislation. While anthropocentric and ecocentric ethical ethics are usually viewed as antagonists, they often function as allies in environmental policy debates. When one wants to save the planet, one should welcome any allies one can find.

There is a festival every year in Puri on the east coast of India in which thousands of worshipers pull through the streets a giant wooden cart bearing an icon of the god Jagannath, the "Lord of the Universe." When the British colonized India they were appalled to see devotees throw themselves under the cart in an attempt to die in sight of their god. This festival gave birth to the English term "juggernaut," meaning the irresistible force of an immense body in motion with vast destructive power. Today, rising human population coupled with the expanding power of the global economy and rising consumer expectations constitutes a true juggernaut that threatens many of the earth's species and ecosystems. The stakes involved in our emerging ecological drama are of such magnitude that securing the earth's ecosystems and climatic order must be recognized as one of our generation's top religious and moral priorities. As Thomas Berry (1999) rightly notes, each age is called to its "great work." Care for the earth and its remarkable species is surely ours.

Bibliography

Alley, K. D. 2000: "Separate Domains: Hinduism, Politics, and Environmental Pollution" in *Hinduism and Ecology: The Intersection of Earth, Sky, and Water*, ed. C. K. Chapple and M. E. Tucker, 355–87. Cambridge, MA: Center for the Study of World Religions, Harvard Divinity School, distributed by Harvard University Press.

Berry, T. 1999: *The Great Work: Our Way Into the Future*. New York: Bell Tower.

Coward, H. 1998: "The Ecological Implications of Karma Theory" in *Purifying the Earthly Body of God*, ed. L. E. Nelson, 39–49. Albany: State University of New York Press.

Derr, T. S., with J. A. Nash and R. J. Neuhaus. 1996: *Environmental Ethics and Christian Humanism*. Nashville, TN: Abingdon Press.

Dwivedi, O. P. 2000: "Dharmic Ecology" in *Hinduism and Ecology*, ed. C. K. Chapple and M. E. Tucker, 3–22. Cambridge, MA: Center for the Study of World Religions, Harvard Divinity School, distributed by Harvard University Press.

Eck, D. L. 1998: *Darśan: Seeing the Divine Image in India*. New York: Columbia University Press.

Guha, R. 1991: *The Unquiet Woods: Ecological Change and Peasant Resistance in the Himalaya*. Delhi: Oxford University Press.

Hessel, D. T. (ed.) 1992: *After Nature's Revolt: Eco-Justice and Theology*. Minneapolis, MN: Fortress Press.

James, G. A. 2000: "Ethical and Religious Dimensions of Chipko Resistance" in *Hinduism and Ecology*, ed. C. K. Chapple and M. E. Tucker, 499–527. Cambridge, MA: Center for the Study of World Religions, Harvard Divinity School, distributed by Harvard University Press.

Kinsley, D. 1995: *Ecology and Religion: Ecological Spirituality in Cross-Cultural Perspective*. Englewood Cliffs, NJ: Prentice-Hall.

Linzey, A. 1994: *Animal Theology*. Urbana: University of Illinois Press.

Mumme, P. Y. 1998: "Models and Images for a Vaiṣṇava Environmental Theology: The Potential Contribution of Śrīvaiṣṇavism" in *Purifying the Earthly Body of God*, ed. L. E. Nelson, 133–61. Albany: State University of New York Press.

Nagarajan, V. R. 1998: "The Earth as Goddess Bhū Devī: Toward a Theory of 'Embedded Ecologies' in Folk Hinduism" in *Purifying the Earthly Body of God*, ed. L. E. Nelson, 269–95. Albany: State University of New York Press.

Narayanan, V. 2001: "Water, Wood, and Wisdom: Ecological Perspectives from the Hindu Traditions." *Daedalus: Journal of the American Academy of Arts and Sciences* 130 (4), 179–206.

Nash, J. A. 1991: *Loving Nature: Ecological Integrity and Christian Responsibility*. Nashville, TN: Abingdon Press.

CHAPTER 48

Nations

Jean Bethke Elshtain

Nations and States

When moderns in the West think of peoples as a collective or communal entity, they think of states, or nation-states. Ours is a post-Westphalian world, dominated by state formations. More sovereign states have come into being in the last forty years than in any comparable period in human history. Peoples who have some sort of collective identity but have not yet been recognized as states, meaning they are not sovereign in a juridical sense, view themselves, and are seen by others, as second-class citizens in the international sphere. Sovereignty attached to state is the ticket that gives a people entry into the community of states. The "nation" designation attached to "state" suggests that a particular people, having a particular sense of nationhood or national identity, is mapped more or less precisely onto that territorial entity known as "the state." In the late modern Western world, this mapping is bound to be imprecise, for few "nations" composed primarily if not exclusively of the historic, linguistic, and, frequently enough, ethnic markers of a single nationality, any longer exist.

Nations are more diffuse than states. They do not entail the hard edges, or borders, that states by definition do, unless or until a political ideology dictates that any "mixing" of the people of one nation with those of another is strictly forbidden. Tests may be devised whereby an ostensibly pure nationhood can be distilled and separated from a tainted, hence inauthentic, national identity. Less defined, nations are more flexible and open ended. They can spread out, as in the case of the diasporic nation of Israel, so much so that the collective identity of a nation may come to be that of "exile" or "in exile." Also, this spreading out may be less diasporic or exilic than aggressive, as one people overruns another and seeks to dominate it. If this occurs, the identity of a particular nation may become that of the "enslaved," or "oppressed," or "colonized."

As soon as nations become nation-states, borders congeal. But borders are not eternal. Some nations are content with historic borders. They are content to confine their collective identity as a nation within received borders, particularly so if the borders seem to correspond to their understanding of who comprises their nation. Other states aspire to extend their borders outwards, perhaps in order to encompass all the members of their "nation" within one political body or "state." Here one thinks of the National Socialist regime's claim that it and it alone was the legitimate container of German identity, a concept that then expanded biologically to incorporate all "Aryans." Under such circumstances nationhood becomes a fighting word and serves as the occasion for a search for *Lebensraum*. Remarkably, considering historic exiles, diasporas, and colonizations, the aspiration to meld "nation" and "state" has never disappeared. All one has to do is to consider the genocides of the twentieth century, a phenomenon that shows little sign of abating in the twenty-first century, to be disabused of that illusion.

If the state is an early modern, Western phenomenon, emerging from the 1648 Treaty of Westphalia, itself preceded by the Peace of Augsburg, 1555, what is the derivation of nation? Does the nation have any moral standing? If so, from what sources does the moral valuation of nations arise? These are complex and by no means easily answered questions, in large part because "nation" is an inherently ambiguous term. If a nation is, as the dictionary insists, an aggregate of persons who are closely associated by common descent, language, or history, so much so as to form a distinct race or people, there is no immediate and stirring valuation of ethical import that attaches *a priori* to such an entity or concept. Nations are worldly entities. Can they in any way be said to partake of the sacral, the holy, the divine? In other words, how does "ethics" get attached to "nation" or "nations"? In order to explain this basic question in religious ethics and also the current challenge of "nations," this chapter explores resources in Jewish and Christian thought. This seems appropriate given the "Western" context of the "nations," but analogies could be found in other traditions as well. Within the Muslim tradition, however, scholars of Islam tell us, the dividing line occurs less between nations than between the "house of Islam" (dar al-Islam) and the non-Muslim world, the "house of war" (dar al-harb). As such, within this tradition, war that is waged to extend "the house of Islam" is legitimate (Tibi 2002). Whereas, we shall see, Jesus of Nazareth rejected earthly dominion, Muḥammad founded a "religiously conceived polity . . . and his successors confronted the realities of the state and, before very long, of a vast and expanding empire. At no time did they create any institution corresponding to, or even remotely resembling, the church in Christendom" (Lewis 2002: 98–9). Exploring the theme of "nations," the task of this chapter is to examine this idea from a distinctly religious ethical perspective in order to demonstrate the contribution of religious ethics to political philosophy.

Nations in Biblical Narratives

In the Hebraic Bible, the God of the Israelites ordains Abraham as the father of nations. In this way it can be said that God is generative of people and of peoples (see Genesis 12:1–3) (see chapter 18). By contrast to "country" or "land" as a place that identifies a region of origin, "nation" in the biblical imagination is far less prosaic, connoting promise, potential, hope, something not yet realized and perhaps not fully realizable on earth. "States" are unknown to scripture. Instead, there are lands, there are kingdoms, and there is Caesar or Rome once one arrives at the Christian New Testament. The world of the Hebraic Bible or Christian Old Testament is a world of peoples and nations. Nations need rulers. Rulers are elders and kings, established in the first instance by divine authority.

If the Old Testament can be said to constitute a political tradition, that tradition is one of kingship and patriarchal rule. The role of elders – of judges, prophets, and kings – is normative. Such elders are personifications of the nation's identity and its fundamental (or first) principles. "Abraham shall become a great and mighty nation," we are told (Gen. 18:17). In the contemporary world, by contrast, patriarchy is a term of derision and virtually synonymous with "the oppression of women," as it is routinely put (see chapter 54). Such a judgment in the context of the Hebrew texts is, at best, anachronistic. Patriarchal authority in scripture helps to bring "the nation" into being and sustain it. The authority lodged in the rule of patriarchs over nations, certainly the nation of Israel, is not derived from our own wills – as we think of political legitimacy in modernity – but, rather, from what Oliver O'Donovan (1996) calls a "theology of divine judgments."

Israel's sense of nationhood or political identity is inseparable from Yahweh's divine kingship and the covenant of God with Israel, a covenant that brings collective identity itself into being. The constitutive role of divinely authorized kingship is central to nationhood. The story of the origination of nations is precisely that – a powerful narrative, so much so that "nations" and "nation" have ever since been imbricated with tales of the coming into being of peoples. The "state," by contrast, is a juridical concept, more abstract, less contextual and storied. It is important to note that nations are *not* voluntaristic entities brought into being by a specific act of human will as in much modern political theory (Hobbes 1998; Locke 1980; Rousseau 1997). Nations are elect and elected: God chooses Abraham. From this moment of election flows the idea that nations embody and carry out the will of God (e.g., John Winthrop's famous "city on a hill" image of the Puritan covenant to be realized on the shores of the new world) (Winthrop 1996).

The coming into being of nations is not presented in exclusively patriarchal terms. The restoration of Jerusalem after exile, for example, is compared to a woman laboring and giving birth. This restoration or "rebirth" is a miracle. Even as a mother nurtures her infant, so God nurtures Jerusalem. Lands and peoples are born and, like a human pregnancy, this takes time to develop and to be made manifest (see Is. 66:7–11). Thus begins a long tradition of thinking of nations in feminine terms. Nations are "she's" that give birth to, and nurture, a people. In many European languages, one speaks a "mother tongue." The potent intermingling of male and female imagery in the iconography, mythology, and political theology of nations helps to account for how and why "the nation" remains so compelling an idea. Nations are sources of uniqueness and particularity. They help to make us distinct. Nation captures our difference, just as familial identity does.

God Governs and Judges the Nations

If, in the biblical "world," Abraham is the Father of Nations, then Moses continues the covenant of nations.

> The Lord said to Moses, "Go down at once! Your people, whom you brought up out of the land of Egypt, have acted perversely; they have been quick to turn aside from the way that I have commanded them . . . Now let me alone, so that my wrath may burn hot against them and I may consume them; and of you I will make a great nation. (Ex. 32:7–10)

The story of nations is often troubled, as this powerful passage indicates. The God of nations makes demands. The people of Israel fail to measure up. God subjects them to severe judgment. Moses pleads with God, following God's articulation of his wrath in the passage cited, and compels God to soften his judgment so as not to bring disaster upon his people. Moses does this, in part, by evoking the Abrahamic founding. An object lesson for the normative evaluation of nations is embodied herein: God judges the nations. This helps to make sense of Thomas Jefferson's pronouncement that he trembled for his nation when he remembered that God was just: the reference point is slavery. It recalls, in the context of the United States, Abraham Lincoln's extraordinary evocation of the inscrutability of divine judgment in his magnificent Second Inaugural:

> The Almighty has His own purposes. "Woe unto the world because of offenses! For it must needs be that offenses come; but woe to that man by whom the offense cometh!" If we shall suppose that American slavery is one of those offenses which, in the providence of God, must needs come, but which, having continued through his appointed time, he now wills to remove, and that he gives to both North and South, this terrible war, as the woe due to those by whom the offense came, shall we discern therein any departure from those divine attributes which the believers in a Living God always ascribe to him? (Lincoln 1990: 333)

Lincoln is securely in the Old Testament tradition as he reflects that God may punish those nations by whom offenses come. This theme has been repeated elsewhere: in the struggle against fascism; the movements against and overthrowing apartheid in South Africa; and the denunciation of oppression in many lands. Through the prophet Amos, we see that nations are subject to judgment, scrutiny, and claims upon their collective conscience. Amos is charged by God with bringing to the Israelites a message they do not want to hear, namely, that they as a nation have abandoned God's ways. Amos links true nationhood with justice and righteousness and calls the nation of Israel back to its founding, even as Martin Luther King, centuries later, called upon Amos' words in simultaneously condemning and lifting-up his nation, charging America to be faithful to her biblically inspired principles (King 1991: 297). The normative thrust of "nation" comes through in such circumstances as an attempt to bring fallen practices into closer harmony with God-sanctioned principles present at the founding, so to speak, when God called the nation into being in the first instance.

This falling away and being recalled is a familiar theme in the narrative of nations. When Amos cries out to the people of Israel; when Dr. King cries out to the would-be "beloved community" of his own nation, it is a call for political righteousness that is unattainable absent divine favor or rectification. Embedded in such prophetic moments in the narrative of nations is the claim that God not only judges between the nations, he also is the governor of nations. It is God who sits on the ultimate throne. Earthly kings can aspire only to the penultimate. "For God is the king of all the earth; sing praises with a psalm. God is king over the nations: God sits on his holy throne" (Ps. 47:8). Only those nations whose God is the Lord are said to be happy.

How does God adjudicate between nations? Israel is the covenanted people and finds favor, and frequently severe judgment, in God's eyes. The story of the rising and falling of Israel's political kingships in God's eyes tells us a great deal about what happens when God's kingship is forgotten or abandoned and earthly kingship becomes idolatrous. Although the promise of being within the Lord's house is lifted up for all nations (Is. 2:2; Mk. 11:17), this condition of universal comity is not attained in biblical history. Indeed, the passage favored by those who seek earthly peace as a possible accomplishment in history (Is. 2:4) is a possibility linked to certain conditions that are never attained. The condition of eschatological peace is one in which the Lord's house has been established everywhere. Human sin, pride, selfishness, and political idolatry stand in the way of such an achievement.

Nations: The Dangers of Political Idolatry, the Requirements of Servitude

The biblical tradition knows little of citizenship in the modern sense. Unlike modern social contract theories, a people is constituted by divine election rather than an act of the will by potential citizens (see Rawls 1999). Loyalty to the nation is thereby more likely thought of as a form of divinely ordained servitude. The patriarch serves God and his people. The people serves God and keeps faith with its tradition. Nations themselves are collective servants, playing a part in God's providential plan. It is God's servant who brings justice to the nations (see Is. 42:1–4) and servants of the nation must seek favor with God through obedience. Human beings cannot help but play a part in a collectivity. They are members of nations by virtue of the fact that they are born. The ethical question is what sort of collectivity is our nation? Does it follow the Lord God in all things? Or has it gone down an idolatrous path? This is the biblical way to think about nation – as that which individuals perpetrate to good or to ill ends. It is a concept with a long history of effects in Western political thought.

If the nation faithfully serves its divinely ordained mandate, if it is governed with justice and righteousness, individual loyalty to nation is enjoined, even required. But a nation that becomes idolatrous is one that should be repudiated, even at risk to the self. The Bible is replete with narratives of dangerous overreach, mostly notably the Tower of Babel that figures so centrally in St. Augustine's *The City of God* (1998). Nations that came together to seek greatness and to reach to God, having succumbed to those temptations of pride that bedevil all nations, are smote by God and the peoples are dispersed and become unintelligible to one another. To become like God is idolatry; to strive to do God's will is the faithful obedience of the good servant, a servant of God, a servant of the nation. Such narratives of the dangers of hubristic striving have been drawn upon by theologians and ethicists historically as they strive to articulate limits to national loyalty and its demands. It has led, for instance, to distinctly Christian conceptions of the "two kingdoms," one religious and one political, and thereby a separation of powers. This idea has been basic to Christian political thought (see chapter 21).

So, if a key political concept emerging from the narrative of the people of Israel is that of "nation" and of an identity called into being through covenant, a key political concept deeded to subsequent generations by Jesus of Nazareth is the need to articulate limits to political identity, loyalty, and definition. There was that fateful moment when Jesus examined a coin and told his followers to render unto Caesar what was Caesar's; unto God, what was God's (Luke 20:24–25). Over time, this evolved into a strong view of the relative autonomy of the governmental order for it, too, is mandated by God and it, too, makes legitimate claims on persons.

Where the line is to be drawn, where "Caesar" illegitimately usurps what is God's varies from one religious tradition and denomination to another. And usurpation might come from the side of religion. Faith may usurp what is properly within the legitimate mandate of government. However, given the power and reach of the modern state, the encroachment by one into the mandate of the other is more likely to flow from structures of governmental power, at least in the West, which has never been hospitable to theocracy. (Close alliances between throne and altar are not the same thing.) The ethical upshot is that, if God is the Father of nations and calls them into being, God, especially through the figure of the second person of the Trinity, separates God and Caesar in such a way that "nations" and "national identity" become inherently ambiguous categories in the ethical sense. The believer as citizen is obliged at each and every point to evaluate what claims are being made on him or her, in whose name, and to what end (see chapter 23).

The eschatological transformation of all politics by the Kingship of Christ is a difficult concept for late moderns mindful of global political realities and the diversity of religions. We can make sense of it only as an "end-time" idea. But if Christ's kingship is removed too far beyond the here and now, what one is called to render to God becomes more abstract, more pallid, than does the far more intrusive immediacy of what we are called to render to "Caesar." Christian ethics is dedicated to making sense of the relationship of the Messianic age to life in what St. Augustine called the *saeculum*, the historic *now* in which we are pinioned during our earthly sojourn. Human self-governance after Christ remains a form of servanthood even as it is tinged by an ever-present temptation toward political idolatry. Jesus, after all, *resists* the temptation to become ruler of worldly kingdoms, as Satan displays the kingdoms before him. His kingdom, Jesus tells his followers, is not of this earth. But we are. And we remain peoples whose earthly sojourn is marked by an ethically promising and problematic immersion in nations. A crucial task of religious ethics in our time is to mine the resources of the religious tradition in order to orient political existence within and among the "nations." But this is just to suggest that one requirement now facing any religious ethics is to provide cultural purchase on political realities rather than simply accepting the terms of debate set by the "nations."

H. Richard Niebuhr, in his modern theological classic *Christ and Culture*, tackles the complex relationship between religious belief and worldly matters as an "enduring problem" for Christians precisely because Jesus articulated a distinction between what is God's and what is Caesar's. For some Christian thinkers, "the injunctions of the Sermon on the Mount concerning anger and resistance to evil, oaths and marriage, anxiety and property, are found incompatible with the duties of life in society," writes

Niebuhr (1959: 9). Can the teachings of Jesus serve as the basis for citizenship duties and responsibilities?

Niebuhr delineates five prototypical responses within the Christian community historically: the Christ against culture; the Christ of culture; the Christ above culture; Christ and culture in paradox; and Christ as transformer of culture. Most of the time, these positions do not exist in pure form as Christians struggle with their life in "the nations," both past and present. An example Niebuhr offers is that of St. Thomas Aquinas, who was faithful as a monk to his vows "against" the culture – poverty, celibacy, and obedience – "even as he belonged to a church that had achieved or accepted full social responsibility for all great institutions" and that had "become the guardian of culture, the fosterer of learning, the judge of nations, the protector of the family, the governor of social religion." For Aquinas, Christianity is, among other things, a structure of practical wisdom "planted among the streets and marketplaces, the houses, palaces, and universities that represent human culture" (Niebuhr 1959: 128–30).

In the matter of "the nations" such a stance commits Christians to taking up political vocations like soldiering, judging, and governing. Such vocations highlight, often in stark ways, the demands of religious faith and the demands of political responsibility. For St. Augustine, for Martin Luther, and for the anti-Nazi martyr Dietrich Bonhoeffer, the harsh demands of civic necessity as well as the command of love require that one may have to commit oneself to the use of force under certain limited conditions, and with certain intentions. There are dangers in taking up worldly vocations. Those who commit themselves to the care of cultural institutions must remain fully aware of just how fragile these institutions are. But to become wholly immersed in social institutions courts a form of presentism and an overly strong commitment to that which is mutable by contrast to that which alone is immutable, namely, God and his Kingdom. The Christ and Caesar distinction sets up a critical tension that simply is the life of the believer-citizen in modernity.

Acknowledgments

The author wishes to acknowledge the vital contributions of John D. Carlson in researching and conceptualizing this chapter.

Bibliography

Augustine, St., Bishop of Hippo. 1998: *The City of God against the Pagans*, trans. R. W. Dyson. Cambridge: Cambridge University Press.

Hobbes, T. 1998: *Leviathan*, ed. J. C. A. Gaskin. Oxford: Oxford University Press.

King, M. L., Jr. 1991: "Letter from Birmingham City Jail" in *A Testament of Hope: The Essential Writings and Speeches of Martin Luther King, Jr.*, ed. J. M. Washington. San Francisco: Harper & Row.

Lewis, B. 2002: *What Went Wrong? Western Impact and Middle Eastern Response*. Oxford: Oxford University Press.

Lincoln, A. 1990: "Second Inaugural Address" in *The Collected Works of Abraham Lincoln*, ed. R. Basler. New Brunswick, NJ: Rutgers University Press.

Locke, J. 1980: *Second Treatise of Government*, ed. C. B. Macpherson. Indianapolis, IN: Hackett.

Niebuhr, H. R. 1959: *Christ and Culture*. New York: Harper Torchbooks.

O'Donovan, O. 1996: *The Desire of the Nations: Rediscovering the Roots of Political Theology*. Cambridge: Cambridge University Press.

Rawls, J. 1999: *A Theory of Justice*, revd. edn. Cambridge, MA: Belknap Press of Harvard University Press.

Rousseau, J.-J. 1997: *The Social Contract and Other Later Political Writings*, trans. V. Gourevitch. Cambridge: Cambridge University Press.

Tibi, B. 2002: "War and Peace in Islam" in *Islamic Political Ethics: Civil Society, Pluralism, and Ethics*. ed. S. H. Hashmi. Princeton, NJ: Princeton University Press.

Winthrop, J. 1996: *The Journal of John Winthrop, 1630–1649*, ed. R. S. Dunn, J. Savage, and L. Yeandle. Cambridge, MA: Harvard University Press.

CHAPTER 49
Global Dynamics

Sallie B. King

Globalization

Globalization is metaphorically explained as the "shrinking of the world." As a descriptive term, globalization refers to the ongoing development of ever more extensive and profound interdependence among the countries, economies, cultures, physical localities, and peoples of the world (see chapter "On Religious Ethics"). Though humankind has seen other times of heightened interdependence (during exploratory, imperial, and colonial eras), the current period of globalization, in the late twentieth and twenty-first centuries, is unique in three respects: (1) it is primarily propelled not by political and military power, but by economic and technological/communication forces; (2) the extent of its reach is virtually planet-wide, as opposed to regional; and (3) it undermines the power of the nation-state – even the most powerful states must accommodate themselves to the imperatives of international trade or suffer the consequences.

One of the problems posed by globalization has to do with concern over the potential "homogenization" of global culture. With the English language, blue jeans, McDonald's, and American movies almost everywhere, globalization seems to be a threat to cultural diversity. Non-dominant cultures seem similar to endangered species, and they have a consciousness of being so. Like an endangered species, the loss of an endangered culture, while worst for itself, would be a loss for humanity. From an instrumental perspective, a culture is a resource for humankind, with potentially valuable resources of wisdom, insight, perspective, lifeways, etc. From a global perspective, it is part of our human heritage. Clearly, some elements of the many cultures will not be of future value and some are reprehensible. However, in the case of cultures whose mores do not violate emerging global norms, contemporary ethical thought cannot justify their demise. Those who admire human cultural creativity and value its flourishing can only mourn the potential widespread and sudden demise of its creations, especially since this potential demise bears no relation to a given culture's inherent worth. What might be done to retard the loss of cultural diversity is an urgent but most difficult question.

Identifying Common Values

Despite the threat to diversity posed by globalization – and conscious of that threat – many people have come to believe that it is important to make a concerted effort to identify points of unity among the peoples of the world, in particular, points of unity on values. Inasmuch as globalization refers to the increasing interdependence among the countries and peoples of the world, it is clear that people share problems and opportunities with each other to a greater degree than was previously the case. Threats of nuclear holocaust, transnational terrorism, global climate change, and the AIDS epidemic, as well as opportunities with problematic implications such as international trade, cannot be resolved by countries working independently. Nor can we recognize and agree upon what *kind* of resolutions would be good without an explicit set of shared ethical values.

Are there absolute norms that transcend the views of particular cultures and religions? How would such a view be justified in an age in which we seem ever more pushed towards relativistic views? (see chapter 2). In the past, many a particular civilization has claimed its own values to be absolute and by virtue of its power imposed them on others. On the other hand, how is it that even those who generally deplore "cultural imperialism" celebrate the end of *sati* in India (prohibited by what was clearly an imperialistic act) and of apartheid in South Africa (to which globalization helped to bring an end)? Perhaps there are some culture-transcending, if not "absolute," norms. But even if that were the case, how could such culture-transcending norms be globally embraced without threatening the diversity of particular cultures?

Important advances have been made on these issues in the past two decades. In *Common Values* Sissela Bok argues for a "minimalist" set of values based upon the observation that certain behaviors are necessary in order for any society of people to survive. Specifically, all societies, in order to survive, have had to (a) require of its members some positive duties of mutual support: duties to care for children and the sick, the duty to honor and obey parents, and a general attitude of reciprocity within the group, expressed in a negative or positive form of the Golden Rule ("do unto others as you would have others do unto you"); (b) prohibit certain actions which, if allowed, would destroy society, especially violence, deceit, and theft within the community; and (c) establish fair procedures for resolving conflicts (Bok 1995). For Bok, these together establish a minimal set of common values found in virtually all cultures, by virtue of their necessity.

Other thinkers nuance the idea of shared values by distinguishing between the core area of ethical agreement, where cross-cultural unity is strongest, and the marginal area, where disagreement is common (see Adams 1993). Thus while the general principle that lying is wrong is found in virtually all cultures and virtually all cultures insist upon its importance in such core contexts as legal disputes, in the marginal area of the "white lie" there is neither agreement among cultures nor strong insistence within a culture on conforming behavior. Similarly, affirmation of the general principle that killing within the group is wrong is near universal, but on matters such as capital punishment and euthanasia there are disputes. We should bear in mind this clarification when considering lists of cross-culturally affirmed common values.

International human rights

The international community has been debating questions of common values, values shared by all humankind, quite intensively since the end of World War II. In these discussions, the United Nations, first, and the Parliament of World Religions, more recently, have played key roles (see chapter 51).

The United Nations was created in an effort to help strengthen international understanding and cooperation. One of its early acts (1948) was to proclaim the Universal Declaration of Human Rights (UDHR). It has become the gold standard for internationally recognized and accepted (if not always acted upon) global norms of behavior. These are expressed in a set of specific "human rights and fundamental freedoms" that are to be respected by all peoples and all nations. The UDHR does not claim that its norms are metaphysically absolute. It states that respect of its norms is necessary for humankind to live together in something approaching a peaceful way. In its preamble, the UDHR declares these rights and freedoms for pragmatic purposes: to promote the development of friendly relations between nations; to avoid the violence to which people will sooner or later turn if their basic rights and freedoms are ignored; and, significantly, because to "enjoy freedom of speech and belief and freedom from fear and want has been proclaimed as the highest aspiration of the common people." Here an empirical claim is made that the people of the world want these protections.

The UDHR has been challenged as a form of cultural imperialism. The idea of a "right" is undeniably a product of Western culture; such an idea does not exist in traditional Asian thought, for example (see chapter 38). It has been recognized that representatives of Western countries played the dominant roles in drawing up the UDHR. However, these have not proven to be fatal objections. Subsequent international documents drawn up under the auspices of the United Nations have emphasized social and economic rights and the group rights of entire peoples. The meetings that produced these subsequent documents emphasized the full participation of the greatest possible diversity of peoples and countries. The documents themselves reflect not only the interests of poorer countries, but also the worldviews of cultures with less stress on individualism.

Early in the 1990s Lee Kuan Yew of Singapore and Mahathir Mohamad of Malaysia ignited debate with their claim that the idea of international human rights is a Western idea that emphasizes individualism and promotes adversarial relationships. Asian societies, they held, place greater emphasis on social harmony and communitarian values. As a response to this challenge, a number of Asian political and social activists denounced the claim that so-called "Asian values" are incompatible with international human rights.

Activists like Aung San Suu Kyi and many others dismiss claims that "Asian values" are incompatible with international human rights as no more than efforts by authoritarian rulers to reject challenges from the international community to their power. Most scholars agree. It remains true that the concept of a "right" is a culturally embedded concept that is alien to many cultures. However, different cultures can and do find ways in their own language and concepts to justify embracing the protections represented by international human rights, protections that those lacking them very much want. Thus, a popular song from the streets of Burma contains the lyric: "I am not among the rice-eating robots . . . Everyone but everyone should be entitled to human rights" (Suu Kyi 1991: 174).

International human rights are quite narrow in scope. They prohibit certain egregious kinds of harm and urge certain specific acts of beneficence; beyond this, international human rights make no claims upon governments, cultures, or people. Thus a country that engaged in *sati* or apartheid would in those respects be in violation of international human rights and subject to possible sanctions from other countries. Simple variations in belief or practice that are non-violent and non-oppressive have nothing to fear from international human rights instruments. The latter represent no threat to cultural diversity, other than forms of diversity associated with violence and oppression.

Global ethic

The Parliament of World Religions, like the United Nations, is both a product and an agent of globalization (see chapter 16). Older than the United Nations, the Parliament of World Religions first met in Chicago in 1893, a milestone globalizing event in which, for the first time, representatives of each of the world religions spoke for themselves on an equally shared platform. In 1993 a centenary celebration and second gathering of the world's religions was held, again in Chicago, and at that time the Parliament was put on a regular footing, with meetings to be held once every five years, in different places around the globe.

In preparation for the 1993 Parliament meeting, Hans Küng was asked to oversee the preparation of a draft of a Global Ethic that could be endorsed by representatives of all the world's religions. The draft was based upon input from a great diversity of religious representatives and adjusted after extensive consultation with a separate set of diverse religious representatives. This draft was approved at the 1993 Parliament as a Declaration "toward" a Global Ethic.

There is significant overlap in content between the Global Ethic and ideas about common values. In the declaration of the Global Ethic, the Parliament affirmed general beneficence, referring to the ubiquity of the Golden Rule. The Global Ethic renders this as its "fundamental demand": "Every human being must be treated humanely." There follow four "irrevocable directives": from the many religions' ethical codes' prohibitions of killing comes "commitment to a culture of non-violence and respect for life"; from prohibitions of stealing comes "commitment to a . . . just economic order"; from prohibitions of lying comes "commitment to a life of truthfulness"; and from prohibitions of sexual immorality, "commitment to a culture of equal rights and partnership between men and women" (Küng 1996: 15–25). These principles should be understood as affirmations of core values, bearing in mind the distinction between core and marginal values mentioned above.

From the beginning, the Global Ethic was conceived not as an external ethical standard to be imposed upon the various religions, but simply as the identification and articulation of the area of moral agreement that already exists among them. It is recognized that it will need to be supplemented by the ethical codes of the religions, rich in narratives, symbols, and ideals. Even so, the Global Ethic is empirical evidence indicating a core area of norms in which the many religions agree with each other. This agreement is put forward by the promoters of the Global Ethic as evidence counting against ethical relativism. Of course, the fact that many religions seem to agree on certain norms of behavior is in fact no evidence that those norms are right in an absolute sense. However, such agreement does provide welcome counter-evidence to the widely held *popular* view (which, while poor philosophy, is nonetheless very influential) that holds that since religions (and cultures) espouse different ethical views, there are no ethical norms that transcend religion and culture and therefore all ethical norms are merely relative to one's religion and culture (see chapter 14). Moreover, it demonstrates in a concrete way to members of one religion that members of other religions hold views in common with them, thereby undercutting absolutist tendencies to think of one's religion as entirely right and in sole possession of Truth, others as entirely wrong (King 1998).

The Global Ethic has had its critics. Some have questioned whether the process of its composition was sufficiently inclusive of diversity. Fundamentalists and exclusivists, though invited, did not participate in the deliberations. Among its four directives, the "commitment to a culture of equal rights and partnership between men and women" has been most controversial. Such concerns as these are by no means fatal, but simply indicate that the Global Ethic needs to be subject to further discussion, as was the UDHR. The result of further discussion in that case was the refinement of the original tenets and greater cross-cultural legitimacy. There is no reason to expect a different outcome for the Global Ethic.

These efforts at constructing common values or global ethics by the United Nations and the Parliament of World Religions take an empirical and pluralistic approach. Their approaches begin from diversity and seek to discover points of overlap or agreement. In retrospect, this move seems inevitable. How, after all, would it be possible to take a non-empirical approach to the effort to construct a global ethic? Any such approach would necessarily entail some metaphysical assumptions which would inevitably privilege one or some worldview(s), religion(s), and culture(s) over others. Any such approach would be guilty of a pernicious and hegemonic absolutism (see chapter 12).

The Challenge to Universal Benevolence

In addition to the precepts and prohibitions that we have been discussing, religions also hold up ethical *ideals* to which they urge their followers to aspire. These are often understood to be at a level of perfection which one may never expect fully to realize, but to which, nevertheless, one aspires to become ever more faithful, or to embody ever more fully. Such ideals in many religions prominently include the ideal of benevolence.

Benevolence is not what it used to be, though. Try to hold to universal benevolence in the context of the contemporary, globalized world, in which, thanks to modern electronic communications and media, we now know current events virtually everywhere in the world. Try to hold to universal benevolence in a world in which, according to current World Bank figures, approximately 24 percent of the world's population (46 percent in sub-Saharan Africa), or 1.2 *billion* people, live in absolute poverty – a figure rejected as too conservative by many observers (World Bank 2002). Hold to universal benevolence in a world in which one's life expectancy varies by decades depending upon the country in which one is born. Think universal benevolence with respect to the urban slums of the Ivory Coast of West Africa, where the population is growing annually by 3.6 percent, meaning that the population will rise from 13.5 million people to 39 million by 2025, much of it living in new urban slums (Kaplan 1994/2000: 38).

What does universal benevolence tell us to do in this world? What guidance do the ethical teachings of our religions give us? If we try to think seriously about the massive problems facing humanity, an ethic of universal benevolence seems to point in a direction that cannot possibly be fulfilled. Must we resort to triage like those development planners who see some countries as so vastly impoverished, so deeply in debt, so ruined ecologically, so lacking in resources and prospects that they write off the entire country as literally hopeless? If we write them off, what becomes of our humanity? On the other hand, what else can we do but put our resources where they can be of best use? Can our religious ethics help us to think through these dilemmas?

Some religious ethics emphasize justice; others, notably the Buddhist, emphasize compassion (see chapter 30). Do these two approaches point us in different directions in the globalizing world? Let us consider. Perhaps we think it straightforward to draw distinctions between ideals and duties; specifically, between caring (or compassion) and responsibility. Traditionally, many religions and moral traditions saw responsibility stopping at the borders of "one's own" community. We may *care* about the whole world and cherish the ideal of serving all humankind, but we only have a *duty*, it seems, to take care of those closest to us. In this view, as one moves concentrically farther and farther from one's immediate circle one seems to move from a duty of beneficence – a responsibility to act for the good of others – to a vague ideal of benevolence, good will to all. There are strong pragmatic and socio-biological reasons for this view. But even in this version there is no clear line between duty and ideal; each seems to fade into the other as one biologically *is* and emotionally *feels* less and less close.

The reality of globalization is precisely this: our idea of who is within "our community" is changing. Today the questions "Who is my brother? Who is my neighbor?" become more and more urgent, the answers less and less clear. If I have traveled, I may care as much about people in another country where I have spent time as I do about people on the other side of my own country. Do I have greater responsibility for people at a distance if I care about them more? If globalization is making us see as artificial such things as national borders, shall we ultimately agree with the Dalai Lama, who argues that globalization is making it easier for us to realize that the lines we human beings have taken as dividing us have always been imaginary, that we always have had a duty to all humankind, and that we should embrace the "universal responsibility" to contribute to the happiness of all humankind (Dalai Lama 1999)?

To the question, "Am I my brother's keeper?" (Genesis 4:9) shall we respond: Can you bear not to be? Since World War II and the Nazi Holocaust, we feel a great urge – a moral duty even – to intervene for humanitarian purposes to prevent the slaughter of innocents in civil war, to stop "ethnic cleansing" and genocide. *Is* this our duty, or just an ideal, which we might or might not embrace in a given case? Perhaps we do see intervention to prevent genocide as a moral duty. Does similar thinking extend to intervention in economic crises which may likewise kill, gravely injure, and uproot vast numbers of people? What about non-crisis situations? John Cobb (2002) argues that the global economic system does daily, systematic violence to the poor, to human community, and to the natural world. If he is right and the global economic system itself is violent, does our moral duty extend to changing it?

Virtually everyone reading these words is a "global winner," one who by virtue of birth in a prosperous country faces continuing prosperity as globalization proceeds. The "global losers," those born in one of the many impoverished, indebted countries, face miserable prospects. Do we "global winners" have a *responsibility* to help the "global losers," since our "winning" has nothing to do with our inherent worth or hard work? Or is such help just an optional good act? Many wealthy countries have programs to help those of its own citizens who, by virtue of birth in a poor family or a race that has been historically oppressed, face a sharply disadvantaged start in the competitions of life; in the United States there are Head Start, welfare, Affirmative Action, federal small business loans, and much more. Many believe that justice requires this of the state. As the world becomes ever more closely interdependent and national boundaries less and less meaningful, will the "global winners" come to feel that justice requires intervention in much more significant ways than heretofore in the plight of the "global losers"? Should they? The question is where to draw the line between "us" and "them" – if, indeed, we can justify drawing it anywhere.

Some institutions, in fact, do not draw the us/them line anywhere. Certain non-government organizations, such as Oxfam and Doctors Without Borders, focus on a single issue and regard it with a globalized perspective that recognizes no real lines dividing humankind. They seem to answer the Dalai Lama's call for "universal responsibility." Motivated by and initially defined in terms of compassion, experience led them to recognize and act on the need to extend compassion into the realm of justice – Oxfam now works to change world trade rules that favor the rich; Doctors Without Borders challenges the economic, political, and military rules that prevent equal access to healthcare. Here, justice ethics – minimally, the ethic of distributive justice – blends with the ethics of compassion. Moreover, at least in these cases, while the task of compassion alone (feeding or healing the world) is infinite, if the rules could be changed to become more just, the task might become possible, though vast. Thus, in the globalized world, skillful compassion may require justice – while sufficient will to change the rules and produce justice will surely require tremendous compassion. Justice and compassion, it seems, are both necessary parts of the picture.

When asked for his advice on what to do about global suffering, Buddhist teacher Thich Nhat Hanh emphasizes that we should not turn our eyes and ears away from suffering, but stay with others' suffering, be present to it, and then some response will come to us; we will feel an imperative to act. Perhaps it is here that compassion ethics and justice ethics meet. Perhaps it is when we feel that we cannot bear to see others suffering that we have a responsibility to take action to help them – a responsibility to our own humanity as well as a responsibility to others. If that is the case, then the Dalai Lama is right: any lines we try to draw to limit our compassion, our responsibility, are artificial. If that is right and our compassion points to a universal responsibility, then our compassion seems to necessitate, minimally, striving for distributive justice. Thus compassion comes to embrace justice without losing its character as compassion, while justice finds its roots in compassion.

Bibliography

Adams, R. M. 1993: "Religious Ethics in a Pluralistic Society" in *Prospects for a Common Morality*, ed. G. Outka and J. P. Reeder, Jr., 93–113. Princeton, NJ: Princeton University Press.

Aung San Suu Kyi. 1991: *Freedom from Fear and Other Writings*. New York: Penguin Books.

Bok, S. 1995: *Common Values*. Columbia: University of Missouri Press.

Cobb, J. 2002: "Economic Aspects of Social and Environmental Violence." *Buddhist–Christian Studies* 22, 3–16.

Dalai Lama. 1999: *Ethics for the New Millennium*. New York: Riverhead Books.

Kaplan, R. D. 1994/2000: "The Coming Anarchy." *Atlantic Monthly*, February. Reprinted in P. O'Meara et al. (eds.), *Globalization and the Challenges of a New Century: A Reader*, 34–60. Bloomington: Indiana University Press.

King, S. 1998: "A Global Ethic in the Light of Comparative Religious Ethics" in *Explorations in Global Ethics: Comparative Religious Ethics and Interreligious Dialogue*, ed. S. B. Twiss and B. Grelle, 188–240. Boulder, CO: Westview Press.

Küng, H. 1996: *Yes to a Global Ethic*. New York: Continuum.

World Bank. 2002: *Global Poverty Monitoring* [cited December 31]. Available from www.worldbank.org/research/povmonitor.

CHAPTER 50

Religious Membership

Robin Gill

One of the important rediscoveries in religious ethics over the last two decades has been the intimate and complex relationship between moral agency and moral communities. This relationship is extremely varied. Sometimes, as in Islam or Judaism, it also involves an intimate connection with a Holy Book. Sometimes, as in Confucianism, it is very closely related to the traditions of a particular society. There is also a wide range of ideas involved, from Buddhist claims about compassion and enlightenment to Christian debates about grace and freedom. Yet, in many religious traditions, a connection is made been moral agency and moral communities that is at odds with much, but not all, modern Western ethical theory. The latter tends to conceive of the moral agent abstracted from communal membership and to focus upon freedom and rational autonomy as the defining feature of moral agency.

This chapter explores some of the implications of this debate about accounts of moral agency. At stake, most basically, is how religious ethics is to understand the importance of religious membership in providing an adequate account of moral agency.

Within the secular post-Enlightenment tradition following Kant, moral agency has characteristically been perceived as being independent of religion and based instead upon autonomous rationality alone (see chapter 3). The individual makes moral choices and decisions based solely upon rational criteria that are available to all competent, rational agents (whether they are themselves privately religious, as Kant was, or not). Moral philosophers like Alasdair MacIntyre (1984) have challenged this understanding of moral agency. At a negative level, moral philosophy – the discipline concerned with autonomous, rational criteria in moral thinking – has been unable to deliver indisputable rational criteria or universally agreed moral decisions. Incommensurable differences remain on key moral issues such as abortion or justice both within the general public of Western societies and (especially and most significantly) among experts in moral philosophy. At a positive level, MacIntyre has argued that virtues molded by moral and religious communities are essential to an adequate understanding of moral agency. Charles Taylor (1989) has also challenged a purely secular understanding of moral agency. Although committed to a notion of autonomy within moral agency, he nevertheless has argued that moral reasoning cannot be properly understood without acknowledging the long history of moral concepts within specific and typically religious communities.

Using insights from MacIntyre and Taylor, this chapter argues that a pluralistic society should recognize not only that religious minorities need to be respected if such a society is to be genuinely inclusive, but also that a number of crucial, but supposedly secular, moral notions have religious roots and may even make full sense only when these roots are explicitly acknowledged. This chapter will begin with the current debate in ethics about agency and membership before moving to specifically religious concerns. Although drawn predominantly from current Western, Christian ethics, there should be implications here for many other forms of religious ethics as well (see chapter 42).

The Debate About Agency

A central part of MacIntyre's critique of moral philosophy is that it makes claims for secular reasoning that it is unable to deliver. Modern ethics as a discipline has tended to claim that it alone, unlike theological ethics, can resolve moral dilemmas in the public realm. Moral reasoning without any divine revelation can be a universal means of reaching moral conclusions. Whereas religion divides people, secular moral philosophy can unite them (see chapter 6). Through the Enlightenment understanding of morality we have been delivered from the bitter religious warfare that characterized Europe during the sixteenth and seventeenth centuries. Decision making based upon moral philosophy offers the prospect of agreement across cultural and ideological divisions. Reason abstracted from religious membership is morally central.

In *After Virtue* MacIntyre subjects such claims to a detailed critique. There is, so the book argues, a clear gap between such claims and their attainment. Within moral philosophy there are very evident and unresolved differences between, for example, deontologists and utilitarians (see chapter 1). These differences become apparent as soon as recent debates are examined about issues such as the rightness of abortion or the nature of justice in society. The book maintains that these differences are actually incommensurable in terms of post-Enlightenment moral philosophy.

So, for example, the differences between pro-life and pro-choice factions in the abortion debate are not, so MacIntyre argues, resolvable in terms of post-Enlightenment moral philosophy. All too often contesting rights of the fetus, on the one hand, or of the woman, on the other, are simply asserted by the different factions without any prospect of rational resolution between them. Vigorous attempts to resolve this contestation have so far failed to convince either faction. Of course, particular power groups within society can ensure that, in the absence of intellectual agreement, one of these factions prevails. In reality this has now happened in much secular bioethics within the West in favor of the pro-choice faction. Although there is still a widespread belief that it is right to have a conscience clause allowing healthcare professionals opposed to abortion not to take a direct part in providing abortions, the same professionals are nevertheless still obliged to refer women requesting an abortion to other professionals who are not opposed. At best this is a conscience clause allowing professionals to opt out of direct action on abortion but not to opt out of abortion provision altogether (akin, perhaps, to ambulance service on the front line in World War I for exemplary pacifists rather than incarceration for thoroughgoing pacifists). A conservative Roman Catholic, Jewish, Muslim, or perhaps Buddhist doctor, opposed on religious grounds to abortion, has no legal alternative but to comply.

Again, a central weakness of much recent moral philosophy is "atomized individualism." It is all too often assumed that moral conclusions are typically reached by individuals through a series of logical steps without reference to others or to tradition until they make a moral decision. The focus here is upon the self as a self-contained island and upon moral decisions reached by an internalized process of logical deduction, as if individuals were not actually part of wider communities embedded in history and tradition. Taylor (1989: 305ff.) seeks to show at length that this is a very impoverished understanding of the moral self. Yet, ironically, it is still an understanding that is implicit within much discussion of autonomy and decision making in applied secular ethics.

In contrast to atomized individualism, some ethicists advocate a return to the moral tradition of virtue ethics and point to the role of moral communities in shaping virtuous individuals. Within this tradition, individuals are trained in virtues within local communities so that, when faced with ethical dilemmas, they do not approach them *de novo* as isolated individuals but as members of communities and as heirs to longstanding sources of moral wisdom. Such individuals depend less upon secular rationality than upon deeply ingrained virtuous habits to resolve moral dilemmas. On this understanding of bioethics – an understanding which is beginning to receive more serious discussion – the primary task of the discipline is to identify virtues which should guide and shape healthcare professionals and patients alike.

Herein lies a central problem. MacIntyre, for one, is highly skeptical about whether Western society is ever again capable of having a unified moral vision. Having deconstructed the universal claims of moral philosophy, he sees only fragmented and changing moral communities in the Western world. He points to the need for a new moral community, but offers little hope that it is actually still possible for any moral community to gain widespread acceptance. At most, presumably, a series of fragmented communities can bring their virtues to areas such as modern medicine, but without any expectation that everyone can accept them.

All of this suggests a serious moral gap that is particularly relevant to religious ethics. There is an evident gap between philosophical claims about virtue within communities and sociological skepticism about actual communities within the modern Western world. If modernity is premised upon individual rationality, it founders upon incommensurable moral conflicts (the very conflicts that moral philosophy was supposed to resolve). A more postmodern vision is premised instead upon local communities shaping virtuous people, but it founders upon the seeming impossibility of achieving general assent today for returning to premodern communities. Moral fragmentation and social conflict seem to be inevitable.

It is at this point that Taylor identifies a second major moral gap. He believes that moral agents are now in an age in which a publicly accessible "cosmic order of meanings" is an impossibility. All that moral agents can rely upon today is "personal resonance" – and that of course will vary from person to person (see chapter 2). He likens us to a crew of car mechanics in a pit-stop, each with four thumbs and with only a very hazy grasp of the wiring used in modern racing cars. We can resort to mundane procedures in an attempt to counter this serious deficiency, but these will not finally obscure the fact that we no longer share a vision of a "cosmic order of meaning" (Taylor 1989: 512). To apply this analysis to bioethics, it is painfully obvious that in ethical discussions about healthcare today we cannot even agree upon a notion of health. For some people, health is concerned narrowly with an absence of disease (itself a term with cultural variants), whereas for others it is concerned with wider well-being (a term with metaethical variants) and for others still with physical, mental, and spiritual health (now with metaphysical variants). Or consider modern warfare: it is often extremely difficult, if not impossible, to get opposing factions to agree about how just-war theory actually applies to them (see chapter 55). For example, one side may see a particular recourse to arms as being a legitimate struggle for liberation, whereas the opposing side may see it instead as an act of terrorism.

Within a detailed discussion of Kantian ethics, John Hare (1996) suggests a third major moral gap. He argues that this is the gap that arises from Kant's high moral demand for individuals combined with his belief that everyone has a propensity not to follow this demand. Specifically, the high moral demand that all people should always behave morally in ways that are universalizable is in clear tension with their propensity to selfishness. For Kant, Hare argues, this gap was particularly acute precisely because he believed that "ought" implies "can": if it is not the case that people can live by the moral demand, then it cannot be the case that they ought to do so. Hare is unconvinced by secular strategies designed to reduce this moral gap. The first seeks to reduce the moral demand itself (perhaps moral demands need not be universalizable) and the second exaggerates our natural propensities (perhaps humans really are not selfish after all). Both of these strategies have also been used at times in bioethics. If the moral demands in bioethics are sufficiently low then we should be able to attain them, or if we can assume that all healthcare professionals and patients will act selflessly then we can keep the demands high. They have also been used in applications of just-war theory. For some, war is inevitable, so they regard the function of just-war theory as simply to limit the worst features of warfare; others maintain that rational moral agents really can consistently reject violent action of any kind and live in a peaceful utopia. Rejecting such strategies, Hare (and, he believes, Kant) argues that this gap can only properly be resolved in terms of specifically religious ethics.

The influence of these moral philosophers upon specifically religious ethics in the last two decades has been immense. Many religious ethicists argue that this philosophical shift away from an individualistic understanding of moral agency gives renewed impetus to their discipline, concerned as it is with providing a critical account of differing ways that particular religious communities respond to moral issues. Some argue that Enlightenment secular moral agency is itself just one ideological tradition among others rather than a privileged mode of moral agency replacing traditional, religiously based moral agency (Hauerwas 1992, 2001; Milbank 1990). What does this really mean? It is at this point that the theme of religious membership becomes significant.

Assumptions About Moral Agency

A number of assumptions lie behind this new understanding of moral agency among religious ethicists. The first is that modernity is characterized by global pluralism rather than by secularity. Modern secularism is not a neutral platform for examining the world, but itself a form of ideology. The second is that, within this global pluralism, differing and sometimes competing religious communities abide and continue to contribute to moral agency. And the third is that such religious communities properly understood – and despite their internal differences – do still have a significant role to play in the public forum, even within secular democracies.

A good illustration of this is the extent to which religious ethicists, both in the United States and in the United Kingdom, and more widely within Europe, have recently been involved in public discussions of the morality of military action following September 11, 2001 and the morality of novel scientific areas such as that of stem cell research. It is now a feature of many national committees established to consider such moral issues that they regularly include a religious ethicist, alongside secular philosophers and lawyers. Politicians within both the United States and the United Kingdom are very wary of basing public policy upon any specific religious teaching (even within the Republic of Ireland such an approach is no longer popular). The same can be said of other, non-Western pluralistic societies, say India. Within many Islamic countries, too, there are similar tensions. In these contexts, secular "law" has increasingly had to navigate religious diversity (see chapter 11). Not the least of the fears is the risk of alienating other religious minorities within their respective countries. Nonetheless, there is now a much wider recognition than there was two decades ago that religious groups may have a distinctive contribution to make to the well-being of society at large.

The appointment in England in July 2002 of the theologian Rowan Williams as archbishop of Canterbury is one example of this increasing recognition. Because the Church of England is still an established church, the prime minister of the United Kingdom has a direct role in the selection process of a new archbishop. This role remains despite the fact that religious attendances across Christian denominations and across faith groups as a whole in England are lower than those elsewhere in the United Kingdom and about half of those in the United States. The new archbishop, in turn, can vote in the House of Lords and thus has a direct role in political decisions and is likely to be especially influential in those involving moral issues. Before his appointment it was already known that Rowan Williams held relatively conservative views on the morality of stem cell research involving human embryos (research which the government supported) and more radical views opposed to the bombing of Afghanistan following September 11, 2001. In addition, to the consternation of evangelicals within the wider Anglican Communion, it was also widely known that he had liberal views on homosexuality and had knowingly ordained as priest someone who was living within a committed same-sex relationship. All of this suggests a very complex pattern of inter-action quite at odds with a separation of public morality from religious traditions. A prime minister, himself with known religious commitments, sanctions the appointment of an archbishop who is likely to exercise a role of public leadership on moral issues, despite evangelical opposition to this appointment from within the Anglican Communion and despite the possibility that once appointed the archbishop might actively oppose government policy in some moral areas (as he did over invading Iraq).

An added twist to this example is that as England increasingly sees itself as a multi-faith society (although in reality the official membership of mosques and synagogues there is relatively small), so the archbishop of Canterbury has sometimes been identi-fied as a spokesperson for religious faith in general. In recent years, a number of key meetings have been sponsored at Lambeth Palace, the London office of the archbishop, involving a broad spectrum of religious leaders. The objective of these meetings has not been simply to promote interreligious friendship and cooperation, but also to present common cause when needed to influence government policy. For example, when Robert Runcie was archbishop, an unsuccessful attempt was made by one of these meetings to influence government to extend the law against public blasphemy to religious tradi-tions beyond Christianity. Inevitably, such an attempt was contentious even within the religious traditions themselves. Some adherents argued that internal contradictions would inevitably arise (especially given the intellectual difficulties in defining what constitutes a "religious" tradition) and in any case free speech was preferable to anachronistic concepts of blasphemy.

Recently there have been a number of religiously inspired empirical studies of public attitudes and moral behavior. One obvious example is *The Family, Religion and Culture Project* directed by the theologian and ethicist Don Browning. Books published as a result of the project have attempted to give an overview of the social and theological debate about the family in modern America. At the heart of this project is a conviction that the family should be defended robustly by Christians, despite the fact that in the name of the Bible it has often been distorted in the past. In the foundation book for the series, the authors argue that the fundamental family issue of our time may be how to retain and honor the intact family without turning it into an object of idolatry and without retaining the inequalities of power, status, and privilege ensconced in its earlier forms (see Browning 1997). Using extensive social statistics they argue that in America today one out of two marriages ends in divorce and almost one in three children is born outside marriage. Yet the United States is still a country of relatively high religious attendance and over two-thirds of all marriages take place in churches and synagogues. Second and even third marriages regularly take place in them in the United States and increasingly within the United Kingdom as well. Those writing for the project are well aware of these facts when they seek to defend what they term the "intact" family – by which they mean families in which children are brought up by both of their biological parents. Not wishing in any way to discriminate against other families, they still believe that it is vital for religious communities to encourage intact families, if necessary with help from the law.

Another approach, which I have set out at length elsewhere, is based less upon a moral campaign than upon an attempt to assess in social scientific terms just how significant religious factors are in moral agency (see Gill 1999). Using extensive international data from social attitude questionnaires, I test whether claimed religious behavior or belief has any demonstrable relationship to more general moral attitudes or action. What emerges is that the religiously active are indeed distinctive in their attitudes and behavior. Some of their attitudes do change over time, especially on issues such as sexuality, and there are obvious moral disagreements between different groups of churchgoers in a number of areas. Nonetheless, there are broad patterns of belief, teleology, and altruism that distinguish those who are religiously active from those who are not. For example, Christian churchgoers have, in addition to their distinctive theistic and Christocentric beliefs, a strong sense of moral order and concern for other people. They are more likely than others to be involved in voluntary service: many childcare groups, youth clubs, charity shops, and care-of-the-elderly services depend heavily upon churchgoers. They see overseas charitable giving as important and are more hesitant about euthanasia and capital punishment and more concerned about the family and civic order than other people. None of these differences is absolute. Analogies could be found in other religions. The values, virtues, moral attitudes, and behavior of churchgoers are shared by many other people as well. The distinctiveness of churchgoers is real but relative.

This evidence is consonant with the argument about moral agency and communal membership. Even in pluralistic American society, there are still religious communities – Catholic Irish, Orthodox Greeks, and Orthodox Jews – which are relatively less fragmented. Yet, as MacIntyre notes, "even however in such communities the need to enter into public debate enforces participation in the cultural *mélange* in the search for a common stock of concepts and norms which all may enjoy and to which all may appeal ... in search of what, if my argument is correct, is a chimaera." This produces a curious mixture of historically and culturally contingent communities misguidedly searching for moral consensus. Further, "moral philosophies, however they may aspire to achieve more than this, always do articulate the morality of some particular social and cultural standpoint." As a result, modern, pluralistic societies cannot hope to achieve moral consensus. Rather, "it is in its historical encounter that any given point of view establishes or fails to establish its rational superiority relative to its particular rivals in some specific contexts" (MacIntyre 1984: 268–9). While moral agency within particular religious communities may be distinctive, it can still overlap with that of other religious and "secular" communities.

Can a causal relationship be established between religious belonging and the distinctive virtues that religious people hold to a greater degree than other people? The strongest evidence for such a relationship involves comparing the responses of two groups of adult non-churchgoers – the one originally brought up going to church almost every week and the other never going in childhood at all. This suggests that the effects of involuntary churchgoing as a child can still be traced in the relative strength of the Christian beliefs of adult non-churchgoers. Compared with non-churchgoers who never went to church as children, those adult non-churchgoers who went regularly as children show twice the level of Christian belief. In addition, the latter are more likely to hold moral attitudes on personal honesty and sexuality that are closer to those of regular churchgoers (see Gill 1999).

Belief and Action

If this evidence is accurate it suggests that for many moral agents there is not the clear separation of morality and religion that the secular post-Enlightenment ethics has claimed. The latter may have underestimated the power of religious belonging/belief to motivate individual moral agents and overestimated its own power to resolve public moral disagreements. In contrast, in a world that is more self-consciously pluralistic, religious traditions may once again be allowed a significant role in public debates about moral issues, even though they are unlikely to be granted the sort of monopoly of ethical decision making more characteristic of theocracies than modern democracies.

Bibliography

Browning, D. S. (ed.) 1997: *From Culture Wars to Common Ground.* Westminster, KY: John Knox Press.

Gill, R. 1999: *Churchgoing and Christian Ethics.* Cambridge: Cambridge University Press.

Gill, R. (ed.) 2001: *The Cambridge Companion to Christian Ethics.* Cambridge: Cambridge University Press.

Hare, J. E. 1996: *The Moral Gap: Kantian Ethics, Human Limits and God's Assistance.* Oxford: Clarendon Press.

Hauerwas, S. 1992: *Against the Nations.* Notre Dame, IN: University of Notre Dame Press.

——2001: *With the Grain of the Universe: The Church's Witness and Natural Theology: being the Gifford Lectures delivered at the University of St. Andrews in 2001.* Grand Rapids, MI: Brazos Press.

Horton, J. and Mendus, S. (eds.) 1994: *After MacIntyre: Critical Perspectives on the Work of Alasdair MacIntyre.* Notre Dame, IN: University of Notre Dame Press.

MacIntyre, A. 1984: *After Virtue: A Study of Moral Theory,* 2nd edn. Notre Dame, IN: University of Notre Dame Press.

Milbank, J. 1990: *Theology and Social Theory: Beyond Secular Reason.* Oxford: Blackwell.

Taylor, C. 1989: *Sources of the Self: The Making of Modern Identity.* Cambridge, MA: Harvard University Press.

2   Persons

CHAPTER 51

Human Rights

Simeon O. Ilesanmi

The contemporary international doctrine of human rights is principally an outgrowth of World War II, arising on the one hand from the statement of allied war aims in the Atlantic Charter (1941) and on the other from persistent pressure brought by individuals and groups outside of governments for a declaration of political principles or an "international bill of rights" for the postwar world. Since then, there has been a progressive evolution and codification of the idea of human rights, with the United Nations serving as the main vehicle through which human rights dreams have been expressed and their projects implemented. Beginning with its Charter of 1946, which affirms in its Preamble "faith in fundamental human rights," the United Nations successively adopted three key documents – the Universal Declaration of Human Rights (1948) and two international covenants, one on Civil and Political Rights and the other on Economic, Social, and Cultural Rights (both 1966) – that today constitute an authoritative catalogue of internationally recognized human rights. Other human rights documents, both regionally inspired, such as the African Charter on Human and People's Rights (1986), and issues-directed, such as the United Nations Declaration on the Elimination of All Forms of Intolerance and Discrimination Based on Religion or Belief (1981), are supplements to the earlier UN instruments.

The inspiration for the understanding of rights, however, antedated the birth of the United Nations. Among other notable sources of human rights ideas are religious traditions, philosophical ideas, legal theories, and revolutionary political and socialist movements, which have articulated moral and humanistic principles that either correspond to or have influenced modern conceptions of human rights. Buddhism and Islam, no less than Christianity, Judaism, and several indigenous religions, portray a vision of universal moral community, in which human beings exist under one transcendent Source, whose will they are to serve for the benefits of all. We find a similar cosmopolitan vision of human interdependence in Cicero's *De Legibus* (52 BCE), where he appeals to human rights laws that transcend customary and civil laws, and endorses the idea of "a citizen of the whole universe, as it were of a single city." Cicero rejected the view that distinctions of race, religion, and opinion are insurmountable barriers to forming an inclusive civic and moral community (see Griffin and Atkins 1991). Enlightenment thinkers bolstered this moral orientation to the world, requiring only that the emerging nation-state be seen as the natural forum for securing civil and political rights against religious establishments (see chapter 48). As women entered the public sphere, militants and thinkers like Olympe de Gouge and Mary Wollstonecraft called for the equal natural rights of women.

While few would dispute the importance of tracing the intellectual history of human rights, the controversy surrounding the use of the term today focuses on what it means to have rights, how they may be justified, and what rights we should have or recognize. For reasons that will become clear, issues of justification and scope of rights have been more contentious than the analytic task of defining human rights (see chapter 2). This chapter explores all three.

The Meaning of Human Rights

Discussions of human rights come up in a variety of contexts, academic and otherwise, which indicate the prominence of the idea in contemporary international society. Accordingly, some scholars suggest that human rights have become a hegemonic political discourse or settled norms within the society of states. While there is much to celebrate in this trend, it can be argued that the global vernacularization of human rights has also contributed to the confusion about their meaning. Conceptually, the word "right" may designate *rectitude* by means of which we talk of something (for example, an action) as being right. This meaning is only tangentially related to what we usually have in mind when talking about human rights, a term that is broadly used to designate *entitlement*. In legal, political, and moral contexts, human rights refer to justifiable claims that individuals and groups can make upon others or upon society, including their governments. The claims may be negative, when they impose constraints upon the actions of others. They may also be positive, requiring active efforts on the part of those against whom they are made to meet the needs embodied in the claims. But are all claims entitled to recognition? What distinguishes "rights" claims from petty claims, and why should we be inclined to take the former seriously while having no qualms about laughing off the latter?

I will identify three different, albeit overlapping, ways of answering these questions. Each answer roughly corresponds to a separate meaning of human rights. First, human rights are taken seriously, or ought to be so taken, because they are expressions of moral identity. They provide normative clues to what a society and its citizens care about. When enacted into law by a democratically elected government, rights often become a means by which important moral values – dignity, respect, and justice – are legally protected. In short, human rights language calls our attention to what it means to be human. It testifies to the goodness of the human who understands himself or herself, and is regarded by others, as a valuable member of the community, and who not only has to be respected but upon whom others can also make similar claims.

Second, human rights function as a meaningful rhetoric for discussing society's response to basic human needs. "A basic need" is anything "in whose absence a person would be harmed in some crucial and fundamental way" (Feinberg 1973: 111). Needs are things required to survive with dignity; they are warrants for protection against potential harm. When someone has a need, that person is not merely entitled to compensation in the event that he or she happens to be deprived of the needed good; one also has a right to the satisfaction of that need even before harm befalls him or her. Rights, then, refer to important human interests, those interests that operate as "trumps" in the sense that they cannot be compromised by reference to collective policies or goals. They denote ultimate and weighty moral concerns that usually override other normative considerations and which persons have a moral duty to respect.

Thus, when we articulate human choices in rights language, we are attributing to those choices a certain peremptory force that is neither derived from, nor can be overridden by, the rules of any municipal legal system. Human rights have a tangible existence and moral force in the world of actions, not because the law or a given received tradition says so (in fact, rights are often the casualties of law and tradition), but because they are the means by which we assess the worth of any tradition or legal system. The capacity of any legal or political order to create moral obligations depends on its conformity with human rights. Unfortunately, this has not always been the case. There has been, in virtually every society, an immense abyss between normative theory and social practice, between constitutional doctrine and constitutive conduct. Slavery, colonialism, sexism, and religious intolerance are among the many indelible deviations from human rights. Thankfully, there have also been progressive efforts toward bridging the gap between our normative aspirations and actual conduct. These efforts are at the core of the rights revolution, in consequence of which many dictators have been tossed out of office and excluded groups enfranchised as bona fide members of their societies. From Africa to Asia, Latin America to Eastern Europe, and in some countries of the Middle East, the language and conceptuality of rights are being incorporated into national constitutions. At the international level, human rights norms and values are also becoming a fashionable subject of bilateral and multilateral diplomacy, largely because of the lexical priority accorded to human rights over actual cultural beliefs and particular social arrangements. Third, these worldwide developments provide a basis for a conceptualization of the idea of human rights, as "an expression of a deep human ability to recognize the other as like oneself; to experience empathy for the other's needs and sufferings; to consent to, support, and rejoice in the fulfillment of the other's human capacities and well-being" (Cahill 1999–2000: 45).

It is conceivable to concede this moral power to rights language but nonetheless argue that its desired goals can be achieved by means of other normative languages. Some have argued that other ideas are more effective than human rights in serving as ethical templates for social and political ordering. A key substitute for human rights is the language of duty, defended by communitarians in the West and by those who ascribe uniqueness to Asian and African cultures. This is the position taken in the African Charter on Human and People's Rights, which Makau Wa Mutua, a

Kenya-born scholar, defends as being consistent with precolonial African emphasis on "communal ties and social cohesiveness," values purportedly undermined by the so-called Western notion of the "individual who is 'utterly free and utterly irresponsible and opposed to society'" (Mutua 1995: 368) (see chapter 41). Similarly, others decry what is caustically referred to as "American rights talk" that "tend[s] to be presented as absolute, individual, and independent of any necessary relation to responsibilities." The near-worship of the individual in the name of rights impoverishes political culture, "promotes unrealistic expectations, heightens social conflict, and inhibits dialogue that might lead towards consensus, accommodation, or at least the discovery of common ground" (Glendon 1991: 12, 14).

American society may be more fragmented than it should ideally be, but it is doubtful that the acceptance and domestication of human rights are the sole culprits. What is more, societies that profess allegiance to the "responsibility language" are no less fragile in their social and political composition than America or other countries of the West. Rather than erecting a false dichotomy between "rights' and "duty," what seems more reasonable is to affirm their correlativeness and mutual entailment. The presumed opposition between the two often arises from confusions and misconceptions, ignoring the fact that some rights have the characteristics claimed for them, and other rights have the features associated with duties or responsibilities. We need the language of duty to enable us to appreciate our sociality and interdependence, and we need rights language to ensure that individual uniqueness is not needlessly sacrificed at the altar of societal convenience.

For example, the right to freedom of speech may be owned by individuals, but it is a precondition for the highly social process of democratic deliberation. That right keeps open the channels of communication; it is emphatically communal in character. Everyone who owns a speech right does so partly so as to contribute to the collectivity; it is this fact that explains the government's inability to "buy" speech rights even when a speaker would like to sell it. So, too, the right to associational freedom is hardly individualistic. In addition to its instrumental value of furthering the rights of the individual – by enabling individual expression and participation in the political process – the right to association is also meant to protect collective action and sociality. Additionally, some rights, even of the most traditional sort, including property, may be necessary conditions for enabling a sense of collective responsibility, even though some understand these rights to be important primarily because they are central to economic growth and material well-being. Yet people without rights to their property may be so dependent on official will that they cannot exercise their responsibilities as citizens (Sunstein 1995; Tuck 1979, see chapter 45).

The danger (and a serious one at that) of dropping the language of rights for other more seemingly attractive, perhaps less fractious and less centrifugal ones is that it would strip people of their *locus standi* for effective and meaningful participation in the deliberative life of their society. The instrumentality of rights is a basis on which the powerless and the marginalized may have some hope of commanding a share of the social and material benefits of their societies. Rights offer us a shield from being coerced or bullied into silence; they draw attention to our voices and our lives – formal attention, informal attention, and the attention of various communities, including attention to oneself (Baier 1993: 159; Feinberg 1973: 58). While no human right is absolute in the sense of being indefeasible, every legitimate claim requires that infringements be justified by morally acceptable reasons.

But should these rights be universally recognized or are they constrained by the dictates of cultures?

Justifying Human Rights

Central to the contemporary doctrine of international human rights is the principle of non-discrimination. "Everyone is entitled to all the rights and freedoms set forth in this Declaration, without distinction of any kind, such as race, color, sex, language, religion, political or other opinion, national or social origin, property, birth or other status" (UN 1948: Art. 2). The non-discrimination principle has become an article of faith for those regarded as universalists in the human rights community, that is, those who argue that a commitment to human rights necessarily implies a rejection of all systems of inequality based upon extrinsic human traits such as age, race, gender, religion, and places of origin. Some proponents of moral universalism appeal to the structure of human action to justify the inclusiveness of the human rights vision (Gewirth 1982). Other proponents ground human rights in the notion of an *a priori* human nature, pre-existing any form of social and political organization (Wiredu 1990: 243). "The whole point of human rights is that they are taken to be binding and available, regardless of any particular identity or conviction" (Little 1999: 157). On this view, rights are the inescapable entailment of the moral status of human beings. The status itself could be predicated on either the value of biological life (Singer 1993: 55–217) or on universal rational agency, the uniquely human capacity for self-consciousness (Korsgaard 1996: 104).

The important question to raise at this juncture is whether religious sensitivities contribute to or undermine the aspirations for a universal recognition of human rights. One stream of scholars believes that it is religion that needs human rights for its preservation, not the other way round. They contend that the morality of historical religious traditions is totalizing and exclusivist (Okin 1999: 9–24). Others argue "human rights are, in substantial part, the modern political fruits of ancient religious beliefs and practices" (Witte 1998: 258). By evoking "a basic sense of fellow humanity, respect for human dignity, and mutual responsibility," religious symbols and beliefs provide a motivational rationale for universalizing and domesticating human rights (Cahill 1999–2000, 47–8). More fundamentally, "the idea of human rights is . . . ineliminably religious" (Perry 1998: 13). The idea of human rights, on this view, requires affirming that each person is "sacred" in relation to a holistic view of the world and its meaning, so that there are certain things that should not be done to and that should be done for any person.

Despite the disagreement between secular (rationalist) universalists and their religious counterparts, both camps agree on the normative understanding of humanity and the defense of human dignity as the primary object of human rights. Neither camp is also completely free of the potential evils that it identifies in the other. Historical religious traditions have perpetrated gruesome atrocities in the name of defending "absolute and universal" truths. Secular philosophical theories are no less sullied by their attribution of "rationality" to some segments of humanity while denying it to others.

The potential for discrimination on both religious and secular grounds has prompted two kinds of skeptical responses. First, cultural relativists see all assertions of universalism as smokescreens for an imperialist moral agenda and contend that morality is a product of historically bound cultures and specific epistemological contexts. They adjudge every society or culture to be a self-contained system that defines its own standard of rationality. Any pretension to the possibility of a transhistorical or universal moral code, applicable to all societies, without regard to time and place, is nothing short of moral dogmatism or idolatry, either of which is both irrational and reactionary. The other response comes from the proponents of "intercultural dialogue," premised on the conviction that the world's religious and philosophical traditions share much in common to enable them overcome their inherited superiority–inferiority complexes. Rather than engaging in a futile pursuit of the "ideal" human, the moral codes found in various societies might produce "a set of standards to which all societies can be held – negative injunctions, most likely, rules against murder, deceit, torture, oppression, and tyranny." These standards would constitute "the moral minimum," not a complete moral code, but rather "reiterated features of particular thick or maximal moralities" (Walzer 1994: 9–10).

Notable contributions to human rights debates in religious ethics seem to share an affirmation of pluralism as the context within which to seek legitimacy and justification for human rights. One historical misjudgment that many people continue to make is the view that contemporary international human rights instruments were produced by a single, principally Western, philosophical ideology. To the contrary, it was in the context of pragmatic, intercultural dialogue that international human rights secure their legitimacy. The concerns to which human rights were addressed are the conditions necessary for personal and communal flourishing (Twiss 1998: 272) (see chapter 16). Against this historical backdrop, it is moot to be asking whether religion can or ought to be part of the conversations about human rights. These conversations are necessarily *public*. As such, religious and secular voices must engage one another as components of a comprehensive cultural milieu.

Scope of Human Rights

The continuing multiplication of human rights instruments at the international and various regional levels shows the ideological fissures to which the human rights community is perennially prone. The dispute about whether the international community should recognize any priorities, either moral or pragmatic, among categories of rights began with adoption of the Universal Declaration of Human Rights. It resulted in the ratification of two different international covenants, one on Civil and Political Rights and the other on Economic, Social, and Cultural Rights representing, respectively, the now moribund ideological blinkers of East and West. Two sub-issues define this debate:

how to classify human rights and whether (or how) to rank them. On classification, it was John Warwick Montgomery who first categorized rights in terms of "generations," by which he meant the chronological appearance and development of rights theory.

For some time, Montgomery's "three generations of rights" provided a structure for discussions of international human rights. Broadly understood, the first generation refers to civil and political rights, the second to social and economic rights, and the third generation designates the right to development insisted upon by the formerly colonized countries of Africa and Asia (Montgomery 1986: 69–70). This classification now has a limited utility. It does not take account of the contemporary concern for "group rights" (see chapter 44). It is thus useful to think of internationally recognized human rights as falling roughly into five categories:

1   Rights of the person (e.g., life, liberty, and security of the person; privacy and freedom of movement; ownership of property; freedom of thought, conscience, and religion, including freedom of religious teaching and practice "in public and private"; prohibition of slavery, torture, and cruel or degrading punishment).
2   Rights associated with the rule of law (equal recognition before the law and equal protection of the law; right to an effective legal remedy for violation of legal rights; impartial hearing and trial; presumption of innocence; prohibition of arbitrary arrest).
3   Political rights (freedom of expression, assembly, and association; rights "to take part in the government of the country" and to "periodic and genuine elections . . . by universal and equal suffrage . . . by secret vote").
4   Economic and social rights (social security, adequate standard of living, free choice of employment, protection against unemployment, "just and favorable remuneration," right to join trade unions, "periodic holidays with pay," free elementary education, and "the right of everyone to the enjoyment of the highest attainable standard of physical and mental health").
5   Rights of communities (self-determination; protection against genocide, slavery and forced labor, racial discrimination, apartheid; protection of minority cultures; and the rights of children).

There is no universal format by which to classify human rights. It is, admittedly, possible to develop a different scheme than the one suggested here.

A far more controversial question is whether we should give priority to some rights over others. The question is raised because rights do conflict, not only because of competing human interests but also because of finite human and societal resources to adequately satisfy all human rights. Up till the early 1990s the dominant orientation was toward prioritization of rights, guided by such considerations as strategy (Hollenbach 1979: 187–202), moral weight (Shue 1980: 155–74), and judicial enforceability (Feinberg 1973). For example, some commonly argued that social, economic, and development rights were unjusticiable, with justiciability defined as the state's obligation to respect, protect, and fulfill a person's right. This characterization rests on the distinction between positive rights and negative rights that I alluded to earlier in the chapter. The former are said to require governmental action; to be resource intensive and therefore expensive to protect; progressive and therefore requiring time to realize; vague in terms of the obligations they mandate; and involve complex, polycentric, and diffuse interests in collective goods (Scott and Macklem 1992: 24). On the other hand, civil and political rights are justifiable because they are, paradigmatically, negative rights and therefore cost-free, immediately satisfiable, precise in the obligations they generate, and comprehensible because they involve discrete clashes of identifiable individual interests (Nozick 1974: 26–53). All that is required to satisfy negative rights is an obligation not beyond the power of both individuals and governments to meet. This of course assumes the existence of propitious social conditions, especially "a set of institutional arrangements for securing legally binding guarantees beneficial to the individual" and "a secure and procedurally regularized legal system" (Claude 1977: 8–10).

The Vienna Declaration and Program of Action adopted on June 25, 1993 by the UN-sponsored World Conference on Human Rights challenges us to move beyond the prioritization paradigm by holding that "all human rights are universal, indivisible, and interdependent and interrelated." This is hardly a novel claim from the standpoint of many religious traditions, with their affirmation of the "fullness of life" as the organizing framework of moral discourse, as well as the belief in the all-encompassing Divine Reality who is related to all realms of life (see chapter "On Religious Ethics"). There is little to celebrate about a society that promotes only one category of rights (e.g., civil/political rights) – that society merely projects an image of truncated humanity. Affirming the *interdependence* of rights is one normative and strategic way to avoid such a distortion of human life. Central to the principle of interdependence is the idea that "values seen as directly related to the full development of personhood cannot be protected and nurtured in isolation" (Scott 1989: 786). It advocates a full conception of human freedom and a full and integrated conception of the self. It thus rejects a related series of fundamental oppositions or dichotomies that can serve to privilege certain conceptions of the self, and to reinforce marginalization.

By affirming the normative unity of all rights, the principle of interdependence dissolves the false dichotomy between the so-called negative rights and positive rights, thereby refuting the attendant claim that only the former are justiciable. This distinction rests on a flawed assumption that for every human right there is only one correlative obligation, rather than seeing all human rights as entailing a complex, multilayered structure of obligations (Raz 1984: 194–200). Using the right to food as an example, Shue (2000) explains that there are four duties corresponding to it: (1) the obligation to respect; (2) the obligation to protect; (3) the obligation to ensure; and (4) the obligation to promote. The first is a classic negative obligation of non-interference, while the other three require varying degrees of positive action or state policy. This moral overlap underscores the need to promote in tandem both categories of rights.

Finally, the principle of interdependence takes into account the social realities of the people: its primary focus is the promotion of being human or of the capacity to be human. Full human flourishing requires material and political empowerment, enjoyed at individual and collective levels, and it is only within a vision of interrelated and interdependent rights that this inclusive ethical good can be secured. By shifting the argument from the *content* of rights per se and locating it at the center of the quest for an understanding of what it means to be human, the principle of interdependence brings a dynamic and sense of urgency to contemporary human rights debates. Amid the mounting global vicissitudes of civil wars, cultural oppression, political autocracy, economic stagnation, natural disasters, population explosion, and refugee crises, to name a few, we need a moral strategy that combines both the aspirations for political liberation with the imperatives of economic sustenance and empowerment. Anything short of this would make life more brutish and alienating.

Bibliography

Baier, A. C. 1993: "Claims, Rights, Responsibilities," in *Prospects for a Common Morality*, ed. G. Outka and J. P. Reeder, 149–69. Princeton, NJ: Princeton University Press.

Cahill, L. S. 1999–2000: "Rights as Religious or Secular: Why Not Both?" *Journal of Law and Religion* 14 (1), 41–52.

Claude, R. P. 1977: "The Western Tradition of Human Rights in Comparative Perspective." *Comparative Judicial Review* 14, 2–12.

Feinberg, J. 1973: *Social Philosophy*. Englewood Cliffs, NJ: Prentice-Hall.

Gewirth, A. 1982: *Human Rights: Essays on Justification and Applications*. Chicago: University of Chicago Press.

Glendon, M. A. 1991: *Rights Talk: The Impoverishment of Political Discourse*. New York: Free Press.

Griffin, M. T. and Atkins, E. M. (eds.) 1991: *Cicero On Duties*. Cambridge: Cambridge University Press.

Hollenbach, D. 1979: *Claims in Conflict: Retrieving and Renewing the Catholic Human Rights Tradition*. New York: Paulist Press.

Korsgaard, C. 1996: *The Sources of Normativity*. Cambridge: Cambridge University Press.

Little, D. 1999: "Rethinking Human Rights: A Review Essay on Religion, Relativism, and Other Matters." *Journal of Religious Ethics* 27 (1), 151–77.

Montgomery, J. W. 1986: *Human Rights and Human Dignity*. Grand Rapids, MI: Zondervan.

Mutua, M. W. 1995: "The Banjul Charter and the African Cultural Fingerprint: An Evaluation of the Language of Duties." *Virginia Journal of International Law* 35 (2), 339–80.

Nozick, R. 1974: *Anarchy, State and Utopia*. New York: Basic Books.

Okin, S. M. 1999: *Is Multiculturalism Bad for Women?* ed. S. M. Okin, J. Cohen, M. Howard, and M. C. Nussbaum. Princeton, NJ: Princeton University Press.

Perry, M. J. 1998: *The Idea of Human Rights: Four Inquiries*. New York: Oxford University Press.

Raz, J. 1984: "Right-Based Moralities" in *Theories of Rights*, ed. J. Waldron, 182–200. Oxford: Oxford University Press.

Scott, C. 1989: "The Interdependence and Permeability of Human Rights Norms: Towards a Partial Fusion of the International Covenants on Human Rights." *Osgoode Hall Law Journal* 27 (4), 768–878.

Scott, C. and Macklem, P. 1992: "Constitutional Ropes of Sand or Justiciable Guarantees? Social Rights in a New South African Constitution." *University of Pennsylvania Law Review* 141 (1): 1–148.

Shue, H. 1980: *Basic Rights: Subsistence, Affluence, and US Foreign Policy*. Princeton, NJ: Princeton University Press.

—— 2000: "Solidarity Among Strangers and the Right to Food" in *Contemporary Moral Issues: Diversity and Consensus*, ed. L. M. Hinman, 471–85. Upper Saddle River, NJ: Prentice-Hall.

Singer, P. 1993: *Practical Ethics*, 2nd edn. Cambridge: Cambridge University Press.

Sunstein, C. 1995: "Rights and Their Critics." *Notre Dame Law Review* 70, 727–68.

Tuck, R. 1979: *Natural Rights Theories: Their Origins and Development*. Cambridge: Cambridge University Press.

Twiss, S. B. 1998: "Moral Grounds and Plural Cultures: Interpreting Human Rights in the International Community." *Journal of Religious Ethics* 26 (2), 271–82.

Walzer, M. 1994: *Thick and Thin: Moral Argument at Home and Abroad*. Notre Dame, IN: University of Notre Dame Press.

Wiredu, K. 1990: "An Akan Perspective on Human Rights" in *Human Rights in Africa: Cross-Cultural Perspectives*, ed. A. A. An-Na'im and F. M. Deng, 243–60. Washington, DC: Brookings Institution.

Witte, J., Jr. 1998: "Law, Religion, and Human Rights: A Historical Protestant Perspective." *Journal of Religious Ethics* 26 (2), 257–62.

CHAPTER 52

Future Generations

Svend Andersen

"Future generations" is the name for an ethical problem. People now living can influence the lives of future people in new ways. Industrial civilization has such an effect on
the natural world that the life conditions of future generations depend upon it. Modern
biotechnology can influence both the very existence of future persons and their properties. Because of the recent emergence of the problem, it is unsurprising that traditional Christian and other religious thinking does not contain obvious resources for
dealing with it. One could even argue that there are important elements in traditional
religious thinking that run counter to moral responsibility for future generations.

The Facts and the Problems

A closer look at the problem of future generations shows that it is not simply one issue,
but several different problems. They can be presented as three questions:

1   Should there be future generations at all? This question presented itself dramati-
    cally from the point in history when it became possible for humans to extinguish
    the whole of humankind. That possibility emerged after the construction of nuclear
    and biochemical weapons, and it was a determining feature of the political climate
    during the Cold War (see chapter 55).
2   What living conditions should future generations have? This question has, first, a
    purely *economic* meaning: how does the handling of contemporary wealth influence
    the economic conditions of future humans? (see chapter 45). This problem is not
    new, but its dimensions are. Second, during the last fifty years the question has
    acquired an *ecological* meaning. In what kind of natural environment will future
    generations find themselves? And third, the question has a *demographic* dimension,
    which is not totally distinct from the previous two aspects. Will the number of
    people on the planet cause grave problems in terms of life conditions?

3   What kind of people should future generations be? Thanks to biotechnology and
the so-called reproduction revolution, it might be possible to an increasing degree
for parents to influence the properties of their offspring (see chapter 46). Prenatal
genetic testing makes possible the negative selection of diseases and handicaps.
Genetic engineering might be used for "enhancing" the genetic makeup of future
children. Reproductive cloning could mean that some future persons will be
(almost) genetically identical with existing persons.

These problems raise different ethical questions, some of which are similar to traditional moral problems. In Western societies these problems are also dealt with in a
secular context with moral philosophy as its form of reflection. It is therefore appropriate to present some arguments in moral philosophy and religious responses. Before
we enter into the ethical field proper, however, it is necessary to mention some
conceptual difficulties.

Conceptual Difficulties

The moral problems related to future generations are in many ways shaped by secular,
Western culture. Their very formulation presupposes that the moral agent is an individual acting against other individuals. Traditionally, future individuals were thought
of as children or grandchildren of now-living persons. The problems of our day,
however, are not only "private" or family problems. Rather, the moral agent is the whole
of humankind, the living inhabitants of the planet. And the moral subjects with whom
they are confronted are future generations as a collective entity. The new issue is
whether and to what degree this collective entity belongs to the sphere of responsibility of the now living (see chapter 49). As to the concept of the future, in secular terms,
its content is not qualitatively different from the present. Future generations are human
beings like us, living in the same physical world we inhabit and in the same empirical
time.

Many traditional religious beliefs do not fit into these concepts of "generation" and
"future." Religions do not regard the future just as an extension of the present. In the
Abrahamic religions (Christianity, Judaism, and Islam) we find ideas about a future
which is transcendent to worldly reality. Cosmic time is one single process beginning
with creation and aiming at the end of the world and the establishment of transcendent reality. Asian religions, on the other hand, see the cosmos as a continuous repetition of stages, even if there is a final state (nirvāna) (see chapter 33). So the very picture
of temporal development and hence of the future in many religious worldviews is
different from the secular picture, and the views in various religions are different from
each other. The same is true of the concept of "generation." According to the "biblical"
religions, children are the same kind of individual humans as their parents. There is
one uniform chain of generations until the end of time and the establishment of a new
transcendent life form. In Asian religions, however, the idea of reincarnation gives a
totally different picture. Children are beings who make rebirth possible.

Related to these cosmological and metaphysical differences are differences in the concept of individual persons. The "biblical" idea of a human agent presupposes the concept of the person in the sense of an identifiable conscious entity who remains the same over time. This concept is far from obvious in Asian religions, where, say in Buddhism, the idea of a stable self is rather regarded as an illusion (see chapter 31). It is therefore not enough to realize differences in various religions' moral teachings about future people. One also has to keep in mind that the very idea of future generations takes its meaning from metaphysical frameworks that vary in different religious traditions.

Future Generations in Traditional Religious Ethics

As an example of traditional religious thinking about future generations we can look at biblical religion (i.e., the Hebrew Bible that is common to Judaism and Christianity, and the New Testament). In the religion of the Hebrew Bible, this-worldly human life has a central place. Humans are created by God as bodily beings. This involves sexual differentiation, sexuality, and procreation: "male and female he created them" (Genesis 1:27). And it is emphasized both as a blessing and a task that humans shall "be fruitful, and multiply, and replenish the earth" (1:28). It is a divine obligation for humans to create future generations.

Even if "future generations" clearly is a central motif in the religion of the Hebrew Bible, one can hardly call it an ethical issue. But the importance of the continuation of the people is reflected in some norms of sexual ethics. Thus, it is emphasized that sexuality should be linked to procreation. Children are regarded as those on whom the future of the parents depends. Hence the obligations of the children are strongly emphasized, as is obvious in the so-called fourth commandment: "Honor thy father and thy mother" (Ex. 20:12).

The "this-worldly" thinking is altered with the appearance of a new understanding of time in apocalyptic thought (i.e., ideas about the end of this time and the beginning of a new era with the establishment of a transcendent, eternal kingdom). Even if this prophetic vision is about a future enacted by God, human responsibility is still emphasized. However, humans are not responsible for the enactment of this "new" future. In the New Testament, apocalyptic thinking plays a dominant role, to such a degree that the end of time will soon occur: "the time is short" and "the fashion of this world passeth away" (1 Cor. 7:29, 31). This of course makes the question of future "worldly" generations quite irrelevant. Marriage and procreation more or less have the character of an interim arrangement: "they that have wives be as though they had none" (1 Cor. 7:29). One could say that according to original Christian belief as we find it in St. Paul, salvation in the transcendent future dominates over the created world. In a way, "future" and "generation" do not really belong together.

Christians soon had to realize that this world would not come to an end immediately. They had to develop an ethics for life in this material world, involving marriage and the raising of children. As an example, consider Martin Luther's interpretation of the fourth commandment. Remarkably, Luther finds in the commandment not only pre-scriptions for children to obey their parents, but also a reminder of the responsibility of parents. Their main task is to raise children to become useful people for God and neigh-bor. This not only means collecting "money and goods" for the children, but also secur-ing their learning and education. The result of good upbringing in this sense would be the flourishing of the worldly and spiritual community of humans. Luther sees the issue of future generations in the framework of his doctrine of social life – both secular and religious – as sustained by God the creator.

Responses in Moral Philosophy

Modern Western ethics has responded to the problem of future generations along the lines of the three questions noted at the beginning of this chapter.

Nuclear deterrence after World War II challenged philosophers from very different camps. Bertrand Russell (1872–1970) saw in it the threat of "extinction of the human species." According to German philosopher Karl Jaspers (1883–1969), the existence of the atomic bomb and the possibility of nuclear war marked a qualitatively new situa-tion: the threat of total annihilation of humankind caused by humans themselves. The risk of nuclear war raised metaphysical or existential questions. Jaspers saw the problem of nuclear war as closely related to the problem of totalitarian government. The West was faced with an alternative: either prepare to defend freedom with the risk of annihilation, or surrender to communist totalitarianism. For Jaspers, this is an alter-native between two sacrifices of not only political–rational, but also religious signifi-cance. The sacrifice of the whole of humanity for the sake of freedom only makes sense if human life is seen in relation to transcendence. Also, the new situation requires a conversion of human beings. The decisions of world politics hence reached dimensions similar to the myths of earlier times (e.g., about the Flood) and the challenge was not only to politics but also to the churches (see Jaspers 1961).

Hans Jonas (1903–93) saw a similar threat in the environmental crisis. His answer is a future-ethics of responsibility (Jonas 1984). Prototypical is the responsibility parents carry for their children. Jonas regards as the most fundamental ethical imper-ative the obligation for there to be future generations – not in the sense of an obliga-tion towards specific humans, but rather as an obligation towards the very idea of humankind.

As to the life conditions of future generations, one question is whether and how the present generation has any responsibility for the economic basis – the wealth – of their descendants. The question can be understood as one of *distributive justice* (i.e., of finding an ethically defensible distribution of the burdens and goods in society). Does it make sense to talk about a just distribution across generations? The concept of distributive justice has a long history within moral philosophy and religious ethics. Two important theories dominate contemporary philosophy: contractarianism and utilitarianism.

American philosopher John Rawls (1921–2002) constructed his theory of justice on the basis of the classical idea about the social contract (Rawls 1973) (see chapter 48). In order for political principles to express fairness, the contracting persons have to choose them under a "veil of ignorance" (i.e., ignorant as to their position – social and otherwise – within the future political order). According to Rawls, under these conditions, two principles of justice would be adopted: (1) equal rights of freedom for all, and (2) unequal distribution of goods and burdens only if all benefit, particularly the worst off. Among the things hidden under the veil of ignorance is the place of each contracting person in the order of generations. The problem of distribution is this: what is a fair share to leave for the following generation? According to Rawls, transmission of the "gains of culture and civilization," maintenance of "just institutions," and the saving of "a suitable amount of real capital accumulation" are required (Rawls 1973: 285). Even if the relation between the present generation and the following is asymmetric and non-reciprocal, just saving mirrors a kind of mutuality. In Rawls, the historical life of a people is seen as cooperation governed by the same principle of justice as that between contemporaries. One generation acting justly for future ones is an essential part of maintaining and improving a just social order.

For utilitarians, the goods to be distributed are amounts of "happiness," nowadays defined as preference satisfaction or interest fulfillment. The utilitarian concept of just distribution is not primarily based on equality, but rather on maximizing: the right way of acting is the one that leads to maximal interest fulfillment for all parties involved. The principle of utility is applied to *environmental* problems by Peter Singer. What kind of environment should the present generation hand over to future ones: should "wilderness," for example, be regarded as "world heritage"? According to utilitarianism, we should leave an environment that will create maximum interest fulfillment, perhaps in terms of enjoyment of nature (Singer 1993). But how can we know which kind of environment will bring enjoyment for future generations? They may have different preferences from ours. This is just one of the difficulties with which a utilitarian ethics for future generations is confronted.

The life conditions of future generations will to a large degree be determined by the number of inhabitants on the earth, hence there is also a *demographic* aspect to our problem. Global population growth will require increased production of food and goods, and will cause further exploitation of natural resources. Hence, it seems to be an obvious requirement to curb the growth of the world's population. Seemingly we have a moral obligation to limit the number of individuals in future generations. However, according to utilitarian ethics, this conclusion is not obvious at all. Utilitarianism has a clear stance on the future of humankind. It regards the extinction of human beings as the gravest crime, because it would entail a vast reduction of the possible sum of happiness. A crucial feature of contemporary ethics, Derek Parfit argues, is that it must take into account that human beings now live in large communities. This means that the negative effects of our acts spread over thousands of millions of people. This is the problem of future generations which, for Parfit, belongs to the most important part of ethics. What is required in this situation is a rational altruism which rejects the self-interest theory of rationality. Rational altruism means radical impartiality. In some cases that requires us to give up our preferential treatment of our own children in favor of acting for the best for all children (Parfit 1985).

Now, if quantity matters, as it essentially does in utilitarianism, a remarkable consequence regarding future generations seems to follow. For any size of the world population, growth would be preferable because that would cause a larger amount of lives worth living. Parfit calls this the "repugnant conclusion" because he admits that the theory he is looking for must avoid it. Even if Parfit has not found the theory required in order to improve non-religious ethics, he has sharpened our awareness of the kind of control we have over future people, and the new kinds of ethical problems that such control brings with it.

Human power over the future also lies in some of the possibilities biotechnology has brought with it. A couple making use of prenatal genetic testing might have the choice of either giving birth to a diseased child or having another child through a new pregnancy. Is this choice about either harming or benefiting a child? In whichever way we answer, the question is an indication of the new kinds of influence people have on future generations. Genetic testing has bearing not only on the parent–child relationship. According to many critics, it can rather be understood as a kind of *eugenics* (i.e., an effort to influence the genetic properties of future generations). Genetic testing and selective abortion would be an instance of negative eugenics. It would improve the genetic quality of the population by selecting away "bad genes." One important argument against this practice is that it contradicts the basic principle of equal human dignity.

Genetics holds promise not only for diagnosis but also for the treatment of diseases. Techniques of so-called gene therapy could not only be applied to diseases, but also be used for improving capacities such as intelligence, longevity, memory, etc. This future possibility for genetic enhancement gives rise to a moral dilemma. On the one hand, it seems natural for parents to give their children the best possible opportunities, and what could be better than the traits mentioned? On the other hand, the determination of crucial properties would give parents a power over the lives of other human beings that contradicts the basic principle of human freedom. This principle has been advanced by Jürgen Habermas in relation to both genetic enhancement and reproductive cloning. The successful application of these techniques would cause the birth of children, the genetic makeup of whom was intentionally designed by other human beings. According to Habermas (2003), this would be an elimination of the chance that is normally connected with reproduction to such a degree that both individual human freedom and a relationship of equality would be violated. This would deeply alter the moral self-understanding of the human species and in this sense influence future generations.

The philosophical theories mentioned in this section fall into three groups. In the first we find a philosopher (Jaspers) who explicitly represents a philosophical religion. Similarly, Jonas could be called a religiously inspired philosopher. In the second group we have philosophers of a Kantian type (Rawls and Habermas), whose theory could not be called religious. Yet they defend liberal positions that leave room for congenial religious arguments. Third, the utilitarian philosophers explicitly emphasize that they seek a non-religious moral theory.

Responses in Global Politics

The environmental threats to the future of humankind – overpopulation, pollution, and resource scarcity – have been on the agenda of global politics since the United

Nations Conference on Human Environment in Stockholm in 1972. In 1983 the UN created the World Commission on Environment and Development (called the Brundtland Commission, after its chairperson). The commission published its report, *Our Common Future*, in 1987. As a follow-up to the report, the UN organized the United Nations Conference on Environment and Development (UNCED) in Rio de Janeiro in 1992, followed by a conference on the same issues in Johannesburg in 2002.

The main ethical idea related to UNCED is "sustainable development." The statement of this idea explicitly mentions future generations: "a sustainable development is a development that fulfills present needs without putting the possibilities of future generations to fulfill their needs in danger." The idea expresses a principle of intra- and intergenerational justice. The primary needs to be met are those of the poor of the present world. The development necessary to achieve this should not, however, unjustly limit the fulfillment of the needs of future generations. The realization of sustainable development would require a universal effort directed at the common (future) good. The UN serves as a political–legal framework, however fragile, to achieve it.

Besides the official UN conference, the Rio summit hosted a great number of nongovernmental organizations (NGOs), among which were several religious communities. The World Council of Churches (WCC) held its own conference, Searching for the New Heaven and the New Earth. In a letter to the churches, the participants of the WCC conference emphasize the uniqueness of the historical situation: for the first time, the life-sustaining systems on the planet can be destroyed by human activity. "And the children, what shall we say to the children and to the future generations?" Christians are to work for a just, peaceful, and ecologically sustainable development in a life-oriented global community. The religious foundation of this global ethics lies in the Christian belief in the Holy Spirit. The power of the Spirit, the authors claim, permeates the whole of creation. Christians should develop a spirituality of creation. A life according to the Spirit would work for all that supports life, such as justice and peace, and fight against poverty and racism, etc. But because the Spirit is present in the whole of creation, spiritual life also means taking care of nature.

Christianity was of course not the only religion present at the 1992 Earth Summit. Among the non-governmental activities was a multi-religious manifestation celebrating the "sacredness of the earth." This event can be seen as an expression of the same idea as the one behind the project of a "world ethic" represented by the Christian theologian Hans Küng. According to Küng (1991), the global threats that put the very survival of humankind into question make necessary the establishment of a common global ethics in which all world religions should play a substantial role.

Conclusion: Why Should Religious People Care?

To skeptical eyes the "world ethic" project could be seen as an effort to instrumentalize religious ethics. The reasoning behind the project seems to be this: because of the grave global problems that threaten the very existence of future generations, we must create a common global ethics with elements from the main religions. Such a pragmatic attitude might conceal some of the theoretical problems inherent in religious ethics. In conclusion, I want to point at two examples of such problems.

1   The emphasis on the obligation to make possible future generations could be seen as an expression of an *anthropocentric* attitude. However, religions such as Hinduism and Buddhism are often regarded as favoring a *biocentric* view, seeing humans as just one kind of entities within the wholeness of being. And even if the Abrahamic religions can be understood in an anthropocentric way, they too think of the whole universe as God's creation and hence question the absolute value of human beings. In any case, the main religious traditions place a caveat on the idea of the survival of humankind as an absolute ethical obligation.

2   As mentioned in the beginning, religious doctrines essentially contain ideas of non-empirical reality and hence forms of existence that transcend the chain of generations. Non-empirical reality can be seen as a spiritual realm behind the illusion of the empirical world or as a future beyond worldly time. In either case, human bodily life is only given a relative position, and the existence of humankind is hardly seen as an end in itself.

The "relativity" of the existence of future generations that follows from both sets of ideas is, however, not the same as moral indifference. Even if this-worldly existence is not the final form of life, it is not without significance. That would be the consequence of asceticism. It is precluded by those religious doctrines that – like creation in Christianity – emphasize the God-givenness and goodness of human life on planet earth. As far as religious ethics is founded in this dual attitude – human life is significant, but not the final good – it could issue in a realistic ethics for the relationship to future generations. Even if religious believers realize that some day there will be no humans any longer, they take on the responsibility for creating the best conditions for their successors. They love their future neighbors as themselves.

Bibliography

Habermas, J. (2003): *The Future of Human Nature*. Oxford: Blackwell.

Jonas, H. (1984): *The Imperative of Responsibility: In Search of an Ethics for the Technological Age.* Chicago: University of Chicago Press.

Jaspers, K. (1961): *The Atom Bomb and the Future of Man*. Chicago: University of Chicago Press.

Küng, H. (1991): *Global Responsibility: In Search of a New World Ethic*. London: SCM Press.

Parfit, D. (1985): *Reasons and Persons*. Oxford: Oxford University Press.

Rawls, J. (1973): *A Theory of Justice*. Oxford: Oxford University Press.

Singer, P. (1993): *Practical Ethics*, 2nd edn. Cambridge: Cambridge University Press.

World Commission on Environment and Development (1987): *Our Common Future*. Oxford: Oxford University Press.

CHAPTER 53
Health

Katherine K. Young

Sickness destabilizes routines and undermines common assumptions. This view from the edge of experience makes people radically question life's meaning and purpose, bringing the spiritual dimension into clear focus. Something has been broken or disrupted – relationships with deities, ancestors, ghosts, demons, or just ordinary people – and must be fixed so that health and harmony are restored. The world is now scarred by massive human suffering: violence and war, widespread poverty and hunger, and also the spread of diseases such as AIDS and SARS on a global scale (see chapter 49). Can religious resources help us to deal ethically with these medical challenges today?

Religion, Health, and Ethics in the Premodern World

The religions of small-scale societies (hunters and gatherers, horticulturalists, and pastoralists), now called "primal," were often characterized by the perception of a shared life force, or power, which was common to people, ancestors, spiritual beings, and even objects of nature, thereby integrating society with both the natural and supernatural. This harmony was based on the kind of behavior (duties, services, and gifts) required for social order and for respecting the environment. If social harmony were not maintained, or if natural disaster were to strike, the result would have been disharmony. Although behavior was guided by sanctions based on collective experience, these sanctions were not formalized as "morality" in terms of commandments, decisions, or principles. When disease struck, people pondered broken taboos and tried to reestablish normal relations with the offended or disturbed powers. Sometimes, the cause of disease or death remained inscrutable. It was attributed to people, ancestors, or spiritual beings who were jealous, capricious, malicious, or aggressive.

    Large-scale societies developed more complex views of space and time (many realms and cycles of time). Some deities became supreme creators, providing the energy for cosmic renewal and prosperity, although they could be jealous and cause harm (such as disease and death), especially if they received no offerings. People believed in their need to sustain the deities by sacrifices (which recycled the power of death to provide health and life) and other rituals.

Gradually, religions developed soteriologies (the idea that ultimate destiny lies in a realm beyond ordinary space and time). Ethics was now related to the welfare of individuals beyond this life and not only to that of the group in this life. People believed that they would be rewarded for their good deeds or punished for their bad ones in another realm. In addition, these societies were more stable than earlier ones; people no longer worried that the sky would fall down if rituals were ignored or covenants broken. They produced more material resources than did earlier societies. This led to specialization, which led in turn to an explosion in knowledge based on observation, classification, and experimentation. The development of empirical medicine was part of this explosion. The ancient civilizations of Egypt and Mesopotamia were characterized by empirical interest in the physical body and its diseases (see the Egyptian "Smith" papyrus, the "Ebers" papyrus, and the Mesopotamian tablets). By the fourth century BCE dramatic advances were made in empirical medicine by the Greeks (the Hippocratic corpus), by the Indians (described in the Hindu Ayurvedic corpus and the Buddhist Pali Canon), and by the Chinese (the Yellow Emperor's Classic of Internal Medicine). These texts classify diseases in ways akin to modern ones (internal medicine; diseases of the eye, nose, ear, and throat; surgery; toxicology; psychology; pediatrics; infectious diseases; surgery; and so forth). Somewhat later, Islamic scholars made major contributions. Ibn Sina (Avicenna, d. 1037), for instance, wrote a monumental encyclopedia on medicine.

Religious communities recognized the effectiveness and power of empirical medicine. They trained physicians and nurses, became custodians of medicines and medical libraries, and eagerly sought out the expertise of other traditions. Greeks borrowed from Egyptian and Mesopotamian medicine, Romans from Greeks, and Hindus and Buddhists from each other. So did Christians, Muslims, and Jews. In the early middle ages, for instance, Jewish and Muslim physicians were trained in Alexandria, Constantinople, and some surviving Roman cities of Italy and southern France. Abu Ya'qub Ishak ibn Sulaiman al-Israeli (ca. 855–955) wrote on medicine. His works were then translated from Arabic into both Hebrew and Latin. Other Jews translated and wrote commentaries on Ibn Sina's Al-Qanun fi al-Tibb. Maimonides (1135–1204) was not only a philosopher and legal authority but also the personal physician of Sultan Saladin, his family, his harem, and his officials in Egypt.

The development of empirical medicine challenged religious explanations of disease and religious treatments and cures. Religious explanations, for example, often said that illness was divine punishment for sin and health the reward for observance of religious rites and moral precepts (although the latter was sometimes internalized as in the Hindu law of karma, which stated "as you sow, so you reap" or the biblical phrase "those who sow the wind shall reap the whirlwind"). By contrast, empirical medicine generally focused on the body and gave material explanations for disease, such as improper diet. There were other conflicts between medicine and religion. In medieval Christianity, for instance, the church considered confession a potential means of cure, so physicians were obliged to call priests. But what could physicians do if patients refused to see priests? And what were patients to think if they realized that their physicians could offer them no hope?

People tried to avoid clashes and to gain the benefits of both approaches, because everyone recognized that medicine had its benefits and its limits. One approach was *metaphoric and practical appropriation*. The practical interest in empirical medicine in Buddhist monasteries, for example, was closely linked with basic Buddhist teachings. The Four Noble Truths were the four principles of medicine: cause, symptom, cure, and non-recurrence. The five basic medicines were the Buddhist concepts of faith, energy, mindfulness, concentration, and wisdom. And enlightenment was the permanent cure for life itself. The spread of Mahāyāna Buddhism into East and Southeast Asia in the first several centuries of the common era was related to its knowledge of empirical medicine. Despite its early emphasis on spiritual healing, Christianity had by the fourth century integrated rudimentary hospitals under the supervision of local bishops. Healing shrines were like hospitals; attending priests had medical skills ranging from rudimentary to expert.

There was also *compartmentalization* – placing a specific medical procedure in a larger religious context of incantations, prayers, rituals, astrology, and so forth. Supreme deities were the ultimate power that defined life and death; the ultimate cause of health and sickness, and the ultimate source of therapies and cures; physicians were agents or servants of the deity. That said, medicine was allowed to operate semi-autonomously.

Yet another approach was *complementary functionalism*. This was used in ancient Mesopotamia and Egypt, Greece, India, and elsewhere. It was based on a functional division between two types of medicine. Empirical medicine dealt with visible, proximate, or natural causes, whereas religious medicine dealt with invisible or supernatural ones. The two were complementary.

Closely related to this approach was *pragmatism*: recognizing all healers and types of medicine as potentially useful. There are many accounts of people seeking both empirical and religious cures.

Finally, there was always *hermeneutical adjustment*: interpreting religious passages by allegory (as Maimonides and Falaquera did in the thirteenth century), simile, levels of meaning, and so forth. In religiously controlled societies, nonetheless, religious approaches trumped empirical ones. During the medieval period, for instance, Christianity – through its clergy, sacraments, and saints – created a chain of dependence for spiritual/miraculous healing. Sacraments became the means by which God's superabundant grace and power were channeled to protect and heal patients. Baptism and exorcism repelled evil spirits that caused sickness. Confession and communion purified people and thus protected them against disease. In medieval India as well, empirical medicine receded to the background as religion came to the foreground.

Attempts to prevent serious conflict between empirical medicine and religion were successful, by and large, in the premodern period. Although both medicine and religion had tried to marginalize magic, it did not disappear completely. Many Christians, Jews, Muslims, and other Near Eastern groups continued to believe in demons or demonesses as causes of illness. Therefore, they continued to use incantations, amulets, magical mirrors, dream interpretations, or astrological, palm, or magic bowl "readings" for cures. Hindus, Buddhists, Taoists, Confucians, and others maintained similar beliefs and practices. These became especially important during individual, familial, or social crises, when all else failed.

It is striking that most of these civilizations considered harmony a key concept of health and well-being. The Greeks, Hindus, and Buddhists, for instance, all believed that good health required a balance of fluids in the body, which in turn had to be balanced with the mind and the environment. The Chinese version was a system of correspondences, harmony requiring the health not only of the body but also that of the state.

Closely related to the topic of health and religion is that of medical ethics. As early as Egypt's Old Kingdom (3400–2474 BCE), problems were debated in the Memphite Drama and the Proverbs of Ptahhotep. Physicians from this time had to deal with both the power and the precariousness of medicine. This involved four basic problems.

First, should physicians offer treatment or not? The common answer was yes, but only for cases that could probably be alleviated or cured; involvement in hopeless cases would make medicine appear ineffective, after all, and thus a form of quackery, or even dangerous. Epidemics were particularly troublesome in this respect: Should physicians flee or stay and care for the sick?

Second, how could physicians distinguish themselves from quacks (of which there were many)? The common solution, both Western and Eastern, was the development of semi-religious professional guilds. These established and monitored standards of education (a good knowledge base, critical approach, precise memory, and perseverance); personal behavior (virtues such as truth, peace, charity, spirituality, and control over anger, envy, and pride); practice (decorum to protect the reputations of women or the privacy of the household); and visible symbols of dress. Finally, they instituted rites of initiation and oaths such as those of Hippocrates (Greek), Asaph (Jewish), Caraka (Hindu), Ahwazi (Islamic), and Enjuin (Japanese Buddhist). One important function of the oath was to check violence (by condemning assisted death, including abortion) and to uphold the foundational principle of the sanctity of life and non-injury (ahiṃsā, for instance, in Hinduism and Buddhism) aside from the few permitted exceptions.

Third, what could be done about the arrogance and greed of physicians? They were warned directly against these vices and taught virtues such as restraint and humility in texts such as the Egyptian Proverbs of Ptahhotep, the Greek Precepts (which advised physicians not to begin consultations by discussing fees, because that would hurt their reputation), and the Buddhist Pali Canon (which eventually prevented the public practice of medicine by monks and nuns because of charges of greed).

Fourth, how could patients be assured of access to medicine? Quite apart from the unwillingness of physicians to treat the dying in order to protect their professional reputations, there were other reasons for denying people access to medical care. Sometimes this was for religious reasons, such as notions of impurity. And sometimes this was for secular reasons, such as punishment of social deviants and political enemies or indifference to the poor. Many states tried to overcome the latter. According to the Mesopotamian Code of Hammurabi, for instance, physicians should charge patients according to type of procedure, economic class, and likelihood of success or failure. The Hippocratic Precepts advised physicians to consider the ability of patients to pay them and extend care to strangers and paupers even if they could pay nothing. And the Hindu Susruta exempted fees from groups such as elders, ascetics, and teachers; moreover, it encouraged care of the indigent out of compassion. Religions encouraged or mandated charity, requesting physicians to treat the poor for minimal costs or without charge, and to look for eternal rewards rather than merely material ones. Religions structured by universalism (Buddhism, Christianity, Islam) sometimes advocated universal medical care (the bodhisattvas in Mahāyāna Buddhism, for instance, were examples of compassion *par excellence*, in the disguise of physicians extending medical care to all or kings building hospitals to help the poor). Though promoted, universal access to medical care was hard to accomplish. By the twelfth century in the West, for instance, despite the admonitions by both ecclesiastical authorities and guilds to treat all patients, many physicians still did not do so. Universal religions increased access also by offering medicine to potential converts, including those of low status.

Any discussion of medical ethics requires some account of gender (see chapter 54). Women were usually barred from the profession of empirical medicine (as physicians or nurses) and often had less access to medical treatment as well. This was probably due to at least four factors.

First, because elite women in traditional societies were often sequestered, they lacked opportunities for education in empirical medicine. Some women had expertise in folk medicine, and some women became midwives, but they are not mentioned in medical works, although we have a few works by men on the medical problems of women. But there were some exceptions to the exclusion of women. Buddhist and Christian nuns were often educated women and interested in medicine; sometimes, they carried the practice of medicine into the secular realm. When Christian women came to India during the colonial period, for instance, many practiced nursing and trained their Indian female converts to do the same, because Hindu women had been restricted by purity and seclusion regulations.

Second, because elite women were often sequestered, in their homes, they could not practice empirical medicine if that involved moving about in public. As a result, male physicians and nurses treated women – but only in the presence of their guardians, to avoid charges of impropriety (which might have made them reluctant to attend to women at all).

Third, because women seldom controlled finances, they lacked the means to obtain medical help for themselves (and their female children). Even when concepts of charity existed, elite women could not access it because of their status.

Fourth, in some societies, women probably received less medical care than boys and men because of "son preference," an idea with religious authority, which might have originated as a way to compensate for the greater loss of male life in pregnancy and early childhood. This still occurs in the rural areas of countries such as India and can have a profound effect on the health (and lives) of girls and women.

Hence, we see both the problem of "access" and the question of the "good physician" found throughout the history of religion and health. Although these premodern civilizations were strikingly similar in some ways when it came to the interaction between religion and health, they were strikingly different in other ways. Two patterns stand out. One is that of "ethnic religions" such as ancient Judaism, Shinto, and elite Hinduism – especially their priestly traditions. These defined identity by birth and by degree of purity. As a result, insiders (those who followed the norms or laws) were separated from outsiders (those who did not). In the context of medicine, this meant that ritual sites or temples were defined as pure, and so the sick or deformed were prevented from defiling them. Priests were carefully distinguished from physicians. In Hinduism, "priestly physicians" who catered to the elite were of ambiguous status because of their contact with the impurity of disease. All this has had profound impact on access to medical care, although most of these religions have either changed to become more accommodating (rabbinic Judaism and bhakti Hinduism) or have developed complementary relations with other religions (as Shinto has with Buddhism, which focuses on "impure" death and dying).

Another general pattern in premodern civilizations is that of "universalistic religions" such as Hellenistic religion, Islam, Christianity, Buddhism (especially Mahāyāna), and Taoism. These emphasized virtues such as charity, love, mercy, or compassion. They often proselytized among marginal groups, including women and the sick, offering access to medical care as a perk of conversion. Consequently, their holy places were sites of healing that provide access to empirical and/or religious cures and therapies. Their religious leaders were often healers.

But these distinctions often blurred in these premodern, complex traditions, because most developed both ethnic and universal traits. In general, we see that as human beings develop more control over life, they worry less about the capriciousness of deities or demons and rely less on magic, although that often changes in periods of warfare, societal breakdown, or natural disasters. Some archaic ideas remain (such as the idea of harmony as health, disharmony as disease), but others gradually decline (viewing sacrifice as a way to tap the power of death to provide health and life).

Religion and Health in the Modern Period

Many themes and challenges found in the premodern world – suffering and human meaning, the relation between empirical medicine and religion, and medical ethics – have continued and intensified in the modern period. This is certainly the case with empirical medicine. The scientific revolution of the seventeenth century emphasized knowledge based on observation, description, classification (which led to new disciplines), reason, experimentation (with verifiable results through repetition), and prediction. But it resulted also in a new worldview, because facts, theories, and truth became separated from ethics, philosophy, and teleology (ultimate human meaning and purpose). The body became only a natural system or, thanks to the Industrial Revolution, a "machine" (see chapter 46). Good health was indicated by a well-functioning body, in other words, and disease or pathology by a malfunctioning one; medicine was now strictly a science and technology, not the functional complement of religion. All this contributed to the view that nature, religion, and society were distinct spheres. Only in nature, however, was truth to be discovered.

Once again, religions tried to come to terms with the conflicts between medicine and religion, even though the conflict was now so extreme that the very value of religion itself was challenged. Many Protestants accepted the virtual autonomy of modern medicine by supporting medical advances and the professionalism of physicians apart from the church, practicing medicine with a general sense of "calling" but without much ecclesiastical control. They understood this new scientific medicine as a way to express the healing ministry of Christ. (Other Protestants, especially those called Charismatics, rejected many claims of modern science and revived the idea of spiritual healings and gifts of the Holy Spirit, which had its basis in the healing ministry of Jesus.) Roman Catholicism accepted a multi-level conceptualization (the reality of scientific explanations but also the idea that God permeates all biochemical and biophysical processes). Religions such as Islam, Hinduism, Buddhism, and Confucianism faced even more problems with modernity in general and the scientific revolution in particular, because these were foreign developments introduced into their countries by colonial powers and their missionaries, who criticized their cultures as scientifically backward, socially unjust, and religiously too other-worldly.

The initial response of most Asian religions was to compartmentalize the two domains under the dictum "Western science, Eastern religion." Hindus – who had already learned about Western medicine under Islamic rule (Muslims, remember, had preserved and refined Western medicine through several centuries) – took other approaches as well. One was syncretism, long a Hindu strategy of dealing with cultural contact and challenge. Another was reconciliation, arguing that Hindu religion and philosophy had prefigured modern science. Still another was that Ayurveda, the traditional medicine, should be kept pure and isolated from foreign influences. As a result, Ayurveda is still practiced in the villages of India and learned in traditional schools. It is professionalizing and modernizing with government support, however, integrating aspects of Western medicine (called allopathy) such as antibiotics, and growing in popularity because of its traditional fluidity between empirical medicine and religion, mind and body, psychology and physiology, physicians and religious healers. Even those Westernized urban and educated Indians who have access to the more expensive allopathy sometimes turn to Ayurveda for chronic and terminal illnesses and culturally specific problems – a modern version of complementary functionalism. The Indian system today is best characterized as pluralistic (Ayurveda and allopathy along with homeopathy and naturopathy).

Contemporary Buddhists, too, have also responded to criticisms. Socially engaged Buddhism has emerged along with a renewed interest in empirical medicine. Some Buddhist countries have developed pluralistic approaches like that of India, whereas others (such as Sri Lanka) have officially chosen Western medicine after independence. As for China, in 1929 the Guomindang government restricted traditional Chinese medicine. But during the Long March of 1934–5, Mao Zedong, the leader of the new communist movement, and his army had to rely on traditional medicine in the countryside. Impressed with its effects, Mao later championed native medicine, which led to research. China operates today with several medical systems (some of which maintain religious explanations for diseases, such as sin, demonic attacks, deviation from norms, or malevolence from the living or the dead).

Religions and Contemporary Challenges in the Period of Globalization

Although it seemed for a while in the West that religion was being marginalized from modern ideas of health and disease, we now find growing interest in religious views. Chronic and terminal illnesses still remain beyond the capacities of modern medicine to "fix," reminding people that life is still finite and therefore raising again perennial questions about its purpose and meaning. Additionally, many secular people want orientations that are personal, holistic, and spiritual, rather than institutional. They see this in some traditional religio-medical practices. This signals a renewed appreciation of religious notions of harmony and integration with nature (often associated with primal religions) and premodern notions of "integral" paths (be they the Sharī'a of Islam, the Halakhah of Judaism, or the many yogas of Hinduism and Buddhism) which place health and ethics within a larger context of meaning and concept of harmony. If this trend continues, then the relation between religion and medicine will be a thing not only of the past but also one of the emerging global, interdependent world.

The ethical question that remains is how to mobilize religious resources to ensure universal access to healthcare. In this context, it is important to remember that, even in societies that were hierarchical in the past (such as Hinduism), there are resources for concepts of reciprocity and human rights (the law of karma, for instance, recognizes capacity for self-determination, agency, and impartial justice); there is a general rule of equal distribution (*sarvam syadasrutitvat*) in the absence of express provision to the contrary; there is a limit to autonomy in the need to prevent harm to others (*ahiṃsā*); and there is a recognition that rights and duties are correlative (although Hinduism, like most premodern religions, prefers to focus on duties and a middle path between radical autonomy and extreme collectivism).

Because suffering and death pose the ultimate questions, which must be given meaning, there will likely always be an attraction to religions and ways will continue to be found for some kind of mutual respect and functional complementarity between religion and empirical medicine, especially in the area of palliative care. Because ethics will always be at the interface of religion and medicine, moreover, the need for creative cooperation between the two will continue. And because most of the world's population still have religious identities and the continuity of identity is important in a postcolonial age of globalization, we can predict that the connection of religion, health, and ethics will remain for this reason too.

Bibliography

Camenisch, P. F. (ed.) 1994: *Religious Methods and Resources in Bioethics*. Chicago: Kluwer Academic Publishers.

Kinsley, D. 1996: *Health, Healing, and Religion: A Cross-Cultural Perspective*. Englewood Cliffs, NJ: Prentice-Hall.

Reich, W. T. (ed.) 1995: *Encyclopedia of Bioethics*. New York: Simon & Schuster/Macmillan.

Unschuld, P. U. 1976–7: "World Views and Concepts of Health Care in China and Europe." *History of Traditional Medicine: Proceedings of the 1st and 2nd International Symposia on the Comparative History of Medicine – East and West*. Susuno-shi, Shizuoka, Japan: Division of Medical History, Taniguchi Foundation.

CHAPTER 54
Body Culture

Regina Ammicht-Quinn

Life Imprisonment

"Plotinus, the philosopher of our day, was a man who was ashamed of being in the body" (Weischedel 1974: 82–106). The founder of the Neoplatonic school of philosophy, Plotinus, we are told, never mentioned his origins, parents, or birthday, the day when the soul entered the body, so that nobody would be tempted to celebrate this unfortunate day. As far as possible he tried to ignore his body and his bodily needs. In consequence, at the end of his life his students left him because his body, putrid and festering, nauseated them.

In the history of philosophy, Plotinus embodies a third-century renaissance and to some degree a simplification of Platonic ideas. True reality and real truth cannot be found in the material world but only in the realm of the spirit. Plotinus, for his part, was a highly respected teacher; even the emperor and his spouse attended his lectures. He must have put a finger on the pulse of his time. And his time was the crucial constituting time for the Christian church. At about the same time, the Christian thinker Origen states: "God created the present world and he chained the soul to the body for punishment." Origen formulates an early Christian version of what is later called *anthropological dualism*. Anthropological dualism teaches not only the gap between body and soul, matter and immateriality, but also an active state of war between those two, with frequent surprise attacks: ascetic attacks on the body by the soul, ecstatic attacks on the soul by the body. The victory is an uncertain one, not finally decided until after death. For the soul is imprisoned in the body.

Contempt of the body can lead to the dissolution of human community. This dissolution is only part – and the lesser part – of a whole conception of life that views bodily life as life imprisonment. The soul only lives behind the body's bars, doomed without domicile. The other, material part of existence is part burden and part threat, sometimes only strange, but normally hostile territory.

Body Project

From the point of view of the Western industrialized world, Plotinus appears strange. It is not only our obsession with hygiene which makes us mentally step back from him. Our time's *zeitgeist* seems to require the opposite to what the third century's *zeitgeist* suggested. In a historically unique way, today the body has shifted to the center of a person's and a society's life plan. In contemporary Western urban culture, churches and museums have been superseded by fitness studios. They are now the privileged places of a self-improvement doctrine which one dutifully visits even if those visits are bound up with troubles and inconveniences (Shusterman 1995: 242).

One of the main features of a contemporary lifestyle is being occupied with the body. This occupation not only generates a whole (media, beauty, and health) industry, but is also inclined to serve needs that traditional religious or secular institutions (churches and museums) increasingly fail to satisfy: needs for wholeness, beauty, salvation. Now all bodies, not only female bodies, are status symbols. To be young, to be beautiful, and to be fit – these are the goals for "good," "successful" embodiment. This represents an essentially new step towards an interpretation of the body. Bodies no longer just exist: they are good or bad, successful or unsuccessful. The body is no longer simply fate, better here, worse there: the body is a result of what I have done or what I have not done but could or should have done, a result of action (see chapter 3). In this way the body as a whole becomes an essential moral issue. Today, the body demands not just attention but also action. It is this action which leads to a body culture, the body culture generates a body cult, and the body cult establishes the body as a project.

This body project has one goal: perfection – specifically, a perfect design. Like every design project, the body design project is concerned with two issues: function and aesthetics. These two basic questions which determine the body design project have a clear gender component: (1) the aesthetic design problem refers, not exclusively but predominantly, to the female body; (2) the functional design problem refers, also not exclusively but predominantly, to the "neutral" body, which is in perception the "normal" and thus the male body.

The functional design project: neutral/male bodies

In 1956 Günther Anders talked about the "Antiquiertheit des Menschen" (antiquity of mankind) (Anders1956). A half-century later he seems to be totally up to date. The human, living, fallible and mortal body proves to be highly inadequate, in need of improvement and with the chance to be improved. The biotechnological goal to diminish human suffering often is suffused with a not-so-explicit goal: human perfection, primarily seen as a body's perfection.

In transportation and communication, the body has been marginalized; in leisure culture the body is centralized: in sports, fitness, wellness, body-based therapies. When the task is important, prostheses as artificial replacements of body parts take over the body functions (Virilio 1994). These are the well-known prostheses of muscular strength, machines and vehicles; these are the prostheses of our sense organs, say microscopes or seismographs; and these are the prostheses of the brain. This prosthetics of the brain occurs when we delegate our ability to calculate and to remember to the computer (see chapter 46). It occurs more radically when organic and artificial nerve systems are neurologically combined, in DNA-based computers or silicon brain implants. While public awareness has focused on bioethical problems, a new line of research has been established. Biophysical research with help of nanotechnology aims at the merging of mind and machine (Brooks 2002). "Imagine a brain," said Peter Cochrane, head of research at British Telecommunications, "which is able to process data at high speed, which won't show symptoms of decline – and which has a delete-key . . . Who could withstand this enhancement of our finally and fundamentally limited humanity?" (*Newsweek* 22/3/99).

In this extensive prosthetic effort the difference between subject and object, between those who act and their auxiliary means, is becoming more and more vague. The body, dependent upon prostheses, can imperceptibly change into a part of the prostheses.

One of the pioneers of theoretical cybernetics, Norbert Wiener, used the formula "one man – one message" (Wiener 1958). This formula is an expression of the idea that there is an "essence" of persons which is based not in the body but in independent bodiless information, stored in genetic material or simply in the brain. This equation of man and unembodied message takes on a new form in cyberspace. "There is no matter here. Our identities have no bodies," wrote John Perry Barlow in his *Declaration of Independence of Cyberspace* (1996). The independence of cyberspace refers especially to one fact: an independence from the unreliable and inadequate meatware. The next and highly desirable evolutionary step will be "to download the brain into the computer and thus liberate it from the weakness of human flesh" (Jastro, cited in Meier-Seethaler 2001).

The distant Plotinus seems to be near. The immortal soul has changed into the spirit floating in the web, liberated from the inadequate, embarrassing body.

The aesthetic design project: female bodies

Although the aesthetic question tends to spread out and concern male bodies, too, we will focus on the female body. Beauty as an (exchange) value on the market, traditionally on the marriage market but today also on the employment market, is a historically new development in the West, dating back to the late eighteenth and the nineteenth centuries. Before the Industrial Revolution, beauty was not simply neglectable, but had a different function in a society's communication. Beauty was an adornment, a pleasant and enchanting ornament that was added to the real criteria for judging women, such as the ability to reproduce, the ability to work, and place in the social hierarchy which indicates the extent of the dowry. Beauty is added to these criteria but does not replace them. Such replacement always has been the fabric that novels and fairy tales are made of.

The more the public and the private sphere are divided since the eighteenth century, the more a new culture of homemaking develops with a cult of beauty. This beauty cult is supported and enforced by the new possibilities of reproducing ideal female images on daguerreotypes, ferrotypes, and photographs – and by the fact that at the end of the nineteenth century middle-class homes were equipped with mirrors. The beauty cult is based on the presupposition that there is such a thing as a universal and objective quality named beauty. For women, striving after this quality named beauty is equally a public task and a natural inclination. Beauty as currency functions when women strive to possess beauty and other people or institutions strive to possess women who possess beauty.

In consequence, the function of what Naomi Wolf (1991) calls the "beauty myth" is neither exclusively nor primarily aesthetic. The beauty myth developed together with the new achievements of middle-class women of the nineteenth and early twentieth centuries, like education, leisure, and relative freedom from material needs. The myth acts as counterpart against those potentially dangerous achievements. The endless Sisyphus-like activity of earning a living and working in the house is replaced or complemented by the endless Sisyphus-like activity of maintaining one's beauty. Thus the energies of educated women who can not at all or only incompletely participate in public life are successfully absorbed.

During the 1920s a new image of the female body emerged in European and Anglo-American cultures: the body became thin. At the same time, in most Western countries women were granted the right to vote. A new part of the world opened up for them. And yet a new and highly individualized prison was established: their bodies. One's own body is not able to achieve the normative standards that become ever more strict. The numbers during puberty are alarming: at age 13, 53 percent of the girls are unhappy with their body; at age 17, 78 percent. A 1984 survey of 33,000 women says that 45 percent of the women between 18 and 35 who were underweight thought of themselves as too fat. A majority of the women said they would prefer to loose 10 or 15 pounds rather than have success at work or satisfaction in love (Wolf 1991: 185–6).

What does "aesthetic" mean in the current body project? Female fat, for a good part of human history a sign and symbol of female eroticism and female sexuality, has become in the industrialized countries a question of morality. Female fat is associated with dirt. The struggle for purity used to take place in the home and in the soul; now it takes place in the body. The body becomes a privileged place for feelings of guilt. As the quest for genital chastity has become weaker, this quest has shifted in a regressive way from the genitals to the oral area. "I'm a girl who just can't say no," says a model in a commercial for a low calorie dessert. Salvation is asked for – and salvation is promised by two of the large women-oriented growing businesses: dietary products and cosmetics. To achieve salvation, quasi-religious rites have to be performed with and on the body. A diet cycle imitates the Christian Easter cycle – or other religious rites of renunciation – with acts of critical self-reflection, self-flagellation, penance, and liberation. The cosmetic industry playfully uses associations of victories over mortality and damnation, promising rebirth and eternity. One of the presuppositions is the ritual anointment with oils whose actual ingredients cost 10 percent of the actual price (Wolf 1991: 107–21). The superfluous value that suggests a certain holiness of those products is a question of belief; overall, the products seem to be new editions of letters of indulgence because in both cases, guilt is settled with money.

Plotinus, and with him some of the early Christian theologians, could not feel more strange than in our department stores' cosmetic departments. And yet there seems to be a subliminal relationship. The aesthetic design project of the body claims, not unlike

Plotinus, that the body itself is bad. But it doesn't help anymore to neglect it; instead, it has to be severely disciplined and tortured, with the slim hope that the results might be deemed "good." The functional design project of the body claims, not unlike Plotinus, that the body in itself is inadequate and useless. Its functions have to be enhanced – or the body, as mortal substance, has to be replaced.

In these ongoing efforts to perfect the body, however, the body cult becomes ambivalent. The body cult whose god is the body that you worship and to whom you sacrifice easily shifts into body contempt or body hate because the body will never succeed in maintaining the standards of a normative aesthetic and, being fallible and mortal, never will achieve the desired standards of functionality. Thus the body cult finally declares the body a handicap.

The Christian Body: Despised and Healed

Visible behind all the worship and all the sacrifices which shape the actual body cult is a profound contempt of the body that allows comparisons to religious traditions and their disciplinary practices. Here we will explore strands in Western Christianity. Emerging in late antiquity, there was a primal fear of the human drives; in those human drives sin itself is incorporated. The visible, touchable, and understandable locus of this struggle with sin is the body. The means and possibilities to act against that sin are based in the body.

Fasting, self-flagellation, practices of mortification, all with a history, are aimed against the individual body and its willful desires. The struggle, however, is not only a struggle *against* something but also a struggle *for* something; namely, the life of the soul. Thus, one level of Christian tradition produces a decided contempt and repression of the body. In order to achieve a higher good, the victory over the body has to be won, in every case a moral sort of victory.

Most post-religious societies know body practices that show a strange similarity to Western practices in Christian tradition, frequently repressing and despising the body. Fasting has become part of an industry and a way of living; certain forms of self-torture are called "exercise" or "fitness." In modern secular societies this structure leads to a circular argumentation. The battle against the body in order to achieve some sort of a higher good is no longer a battle in favor of the soul, but a battle in favor of the body – in favor of the new and perfect body. This new and perfect body bears expectations for salvation that formerly belonged to the soul. The postmodern secular body cult seemingly views the fallible, aging, and coveting body as an object of loathing and rejection, as enemy. The body must be controlled, tamed, toned, and upgraded in order to become a new, quasi-reincarnated body. The struggle against the body in favor of the body is a never ending one, a never ending story of remorse, penance, and new beginnings based on a far away utopia of a better and finally good life.

This Christian tradition that perceives the body as a soul's dungeon is not the only Christian tradition we have, nor is every form of asceticism to be perceived as repressing or despising the body. It is time to reconsider the strong connection between asceticism and pleasure. The question is why the structure of a body-repressing tradition has emerged in the postmodern culture – and not other, equally or more important structures.

Living in a culture that has established a body cult and within that body cult a view of the body as handicap, we might be able to read biblical texts in a new way. Only on a second reading do we discover how deeply concerned the biblical texts are with the integrity and the well-being of bodies. For instance, 31 percent of the text of the gospel of Matthew (209 out of 660 verses) speaks of miracles and those miracle stories are mostly healing stories. Our modern Western difficulties with healing stories as miracles often overshadow the picture that seems to be central for the texts themselves: Jesus healing people.

Jesus' healings take place amid a culture where such healings and such healers are common. The healings achieve their specific meaning as they combine apocalyptic thinking and miracle charisma, the apocalyptic expectation of future salvation and this salvation's episodic realization (Theißen 1974: 276). "If I cast out devils by the Spirit of God [Lk.: with the finger of God], then the Kingdom of God is come unto you" (Mt. 12:8; Lk. 11:20). This logion is in historical critical research widely considered as authentic (Bultmann 1964: 174). More interesting, however, are its rhetorical implications: the logion provides the reader with an interpretation of the act by the actor. Deciphering this hermeneutical "code," it becomes obvious that the connection between healing and the Kingdom of God, healing and salvation, is a direct and a necessary one. Healings are the manifestations of God's kingdom which has begun now and which is revealed in who Jesus is and in what he does.

The *context* which makes the *text* of Jesus' healings understandable is an eschatological context. And inversely this eschatological *context* is specified, stamped, and concretized by the *text* of the healings. Healings and the salutariness which they provide are the concrete and body-based aspect of the promised salvation. That there is a concrete and body-based aspect of salvation at all might be no surprise for those whose faith is rooted in an Exodus tradition; for a Christian tradition colored in large part by an anthropological dualism, it is surprising news until today, immediately evident maybe only for those who are – then and today – blind and bent, lame and leprous, deaf, sick, bleeding, and possessed with demons.

This shows a characteristic feature of the healings' text: healings are not forced or violent acts, but a specific answer to a specific question. They do not create faith, but they presuppose faith. Already in the New Testament we discover a tendency to split *text* and *context*, healing and teaching and therefore healing and salvation. If we look at the healings no longer as the apocalyptic restoration of the creation in and for persons, but primarily as miracles, the hermeneutical point and the possible understanding are changing. The Kingdom of God, as the *context* for the teaching, loses its body-based aspect and its bodily roots and tends to present itself in an abstract way. The *texts* function as proof and legitimation and tend to be functionalized beyond men and women's bodies.

Body Ethics

On this background and in this horizon of meaning the question about body and ethics reappears in a new way. On different levels this is a central question, most obvious since in Western societies there is a precarious social and cultural development. We experience the functional deficiency and the resulting marginalization of the body in many fields of everyday life, while at the same time the body cult strives for perfection. This is – in theory and practice – a fragile construction: the search for perfection can easily end in destruction. Massive somatic and psychosomatic disorders result from an almost epidemic discontent with the body. On another level compassion with another's fallible and mortal bodily life can easily – by means of politics, research or simple, social pressure – be outdated and replaced by a despising moral reproach: You – or your parents – could have known and done better; nobody to blame but yourself.

In this situation ethical reflection is confronted with unsolved questions which ask for reflection, critique, and projection of new images of embodied human life. At the metaethical level we discover that the body always was central in moral praxis and ethical reflection. The central ethical questions are the questions of what stimulates life and what destroys life. If this central status of the body in ethical reflection is recognized we regain basic ethical categories which are bodily categories: birth – pleasure – pain – death. These coordinates of embodied human life are not only phenomenological but also ethical categories. They are ethical categories insofar as they increasingly become the focus of individual and social action with an increasingly louder question: Do we need those categories to describe human life or could it be nicer, more convenient, more promising, if humankind would succeed in severely controlling and finally abolishing them? Birth, pleasure, pain and death are ethical categories because they reveal something about us; they "talk" about the locus where humankind has to decide what is human, and they "talk" about the price human societies and human individuals would have to pay in denying them.

The urgent actual ethical questions are in a vast part connected with and related to the body. This is true not only for problems of sexuality, the beginning and ending of life, and all bioethical questions, but also beyond these, questions about work, technologies, and communication, and the question of justice and distribution.

Within a situation where the cause of insecurity and profound unhappiness is increasingly seldom moral repression and quite often moral arbitrariness or relativism – relativism that can present itself as cultural sensibility – we have the chance to preserve ethical universalism without denying the postmodern context if we take recourse to bodily ethical categories (see chapter 14). Moral responsibility is no longer bound to the question: "Do you look how I think you should? Do you function how I assume?" And not even to the question: "Do you believe and desire what I believe and desire?" The crucial question to take regarding moral responsibility would be: "Are you suffering?" (Rorty 1989: 198).

What is the Ethical Task?

Ethical reflection on the body and bodily life is an exercise in ambivalence. One cannot outrun the ambivalence because it permeates personal experience, social analysis, moral and theological reflection, a tradition's past and present. Thus the exercise in ambivalence can't be an exercise against ambivalence; it is rather an exercise in giving meaning to ambivalence and therefore being able to live with ambivalence.

The Christian tradition provides us with a strong guiding idea. Christianity's basic truth, its essence, is incarnation. God becomes man – or, more precisely, God becomes flesh. Only when one removes the haze, the aestheticizing filter from centuries of theological and liturgical speech about this word can one rediscover that it is an offensive, even shocking word. First of all, it was said during a time when the surrounding cultures emphasized the spirit, immateriality. During Jesus' time, "salvation" would have been expected to overcome the world, the body, the material. Salvation was to be experienced in overcoming everything worldly. Secondly, the word is drastic. The center of the gospel tells us not – like some later theologians – that God puts on a body and takes it off again like some piece of useful but discardable clothing. God does not put on a bodily cover in order to temporarily meet humankind in a human way. God becomes flesh. The occidental Christian suspicion and mistrust toward the body seem to be the huge and tragic misunderstanding in Christianity.

Today, the ethical task is to outline new images of men's and women's bodies, images which are alive, not machine-like and not eternal, not hurt, not damaged, not disabled by aesthetic or functional myths, but healed. If we realize the actual body cult's theological background it would no longer be necessary to stylize fitness studios as new churches of self-improvement, to reactualize the questions of sin, repentance, atonement, and resurrection using diet recipes and beauty myths. In theological terms, salvation would not take place beyond our heads and not beyond our bodies. The old and new shame of being in the body could gradually give way, despite and because of our mortality, to the pleasure of being in the body.

Bibliography

Ammicht Quinn, R. 2003: *Koerper – Religion – Sexualitaet. Theologische Reflexion zur Ethik der Geschlechter*. Mainz: Gruenewald.

Anders, G. 1956: *Die Antiquiertheit des Menschen, Vol. 2: Ueber die Zerstoerung des Lebens in der dritten industriellen Revolution*. Munich: Beck.

Ariès, P. and Duby, G. (eds.) 1989–93: *Geschichte des privaten Lebens*, 5 vols. Frankfurt am Main: Fischer.

Barlow, J. P. 1996: *A Declaration of Independence of Cyberspace* [cited December 1, 2001]. Available from www.eff.org/~barlow.

Bordo, S. 1993: *Unbearable Weight: Feminism, Western Culture, and the Body*. Berkeley: University of California Press.

Brooks, R. 2002: *Flesh and Machines*. New York: Pantheon Books.

Brown, P. 1988: *The Body and Society: Men, Women and Sexual Renunciation in Early Christianity*. New York: Columbia University Press.

Bultmann, R. 1964 [1921]: *Die Geschichte der synoptischen Tradition*. Goettingen: Vandenhoeck und Ruprecht.

Foucault, M. 1983–9: *Sexualitaet und Wahrheit*, Vols. 1–3. Frankfurt am Main: Suhrkamp.

Jacobs Brumberg, J. 1997: *The Body Project: An Intimate History of American Girls*. New York: Random House.

Johnson, M. 1987: *The Body in Mind*. Chicago: University of Chicago Press.

Kamper, D. and Wulf, C. (eds.) 1982: *Die Wiederkehr des Koerpers*. Frankfurt am Main: Suhrkamp.

Laqueur, T. 1990: *Making Sex: Body and Gender from the Greeks to Freud*. Cambridge, MA: Harvard University Press.

List, E. 1993: *Die Praesenz des Anderen. Theorie und Geschlechterpolitik*. Frankfurt am Main: Suhrkamp.

Meier-Seethaler, C. 2001: *Gefuehl und Urteilskraft: Ein Plaedoyer fuer die emotionale Vernunft*. Munich: Beck.

Moltmann-Wendel, E. 1989: *Wenn Gott und Koerper sich begegnen. Feministische Perspektiven zur Leiblichkeit*. Gütersloh: Siebenstern.

Rorty, R. 1989: *Contingency, Irony, and Solidarity*. Cambridge, MA: Cambridge University Press.

Shusterman, R. 1995: "Die Sorge um den Koerper in der heutigen Kultur" in *Philosophische Ansichten der Kultur der Moderne*, ed. A. Kuhlmann, 241–77. Frankfurt am Main: Fischer.

Theißen, G. 1974: *Urchristliche Wundergeschichten. Ein Beitrag zur formgeschichtlichen Erforschung der synoptischen Evangelien*. Guetersloh: Mohn.

Theweleit, K. 1987: *Maennerphantasien, Vol. 1: Frauen, Fluten, Koerper, Geschichte; Vol. 2: Maennerkoerper – Zur Psychoanalyse des weißen Terrors*. Reinbek: Rohwolt.

Virilio, P. 1994: *Die Eroberung des Koerpers: Vom Uebermenschen zum ueberreizten Menschen*. Munich: Hanser.

Walker Bynum, C. 1992: *Fragmentation and Redemption: Essays on Gender and the Human Body in Medieval Religion*. Cambridge: Zone Books.

Weischedel, W. 1974: *Die philosophische Hintertreppe*. Munich: Nymphenburger Verlagshandlung.

Wiener, N. 1958: *Mensch und Menschmaschine*. Frankfurt am Main: Ullstein.

Wolf, N. 1991: *The Beauty Myth*. New York: Anchor Books.

CHAPTER 55

Religion and Religious War

John Kelsay

The Political Context of War

Human beings are reason seekers and reason givers. Moral discourse seems to require that people engaged in certain behaviors respond to queries by giving reasons that justify their actions (see chapter 6).

War provides a particularly good example of this seeking and giving of reasons. The term is most properly used in connection with violence between established political communities. With some qualifications, it may also be used to describe violence within political communities ("civil" war) or conflicts between established communities and "non-state" actors (for example, terrorist groups.) Given this connection with politics, it is not surprising that the reason seeking and reason giving connected with war typically reflect political interests. Those who engage in war usually seek to fulfill political aims; for example, defending territory or protecting citizens' rights. Augustine of Hippo wrote: "No one goes to war except with the goal of attaining peace." For Augustine, all human communities may be described as the embodiment of some balance between peace, order, and justice. War is thus a political activity, carried out with the aim of establishing, maintaining, or defending the *pax-ordo-iustitia* connected with particular political communities.

The Ancient Connections Between Religion and War

With this in mind, the ancient association of religion and war hardly seems strange. Religious activity, like war, has political dimensions. War is a means to political ends, while religion provides a kind of cosmic foundation to political life. Images of the divine as king, judge, or warrior point to the relation of religion and politics. As one of the oldest texts in the Bible has it, "The Lord is a man of war." Or, in a very different cosmic setting, the Ṛg Veda speaks of Indra, "best of warriors," the "thunder-armed." Phrases like these depict deities as defenders of justice. As such, notions of divinity provide models for human agents who strive on behalf of a just social order. Even as war is a political act, it also becomes a matter of religious practice (see chapter 8).

Examples of "religious war" abound in ancient religious texts. Some of the most important in shaping discussions of religion and war occur in the biblical story of the Israelite exodus from Egypt and the conquest of the "promised land." The book of Exodus relates the story by which God delivers an enslaved people from oppression. In Exodus 15, the people celebrate God's victory over Pharaoh:

> I will sing to the Lord,
> For he has triumphed gloriously;
> Horse and rider he has thrown into the sea . . .

As the story continues, the people of Israel wander through the wilderness, struggling yet protected by their divine defender. When they finally enter Canaan, the land promised to their ancestors, the Israelites fight to take possession from the inhabitants. It is crucial that they do so at the order of God, who fights for and with them, so long as they honor God's directive. As each city is taken, "all that is in it shall be devoted to the Lord for destruction" (Joshua 6:17). The book of Joshua presents this "ban" as an aspect of worship (see Niditch 1993). The lives and property of the enemy are thus offered as a sacrifice, which is considered God's "portion" as the protector of the people. In other traditions, the ban seems more a condition for the preservation of a just political order. Deuteronomy 20, for example, sets forth rules of war that distinguish between "the towns that are very far from you" and those "that the Lord your God is giving you as an inheritance . . . [in which] you must not let anything that breathes remain alive . . . so that they may not teach you to do all the abhorrent things that they do for their gods, and you thus sin against the Lord your God."

Such stories did much to entrench the notion that religion and war should be intimately related. For Christian theologians like Ambrose and Augustine, the Hebrew or Old Testament traditions seemed in one sense the prototype of a *just war*. In another sense, however, the Israelite stories presented a problem. For the New Testament depicted Christ as saying: "Do not resist an evildoer . . . Love your enemies and pray for those who persecute you . . . Be perfect, therefore, even as your heavenly Father is perfect" (Matthew 5: 38–48). In the writings of these Christians, we find the beginnings of a way of thinking about war that specifies considerations governing the justification of war (the *ius ad bellum*) and the conduct of war (the *ius in bello*.)

A full and formal statement of "just war criteria" would not be developed until some centuries later. Even at this point, however, one may consider that the justification of war required such things as (1) authorization by legitimate public officials; (2) a just cause; (3) righteous intent; and (4) a conscientious estimate with respect to (a) the proportionality of damages done to the good achieved or the evil avoided, (b) the prospects for success, (c) the possibility that means other than war might attain the desired goal, and (d) the likelihood that war will establish, maintain, or defend peace (that is, the *pax-ordo-iustitia* of a political community). With respect to the conduct of war, one may further consider that just fighting required (1) avoiding direct attacks against

noncombatants and (2) avoidance of weapons or war strategies that inflict disproportionate harm. In expressing such concerns, Ambrose and Augustine helped to found a
tradition that informs Christian practice to the present. Historical studies trace developments by which the various criteria governing the justification and limitation of war
received specification through the efforts of canon lawyers, church councils, political
leaders, military commanders, diplomats, and other contributors to Western civilization (see Russell 1975; Johnson 1999).

War in the Modern Age: A Plurality of Traditions

The just war tradition first emerged in the West as an aspect of Christian practice, specifically with respect to the civilizing mission of the church in Europe. As the church
divided into the churches, and Christendom into the nations of Western Europe, just
war thinking took its place as one of several ways of reflecting on the morality of war.
Of these, the set of concerns associated with international law present the closest analogue to just war tradition. But various forms of pacifism are also important, as is the
just war thinking of non-Christian religious and cultural traditions (Kelsay 1993;
Bartholomeusz 2002).

International law

The modern notion of international law owes much to ancient and medieval ideas
about the *jus gentium* or "law of nations." The idea was that the practice of existing
communities reflected a set of norms that should guide thinking about the justification
and conduct of war. Formal treaties were one source of the law of nations, as was the
less formal "customary practice" observed among the nations of Europe (see chapter
48). These sources speak to the possibility of third-party mediation as means of avoiding war, of agreements to forego the use of certain types of weaponry, and of conventions governing attacks on cities and the treatment of prisoners of war. In the sixteenth
and seventeenth centuries, writers like the Protestant Grotius and the Catholic Vitoria
argued for the extension of these notions to the world as a whole. Vitoria in particular
made the case that considerations of justice developed among Christians should be relevant to dealings with the natives of the Americas. For him, as for Grotius, the law of
nations had universal significance and should guide relations between all the peoples
of the world.

Many contemporary writers agree. One of the strongest trends in modern political
thought focuses on the development of international institutions able to put into practice the ideal of a universal law of nations (see chapter 49). Following World War II,
the Charter of the United Nations expressed this hope, reserving the right of war to the
international community, except in cases of national self-defense. The Geneva Conventions and attached protocols codified norms governing the protection of noncombatants, treatment of prisoners of war, and the use of weapons of mass destruction.
Representatives of all major religious and cultural traditions have expressed ideas con-

sonant with the judgment that disputes among nations should be referred to international authorities whenever possible, and that war should only be justified as a last resort: for individual states, in cases where established borders are violated or threatened; for all other cases, as determined by the UN or its Security Council.

Despite such support, many questions remain unanswered. Some of these bear on the relationship between just war and international law traditions. Some argue that just war tradition assigns the right of war to particular political communities, each embodying a particular *pax-ordo-iustitia* (Ramsey 1983). While the UN provides a useful forum for these communities to deliberate about common interests, and for diplomacy intended to mediate disputes, it does not embody an actual order capable of replacing the *pax-ordo-iustitia* of particular communities. Until it does (Ramsey argued) no state can or should give up the right to employ military force in order to secure its interests, defined in terms of the *pax-ordo-iustitia* it embodies.

Paul Ramsey made this argument in the context of the Cold War, when US–Soviet competition often rendered the UN unable to act in accord with the mandate expressed in its Charter. However, even after the end of the Cold War, many express similar judgments. US-led action aimed at regime change in Iraq in 2003 is but one of a number of events that raise questions regarding the possibility of the UN as the *locus* of authority for an international rule of law. Arguments regarding humanitarian intervention and the proper means of dealing with international terrorism also indicate important points of contention between the just war and international law traditions.

Pacifism

Pacifist perspectives also present an alternative to the just war tradition. Here, one should note that the term "pacifism" is apparently a modern invention, dating from political debates in Edwardian England ca. 1900. It has come, however, to stand in general for attitudes of opposition to war or to participation in war. In that sense, the phenomenon is longstanding, and many contemporary pacifists find inspiration in early Christian or other religious texts (see chapter 30).

Many such ancient examples are controversial, in the sense that it is often unclear whether opposition to war is based on the judgment that killing is wrong, or whether it is really based on other factors (for example, early Christian judgments that service in the Roman army involved idolatry). A later Christian writer like Erasmus of Rotterdam, whose arguments focus on the terrible waste engendered by war, presents a similarly "qualified" pacifism, in the sense that his opposition to war is not absolute. Contemporary opposition to war is often of this type. It rejects war for most purposes, but preserves military action as a last resort for national self-defense or the prevention of genocide, albeit only with international authorization.

More thoroughgoing forms of pacifism may be found, first, among advocates of nonviolent political action, and second, among Christian writers who find inspiration in the political ethics of the Radical Reformation of the sixteenth century. With respect to the first, the examples of Mohandas K. Gandhi and Martin Luther King, Jr. provide important guides. Here, the idea is that action for justice should involve "strong persuasion" in the form of an appeal to the conscience of those involved in injustice. This action should be non-violent, since military force does not appeal to conscience, but to fear. In the short run, non-violent action may not yield the desirable results, but the "long arc of the universe" is on the side of those who consider it better to suffer injustice than to inflict it. With respect to Radical Reformation pacifism, some writers insist that the refusal to bear arms is a constitutive aspect of Christian discipleship. The way of Jesus is the way of suffering love. Any use of military force violates Christian vocation, as the example of Jesus shows that the proper role for human beings involves the practice of suffering love in humble reliance on God (Hauerwas 1992; Yoder 1994).

In their 1983 pastoral letter *The Challenge of Peace*, the US Catholic bishops said that both pacifism and just war tradition are valid expressions of Christian discipleship. Nevertheless, the bishops' argument suggests that just war tradition remains primary, for at least the following reasons: (1) the peace for which Christians hope is eschatological, meaning that it is fully revealed at the end of days, when the Kingdom of God is fully revealed; (2) until the end, political action takes place in a world where justice requires the defense of innocents against aggressors; (3) while non-violent forms of defense have a certain prima facie desirability, those who would act for justice must be prepared to use armed force, or else become complicit in the suffering of victims of aggression; (4) when force is required, it should be governed by norms of justice, as indicated by the just war tradition (National Conference of Catholic Bishops 1983).

Islamic thinking

Non-Christian traditions also provide an important source for thinking about war in the modern age. Recent studies indicate the strong affinities of the Islamic "judgments concerning armed force" with just war tradition (see Kelsay 1993; Johnson 1997). Historic judgments by Islamic scholars indicate that war should be considered in the context of political ethics and that it should be authorized by legitimate public authorities for the cause of establishing, defending, or maintaining a just public order. The tradition also requires righteous intention on the part of those fighting. Further judgments indicate that war should be undertaken following an assessment of the likelihood that other measures will not work, that costs will be proportionate to benefits, and that there is a reasonable hope of success, in the sense that fighting will yield a more satisfactory balance between peace, order, and justice. *Ius in bello* criteria are reflected as well: Muslim fighters are to avoid direct attacks on noncombatants, and discussion of particular weapons and tactics indicates a concern to avoid disproportionate damage to one's enemy. As with the just war tradition, Islamic judgments concerning armed force develop over time, in connection with specific military and political contexts. It seems clear that the Islamic and just war traditions have much in common, however, which makes it all the more critical to understand why, at the beginning of the twenty-first century, conflict between Western and Islamic societies seems so ubiquitous. We shall return to this point in a moment.

It is worth noting that inquiry into the war thinking of a number of other traditions is only beginning. The work of the late Tessa Bartholomeusz (2002) suggests some directions for inquiries into a Buddhist just war tradition. More systematic inquiries with respect to Hindu, Confucian, and other great traditions are sorely needed to provide a more complete picture of the relations between religion, politics, and war.

Contemporary Issues

For most of the twentieth century, advocates of the just war and other traditions were preoccupied with conflicts related to the Cold War rivalry between the US and the Soviet Union. In this context, discussions of ethics focused on policies of deterrence, especially those involving nuclear weapons, or on counter-intervention, for example in Vietnam. In the post-Cold War era, discussion quickly turned to the occurrence of an exceptional number of bloody "civil" wars. In some cases, these seemed an ironic result of the end of the US–USSR competition for influence. In Yugoslavia, for example, Soviet influence had been important in sustaining policies intended to suppress religious and ethnic rivalries. For a variety of reasons, these lost strength in the early 1980s. Shortly after the 1991 collapse of the USSR old rivalries between Serbs, Croats, and Muslims reemerged, at times with genocidal intent, as Yugoslavia dissolved into a number of independent states.

In this and similar cases, most discussion focused on questions of intervention. According to the UN Charter, intervention within the borders of a sovereign state should only be undertaken when internal conflicts threaten to "spill over" into neighboring states. Even in these cases, UN authorization is required. The Soviet–US rivalry rendered this point moot during the Cold War, as each power possessed the right to veto any intervention contrary to its interests. With the end of the Cold War, however, the UN sent forces into one part of the former Yugoslavia (Bosnia-Hercegovina). While the forces were constrained by rules of engagement in ways that led to much criticism, they were nevertheless critical in separating the warring parties and beginning a process of disarmament. In another sector (Kosovo/a), however, a threatened veto by Russia prevented UN action, and the US turned to NATO in order to orchestrate an effective intervention. While many questioned the legality of this action, in the end most agreed that intervention was necessary to prevent genocide, and that the result (regime change in Serbia) was a desirable end. As the discussion about US-led action aimed at regime change in Iraq shows, questions about intervention (when it is appropriate, how it should be organized, and, above all, who authorizes it) remain critical matters for religious and moral reflection.

The attacks on New York and Washington, DC on September 11, 2001, seem to put discussions of intervention in a different light. In particular, the statement on national security strategy issued by the Bush administration in October 2002 indicated that US policy will include an option of preemptive military action in cases where states may be considered hostile and are known to have programs for the development of weapons of mass destruction. Advocates of just war, international law, and other traditions responded by indicating that preemptive action requires that the threat from an enemy be imminent. The arguments of the Bush Administration make clear, however, that the events of September 11, 2001 mean that US policy must be set in the context of an ongoing struggle with "terrorist groups of global reach." This means that the enemy is not confined to or governed by the political–territorial institutions of an established state. Rather, groups like al-Qa'ida view the world as a battlefield, so that the various states are really more or less useable "centers for operations" in an ongoing war against the United States and its allies. Given this, the Bush "doctrine" of preemption appears to mean "striking while there is time" to prevent al-Qa'ida and other groups from taking advantage of the resources provided by states hostile to the US. Defenders of the Bush administration's policy stress that at a time when hostile forces have the capacity to use chemical, biological, or nuclear weapons, the notion of imminent threat takes on a new meaning (see Elshtain 2003).

Post-Cold War conflicts also raise important questions with respect to what might be called "the return of religious war." Fighting in the former Yugoslavia and ongoing struggles with al-Qa'ida seem to many to bring back the kind of warfare where fighting is commanded by a deity which itself joins in the fighting. Thus much evidence suggests that Serbs understood themselves as the protectors of the borders of Christian civilization, seeking to rid their land of a Muslim intruder. Al-Qa'ida's rhetoric suggests that policies advocated by the US are understood to violate Islamic tradition. Even in cases where the role of deity is quite different, the return of religious war seems evident. In Sri Lanka, for example, the Sinhala majority construes struggles with Tamil rebels as a defense of territory necessary for the preservation of true Buddhist practice. In the conflict between Israelis and Palestinians, Israelis who settle in Palestinian territory often speak in ways that suggest they are reclaiming the land promised to their (biblical) ancestors. Some Palestinians, in turn, speak of the land from the Red Sea to the Jordan as a trust given by God to the Muslims until the Day of Judgment, and say that no human being has the right to negotiate or otherwise give it away.

Religion and Total War?

Given the longstanding relations between religion and war outlined in this chapter, such arguments are not surprising. Religion and war meet in connection with the drive to establish, maintain, and protect the order associated with particular political communities. War is a means to attain such goals. Religion provides an important source of legitimation for the *pax-ordo-iusititia* embodied by particular communities.

Despite such ancient links, many find the association of religion and war disturbing. For example, Pope John Paul II speaks of religious war as the worst form of idolatry. The pope's judgment certainly points to changes in the conception of deity from ancient to modern times. It also points to shifts in Christian political thought, whereby the spiritual aims of faith and the temporal purposes of political order are distinguished more clearly than in ancient times. The pope's statement also resonates with a judgment common to modern thought: that "war is more humane when God is left out." Modern thinking about war is built on the memory of Europe's Wars of Religion, in which the tactics of various groups mirrored the biblical "ban." Given this, many interpreters of just war and other religious–moral traditions consider that those who believe themselves fighters for God are prone to war without mercy.

Whether the judgment "religious war equals total war" is justified is a matter for further inquiry. Much Islamic thought suggests that placing war in a religious context, in which those who fight for God's cause must observe God's limits, is the surest way to attain the goals of honorable combat. And even the biblical notion of the ban must be read in the context of rules that indicate that most wars are fought according to *ius in bello* limits (as, for example, in engagements with cities "far off" in Deuteronomy 20, or in the pronouncement of judgments against those who kill indiscriminately in war in Amos 1 and 2.) Even the 1998 *Declaration concerning armed struggle against Jews and Crusaders*, in which leaders of al-Qa'ida and other groups argued that contemporary political conditions require Muslims to fight Americans and their allies without distinguishing civilian and military targets, probably does not provide evidence for a simple equation between religious war and total war. If this is the case, there may be reason for advocates of *ius in bello* restraints to focus less on the fact of religious justifications for war, and more on the limits that particular religious traditions stress must always be an aspect of the conduct of just and limited war.

Bibliography

Bartholomeusz, T. 2002: *In Defense of Dharma: Just War Ideology in Buddhist Sri Lanka*. New York: Routledge-Curzon.

Elshtain, J. B. 2003: *Just War against Terror: The Burden of American Power in a Violent World*. New York: Basic Books.

Hauerwas, S. 1992: *Against the Nations: War and Survival in a Liberal Society*. Notre Dame, IN: University of Notre Dame Press.

Johnson, J. T. 1997: *The Holy War Idea in Western and Islamic Traditions*. University Park: Pennsylvania State University Press.

—— 1999: *Morality and Contemporary Warfare*. New Haven, CT: Yale University Press.

Kelsay, J. 1993: *Islam and War: A Study in Comparative Ethics*. Louisville, KY: Westminster/John Knox Press.

National Conference of Catholic Bishops. 1983: *The Challenge of Peace: God's Promise and Our Response*. Washington, DC: United States Catholic Conference.

Niditch, S. 1993: *War in the Hebrew Bible: A Study in the Ethics of Violence*. Oxford: Oxford University Press.

Ramsey, P. 1983: *The Just War: Force and Political Responsibility*. Savage, MD: Rowman & Littlefield.

Russell, F. 1975: *The Just War in the Middle Ages*. Cambridge: Cambridge University Press.

Yoder, J. 1994: *The Politics of Jesus*, revd. edn. Grand Rapids, MI: William B. Eerdmans.

CHAPTER 56

Moral Development

Don S. Browning

The phrase "moral development" suggests to many educated people the field of moral psychology. This is the academic discipline that is often thought to have the most profound insight into the processes of moral formation. Others, however, think of traditional religion; religious communities, they think, are the primary carriers of the ethical truths and processes of socialization needed to create moral people. Immediately, then, the term moral development raises the specter of the conflict between religion and science. Psychology, it is thought, is a science; religion, it is held, is about our relation to the ultimate about which science, some believe, can tell us very little (see chapter 3).

Science versus Tradition

Behind the conflict between science and religion on the moral development of persons is the deeper philosophical conflict between what is generally called "foundationalism" and "non-foundationalism." This is a conflict about how genuine knowledge, both moral and scientific, should be acquired. Foundationalists believe that it comes from rejecting or bracketing tradition and building knowledge on the basis of objective sense data, scientific experiment, or certain irrefutable *a priori* ideas. The foundationalists believe that true knowledge about the moral development of persons will be discovered scientifically, most likely from the various fields of psychology, whether psychoanalytic, humanistic, cognitive, or evolutionary psychological. Non-foundationalists believe that cultural and religious traditions are the carriers of reliable knowledge and that, at best, science or *a priori* intuitions add only certain minor clarifications to what our traditions already tell us (Bernstein 1983: 1–20). They believe that our religious and cultural traditions have already discovered both what moral persons are and how to form them. This chapter argues that the non-foundationalists are right, but only if they acknowledge the important role the sciences can play in the criticism, refinement, and appropriation of the moral wisdom of our traditions. This opens new directions for work in religious ethics.

Modern Psychology and Moral Development

Most of the modern psychologies of moral development have been foundationalist to the core. They have aspired to find an objective, value free, and tradition-free way of talking about moral development. Because of its scientific aspirations toward objectivity, much modern psychological research is now thought to have been incomplete. It did its research with inadequate prescientific models of what mature moral action and reflection are really like. For instance, Sigmund Freud believed that his psychoanalytic insights into moral development were scientific and value free. Morality is formed, he taught, by infants and children emotionally identifying with powerful parental figures in their lives, especially the father. In order to retain the father's love, children identify with the negative prohibitions of the father and internalize them into their inner psychological lives, what Freud called the superego (1957: 34–53). But this made moral development primarily an unconscious process of internalizing the values – and often the prejudices – of parents. It gave us no account of how mature persons learn to evaluate their parents' morality in light of classical moral insights found either in their cultural traditions or in recognized philosophical moral principles.

Humanistic psychology also wanted to find a ground for moral development that was scientific and liberated from religious and cultural traditions (Browning 1987; van der Ven 1998: 235). It is an approach to personality development and psychotherapy that held moral development of persons was a matter of learning how to listen to, reflect on, and evaluate one's own organismic experience and capacity for self-actualization (Rogers 1951; Maslow 1954; Perls, Hefferline, and Goodman 1951). Religious and cultural traditions – whether mediated by parents or local communities – were at best advisory to the final center of authority found in the biologically grounded self-actualization tendencies of the individual person. Only gradually did it become apparent that this view of morality was a form of "ethical egoism"; morality was what satisfied and fulfilled the individual (Browning 1987: 72). This implicit moral principle lacked the main feature of genuine morality: the capacity to mediate conflicts between the needs and desires of the individual and the needs and desires of others. In spite of this striking inadequacy, humanistic psychology has influenced the images of health and human fulfillment of much of modern psychotherapy and even the program in moral education called "values clarification" – an approach widely used in schools, prisons, and churches throughout the United States and in other countries as well (see, for example, Simon, Howe, and Kirchenbaum 1971).

The humanistic psychologies, with their biologistic understanding of moral development, have affinities with the more recent claims of evolutionary psychology. This school of psychology believes that moral values are embedded in the biological processes of sexual selection (kin altruism, inclusive fitness, and natural selection). Kin altruism is the primate inclination to protect, care for, and even empathize with those beings (principally offspring and relatives) who carry and extend his or her genes (see

Wright 1994: 158–61). The concept of inclusive fitness claims that creatures that pro-create through sexual selection are concerned about the survival and well-being of not only their own genes but also the offspring and relatives that carry their genes. This is not just a selfish process. It can also be seen as the ground of sympathy and identification with others (see de Waal 1996: 78–83; cf. Dawkins 1976). The processes of natural selection, the theory goes, have tended to retain creatures with these sympathetic capacities because of their adaptive qualities for themselves and their genetic family line. James Q. Wilson in *The Moral Sense* (1993) has developed a link between evolutionary psychology and the moral sentiment theories of Scottish philosophers Francis Hutcheson, David Hume, and Adam Smith. Kin altruism and inclusive fitness give rise to moral sentiments that can become elaborated into an adult sense of sympathy, fairness, self-control, and even duty (1993: 29–120). These sentiments develop and mature within the context of the deep investments of family life, but can gradually be analogically extended and universalized to others outside the family (1993: 192–200).

Evolutionary psychology and humanistic psychology are doubtless correct in holding that our organismic experience or deep inclinations toward gene immortality, kin altruism, and inclusive fitness *under certain conditions* contribute to morally relevant inclinations and sentiments. However, neither school of moral development understands the difference between such premoral inclinations and more properly moral inclinations, sentiments, and values. They do not understand the social, cultural, and hermeneutic conditions under which morally relevant (yet still premoral) biological inclinations are selected, nourished, and enhanced and inclinations and sentiments are channeled, sometimes suppressed, but finally redirected toward morally worthy ends.

The most powerful contemporary psychological perspective on moral development can be found in the cognitive theories of Lawrence Kohlberg. Along with the Swiss psychologist Jean Piaget, Kohlberg believed that moral development employed in the realm of moral conflict and deliberation used the same cognitive capacities as in science and mathematics (Piaget 1965; Kohlberg 1981). Kohlberg was stimulated to do his work because of accumulating evidence that moral training of the kinds associated with Boy Scout merit badges and Sunday School moral instruction did not help young people learn to cope with moral conflict and new moral dilemmas. He realized that social scientists cannot adequately do empirical work in moral development unless they make some important prescientific decisions about the nature of morality. Kohlberg decided that the moral theories of Immanuel Kant and the neo-Kantian perspective of John Rawls provide the most adequate philosophical framework for the scientific study of the moral development of persons (Rawls 1971; Kant 1959). Morality is primarily a matter of *moral thinking*; it is the capacity to guide one's actions by maxims that one can will to be universal law – a law for all humans to follow, both in your action toward them and their action toward you (see chapter 1). To think morally means to be able to place oneself in the shoes of the other and think what one's actions might mean to them as well as oneself. It also means being blind to how one's action might benefit oneself in light of certain characteristics such as race, wealth, class, abilities, gender, education, or age.

Given these philosophical precommitments, what did Kohlberg actually learn from his scientific observations? Development of moral thinking, he showed, is measurable. One can find people thinking with some approximation to Kant and Rawls' view of morality, and that there is a developmental timetable for the emergence of one's capacity for such moral thinking. Moral thinking moves from the *preconventional* and egocentric stage of early childhood (the right thing to do is that which is satisfying and avoids pain and punishment), to the *conventional* thinking of late childhood and early teens (right action is what parents and the community say we should do), to *postconventional* thinking of late teens and adulthood (right action is the greatest good for the largest number or, higher still, truly universal and reversible moral thinking of the kind Kant and Rawls describe) (Kohlberg 1981: 17–18). Of course, not everyone moves to the higher stages. Most do not get beyond conventionality and some are arrested at preconventional levels. Kohlberg believed his empirical studies demonstrated that moral development parallels, and is aided by, the natural sequence of human cognitive development. Finally, he claimed to learn some of the empirical conditions that facilitate the growth, elaboration, and complexification of higher levels of moral thinking. Moral development is provoked by diverse and conflicting social experiences that compel us to restructure our moral cognitive categories so that they become more attentive to and inclusive of the claims of other people, even those outside our traditional circles.

Today, it is widely believed that Kohlberg's view of moral development was far too narrow. He confined morality to moral thinking and paid no systematic attention to the premoral goods that moral thinking should order. Closely related to this point is the feminist critique. Carol Gilligan (1982) has argued that it is a model of moral thinking that fits men more than women. Hence, it was a gender-biased model. Kohlberg's view of moral thinking emphasizes justice and rights and neglects elements of care and nurture, features that Gilligan believes, at least in Western societies, are more often found in the way women approach moral issues (1982: 62). Communitarian ethicists have advanced criticisms as well. They complain that Kohlberg neglects other aspects of morality, principally the role of virtue, narrative, tradition, and community (MacIntyre 1981). The field of psychology has been influenced by this line of thinking. Owen Flanagan (1991) argues for the importance in psychology and moral philosophy of the narrative formation of moral character and virtue.

Associated with the turn to virtue and narrative in modern theology, philosophy, and psychology is the emergence of character education in schools and communities in the US and other countries. In the early 1990s the general public in several countries became concerned about the increase in crime, cheating, out-of-wedlock pregnancies, sexually transmitted diseases, and alcohol and drug consumption among school-age populations. The leading approach centered around various programs in character education; these initiatives generally entailed school or community-wide discussions about the meaning of such virtues as truth, honesty, commitment, duty, etc. Although apparently powerful in producing a higher level of civility among students and community members, some critics believe that this approach to character education does little to illuminate either the goods at stake in moral issues or the principles of obligation that should guide deliberation and action in new situations. Furthermore, some sociologists believe that character education's concentration on lists of specific virtues may produce only superficial conformity rather than a vital and transformative moral life (Hunter 2000).

A Hermeneutic Understanding of Moral Development

Modern psychology has contributed bits and pieces of insight into the nature of the moral development of persons. It has not, however, delivered a dominant model that has been accepted widely or that has improved decisively our understanding of moral development beyond the wisdom of inherited religious and philosophical resources. Yet, the bits and pieces – the partial insights – can prove valuable if we resist the temptation to inflate a limited finding into representing the entire field of moral deliberation and action. The problem with social scientific research into moral development is this: it has been guided by inadequate prescientific models of morality.

Recently, new philosophical models of ethics and morality have emerged that should be examined for their usefulness for understanding the fullness of moral development. They also may have much to contribute to the social scientific study of moral development. I will illustrate these new prescientific models by outlining the hermeneutic view of ethics and morality found in the writings of Paul Ricoeur. Ricoeur's model can be found in what he calls his "little ethics" (1992: chs. 5–10). According to him, development toward mature moral reflection and action, when fully described, *both includes and yet is more than* the internalization of parental prohibitions (Freud), deepened trust in one's own valuing process (humanistic psychology), kin altruism analogically applied to non-kin (evolutionary psychology), universalizable moral thinking (Kohlberg), and the uncritical assimilation of virtues (character education). For Ricoeur, the development of persons toward moral maturity reflects the full structure of the self in its interpretive and dialogical action with the world. Ricoeur believes that the self in dialogue with its world has a three-step rhythm: the steps of *describing, narrating,* and *prescribing* (Ricoeur 1992: 20). When confronting a moral problem, we first describe it, then bring it into contact with our fund of narratives about the meaning of life and our place in it, and then prescribe some kind of moral response. This happy formula about the moral self will help us understand the full complexity of moral maturity.

Mature moral thinking and action develops along the following lines. First, Ricoeur makes a distinction between ethics and morality. In fact, he asserts the logical and developmental priority of "ethics" over "morality." "Ethics," he claims, springs from our desiring selves and from our efforts to realize some good in our lives. Here is where Freud, the humanistic psychologies, and evolutionary psychology throw some light on moral development; all of them taught that ethics springs from our desires, needs, and strivings for self-actualization (Ricoeur 1970). Morality, on the other hand, has more to do with duties and obligations to others. According to Ricoeur, morality builds on, tries to fulfill, yet properly orders our ethical striving toward the good and does this in light of the needs and reality of other people.

How do we understand and learn about these aspirations toward the good? Do we learn about them by directly feeling and following our raw desires and actualization tendencies? Ricoeur says no. We should instead *describe* (the first of the three steps) our culture and tradition's classic *practices* for pursuing these goods. Such practices crystallize our enduring goods and the appropriate means to acquire them. In this emphasis on practices as revealing the goods of our ethical strivings, Ricoeur affirms the importance to ethics of the teleological concerns of the modern psychologies (desire, organismic experience, self-actualization) but now places these strivings within a communitarian context. This view says, in effect, that the truly tested and lasting goods of life are discovered through the inherited practices of a community and its traditions (MacIntyre 1981: 177).

Teaching persons how to *describe* the inherited practices of a tradition is just the first step toward the moral development of persons. If we are socialized beings, the more excellent forms of our desires are projected into hierarchies of linguistic codes that give intelligibility to our practices: (1) codes of coordination (simple patterns of means to various ends); (2) codes of subordination (such as plowing in order to farm); (3) constitutive rules (moving the pawn to play the game of chess); (4) plans of life (far reaching goals and aspirations); (5) images of the "good life" (models as to what are truly valuable aspirations for life as a whole); and (6) larger narratives that give unity and meaning to our life in the midst of its disappointments and conflicts. All of these layers of language pattern our desires and practices at their very core, carry us toward more fully ethical action, and *lead us to the doorstep of morality*. Ethics understood as the pursuit of the goods of life requires a grand and complex process of education, socialization, and critical interpretation on the excellent practices of a tested and established tradition.

"Narratives" was the last of the long list of ways that our practices, which embody the goods we seek, are encoded by language and tradition. *Narration* was also the second step in Ricoeur's threefold understanding of the interpretive and dialogical self. Some narrative – some story – always integrates the hierarchies of encoded "ethical" practices. Some narrative gives the final meaning to our means–end actions, our if–then actions, our plans of life, and our images of the good life. To develop as a moral person, one must assimilate the classic narratives of one's tradition – those that over time have proved most capable of giving meaning to our ethical struggles and losses. In the words of Hans-Georg Gadamer (1989), from whom Ricoeur has learned so much, development toward morality requires learning to interpret the "classics" of a tradition.

In spite of this emphasis on the role in "ethics" of inherited communal practices and traditions, Ricoeur would have us go beyond the traditionalism of communitarianism. Action at this ethical stage only deals with communally patterned aspirations; we have not yet arrived in the arena of full "morality." Why is it that our ethical aspirations toward the goods of life do not, in themselves, deal with the core of genuine moral maturity for persons? The answer is that the goods of life conflict and thereby produce various forms of violence. The field of ethics, in contrast to the arena of morality, is born out of our purposive search for the good. "Morality" itself assumes and builds on our ethical and teleological aspirations, but it also goes beyond them. Morality in the proper sense of the word is born out of the tragic conflict between the goods of life. Morality mediates conflicts between goods and the different people and communities seeking these goods. Morality does this by employing tests about which of the maxims guiding our ethical striving are actually universalizable. Such tests can be found in Kant's second formulation of the categorical imperative: "Act so that you treat humanity, whether in your own person or in that of another, always as an end and never as a means only" (Kant 1959: 47). In the context of religions such as Judaism and Christianity, and other religions as well, one finds similar tests in the Golden Rule (see chapters 18 and 22). In Christianity, we find the principle of neighbor love: "You shall love your neighbor as yourself" (Mt. 22:39). These principles show solicitude and respect for both other and self, tell us to treat all persons as ends and never as means alone, and require us to recognize that in their humanity alone *all* individuals are deserving of just access to the goods of life. Actions pursuing goods that pass this test of universalization are moral actions in contrast to simple ethical aspirations.

It is at the moment of this test that Kohlberg's model of moral development and his emphasis on universalization as the highest level of moral thinking would find a limited place within Ricoeur's fuller hermeneutic theory of morality. In discussing the test of universalization, however, one has already moved into Ricoeur's third step: the moment of *prescription*. But prescription has several dimensions to it. First, as we have seen, an ethics of desire, habit, virtue, and community formation (Aristotle) is tested by the categorical imperative and similar principles of universalization (Kant). Second, the tests of our ethical strivings that come from using the universalization principle of the categorical imperative, the Golden Rule, or the love commandment must now be fine-tuned to assess the concrete goods at stake in specific situations. Ordering and ranking these conflicting goods requires wisdom, or practical reason. It requires taking seriously the situation in all of its complications and ambiguity.

The Aim of Moral Development

This critical hermeneutic perspective points to a fuller and more adequate model of development toward mature moral reflection and action. We should help children, young people, and adults understand that they are moral interpreters who inherit traditions of moral practice. Parents, schools, and religious institutions should help them understand that the first step of a moral decision is an act of interpretation; it involves asking, what is the meaning of the deeply coded practices that they have inherited? They should learn to inquire into the proper way to interpret these practices. They should learn to ask, "Do I understand these traditions of practices correctly? What are the images of the good life and the narratives that give them meaning?" They should be taught to be sensitive about whether their practices and the goods they embody conflict within themselves and conflict with, and perhaps destroy, the practices and goods of others. They should then learn to exercise some version of the principle of universalization. Finally, they should learn how to return to the original situation to determine how their narratives and the principle of universalization help reorder the conflicting goods that engendered the original violence. The aim of moral development should be wisdom.

Conclusion

Moral deliberation is inextricably related to understanding and interpretation. Something like this model of moral reflection and action should guide our social, cultural, and religious effort to develop moral persons. Something like this model should guide our human and social sciences in their research to grasp the more detailed conditions for moral development.

Bibliography

Bernstein, R. 1983: *Beyond Objectivism and Relativism*. Philadelphia: University of Pennsylvania Press.

Browning, D. 1987: *Religious Thought and the Modern Psychologies*. Minneapolis, MN: Fortress Press.

Dawkins, R. 1976: *The Selfish Gene*. New York: Oxford University Press.

de Waal, F. 1996: *Good Natured: The Origins of Right and Wrong in Humans and Other Animals*. Cambridge, MA: Harvard University Press.

Flanagan, O. 1991: *The Varieties of Moral Personality: Ethics and Psychological Realism*. Cambridge, MA: Harvard University Press.

Freud, S. 1957: *The Ego and the Id*. London: Hogarth Press.

Gadamer, H.-G. 1989: *Truth and Method*, 2nd revd. edn., trans. J. Weinsheimer and D. G. Marshall. New York: Crossroad.

Gilligan, C. 1982: *In a Different Voice*. Cambridge, MA: Harvard University Press.

Hunter, J. D. 2000: *The Death of Character*. New York: Basic Books.

Kant, I. 1959: *Foundations of the Metaphysics of Morals*. New York: Bobbs-Merrill.

Kohlberg, L. 1981: *The Philosophy of Moral Development I*. New York: Harper & Row.

MacIntyre, A. 1981: *After Virtue*. Notre Dame, IN: University of Notre Dame Press.

Maslow, A. 1954: *Motivation and Personality*. New York: Harper & Brothers.

Perls, F., Hefferline, R., and Goodman, P. 1951: *Gestalt Therapy*. New York: Dell Publishing.

Piaget, J. 1965: *The Moral Judgment of the Child*. New York: Free Press.

Rawls, J. 1971: *A Theory of Justice*. Cambridge, MA: Harvard University Press.

Ricoeur, P. 1970: *Freud and Philosophy*. New Haven, CT: Yale University Press.

——1992: *Oneself as Another*, trans. K. Blamey. Chicago: University of Chicago Press.

Rogers, C. 1951: *Client-Centered Therapy*. Boston, MA: Houghton Mifflin.

Simon, S., Howe, L., and Kirchenbaum, H. 1971: *Values Clarification: A Handbook of Practical Strategies for Teachers and Students*. New York: Hart Publishing.

van der Ven, J. 1998: *Formation of the Moral Self*. Grand Rapids, MN: William. B. Eerdmans.

Wilson, J. Q. 1993: *The Moral Sense*. New York: Free Press.

Wright, R. 1994: *The Moral Animal*. New York: Pantheon Books.

CHAPTER 57

Indigenous Peoples

Vine Deloria, Jr.

Religion as a distinct and separate activity of life does not exist for most indigenous peoples. They are a wholly empirical people, deriving their understanding of life from their experiences and the traditions of previous experience handed down in stories and practices. They formulate a general perspective on the rhythms of the natural world and derive practical principles to serve as guidelines for human behavior. From observation they know that everything in the universe has life and they set as their goal achieving a knowledge that will enable them to blend with other forms of life within the cosmos (see chapter 43). They do not, as a rule, distinguish between things wholly physical and intangible experiences that we may call fantasy, hallucination, or even spiritual revelations. Dreams, apparitions, and unusual events that they may experience in the course of living are regarded as essential elements in their lives, a valuable source of information that can be obtained in no other way. Yet in their daily lives much care is taken to distinguish between purely secular behavior and the unusual event that reveals the sacred dimension of life.

This chapter explores the moral outlook of indigenous people in North America. Of course, one must realize that crucial distinctions among these communities and other indigenous people around the world would need further attention. Yet by drawing on the resources of Native-American tribes, the wisdom and also present challenges facing indigenous people can be discerned and explained. The chapter concludes with the threat posed to these peoples.

Moral Identity and Moral Order

Concern for moral identity seems to be grounded in the conception they hold about the creation of the world (see chapter 13). Yet even in the simplest stories of the creation event one finds that the narratives are already structured by a sense of morality and purpose. The Creator and his/her assisting spirits are already bound to respect certain limitations on the exercise of their powers. We often find the kinship patterns directing the behavior of the major divine actors in the creation drama so that the universe cannot exist unless there is already an orderly structure within which the supernaturals can act. These relationships are not restricted to humans, but assist in defining the manner in which birds, animals, and other forms of life behave and relate to each other.

For an impressive number of indigenous communities, humans are regarded as the last creatures to be created. The other creatures have already arrived or have been created and know how to live in the physical world using the special talents and knowledge given them before humans enter the picture. Sometimes, without any antecedent, the birds and animals themselves create the world or act as cooperative partners with the spirits to do so. We are, therefore, the junior members of the web of life and we must learn from all other creatures. Some of the songs of indigenous peoples recite and celebrate the strength and knowledge of the animals, the wisdom of the birds, the rhythmic growth of the plants, and other attributes in which other forms of life have faculties superior to our own.

A primary talent, it seems, of indigenous peoples consists in the ability to describe the cycles of life experience in spoken words and ceremonies that express what all creatures feel at a given moment. We can also reflect on the nature of the world and seek cooperative relationships with animals and plants that enable them to reach their highest possibility of fulfillment (see chapter 47). Our role becomes apparent to us when, in a great catastrophic event, such as an earthquake or flood, we find the birds and animals coming to us, looking for guidance and safety, as if we were capable of resolving the crisis.

The other creatures provide us with examples of how to live in different landscapes as individuals, families, and groups of families. By watching how birds and animals feed themselves we can find food in the most obscure places. The Sonoran desert of Mexico and southern Arizona, for example, appears to be without redeeming qualities as a food supply, yet the Indians who lived in the area knew over a hundred plants that were nutritious and edible by closely observing what the birds and animals ate and, most important, when they harvested their food. In the deep forests, adopting the diet of the bears and small water animals led to the discovery of edible foods and medicines. We have always relied on the examples of other creatures to show us how to live productively on the earth. Today, these practices are being formalized in a new science, zoopharmacognosy, the effort to learn how animals use different roots and plants to cure their illnesses.

Indigenous peoples particularly noted the social behavior of other creatures. Buffalo, for example, graze in certain set patterns with the adult bulls in advance of the buffalo family, younger males always on the outside of the family group, and the cows and young calves in the center. In the harshest blizzard the buffalo will form a wedge with the older animals on the outside of the group, the younger in the center, with the animals most in jeopardy from the blizzard changing places occasionally so that no single animal must bear the brunt of the icy wind beyond limits of endurance. In migrating, this pattern is always used so that the younger animals are protected from predators. When an individual is injured, buffalo – like elephants and other animals – gather around and try to assist the stricken member of the family. The Plains Indians copied this pattern in their hunting migrations with but one change. The elder men having experience and powers led the tribe so that their advice could immediately be sought should trouble occur.

While some animals seem to cede the leadership of the group to the male who demonstrates physical superiority, the real leader of the herd or group is not always the strongest male but often the male that has some kind of charismatic status within the herd. Close and continued observation of a herd can reveal this nearly hidden phenomenon. From this behavior we learn that in the animal world it is the appropriate behavior, considering all conditions, that provides the real leadership. We also learn that animals on the outside of the herd or on the edges of the prairie dog town are sentinels or scouts whose duty it is to alert the group in case of danger. Many indigenous peoples pattern their social and political activities after these ways of the animals, and often they come to believe that they and the animal are one spirit because they can harmonize with the animals so well. One level of their moral vision is that of *imitation*.

Moral Understanding and Interspecies Communication

Mere imitation is sufficient to ensure that humans fit into the environmental food chain with the animals. But the question arises how the non-human creatures *know* the things they do. How do their actions and reactions mirror the experiences we have? How do they have the same kinds of emotions, love, loyalty, jealousy, and sacrifice that we have? Do we gain their knowledge only by imitation or is there another way to establish a personal relationship with other forms of life? Eventually, indigenous people concluded that other creatures were peoples also, distinguishable from us primarily by a different physical shape and apparent destiny but capable of enjoying a great variety of emotional experiences that we recognize in ourselves.

Here the quest for a better understanding, the distinctive characteristic of our species, comes into play. Indigenous peoples sought to learn the most closely held secrets of the birds and animals, so they spent a great deal of time watching them and meditating on what they had observed. How did animals respond to certain life-threatening situations? How did they protect their young? How did the burrowing animals store food for the winter? How could animals identify minute changes in the weather and take precautions long before humans became aware of the changes? Often, meditation laid the groundwork for an encounter with a bird or animal. In dreams, animals and birds might appear and give humans a song, instruct them in how to gather medicines, or offer to provide protection in dangerous ventures. These communications were as real as if they had been experienced in the secular daytime event. They were always empirically verified when the human sought to make use of the information given in a dream.

The understanding of the nature of the organic world is radically changed when a bird, animal, or plant speaks to a human. While this event could occur in dreams or visions, it was also possible to encounter another creature during the daily chores and receive instructions that could immediately be put into motion. A woman might be out gathering roots and berries and hear a voice calling to her, a voice she had never heard before. After searching diligently to locate the source of the communication she might find a plant that she had not known previously. The plant might express its desire to help her. It might tell her how to harvest its fruit, how to make it edible, or how to prepare a broth or soup for nutrition or medicinal purposes. There was a berry bush on the Great Plains that produced sweet berries when approached downwind but sour berries when the harvester approached upwind. Such a radical change in the usefulness of the fruit of the plant might be discovered accidentally, but it also might be part of the instructions given by the berry bush.

In most episodes of interspecies communication, the non-human participant tells the human that he or she has been under observation for some time and has proven worthy of the bird or plant's friendship. The human must have shown a morality consonant with the morality of the cosmos, a morality recognized and cherished by other creatures: the practice of showing respect for the non-human. The non-human therefore trusts the human to use its knowledge or assistance in the proper way. At the deepest level of life, and with a strict adherence to the cosmic order, other creatures seem to have a great affection for us and are always ready to communicate with us. If we are worthy in their eyes, they adopt us.

Countless stories describe how humans came to have a natural technology through the intercession of non-human beings that taught the humans how best to use them or call upon them. Thus, the cedar told the Pacific Northwest peoples how to make canoes, the ground turnip and camas root told the women how to harvest and cook them, remembering always to place a pinch of tobacco in the hole where they had once taken root. Squash, corn, and beans, the Three Sisters, told the Iroquois that they must be planted together if they were to blossom and bear a plentiful harvest. The cottonwood told some young boys to advise their parents to use its leaf as a pattern for the tipi. The buffalo told the Blackfeet to change their way of hunting lest their numbers decrease and they disappear.

From Imitation to Participation

At the stage where there is interspecies communication the morality that had once existed at the level of *imitation* now becomes a *participatory morality* in which humans and non-humans are fulfilled. The occasional confrontation with the non-human beings proved such a benefit that the people looked for other ways of opening themselves to more communications with the other creatures. This desire was expressed in the practice of the vision quest, which became almost universal among indigenous peoples in North America. Here humans humbled themselves before the living universe, fasted for days asking for guidance in the life ahead, and sought friendship with whatever creature might take pity on them.

During this experience the petitioner might simply hear a voice announcing that the higher powers were pleased with the human's effort and encouraging one to live a good life. Sometimes an animal or bird would tell the human that his or her sincerity had touched their hearts and so they would give a song to sing when needing their assistance. Thereafter, unless the gift was misused, the human could call upon the other creature for help and guidance. The human receiving this gift has all the positive powers that are innate to humans and the capability of calling on an animal helper to solve problems that humans alone cannot solve. A human with a spiritual helper, then, is held to a higher standard of morality than a person lacking such a relationship. But the power was always exercised on behalf of the community.

Often, people would create societies composed of other people who shared experiences with a certain animal. Thus the Fox society had members who had enjoyed a positive relationship with that animal and sought to display his observed virtues in their own lives. They were forbidden to kill or eat the animal that was helping them and therefore had to trade for furs, hides and other body parts with those hunters who had no relationship with the fox. In a typical village all the local animals would be represented by humans who had personal relationships so that the community as a whole benefited.

This benefit included those people who had special relationships with the winds, thunders, and powers of the four directions. It was therefore necessary for the community to be aware of the limitations placed on them by these relationships and not to cause undue harm by violating one of the prohibitions. The non-humans could punish the humans when an agreed boundary was violated, when the plant or animal was not accorded respect, or when the powers were misused. Since the community benefited from the positive side of the relationship it could also suffer from a violation by an individual. At such a time the injured non-human of the incident would usually inform a spiritual elder of the community and measures would be taken to resolve the issue. Since climatic elements had immense power, the people took special care not to offend them or to repair the damage of the relationship as quickly as possible.

Most important in understanding this web of life and the sharing of knowledge is that the individual bird or animal knew the limits of their relationship and judged the human accordingly. Strangely, individuals of the species seemed to have an intimate knowledge of the promises made earlier to a human by another member of the same species. We seem to have here a variant of the 100th monkey phenomenon in that when a human desired assistance from one of his non-human friends, spiritual help came from a local individual of that particular species. Otherwise, birds and animals pursued their normal lives. Sometimes a different bird or animal would appear and inform the human that it also carried the responsibility for performing certain tasks and therefore had come to perform the promise. We are here undoubtedly talking about a higher spirit manifesting itself through the medium of a bird or animal, rather than those creatures themselves having superior minds or the inclination to deal with human necessities.

The Spiritual Lives of Sacred Places

Mountains, lakes, rivers, buttes, and mesas were found to have spiritual lives of their own and a superior knowledge of what had come before. When humans approached a natural feature they would often meet, in human form, the spirit of that place. They would be told the limits of their relationship with the location. Finding sacred locations was not difficult because geological uniqueness seemed to be part of the sacred nature of things, indicating that there was individuality in physical features also. Thus, the spectacular Spider Women's Rock in Canyon de Chelly attracted the Navajos and was recognized as a sacred site, the Hopis held springs sacred, and the Bear's Lodge (Devil's Tower) was understood as a sacred location for many Plains tribes.

The actual listing of these locations in North America would be quite long, although many tribes shared sites for ceremonial purposes. The Cheyennes and Sioux both regarded Bear Butte near the Black Hills as a special place to do vision quests and seek spiritual guidance. The Medicine Wheel in Wyoming was a special location for many of the local tribes and they marked this spot of primary power by creating a large circle with spokes to indicate the center. Other sacred locations were so ordinary that unless a human knew the history and geographical boundaries of the site, they could not be located by guesswork. Over many generations, then, it was possible to understand a vast landscape and how different sites related to each other. Four impressive mountains marked the boundaries of Navajo land and it was known that a special "dome" of sacred power existed within these boundaries.

There were, by the same token, places where the people discerned and avoided some kind of evil or forbidding force. The Yellowstone geysers of Wyoming, the Badlands of North and South Dakota, and several canyons in Utah immediately come to mind as sites where people discerned a negative presence. In the Pacific Northwest some lakes were regarded as extremely dangerous and to be avoided at all costs. There were many stories of how people disappeared while using the lake and these were sufficient in warning people of the dangers at some locations. Often these lakes were the places where water monsters appeared, so that it is difficult to tell whether it was the story of the monster or the lake itself that was hostile.

Medicine men relate that special piles of stone were placed around the perimeter of bad places to warn people away from them. Sites could also attract ghosts of people long dead who had suffered a tragic fate at a particular location. As a consequence of the ability to discern evil locations and spirits, the people had to become intimately acquainted with the complete powers of a particular landscape and limit their activities accordingly. A location where some great tragedy had occurred might be avoided because that tragedy might be reenacted by the spirits of the people who died there. Ghostly reenactments of a tragic event were not unusual.

Elders say that in very early times the spiritual leaders of their tribes were introduced into the secrets of sacred places by learning special ceremonies that enabled them to go inside mountains and rivers as if they were a normal part of the physical world in which they lived. The Cheyennes spoke of a cave at Bear Butte into which they could go to converse with the spirits. Secular observers could not find the cave and there was no physical evidence of its existence. However, when a certain ceremony was performed, the Cheyenne medicine men seeking advice from the spirits could easily find the cave. It did not otherwise exist in our physical world. The Sioux had a similar experience with the Bear's Lodge (Devil's Tower) and medicine men maintained that another world with trees, lakes, and rivers existed within that structure.

Many tribes related how the Little People lived in springs and waterfalls and could take humans to their homes underwater without injuring them. Since people abducted by the Little People could not return except under unusual circumstances, people were generally afraid to risk themselves at these locations. The Little People could come out of their world into ours and perform most of the daily routine functions that we do. Indeed, some Crows and Shoshones relate how they have encountered Little People while hunting in the Wind River Mountains in Wyoming. They seem to have a physical reality in these encounters.

That large inanimate natural features could have a sentient existence and intellectual life created yet another level of morality to which people were bound. The Black Hills, for example, were set aside for the benefit of the animals and they were believed to gather there on occasion to celebrate their existence. People could go into the Hills to gather lodge poles and foods, but they were not supposed to disrupt the other creatures in their use of the place. This higher morality of the *unity of life* is characterized by the requirement humans exercise *self-discipline* and *provide* for the birds and animals. It was roughly the equivalent of our game preserves today, but had considerably more status in the eyes of the people.

An Ethics of Life and Current Challenges

What were the forces in the natural world that possessed such power as to change, in an instant, the lives of all the living beings? Noting wind, rain, snow, and fire, observing the infinitude of the starry heavens, and finding there energetic powers of immense intensity, humans sought to understand the larger cosmos. Remembering the place where wind and snows originated they identified the four directions as having immense powers and in large part determining the fortunes of human beings. Even these directions seemed to possess personality and thus it was that they personified the directions, often representing them as human figures and personalities. Since these powers were far superior to those of the most knowledgeable humans, rituals were structured so that the powers of the universe were first addressed before human concerns were voiced. In the Southwestern United States the people created the sand painting that reproduced the bounded cosmos in miniature. In the Plains and woodlands the ceremonial pipe was raised and pointed to the four directions, then to the sky and finally to the earth. By recognizing the spiritual context in which appeals for help and prayers of thanksgiving were made, the people conformed to the requirements of a *moral universe* (see chapters "On Religious Ethics" and 2).

The power that was first discerned to exist in every entity in the world and enabled them to move was understood as representing an ultimate *unity of life*. The difference between species was one of structure only and people classified the organic world by the means of locomotion – flying, crawling, creeping, and walking creatures. Birds and animals seen together in benign relationships gave testimony that among the other beings friendships existed similar to the benefits that people received from each other. Each apprehension of non-human relationships revealed the deeper life of the spirit.

Morality, then, was a function of the universe but manifested in the knowledge and behavior of all living things. The "ethics" of indigenous peoples thereby includes within its vision *imitation*, *participation*, *self-discipline*, and *unity of life* wherein human existence is set within a wider reality of sacred places, interspecies communication, and manifold powers. The point of this "ethics of life" was to allow all creatures to fulfill their destiny insofar as they could do so without disruption of other forms of life. There were, to be sure, predator–prey relationships in the food chain, but they were understood as having been reached by mutual consent between humans and the other creatures. We live on the game animals but we contribute our bodies to the earth to become soil in which grasses grow to feed the animals.

Once this chain of being was disrupted, indigenous peoples were unable to fulfill their duties toward the rest of creation. It was and is disruption by conquest, social displacement, racial and ethnic bias, and economic and technological development that threatens indigenous ways of life around the world. The only morality that has become adopted in this threatening situation is from the civilized invader, a morality wholly foreign to the world in which we really live.

Bibliography

Basso, K. *Wisdom Sits in High Places*. Albuquerque, NM: University of New Mexico Press.
Eastman, C. *The Soul of the Indian*. Lincoln: University of Nebraska Press.
Irwin, L. *The Dream Seekers*. Norman: University of Oklahoma Press.
Neihardt, J. *Black Elk Speaks*. Lincoln: University of Nebraska Press.
Standing Bear, L. *My People the Sioux*. Lincoln: University of Nebraska Press.
Waters, F. *Masked Gods*. Denver, CO: Sage.

Standard English Usage Words

The following is a list of frequently used terms that have developed instances of standard English usage. The spellings in the left hand column are those given in the Oxford English Dictionary. The spellings in the right hand column reflect the scholarly conventions for transliteration into Roman characters employed by the contributors to this volume.

Standard usage	*Actual transliteration*
ahimsa	ahiṃsā
Allah	Allāh
Asoka	Aśoka
atman	ātman
Bhagavadgita	Bhagavad Gītā
brahmin	brahman
hadith	Ḥadīth
jihad	jihād
Krishna	Kṛṣṇa
moksha	mokṣa
Muhammad	Muḥammad
nirvana	nirvāna
Quran	Qur'ān
Rig Veda	Ṛg Veda
samsara	saṃsāra
sharia	Sharī'a
shiite	Shī'ite
sudra	śūdra
Sufi	Sūfī

Standard usage	Actual transliteration
Sunni	Sunnī
Tripitaka	Tripiṭaka
Upanisad	Upaniṣad
Vedanta	Vedānta
Vishnu	Viṣṇu

Glossary of Basic Terms

David A. Clairmont

A

ācāra
(Skt.) Right conduct in accordance with conventional observance; an *ācārya* is one who teaches these rules of conduct, particularly as they relate to handing on religious law and ritual.

adab
(Arb.) Civility, etiquette, right norms of conduct; norms and customs; can indicate both laudatory personal traits as well as the disciplines necessary to inculcate these traits into personal behaviors.

agape
(Gk.) Love or charity, often seen as the primary requirement and guide for conduct and character in Christian life (Mt. 22:37); in traditional Catholic moral theology, infused supernatural virtue (*caritas*)

that directs the human person (will and action) to his or her supernatural end (the love of God inclusive of neighbor love); in contemporary Christian ethics variously interpreted as (a) unconditional other-regard or (b) equal regard for all human beings, including oneself.

aggadah (Heb.) That portion of the Talmud containing narrative, sermons, and speculative explanations of rabbinic philosophy; often recasts biblical stories and accounts of the activities of rabbis in order to illustrate good behaviors and right thinking about problems.

ahiṃsā (Skt.) Non-violence, not desiring injury or harm of another; a notion shared by Jainism, Buddhism, and Hinduism in different ways; also denotes correlative feelings for the well-being or flourishing of other people.

àjé (Yr.) Witches; more generally, those who have contact with destructive spirits.

akrasia (Gk.) "Weakness of will" exhibited primarily in intentional behavior that conflicts with the agent's values or principles; contrasted with *enkrasia* (continence; strong will).

Allāh (Arb.) God or the supreme being; used specifically in relation to the belief in the single God of Islamic faith but also in reference to the generic term for a divine being.

Amma (Dg.) In the cosmology of the Dogon of Mali, the god responsible for initiating creation and through whose children the earth was created.

anātman (Skt.) Not-self; according to Buddhist teaching, this is one of the three characteristics (along with impermanence [*anitya*] and unsatisfactoriness [*duḥkha*]) of all existence in human and divine realms.

anthropocentric (En.) Centered on the human, often used to describe an ethical system exclusively concerned with the human good.

apocalyptic, apocalypticism (En.) A pattern of thought centering on dramatic transitions, whether from one "age" or mode of existence to another (often eschatological or soteriological in significance).

Apocrypha/apocryphal (Gk./En.) Literally, "hidden things"; certain books that were written around the time of the canonical books of the Hebrew Bible but not accepted as part of the canon proper; accepted as part of the Christian biblical canon for some but not all Christian denominations.

apology
(En.) A reasoned defense or recommendation of some religious or moral position or way of life.

apostle/apostolic
(Gk./En.) One of the original twelve followers of Jesus of Nazareth called by him to be his companions during his lifetime; also refers to those who spread the teachings of Jesus of Nazareth and the early Christian community.

arete
(Gk.) Excellence or qualitative goodness, translated as "virtue."

artha
(Skt.) Literally "goal" or "advantage"; traditionally, there are four *arthas* expounded in Hindu Indian thought: *dharma* (law and proper ordering of society), *artha* (material prosperity), *kāma* (sensual or erotic pleasure), and *mokṣa* (liberation from the cycle of rebirth); also the name of the particular Hindu *śāstra* concerned with the ends proper to one of the ruling class (*kṣatriyas*).

ase
(Yr.) The life sustaining power of the universe which has the potential to be used for both good and evil purposes.

Ash'arite
(Arb.) Related to the teaching and interpretive methods of Abū al-Ḥasan al-Ash'ari (d. 935 CE); respected the use of reason to prove the existence of God and the basic characteristics of God, but acknowledged the limits of reason and were more conservative in their judgment about the extent of reason's power than the Mu'tazilites; also attributed to God the possibility for all human action while still maintaining the importance of human responsibility and accountability.

askesis/asceticism
(Gk./En.) A system of practices of self-abnegation meant to combat vice and develop virtue.

āśrama
(Skt.) Stage of life of one who is a householder (specifically for the *brahman* and *kṣatriya* classes); as discussed in the *Manusmṛti* (Laws of Manu), there are four *āśramas* (student, householder, forest dweller, and ascetic wanderer).

ātman
(Skt.) In Indian religions, the concept of the individual self or soul, which is eternal and is identical with Brahmā (the single creative force in the universe).

autonomy
(En.) Self-rule; specifically, the capacity for moral self-determination.

avidyā	(Skt.) Ignorance; in Indian cosmologies, that quality of the mind which prevents an individual from bring released from the cycle of death and rebirth (saṃsāra).
axiology	(En.) Theory of value or the good.

B

babalaow	(Yr.) Literally "father of secrets"; the individual who performs a divination in a traditional Yoruba ceremony.
baraka	(Arb.) Blessing; denotes the grace, favor, or virtue which is bestowed by Allāh on people or on sacred places or objects (for instance, burial sites of holy persons).
bhakti	(Skt.) In Indian religions, devotional practices often directed at gods but also to other persons.
Brahmā	(Skt.) In Hinduism, the one supreme creative power of the universe; also the force underlying Vedic ritual practices.
brahman	(Skt.) One of the four groups (*varṇas*) in traditional Hindu society, based on ritual purity; the priestly class responsible for passing on religious knowledge and for performing sacrificial rituals that mediate between gods and human beings.
Buddha	(Skt.) "Awakened one," usually used in reference to the historical figure Siddhārtha Gautama and also in reference to other enlightened beings in Buddhist cosmology; in Mahāyāna Buddhism, refers both to the historical figure and to the quality existing in all beings, giving them the potential to achieve enlightenment (*tathāgatagarbha* or "Buddha Nature").
byaruhanga	(Ba.) Property of the gods; also used to refer to children.

C

caliph	(Arb.) Literally, "representative"; in a general sense referring to one who participates in the good fortune enjoyed by one's ancestors; specifically referring to a legitimate successor of Muḥammad.
canon/canonical	(En.) Officially recognized sacred texts (e.g., the complete Christian Bible, including the Hebrew scriptures and New Testament).
casuistry	(En.) The determination of the rightness or wrongness of actions by the application of general

moral principles to particular situations or individual cases.

catholic
(En.) Literally, "universal," meaning the quality of the Christian church whereby its message pertains to all people at all times; also Catholic, specifically used to refer to the Roman Catholic Church.

ceyin
(Ch.) Compassion

Christology
(En.) The doctrine of the person and the work of Jesus Christ in Christian theology.

cirang
(Ch.) Yielding, deference.

cognitivism
(En.) The view that moral judgments express beliefs that can be true or false, and that true beliefs ("moral facts") can be apprehended by the mind.

conscience
(En.) The natural human capacity for knowledge of moral norms and values necessary for moral judgment in general and particular cases.

conscientia
(Lt.) Translation of the Greek *syneidesis*, generally denoting the capacity for making specific moral judgments in particular situations; in Christian theology, that dimension of conscience most affected by error and sin.

consequentialist
(En.) Those moral theories which judge an action based on the desirability of the outcome or consequences.

cosmogony
(En.) Theory of the origin of the universe; often refers to the narratives found in religious traditions about the origins of the universe and the beginnings of human life.

cosmology
(En.) Theory of the order of the universe and the proper activities of each kind of creature within it.

cupiditas
(Lt.) Cupidity or concupiscence; the inordinate love of finite or creaturely ends, usually contrasted with charity (*caritas*).

D

dao
(Ch.) Literally, "way" or "path"; refers to the ultimate truth within Chinese philosophies and religions, in particular within Daoism; also the ways this truth permeates the diverse spheres of the universe and human life.

ḍarūriyāt
(Arb.) Level of Sharīʿa directives indicating compelling interest.

de
(Ch.) Virtue; more specifically, that power accrued by one who acts favorably to another; in the teachings of Confucius, virtue that was gained both through

	practices of moral formation and through the proper performance of ritual.
Decalogue	(En.) Ten Commandments given to Moses by Yahweh at Sinai (Ex. 20).
deontological	(Gk./En.) From the Greek *deon* meaning "duty," relates to theories of ethics holding that the basic standards for morally right action are independent of the good or evil ends produced or pursued; these standards identify duties or obligations.
Dependent co-arising	(Skt./pratītyasamutpāda) The central Buddhist doctrine of the interrelated nature of all causal phenomena, enumerated in twelve steps (ignorance, mental formations, consciousness, mind and body, six sense bases, contact, feeling, craving, grasping, becoming, birth, old age and death).
dexing	(Ch.) Moral conduct; the means by which the *Dao* is brought into being.
dharma	(Skt.) Law, truth, way, morality, social convention; natural order of the world; in Indian traditions generally, the ordering of human affairs in accordance with the preexisting order of the universe; in Buddhism, refers specifically to the teachings of the Buddha.
dhawq	(Arb.) Aesthetic sensibility.
dogmatics	(En.) Systematic presentation and examination of all Christian doctrines, sometimes distinguished from ethics or moral theology; the precise meaning of the term depends on a theological position.
Dogon	[Dg.] The people inhabiting what is now the African region of Mali; also refers to the group of languages spoken in that region.

E

ecclesial/ecclesiastical	(En.) Of or having to do with the Christian church.
ecumenical council	(En.) In Christianity, a worldwide gathering of bishops to determine authoritatively matters of doctrine and practice.
Eightfold Path	(Skt./Aṣṭangika-mārga) In Buddhism, the path leading to the cessation of unsatisfactoriness; these are (1) right view, (2) right intention, (3) right speech, (4) right action, (5) right livelihood, (6) right effort, (7) right mindfulness, (8) right concentration.
encyclical	(En.) A letter, or circular, sent to all Christian churches of a given area; in modern Roman Catholic usage the term is restricted to letters sent out by the pope.

epistemology	(En.) The theory of knowledge.
eschatology	(En.) Teachings about the *eschaton*, or end of the world.
ethic/ethical	(En.) Originally, related to character or customary values; also, pertaining to any sort of reflection on morals or moral questions.
ethics	(En.) A discipline of thought (i.e., a science of morals), found within both philosophy and theology.
eudaimonia	(Gk.) Human happiness or "flourishing"; in ethical theory, forms of eudaimonistic ethics include hedonism, the view that feeling good or pleasure is the essence of human well-being, and perfectionism, the view that doing well or excelling at things worth doing is the essence of human well-being.
evangelical	(En.) In Christian thought of or related to the gospel or Word or the good news as the core of Christian faith.
existentialism	(En.) Any school of thought stressing the priority of the problem of existence (particularly, authentic individual being) over that of human essence.

F

fatwā	(Arb.) In Islam, an official opinion on a legal matter; a response given to a question about a matter of law about which existing interpretation seems inconclusive; an authoritative but not infallible opinion issued by a *muftī*.
fideism	(En.) A religious view that holds to the incapacity of the intellect to attain knowledge of divine matters and correspondingly puts exclusive emphasis on faith based on revelation.
fiqh	(Arb.) Literally, "knowledge," but more generally the study of legal matters in Islam; discernment or interpretation of legal matters based on the Qur'ān (scripture), Sunna (custom or tradition), Ijmā' (convergence of opinion or consistency), and Qiyās (use of analogy in reasoning about specific cases not covered in the former three sources).
Four Noble Truths	(Skt./Catvāri-ārya-satyāni) In Buddhism, the teaching that (1) all life is unsatisfactory, (2) that the origin of unsatisfactoriness consists in craving, (3) that the cessation of craving is the cessation of unsatisfactoriness, and (4) the *Aṣṭangika-mārga* (Eightfold Path) is the way leading to the cessation of unsatisfactoriness.

G

Gemara	(Arm./Heb.) The next layer or level of the Talmud after Mishnah; an interpretation of the Mishnah.
Golden Rule	(En.) Name for the precept found in the Christian Bible, specifically the Sermon on the Mount and elsewhere: "In everything do to others as you would have them do to you" (Mt. 7:12 and parallels).
gospel	(En.) Literally, "good news"; more specifically, the central content of the Christian revelation, the glad tidings of redemption; it also designates a specifically Christian textual genre containing different accounts of Jesus' life and teachings; four of these texts (Matthew, Mark, Luke, and John) were chosen for inclusion in the New Testament and assigned unique authority and canonical status.
grace	(En.) According to Christian faith, the gift or assistance of God in creation and salvation.
guru	(Skt.) A teacher or instructor who trains one according to a particular way of life.

H

habit	(En.) A disposition, innate or formed, to act in a certain way, often associated with virtues and vices.
Ḥadīth	(Arb.) The deeds of the prophet Muḥammad; used specifically about a series of narratives about the Prophet and his followers and generally to denote tradition.
ḥājiyāt	(Arb.) Level of Sharī'a directives indicating the level of needs.
Halakhah	(Heb.) The body of Jewish religious law; consists of the commandments enumerated in the Pentateuch, the statements recorded in the prophetic writings, precedents handed down orally as authoritative interpretations of the written laws, as well as collected sayings.
Hasidism	(Heb./En.) An eighteenth-century Jewish reformed movement, founded by Rabbi Israel ben Eliezer.
hedonism	(En.) Any school of thought which defines human happiness (*see* eudaimonia) in terms of pleasure; in Western ethics associated with Epicureanism, Hobbesianism, and later utilitarianism (e.g., Bentham).
Hellenistic	(En.) Having do with the ancient Greek and Roman world, its philosophy, civilization, etc.; more specifically, the period of Greek literature and culture from

the death of Alexander the Great (323 BCE) to that of Cleopatra (31 BCE).

hermeneutics (Gk./En.) The science of the methods of interpretation, especially (but not exclusively) textual interpretation; generally, the philosophy of human understanding.

heteronomy (En.) Generally, rule by another; in ethics, used to specify a state of affairs where moral demands come from outside an agent's own person; e.g., theonomy (rule by God)

Hīnayāna (Skt.) Literally, "little vehicle"; a pejorative term used by the Mahāyāna to refer to those Buddhist traditions (most notably the Theravāda – "way of the elders") with a strong monastic community that take the Pali canonical texts (Tipiṭaka or "three-fold basket") as authoritative; these communities are still vibrant in Sri Lanka, Burma/Myanmar, Cambodia, Laos, and Thailand, among others.

I

ideology (En.) Generally, any set of ideas associated with a particular view of social, natural, or supernatural reality; specifically, in Marxist discourse, the intellectual product of relations of production and consumption which systematically distorts and conceals those relations.

ifa (Yr.) The practice of divination.

ijmā' (Arb.) Legal consensus in Islam denoting convergence or consistency of opinion.

ijtihād (Arb.) Literally, "striving" used in Islam to refer to the act of interpreting a law through individual effort and the consultation of proper theological sources.

imago dei (Lt.) Literally, "image of God"; according to the Hebrew Bible, humanity is created in the "image and likeness of God (Gen. 1:26–27).

imām (Arb.) The leader of a group of Muslims; among Shī'ite Muslims, an *imām* has the status of a *caliph* and is regarded as having a special relationship with the divine.

īmān (Arb.) Faith; specifically, confidence in Allāh and in the truth of the message of his prophet, Moḥammad.

imitatio dei (Lt.) "Imitation of God."

imperative (En.) A statement about what ought to be done.

Islam	(Arb.) To surrender or submit to the will of God; denotes those traditions taking the teachings of the Prophet Muḥammad.
ius gentium	(Lt.) "Law of the people"; the civil laws of particular societies.
ius ad bellum	(Lt.) In the Christian "just war" tradition, those criteria that specify the conditions under which it is acceptable to initiate military action; these include just cause, proper authority, last resort, and reasonable likelihood of success.
ius in bello	(Lt.) In the Christian "just war" tradition, those criteria that specify the proper actions of those in the midst of combat; these include proportional response and non-combatant immunity.
ius naturale	(Lt) "Natural law"; the universal moral law common to all rational creatures.
iwa	(Yr.) Character; existence or the totality of a person's being.

J

Jesus of Nazareth	(En.) The Jewish teacher and itinerant preacher (ca. 0–33 CE) whose life, death, and resurrection serve as the seminal events upon which Christian belief and practice are based; the one whom Christians worship as savior and lord, the Christ.
jñāna	(Skt.) In Indian religions, generally denotes any kind of knowledge, including all forms of spiritual knowledge; specifically, it denotes that element of cognition in which a specific cognitive event occurs.
jihād	(Arb.) A particular kind of striving against any internal or external evil (particularly striving against impulses in oneself or temptation outside oneself); strictly speaking, a defense of Islam against aggression which may take the form of speech, writing, or physical conflict.
Judaism	(En.) Referring to the monotheistic religion of the Jewish people, having Abraham, Moses, and King David as its founding figures, and counting the Torah as its book of divine revelation.
justification	(En.) (a) In Christian theology, the act whereby God makes or pronounces persons righteous and/or acquits punishment and mercifully forgives sins; also, the change in the human condition whereby persons pass from a state of sin into a state of

righteousness; (b) in moral theory, a procedure for establishing the validity of moral theories, actions, or principles.

'itāb
(Arb.) Blame.

K

kabbalah
(Heb.) Refers to a certain body of mystical teachings and practices in Judaism which focus on the immanent as well as the transcendent aspects of the divine that are perceived through the process of contemplation.

karma
(Skt.) Action; more broadly, it refers to the cumulative effects of good or bad moral action which affects the status in future rebirths.

khuluq
(Arb.) Character.

kṣatriya
(Skt.) One of the four groups (varṇas) in traditional Hindu society, based on ritual purity; the warrior, noble, or ruling class

kuśala
(Skt.) "Good" in the sense of skillful, beneficial, or expedient; refers both to what enables one to perform a particular kind of beneficial action and also how a teaching is tailored to the stage of advancement of the one who is receiving it; the opposite is *akuśala*, which indicates "bad" in the sense of not beneficial.

kuwa na
(Sw.) To be with in the sense of a relationship of one thing to another.

L

li
(Ch.) Ritual; propriety as one of the five essential virtues proposed by Confucius, ritual practice as the best place to manifest propriety; in traditional Chinese thought, believed to be one aspect of knowledge passed on from one generation to the next and through which much of the ancient wisdom of the sages was codified.

liuyi
(Ch.) Division of traditional Chinese learning into six arts: *shu* (history), *shi* (poetry), *yi* (changes), *li* (ritual), *chunqiu* (spring and autumn annals), and *yue* (music).

logos
(Gk.) "Word" or "reason"; in Western antiquity, often associated with universal reason governing and permeating the world (cf. Stoicism); in Christian theology, often associated with the second person of the Trinity and the figure of Wisdom.

lokottara
(Skt.) Other-worldly; that aspect of Buddhist teaching that aims at a higher achievement, namely

	nirvāna; in contrast to *lokiya* (this-worldly) or what pertains to the world of ordinary interactions.
love	(En.) In Christian theology, a good principle of both divine and human action, often specified as *agape* (unconditional other-regard or universal equal-regard), often in distinction from *eros* (desire) or *philia* (friendship or mutual care); the term *caritas*, meaning charity or love, was used in classical theological ethics to denote the source of all virtues and the proper disposition toward God and neighbor.
M	
magisterium	(Lat.) The teaching authority of the Roman Catholic Church, comprised of the college of bishops.
Mahābhārata	(Skt.) One of the great ancient Indian epics (along with the Rāmāyana) which chronicles the incarnation of the god Visnu as Krsna and the great struggle between the Pāndava and Kaurava families; the Bhagavad Gītā (or "song of the blessed one") is a part of this longer epic.
Mahāyāna	(Skt.) In Buddhism, the "great vehicle," which emphasizes the potential for enlightenment found in all beings; the predominant form of Buddhism in China, Japan, Korea, and other East Asian countries.
Manusmrti	(Skt.) One of the foundational Hindu texts, *Laws of Manu* details many of the social and ceremonial aspects of life incumbent upon practitioners on a wide array of topics; notable is the explication of kinds of law, the dynamics of karma, and the origins of the caste system.
martyr	(En.) Literally, "witness"; person who suffers death for their conviction.
maslaha	(Arb.) Public interest.
Messiah	(Heb.) "Anointed one" (in Greek, *Christos*); the term came to mean a royal descendent of the dynasty of David who would restore the united kingdom of Israel and Judah and usher in an age of peace, justice, and prosperity; the title *Christos* came to be applied in Christianity to Jesus of Nazareth by his followers.
messianism	(En.) Generally, the belief that a religio-political figure will appear at some time to lead society to justice, shared by Judaism, Christianity, and Islam.
metaethics	(En.) The analysis of the meaning, nature, or ground of basic moral concepts, beliefs, or judgments; not directly concerned with particular questions of

normative or applied ethics but with the form, validity, and justification of moral theory in general.

metaphysics   (En.) A philosophical theory of the most fundamental constituents or the most general characteristics of reality as such.

Midrash   (Heb.) "Interpretation"; in Judaism, a general term for rabbinic interpretation of scripture, as well as for specific collections of rabbinic literature.

Mishnah   (Heb.) "Teaching" or "repetition"; the oral part of the Torah law (as found in the Talmud); an authorized compilation of rabbinic law, promulgated ca. 210 CE.

mitzvah   (Heb.) "Command" or "precept"; a religious commandment or religious obligation; there are ten main ones (*see* Decalogue) and traditionally there are said to be 613 precepts, 365 negative ("do not do this") and 248 positive ("do this").

mokṣa   (Skt.) Liberation, release; the final cessation of the rounds of rebirth.

moral   (En.) [adj.] (a) Generally, relating to any claim or statement which involves a distinction between rightness and wrongness and/or goodness and badness (of character, disposition, action, rule, principle); (b) specifically, an approving description of something virtuous; [n.] (c) a custom or guide for action which influences acceptable social behavior in a specific community; also, a quality or characteristic of the individual person which directs action.

moral anthropology   (En.) Account of the moral features of human nature or the human condition.

moral predication   (En.) The task of using language to name, classify, or label the moral status of objects, persons, actions, intentions, relations, ends, consequences, etc.

moral realism   (En.) The view that moral truths are grounded in the nature of things ("objectively") rather than in subjective and variable human reactions to things or social conventions.

moral sense   (En.) A supposedly innate faculty (analogous to the sense of beauty) for detecting moral properties; in Western ethics, some forms of eighteenth-century intuitionism claimed that the perception of certain actions aroused distinctive feelings of pleasure (approval) and pain (disapproval) in spectators and that these feelings in turn motivated moral behavior.

Muḥammad   (Arb.) The prophet from whose life and teachings are formed the foundations of Islam; lived ca. 570–632

	CE; his inspired speech is recorded in the verses of the Qur'ān.
muḥāsaba	(Arb.) Self-examination.
mujāhada	(Arb.) Ascetic practices.
Muslim	(Arb.) "One who submits to the will of God"; more specifically, to be a Muslim, one must recite the *shahadah*.
Muʻtazilite	(Arb.) Form of Shīʻite Muslim theology; holds that God can be known through the natural power of human reason.

N

natural law	(En.) (a) In ancient Greek and Roman thought, a moral principle or rule which applies universally and is not based on custom or convention but rather on the inherent structure of reality to which rational creatures have access; (b) in a Christian context, the law implanted in human beings by the Creator which allows them to know moral principles through the light of natural moral reason; often contrasted with the revealed law.
nirvāna	(Skt.) Literally, "extinguishing" or "blowing out" of the flame of desire; the conclusion of Buddhist practice in which all craving and attachment cease.
Noahide laws	(En.) According to rabbinic interpretations, seven laws were given to Noah (see Genesis 9) and were incumbent upon all humanity (i.e., descendants of Noah); a gentile who follows the Noahide laws is considered righteous; parallel to the idea of natural law. The Noahide laws include (1) mandate for all societies to establish courts of justice; (2) prohibition of blasphemy; (3) prohibition of idolatry; (4) prohibition of killing innocent human life; (5) prohibition against sexual practices of incest, adultery, homosexuality, and bestiality; (6) prohibition of robbery; (7) prohibition of tearing a limb from a living animal for food.
non-moral	(En.) A term used to identify a class of values not involving ethical judgments about the human person or human action (e.g., "This is a good car").
norm/normative	(En.) Standard, rule, or principle.

O

Obatala	(Yr.) The chief divinity in the Yoruba cosmological system.

Ogo   (Dg.) One of the first two created cosmic beings who effected the creation of the world; child of Amma.

Olodumare   (Yr.) Supreme being.

ontology   (En.) Reflection in philosophy and metaphysics on what truly exists, what persists throughout time, or what underlies appearance by way of existent reality.

orí   (Yr.) Head; the location of personality and individual destiny discovered through divination.

orthodox   (En.) (a) Related to right belief, as contrasted with heterodox or heretical; also a level of strictness in belief and practice, often characterized by very close adherence to religious rules and standards; (b) a name used to specify certain communities within Judaism and Christianity.

òrun   (Yr.) Heaven.

Orunmila   (Yr.) Divinity of wisdom.

P

palaver   (En.) In the context of African religions, a council convened to address matters of concern to the community.

papacy/papal/pope   (En.) The office of the head of the Roman Catholic Church; traditionally understood to be the successor of Peter, one of the original twelve apostles of Jesus.

pāpa   (Skt.) Detrimental, evil, wretched; denoting both wrong moral acts and also destructive natural occurrences which affect human beings negatively.

pāramitā   (Skt.) In Mahāyāna Buddhism, the perfections or virtues developed by a Bodhisattva.

patristic   (En.) Of or related to the so-called Christian Church Fathers, those Christian writers between the end of the first century CE and the close of the eighth century CE.

penance   (En.) Literally, "punishment"; (a) an act performed to show sorrow for sin, to atone for the sin by one's own act, and to avert punishment remaining after remission; (b) in Christian practice the sacrament consisting of such acts, including repentance, confession, satisfaction, and absolution.

phronesis   (Gk.) "Prudence"; practical wisdom, or knowledge of the proper ends of life; (a) distinguished by Aristotle from theoretical knowledge and mere means–end reasoning, or craft, and itself a necessary and sufficient condition of virtue (*see* practical reason); (b) for Christian ethics, the first principles of practical reason (commandments, natural law) are seen as analogous to the first principles of speculative reason (*see* synteresis).

piety
(En.) Generally, the affective or experiential dimension of religious faith.

pneumatology
(En.) Christian doctrine of the Holy Spirit, or thought and discourse about the Holy Spirit.

practical reason
(En.) Reasoning that justifies action, either in the pragmatic sense that if one desires x and performing action y is the means to x, then one should do y; or in the moral sense that if x ought to be done, then one ought to do x whatever one's desires. Greek philosophers called practical reasoning *phronesis*.

prajñā
(Skt.) Wisdom; the highest knowledge which leads to liberation; also the final stage and culmination of Buddhist practice.

premoral
(En.) Term used to differentiate prima facie values or disvalues (e.g., self-preservation, food, shelter, etc.) relevant to or significant for the moral life. (*See also* non-moral; moral.)

proairesis
(Gk.) "Choice" or "deliberative desire"; a decision issuing from desiring in accordance with rational deliberation.

proportionalism
(En.) Generally, a view in Roman Catholic moral theology that the moral judgment of a human act must consider the proportionality of the means to achieve its final end as well as the intention of the act; in contemporary Christian ethics, it is often discussed as a form of consequentialism that seeks to bring about greater benefits than harms.

Protestant
(En.) The word describing those Christian communities whose theological orientation derives from the Protestant Reformation which sought to purify the Christian church from excessive reliance on institutional authority and attempts at self-justification through the performance of works, emphasizing instead the centrality of scripture and the primacy of faith.

pūjā
(Skt.) Reverence, devotion, an offering of respect.

Purāṇa
(Skt.) Those texts of traditional Hindu belief which give mythological account of early communities; central devotional texts for certain kinds of Hinduism.

Q

qadar   (Arb.) "Destiny"; in Islam, the individual's fate, which is largely dependent upon free individual choices the human agent makes between good and evil; God determines the outcomes of events on a universal level.

qi   (Ch.) Energy or vital principle; what animates and motivates all things; the subject of defined breathing exercises intended to bring the human body back into balance in itself and with its surrounding environment.

qiyās   (Arb.) Analogical reasoning about specific cases; one of the traditional four sources of Islamic law (along with the Qur'ān, Sunna and Ijmā').

Qur'ān   (Arb.) "Recitation"; the holy book of Islam, which Muslims believe is a divinely revealed scripture sent to Muḥammad from God through the angel Gabriel in the Arabic language.

R

rabbi/rabbinic   (Hb.) An elder and/or teacher in the Jewish tradition.

Rāmāyaṇa   (Skt.) One of the great ancient Indian epics (along with the *Mahābhārata*); it chronicles the incarnation of the god Viṣṇu as the hero Rāma.

reformed   (En.) (a) Of or related to the teachings of John Calvin and later Calvinism (compare "Reformation," which describes the teachings and traditions of Protestantism in general, as well as the historical event through which various Protestant communities were differentiated); (b) in the Jewish tradition, a level of strictness in belief and practice, often characterized by an openness to change and modernity.

ren   (Ch.) Benevolence, humaneness.

renyi   (Ch.) Righteous conduct.

S

samādhi   (Skt.) Concentration, meditation; that form of meditation centered on calming and focusing the mind (in distinction from *vipassanā* which aims at insight); also the second stage of Buddhist practice.

saṃsāra   (Skt.) The cycle or round of rebirth.

saṃskāras   (Skt.) Rites of passage or life-cycle rites such as birth and marriage ceremonies.

śāstra   (Skt.) Genre of Indian literature, collecting teachings on particular topics of morality and learning.

sattva	(Skt.) Goodness, purity, brightness, intelligence, being.
shahadah	(Arb.) "Act of bearing witness"; the declaration of faith that there is no deity except God and Muḥammad is his messenger.
shan	(Ch.) Goodness.
Sharī'a	(Arb.) Islamic law, a complex code of life grounded in divine revelation; the sources of Sharīa are both revealed and non-revealed, including the Qur'ān, the Sunna, and independent juristic reasoning (*ijtihād*) that takes a variety of forms, including analogical reasoning (*qiyās*), juristic preference (*istiḥsān*), considerations of public interest (*istiṣlāh*), and general consensus (*ijmā'*) of the learned.
shengren	(Ch.) Sages; teachers of past memory in whom there were the best expressions of right conduct.
shifei	(Ch.) Right and wrong.
Shī'ite	(Arb.) One of the main traditions within Islam, taking Ali, cousin to the Prophet Muḥammad, as the Prophet's intended successor, and rejecting other caliphs and Sunnī legal institutions as proper authorities.
Siddhārtha Gautama	(Skt.) The historical prince of the Sakya clan in India (490–410 BCE/566–486 BCE?) whose reflection on his enlightenment experience and his subsequent teaching became the basis of Buddhism.
śīla	(Skt.) Virtue, morality; in Buddhism, those behaviors which express good action and are the foundation and prerequisite for the practice of meditation.
Sinai	(Hb.) According to the Hebrew Bible, the mountain on which Moses was given the Ten Commandments which would guide the moral life of the Israelites.
śūdra	(Skt.) One of the four groups in traditional Hindu society, representing the servant class; not normally enumerated based on the distinction of ritual purity because this class was considered to be impure.
Sūfī	(Arb.) Islamic tradition and communities of ascetic/spiritual practices.
summum bonum	(Lt.) "Highest good."
sunna	(Arb.) The paradigm of behavior every Muslim must follow; the concept of the *sunna* is based on the belief that the Prophet Muḥammad is a role model for all Muslims; *sunna* is based on the teachings of the Qur'ān and supplemented by the corpus of *ḥadīth*, the recorded sayings and doings of Muḥammad

explaining and demonstrating how the teachings of the Qur'ān are put into effect; thus, Muḥammad acts as both exemplar and legislator for the Muslim community.

Sunnī   (Arb.) One of the main traditions within Islam, holding the first four caliphs to succeed the Prophet Muḥammad as the authoritative interpreters of the Prophet's teaching.

śūnyatā   (Skt.) Emptiness; a central teaching of Mahāyāna Buddhism which states that all phenomena are empty of a substantial nature.

supererogatory   (En.) Those acts considered to be above and beyond what is required by morality.

suru   (Yr.) Patience.

syllogism, practical   (En.) A logical form in which the major premise states a general rule for conduct, the minor premise specifies the salient features of a particular situation, and the conclusion is a judgment that results in action about what ought to be done.

syneidesis   (Gk.) "Conscience", knowledge, consciousness of wrong doing (*see* conscientia).

synteresis   (Gk.) A technical term used in classical Western moral thought to denote human knowledge of the first principles of moral action; the use of this term originated from Jerome's election, in his Commentary on Ezekiel, to use this word (meaning 'preservation') instead of the Greek term *syneidesis*, to indicate that part of the soul which, though damaged by sin, still maintains the capacity to distinguish between good and evil.

T

taḥsīnāt   (Arb.) Level of Sharī'a directives indicating the level of improvements.

Talmud   (Hb.) "Study" or "learning"; the basic compendium of Jewish law, thought, and biblical commentary; a compilation of Jewish oral Torah made between the second and fifth centuries. Rabbinic Judaism produced two Talmuds: (a) the "Babylonian" Talmud, or Talmud Bavli, the edition developed in Babylonia, and edited at the end of the fifth century CE; and (b) the "Palestinian" or "Jerusalem" Talmud, or Talmud Yerushalmi, the edition compiled in the land of Israel at the end of the fourth century CE. Both Talmuds tamas include the Mishnah and Gemara.

tamas   (Skt.) Darkness, inertia, gloom, ignorance.

tṛṣṇā	(Skt.) Thirst, craving; in Buddhism, considered to be the root of attachment.
teleological	(En.) Generally refers to end-seeking; specifically, any system of thought which focuses on the ends proper to particular beings and their activity in seeking those ends as the means by which to judge proper behavior.
theocentric	(En.) Centered on God; often used to describe an ethical system which is mainly concerned about divine agency, divine purposes, and the human relationship to the divine.
Theravāda	(Pa.) One branch of so-called Hīnayāna Buddhism known as the "way of the elders"; emphasizing a strong monastic community and taking Pali canonical texts (Tipiṭaka or "three-fold basket") as authoritative; these communities are still vibrant in the countries of Sri Lanka, Burma/Myanmar, Cambodia, Laos, and Thailand, among others.
tianming	(Ch.) Mandate of heaven; central to the justification of Chinese emperors who held power.
Torah	(Hb.) The law, teaching, or wisdom handed down in both written and oral form to Moses on Sinai; identified in written form with the Pentateuch, the first five books of the Hebrew and Christian Bibles.
Trinity	(En.) In Christianity, referring to three distinct persons (Father, Son, and Holy Spirit) in a single divine being.

U

ummah	(Arb.) The worldwide community of Muslims.
universalism	(En.) In moral theory, the status of truths or rules that apply at all times in all places, regardless of social and historical context.
Upaniṣad	(Skt.) Genre of ancient Indian (Hindu) literature of stories, prayers, and speculative investigation into the nature of the self (ātman) and its unity with the creative power of the universe (brahmā).
utilitarianism	(En.) A moral theory according to which an action is right if and only if its performance will be more productive of pleasure or happiness, or more preventive of pain or unhappiness, for the greatest number of relevant beings than any alternative.

V

vaiśya	(Skt.) One of the four groups (varṇa) in traditional Hindu society, based on ritual purity; the merchant class.

Vajrayāna (Skt.) In Buddhism, the "thunderbolt" or "diamond" vehicle; often called the esoteric or tantric traditions of Mahāyāna Buddhism; refers to the many schools of Tibetan Buddhism.

value (En.) The quality of being good, important, or of human concern, or an entity which possesses this quality.

varṇa (Skt.) The four social classes in ancient Indian society.

Veda (Skt.) Originally oral hymns and chants, these became the primary texts of early Vedic Indian religion; includes the Ṛg Veda, the Yajur Veda, the Sāma Veda and the Atharva Veda.

Vedānta (Skt.) Traditions of theological and philosophical thought stemming from commentary on the Upaniṣads; comprising, the Dvaita (dual) and Advaita (non-dual) branches.

venial sin (En.) In Roman Catholic moral theology a sin which, unlike mortal sin, does not wholly remove the soul from sanctifying grace.

virtue (En.) Generally, an excellence or good quality; a good quality inhering in a human disposition to act.

W

walī (Arb.) Saint, friend, patron.

X

xiao (Ch.) Filial piety.

xin (Ch.) Belief, trust.

xing (Ch.) Original nature.

xiu'wu (Ch.) Shame.

xue (Ch.) Learning.

Y

yajña (Skt.) Sacrifice; refers in particular to the early Vedic fire sacrifice, but is used more broadly in Indian religion to refer to acts of reverence, devotion, and worship.

yi (Ch.) Righteousness; more specifically, fulfilling one's obligations.

yoga (Skt.) Literally, "work"; self-discipline or practices of self-mastery.

yogin/yoginī (Skt.) Practitioner; male/female devotee or ascetic.

Yoruba (Yr.) The people inhabiting the Western African country of Nigeria; also referring to the language of this people which belongs to Kwa group of languages.

Z

zhen   (Ch.) Truth.

zhi   (Ch.) Wisdom; also aims or goals (usually in reference to the ancient sages).

zi   (Ch.) Master or teacher.

Acknowledgments

The project assistant wishes to thank the following people for their assistance in compiling this glossary: Kelly Brotzman, Mihwa Choi, Michael Johnson, Kevin Jung, William Schweiker, and Rebecca Waltenberger. All entries were developed from the bibliographical sources listed below and from the adaptations made to definitions given in essays of this volume's contributors.

Bibliography

Bowker, John (ed.) (1997). *The Oxford Dictionary of World Religions*. New York: Oxford University Press.

Donigar, Wendy (ed.) (1999). *Mirriam-Webster's Encyclopedia of World Religions*. Springfield, MA: Merriam-Webster.

Eliade, Mircea (ed.) (1987). *The Encyclopedia of Religion*, 16 vols. New York: Macmillan.

Hastings, James (ed.) (1926) [1908]. *Encyclopedia of Religion and Ethics*, 13 vols. New York: Charles Scribner's Sons.

Smith, Jonathan Z. (ed.) (1995). *The Harper Collins Dictionary of Religion*. San Francisco: Harper San Francisco.

Index